Introduction to Natural Language Processing

Introduction to Natural Language Processing

Jacob Eisenstein

The MIT Press
Cambridge, Massachusetts
London, England

This book was set in Times New Roman by Westchester Publishing Services. Printed and bound in the United States of America.

Library of Congress Cataloging-in-Publication Data

Names: Eisenstein, Jacob, author.
Title: Introduction to natural language processing / Jacob Eisenstein.
Description: Cambridge, MA : The MIT Press, [2019] | Series: Adaptive computation and machine learning | Includes bibliographical references and index.
Identifiers: LCCN 2018059552 | ISBN 9780262042840 (hardcover : alk. paper)
Subjects: LCSH: Natural language processing (Computer science)
Classification: LCC QA76.9.N38 E46 2019 | DDC 006.3/5—dc23
LC record available at https://lccn.loc.gov/2018059552

10 9 8 7 6 5 4 3 2

Contents

Preface

The goal of this text is focus on a core subset of the natural language processing, unified by the concepts of learning and search. A remarkable number of problems in natural language processing can be solved by a compact set of methods:

Search Viterbi, CKY, minimum spanning tree, shift-reduce, integer linear programming, beam search.

Learning Maximum likelihood estimation, logistic regression, perceptron, expectation-maximization, matrix factorization, backpropagation.

This text explains how these methods work and how they can be applied to a wide range of tasks: document classification, word sense disambiguation, part-of-speech tagging, named entity recognition, parsing, coreference resolution, relation extraction, discourse analysis, language modeling, and machine translation.

Background

Because natural language processing draws on many different intellectual traditions, almost everyone who approaches it feels underprepared in one way or another. Here is a summary of what is expected, and where you can learn more:

Mathematics and machine learning The text assumes a background in multivariate calculus and linear algebra: vectors, matrices, derivatives, and partial derivatives. You should also be familiar with probability and statistics. A review of basic probability is found in Appendix A, and a minimal review of numerical optimization is found in Appendix B. For linear algebra, the online course and textbook from Strang (2016) provide an excellent review. Deisenroth et al. (2018) are currently preparing a textbook on *Mathematics for Machine Learning*, a draft can be found online.[1] For an introduction to probabilistic modeling and estimation, see James et al. (2013); for a more advanced and comprehensive discussion of the same material, the classic reference is Hastie et al. (2009).

1. https://mml-book.github.io/.

Linguistics This book assumes no formal training in linguistics, aside from elementary concepts likes nouns and verbs, which you have probably encountered in the study of English grammar. Ideas from linguistics are introduced throughout the text as needed, including discussions of morphology and syntax (chapter 9), semantics (chapters 12 and 13), and discourse (chapter 16). Linguistic issues also arise in the application-focused chapters 4, 8, and 18. A short guide to linguistics for students of natural language processing is offered by Bender (2013); you are encouraged to start there and then pick up a more comprehensive introductory textbook (e.g., Akmajian et al., 2010; Fromkin et al., 2013).

Computer science The book is targeted at computer scientists, who are assumed to have taken introductory courses on the analysis of algorithms and complexity theory. In particular, you should be familiar with asymptotic analysis of the time and memory costs of algorithms and with the basics of dynamic programming. The classic text on algorithms is offered by Cormen et al. (2009); for an introduction to the theory of computation, see Arora and Barak (2009) and Sipser (2012).

How to Use This Book

After the introduction, the textbook is organized into four main units:

Learning This section builds up a set of machine learning tools that will be used throughout the other sections. Because the focus is on machine learning, the text representations and linguistic phenomena are mostly simple: "bag-of-words" text classification is treated as a model example. Chapter 4 describes some of the more linguistically interesting applications of word-based text analysis.

Sequences and trees This section introduces the treatment of language as a structured phenomena. It describes sequence and tree representations and the algorithms that they facilitate, as well as the limitations that these representations impose. Chapter 9 introduces finite-state automata and briefly overviews a context-free account of English syntax.

Meaning This section takes a broad view of efforts to represent and compute meaning from text, ranging from formal logic to neural word embeddings. It also includes two topics that are closely related to semantics: resolution of ambiguous references and analysis of multi sentence discourse structure.

Applications The final section offers chapter-length treatments on three of the most prominent applications of natural language processing: information extraction, machine translation, and text generation. Each of these applications merits a textbook length treatment of its own (Koehn, 2009; Grishman, 2012; Reiter and Dale, 2000); the chapters here explain some of the most well-known systems using the formalisms and methods built up earlier in the book, while introducing methods such as neural attention.

Each chapter contains some advanced material, which is marked with an asterisk. This material can be safely omitted without causing misunderstandings later on. But even without these advanced sections, the text is too long for a single semester course, so instructors will have to pick and choose among the chapters.

Chapters 1 to 3 provide building blocks that will be used throughout the book, and chapter 4 describes some critical aspects of the practice of language technology. Language models (chapter 6), sequence labeling (chapter 7), and parsing (chapters 10 and 11) are canonical topics in natural language processing, and distributed word embeddings (chapter 14) have become ubiquitous. Of the applications, machine translation (chapter 18) is the best choice: it is more cohesive than information extraction and more mature than text generation. Many students will benefit from the review of probability in appendix A.

- A course focusing on machine learning should add the chapter on unsupervised learning (chapter 5). The chapters on predicate-argument semantics (chapter 13), reference resolution (chapter 15), and text generation (chapter 19) are particularly influenced by recent progress in machine learning, including deep neural networks and learning to search.
- A course with a more linguistic orientation should add the chapters on applications of sequence labeling (chapter 8), formal language theory (chapter 9), semantics (chapters 12 and 13), and discourse (chapter 16).
- For a course with a more applied focus, I recommend the chapters on applications of sequence labeling (chapter 8), predicate-argument semantics (chapter 13), information extraction (chapter 17), and text generation (chapter 19).

Acknowledgments

Several colleagues, students, and friends read early drafts of chapters in their areas of expertise, including Yoav Artzi, Kevin Duh, Heng Ji, Jessy Li, Brendan O'Connor, Yuval Pinter, Shawn Ling Ramirez, Nathan Schneider, Pamela Shapiro, Noah A. Smith, Sandeep Soni, and Luke Zettlemoyer. I also thank the anonymous reviewers, particularly reviewer 4, who provided detailed line-by-line edits and suggestions. The text benefited from high-level discussions with my editor Marie Lufkin Lee, as well as Kevin Murphy, Shawn Ling Ramirez, and Bonnie Webber. In addition, there are many people to thank for finding mistakes in early drafts or for recommending key references. These include: Parminder Bhatia, Kimberly Caras, Jiahao Cai, Justin Chen, Rodolfo Delmonte, Murtaza Dhuliawala, Yantao Du, Barbara Eisenstein, Luiz C. F. Ribeiro, Chris Gu, Joshua Killingsworth, Jonathan May, Taha Merghani, Gus Monod, Raghavendra Murali, Nidish Nair, Brendan O'Connor, Dan Oneata, Brandon Peck, Yuval Pinter, Nathan Schneider, Jianhao Shen, Zhewei Sun, Rubin Tsui, Ashwin Cunnapakkam Vinjimur, Denny Vrandečić, William Yang Wang, Clay Washington, Ishan Waykul, Aobo Yang, Xavier Yao, Yuyu Zhang, and several anonymous commenters. Clay Washington tested some of the programming exercises, and Varun Gupta tested some of the written exercises. Thanks to Kelvin Xu for sharing a high-resolution version of figure 19.3.

Most of the book was written while I was at Georgia Tech's School of Interactive Computing. I thank the School for its support of this project, and I thank my colleagues there for their help and support at the beginning of my faculty career. I also thank (and apologize to) the many students in Georgia Tech's CS 4650 and 7650 who suffered through early versions of the text. The book is dedicated to my parents.

Notation

As a general rule, words, word counts, and other types of observations are indicated with Roman letters (a, b, c); parameters are indicated with Greek letters (α, β, θ). Vectors are indicated with bold script for both random variables $\boldsymbol{x}$ and parameters $\boldsymbol{\theta}$. Other useful notations are indicated in the table below.

Basics

$\exp x$	the base-2 exponent, 2^x
$\log x$	the base-2 logarithm, $\log_2 x$
$\{x_n\}_{n=1}^N$	the set $\{x_1, x_2, \ldots, x_N\}$
x_i^j	x_i raised to the power j
$x_i^{(j)}$	indexing by both i and j

Linear algebra

$\boldsymbol{x}^{(i)}$	a column vector of feature counts for instance i, often word counts
$\boldsymbol{x}_{j:k}$	elements j through k (inclusive) of a vector $\boldsymbol{x}$
$[\boldsymbol{x}; \boldsymbol{y}]$	vertical concatenation of two column vectors
$[\boldsymbol{x}, \boldsymbol{y}]$	horizontal concatenation of two column vectors
$\boldsymbol{e}_n$	a "one-hot" vector with a value of 1 at position n, and zero everywhere else
$\boldsymbol{\theta}^\top$	the transpose of a column vector $\boldsymbol{\theta}$
$\boldsymbol{\theta} \cdot \boldsymbol{x}^{(i)}$	the dot product $\sum_{j=1}^N \theta_j \times x_j^{(i)}$
$\mathbf{X}$	a matrix
$x_{i,j}$	row i, column j of matrix $\mathbf{X}$
$\text{Diag}(\boldsymbol{x})$	a matrix with $\boldsymbol{x}$ on the diagonal, e.g., $\begin{pmatrix} x_1 & 0 & 0 \\ 0 & x_2 & 0 \\ 0 & 0 & x_3 \end{pmatrix}$
$\mathbf{X}^{-1}$	the inverse of matrix $\mathbf{X}$

Text datasets

w_m	word token at position m
N	number of training instances
M	length of a sequence (of words or tags)
V	number of words in vocabulary
$y^{(i)}$	the true label for instance i
$\hat{y}$	a predicted label
$\mathcal{Y}$	the set of all possible labels
K	number of possible labels $K = \|\mathcal{Y}\|$
□	the start token
■	the stop token
$\boldsymbol{y}^{(i)}$	a structured label for instance i, such as a tag sequence
$\mathcal{Y}(\boldsymbol{w})$	the set of possible labelings for the word sequence $\boldsymbol{w}$
◊	the start tag
♦	the stop tag

Probabilities

$\Pr(A)$	probability of event A
$\Pr(A \mid B)$	probability of event A, conditioned on event B
$\mathrm{p}_B(b)$	the marginal probability of random variable B taking value b; written $\mathrm{p}(b)$ when the choice of random variable is clear from context
$\mathrm{p}_{B\|A}(b \mid a)$	the probability of random variable B taking value b, conditioned on A taking value a; written $\mathrm{p}(b \mid a)$ when clear from context
$A \sim p$	the random variable A is distributed according to distribution p; for example, $X \sim \mathcal{N}(0, 1)$ states that the random variable X is drawn from a normal distribution with zero mean and unit variance
$A \mid B \sim p$	conditioned on the random variable B, A is distributed according to p.

Machine learning

$\Psi(\boldsymbol{x}^{(i)}, y)$	the score for assigning label y to instance i
$\boldsymbol{f}(\boldsymbol{x}^{(i)}, y)$	the feature vector for instance i with label y
$\boldsymbol{\theta}$	a (column) vector of weights
$\ell^{(i)}$	loss on an individual instance i
L	objective function for an entire dataset
$\mathcal{L}$	log-likelihood of a dataset
λ	the amount of regularization

1 Introduction

Natural language processing is the set of methods for making human language accessible to computers. In the past decade, natural language processing has become embedded in our daily lives: automatic machine translation is ubiquitous on the web and in social media; text classification keeps our email inboxes from collapsing under a deluge of spam; search engines have moved beyond string matching and network analysis to a high degree of linguistic sophistication; dialog systems provide an increasingly common and effective way to get and share information.

These diverse applications are based on a common set of ideas, drawing on algorithms, linguistics, logic, statistics, and more. The goal of this text is to provide a survey of these foundations. The technical fun starts in the next chapter; the rest of this current chapter situates natural language processing with respect to other intellectual disciplines, identifies some high-level themes in contemporary natural language processing, and advises the reader on how best to approach the subject.

1.1 Natural Language Processing and Its Neighbors

Natural language processing draws on many other intellectual traditions, from formal linguistics to statistical physics. This section briefly situates natural language processing with respect to some of its closest neighbors.

Computational linguistics

Most of the meetings and journals that host natural language processing research bear the name "computational linguistics," and the terms may be thought of as essentially synonymous. But while there is substantial overlap, there is an important difference in focus. In linguistics, language is the object of study. Computational methods may be brought to bear, just as in scientific disciplines like computational biology and computational astronomy, but they play only a supporting role. In contrast, natural language processing is focused on the design and analysis of computational algorithms and representations for processing natural human language. The goal of natural language processing is to provide new computational capabilities around human language: for example, extracting information from texts, translating between languages, answering questions, holding a conversation, taking instructions, and so on. Fundamental linguistic insights may be crucial for accomplishing these tasks, but success is ultimately measured by whether and how well the job gets done.

Machine learning

Contemporary approaches to natural language processing rely heavily on machine learning, which makes it possible to build complex computer programs from examples. Machine learning provides an array of general techniques for tasks like converting a sequence of discrete tokens in one vocabulary to a sequence of discrete tokens in another vocabulary—a generalization of what one might informally call "translation." Much of today's natural language processing research can be thought of as applied machine learning. However, natural language processing has characteristics that distinguish it from many of machine learning's other application domains.

- Unlike images or audio, text data is fundamentally discrete, with meaning created by combinatorial arrangements of symbolic units. This is particularly consequential for applications in which text is the output, such as translation and summarization, because it is not possible to gradually approach an optimal solution.
- Although the set of words is discrete, new words are always being created. Furthermore, the distribution over words (and other linguistic elements) resembles that of a **power law**[1] (Zipf, 1949): there will be a few words that are very frequent, and a long tail of words that are rare. A consequence is that natural language processing algorithms must be especially robust to observations that do not occur in the training data.
- Language is **compositional**: units such as words can combine to create phrases, which can combine by the very same principles to create larger phrases. For example, a **noun phrase** can be created by combining a smaller noun phrase with a **prepositional phrase**, as in *the whiteness of the whale*. The prepositional phrase is created by combining a preposition (in this case, *of*) with another noun phrase (*the whale*). In this way, it is possible to create arbitrarily long phrases, such as,

(1.1) … huge globular pieces of the whale of the bigness of a human head.[2]

The meaning of such a phrase must be analyzed in accord with the underlying hierarchical structure. In this case, *huge globular pieces of the whale* acts as a single noun phrase, which is conjoined with the prepositional phrase *of the bigness of a human head*. The interpretation would be different if instead, *huge globular pieces* were conjoined with the prepositional phrase *of the whale of the bigness of a human head*—implying a disappointingly small whale. Even though text appears as a sequence, machine learning methods must account for its implicit recursive structure.

1. Throughout the text, **boldface** will be used to indicate keywords that appear in the index.
2. Throughout the text, this notation will be used to introduce linguistic examples.

Artificial intelligence

The goal of artificial intelligence is to build software and robots with the same range of abilities as humans (Russell and Norvig, 2009). Natural language processing is relevant to this goal in several ways. On the most basic level, the capacity for language is one of the central features of human intelligence, and is therefore a prerequisite for artificial intelligence.[3] Second, much of artificial intelligence research is dedicated to the development of systems that can reason from premises to a conclusion, but such algorithms are only as good as what they know (Dreyfus, 1992). Natural language processing is a potential solution to the "knowledge bottleneck," by acquiring knowledge from texts, and perhaps also from conversations. This idea goes all the way back to Turing's 1949 paper "Computing Machinery and Intelligence", which proposed the **Turing test** for determining whether artificial intelligence had been achieved (Turing, 2009).

Conversely, reasoning is sometimes essential for basic tasks of language processing, such as resolving a pronoun. **Winograd schemas** are examples in which a single word changes the likely referent of a pronoun, in a way that seems to require knowledge and reasoning to decode (Levesque et al., 2011). For example,

(1.2) The trophy doesn't fit into the brown suitcase because it is too [small/large].

When the final word is *small*, then the pronoun *it* refers to the suitcase; when the final word is *large*, then *it* refers to the trophy. Solving this example requires spatial reasoning; other schemas require reasoning about actions and their effects, emotions and intentions, and social conventions.

Such examples demonstrate that natural language understanding cannot be achieved in isolation from knowledge and reasoning. Yet the history of artificial intelligence has been one of increasing specialization: with the growing volume of research in subdisciplines such as natural language processing, machine learning, and computer vision, it is difficult for anyone to maintain expertise across the entire field. Still, recent work has demonstrated interesting connections between natural language processing and other areas of AI, including computer vision (e.g., Antol et al., 2015) and game playing (e.g., Branavan et al., 2009a). The dominance of machine learning throughout artificial intelligence has led to a broad consensus on representations such as graphical models and computation graphs, and on algorithms such as backpropagation and combinatorial optimization. Many of the algorithms and representations covered in this text are part of this consensus.

3. This view is shared by some, but not all, prominent researchers in artificial intelligence. Michael Jordan, a specialist in machine learning, has said that if he had a billion dollars to spend on any large research project, he would spend it on natural language processing (https://www.reddit.com/r/MachineLearning/comments/2fxi6v/ama_michael_i_jordan/). On the other hand, in a public discussion about the future of artificial intelligence in February 2018, computer vision researcher Yann Lecun argued that despite its many practical applications, language is perhaps "number 300" in the priority list for artificial intelligence research, and that it would be a great achievement if artificial intelligence could attain the capabilities of an orangutan, which do not include language (http://www.abigailsee.com/2018/02/21/deep-learning-structure-and-innate-priors.html).

Computer science

The discrete and recursive nature of natural language invites the application of theoretical ideas from computer science. Linguists such as Chomsky and Montague have shown how formal language theory can help to explain the syntax and semantics of natural language. Theoretical models such as finite-state and pushdown automata are the basis for many practical natural language processing systems. Algorithms for searching the combinatorial space of analyses of natural language utterances can be analyzed in terms of their computational complexity, and theoretically motivated approximations can sometimes be applied.

The study of computer systems is also relevant to natural language processing. Large datasets of unlabeled text can be processed more quickly by parallelization techniques like MapReduce (Dean and Ghemawat, 2008; Lin and Dyer, 2010); high-volume data sources such as social media can be summarized efficiently by approximate streaming and sketching techniques (Goyal et al., 2009). When deep neural networks are implemented in production systems, it is possible to eke out speed gains using techniques such as reduced-precision arithmetic (Wu et al., 2016). Many classical natural language processing algorithms are not naturally suited to graphics processing unit (GPU) parallelization, suggesting directions for further research at the intersection of natural language processing and computing hardware (Yi et al., 2011).

Speech processing

Natural language is often communicated in spoken form, and speech recognition is the task of converting an audio signal to text. From one perspective, this is a signal processing problem, which might be viewed as a preprocessing step before natural language processing can be applied. However, context plays a critical role in speech recognition by human listeners: knowledge of the surrounding words influences perception and helps to correct for noise (Miller et al., 1951). For this reason, speech recognition is often integrated with text analysis, particularly with statistical **language models**, which quantify the probability of a sequence of text (see chapter 6). Beyond speech recognition, the broader field of speech processing includes the study of speech-based dialogue systems, which are briefly discussed in chapter 19. Historically, speech processing has often been pursued in electrical engineering departments, while natural language processing has been the purview of computer scientists. For this reason, the extent of interaction between these two disciplines is less than it might otherwise be.

Ethics

As machine learning and artificial intelligence become increasingly ubiquitous, it is crucial to understand how their benefits, costs, and risks are distributed across different kinds of people. Natural language processing raises some particularly salient issues around ethics, fairness, and accountability:

Access Who is natural language processing designed to serve? For example, whose language is translated *from*, and whose language is translated *to*?

Bias Does language technology learn to replicate social biases from text corpora, and does it reinforce these biases as seemingly objective computational conclusions?

Labor Whose text and speech comprise the datasets that power natural language processing, and who performs the annotations? Are the benefits of this technology shared with all the people whose work makes it possible?

Privacy and internet freedom What is the impact of large-scale text processing on the right to free and private communication? What is the potential role of natural language processing in regimes of censorship or surveillance?

This text lightly touches on issues related to fairness and bias in § 14.6.3 and § 18.1.1, but these issues are worthy of a book of their own. For more from within the field of computational linguistics, see the papers from the annual workshop on Ethics in Natural Language Processing (Hovy et al., 2017; Alfano et al., 2018). For an outside perspective on ethical issues relating to data science at large, see boyd and Crawford (2012).

Others

Natural language processing plays a significant role in emerging interdisciplinary fields like **computational social science** and the **digital humanities**. Text classification (chapter 4), clustering (chapter 5), and information extraction (chapter 17) are particularly useful tools; another is **probabilistic topic models** (Blei, 2012), which are not covered in this text. **Information retrieval** (Manning et al., 2009) makes use of similar tools, and conversely, techniques such as latent semantic analysis (§ 14.3) have roots in information retrieval. **Text mining** is sometimes used to refer to the application of data mining techniques, especially classification and clustering, to text. While there is no clear distinction between text mining and natural language processing (nor between data mining and machine learning), text mining is typically less concerned with linguistic structure, and more interested in fast, scalable algorithms.

1.2 Three Themes in Natural Language Processing

Natural language processing covers a diverse range of tasks, methods, and linguistic phenomena. But despite the apparent incommensurability between, say, the summarization of scientific articles (§ 16.3.4) and the identification of suffix patterns in Spanish verbs (§ 9.1.4), some general themes emerge. The remainder of the introduction focuses on these themes, which will recur in various forms through the text. Each theme can be expressed as an opposition between two extreme viewpoints on how to process natural language. The methods discussed in the text can usually be placed somewhere on the continuum between these two extremes.

1.2.1 Learning and Knowledge

A recurring topic of debate is the relative importance of machine learning and linguistic knowledge. On one extreme, advocates of "natural language processing from scratch" (Collobert et al., 2011b) propose to use machine learning to train end-to-end systems that transmute raw text into any desired output structure: such as a summary, database, or translation. On the other extreme, the core work of natural language processing is sometimes taken to be transforming text into a stack of general-purpose linguistic structures: from subword units called **morphemes**, to word-level **parts-of-speech**, to tree-structured representations of grammar, and beyond, to logic-based representations of meaning. In theory, these general-purpose structures should then be able to support any desired application.

The end-to-end approach has been buoyed by recent results in computer vision and speech recognition, in which advances in machine learning have swept away expert-engineered representations based on the fundamentals of optics and phonology (Krizhevsky et al., 2012; Graves and Jaitly, 2014). But while machine learning is an element of nearly every contemporary approach to natural language processing, linguistic representations such as syntax trees have not yet gone the way of the visual edge detector or the auditory triphone. Linguists have argued for the existence of a "language faculty" in all human beings, which encodes a set of abstractions specially designed to facilitate the understanding and production of language. The argument for the existence of such a language faculty is based on the observation that children learn language faster and from fewer examples than would be possible if language was learned from experience alone.[4] From a practical standpoint, linguistic structure seems to be particularly important in scenarios where training data is limited.

There are a number of ways in which knowledge and learning can be combined in natural language processing. Many supervised learning systems make use of carefully engineered **features**, which transform the data into a representation that can facilitate learning. For example, in a task like search, it may be useful to identify each word's **stem**, so that a system can more easily generalize across related terms such as *whale*, *whales*, *whalers*, and *whaling*. (This issue is relatively benign in English, as compared to the many languages that include much more elaborate systems of prefixed and suffixes.) Such features could be obtained from a hand-crafted resource, like a dictionary that maps each word to a single root form. Alternatively, features can be obtained from the output of a general-purpose language processing system, such as a parser or part-of-speech tagger, which may itself be built on supervised machine learning.

Another synthesis of learning and knowledge is in model structure: building machine learning models whose architectures are inspired by linguistic theories. For example, the

4. *The Language Instinct* (Pinker, 2003) articulates these arguments in an engaging and popular style. For arguments against the innateness of language, see Elman et al. (1998).

organization of sentences is often described as **compositional**, with meaning of larger units gradually constructed from the meaning of their smaller constituents. This idea can be built into the architecture of a deep neural network, which is then trained using contemporary deep learning techniques (Dyer et al., 2016).

The debate about the relative importance of machine learning and linguistic knowledge sometimes becomes heated. No machine learning specialist likes to be told that their engineering methodology is unscientific alchemy;[5] nor does a linguist want to hear that the search for general linguistic principles and structures has been made irrelevant by big data. Yet there is clearly room for both types of research: we need to know how far we can go with end-to-end learning alone, while at the same time, we continue the search for linguistic representations that generalize across applications, scenarios, and languages. For more on the history of this debate, see Church (2011); for an optimistic view of the potential symbiosis between computational linguistics and deep learning, see Manning (2015).

1.2.2 Search and Learning

Many natural language processing problems can be written mathematically in the form of optimization,[6]

$$\hat{y} = \underset{y \in \mathcal{Y}(\boldsymbol{x})}{\operatorname{argmax}} \Psi(\boldsymbol{x}, y; \boldsymbol{\theta}), \qquad [1.1]$$

where,

- $\boldsymbol{x}$ is the input, which is an element of a set $\mathcal{X}$;
- y is the output, which is an element of a set $\mathcal{Y}(\boldsymbol{x})$;
- Ψ is a scoring function (also called the **model**), which maps from the set $\mathcal{X} \times \mathcal{Y}$ to the real numbers;
- $\boldsymbol{\theta}$ is a vector of parameters for Ψ; and
- $\hat{y}$ is the predicted output, which is chosen to maximize the scoring function.

This basic structure can be applied to a huge range of problems. For example, the input $\boldsymbol{x}$ might be a social media post, and the output y might be a labeling of the emotional sentiment expressed by the author (chapter 4); or $\boldsymbol{x}$ could be a sentence in French, and the output y could be a sentence in Tamil (chapter 18); or $\boldsymbol{x}$ might be a sentence in English, and y might be a representation of the syntactic structure of the sentence (chapter 10); or

5. Ali Rahimi argued that much of deep learning research was similar to "alchemy" in a presentation at the 2017 Conference on Neural Information Processing Systems. He was advocating for more learning theory, not more linguistics.

6. Throughout this text, equations will be numbered by square brackets, and linguistic examples will be numbered by parentheses.

$\boldsymbol{x}$ might be a news article and $\boldsymbol{y}$ might be a structured record of the events that the article describes (chapter 17).

This formulation reflects an implicit decision that language processing algorithms will have two distinct modules:

Search The search module is responsible for computing the argmax of the function Ψ. In other words, it finds the output $\hat{\boldsymbol{y}}$ that gets the best score with respect to the input $\boldsymbol{x}$. This is easy when the search space $\mathcal{Y}(\boldsymbol{x})$ is small enough to enumerate, or when the scoring function Ψ has a convenient decomposition into parts. In many cases, we will want to work with scoring functions that do not have these properties, motivating the use of more sophisticated search algorithms, such as bottom-up dynamic programming (§ 10.1) and beam search (§ 11.3.1). Because the outputs are usually discrete in language processing problems, search often relies on the machinery of **combinatorial optimization**.

Learning The learning module is responsible for finding the parameters $\boldsymbol{\theta}$. This is typically (but not always) done by processing a large dataset of labeled examples, $\{(\boldsymbol{x}^{(i)}, \boldsymbol{y}^{(i)})\}_{i=1}^{N}$. Like search, learning is also approached through the framework of optimization, as we will see in chapter 2. Because the parameters are usually continuous, learning algorithms generally rely on **numerical optimization** to identify vectors of real-valued parameters that optimize some function of the model and the labeled data. Some basic principles of numerical optimization are reviewed in appendix B.

The division of natural language processing into separate modules for search and learning makes it possible to reuse generic algorithms across many tasks and models. Much of the work of natural language processing can be focused on the design of the model Ψ—identifying and formalizing the linguistic phenomena that are relevant to the task at hand—while reaping the benefits of decades of progress in search, optimization, and learning. This textbook will describe several classes of scoring functions, and the corresponding algorithms for search and learning.

When a model is capable of making subtle linguistic distinctions, it is said to be *expressive*. Expressiveness is often traded off against efficiency of search and learning. For example, a word-to-word translation model makes search and learning easy, but it is not expressive enough to distinguish good translations from bad ones. Many of the most important problems in natural language processing seem to require expressive models, in which the complexity of search grows exponentially with the size of the input. In these models, exact search is usually impossible. Intractability threatens the neat modular decomposition between search and learning: if search requires a set of heuristic approximations, then it may be advantageous to learn a model that performs well under these specific heuristics. This has motivated some researchers to take a more integrated approach to search and learning, as briefly mentioned in chapters 11 and 15.

1.2.3 Relational, Compositional, and Distributional Perspectives

Any element of language—a word, a phrase, a sentence, or even a sound—can be described from at least three perspectives. Consider the word *journalist*. A *journalist* is a subcategory of a *profession*, and an *anchorwoman* is a subcategory of *journalist*; furthermore, a *journalist* performs *journalism*, which is often, but not always, a subcategory of *writing*. This relational perspective on meaning is the basis for semantic **ontologies** such as **WordNet** (Fellbaum, 2017), which enumerate the relations that hold between words and other elementary semantic units. The power of the relational perspective is illustrated by the following example:

(1.3) Umashanthi interviewed Ana. She works for the college newspaper.

Who works for the college newspaper? The word *journalist*, while not stated in the example, implicitly links the *interview* to the *newspaper*, making *Umashanthi* the most likely referent for the pronoun. (A general discussion of how to resolve pronouns is found in chapter 15.)

Yet despite the inferential power of the relational perspective, it is not easy to formalize computationally. Exactly which elements are to be related? Are *journalists* and *reporters* distinct, or should we group them into a single unit? Is the kind of *interview* performed by a journalist the same as the kind that one undergoes when applying for a job? Ontology designers face many such thorny questions, and the project of ontology design hearkens back to Borges's (1993) *Celestial Emporium of Benevolent Knowledge*, which divides animals into:

> (a) belonging to the emperor; (b) embalmed; (c) tame; (d) suckling pigs; (e) sirens; (f) fabulous; (g) stray dogs; (h) included in the present classification; (i) frenzied; (j) innumerable; (k) drawn with a very fine camelhair brush; (l) et cetera; (m) having just broken the water pitcher; (n) that from a long way off resemble flies.

Difficulties in ontology construction have led some linguists to argue that there is no task-independent way to partition up word meanings (Kilgarriff, 1997).

Some problems are easier. Each member in a group of *journalists* is a *journalist*: the *-s* suffix distinguishes the plural meaning from the singular in most of the nouns in English. Similarly, a *journalist* can be thought of, perhaps colloquially, as someone who produces or works on a *journal*. (Taking this approach even further, the word *journal* derives from the French *jour+nal*, or *day+ly* = *daily*.) In this way, the meaning of a word is constructed from the constituent parts—the principle of **compositionality**. This principle can be applied to larger units: phrases, sentences, and beyond. Indeed, one of the great strengths of the compositional view of meaning is that it provides a roadmap for understanding entire texts and dialogues through a single analytic lens, grounding out in the smallest parts of individual words.

But alongside *journalists* and *antiparliamentarians*, there are many words that seem to be linguistic atoms: think, for example, of *whale*, *blubber*, and *Nantucket*. Idiomatic phrases like *kick the bucket* and *shoot the breeze* have meanings that are quite different from the sum of their parts (Sag et al., 2002). Composition is of little help for such words and expressions, but their meanings can be ascertained—or at least approximated—from the contexts in which they appear. Take, for example, *blubber*, which appears in such contexts as:

(1.4) a. The blubber served them as fuel.
b. … extracting it from the blubber of the large fish …
c. Amongst oily substances, blubber has been employed as a manure.

These contexts form the **distributional properties** of the word *blubber*, and they link it to words that can appear in similar constructions: *fat*, *pelts*, and *barnacles*. This distributional perspective makes it possible to learn about meaning from unlabeled data alone; unlike relational and compositional semantics, no manual annotation or expert knowledge is required. Distributional semantics is thus capable of covering a huge range of linguistic phenomena. However, it lacks precision: *blubber* is similar to *fat* in one sense, to *pelts* in another sense, and to *barnacles* in still another. The question of *why* all these words tend to appear in the same contexts is left unanswered.

The relational, compositional, and distributional perspectives all contribute to our understanding of linguistic meaning, and all three appear to be critical to natural language processing. Yet they are uneasy collaborators, requiring seemingly incompatible representations and algorithmic approaches. This text presents some of the best known and most successful methods for working with each of these representations, but future research may reveal new ways to combine them.

I LEARNING

2 Linear Text Classification

We begin with the problem of **text classification**: given a text document, assign it a discrete label $y \in \mathcal{Y}$, where $\mathcal{Y}$ is the set of possible labels. Text classification has many applications, from spam filtering to the analysis of electronic health records. This chapter describes some of the most well-known and effective algorithms for text classification, from a mathematical perspective that should help you understand what they do and why they work. Text classification is also a building block in more elaborate natural language processing tasks. For readers without a background in machine learning or statistics, the material in this chapter will take more time to digest than most of the subsequent chapters. But this investment will pay off as the mathematical principles behind these basic classification algorithms reappear in other contexts throughout the book.

2.1 The Bag of Words

To perform text classification, the first question is how to represent each document, or instance. A common approach is to use a column vector of word counts: for example, $\boldsymbol{x} = [0, 1, 1, 0, 0, 2, 0, 1, 13, 0 \dots]^\top$, where x_j is the count of word j. The length of $\boldsymbol{x}$ is $V \triangleq |\mathcal{V}|$, where $\mathcal{V}$ is the set of possible words in the vocabulary. In linear classification, the classification decision is based on a weighted sum of individual feature counts, such as word counts.

The object $\boldsymbol{x}$ is a vector, but it is often called a **bag of words**, because it includes only information about the count of each word, and not the order in which the words appear. With the bag-of-words representation, we are ignoring grammar, sentence boundaries, paragraphs—everything but the words. Yet the bag-of-words model is surprisingly effective for text classification. If you see the word *whale* in a document, is it fiction or nonfiction? What if you see the word *molybdenum*? For many labeling problems, individual words can be strong predictors.

To predict a label from a bag of words, we can assign a score to each word in the vocabulary, measuring the compatibility with the label. For example, for the label FICTION, we might assign a positive score to the word *whale* and a negative score to the word *molybdenum*. These scores are called **weights**, and they are arranged in a column vector $\boldsymbol{\theta}$.

Suppose that you want a multiclass classifier, where $K \triangleq |\mathcal{Y}| > 2$. For example, you might want to classify news stories about sports, celebrities, music, and business. The goal is to predict a label $\hat{y}$, given the bag of words $\boldsymbol{x}$, using the weights $\boldsymbol{\theta}$. For each label $y \in \mathcal{Y}$, we compute a score $\Psi(\boldsymbol{x}, y)$, which is a scalar measure of the compatibility between the bag of words $\boldsymbol{x}$ and the label y. In a linear bag-of-words classifier, this score is the vector inner product between the weights $\boldsymbol{\theta}$ and the output of a **feature function** $\boldsymbol{f}(\boldsymbol{x}, y)$,

$$\Psi(\boldsymbol{x}, y) = \boldsymbol{\theta} \cdot \boldsymbol{f}(\boldsymbol{x}, y) = \sum_j \theta_j f_j(\boldsymbol{x}, y). \tag{2.1}$$

As the notation suggests, $\boldsymbol{f}$ is a function of two arguments, the word counts $\boldsymbol{x}$ and the label y, and it returns a vector output. For example, given arguments $\boldsymbol{x}$ and y, element j of this feature vector might be,

$$f_j(\boldsymbol{x}, y) = \begin{cases} x_{whale}, & \text{if } y = \textsc{Fiction} \\ 0, & \text{otherwise} \end{cases} \tag{2.2}$$

This function returns the count of the word *whale* if the label is FICTION, and it returns zero otherwise. The index j depends on the position of *whale* in the vocabulary and of FICTION in the set of possible labels. The corresponding weight θ_j then scores the compatibility of the word *whale* with the label FICTION.[1] A positive score means that this word makes the label more likely.

The output of the feature function can be formalized as a vector:

$$\boldsymbol{f}(\boldsymbol{x}, y=1) = [\boldsymbol{x}; \underbrace{0; 0; \ldots; 0}_{(K-1)\times V}] \tag{2.3}$$

$$\boldsymbol{f}(\boldsymbol{x}, y=2) = [\underbrace{0; 0; \ldots; 0}_{V}; \boldsymbol{x}; \underbrace{0; 0; \ldots; 0}_{(K-2)\times V}] \tag{2.4}$$

$$\boldsymbol{f}(\boldsymbol{x}, y=K) = [\underbrace{0; 0; \ldots; 0}_{(K-1)\times V}; \boldsymbol{x}], \tag{2.5}$$

where $[\underbrace{0; 0; \ldots; 0}_{(K-1)\times V}]$ is a column vector of $(K-1) \times V$ zeros, and the semicolon indicates vertical concatenation. For each of the K possible labels, the feature function returns a vector that is mostly zeros, with a column vector of word counts $\boldsymbol{x}$ inserted in a location

1. In practice, both $\boldsymbol{f}$ and $\boldsymbol{\theta}$ may be implemented as dictionaries rather than vectors, so that it is not necessary to explicitly identify j. In such an implementation, the tuple (*whale*, FICTION) acts as a key in both dictionaries; the values in $\boldsymbol{f}$ are feature counts, and the values in $\boldsymbol{\theta}$ are weights.

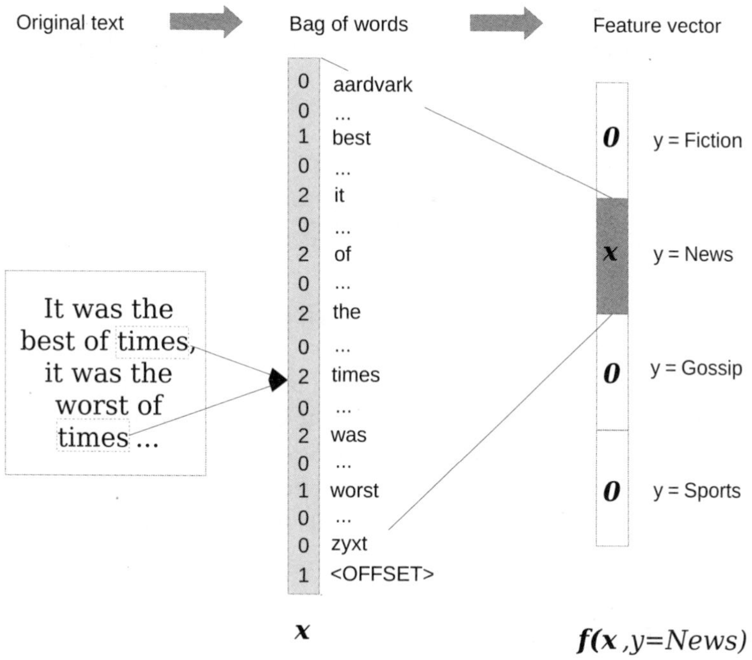

Figure 2.1
The bag-of-words and feature vector representations, for a hypothetical text classification task.

that depends on the specific label y. This arrangement is shown in figure 2.1. The notation may seem awkward at first, but it generalizes to an impressive range of learning settings, particularly **structure prediction**, which is the focus of chapters 7 to 11.

Given a vector of weights, $\boldsymbol{\theta} \in \mathbb{R}^{VK}$, we can now compute the score $\Psi(\boldsymbol{x}, y)$ by equation 2.1. This inner product gives a scalar measure of the compatibility of the observation $\boldsymbol{x}$ with label y.[2] For any document $\boldsymbol{x}$, we predict the label $\hat{y}$,

$$\hat{y} = \underset{y \in \mathcal{Y}}{\operatorname{argmax}} \Psi(\boldsymbol{x}, y) \quad [2.6]$$

$$\Psi(\boldsymbol{x}, y) = \boldsymbol{\theta} \cdot \boldsymbol{f}(\boldsymbol{x}, y). \quad [2.7]$$

This inner product notation gives a clean separation between the *data* ($\boldsymbol{x}$ and y) and the *parameters* ($\boldsymbol{\theta}$).

2. Only $V \times (K-1)$ features and weights are necessary. By stipulating that $\Psi(\boldsymbol{x}, y = K) = 0$ regardless of $\boldsymbol{x}$, it is possible to implement any classification rule that can be achieved with $V \times K$ features and weights. This is the approach taken in binary classification rules like $y = \text{Sign}(\boldsymbol{\beta} \cdot \boldsymbol{x} + a)$, where $\boldsymbol{\beta}$ is a vector of weights, a is an offset, and the label set is $\mathcal{Y} = \{-1, 1\}$. However, for multiclass classification, it is more concise to write $\boldsymbol{\theta} \cdot \boldsymbol{f}(\boldsymbol{x}, y)$ for all $y \in \mathcal{Y}$.

While vector notation is used for presentation and analysis, in code the weights and feature vector can be implemented as dictionaries. The inner product can then be computed as a loop. In Python:

```
def compute_score(x,y,weights):
    total = 0
    for feature,count in feature_function(x,y).items():
        total += weights[feature] * count
    return total
```

This representation is advantageous because it avoids storing and iterating over the many features whose counts are zero.

It is common to add an **offset feature** at the end of the vector of word counts $\boldsymbol{x}$, which is always 1. We then have to also add an extra zero to each of the zero vectors, to make the vector lengths match. This gives the entire feature vector $\boldsymbol{f}(\boldsymbol{x}, y)$ a length of $(V+1) \times K$. The weight associated with this offset feature can be thought of as a bias for or against each label. For example, if we expect most emails to be spam, then the weight for the offset feature for $y = \text{SPAM}$ should be larger than the weight for the offset feature for $y = \text{NOT-SPAM}$.

Returning to the weights $\boldsymbol{\theta}$, where do they come from? One possibility is to set them by hand. If we wanted to distinguish, say, English from Spanish, we can use English and Spanish dictionaries and set the weight to one for each word that appears in the associated dictionary. For example,[3]

$$
\begin{aligned}
\theta_{(E,bicycle)} &= 1 & \theta_{(S,bicycle)} &= 0 \\
\theta_{(E,bicicleta)} &= 0 & \theta_{(S,bicicleta)} &= 1 \\
\theta_{(E,con)} &= 1 & \theta_{(S,con)} &= 1 \\
\theta_{(E,ordinateur)} &= 0 & \theta_{(S,ordinateur)} &= 0.
\end{aligned}
$$

Similarly, if we want to distinguish positive and negative sentiment, we could use positive and negative **sentiment lexicons** (see § 4.1.2), which are defined by social psychologists (Tausczik and Pennebaker, 2010).

But it is usually not easy to set classification weights by hand, due to the large number of words and the difficulty of selecting exact numerical weights. Instead, we will learn the weights from data. Email users manually label messages as SPAM; newspapers label their own articles as BUSINESS or STYLE. Using such **instance labels**, we can automatically acquire weights using **supervised machine learning**. This chapter will discuss several machine learning approaches for classification. The first is based on probability. For a review of probability, consult appendix A.

3. In this notation, each tuple (language, word) indexes an element in $\boldsymbol{\theta}$, which remains a vector.

2.2 Naïve Bayes

The **joint probability** of a bag of words $\boldsymbol{x}$ and its true label y is written $p(\boldsymbol{x}, y)$. Suppose we have a dataset of N labeled instances, $\{(\boldsymbol{x}^{(i)}, y^{(i)})\}_{i=1}^{N}$, which we assume are **independent and identically distributed** (see § A.3). Then the joint probability of the entire dataset, written $p(\boldsymbol{x}^{(1:N)}, y^{(1:N)})$, is equal to $\prod_{i=1}^{N} p_{X,Y}(\boldsymbol{x}^{(i)}, y^{(i)})$.[4]

What does this have to do with classification? One approach to classification is to set the weights $\boldsymbol{\theta}$ so as to maximize the joint probability of a **training set** of labeled documents. This is known as **maximum likelihood estimation**:

$$\hat{\boldsymbol{\theta}} = \underset{\boldsymbol{\theta}}{\operatorname{argmax}}\, p(\boldsymbol{x}^{(1:N)}, y^{(1:N)}; \boldsymbol{\theta}) \tag{2.8}$$

$$= \underset{\boldsymbol{\theta}}{\operatorname{argmax}} \prod_{i=1}^{N} p(\boldsymbol{x}^{(i)}, y^{(i)}; \boldsymbol{\theta}) \tag{2.9}$$

$$= \underset{\boldsymbol{\theta}}{\operatorname{argmax}} \sum_{i=1}^{N} \log p(\boldsymbol{x}^{(i)}, y^{(i)}; \boldsymbol{\theta}). \tag{2.10}$$

The notation $p(\boldsymbol{x}^{(i)}, y^{(i)}; \boldsymbol{\theta})$ indicates that $\boldsymbol{\theta}$ is a *parameter* of the probability function. The product of probabilities can be replaced by a sum of log-probabilities because the log function is monotonically increasing over positive arguments, and so the same $\boldsymbol{\theta}$ will maximize both the probability and its logarithm. Working with logarithms is desirable because of numerical stability: on a large dataset, multiplying many probabilities can **underflow** to zero.[5]

The probability $p(\boldsymbol{x}^{(i)}, y^{(i)}; \boldsymbol{\theta})$ is defined through a **generative model**—an idealized random process that has generated the observed data.[6] Algorithm 1 describes the generative model underlying the **Naïve Bayes** classifier, with parameters $\boldsymbol{\theta} = \{\boldsymbol{\mu}, \boldsymbol{\phi}\}$.

- The first line of this generative model encodes the assumption that the instances are mutually independent: neither the label nor the text of document i affects the label or text of document j.[7] Furthermore, the instances are identically distributed: the distributions over

4. The notation $p_{X,Y}(\boldsymbol{x}^{(i)}, y^{(i)})$ indicates the joint probability that random variables X and Y take the specific values $\boldsymbol{x}^{(i)}$ and $y^{(i)}$ respectively. The subscript will often be omitted when it is clear from context. For a review of random variables, see appendix A.

5. Throughout this text, you may assume all logarithms and exponents are base 2, unless otherwise indicated. Any reasonable base will yield an identical classifier, and base 2 is most convenient for working out examples by hand.

6. Generative models will be used throughout this text. They explicitly define the assumptions underlying the form of a probability distribution over observed and latent variables. For a readable introduction to generative models in statistics, see Blei (2014).

7. Can you think of any cases in which this assumption is too strong?

Algorithm 1
Generative process for the Naïve Bayes classification model.

---

for instance $i \in \{1, 2, \ldots, N\}$ **do**:
    Draw the label $y^{(i)} \sim \text{Categorical}(\boldsymbol{\mu})$;
    Draw the word counts $\boldsymbol{x}^{(i)} \mid y^{(i)} \sim \text{Multinomial}(\boldsymbol{\phi}_{y^{(i)}})$.

---

the label $y^{(i)}$ and the text $\boldsymbol{x}^{(i)}$ (conditioned on $y^{(i)}$) are the same for all instances i. In other words, we make the assumption that every document has the same distribution over labels and that each document's distribution over words depends only on the label, and not on anything else about the document. We also assume that the documents don't affect each other: if the word *whale* appears in document $i = 7$, that does not make it any more or less likely that it will appear again in document $i = 8$.

- The second line of the generative model states that the random variable $y^{(i)}$ is drawn from a categorical distribution with parameter $\boldsymbol{\mu}$. Categorical distributions are like weighted dice: the column vector $\boldsymbol{\mu} = [\mu_1; \mu_2; \ldots; \mu_K]$ gives the probabilities of each label, so that the probability of drawing label y is equal to μ_y. For example, if $\mathcal{Y} = \{\text{POSITIVE}, \text{NEGATIVE}, \text{NEUTRAL}\}$, we might have $\boldsymbol{\mu} = [0.1; 0.7; 0.2]$. We require $\sum_{y \in \mathcal{Y}} \mu_y = 1$ and $\mu_y \geq 0, \forall y \in \mathcal{Y}$: each label's probability is nonnegative, and the sum of these probabilities is equal to one. [8]
- The third line describes how the bag-of-words counts $\boldsymbol{x}^{(i)}$ are generated. By writing $\boldsymbol{x}^{(i)} \mid y^{(i)}$, this line indicates that the word counts are conditioned on the label, so that the joint probability is factored using the chain rule,

$$\text{p}_{X,Y}(\boldsymbol{x}^{(i)}, y^{(i)}) = \text{p}_{X|Y}(\boldsymbol{x}^{(i)} \mid y^{(i)}) \times \text{p}_Y(y^{(i)}). \quad [2.11]$$

The specific distribution $\text{p}_{X|Y}$ is the **multinomial**, which is a probability distribution over vectors of nonnegative counts. The probability mass function for this distribution is:

$$\text{p}_{\text{mult}}(\boldsymbol{x}; \boldsymbol{\phi}) = B(\boldsymbol{x}) \prod_{j=1}^{V} \phi_j^{x_j} \quad [2.12]$$

$$B(\boldsymbol{x}) = \frac{\left(\sum_{j=1}^{V} x_j\right)!}{\prod_{j=1}^{V} (x_j!)}. \quad [2.13]$$

8. Formally, we require $\boldsymbol{\mu} \in \Delta^{K-1}$, where Δ^{K-1} is the $K-1$ **probability simplex**, the set of all vectors of K nonnegative numbers that sum to one. Because of the sum-to-one constraint, there are $K-1$ degrees of freedom for a vector of size K.

As in the categorical distribution, the parameter ϕ_j can be interpreted as a probability: specifically, the probability that any given token in the document is the word j. The multinomial distribution involves a product over words, with each term in the product equal to the probability ϕ_j, exponentiated by the count x_j. Words that have zero count play no role in this product, because $\phi_j^0 = 1$. The term $B(\boldsymbol{x})$ is called the **multinomial coefficient**. It doesn't depend on $\boldsymbol{\phi}$ and can usually be ignored. Can you see why we need this term at all?[9]

The notation $\text{p}(\boldsymbol{x} \mid y; \boldsymbol{\phi})$ indicates the conditional probability of word counts $\boldsymbol{x}$ given label y, with parameter $\boldsymbol{\phi}$, which is equal to $\text{p}_{\text{mult}}(\boldsymbol{x}; \boldsymbol{\phi}_y)$. By specifying the multinomial distribution, we describe the **multinomial Naïve Bayes** classifier. Why "naïve"? Because the multinomial distribution treats each word token independently, conditioned on the class: the probability mass function factorizes across the counts.[10]

2.2.1 Types and Tokens

A slight modification to the generative model of Naïve Bayes is shown in algorithm 2. Instead of generating a vector of counts of **types**, $\boldsymbol{x}$, this model generates a *sequence* of **tokens**, $\boldsymbol{w} = (w_1, w_2, \ldots, w_M)$. The distinction between types and tokens is critical: $x_j \in \{0, 1, 2, \ldots, M\}$ is the count of word type j in the vocabulary (e.g., the number of times the word *cannibal* appears); $w_m \in \mathcal{V}$ is the identity of token m in the document (e.g., $w_m =$ *cannibal*).

The probability of the sequence $\boldsymbol{w}$ is a product of categorical probabilities. Algorithm 2 makes a conditional independence assumption: each token $w_m^{(i)}$ is independent of all other tokens $w_{n \neq m}^{(i)}$, conditioned on the label $y^{(i)}$. This is identical to the "naïve" independence assumption implied by the multinomial distribution, and as a result, the optimal parameters for this model are identical to those in multinomial Naïve Bayes. For any instance, the probability assigned by this model is proportional to the probability under multinomial Naïve Bayes. The constant of proportionality is the multinomial coefficient $B(\boldsymbol{x})$. Because $B(\boldsymbol{x}) \geq 1$, the probability for a vector of counts $\boldsymbol{x}$ is at least as large as the probability for a list of words $\boldsymbol{w}$ that induces the same counts: there can be many word sequences that correspond to a single vector of counts. For example, *man bites dog* and *dog bites man* correspond to an identical count vector, $\{\textit{bites}: 1, \textit{dog}: 1, \textit{man}: 1\}$, and $B(\boldsymbol{x})$ is equal to the total number of possible word orderings for count vector $\boldsymbol{x}$.

Sometimes it is useful to think of instances as counts of types, $\boldsymbol{x}$; other times, it is better to think of them as sequences of tokens, $\boldsymbol{w}$. If the tokens are generated from a model

9. Technically, a multinomial distribution requires a second parameter, the total number of word counts in $\boldsymbol{x}$. In the bag-of-words representation, x is equal to the number of words in the document. However, this parameter is irrelevant for classification.

10. You can plug in any probability distribution to the generative story and it will still be Naïve Bayes, as long as you are making the "naïve" assumption that the features are conditionally independent, given the label. For example, a multivariate Gaussian with diagonal covariance is naïve in exactly the same sense.

Algorithm 2
Alternative generative process for the Naïve Bayes classification model.

---

for instance $i \in \{1, 2, \ldots, N\}$ **do**:
  Draw the label $y^{(i)} \sim \text{Categorical}(\boldsymbol{\mu})$;
  for token $m \in \{1, 2, \ldots, M_i\}$ **do**:
    Draw the token $w_m^{(i)} \mid y^{(i)} \sim \text{Categorical}(\boldsymbol{\phi}_{y^{(i)}})$.

---

that assumes conditional independence, then these two views lead to probability models that are identical, except for a scaling factor that does not depend on the label or the parameters.

2.2.2 Prediction

The Naïve Bayes prediction rule is to choose the label y that maximizes $\log \mathrm{p}(\boldsymbol{x}, y; \boldsymbol{\mu}, \boldsymbol{\phi})$:

$$\hat{y} = \underset{y}{\operatorname{argmax}} \log \mathrm{p}(\boldsymbol{x}, y; \boldsymbol{\mu}, \boldsymbol{\phi}) \tag{2.14}$$

$$= \underset{y}{\operatorname{argmax}} \log \mathrm{p}(\boldsymbol{x} \mid y; \boldsymbol{\phi}) + \log \mathrm{p}(y; \boldsymbol{\mu}) \tag{2.15}$$

Now we can plug in the probability distributions from the generative story.

$$\log \mathrm{p}(\boldsymbol{x} \mid y; \boldsymbol{\phi}) + \log \mathrm{p}(y; \boldsymbol{\mu}) = \log \left[B(\boldsymbol{x}) \prod_{j=1}^{V} \phi_{y,j}^{x_j} \right] + \log \mu_y \tag{2.16}$$

$$= \log B(\boldsymbol{x}) + \sum_{j=1}^{V} x_j \log \phi_{y,j} + \log \mu_y \tag{2.17}$$

$$= \log B(\boldsymbol{x}) + \boldsymbol{\theta} \cdot \boldsymbol{f}(\boldsymbol{x}, y), \tag{2.18}$$

where

$$\boldsymbol{\theta} = [\boldsymbol{\theta}^{(1)}; \boldsymbol{\theta}^{(2)}; \ldots; \boldsymbol{\theta}^{(K)}] \tag{2.19}$$

$$\boldsymbol{\theta}^{(y)} = [\log \phi_{y,1}; \log \phi_{y,2}; \ldots; \log \phi_{y,V}; \log \mu_y]. \tag{2.20}$$

The feature function $\boldsymbol{f}(\boldsymbol{x}, y)$ is a vector of V word counts and an offset, padded by zeros for the labels not equal to y (see equations 2.3–2.5 and figure 2.1). This construction ensures that the inner product $\boldsymbol{\theta} \cdot \boldsymbol{f}(\boldsymbol{x}, y)$ only activates the features whose weights are in $\boldsymbol{\theta}^{(y)}$. These features and weights are all we need to compute the joint log-probability $\log \mathrm{p}(\boldsymbol{x}, y)$ for each y. This is a key point: through this notation, we have converted the problem of computing the log-likelihood for a document-label pair $(\boldsymbol{x}, y)$ into the computation of a vector inner product.

2.2.3 Estimation

The parameters of the categorical and multinomial distributions have a simple interpretation: they are vectors of expected frequencies for each possible event. Based on this interpretation, it is tempting to set the parameters empirically,

$$\phi_{y,j} = \frac{\text{count}(y,j)}{\sum_{j'=1}^{V} \text{count}(y,j')} = \frac{\sum_{i:y^{(i)}=y} x_j^{(i)}}{\sum_{j'=1}^{V} \sum_{i:y^{(i)}=y} x_{j'}^{(i)}}, \qquad [2.21]$$

where count(y,j) refers to the count of word j in documents with label y.

Equation 2.21 defines the **relative frequency estimate** for $\boldsymbol{\phi}$. It can be justified as a **maximum likelihood estimate**: the estimate that maximizes the probability $\text{p}(\boldsymbol{x}^{(1:N)}, y^{(1:N)}; \boldsymbol{\theta})$. Based on the generative model in algorithm 1, the log-likelihood is,

$$\mathcal{L}(\boldsymbol{\phi}, \boldsymbol{\mu}) = \sum_{i=1}^{N} \log \text{p}_{\text{mult}}(\boldsymbol{x}^{(i)}; \boldsymbol{\phi}_{y^{(i)}}) + \log \text{p}_{\text{cat}}(y^{(i)}; \boldsymbol{\mu}), \qquad [2.22]$$

which is now written as a function $\mathcal{L}$ of the parameters $\boldsymbol{\phi}$ and $\boldsymbol{\mu}$. Let's continue to focus on the parameters $\boldsymbol{\phi}$. Because p(y) is constant with respect to $\boldsymbol{\phi}$, we can drop it:

$$\mathcal{L}(\boldsymbol{\phi}) = \sum_{i=1}^{N} \log \text{p}_{\text{mult}}(\boldsymbol{x}^{(i)}; \boldsymbol{\phi}_{y^{(i)}}) = \sum_{i=1}^{N} \log B(\boldsymbol{x}^{(i)}) + \sum_{j=1}^{V} x_j^{(i)} \log \phi_{y^{(i)},j}, \qquad [2.23]$$

where $B(\boldsymbol{x}^{(i)})$ is constant with respect to $\boldsymbol{\phi}$.

Maximum likelihood estimation chooses $\boldsymbol{\phi}$ to maximize the log-likelihood $\mathcal{L}$. However, the solution must obey the following constraints:

$$\sum_{j=1}^{V} \phi_{y,j} = 1 \quad \forall y. \qquad [2.24]$$

These constraints can be incorporated by adding a set of Lagrange multipliers to the objective (see appendix B for more details). To solve for each $\boldsymbol{\theta}_y$, we maximize the Lagrangian,

$$\ell(\boldsymbol{\phi}_y) = \sum_{i:y^{(i)}=y} \sum_{j=1}^{V} x_j^{(i)} \log \phi_{y,j} - \lambda(\sum_{j=1}^{V} \phi_{y,j} - 1). \qquad [2.25]$$

Differentiating with respect to the parameter $\phi_{y,j}$ yields

$$\frac{\partial \ell(\boldsymbol{\phi}_y)}{\partial \phi_{y,j}} = \sum_{i:y^{(i)}=y} x_j^{(i)} / \phi_{y,j} - \lambda. \qquad [2.26]$$

The solution is obtained by setting each element in this vector of derivatives equal to zero:

$$\lambda \phi_{y,j} = \sum_{i:y^{(i)}=y} x_j^{(i)}$$ [2.27]

$$\phi_{y,j} \propto \sum_{i:y^{(i)}=y} x_j^{(i)} = \sum_{i=1}^{N} \delta\left(y^{(i)}=y\right) x_j^{(i)} = \text{count}(y,j),$$ [2.28]

where $\delta\left(y^{(i)}=y\right)$ is a **delta function**, also sometimes called an indicator function, which returns one if $y^{(i)}=y$. The symbol $\propto$ indicates that $\phi_{y,j}$ is **proportional to** the right-hand side of the equation.

Equation 2.28 shows three different notations for the same thing: a sum over the word counts for all documents i such that the label $y^{(i)}=y$. This gives a solution for each $\boldsymbol{\phi}_y$ up to a constant of proportionality. Now recall the constraint $\sum_{j=1}^{V} \boldsymbol{\phi}_{y,j}=1$, which arises because $\boldsymbol{\phi}_y$ represents a vector of probabilities for each word in the vocabulary. This constraint leads to an exact solution, which does not depend on λ:

$$\phi_{y,j} = \frac{\text{count}(y,j)}{\sum_{j'=1}^{V} \text{count}(y,j')}.$$ [2.29]

This is equal to the relative frequency estimator from equation 2.21. A similar derivation gives $\mu_y \propto \sum_{i=1}^{N} \delta\left(y^{(i)}=y\right)$.

2.2.4 Smoothing

With text data, there are likely to be pairs of labels and words that never appear in the training set, leaving $\phi_{y,j}=0$. For example, the word *molybdenum* may have never yet appeared in a work of fiction. But choosing a value of $\phi_{\text{FICTION},molybdenum}=0$ would allow this single feature to completely veto a label, because $\text{p}(\text{FICTION} \mid \boldsymbol{x})=0$ if $\boldsymbol{x}_{molybdenum}>0$.

This is undesirable, because it imposes high **variance**: depending on what data happens to be in the training set, we could get vastly different classification rules. One solution is to **smooth** the probabilities, by adding a "pseudocount" of α to each count, and then normalizing:

$$\phi_{y,j} = \frac{\alpha + \text{count}(y,j)}{V\alpha + \sum_{j'=1}^{V} \text{count}(y,j')}.$$ [2.30]

This is called **Laplace smoothing.**[11] The pseudocount α is a **hyperparameter**, because it controls the form of the log-likelihood function, which in turn drives the estimation of $\boldsymbol{\phi}$.

11. Laplace smoothing has a Bayesian justification, in which the generative model is extended to include $\boldsymbol{\phi}$ as a random variable. The resulting distribution over $\boldsymbol{\phi}$ depends on both the data ($\boldsymbol{x}$ and y) and the **prior probability** $\text{p}(\boldsymbol{\phi};\alpha)$. The corresponding estimate of $\boldsymbol{\phi}$ is called **maximum a posteriori**, or MAP. This is in contrast with maximum likelihood, which depends only on the data.

Smoothing reduces variance, but moves us away from the maximum likelihood estimate: it imposes a **bias**. In this case, the bias points toward uniform probabilities. Machine learning theory shows that errors on heldout data can be attributed to the sum of bias and variance (Mohri et al., 2012). In general, techniques for reducing variance often increase the bias, leading to a **bias-variance tradeoff**.

- Unbiased classifiers may **overfit** the training data, yielding poor performance on unseen data.
- But if the smoothing is too large, the resulting classifier can **underfit** instead. In the limit of $\alpha \to \infty$, there is zero variance: you get the same classifier, regardless of the data. However, the bias is likely to be large.

Similar issues arise throughout machine learning. Later in this chapter we will encounter **regularization**, which controls the bias-variance tradeoff for logistic regression and large-margin classifiers (§ 2.5.1); § 3.3.2 describes techniques for controlling variance in deep learning; chapter 6 describes more elaborate methods for smoothing empirical probabilities.

2.2.5 Setting Hyperparameters

Returning to Naïve Bayes, how should we choose the best value of hyperparameters like α? Maximum likelihood will not work: the maximum likelihood estimate of α on the training set will always be $\alpha = 0$. In many cases, what we really want is **accuracy**: the number of correct predictions, divided by the total number of predictions. (Other measures of classification performance are discussed in § 4.4.) As we will see, it is hard to optimize for accuracy directly. But for scalar hyperparameters like α, tuning can be performed by a simple heuristic called **grid search**: try a set of values (e.g., $\alpha \in \{0.001, 0.01, 0.1, 1, 10\}$), compute the accuracy for each value, and choose the setting that maximizes the accuracy.

The goal is to tune α so that the classifier performs well on *unseen* data. For this reason, the data used for hyperparameter tuning should not overlap the training set, where very small values of α will be preferred. Instead, we hold out a **development set** (also called a **tuning set**) for hyperparameter selection. This development set may consist of a small fraction of the labeled data, such as 10%.

We also want to predict the performance of our classifier on unseen data. To do this, we must hold out a separate subset of data, called the **test set**. It is critical that the test set not overlap with either the training or development sets, or else we will overestimate the performance that the classifier will achieve on unlabeled data in the future. The test set should also not be used when making modeling decisions, such as the form of the feature function, the size of the vocabulary, and so on (these decisions are reviewed in chapter 4.) The ideal practice is to use the test set only once—otherwise, the test set is used to guide the classifier design, and test set accuracy will diverge from accuracy on truly unseen data. Because annotated data is expensive, this ideal can be hard to follow in practice, and many test sets have been used for decades. But in some high-impact applications like machine translation and information extraction, new test sets are released every year.

When only a small amount of labeled data is available, the test set accuracy can be unreliable. K-fold **cross-validation** is one way to cope with this scenario: the labeled data is divided into K folds, and each fold acts as the test set, while training on the other folds. The test set accuracies are then aggregated. In the extreme, each fold is a single data point; this is called **leave-one-out cross-validation**. To perform hyperparameter tuning in the context of cross-validation, another fold can be used for grid search. It is important not to repeatedly evaluate the cross-validated accuracy while making design decisions about the classifier, or you will overstate the accuracy on truly unseen data.

2.3 Discriminative Learning

Naïve Bayes is easy to work with: the weights can be estimated in closed form, and the probabilistic interpretation makes it relatively easy to extend. However, the assumption that features are independent can seriously limit its accuracy. Thus far, we have defined the feature function $\boldsymbol{f}(\boldsymbol{x}, y)$ so that it corresponds to bag-of-words features: one feature per word in the vocabulary. In natural language, bag-of-words features violate the assumption of conditional independence—for example, the probability that a document will contain the word *naïve* is surely higher given that it also contains the word *Bayes*—but this violation is relatively mild.

However, good performance on text classification often requires features that are richer than the bag of words:

- To better handle out-of-vocabulary terms, we want features that apply to multiple words, such as prefixes and suffixes (e.g., *anti-*, *un-*, *-ing*) and capitalization.
- We also want n-**gram** features that apply to multiword units: **bigrams** (e.g., *not good*, *not bad*), **trigrams** (e.g., *not so bad*, *lacking any decency*, *never before imagined*), and beyond.

These features flagrantly violate the Naïve Bayes independence assumption. Consider what happens if we add a prefix feature. Under the Naïve Bayes assumption, the joint probability of a word and its prefix are computed with the following approximation:[12]

$$\Pr(\text{word} = \textit{unfit}, \text{prefix} = \textit{un-} \mid y) \approx \Pr(\text{prefix} = \textit{un-} \mid y) \times \Pr(\text{word} = \textit{unfit} \mid y).$$

To test the quality of the approximation, we can manipulate the left-hand side by applying the chain rule:

$$\Pr(\text{word} = \textit{unfit}, \text{prefix} = \textit{un-} \mid y) = \Pr(\text{prefix} = \textit{un-} \mid \text{word} = \textit{unfit}, y). \quad [2.31]$$

$$\times \Pr(\text{word} = \textit{unfit} \mid y). \quad [2.32]$$

12. The notation $\Pr(\cdot)$ refers to the probability of an event, and $\mathrm{p}(\cdot)$ refers to the probability density or mass for a random variable (see appendix A).

But Pr(prefix = *un-* | word = *unfit*, y) = 1, because *un-* is guaranteed to be the prefix for the word *unfit*. Therefore,

$$\begin{aligned}\Pr(\text{word}=\textit{unfit},\text{prefix}=\textit{un-}\mid y)=&1 && \times\Pr(\text{word}=\textit{unfit}\mid y) && [2.33]\\ \gg&\Pr(\text{prefix}=\textit{un-}\mid y) && \times\Pr(\text{word}=\textit{unfit}\mid y), && [2.34]\end{aligned}$$

because the probability of any given word starting with the prefix *un-* is much less than one. Naïve Bayes will systematically underestimate the true probabilities of conjunctions of positively correlated features. To use such features, we need learning algorithms that do not rely on an independence assumption.

The origin of the Naïve Bayes independence assumption is the learning objective, $p(\boldsymbol{x}^{(1:N)}, y^{(1:N)})$, which requires modeling the probability of the observed text. In classification problems, we are always given $\boldsymbol{x}$ and are only interested in predicting the label y. In this setting, modeling the probability of the text $\boldsymbol{x}$ seems like a difficult and unnecessary task. **Discriminative learning** algorithms avoid this task and focus directly on the problem of predicting y.

2.3.1 Perceptron

In Naïve Bayes, the weights can be interpreted as parameters of a probabilistic model. But this model requires an independence assumption that usually does not hold and limits our choice of features. Why not forget about probability and learn the weights in an error-driven way? The **perceptron** algorithm, shown in algorithm 3, is one way to do this.

The algorithm is simple: if you make a mistake, increase the weights for features that are active with the correct label $y^{(i)}$ and decrease the weights for features that are active with the guessed label $\hat{y}$. Perceptron is an **online learning** algorithm, because the classifier weights change after every example. This is different from Naïve Bayes, which is a **batch learning** algorithm: it computes statistics over the entire dataset and then sets the weights in a single operation. Algorithm 3 is vague about when this online learning procedure terminates. We will return to this issue shortly.

The perceptron algorithm may seem like an unprincipled heuristic: Naïve Bayes has a solid foundation in probability, but the perceptron is just adding and subtracting constants from the weights every time there is a mistake. Will this really work? In fact, there is some nice theory for the perceptron, based on the concept of **linear separability**. Informally, a dataset with binary labels ($y \in \{0, 1\}$) is linearly separable if it is possible to draw a hyperplane (a line in many dimensions), such that on each side of the hyperplane, all instances have the same label. This definition can be formalized and extended to multiple labels:

Definition 1 (Linear separability). *The dataset* $\mathcal{D} = \{(\boldsymbol{x}^{(i)}, y^{(i)})\}_{i=1}^{N}$ *is linearly separable iff (if and only if) there exists some weight vector* $\boldsymbol{\theta}$ *and some* ***margin*** ρ *such that for every*

Algorithm 3
Perceptron learning algorithm.

---

procedure PERCEPTRON($\boldsymbol{x}^{(1:N)}, y^{(1:N)}$)
  $t \leftarrow 0$
  $\boldsymbol{\theta}^{(0)} \leftarrow \mathbf{0}$
  repeat
    $t \leftarrow t + 1$
    Select an instance i
    $\hat{y} \leftarrow \text{argmax}_y\, \boldsymbol{\theta}^{(t-1)} \cdot \boldsymbol{f}(\boldsymbol{x}^{(i)}, y)$
    if $\hat{y} \neq y^{(i)}$ **then**
      $\boldsymbol{\theta}^{(t)} \leftarrow \boldsymbol{\theta}^{(t-1)} + \boldsymbol{f}(\boldsymbol{x}^{(i)}, y^{(i)}) - \boldsymbol{f}(\boldsymbol{x}^{(i)}, \hat{y})$
    else
      $\boldsymbol{\theta}^{(t)} \leftarrow \boldsymbol{\theta}^{(t-1)}$
  until tired
  return $\boldsymbol{\theta}^{(t)}$

---

instance $(\boldsymbol{x}^{(i)}, y^{(i)})$*, the inner product of* $\boldsymbol{\theta}$ *and the feature function for the true label,* $\boldsymbol{\theta} \cdot \boldsymbol{f}(\boldsymbol{x}^{(i)}, y^{(i)})$*, is at least* ρ *greater than inner product of* $\boldsymbol{\theta}$ *and the feature function for every other possible label,* $\boldsymbol{\theta} \cdot \boldsymbol{f}(\boldsymbol{x}^{(i)}, y')$*:*

$$\exists \boldsymbol{\theta}, \rho > 0 : \forall (\boldsymbol{x}^{(i)}, y^{(i)}) \in \mathcal{D}, \quad \boldsymbol{\theta} \cdot \boldsymbol{f}(\boldsymbol{x}^{(i)}, y^{(i)}) \geq \rho + \max_{y' \neq y^{(i)}} \boldsymbol{\theta} \cdot \boldsymbol{f}(\boldsymbol{x}^{(i)}, y'). \qquad [2.35]$$

Linear separability is important because of the following guarantee: if your data is linearly separable, then the perceptron algorithm will find a separator (Novikoff, 1962).[13] So while the perceptron may seem heuristic, it is guaranteed to succeed, if the learning problem is easy enough.

How useful is this proof? Minsky and Papert (1969) famously proved that the simple logical function of *exclusive-or* is not separable and that a perceptron is therefore incapable of learning this function. But this is not just an issue for the perceptron: any linear classification algorithm, including Naïve Bayes, will fail on this task. Text classification problems usually involve high-dimensional feature spaces, with thousands or millions of features. For these problems, it is very likely that the training data is indeed separable. And even if the dataset is not separable, it is still possible to place an upper bound on the number of errors that the perceptron algorithm will make (Freund and Schapire, 1999).

13. It is also possible to prove an upper bound on the number of training iterations required to find the separator. Proofs like this are part of the field of **machine learning theory** (Mohri et al., 2012).

Algorithm 4
Averaged perceptron learning algorithm.

---

procedure AVG-PERCEPTRON($\boldsymbol{x}^{(1:N)}, \boldsymbol{y}^{(1:N)}$)
    $t \leftarrow 0$
    $\boldsymbol{\theta}^{(0)} \leftarrow 0$
    repeat
        $t \leftarrow t + 1$
        Select an instance i
        $\hat{y} \leftarrow \text{argmax}_y \, \boldsymbol{\theta}^{(t-1)} \cdot \boldsymbol{f}(\boldsymbol{x}^{(i)}, y)$
        if $\hat{y} \neq y^{(i)}$ **then**
            $\boldsymbol{\theta}^{(t)} \leftarrow \boldsymbol{\theta}^{(t-1)} + \boldsymbol{f}(\boldsymbol{x}^{(i)}, y^{(i)}) - \boldsymbol{f}(\boldsymbol{x}^{(i)}, \hat{y})$
        else
            $\boldsymbol{\theta}^{(t)} \leftarrow \boldsymbol{\theta}^{(t-1)}$
        $\boldsymbol{m} \leftarrow \boldsymbol{m} + \boldsymbol{\theta}^{(t)}$
    until tired
    $\overline{\boldsymbol{\theta}} \leftarrow \frac{1}{t}\boldsymbol{m}$
    return $\overline{\boldsymbol{\theta}}$

2.3.2 Averaged Perceptron

The perceptron iterates over the data repeatedly—until "tired," as described in algorithm 3. If the data is linearly separable, the perceptron will eventually find a separator, and we can stop once all training instances are classified correctly. But if the data is not linearly separable, the perceptron can *thrash* between two or more weight settings, never converging. In this case, how do we know that we can stop training, and how should we choose the final weights? An effective practical solution is to *average* the perceptron weights across all iterations.

This procedure is shown in algorithm 4. The learning algorithm is nearly identical, but we also maintain a vector of the sum of the weights, $\boldsymbol{m}$. At the end of the learning procedure, we divide this sum by the total number of updates, t, to compute the average weights, $\overline{\boldsymbol{\theta}}$. These average weights are then used for prediction. In the algorithm sketch, the average is computed from a running sum, $\boldsymbol{m} \leftarrow \boldsymbol{m} + \boldsymbol{\theta}$. However, this is inefficient, because it requires $|\boldsymbol{\theta}|$ operations to update the running sum. When $\boldsymbol{f}(\boldsymbol{x}, y)$ is sparse, $|\boldsymbol{\theta}| \gg |\boldsymbol{f}(\boldsymbol{x}, y)|$ for any individual $(\boldsymbol{x}, y)$. This means that computing the running sum will be much more expensive than computing of the update to $\boldsymbol{\theta}$ itself, which requires only $2 \times |\boldsymbol{f}(\boldsymbol{x}, y)|$ operations. One of the exercises is to sketch a more efficient algorithm for computing the averaged weights.

Even if the dataset is not separable, the averaged weights will eventually converge. One possible stopping criterion is to check the difference between the average weight vectors after each pass through the data: if the norm of the difference falls below some predefined threshold, we can stop training. Another stopping criterion is to hold out some data, and to measure the predictive accuracy on this heldout data. When the accuracy on the heldout data starts to decrease, the learning algorithm has begun to **overfit** the training set. At this point, it is probably best to stop; this stopping criterion is known as **early stopping**.

Generalization is the ability to make good predictions on instances that are not in the training data. Averaging can be proven to improve generalization, by computing an upper bound on the generalization error (Freund and Schapire, 1999; Collins, 2002).

2.4 Loss Functions and Large-Margin Classification

Naïve Bayes chooses the weights $\boldsymbol{\theta}$ by maximizing the joint log-likelihood $\log \mathrm{p}(\boldsymbol{x}^{(1:N)}, y^{(1:N)})$. By convention, optimization problems are generally formulated as minimization of a **loss function**. The input to a loss function is the vector of weights $\boldsymbol{\theta}$, and the output is a nonnegative number, measuring the performance of the classifier on a training instance. Formally, the loss $\ell(\boldsymbol{\theta}; \boldsymbol{x}^{(i)}, y^{(i)})$ is then a measure of the performance of the weights $\boldsymbol{\theta}$ on the instance $(\boldsymbol{x}^{(i)}, y^{(i)})$. The goal of learning is to minimize the sum of the losses across all instances in the training set.

We can trivially reformulate maximum likelihood as a loss function by defining the loss function to be the *negative* log-likelihood:

$$\log \mathrm{p}(\boldsymbol{x}^{(1:N)}, y^{(1:N)}; \boldsymbol{\theta}) = \sum_{i=1}^{N} \log \mathrm{p}(\boldsymbol{x}^{(i)}, y^{(i)}; \boldsymbol{\theta}) \qquad [2.36]$$

$$\ell_{\mathrm{NB}}(\boldsymbol{\theta}; \boldsymbol{x}^{(i)}, y^{(i)}) = -\log \mathrm{p}(\boldsymbol{x}^{(i)}, y^{(i)}; \boldsymbol{\theta}) \qquad [2.37]$$

$$\hat{\boldsymbol{\theta}} = \underset{\boldsymbol{\theta}}{\operatorname{argmin}} \sum_{i=1}^{N} \ell_{\mathrm{NB}}(\boldsymbol{\theta}; \boldsymbol{x}^{(i)}, y^{(i)}) \qquad [2.38]$$

$$= \underset{\boldsymbol{\theta}}{\operatorname{argmax}} \sum_{i=1}^{N} \log \mathrm{p}(\boldsymbol{x}^{(i)}, y^{(i)}; \boldsymbol{\theta}). \qquad [2.39]$$

The problem of minimizing ℓ_{NB} is thus identical to maximum likelihood estimation.

Loss functions provide a general framework for comparing learning objectives. For example, an alternative loss function is the **zero-one loss**:

$$\ell_{0\text{-}1}(\boldsymbol{\theta}; \boldsymbol{x}^{(i)}, y^{(i)}) = \begin{cases} 0, & y^{(i)} = \operatorname{argmax}_y \boldsymbol{\theta} \cdot \boldsymbol{f}(\boldsymbol{x}^{(i)}, y) \\ 1, & \text{otherwise} \end{cases}. \qquad [2.40]$$

The zero-one loss is zero if the instance is correctly classified and one otherwise. The sum of zero-one losses is proportional to the error rate of the classifier on the training data. Because a low error rate is often the ultimate goal of classification, this may seem ideal. But the zero-one loss has several problems. One is that it is **nonconvex**,[14] which means that there is no guarantee that gradient-based optimization will be effective. A more serious problem is that the derivatives are useless: the partial derivative with respect to any parameter is zero everywhere, except at the points where $\boldsymbol{\theta} \cdot \boldsymbol{f}(\boldsymbol{x}^{(i)}, y) = \boldsymbol{\theta} \cdot \boldsymbol{f}(\boldsymbol{x}^{(i)}, \hat{y})$ for some $\hat{y}$. At those points, the loss is discontinuous, and the derivative is undefined.

The perceptron optimizes a loss function that has better properties for learning:

$$\ell_{\text{PERCEPTRON}}(\boldsymbol{\theta}; \boldsymbol{x}^{(i)}, y^{(i)}) = \max_{y \in \mathcal{Y}} \boldsymbol{\theta} \cdot \boldsymbol{f}(\boldsymbol{x}^{(i)}, y) - \boldsymbol{\theta} \cdot \boldsymbol{f}(\boldsymbol{x}^{(i)}, y^{(i)}). \qquad [2.41]$$

When $\hat{y} = y^{(i)}$, the loss is zero; otherwise, it increases linearly with the gap between the score for the predicted label $\hat{y}$ and the score for the true label $y^{(i)}$. Plotting this loss against the input $\max_{y \in \mathcal{Y}} \boldsymbol{\theta} \cdot \boldsymbol{f}(\boldsymbol{x}^{(i)}, y) - \boldsymbol{\theta} \cdot \boldsymbol{f}(\boldsymbol{x}^{(i)}, y^{(i)})$ gives a hinge shape, motivating the name **hinge loss**.

To see why this is the loss function optimized by the perceptron, take the derivative with respect to $\boldsymbol{\theta}$:

$$\frac{\partial}{\partial \boldsymbol{\theta}} \ell_{\text{PERCEPTRON}}(\boldsymbol{\theta}; \boldsymbol{x}^{(i)}, y^{(i)}) = \boldsymbol{f}(\boldsymbol{x}^{(i)}, \hat{y}) - \boldsymbol{f}(\boldsymbol{x}^{(i)}, y^{(i)}). \qquad [2.42]$$

At each instance, the perceptron algorithm takes a step of magnitude one in the opposite direction of this **gradient**, $\nabla_{\boldsymbol{\theta}} \ell_{\text{PERCEPTRON}} = \frac{\partial}{\partial \boldsymbol{\theta}} \ell_{\text{PERCEPTRON}}(\boldsymbol{\theta}; \boldsymbol{x}^{(i)}, y^{(i)})$. As we will see in § 2.6, this is an example of the optimization algorithm **stochastic gradient descent**, applied to the objective in equation 2.41.

***Breaking ties with subgradient descent**[15] Careful readers will notice the tacit assumption that there is a unique $\hat{y}$ that maximizes $\boldsymbol{\theta} \cdot \boldsymbol{f}(\boldsymbol{x}^{(i)}, y)$. What if there are two or more labels that maximize this function? Consider binary classification: if the maximizer is $y^{(i)}$, then the gradient is zero, and so is the perceptron update; if the maximizer is $\hat{y} \neq y^{(i)}$, then the update is the difference $\boldsymbol{f}(\boldsymbol{x}^{(i)}, y^{(i)}) - \boldsymbol{f}(\boldsymbol{x}^{(i)}, \hat{y})$. The underlying issue is that the perceptron loss is not **smooth**, because the first derivative has a discontinuity at the hinge point, where the score for the true label $y^{(i)}$ is equal to the score for some other label $\hat{y}$. At this point, there is no unique gradient; rather, there is a set of **subgradients**. A vector $\boldsymbol{v}$ is a subgradient of the function g at $\boldsymbol{u}_0$ iff $g(\boldsymbol{u}) - g(\boldsymbol{u}_0) \geq \boldsymbol{v} \cdot (\boldsymbol{u} - \boldsymbol{u}_0)$ for all $\boldsymbol{u}$. Graphically, this defines the set of hyperplanes that include $g(\boldsymbol{u}_0)$ and do not intersect g at any other

14. A function f is **convex** iff $\alpha f(x_i) + (1-\alpha) f(x_j) \geq f(\alpha x_i + (1-\alpha) x_j)$, for all $\alpha \in [0, 1]$ and for all x_i and x_j on the domain of the function. In words, any weighted average of the output of f applied to any two points is larger than the output of f when applied to the weighted average of the same two points. Convexity implies that any local minimum is also a global minimum, and there are many effective techniques for optimizing convex functions (Boyd and Vandenberghe, 2004). See appendix B for a brief review.

15. Throughout this text, advanced topics will be marked with an asterisk.

point. As we approach the hinge point from the left, the gradient is $\boldsymbol{f}(\boldsymbol{x},\hat{y}) - \boldsymbol{f}(\boldsymbol{x},y)$; as we approach from the right, the gradient is $\mathbf{0}$. At the hinge point, the subgradients include all vectors that are bounded by these two extremes. In subgradient descent, *any* subgradient can be used (Bertsekas, 2012). Because both $\mathbf{0}$ and $\boldsymbol{f}(\boldsymbol{x},\hat{y}) - \boldsymbol{f}(\boldsymbol{x},y)$ are subgradients at the hinge point, either one can be used in the perceptron update. This means that if multiple labels maximize $\boldsymbol{\theta} \cdot \boldsymbol{f}(\boldsymbol{x}^{(i)},y)$, any of them can be used in the perceptron update.

Perceptron versus Naïve Bayes The perceptron loss function has some pros and cons with respect to the negative log-likelihood loss implied by Naïve Bayes.

- Both ℓ_{NB} and $\ell_{\text{PERCEPTRON}}$ are convex, making them relatively easy to optimize. However, ℓ_{NB} can be optimized in closed form, while $\ell_{\text{PERCEPTRON}}$ requires iterating over the dataset multiple times.
- ℓ_{NB} can suffer *infinite* loss on a single example, because the logarithm of zero probability is negative infinity. Naïve Bayes will therefore overemphasize some examples and underemphasize others.
- The Naïve Bayes classifier assumes that the observed features are conditionally independent, given the label, and the performance of the classifier depends on the extent to which this assumption holds. The perceptron requires no such assumption.
- $\ell_{\text{PERCEPTRON}}$ treats all correct answers equally. Even if $\boldsymbol{\theta}$ only gives the correct answer by a tiny margin, the loss is still zero.

2.4.1 Online Large-Margin Classification

This last comment suggests a potential problem with the perceptron. Suppose a test example is very close to a training example, but not identical. If the classifier only gets the correct answer on the training example by a small amount, then it may give a different answer on the nearby test instance. To formalize this intuition, define the **margin** as

$$\gamma(\boldsymbol{\theta};\boldsymbol{x}^{(i)},y^{(i)}) = \boldsymbol{\theta} \cdot \boldsymbol{f}(\boldsymbol{x}^{(i)},y^{(i)}) - \max_{y \neq y^{(i)}} \boldsymbol{\theta} \cdot \boldsymbol{f}(\boldsymbol{x}^{(i)},y). \tag{2.43}$$

The margin represents the difference between the score for the correct label $y^{(i)}$, and the score for the highest-scoring incorrect label. The intuition behind **large-margin classification** is that it is not enough to label the training data correctly—the correct label should be separated from other labels by a comfortable margin. This idea can be encoded into a loss function:

$$\ell_{\text{MARGIN}}(\boldsymbol{\theta};\boldsymbol{x}^{(i)},y^{(i)}) = \begin{cases} 0, & \gamma(\boldsymbol{\theta};\boldsymbol{x}^{(i)},y^{(i)}) \geq 1, \\ 1 - \gamma(\boldsymbol{\theta};\boldsymbol{x}^{(i)},y^{(i)}), & \text{otherwise} \end{cases} \tag{2.44}$$

$$= \left(1 - \gamma(\boldsymbol{\theta};\boldsymbol{x}^{(i)},y^{(i)})\right)_+, \tag{2.45}$$

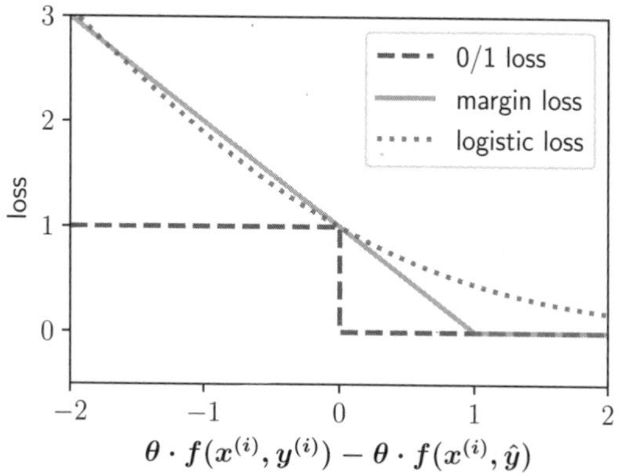

Figure 2.2
Margin, zero-one, and logistic loss functions.

where $(x)_+ = \max(0, x)$. The loss is zero if there is a margin of at least 1 between the score for the true label and the best-scoring alternative $\hat{y}$. This is almost identical to the perceptron loss, but the hinge point is shifted to the right, as shown in figure 2.2. The margin loss is a convex upper bound on the zero-one loss.

The margin loss can be minimized using an online learning rule that is similar to perceptron. We will call this learning rule the **online support vector machine**, for reasons that will be discussed in the derivation. Let us first generalize the notion of a classification error with a **cost function** $c(y^{(i)}, y)$. We will focus on the simple cost function,

$$c(y^{(i)}, y) = \begin{cases} 1, & y^{(i)} \neq \hat{y} \\ 0, & \text{otherwise,} \end{cases} \qquad [2.46]$$

but it is possible to design specialized cost functions that assign heavier penalties to especially undesirable errors (Tsochantaridis et al., 2004). This idea is revisited in chapter 7.

Using the cost function, we can now define the online support vector machine as the following classification rule:

$$\hat{y} = \underset{y \in \mathcal{Y}}{\operatorname{argmax}}\, \boldsymbol{\theta} \cdot \boldsymbol{f}(\boldsymbol{x}^{(i)}, y) + c(y^{(i)}, y) \qquad [2.47]$$

$$\boldsymbol{\theta}^{(t)} \leftarrow (1 - \lambda)\boldsymbol{\theta}^{(t-1)} + \boldsymbol{f}(\boldsymbol{x}^{(i)}, y^{(i)}) - \boldsymbol{f}(\boldsymbol{x}^{(i)}, \hat{y}). \qquad [2.48]$$

This update is similar in form to the perceptron, with two key differences:

- Rather than selecting the label $\hat{y}$ that maximizes the score of the current classification model, the argmax searches for labels that are both *strong*, as measured by $\boldsymbol{\theta} \cdot \boldsymbol{f}(\boldsymbol{x}^{(i)}, y)$, and *wrong*, as measured by $c(y^{(i)}, y)$. This maximization is known as **cost-augmented decoding**, because it augments the maximization objective to favor high-cost labels. If the highest-scoring label is $y = y^{(i)}$, then the margin loss for this instance is zero, and no update is needed. If not, then an update is required to reduce the margin loss—even if the current model classifies the instance correctly. Cost augmentation is only done while learning; it is not applied when making predictions on unseen data.

- The previous weights $\boldsymbol{\theta}^{(t-1)}$ are scaled by $(1 - \lambda)$, with $\lambda \in (0, 1)$. The effect of this term is to cause the weights to "decay" back toward zero. In the support vector machine, this term arises from the minimization of a specific form of the margin, as described below. However, it can also be viewed as a form of **regularization**, which can help to prevent overfitting (see § 2.5.1). In this sense, it plays a role that is similar to smoothing in Naïve Bayes (see § 2.2.4).

2.4.2 *Derivation of the Online Support Vector Machine

The derivation of the online support vector machine is somewhat involved, but gives further intuition about why the method works. Begin by returning the idea of linear separability (definition 1): if a dataset is linearly separable, then there is some hyperplane $\boldsymbol{\theta}$ that correctly classifies all training instances with margin ρ. This margin can be increased to any desired value by multiplying the weights by a constant.

Now, for any datapoint $(\boldsymbol{x}^{(i)}, y^{(i)})$, the geometric distance to the separating hyperplane is given by $\frac{\gamma(\boldsymbol{\theta}; \boldsymbol{x}^{(i)}, y^{(i)})}{||\boldsymbol{\theta}||_2}$, where the denominator is the norm of the weights, $||\boldsymbol{\theta}||_2 = \sqrt{\sum_j \theta_j^2}$. The geometric distance is sometimes called the **geometric margin**, in contrast to the **functional margin** $\gamma(\boldsymbol{\theta}; \boldsymbol{x}^{(i)}, y^{(i)})$. Both are shown in figure 2.3. The geometric margin is a good measure of the robustness of the separator: if the functional margin is large, but the norm $||\boldsymbol{\theta}||_2$ is also large, then a small change in $\boldsymbol{x}^{(i)}$ could cause it to be misclassified. We therefore seek to maximize the minimum geometric margin across the dataset, subject to the constraint that the margin loss is always zero:

$$\begin{aligned}
\max_{\boldsymbol{\theta}} \quad & \min_{i=1,2,\ldots N} \quad \frac{\gamma(\boldsymbol{\theta}; \boldsymbol{x}^{(i)}, y^{(i)})}{||\boldsymbol{\theta}||_2} \\
\text{s.t.} \quad & \gamma(\boldsymbol{\theta}; \boldsymbol{x}^{(i)}, y^{(i)}) \geq 1, \quad \forall i.
\end{aligned} \qquad [2.49]$$

This is a **constrained optimization** problem, where the second line describes constraints on the space of possible solutions $\boldsymbol{\theta}$. In this case, the constraint is that the functional margin must always be at least one, and the objective is that the minimum geometric margin be as large as possible.

Constrained optimization is reviewed in appendix B. In this case, further manipulation yields an unconstrained optimization problem. First, note that the norm $||\boldsymbol{\theta}||_2$ scales linearly: $||a\boldsymbol{\theta}||_2 = a||\boldsymbol{\theta}||_2$. Furthermore, the functional margin γ is a linear function of $\boldsymbol{\theta}$, so that $\gamma(a\boldsymbol{\theta}; \boldsymbol{x}^{(i)}, y^{(i)}) = a\gamma(\boldsymbol{\theta}; \boldsymbol{x}^{(i)}, y^{(i)})$. As a result, any scaling factor on $\boldsymbol{\theta}$ will cancel in the numerator and denominator of the geometric margin. If the data is linearly separable at any $\rho > 0$, it is always possible to rescale the functional margin to 1 by multiplying $\boldsymbol{\theta}$ by a scalar constant. We therefore need only minimize the denominator $||\boldsymbol{\theta}||_2$, subject to the constraint on the functional margin. The minimizer of $||\boldsymbol{\theta}||_2$ is also the minimizer of $\frac{1}{2}||\boldsymbol{\theta}||_2^2 = \frac{1}{2}\sum \theta_j^2$,

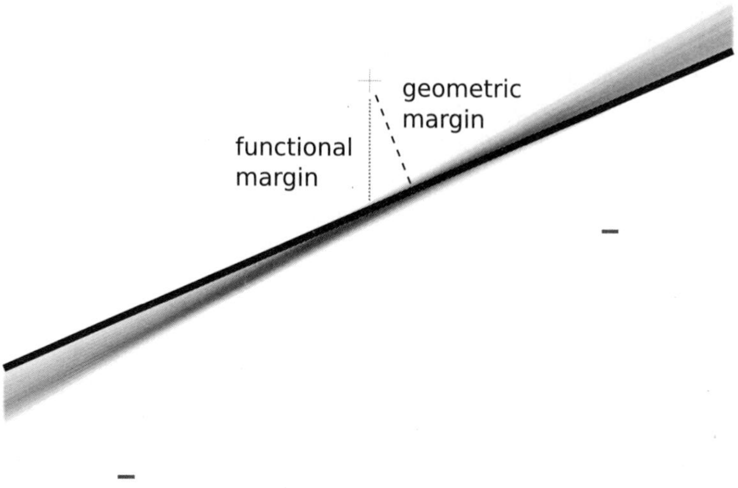

Figure 2.3
Functional and geometric margins for a binary classification problem. All separators that satisfy the margin constraint are shown. The separator with the largest geometric margin is shown in bold.

which is easier to work with. This yields a simpler optimization problem:

$$\begin{aligned}\min_{\boldsymbol{\theta}}. \quad & \frac{1}{2}||\boldsymbol{\theta}||_2^2 \\ \text{s.t.} \quad & \gamma(\boldsymbol{\theta}; \boldsymbol{x}^{(i)}, y^{(i)}) \geq 1, \quad \forall_i.\end{aligned} \tag{2.50}$$

This problem is a **quadratic program**: the objective is a quadratic function of the parameters, and the constraints are all linear inequalities. One solution to this problem is to incorporate the constraints through Lagrange multipliers $\alpha_i \geq 0, i = 1, 2, \ldots, N$. The instances for which $\alpha_i > 0$ are called **support vectors**; other instances are irrelevant to the classification boundary. This motivates the name **support vector machine**.

Thus far we have assumed linear separability, but many datasets of interest are not linearly separable. In this case, there is no $\boldsymbol{\theta}$ that satisfies the margin constraint. To add more flexibility, we can introduce a set of **slack variables**, $\xi_i \geq 0$. Instead of requiring that the functional margin be greater than or equal to one, we require that it be greater than or equal to $1 - \xi_i$. Ideally there would not be any slack, so the slack variables are penalized in the objective function:

$$\begin{aligned}\min_{\boldsymbol{\theta}, \xi} \quad & \frac{1}{2}||\boldsymbol{\theta}||_2^2 + C\sum_{i=1}^{N} \xi_i \\ \text{s.t.} \quad & \gamma(\boldsymbol{\theta}; \boldsymbol{x}^{(i)}, y^{(i)}) + \xi_i \geq 1, \quad \forall i \\ & \xi_i \geq 0, \quad \forall_i.\end{aligned} \tag{2.51}$$

The hyperparameter C controls the tradeoff between violations of the margin constraint and the preference for a low norm of $\boldsymbol{\theta}$. As $C \to \infty$, slack is infinitely expensive, and there is only a solution if the data is separable. As $C \to 0$, slack becomes free, and there is a trivial solution at $\boldsymbol{\theta} = \mathbf{0}$. Thus, C plays a similar role to the smoothing parameter in Naïve Bayes (§ 2.2.4), trading off between a close fit to the training data and better generalization. Like the smoothing parameter of Naïve Bayes, C must be set by the user, typically by maximizing performance on a heldout development set.

To solve the constrained optimization problem defined in equation 2.51, we can first solve for the slack variables,

$$\xi_i \geq (1 - \gamma(\boldsymbol{\theta}; \boldsymbol{x}^{(i)}, y^{(i)}))_+. \tag{2.52}$$

The inequality is tight: the optimal solution is to make the slack variables as small as possible, while still satisfying the constraints (Ratliff et al., 2007; Smith, 2011). By plugging the minimum slack variables back into equation 2.51, the problem can be transformed into the unconstrained optimization,

$$\min_{\boldsymbol{\theta}} \quad \frac{\lambda}{2}||\boldsymbol{\theta}||_2^2 + \sum_{i=1}^{N} (1 - \gamma(\boldsymbol{\theta}; \boldsymbol{x}^{(i)}, y^{(i)}))_+, \tag{2.53}$$

where each ξ_i has been substituted by the right-hand side of equation 2.52, and the factor of C on the slack variables has been replaced by an equivalent factor of $\lambda = \frac{1}{C}$ on the norm of the weights.

Equation 2.53 can be rewritten by expanding the margin,

$$\min_{\boldsymbol{\theta}} \quad \frac{\lambda}{2}||\boldsymbol{\theta}||_2^2 + \sum_{i=1}^{N} \left(\max_{y \in \mathcal{Y}} \left(\boldsymbol{\theta} \cdot \boldsymbol{f}(\boldsymbol{x}^{(i)}, y) + c(y^{(i)}, y) \right) - \boldsymbol{\theta} \cdot \boldsymbol{f}(\boldsymbol{x}^{(i)}, y^{(i)}) \right)_+, \tag{2.54}$$

where $c(y, y^{(i)})$ is the cost function defined in equation 2.46. We can now differentiate with respect to the weights,

$$\nabla_{\boldsymbol{\theta}} L_{\text{SVM}} = \lambda \boldsymbol{\theta} + \sum_{i=1}^{N} \boldsymbol{f}(\boldsymbol{x}^{(i)}, \hat{y}) - \boldsymbol{f}(\boldsymbol{x}^{(i)}, y^{(i)}), \tag{2.55}$$

where L_{SVM} refers to minimization objective in equation 2.54 and $\hat{y} = \text{argmax}_{y \in \mathcal{Y}} \boldsymbol{\theta} \cdot \boldsymbol{f}(\boldsymbol{x}^{(i)}, y) + c(y^{(i)}, y)$. The online support vector machine update arises from the application of **stochastic gradient descent** (described in § 2.6.2) to this gradient.

2.5 Logistic Regression

Thus far, we have seen two broad classes of learning algorithms. Naïve Bayes is a probabilistic method, where learning is equivalent to estimating a joint probability distribution. The perceptron and support vector machine are discriminative, error-driven algorithms: the learning objective is closely related to the number of errors on the training data. Probabilistic and error-driven approaches each have advantages: probability makes it possible to quantify uncertainty about the predicted labels, but the probability model of Naïve Bayes makes unrealistic independence assumptions that limit the features that can be used.

Logistic regression combines advantages of discriminative and probabilistic classifiers. Unlike Naïve Bayes, which starts from the **joint probability** $p_{X,Y}$, logistic regression defines the desired **conditional probability** $p_{Y|X}$ directly. Think of $\boldsymbol{\theta} \cdot \boldsymbol{f}(\boldsymbol{x}, y)$ as a scoring function for the compatibility of the base features $\boldsymbol{x}$ and the label y. To convert this score into a probability, we first exponentiate, obtaining $\exp(\boldsymbol{\theta} \cdot \boldsymbol{f}(\boldsymbol{x}, y))$, which is guaranteed to be nonnegative. Next, we normalize, dividing over all possible labels $y' \in \mathcal{Y}$. The resulting conditional probability is defined as

$$p(y \mid \boldsymbol{x}; \boldsymbol{\theta}) = \frac{\exp(\boldsymbol{\theta} \cdot \boldsymbol{f}(\boldsymbol{x}, y))}{\sum_{y' \in \mathcal{Y}} \exp(\boldsymbol{\theta} \cdot \boldsymbol{f}(\boldsymbol{x}, y'))}. \qquad [2.56]$$

Given a dataset $\mathcal{D} = \{(\boldsymbol{x}^{(i)}, y^{(i)})\}_{i=1}^{N}$, the weights $\boldsymbol{\theta}$ are estimated by **maximum conditional likelihood**:

$$\log p(\boldsymbol{y}^{(1:N)} \mid \boldsymbol{x}^{(1:N)}; \boldsymbol{\theta}) = \sum_{i=1}^{N} \log p(y^{(i)} \mid \boldsymbol{x}^{(i)}; \boldsymbol{\theta}) \qquad [2.57]$$

$$= \sum_{i=1}^{N} \boldsymbol{\theta} \cdot \boldsymbol{f}(\boldsymbol{x}^{(i)}, y^{(i)}) - \log \sum_{y' \in \mathcal{Y}} \exp\left(\boldsymbol{\theta} \cdot \boldsymbol{f}(\boldsymbol{x}^{(i)}, y')\right). \qquad [2.58]$$

The final line is obtained by plugging in equation 2.56 and taking the logarithm.[16] Inside the sum, we have the (additive inverse of the) **logistic loss**:

$$\ell_{\text{LOGREG}}(\boldsymbol{\theta}; \boldsymbol{x}^{(i)}, y^{(i)}) = -\boldsymbol{\theta} \cdot \boldsymbol{f}(\boldsymbol{x}^{(i)}, y^{(i)}) + \log \sum_{y' \in \mathcal{Y}} \exp(\boldsymbol{\theta} \cdot \boldsymbol{f}(\boldsymbol{x}^{(i)}, y')). \qquad [2.59]$$

The logistic loss is shown in figure 2.2 on page 31. A key difference from the zero-one and hinge losses is that logistic loss is never zero. This means that the objective function can always be improved by assigning higher confidence to the correct label.

2.5.1 Regularization

As with the support vector machine, better generalization can be obtained by penalizing the norm of $\boldsymbol{\theta}$. This is done by adding a multiple of the squared norm $\frac{\lambda}{2}||\boldsymbol{\theta}||_2^2$ to the minimization objective. This is called L_2 regularization, because $||\boldsymbol{\theta}||_2^2$ is the squared L_2 norm of the

16. The log-sum-exp term is a common pattern in machine learning. It is numerically unstable, because it will underflow if the inner product is small and overflow if the inner product is large. Scientific computing libraries usually contain special functions for computing `logsumexp`, but with some thought, you should be able to see how to create an implementation that is numerically stable.

vector $\boldsymbol{\theta}$. Regularization forces the estimator to trade off performance on the training data against the norm of the weights, and this can help to prevent overfitting. Consider what would happen to the unregularized weight for a base feature j that is active in only one instance $\boldsymbol{x}^{(i)}$: the conditional log-likelihood could always be improved by increasing the weight for this feature, so that $\boldsymbol{\theta}_{(j,y^{(i)})} \to \infty$ and $\boldsymbol{\theta}_{(j,\tilde{y} \neq y^{(i)})} \to -\infty$, where (j, y) is the index of feature associated with $x_j^{(i)}$ and label y in $\boldsymbol{f}(\boldsymbol{x}^{(i)}, y)$.

In § 2.2.4 (footnote 11), we saw that smoothing the probabilities of a Naïve Bayes classifier can be justified as a form of maximum *a posteriori* estimation, in which the parameters of the classifier are themselves random variables, drawn from a **prior distribution**. The same justification applies to L_2 regularization. In this case, the prior is a zero-mean Gaussian on each term of $\boldsymbol{\theta}$. The log-likelihood under a zero-mean Gaussian is

$$\log N(\theta_j; 0, \sigma^2) \propto -\frac{1}{2\sigma^2}\theta_j^2, \qquad [2.60]$$

so that the regularization weight λ is equal to the inverse variance of the prior, $\lambda = \frac{1}{\sigma^2}$.

2.5.2 Gradients

Logistic loss is minimized by optimization along the gradient. Specific algorithms are described in the next section, but first let's compute the gradient with respect to the logistic loss of a single example:

$$\ell_{\text{LOGREG}} = -\boldsymbol{\theta} \cdot \boldsymbol{f}(\boldsymbol{x}^{(i)}, y^{(i)}) + \log \sum_{y' \in \mathcal{Y}} \exp\left(\boldsymbol{\theta} \cdot \boldsymbol{f}(\boldsymbol{x}^{(i)}, y')\right) \qquad [2.61]$$

$$\frac{\partial \ell}{\partial \boldsymbol{\theta}} = -\boldsymbol{f}(\boldsymbol{x}^{(i)}, y^{(i)}) + \frac{1}{\sum_{y'' \in \mathcal{Y}} \exp\left(\boldsymbol{\theta} \cdot \boldsymbol{f}(\boldsymbol{x}^{(i)}, y'')\right)} \times \sum_{y' \in \mathcal{Y}} \exp\left(\boldsymbol{\theta} \cdot \boldsymbol{f}(\boldsymbol{x}^{(i)}, y')\right) \times \boldsymbol{f}(\boldsymbol{x}^{(i)}, y') \qquad [2.62]$$

$$= -\boldsymbol{f}(\boldsymbol{x}^{(i)}, y^{(i)}) + \sum_{y' \in \mathcal{Y}} \frac{\exp\left(\boldsymbol{\theta} \cdot \boldsymbol{f}(\boldsymbol{x}^{(i)}, y')\right)}{\sum_{y'' \in \mathcal{Y}} \exp\left(\boldsymbol{\theta} \cdot \boldsymbol{f}(\boldsymbol{x}^{(i)}, y'')\right)} \times \boldsymbol{f}(\boldsymbol{x}^{(i)}, y') \qquad [2.63]$$

$$= -\boldsymbol{f}(\boldsymbol{x}^{(i)}, y^{(i)}) + \sum_{y' \in \mathcal{Y}} \mathrm{p}(y' \mid \boldsymbol{x}^{(i)}; \boldsymbol{\theta}) \times \boldsymbol{f}(\boldsymbol{x}^{(i)}, y') \qquad [2.64]$$

$$= -\boldsymbol{f}(\boldsymbol{x}^{(i)}, y^{(i)}) + E_{Y|X}[\boldsymbol{f}(\boldsymbol{x}^{(i)}, y)]. \qquad [2.65]$$

The final step employs the definition of a conditional expectation (§ A.5). The gradient of the logistic loss is equal to the difference between the expected counts under the current model, $E_{Y|X}[\boldsymbol{f}(\boldsymbol{x}^{(i)}, y)]$, and the observed feature counts, $\boldsymbol{f}(\boldsymbol{x}^{(i)}, y^{(i)})$. When these two vectors are equal for a single instance, there is nothing more to learn from it; when they are equal in sum over the entire dataset, there is nothing more to learn from the dataset as a whole. The gradient of the hinge loss is nearly identical, but it involves the features of the predicted label under the current model, $\boldsymbol{f}(\boldsymbol{x}^{(i)}, \hat{y})$, rather than the expected features, $E_{Y|X}[\boldsymbol{f}(\boldsymbol{x}^{(i)}, y)]$, under the conditional distribution, $\mathrm{p}(y \mid \boldsymbol{x}; \boldsymbol{\theta})$.

The regularizer contributes $\lambda\boldsymbol{\theta}$ to the overall gradient:

$$L_{\text{LOGREG}} = \frac{\lambda}{2}||\boldsymbol{\theta}||_2^2 - \sum_{i=1}^{N}\left(\boldsymbol{\theta}\cdot\boldsymbol{f}(\boldsymbol{x}^{(i)}, y^{(i)}) - \log\sum_{y'\in\mathcal{Y}}\exp\boldsymbol{\theta}\cdot\boldsymbol{f}(\boldsymbol{x}^{(i)}, y')\right) \quad [2.66]$$

$$\nabla_{\boldsymbol{\theta}} L_{\text{LOGREG}} = \lambda\boldsymbol{\theta} - \sum_{i=1}^{N}\left(\boldsymbol{f}(\boldsymbol{x}^{(i)}, y^{(i)}) - E_{y|\boldsymbol{x}}[\boldsymbol{f}(\boldsymbol{x}^{(i)}, y)]\right). \quad [2.67]$$

2.6 Optimization

Each of the classification algorithms in this chapter can be viewed as an optimization problem:

- In Naïve Bayes, the objective is the joint likelihood $\log \mathrm{p}(\boldsymbol{x}^{(1:N)}, \boldsymbol{y}^{(1:N)})$. Maximum likelihood estimation yields a closed-form solution for $\boldsymbol{\theta}$.
- In the support vector machine, the objective is the regularized margin loss,

$$L_{\text{SVM}} = \frac{\lambda}{2}||\boldsymbol{\theta}||_2^2 + \sum_{i=1}^{N}(\max_{y\in\mathcal{Y}}(\boldsymbol{\theta}\cdot\boldsymbol{f}(\boldsymbol{x}^{(i)}, y) + c(y^{(i)}, y)) - \boldsymbol{\theta}\cdot\boldsymbol{f}(\boldsymbol{x}^{(i)}, y^{(i)}))_+. \quad [2.68]$$

There is no closed-form solution, but the objective is convex. The perceptron algorithm minimizes a similar objective.

- In logistic regression, the objective is the regularized negative log-likelihood,

$$L_{\text{LOGREG}} = \frac{\lambda}{2}||\boldsymbol{\theta}||_2^2 - \sum_{i=1}^{N}\left(\boldsymbol{\theta}\cdot\boldsymbol{f}(\boldsymbol{x}^{(i)}, y^{(i)}) - \log\sum_{y\in\mathcal{Y}}\exp\left(\boldsymbol{\theta}\cdot\boldsymbol{f}(\boldsymbol{x}^{(i)}, y)\right)\right). \quad [2.69]$$

Again, there is no closed-form solution, but the objective is convex.

These learning algorithms are distinguished by *what* is being optimized, rather than *how* the optimal weights are found. This decomposition is an essential feature of contemporary machine learning. The domain expert's job is to design an objective function—or more generally, a **model** of the problem. If the model has certain characteristics, then generic optimization algorithms can be used to find the solution. In particular, if an objective function is differentiable, then gradient-based optimization can be employed; if it is also convex, then gradient-based optimization is guaranteed to find the globally optimal solution. The support vector machine and logistic regression have both of these properties and so are amenable to generic **convex optimization** techniques (Boyd and Vandenberghe, 2004).

2.6.1 Batch Optimization

In **batch optimization**, each update to the weights is based on a computation involving the entire dataset. One such algorithm is **gradient descent**, which iteratively updates the weights,

$$\boldsymbol{\theta}^{(t+1)} \leftarrow \boldsymbol{\theta}^{(t)} - \eta^{(t)} \nabla_{\boldsymbol{\theta}} L, \qquad [2.70]$$

where $\nabla_{\boldsymbol{\theta}} L$ is the gradient computed over the entire training set and $\eta^{(t)}$ is the **learning rate** at iteration t. If the objective L is a convex function of $\boldsymbol{\theta}$, then this procedure is guaranteed to terminate at the global optimum, for appropriate schedule of learning rates, $\eta^{(t)}$.[17]

In practice, gradient descent can be slow to converge, as the gradient can become infinitesimally small. Faster convergence can be obtained by second-order Newton optimization, which incorporates the inverse of the **Hessian matrix**,

$$H_{i,j} = \frac{\partial^2 L}{\partial \theta_i \partial \theta_j}. \qquad [2.71]$$

The size of the Hessian matrix is quadratic in the number of features. In the bag-of-words representation, this is usually too big to store, let alone invert. **Quasi-Newton optimization** techniques maintain a low-rank approximation to the inverse of the Hessian matrix. Such techniques usually converge more quickly than gradient descent, while remaining computationally tractable even for large feature sets. A popular quasi-Newton algorithm is L-BFGS (Liu and Nocedal, 1989), which is implemented in many scientific computing environments, such as SCIPY and MATLAB.

For any gradient-based technique, the user must set the learning rates $\eta^{(t)}$. While convergence proofs usually employ a decreasing learning rate, in practice, it is common to fix $\eta^{(t)}$ to a small constant, like 10^{-3}. The specific constant can be chosen by experimentation, although there is research on determining the learning rate automatically (Schaul et al., 2013; Wu et al., 2018).

2.6.2 Online Optimization

Batch optimization computes the objective on the entire training set before making an update. This may be inefficient, because at early stages of training, a small number of training examples could point the learner in the correct direction. **Online learning** algorithms make updates to the weights while iterating through the training data. The theoretical basis for this approach is a stochastic approximation to the true objective function,

17. Convergence proofs typically require the learning rate to satisfy the following conditions: $\sum_{t=1}^{\infty} \eta^{(t)} = \infty$ and $\sum_{t=1}^{\infty} (\eta^{(t)})^2 < \infty$ (Bottou et al., 2018). These properties are satisfied by any learning rate schedule $\eta^{(t)} = \eta^{(0)} t^{-\alpha}$ for $\alpha \in [1, 2]$.

Algorithm 5

Generalized gradient descent. The function BATCHER partitions the training set into B batches such that each instance appears in exactly one batch. In gradient descent, $B = 1$; in stochastic gradient descent, $B = N$; in minibatch stochastic gradient descent, $1 < B < N$.

---

procedure GRADIENT-DESCENT($\boldsymbol{x}^{(1:N)}, \boldsymbol{y}^{(1:N)}, L, \eta^{(1\ldots\infty)}$, BATCHER, $T_{\max}$)
    $\boldsymbol{\theta} \leftarrow \boldsymbol{0}$
    $t \leftarrow 0$
    repeat
        $(\boldsymbol{b}^{(1)}, \boldsymbol{b}^{(2)}, \ldots, \boldsymbol{b}^{(B)}) \leftarrow$ BATCHER(N)
        for $n \in \{1, 2, \ldots, B\}$ **do**
            $t \leftarrow t + 1$
            $\boldsymbol{\theta}^{(t)} \leftarrow \boldsymbol{\theta}^{(t-1)} - \eta^{(t)} \nabla_{\boldsymbol{\theta}} L(\boldsymbol{\theta}^{(t-1)}; \boldsymbol{x}^{(b_1^{(n)}, b_2^{(n)}, \ldots)}, \boldsymbol{y}^{(b_1^{(n)}, b_2^{(n)}, \ldots)})$
            if Converged($\boldsymbol{\theta}^{(1,2,\ldots,t)}$) **then**
                return $\boldsymbol{\theta}^{(t)}$
    until $t = T_{\max}$
    return $\boldsymbol{\theta}^{(t)}$

$$\sum_{i=1}^{N} \ell(\boldsymbol{\theta}; \boldsymbol{x}^{(i)}, y^{(i)}) \approx N \times \ell(\boldsymbol{\theta}; \boldsymbol{x}^{(j)}, y^{(j)}), \qquad (\boldsymbol{x}^{(j)}, y^{(j)}) \sim \{(\boldsymbol{x}^{(i)}, y^{(i)})\}_{i=1}^{N}, \qquad [2.72]$$

where the instance $(\boldsymbol{x}^{(j)}, y^{(j)})$ is sampled at random from the full dataset.

In **stochastic gradient descent**, the approximate gradient is computed by randomly sampling a single instance, and an update is made immediately. This is similar to the perceptron algorithm, which also updates the weights one instance at a time. In **minibatch** stochastic gradient descent, the gradient is computed over a small set of instances. A typical approach is to set the minibatch size so that the entire batch fits in memory on a graphics processing unit (Neubig et al., 2017a). It is then possible to speed up learning by parallelizing the computation of the gradient over each instance in the minibatch.

Algorithm 5 offers a generalized view of gradient descent. In standard gradient descent, the batcher returns a single batch with all the instances. In stochastic gradient descent, it returns N batches with one instance each. In minibatch settings, the batcher returns B minibatches, $1 < B < N$.

There are many other techniques for online learning, and research in this area is ongoing (Bottou et al., 2018). Some algorithms use an adaptive learning rate, which can be different for every feature (Duchi et al., 2011). Features that occur frequently are likely to be updated frequently, so it is best to use a small learning rate; rare features will be updated infrequently, so it is better to take larger steps. The **AdaGrad** (adaptive gradient) algorithm achieves this behavior by storing the sum of the squares of the gradients for each feature, and rescaling the learning rate by its inverse:

$$g_t = \nabla_{\boldsymbol{\theta}} L(\boldsymbol{\theta}^{(t)}; \boldsymbol{x}^{(i)}, y^{(i)}) \tag{2.73}$$

$$\theta_j^{(t+1)} \leftarrow \theta_j^{(t)} - \frac{\eta^{(t)}}{\sqrt{\sum_{t'=1}^{t} g_{t,j}^2}} g_{t,j}, \tag{2.74}$$

where j iterates over features in $\boldsymbol{f}(\boldsymbol{x}, y)$.

In most cases, the number of active features for any instance is much smaller than the number of weights. If so, the computation cost of online optimization will be dominated by the update from the regularization term, $\lambda\boldsymbol{\theta}$. The solution is to be "lazy," updating each θ_j only as it is used. To implement lazy updating, store an additional parameter τ_j, which is the iteration at which θ_j was last updated. If θ_j is needed at time t, the $t - \tau$ regularization updates can be performed all at once. This strategy is described in detail by Kummerfeld et al. (2015).

2.7 *Additional Topics in Classification

This section presents some additional topics in classification that are particularly relevant for natural language processing, especially for understanding the research literature.

2.7.1 Feature Selection by Regularization

In logistic regression and large-margin classification, generalization can be improved by regularizing the weights toward 0, using the L_2 norm. But rather than encouraging weights to be small, it might be better for the model to be **sparse**: it should assign weights of exactly zero to most features, and only assign nonzero weights to features that are clearly necessary. This idea can be formalized by the L_0 norm, $L_0 = ||\boldsymbol{\theta}||_0 = \sum_j \delta\left(\theta_j \neq 0\right)$, which applies a constant penalty for each nonzero weight. This norm can be thought of as a form of **feature selection**: optimizing the L_0-regularized conditional likelihood is equivalent to trading off the log-likelihood against the number of active features. Reducing the number of active features is desirable because the resulting model will be fast and low memory, and should generalize well, since irrelevant features will be pruned away. Unfortunately, the L_0 norm is nonconvex and nondifferentiable. Optimization under L_0 regularization is **NP-hard**, meaning that it can be solved efficiently only if P = NP (Ge et al., 2011).

A useful alternative is the L_1 norm, which is equal to the sum of the absolute values of the weights, $||\boldsymbol{\theta}||_1 = \sum_j |\theta_j|$. The L_1 norm is convex and can be used as an approximation to L_0 (Tibshirani, 1996). Conveniently the L_1 norm also performs feature selection, by driving many of the coefficients to zero; it is therefore known as a **sparsity-inducing regularizer**. The L_1 norm does not have a gradient at $\theta_j = 0$, so we must instead optimize the L_1-regularized objective using **subgradient** methods. The associated stochastic subgradient descent algorithms are only somewhat more complex than conventional stochastic gradient descent; Sra et al. (2012) survey approaches for estimation under L_1 and other regularizers.

Gao et al. (2007) compare L_1 and L_2 regularization on a suite of natural language processing problems, finding that L_1 regularization generally gives similar accuracy to L_2 regularization, but that L_1 regularization produces models that are between 10 and 50 times smaller, because more than 90 percent of the feature weights are set to zero.

2.7.2 Other Views of Logistic Regression

In binary classification, we can dispense with the feature function and choose y based on the inner product of $\boldsymbol{\theta} \cdot \boldsymbol{x}$. The conditional probability $\mathrm{p}_{Y|X}$ is obtained by passing this inner product through a **logistic function**:

$$\sigma(a) \triangleq \frac{\exp(a)}{1+\exp(a)} = (1+\exp(-a))^{-1} \quad [2.75]$$

$$\mathrm{p}(y \mid \boldsymbol{x}; \boldsymbol{\theta}) = \sigma(\boldsymbol{\theta} \cdot \boldsymbol{x}). \quad [2.76]$$

This is the origin of the name "logistic regression." Logistic regression can be viewed as part of a larger family of **generalized linear models** (GLMs), in which various other **link functions** convert between the inner product $\boldsymbol{\theta} \cdot \boldsymbol{x}$ and the parameter of a conditional probability distribution.

Logistic regression and related models are sometimes referred to as **log-linear**, because the log-probability is a linear function of the features. But in the early NLP literature, logistic regression was often called **maximum entropy** classification (Berger et al., 1996). This name refers to an alternative formulation, in which the goal is to find the maximum entropy probability function that satisfies **moment-matching** constraints. These constraints specify that the empirical count of each feature should match the expected count under the induced probability distribution $\mathrm{p}_{Y|X;\boldsymbol{\theta}}$:

$$\sum_{i=1}^{N} f_j(\boldsymbol{x}^{(i)}, y^{(i)}) = \sum_{i=1}^{N} \sum_{y \in \mathcal{Y}} \mathrm{p}(y \mid \boldsymbol{x}^{(i)}; \boldsymbol{\theta}) f_j(\boldsymbol{x}^{(i)}, y), \quad \forall j. \quad [2.77]$$

The moment-matching constraint is satisfied exactly when the derivative of the conditional log-likelihood function (equation 2.65) is equal to zero. However, the constraint can be met by many values of $\boldsymbol{\theta}$, so which should we choose?

The **entropy** of the conditional probability distribution $\mathrm{p}_{Y|X}$ is

$$H(\mathrm{p}_{Y|X}) = -\sum_{\boldsymbol{x} \in \mathcal{X}} \mathrm{p}_X(\boldsymbol{x}) \sum_{y \in \mathcal{Y}} \mathrm{p}_{Y|X}(y \mid \boldsymbol{x}) \log \mathrm{p}_{Y|X}(y \mid \boldsymbol{x}), \quad [2.78]$$

where $\mathcal{X}$ is the set of all possible feature vectors and $\mathrm{p}_X(\boldsymbol{x})$ is the probability of observing the base features $\boldsymbol{x}$. The distribution p_X is unknown, but it can be estimated by summing over all the instances in the training set:

$$\tilde{H}(p_{Y|X}) = -\frac{1}{N}\sum_{i=1}^{N}\sum_{y\in\mathcal{Y}} p_{Y|X}(y \mid \boldsymbol{x}^{(i)}) \log p_{Y|X}(y \mid \boldsymbol{x}^{(i)}). \quad [2.79]$$

If the entropy is large, the likelihood function is smooth across possible values of y; if it is small, the likelihood function is sharply peaked at some preferred value; in the limiting case, the entropy is zero if $p(y \mid x) = 1$ for some y. The maximum entropy criterion chooses to make the weakest commitments possible, while satisfying the moment-matching constraints from equation 2.77. The solution to this constrained optimization problem is identical to the maximum conditional likelihood (logistic-loss) formulation that was presented in § 2.5.

2.8 Summary of Learning Algorithms

It is natural to ask which learning algorithm is best, but the answer depends on what characteristics are important to the problem you are trying to solve.

Naïve Bayes *Pros*: easy to implement; estimation is fast, requiring only a single pass over the data; assigns probabilities to predicted labels; controls overfitting with smoothing parameter. *Cons*: often has poor accuracy, especially with correlated features.

Perceptron *Pros*: easy to implement; online; error-driven learning means that accuracy is typically high, especially after averaging. *Cons*: not probabilistic; hard to know when to stop learning; lack of margin can lead to overfitting.

Support vector machine *Pros*: optimizes an error-based metric, usually resulting in high accuracy; overfitting is controlled by a regularization parameter. *Cons*: not probabilistic.

Logistic regression *Pros*: error driven and probabilistic; overfitting is controlled by a regularization parameter. *Cons*: batch learning requires black-box optimization; logistic loss can "overtrain" on correctly labeled examples.

One of the main distinctions is whether the learning algorithm offers a probability over labels. This is useful in modular architectures, where the output of one classifier is the input for some other system. In cases where probability is not necessary, the support vector machine is usually the right choice, since it is no more difficult to implement than the perceptron and is often more accurate. When probability is necessary, logistic regression is usually more accurate than Naïve Bayes.

Additional Resources

A machine learning textbook will offer more classifiers and more details (e.g., Murphy, 2012), although the notation will differ slightly from what is typical in natural language processing. Probabilistic methods are surveyed by Hastie et al. (2009), and Mohri et al.

(2012) emphasize theoretical considerations. Bottou et al. (2018) survey the rapidly moving field of online learning, and Kummerfeld et al. (2015) empirically review several optimization algorithms for large-margin learning. The Python toolkit SCIKIT-LEARN includes implementations of all of the algorithms described in this chapter (Pedregosa et al., 2011).

Appendix B describes an alternative large-margin classifier, called **passive-aggressive**. Passive-aggressive is an online learner that seeks to make the smallest update that satisfies the margin constraint at the current instance. It is closely related to MIRA, which was used widely in NLP in the 2000s (Crammer and Singer, 2003).

Exercises

There will be exercises at the end of each chapter. In this chapter, the exercises are mostly mathematical, matching the subject material. In other chapters, the exercises will emphasize linguistics or programming.

1. Let $\boldsymbol{x}$ be a bag-of-words vector such that $\sum_{j=1}^{V} x_j = 1$. Verify that the multinomial probability $\text{p}_{\text{mult}}(\boldsymbol{x}; \boldsymbol{\phi})$, as defined in equation 2.12, is identical to the probability of the same document under a categorical distribution, $\text{p}_{\text{cat}}(\boldsymbol{w}; \boldsymbol{\phi})$.
2. Suppose you have a single feature x, with the following conditional distribution:

$$\text{p}(x \mid y) = \begin{cases} \alpha, & X=0, Y=0 \\ 1-\alpha, & X=1, Y=0 \\ 1-\beta, & X=0, Y=1 \\ \beta, & X=1, Y=1. \end{cases} \qquad [2.80]$$

   Further suppose that the prior is uniform, $\Pr(Y=0) = \Pr(Y=1) = \frac{1}{2}$, and that both $\alpha > \frac{1}{2}$ and $\beta > \frac{1}{2}$. Given a Naïve Bayes classifier with accurate parameters, what is the probability of making an error?
3. Derive the maximum likelihood estimate for the parameter $\boldsymbol{\mu}$ in Naïve Bayes.
4. The classification models in the text have a vector of weights for each possible label. Although this is notationally convenient, it is overdetermined: for any linear classifier that can be obtained with $K \times V$ weights, an equivalent classifier can be constructed using $(K-1) \times V$ weights.

   a) Describe how to construct this classifier. Specifically, if given a set of weights $\boldsymbol{\theta}$ and a feature function $\boldsymbol{f}(\boldsymbol{x}, y)$, explain how to construct alternative weights and feature function $\boldsymbol{\theta}'$ and $\boldsymbol{f}'(\boldsymbol{x}, y)$, such that

$$\forall y, y' \in \mathcal{Y}, \boldsymbol{\theta} \cdot \boldsymbol{f}(\boldsymbol{x}, y) - \boldsymbol{\theta} \cdot \boldsymbol{f}(\boldsymbol{x}, y') = \boldsymbol{\theta}' \cdot \boldsymbol{f}'(\boldsymbol{x}, y) - \boldsymbol{\theta}' \cdot \boldsymbol{f}'(\boldsymbol{x}, y'). \qquad [2.81]$$

b) Explain how your construction justifies the well-known alternative form for binary logistic regression, $\Pr(Y=1 \mid \boldsymbol{x};\boldsymbol{\theta}) = \frac{1}{1+\exp(-\boldsymbol{\theta}' \cdot \boldsymbol{x})} = \sigma(\boldsymbol{\theta}' \cdot \boldsymbol{x})$, where σ is the sigmoid function.

5. Suppose you have two labeled datasets D_1 and D_2, with the same features and labels.
   - Let $\boldsymbol{\theta}^{(1)}$ be the unregularized logistic regression (LR) coefficients from training on dataset D_1.
   - Let $\boldsymbol{\theta}^{(2)}$ be the unregularized LR coefficients (same model) from training on dataset D_2.
   - Let $\boldsymbol{\theta}^*$ be the unregularized LR coefficients from training on the combined dataset $D_1 \cup D_2$.

   Under these conditions, prove that for any feature j,

   $$\theta_j^* \geq \min(\theta_j^{(1)}, \theta_j^{(2)})$$
   $$\theta_j^* \leq \max(\theta_j^{(1)}, \theta_j^{(2)}). \qquad [2.82]$$

6. Let $\hat{\boldsymbol{\theta}}$ be the solution to an unregularized logistic regression problem, and let $\boldsymbol{\theta}^*$ be the solution to the same problem, with L_2 regularization. Prove that $||\boldsymbol{\theta}^*||_2^2 \leq ||\hat{\boldsymbol{\theta}}||_2^2$.

7. As noted in the discussion of averaged perceptron in § 2.3.2, the computation of the running sum $\boldsymbol{m} \leftarrow \boldsymbol{m} + \boldsymbol{\theta}$ is unnecessarily expensive, requiring $K \times V$ operations. Give an alternative way to compute the averaged weights $\overline{\boldsymbol{\theta}}$, with complexity that is independent of V and linear in the sum of feature sizes $\sum_{i=1}^{N} |\boldsymbol{f}(\boldsymbol{x}^{(i)}, y^{(i)})|$.

8. Consider a dataset that is comprised of two identical instances $\boldsymbol{x}^{(1)} = \boldsymbol{x}^{(2)}$ with distinct labels $y^{(1)} \neq y^{(2)}$. Assume all features are binary, $x_j \in \{0, 1\}$ for all j.

   Now suppose that the averaged perceptron always trains on the instance $(\boldsymbol{x}^{i(t)}, y^{i(t)})$, where $i(t) = 2 - (t \mod 2)$, which is 1 when the training iteration t is odd and 2 when t is even. Further suppose that learning terminates under the following condition:

   $$\epsilon \geq \max_j \left| \frac{1}{t} \sum_t \theta_j^{(t)} - \frac{1}{t-1} \sum_t \theta_j^{(t-1)} \right|. \qquad [2.83]$$

   In words, the algorithm stops when the largest change in the averaged weights is less than or equal to ϵ. Compute the number of iterations before the averaged perceptron terminates.

9. Prove that the margin loss is convex in $\boldsymbol{\theta}$. Use this definition of the margin loss:

   $$L(\boldsymbol{\theta}) = -\boldsymbol{\theta} \cdot \boldsymbol{f}(\boldsymbol{x}, y^*) + \max_y \boldsymbol{\theta} \cdot \boldsymbol{f}(\boldsymbol{x}, y) + c(y^*, y), \qquad [2.84]$$

   where y^* is the gold label. As a reminder, a function f is convex iff

   $$f(\alpha x_1 + (1-\alpha)x_2) \leq \alpha f(x_1) + (1-\alpha) f(x_2), \qquad [2.85]$$

   for any x_1, x_2 and $\alpha \in [0, 1]$.

10. If a function f is m-strongly convex, then for some $m > 0$, the following inequality holds for all x and x' on the domain of the function:

$$f(x') \leq f(x) + (\nabla_x f) \cdot (x' - x) + \frac{m}{2}||x' - x||_2^2. \quad [2.86]$$

Let $f(x) = L(\boldsymbol{\theta}^{(t)})$, representing the loss of the classifier at iteration t of gradient descent; let $f(x') = L(\boldsymbol{\theta}^{(t+1)})$. Assuming the loss function is m-convex, prove that $L(\boldsymbol{\theta}^{(t+1)}) \leq L(\boldsymbol{\theta}^{(t)})$ for an appropriate constant learning rate η, which will depend on m. Explain why this implies that gradient descent converges when applied to an m-strongly convex loss function with a unique minimum.

3 Nonlinear Classification

Linear classification may seem like all we need for natural language processing. The bag-of-words representation is inherently high dimensional, and the number of features is often larger than the number of labeled training instances. This means that it is usually possible to find a linear classifier that perfectly fits the training data, or even to fit any arbitrary labeling of the training instances! Moving to nonlinear classification may therefore only increase the risk of overfitting. Furthermore, for many tasks, **lexical features** (words) are meaningful in isolation and can offer independent evidence about the instance label—unlike computer vision, where individual pixels are rarely informative, and must be evaluated holistically to make sense of an image. For these reasons, natural language processing has historically focused on linear classification.

But in recent years, nonlinear classifiers have swept through natural language processing and are now the default approach for many tasks (Manning, 2015). There are at least three reasons for this change.

- There have been rapid advances in **deep learning**, a family of nonlinear methods that learn complex functions of the input through multiple layers of computation (Goodfellow et al., 2016).
- Deep learning facilitates the incorporation of **word embeddings**, which are dense vector representations of words. Word embeddings can be learned from large amounts of unlabeled data and enable generalization to words that do not appear in the annotated training data (word embeddings are discussed in detail in chapter 14).
- While CPU speeds have plateaued, there have been rapid advances in specialized hardware called graphics processing units (GPUs), which have become faster, cheaper, and easier to program. Many deep learning models can be implemented efficiently on GPUs, offering substantial performance improvements over CPU-based computing.

This chapter focuses on **neural networks**, which are the dominant approach for nonlinear classification in natural language processing today.[1] Historically, a few other nonlinear learning methods have been applied to language data.

- **Kernel methods** are generalizations of the **nearest-neighbor** classification rule, which classifies each instance by the label of the most similar example in the training set. The application of the **kernel support vector machine** to information extraction is described in chapter 17.
- **Decision trees** classify instances by checking a set of conditions. Scaling decision trees to bag-of-words inputs is difficult, but decision trees have been successful in problems such as coreference resolution (chapter 15), where more compact feature sets can be constructed (Soon et al., 2001).
- **Boosting** and related **ensemble methods** work by combining the predictions of several "weak" classifiers, each of which may consider only a small subset of features. Boosting has been successfully applied to text classification (Schapire and Singer, 2000) and syntactic analysis (Abney et al., 1999) and remains one of the most successful methods on machine learning competition sites such as Kaggle (Chen and Guestrin, 2016).

Hastie et al. (2009) provide an excellent overview of these techniques.

3.1 Feedforward Neural Networks

Consider the problem of building a classifier for movie reviews. The goal is to predict a label $y \in \{\text{GOOD}, \text{BAD}, \text{OKAY}\}$ from a representation of the text of each document, $\boldsymbol{x}$. But what makes a good movie? The story, acting, cinematography, editing, soundtrack, and so on. Now suppose the training set contains labels for each of these additional features, $\boldsymbol{z} = [z_1, z_2, \ldots, z_{K_z}]^\top$. With such a training set, we could build a two-step classifier:

1. **Use the text $\boldsymbol{x}$ to predict the features $\boldsymbol{z}$.** Specifically, train a logistic regression classifier to compute $\mathrm{p}(z_k \mid \boldsymbol{x})$, for each $k \in \{1, 2, \ldots, K_z\}$.
2. **Use the features $\boldsymbol{z}$ to predict the label y.** Again, train a logistic regression classifier to compute $\mathrm{p}(y \mid \boldsymbol{z})$. On test data, $\boldsymbol{z}$ is unknown, so we will use the probabilities $\mathrm{p}(\boldsymbol{z} \mid \boldsymbol{x})$ from the first layer as the features.

This setup is shown in figure 3.1, which describes the proposed classifier in a **computation graph**: the text features $\boldsymbol{x}$ are connected to the middle layer $\boldsymbol{z}$, which is connected to the label y.

If we assume that each z_k is binary, $z_k \in \{0, 1\}$, then the probability $\mathrm{p}(z_k \mid \boldsymbol{x})$ can be modeled using binary logistic regression:

1. I will use "deep learning" and "neural networks" interchangeably.

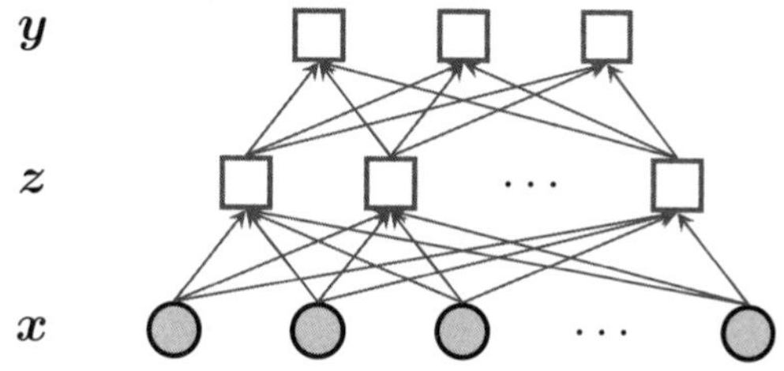

Figure 3.1
A feedforward neural network. Shaded circles indicate observed features, usually words; squares indicate nodes in the computation graph, which are computed from the information carried over the incoming arrows.

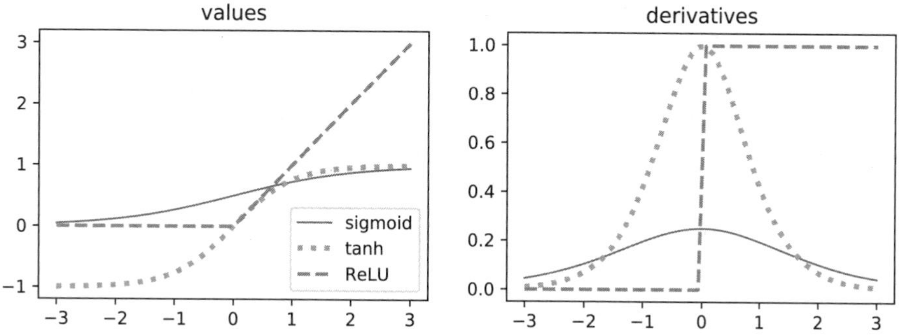

Figure 3.2
The sigmoid, tanh, and ReLU activation functions.

$$\Pr(z_k = 1 \mid \boldsymbol{x}; \Theta^{(x\to z)}) = \sigma(\boldsymbol{\theta}_k^{(x\to z)} \cdot \boldsymbol{x}) = (1 + \exp(-\boldsymbol{\theta}_k^{(x\to z)} \cdot \boldsymbol{x}))^{-1}, \tag{3.1}$$

where σ is the **sigmoid** function (shown in figure 3.2), and the matrix $\Theta^{(x\to z)} \in \mathbb{R}^{K_z \times V}$ is constructed by stacking the weight vectors for each z_k,

$$\Theta^{(x\to z)} = [\boldsymbol{\theta}_1^{(x\to z)}, \boldsymbol{\theta}_2^{(x\to z)}, \ldots, \boldsymbol{\theta}_{K_z}^{(x\to z)}]^\top. \tag{3.2}$$

We will assume that $\boldsymbol{x}$ contains a term with a constant value of 1, so that a corresponding offset parameter is included in each $\boldsymbol{\theta}_k^{(x\to z)}$.

The output layer is computed by the multiclass logistic regression probability,

$$\Pr(y = j \mid \boldsymbol{z}; \Theta^{(z\to y)}, \boldsymbol{b}) = \frac{\exp(\boldsymbol{\theta}_j^{(z\to y)} \cdot \boldsymbol{z} + b_j)}{\sum_{j' \in \mathcal{Y}} \exp(\boldsymbol{\theta}_{j'}^{(z\to y)} \cdot \boldsymbol{z} + b_{j'})}, \tag{3.3}$$

where b_j is an offset for label j, and the output weight matrix $\Theta^{(z\to y)} \in \mathbb{R}^{K_y \times K_z}$ is again constructed by concatenation,

$$\Theta^{(z\to y)} = [\boldsymbol{\theta}_1^{(z\to y)}, \boldsymbol{\theta}_2^{(z\to y)}, \ldots, \boldsymbol{\theta}_{K_y}^{(z\to y)}]^\top. \tag{3.4}$$

The vector of probabilities over each possible value of y is denoted as

$$p(\boldsymbol{y} \mid z; \Theta^{(z\to y)}, \boldsymbol{b}) = \text{softmax}(\Theta^{(z\to y)} z + \boldsymbol{b}), \quad [3.5]$$

where element j in the output of the **softmax** function is computed as in equation 3.3.

This set of equations defines a multilayer classifier, which can be summarized as

$$p(z \mid \boldsymbol{x}; \Theta^{(x\to z)}) = \sigma(\Theta^{(x\to z)} \boldsymbol{x}) \quad [3.6]$$

$$p(\boldsymbol{y} \mid z; \Theta^{(z\to y)}, \boldsymbol{b}) = \text{softmax}(\Theta^{(z\to y)} z + \boldsymbol{b}), \quad [3.7]$$

where the function σ is now applied **elementwise** to the vector of inner products,

$$\sigma(\Theta^{(x\to z)} \boldsymbol{x}) = [\sigma(\boldsymbol{\theta}_1^{(x\to z)} \cdot \boldsymbol{x}), \sigma(\boldsymbol{\theta}_2^{(x\to z)} \cdot \boldsymbol{x}), \ldots, \sigma(\boldsymbol{\theta}_{K_z}^{(x\to z)} \cdot \boldsymbol{x})]^\top. \quad [3.8]$$

Now suppose that the hidden features z are never observed, even in the training data. We can still construct the architecture in figure 3.1. Instead of predicting y from a discrete vector of predicted values z, we use the probabilities $\sigma(\boldsymbol{\theta}_k \cdot \boldsymbol{x})$. The resulting classifier is barely changed:

$$z = \sigma(\Theta^{(x\to z)} \boldsymbol{x}) \quad [3.9]$$

$$p(y \mid \boldsymbol{x}; \Theta^{(z\to y)}, \boldsymbol{b}) = \text{softmax}(\Theta^{(z\to y)} z + \boldsymbol{b}). \quad [3.10]$$

This defines a classification model that predicts the label $y \in \mathcal{Y}$ from the base features $\boldsymbol{x}$, through a "hidden layer" z. This is a **feedforward neural network**.[2]

3.2 Designing Neural Networks

There several ways to generalize the feedforward neural network.

3.2.1 Activation Functions

If the hidden layer is viewed as a set of latent features, then the sigmoid function in equation 3.9 represents the extent to which each of these features is "activated" by a given input. However, the hidden layer can be regarded more generally as a nonlinear transformation of the input. This opens the door to many other activation functions, some of which are shown in figure 3.2. At the moment, the choice of activation functions is more art than science, but a few points can be made about the most popular varieties:

- The range of the sigmoid function is $(0, 1)$. The bounded range ensures that a cascade of sigmoid functions will not "blow up" to a huge output, and this is important for deep networks with several hidden layers. The derivative of the sigmoid is

2. The architecture is sometimes called a **multilayer perceptron**, but this is misleading, because each layer is not a perceptron as defined in the previous chapter.

$\frac{\partial}{\partial a}\sigma(a) = \sigma(a)(1 - \sigma(a))$. This derivative becomes small at the extremes, which can make learning slow; this is called the **vanishing gradient** problem.

- The range of the **tanh activation function** is $(-1, 1)$: like the sigmoid, the range is bounded, but unlike the sigmoid, it includes negative values. The derivative is $\frac{\partial}{\partial a}\tanh(a) = 1 - \tanh(a)^2$, which is steeper than the logistic function near the origin (LeCun et al., 2012). The tanh function can also suffer from vanishing gradients at extreme values.
- The **rectified linear unit (ReLU)** is zero for negative inputs and linear for positive inputs (Glorot et al., 2011):

$$\text{ReLU}(a) = \begin{cases} a, & a \geq 0 \\ 0, & \text{otherwise.} \end{cases} \qquad [3.11]$$

The derivative is a step function, which is 1 if the input is positive, and zero otherwise. Once the activation is zero, the gradient is also zero. This can lead to the problem of "dead neurons," where some ReLU nodes are zero for all inputs, throughout learning. A solution is the **leaky ReLU**, which has a small positive slope for negative inputs (Maas et al., 2013),

$$\text{Leaky-ReLU}(a) = \begin{cases} a, & a \geq 0 \\ .0001a, & \text{otherwise.} \end{cases} \qquad [3.12]$$

Sigmoid and tanh are sometimes described as **squashing functions**, because they squash an unbounded input into a bounded range. Glorot and Bengio (2010) recommend against the use of the sigmoid activation in deep networks, because its mean value of $\frac{1}{2}$ can cause the next layer of the network to be saturated, leading to small gradients on its own parameters. Several other activation functions are reviewed in the textbook by Goodfellow et al. (2016), who recommend ReLU as the "default option."

3.2.2 Network Structure

Deep networks stack up several hidden layers, with each $z^{(d)}$ acting as the input to the next layer, $z^{(d+1)}$. As the total number of nodes in the network increases, so does its capacity to learn complex functions of the input. Given a fixed number of nodes, one must decide whether to emphasize width (large K_z at each layer) or depth (many layers). At present, this tradeoff is not well understood.[3]

It is also possible to "short circuit" a hidden layer, by propagating information directly from the input to the next higher level of the network. This is the idea behind **residual**

3. With even a single hidden layer, a neural network can approximate any continuous function on a closed and bounded subset of $\mathbb{R}^N$ to an arbitrarily small nonzero error; see section 6.4.1 of Goodfellow et al. (2016) for a survey of these theoretical results. However, depending on the function to be approximated, the width of the hidden layer may need to be arbitrarily large. Furthermore, the fact that a network has the *capacity* to approximate any given function does not imply that it is possible to *learn* the function using gradient-based optimization.

networks, which propagate information directly from the input to the subsequent layer (He et al., 2016),

$$z = f(\Theta^{(x \to z)} \boldsymbol{x}) + \boldsymbol{x}, \tag{3.13}$$

where f is any nonlinearity, such as sigmoid or ReLU. A more complex architecture is the **highway network** (Srivastava et al., 2015; Kim et al., 2016), in which an addition **gate** controls an interpolation between $f(\Theta^{(x \to z)} \boldsymbol{x})$ and $\boldsymbol{x}$,

$$\boldsymbol{t} = \sigma(\Theta^{(t)} \boldsymbol{x} + \boldsymbol{b}^{(t)}) \tag{3.14}$$

$$z = \boldsymbol{t} \odot f(\Theta^{(x \to z)} \boldsymbol{x}) + (\boldsymbol{1} - \boldsymbol{t}) \odot \boldsymbol{x}, \tag{3.15}$$

where $\odot$ refers to an elementwise vector product, and **1** is a column vector of ones. As before, the sigmoid function is applied elementwise to its input; recall that the output of this function is restricted to the range (0, 1). Gating is also used in the **long short-term memory (LSTM)**, which is discussed in chapter 6. Residual and highway connections address a problem with deep architectures: repeated application of a nonlinear activation function can make it difficult to learn the parameters of the lower levels of the network, which are too distant from the supervision signal.

3.2.3 Outputs and Loss Functions

In the multiclass classification example, a softmax output produces probabilities over each possible label. This aligns with a negative **conditional log-likelihood**,

$$-\mathcal{L} = -\sum_{i=1}^{N} \log p(y^{(i)} \mid \boldsymbol{x}^{(i)}; \Theta), \tag{3.16}$$

where $\Theta = \{\Theta^{(x \to z)}, \Theta^{(z \to y)}, \boldsymbol{b}\}$ is the entire set of parameters.

This loss can be written alternatively as follows:

$$\tilde{y}_j \triangleq \Pr(y = j \mid \boldsymbol{x}^{(i)}; \Theta) \tag{3.17}$$

$$-\mathcal{L} = -\sum_{i=1}^{N} \boldsymbol{e}_{y^{(i)}} \cdot \log \tilde{\boldsymbol{y}}, \tag{3.18}$$

where $\boldsymbol{e}_{y^{(i)}}$ is a **one-hot vector** of zeros with a value of 1 at position $y^{(i)}$. The inner product between $\boldsymbol{e}_{y^{(i)}}$ and $\log \tilde{\boldsymbol{y}}$ is also called the multinomial **cross-entropy**, and this terminology is preferred in many neural networks papers and software packages.

It is also possible to train neural networks from other objectives, such as a margin loss. In this case, it is not necessary to use softmax at the output layer—an affine transformation of the hidden layer is enough:

$$\Psi(y; \boldsymbol{x}^{(i)}, \Theta) = \boldsymbol{\theta}_y^{(z \to y)} \cdot z + b_y \tag{3.19}$$

$$\ell_{\text{MARGIN}}(\Theta; \boldsymbol{x}^{(i)}, y^{(i)}) = \max_{y \neq y^{(i)}} \left(1 + \Psi(y; \boldsymbol{x}^{(i)}, \Theta) - \Psi(y^{(i)}; \boldsymbol{x}^{(i)}, \Theta)\right)_+. \quad [3.20]$$

In regression problems, the output is a scalar or vector (see § 4.1.2). For these problems, a typical loss function is the squared error $(y - \hat{y})^2$ or squared norm $||\boldsymbol{y} - \hat{\boldsymbol{y}}||_2^2$.

3.2.4 Inputs and Lookup Layers

In text classification, the input layer $\boldsymbol{x}$ can refer to a bag-of-words vector, where x_j is the count of word j. The input to the hidden unit z_k is then $\sum_{j=1}^{V} \theta_{j,k}^{(x \to z)} x_j$, and word j is represented by the vector $\boldsymbol{\theta}_j^{(x \to z)}$. This vector is sometimes described as the **embedding** of word j and can be learned from unlabeled data, using techniques discussed in chapter 14. The columns of $\Theta^{(x \to z)}$ are each K_z-dimensional word embeddings.

Chapter 2 presented an alternative view of text documents, as sequences of word tokens, $w_1, w_2, \ldots, w_M$. In a neural network, each word token w_m is represented with a one-hot vector, $\boldsymbol{e}_{w_m}$, with dimension V. The matrix-vector product $\Theta^{(x \to z)} \boldsymbol{e}_{w_m}$ returns the embedding of word w_m. The complete document can be represented by horizontally concatenating these one-hot vectors, $\mathbf{W} = [\boldsymbol{e}_{w_1}, \boldsymbol{e}_{w_2}, \ldots, \boldsymbol{e}_{w_M}]$, and the bag-of-words representation can be recovered from the matrix-vector product $\mathbf{W}[1, 1, \ldots, 1]^\top$, which sums each row over the tokens $m = \{1, 2, \ldots, M\}$. The matrix product $\Theta^{(x \to z)} \mathbf{W}$ contains the horizontally concatenated embeddings of each word in the document, which will be useful as the starting point for **convolutional neural networks** (see § 3.4). This is sometimes called a **lookup layer**, because the first step is to look up the embeddings for each word in the input text.

3.3 Learning Neural Networks

The feedforward network in figure 3.1 can now be written as

$$\boldsymbol{z} \leftarrow f(\Theta^{(x \to z)} \boldsymbol{x}^{(i)}) \quad [3.21]$$

$$\tilde{\boldsymbol{y}} \leftarrow \text{softmax}\left(\Theta^{(z \to y)} \boldsymbol{z} + \boldsymbol{b}\right) \quad [3.22]$$

$$\ell^{(i)} \leftarrow -\boldsymbol{e}_{y^{(i)}} \cdot \log \tilde{\boldsymbol{y}}, \quad [3.23]$$

where f is an elementwise activation function, such as σ or ReLU, and $\ell^{(i)}$ is the loss at instance i. The parameters $\Theta^{(x \to z)}$, $\Theta^{(z \to y)}$, and $\boldsymbol{b}$ can be estimated using online gradient-based optimization. The simplest such algorithm is stochastic gradient descent, which was discussed in § 2.6. Each parameter is updated by the gradient of the loss,

$$\boldsymbol{b} \leftarrow \boldsymbol{b} - \eta^{(t)} \nabla_{\boldsymbol{b}} \ell^{(i)} \quad [3.24]$$

$$\boldsymbol{\theta}_k^{(z \to y)} \leftarrow \boldsymbol{\theta}_k^{(z \to y)} - \eta^{(t)} \nabla_{\boldsymbol{\theta}_k^{(z \to y)}} \ell^{(i)} \quad [3.25]$$

$$\boldsymbol{\theta}_n^{(x \to z)} \leftarrow \boldsymbol{\theta}_n^{(x \to z)} - \eta^{(t)} \nabla_{\boldsymbol{\theta}_n^{(x \to z)}} \ell^{(i)}, \quad [3.26]$$

where $\eta^{(t)}$ is the learning rate on iteration t, $\ell^{(i)}$ is the loss on instance (or minibatch) i, $\boldsymbol{\theta}_n^{(x\rightarrow z)}$ is column n of the matrix $\Theta^{(x\rightarrow z)}$, and $\boldsymbol{\theta}_k^{(z\rightarrow y)}$ is column k of $\Theta^{(z\rightarrow y)}$.

The gradients of the negative log-likelihood on $\boldsymbol{b}$ and $\boldsymbol{\theta}_k^{(z\rightarrow y)}$ are similar to the gradients in logistic regression. For $\boldsymbol{\theta}^{(z\rightarrow y)}$, the gradient is

$$\nabla_{\boldsymbol{\theta}_k^{(z\rightarrow y)}} \ell^{(i)} = \left[\frac{\partial \ell^{(i)}}{\partial \theta_{k,1}^{(z\rightarrow y)}}, \frac{\partial \ell^{(i)}}{\partial \theta_{k,2}^{(z\rightarrow y)}}, \ldots, \frac{\partial \ell^{(i)}}{\partial \theta_{k,K_y}^{(z\rightarrow y)}} \right]^\top \qquad [3.27]$$

$$\frac{\partial \ell^{(i)}}{\partial \theta_{k,j}^{(z\rightarrow y)}} = -\frac{\partial}{\partial \theta_{k,j}^{(z\rightarrow y)}} \left(\boldsymbol{\theta}_{y^{(i)}}^{(z\rightarrow y)} \cdot \boldsymbol{z} - \log \sum_{y \in \mathcal{Y}} \exp \boldsymbol{\theta}_y^{(z\rightarrow y)} \cdot \boldsymbol{z} \right) \qquad [3.28]$$

$$= \left(\Pr(y=j \mid \boldsymbol{z}; \Theta^{(z\rightarrow y)}, \boldsymbol{b}) - \delta\left(j=y^{(i)}\right) \right) z_k, \qquad [3.29]$$

where $\delta\left(j=y^{(i)}\right)$ is a function that returns one when $j=y^{(i)}$, and zero otherwise. The gradient $\nabla_{\boldsymbol{b}} \ell^{(i)}$ is similar to equation 3.29.

The gradients on the input layer weights $\Theta^{(x\rightarrow z)}$ are obtained by the chain rule of differentiation:

$$\frac{\partial \ell^{(i)}}{\partial \theta_{n,k}^{(x\rightarrow z)}} = \frac{\partial \ell^{(i)}}{\partial z_k} \frac{\partial z_k}{\partial \theta_{n,k}^{(x\rightarrow z)}} \qquad [3.30]$$

$$= \frac{\partial \ell^{(i)}}{\partial z_k} \frac{\partial f(\boldsymbol{\theta}_k^{(x\rightarrow z)} \cdot \boldsymbol{x})}{\partial \theta_{n,k}^{(x\rightarrow z)}} \qquad [3.31]$$

$$= \frac{\partial \ell^{(i)}}{\partial z_k} \times f'(\boldsymbol{\theta}_k^{(x\rightarrow z)} \cdot \boldsymbol{x}) \times x_n, \qquad [3.32]$$

where $f'(\boldsymbol{\theta}_k^{(x\rightarrow z)} \cdot \boldsymbol{x})$ is the derivative of the activation function f, applied at the input $\boldsymbol{\theta}_k^{(x\rightarrow z)} \cdot \boldsymbol{x}$. For example, if f is the sigmoid function, then the derivative is

$$\frac{\partial \ell^{(i)}}{\partial \theta_{n,k}^{(x\rightarrow z)}} = \frac{\partial \ell^{(i)}}{\partial z_k} \times \sigma(\boldsymbol{\theta}_k^{(x\rightarrow z)} \cdot \boldsymbol{x}) \times (1 - \sigma(\boldsymbol{\theta}_k^{(x\rightarrow z)} \cdot \boldsymbol{x})) \times x_n \qquad [3.33]$$

$$= \frac{\partial \ell^{(i)}}{\partial z_k} \times z_k \times (1 - z_k) \times x_n. \qquad [3.34]$$

For intuition, consider each of the terms in the product.

- If the negative log-likelihood $\ell^{(i)}$ does not depend much on z_k, then $\frac{\partial \ell^{(i)}}{\partial z_k} \approx 0$. In this case, it doesn't matter how z_k is computed, and so $\frac{\partial \ell^{(i)}}{\partial \theta_{n,k}^{(x\rightarrow z)}} \approx 0$.

- If z_k is near 1 or 0, then the curve of the sigmoid function is nearly flat (figure 3.2), and changing the inputs will make little local difference. The term $z_k \times (1 - z_k)$ is maximized at $z_k = \frac{1}{2}$, where the slope of the sigmoid function is steepest.
- If $x_n = 0$, then it does not matter how we set the weights $\theta_{n,k}^{(x \to z)}$, so $\frac{\partial \ell^{(i)}}{\partial \theta_{n,k}^{(x \to z)}} = 0$.

3.3.1 Backpropagation

The equations above rely on the chain rule to compute derivatives of the loss with respect to each parameter of the model. Furthermore, local derivatives are frequently reused: for example, $\frac{\partial \ell^{(i)}}{\partial z_k}$ is reused in computing the derivatives with respect to each $\theta_{n,k}^{(x \to z)}$. These terms should therefore be computed once and then cached. Furthermore, we should only compute any derivative once we have already computed all of the necessary "inputs" demanded by the chain rule of differentiation. This combination of sequencing, caching, and differentiation is known as **backpropagation**. It can be generalized to any directed acyclic **computation graph**.

A computation graph is a declarative representation of a computational process. At each node t, compute a value v_t by applying a function f_t to a (possibly empty) list of parent nodes $\boldsymbol{\pi}_t$. Figure 3.3 shows the computation graph for a feedforward network with one hidden layer. There are nodes for the input $\boldsymbol{x}^{(i)}$, the hidden layer z, the predicted output $\hat{\boldsymbol{y}}$, and the parameters Θ. During training, there is also a node for the ground truth label $y^{(i)}$ and the loss $\ell^{(i)}$. The predicted output $\hat{\boldsymbol{y}}$ is one of the parents of the loss (the other is the label $y^{(i)}$); *its* parents include Θ and z, and so on.

Computation graphs include three types of nodes:

Variables. In the feedforward network of figure 3.3, the variables include the inputs $\boldsymbol{x}$, the hidden nodes z, the outputs $\boldsymbol{y}$, and the loss function. Inputs are variables that do not have parents. Backpropagation computes the gradients with respect to all variables except the inputs and propagates these gradients backward to the parameters.

Parameters. In a feedforward network, the parameters include the weights and offsets. In figure 3.3, the parameters are summarized in the node Θ, but we could have separate nodes for $\Theta^{(x \to z)}$, $\Theta^{(z \to y)}$, and any offset parameters. Parameter nodes do not have parents; they are not computed from other nodes but, rather, are learned by gradient descent.

Loss. The loss $\ell^{(i)}$ is the quantity that is to be minimized during training. The node representing the loss in the computation graph is not the parent of any other node; its parents are typically the predicted label $\hat{\boldsymbol{y}}$ and the true label $\boldsymbol{y}^{(i)}$. Backpropagation begins by computing the gradient of the loss and then propagating this gradient backward to its immediate parents.

If the computation graph is a directed acyclic graph, then it is possible to order the nodes with a topological sort, so that if node t is a parent of node t', then $t < t'$. This means that the values $\{v_t\}_{t=1}^{T}$ can be computed in a single forward pass. The topological sort is reversed

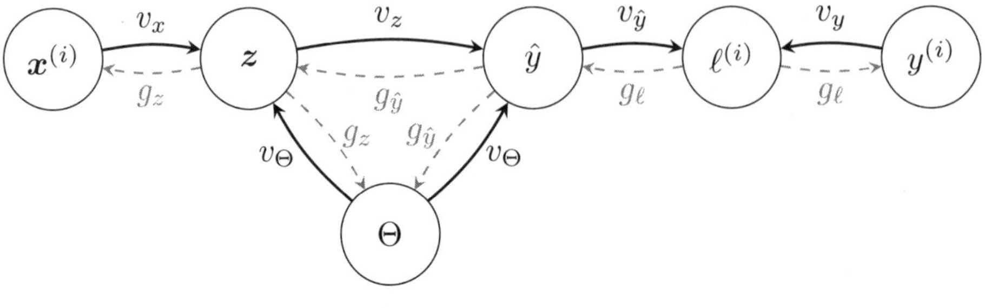

Figure 3.3
A computation graph for the feedforward neural network shown in figure 3.1.

when computing gradients: each gradient g_t is computed from the gradients of the children of t, implementing the chain rule of differentiation. The general backpropagation algorithm for computation graphs is shown in algorithm 6.

While the gradients with respect to each parameter may be complex, they are composed of products of simple parts. For many networks, all gradients can be computed through **automatic differentiation**. This means that you need only specify the feedforward computation, and the gradients necessary for learning can be obtained automatically. There are many software libraries that perform automatic differentiation on computation graphs, such as TORCH (Collobert et al., 2011a), TENSORFLOW (Abadi et al., 2016), and DYNET (Neubig et al., 2017b). One important distinction between these libraries is whether they support **dynamic computation graphs**, in which the structure of the computation graph varies across instances. Static computation graphs are compiled in advance and can be applied to fixed-dimensional data, such as bag-of-words vectors. In many natural language processing problems, each input has a distinct structure, requiring a unique computation graph. A simple case occurs in recurrent neural network language models (see chapter 6), in which there is one node for each word in a sentence. More complex cases include recursive neural networks (see chapter 14), in which the network is a tree structure matching the syntactic organization of the input.

3.3.2 Regularization and Dropout

In linear classification, overfitting was addressed by augmenting the objective with a regularization term, $\lambda||\boldsymbol{\theta}||_2^2$. This same approach can be applied to feedforward neural networks, penalizing each matrix of weights:

$$L = \sum_{i=1}^{N} \ell^{(i)} + \lambda_{z\rightarrow y}||\Theta^{(z\rightarrow y)}||_F^2 + \lambda_{x\rightarrow z}||\Theta^{(x\rightarrow z)}||_F^2, \qquad [3.35]$$

where $||\Theta||_F^2 = \sum_{i,j} \theta_{i,j}^2$ is the squared **Frobenius norm**, which generalizes the L_2 norm to matrices. The bias parameters $\boldsymbol{b}$ are not regularized, as they do not contribute to the

Algorithm 6

General backpropagation algorithm. In the computation graph G, every node contains a function f_t and a set of parent nodes $\boldsymbol{\pi}_t$; the inputs to the graph are $\boldsymbol{x}^{(i)}$.

---

procedure BACKPROP($G = \{f_t, \boldsymbol{\pi}_t\}_{t=1}^{T}\}, \boldsymbol{x}^{(i)}$)

  $v_{t(n)} \leftarrow x_n^{(i)}$ for all n and associated computation nodes $t(n)$.

  for $t \in$ TOPOLOGICALSORT(G) **do** ▷ Forward pass: compute value at each node

    if $|\boldsymbol{\pi}_t| > 0$ **then**

      $v_t \leftarrow f_t(v_{\pi_{t,1}}, v_{\pi_{t,2}}, \ldots, v_{\pi_{t,N_t}})$

  $g_{\text{objective}} \leftarrow 1$ ▷ Backward pass: compute gradients at each node

  for $t \in$ REVERSE(TOPOLOGICALSORT(G)) **do**

    $g_t \leftarrow \sum_{t':t \in \boldsymbol{\pi}_{t'}} g_{t'} \times \nabla_{v_t} v_{t'}$ ▷ Sum over all t' that are children of t, propagating the gradient $g_{t'}$, scaled by the local gradient $\nabla_{v_t} v_{t'}$

  return $\{g_1, g_2, \ldots, g_T\}$

---

sensitivity of the classifier to the inputs. In gradient-based optimization, the practical effect of Frobenius norm regularization is that the weights "decay" toward zero at each update, motivating the alternative name **weight decay**.

Another approach to controlling model complexity is **dropout**, which involves randomly setting some computation nodes to zero during training (Srivastava et al., 2014). For example, in the feedforward network, on each training instance, with probability ρ, we set each input x_n and each hidden layer node z_k to zero. Srivastava et al. (2014) recommend $\rho = 0.5$ for hidden units and $\rho = 0.2$ for input units. Dropout is also incorporated in the gradient computation, so if node z_k is dropped, then none of the weights $\boldsymbol{\theta}_k^{(x \to z)}$ will be updated for this instance. Dropout prevents the network from learning to depend too much on any one feature or hidden node and prevents **feature co-adaptation**, in which a hidden unit is only useful in combination with one or more other hidden units. Dropout is a special case of **feature noising**, which can also involve adding Gaussian noise to inputs or hidden units (Holmstrom and Koistinen, 1992). Wager et al. (2013) show that dropout is approximately equivalent to "adaptive" L_2 regularization, with a separate regularization penalty for each feature.

3.3.3 *Learning Theory

Chapter 2 emphasized the importance of **convexity** for learning: for convex objectives, the global optimum can be found efficiently. The negative log-likelihood and hinge loss are convex functions of the parameters of the output layer. However, the output of a feedforward network is generally not a convex function of the parameters of the input layer, $\Theta^{(x \to z)}$. Feedforward networks can be viewed as function composition, where each layer is a function that is applied to the output of the previous layer. Convexity is generally not preserved in the composition of two convex functions—and furthermore, "squashing" activation functions like tanh and sigmoid are not convex.

The nonconvexity of hidden layer neural networks can also be seen by permuting the elements of the hidden layer, from $\boldsymbol{z} = [z_1, z_2, \ldots, z_{K_z}]$ to $\tilde{\boldsymbol{z}} = [z_{\pi(1)}, z_{\pi(2)}, \ldots, z_{\pi(K_z)}]$. This corresponds to applying π to the rows of $\Theta^{(x \to z)}$ and the columns of $\Theta^{(z \to y)}$, resulting in permuted parameter matrices $\Theta_\pi^{(x \to z)}$ and $\Theta_\pi^{(z \to y)}$. As long as this permutation is applied consistently, the loss will be identical, $L(\Theta) = L(\Theta_\pi)$: it is *invariant* to this permutation. However, the loss of the linear combination $L(\alpha\Theta + (1-\alpha)\Theta_\pi)$ will generally not be identical to the loss under Θ or its permutations. If $L(\Theta)$ is better than the loss at any points in the immediate vicinity, and if $L(\Theta) = L(\Theta_\pi)$, then the loss function does not satisfy the definition of convexity (see § 2.4). One of the exercises asks you to prove this more rigorously.

In practice, the existence of multiple optima is not necessary problematic, if all such optima are permutations of the sort described in the previous paragraph. In contrast, "bad" local optima are better than their neighbors, but much worse than the global optimum. Fortunately, in large feedforward neural networks, most local optima are nearly as good as the global optimum (Choromanska et al., 2015). More generally, a **critical point** is one at which the gradient is zero. Critical points may be local optima, but they may also be **saddle points**, which are local minima in some directions, but local *maxima* in other directions. For example, the equation $x_1^2 - x_2^2$ has a saddle point at $\boldsymbol{x} = (0, 0)$. In large networks, the overwhelming majority of critical points are saddle points, rather than local minima or maxima (Dauphin et al., 2014). Saddle points can pose problems for gradient-based optimization, because learning will slow to a crawl as the gradient goes to zero. However, the noise introduced by stochastic gradient descent, and by feature noising techniques such as dropout, can help online optimization to escape saddle points and find high-quality optima (Ge et al., 2015). Other techniques address saddle points directly, using local reconstructions of the Hessian matrix (Dauphin et al., 2014) or higher-order derivatives (Anandkumar and Ge, 2016).

Another theoretical puzzle about neural networks is how they are able to **generalize** to unseen data. Given enough parameters, a two-layer feedforward network can "memorize" its training data, attaining perfect accuracy on any training set. A particularly salient demonstration was provided by Zhang et al. (2017), who showed that neural networks can learn to perfectly classify a training set of images, even when the labels are replaced with random values! Of course, this network attains only chance accuracy when applied to heldout data. The concern is that when such a powerful learner is applied to real training data, it may learn a pathological classification function, which exploits irrelevant details of the training data and fails to generalize. Yet this extreme **overfitting** is rarely encountered in practice, and can usually be prevented by regularization, dropout, and early stopping (see § 3.3.4). Recent papers have derived generalization guarantees for specific classes of neural networks (e.g., Kawaguchi et al., 2017; Brutzkus et al., 2018), but theoretical work in this area is ongoing.

3.3.4 Tricks

Getting neural networks to work sometimes requires heuristic "tricks" (Bottou, 2012; Goodfellow et al., 2016; Goldberg, 2017). This section presents some tricks that are especially important.

Initialization Initialization is not especially important for linear classifiers, because convexity ensures that the global optimum can usually be found quickly. But for multilayer neural networks, it is helpful to have a good starting point. One reason is that if the magnitude of the initial weights is too large, a sigmoid or tanh nonlinearity will be saturated, leading to a small gradient, and slow learning. Large gradients can cause training to diverge, with the parameters taking increasingly extreme values until reaching the limits of the floating point representation.

Initialization can help avoid these problems by ensuring that the variance over the initial gradients is constant and bounded throughout the network. For networks with tanh activation functions, this can be achieved by sampling the initial weights from the following uniform distribution (Glorot and Bengio, 2010),

$$\theta_{i,j} \sim U\left[-\frac{\sqrt{6}}{\sqrt{d_{\text{in}}(n)+d_{\text{out}}(n)}}, \frac{\sqrt{6}}{\sqrt{d_{\text{in}}(n)+d_{\text{out}}(n)}}\right]. \quad [3.36]$$

For the weights leading to a ReLU activation function, He et al. (2015) use similar argumentation to justify sampling from a zero-mean Gaussian distribution,

$$\theta_{i,j} \sim N(0, \sqrt{2/d_{\text{in}}(n)}). \quad [3.37]$$

Rather than initializing the weights independently, it can be beneficial to initialize each layer jointly as an **orthonormal matrix**, ensuring that $\Theta^\top\Theta = \mathbb{I}$ (Saxe et al., 2014). Orthonormal matrices preserve the norm of the input, so that $||\Theta \boldsymbol{x}|| = ||\boldsymbol{x}||$, which prevents the gradients from exploding or vanishing. Orthogonality ensures that the hidden units are uncorrelated, so that they correspond to different features of the input. Orthonormal initialization can be performed by applying **singular-value decomposition** to a matrix of values sampled from a standard normal distribution:

$$a_{i,j} \sim N(0,1) \quad [3.38]$$

$$\mathbf{A} = \{a_{i,j}\}_{i=1,j=1}^{d_{\text{in}}(j),d_{\text{out}}(j)} \quad [3.39]$$

$$\mathbf{U}, \mathbf{S}, \mathbf{V}^\top = \text{SVD}(\mathbf{A}) \quad [3.40]$$

$$\Theta^{(j)} \leftarrow \mathbf{U}. \quad [3.41]$$

The matrix **U** contains the **singular vectors** of **A** and is guaranteed to be orthonormal. For more on singular-value decomposition, see chapter 14.

Even with careful initialization, there can still be significant variance in the final results. It can be useful to make multiple training runs and select the one with the best performance on a heldout development set.

Clipping and normalization Learning can be sensitive to the magnitude of the gradient: too large, and learning can diverge, with successive updates thrashing between increasingly extreme values; too small, and learning can grind to a halt. Several heuristics have been proposed to address this issue.

- In **gradient clipping** (Pascanu et al., 2013), an upper limit is placed on the norm of the gradient, and the gradient is rescaled when this limit is exceeded:

$$\text{CLIP}(\tilde{\boldsymbol{g}}) = \begin{cases} \boldsymbol{g} & ||\hat{\boldsymbol{g}}|| < \tau \\ \frac{\tau}{||\boldsymbol{g}||}\boldsymbol{g} & \text{otherwise.} \end{cases} \quad [3.42]$$

- In **batch normalization** (Ioffe and Szegedy, 2015), the inputs to each computation node are recentered by their mean and variance across all of the instances in the minibatch $\mathcal{B}$ (see § 2.6.2). For example, in a feedforward network with one hidden layer, batch normalization would tranform the inputs to the hidden layer as follows:

$$\boldsymbol{\mu}^{(\mathcal{B})} = \frac{1}{|\mathcal{B}|}\sum_{i \in \mathcal{B}} \boldsymbol{x}^{(i)} \quad [3.43]$$

$$\boldsymbol{s}^{(\mathcal{B})} = \frac{1}{|\mathcal{B}|}\sum_{i \in \mathcal{B}} (\boldsymbol{x}^{(i)} - \boldsymbol{\mu}^{(\mathcal{B})})^2 \quad [3.44]$$

$$\overline{\boldsymbol{x}}^{(i)} = (\boldsymbol{x}^{(i)} - \boldsymbol{\mu}^{(\mathcal{B})})/\sqrt{\boldsymbol{s}^{(\mathcal{B})}}. \quad [3.45]$$

Empirically, this speeds convergence of deep architectures. One explanation is that it helps to correct for changes in the distribution of activations during training.

- In **layer normalization** (Ba et al., 2016), the inputs to each nonlinear activation function are recentered across the layer:

$$\boldsymbol{a} = \Theta^{(x \to z)}\boldsymbol{x} \quad [3.46]$$

$$\mu = \frac{1}{K_z}\sum_{k=1}^{K_z} a_k \quad [3.47]$$

$$s = \frac{1}{K_z}\sum_{k=1}^{K_z} (a_k - \mu)^2 \quad [3.48]$$

$$\boldsymbol{z} = (\boldsymbol{a} - \mu)/\sqrt{s}. \quad [3.49]$$

Layer normalization has similar motivations to batch normalization, but it can be applied across a wider range of architectures and training conditions.

Online optimization There is a cottage industry of online optimization algorithms that attempt to improve on stochastic gradient descent. **AdaGrad** was reviewed in § 2.6.2; its main innovation is to set adaptive learning rates for each parameter by storing the sum of squared gradients. Rather than using the sum over the entire training history, we can keep a running estimate,

$$v_j^{(t)} = \beta v_j^{(t-1)} + (1 - \beta) g_{t,j}^2, \tag{3.50}$$

where $g_{t,j}$ is the gradient with respect to parameter j at time t, and $\beta \in [0, 1]$. This term places more emphasis on recent gradients and is employed in the AdaDelta (Zeiler, 2012) and Adam (Kingma and Ba, 2014) optimizers. Online optimization and its theoretical background are reviewed by Bottou et al. (2018). **Early stopping**, mentioned in § 2.3.2, can help to avoid overfitting by terminating training after reaching a plateau in the performance on a heldout validation set.

Practical advice The bag of tricks for training neural networks continues to grow, and it is likely that there will be several new ones by the time you read this. Today, it is standard practice to use gradient clipping, early stopping, and a sensible initialization of parameters to small random values. More bells and whistles can be added as solutions to specific problems—for example, if it is difficult to find a good learning rate for stochastic gradient descent, then it may help to try a fancier optimizer with an adaptive learning rate. Alternatively, if a method such as layer normalization is used by related models in the research literature, you should probably consider it, especially if you are having trouble matching published results. As with linear classifiers, it is important to evaluate these decisions on a held-out development set, and not on the test set that will be used to provide the final measure of the model's performance (see § 2.2.5).

3.4 Convolutional Neural Networks

A basic weakness of the bag-of-words model is its inability to account for the ways in which words combine to create meaning, including even simple reversals such as *not pleasant*, *hardly a generous offer*, and *I wouldn't mind missing the flight*. Computer vision faces the related challenge of identifying the semantics of images from pixel features that are uninformative in isolation. An earlier generation of computer vision research focused on designing *filters* to aggregate local pixel-level features into more meaningful representations, such as edges and corners (e.g., Canny, 1986). Similarly, earlier NLP research attempted to capture multiword linguistic phenomena by hand-designed lexical patterns (Hobbs et al., 1997). In both cases, the output of the filters and patterns could then act as base features in a linear classifier. But rather than designing these feature extractors by hand, a better approach is to learn them, using the magic of backpropagation. This is the idea behind **convolutional neural networks**.

Following § 3.2.4, define the base layer of a neural network as

$$\mathbf{X}^{(0)} = \Theta^{(x \to z)}[\boldsymbol{e}_{w_1}, \boldsymbol{e}_{w_2}, \ldots, \boldsymbol{e}_{w_M}], \tag{3.51}$$

where $\boldsymbol{e}_{w_m}$ is a column vector of zeros, with a 1 at position w_m. The base layer has dimension $\mathbf{X}^{(0)} \in \mathbb{R}^{K_e \times M}$, where K_e is the size of the word embeddings. To merge information across adjacent words, we *convolve* $\mathbf{X}^{(0)}$ with a set of filter matrices $\mathbf{C}^{(k)} \in \mathbb{R}^{K_e \times h}$. Convolution is indicated by the symbol $*$, and is defined as

$$\mathbf{X}^{(1)} = f(\boldsymbol{b} + \mathbf{C} * \mathbf{X}^{(0)}) \quad \Longrightarrow \quad x_{k,m}^{(1)} = f\left(b_k + \sum_{k'=1}^{K_e} \sum_{n=1}^{h} c_{k',n}^{(k)} \times x_{k',m+n-1}^{(0)}\right), \tag{3.52}$$

where f is an activation function such as tanh or ReLU, and $\boldsymbol{b}$ is a vector of offsets. The convolution operation slides the matrix $\mathbf{C}^{(k)}$ across the columns of $\mathbf{X}^{(0)}$. At each position m, we compute the elementwise product $\mathbf{C}^{(k)} \odot \mathbf{X}_{m:m+h-1}^{(0)}$, and take the sum.

A simple filter might compute a weighted average over nearby words,

$$\mathbf{C}^{(k)} = \begin{bmatrix} 0.5 & 1 & 0.5 \\ 0.5 & 1 & 0.5 \\ \ldots & \ldots & \ldots \\ 0.5 & 1 & 0.5 \end{bmatrix}, \tag{3.53}$$

thereby representing trigram units like *not so unpleasant*. In **one-dimensional convolution**, each filter matrix $\mathbf{C}^{(k)}$ is constrained to have nonzero values only at row k (Kalchbrenner et al., 2014). This means that each dimension of the word embedding is processed by a separate filter, and it implies that $K_f = K_e$.

To deal with the beginning and end of the input, the base matrix $\mathbf{X}^{(0)}$ may be padded with h column vectors of zeros at the beginning and end; this is known as **wide convolution**. If padding is not applied, then the output from each layer will be $h-1$ units smaller than the input; this is known as **narrow convolution**. The filter matrices need not have identical filter widths, so more generally we could write h_k to indicate to width of filter $\mathbf{C}^{(k)}$. As suggested by the notation $\mathbf{X}^{(0)}$, multiple layers of convolution may be applied, so that $\mathbf{X}^{(d)}$ is the input to $\mathbf{X}^{(d+1)}$.

After D convolutional layers, we obtain a matrix representation of the document $\mathbf{X}^{(D)} \in \mathbb{R}^{K_z \times M}$. If the instances have variable lengths, it is necessary to aggregate over all M word positions to obtain a fixed-length representation. This can be done by a **pooling** operation, such as max pooling (Collobert et al., 2011b) or average pooling,

$$z = \text{MaxPool}(\mathbf{X}^{(D)}) \quad \Longrightarrow \quad z_k = \max\left(x_{k,1}^{(D)}, x_{k,2}^{(D)}, \ldots x_{k,M}^{(D)}\right) \tag{3.54}$$

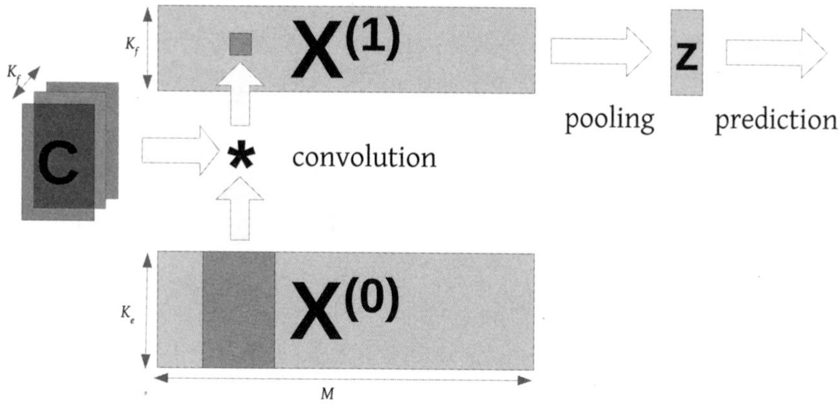

Figure 3.4
A convolutional neural network for text classification.

$$z = \text{AvgPool}(\mathbf{X}^{(D)}) \quad \Longrightarrow \quad z_k = \frac{1}{M}\sum_{m=1}^{M} x_{k,m}^{(D)}. \qquad [3.55]$$

The vector z can now act as a layer in a feedforward network, culminating in a prediction $\hat{y}$ and a loss $\ell^{(i)}$. The setup is shown in figure 3.4.

Just as in feedforward networks, the parameters $(\mathbf{C}^{(k)}, \boldsymbol{b}, \Theta)$ can be learned by backpropagating from the classification loss. This requires backpropagating through the max-pooling operation, which is a discontinuous function of the input. But because we need only a local gradient, backpropagation flows only through the argmax m:

$$\frac{\partial z_k}{\partial x_{k,m}^{(D)}} = \begin{cases} 1, & x_{k,m}^{(D)} = \max\left(x_{k,1}^{(D)}, x_{k,2}^{(D)}, \ldots x_{k,M}^{(D)}\right) \\ 0, & \text{otherwise.} \end{cases} \qquad [3.56]$$

The computer vision literature has produced a huge variety of convolutional architectures, and many of these innovations can be applied to text data. One avenue for improvement is more complex pooling operations, such as k-max pooling (Kalchbrenner et al., 2014), which returns a matrix of the k largest values for each filter. Another innovation is the use of **dilated convolution** to build multiscale representations (Yu and Koltun, 2016). At each layer, the convolutional operator applied in *strides*, skipping ahead by s steps after each feature. As we move up the hierarchy, each layer is s times smaller than the layer below it, effectively summarizing the input (Kalchbrenner et al., 2016; Strubell et al., 2017). This idea is shown in figure 3.5. Multilayer convolutional networks can also be augmented with "shortcut" connections, as in the residual network from § 3.2.2 (Johnson and Zhang, 2017).

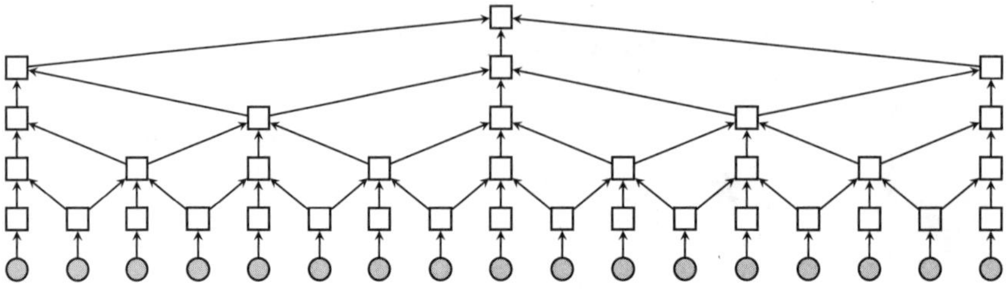

Figure 3.5
A dilated convolutional neural network captures progressively larger context through recursive application of the convolutional operator.

Additional Resources

The deep learning textbook by Goodfellow et al. (2016) covers many of the topics in this chapter in more detail. For a comprehensive review of neural networks in natural language processing, see Goldberg (2017). A seminal work on deep learning in natural language processing is the aggressively titled "Natural Language Processing (Almost) from Scratch," which uses convolutional neural networks to perform a range of language processing tasks (Collobert et al., 2011b), although there is earlier work (e.g., Henderson, 2004). This chapter focuses on feedforward and convolutional neural networks, but recurrent neural networks are one of the most important deep learning architectures for natural language processing, They are covered extensively in chapters 6 and 7.

The role of deep learning in natural language processing research has provoked angst in some parts of the natural language processing research community (e.g., Goldberg, 2017 (accessed February 6, 2019)), especially as some of the more zealous deep learning advocates have argued that end-to-end learning from "raw" text can eliminate the need for linguistic constructs such as sentences, phrases, and even words (Zhang et al., 2015, originally titled "Text Understanding from Scratch"). These developments were surveyed by Manning (2015). While reports of the demise of linguistics in natural language processing remain controversial at best, deep learning and backpropagation have become ubiquitous in both research and applications.

Exercises

1. Figure 3.3 shows the computation graph for a feedforward neural network with one layer.
   a) Update the computation graph to include a residual connection between $\boldsymbol{x}$ and $\boldsymbol{z}$.
   b) Update the computation graph to include a highway connection between $\boldsymbol{x}$ and $\boldsymbol{z}$.

2. Prove that the softmax and sigmoid functions are equivalent when the number of possible labels is two. Specifically, for any $\Theta^{(z \rightarrow y)}$ (omitting the offset $\boldsymbol{b}$ for simplicity), show how to construct a vector of weights $\boldsymbol{\theta}$ such that

$$\text{softmax}(\Theta^{(z \rightarrow y)} z)[0] = \sigma(\boldsymbol{\theta} \cdot z). \quad [3.57]$$

3. Convolutional neural networks often aggregate across words by using max **pooling** (equation 3.54 in § 3.4). A potential concern is that there is zero gradient with respect to the parts of the input that are not included in the maximum. The following questions consider the gradient with respect to an element of the input, $x_{m,k}^{(0)}$, and they assume that all parameters are independently distributed.
   a) First consider a minimal network, with $z = \text{MaxPool}(\mathbf{X}^{(0)})$. What is the probability that the gradient $\frac{\partial \ell}{\partial x_{m,k}^{(0)}}$ is nonzero?
   b) Now consider a two-level network, with $\mathbf{X}^{(1)} = f(\boldsymbol{b} + \mathbf{C} * \mathbf{X}^{(0)})$. Express the probability that the gradient $\frac{\partial \ell}{\partial x_{m,k}^{(0)}}$ is nonzero, in terms of the input length M, the filter size n, and the number of filters K_f.
   c) Using a calculator, work out the probability for the case $M = 128, n = 4, K_f = 32$.
   d) Now consider a three-level network, $\mathbf{X}^{(2)} = f(\boldsymbol{b} + \mathbf{C} * \mathbf{X}^{(1)})$. Give the general equation for the probability that $\frac{\partial \ell}{\partial x_{m,k}^{(0)}}$ is nonzero, and compute the numerical probability for the scenario in the previous part, assuming $K_f = 32$ and $n = 4$ at both levels.
4. Design a feedforward network to compute the XOR function:

$$f(x_1, x_2) = \begin{cases} -1, & x_1 = 1, x_2 = 1 \\ 1, & x_1 = 1, x_2 = 0 \\ 1, & x_1 = 0, x_2 = 1 \\ -1, & x_1 = 0, x_2 = 0 \end{cases}. \quad [3.58]$$

   Your network should have a single output node that uses the "Sign" activation function, $f(x) = \begin{cases} 1, & x > 0 \\ -1, & x \leq 0. \end{cases}$. Use a single hidden layer, with ReLU activation functions. Describe all weights and offsets.
5. Consider the same network as above (with ReLU activations for the hidden layer), with an arbitrary differentiable loss function $\ell(y^{(i)}, \tilde{y})$, where $\tilde{y}$ is the activation of the output node. Suppose all weights and offsets are initialized to zero. Show that gradient descent will not learn the desired function from this initialization.
6. The simplest solution to the previous problem relies on the use of the ReLU activation function at the hidden layer. Now consider a network with arbitrary activations on the hidden layer. Show that if the initial weights are any uniform constant, then gradient descent will not learn the desired function from this initialization.

7. Consider a network in which the base features are all binary, $\boldsymbol{x} \in \{0, 1\}^M$; the hidden layer activation function is sigmoid, $z_k = \sigma(\boldsymbol{\theta}_k \cdot \boldsymbol{x})$; and the initial weights are sampled independently from a standard normal distribution, $\theta_{j,k} \sim N(0, 1)$.
   - Show how the probability of a small initial gradient on any weight, $\frac{\partial z_k}{\partial \boldsymbol{\theta}_{j,k}} < \alpha$, depends on the size of the input M. **Hint**: use the lower bound,
   $$\Pr(\sigma(\boldsymbol{\theta}_k \cdot \boldsymbol{x}) \times (1 - \sigma(\boldsymbol{\theta}_k \cdot \boldsymbol{x})) < \alpha) \quad \geq \quad 2\Pr(\sigma(\boldsymbol{\theta}_k \cdot \boldsymbol{x}) < \alpha), \tag{3.59}$$
   and relate this probability to the variance $V[\boldsymbol{\theta}_k \cdot \boldsymbol{x}]$.
   - Design an alternative initialization that removes this dependence.
8. The ReLU activation function can lead to "dead neurons," which can never be activated on any input. Consider the following two-layer feedforward network with a scalar output y:
   $$z_i = \text{ReLU}(\boldsymbol{\theta}_i^{(x \to z)} \cdot \boldsymbol{x} + b_i) \tag{3.60}$$
   $$y = \boldsymbol{\theta}^{(z \to y)} \cdot \boldsymbol{z}. \tag{3.61}$$
   Suppose that the input is a binary vector of observations, $\boldsymbol{x} \in \{0, 1\}^D$.
   a) Under what condition is node z_i "dead"? Your answer should be expressed in terms of the parameters $\boldsymbol{\theta}_i^{(x \to z)}$ and b_i.
   b) Suppose that the gradient of the loss on a given instance is $\frac{\partial \ell}{\partial y} = 1$. Derive the gradients $\frac{\partial \ell}{\partial b_i}$ and $\frac{\partial \ell}{\partial \theta_{j,i}^{(x \to z)}}$ for such an instance.
   c) Using your answers to the previous two parts, explain why a dead neuron can never be brought back to life during gradient-based learning.
9. Suppose that the parameters $\Theta = \{\Theta^{(x \to z)}, \Theta(z \to y), \boldsymbol{b}\}$ are a local optimum of a feedforward network in the following sense: there exists some $\epsilon > 0$ such that
   $$\left(||\tilde{\Theta}^{(x \to z)} - \Theta^{(x \to z)}||_F^2 + ||\tilde{\Theta}^{(z \to y)} - \Theta^{(z \to y)}||_F^2 + ||\tilde{\boldsymbol{b}} - \boldsymbol{b}||_2^2 < \epsilon \right)$$
   $$\Rightarrow \left(L(\tilde{\Theta}) > L(\Theta) \right). \tag{3.62}$$
   Define the function π as a permutation on the hidden units, as described in § 3.3.3, so that for any Θ, $L(\Theta) = L(\Theta_\pi)$. Prove that if a feedforward network has a local optimum in the sense of item 3.62, then its loss is not a convex function of the parameters Θ, using the definition of convexity from § 2.4
10. Consider a network with a single hidden layer, and a single output,
   $$y = \boldsymbol{\theta}^{(z \to y)} \cdot g(\Theta^{(x \to z)} \boldsymbol{x}). \tag{3.63}$$
   Assume that g is the ReLU function. Show that for any matrix of weights $\Theta^{(x \to z)}$, it is permissible to rescale each row to have a norm of one, because an identical output can be obtained by finding a corresponding rescaling of $\boldsymbol{\theta}^{(z \to y)}$.

4 Linguistic Applications of Classification

Having covered several techniques for classification, this chapter shifts the focus from mathematics to linguistic applications. Later in the chapter, we will consider the design decisions involved in text classification, as well as best practices for evaluation.

4.1 Sentiment and Opinion Analysis

A popular application of text classification is to automatically determine the **sentiment** or **opinion polarity** of documents such as product reviews and social media posts. For example, marketers are interested to know how people respond to advertisements, services, and products (Hu and Liu, 2004), and social scientists are interested in how emotions are affected by phenomena such as the weather (Hannak et al., 2012) and how both opinions and emotions spread over social networks (Coviello et al., 2014; Miller et al., 2011). In the field of **digital humanities**, literary scholars track plot structures through the flow of sentiment across a novel (Jockers, 2015).[1]

Sentiment analysis can be framed as a direct application of document classification, assuming reliable labels can be obtained. In the simplest case, sentiment analysis is a two- or three-class problem, with sentiments of POSITIVE, NEGATIVE, and possibly NEUTRAL. Such labels could be annotated by hand, or obtained automatically through a variety of means:

- Tweets containing happy emoticons can be marked as positive and sad emoticons as negative (Read, 2005; Pak and Paroubek, 2010).
- Reviews with four or more stars can be marked as positive and three or fewer stars as negative (Pang et al., 2002).
- Statements from politicians who are voting for a given bill are marked as positive (toward that bill); statements from politicians voting against the bill are marked as negative (Thomas et al., 2006).

1. Comprehensive surveys on sentiment analysis and related problems are offered by Pang and Lee (2008) and Liu (2015).

The bag-of-words model is a good fit for sentiment analysis at the document level: if the document is long enough, we would expect the words associated with its true sentiment to overwhelm the others. Indeed, **lexicon-based sentiment analysis** avoids machine learning altogether, and classifies documents by counting words against positive and negative sentiment word lists (Taboada et al., 2011).

Lexicon-based classification is less effective for short documents, such as single-sentence reviews or social media posts. In these documents, linguistic issues like **negation** and **irrealis** (Polanyi and Zaenen, 2006)—events that are hypothetical or otherwise nonfactual—can make bag-of-words classification ineffective. Consider the following examples:

(4.1) a. That's not bad for the first day.
b. This is not the worst thing that can happen.
c. It would be nice if you acted like you understood.
d. There is no reason at all to believe that the polluters are suddenly going to become reasonable (Wilson et al., 2005).
e. This film should be brilliant. The actors are first grade. Stallone plays a happy, wonderful man. His sweet wife is beautiful and adores him. He has a fascinating gift for living life fully. It sounds like a great plot, **however**, the film is a failure (Pang et al., 2002).

A minimal solution is to move from a bag-of-words model to a bag-of-**bigrams** model, where each base feature is a pair of adjacent words, for example,

$$(\textit{that's}, \textit{not}), (\textit{not}, \textit{bad}), (\textit{bad}, \textit{for}), \ldots \qquad [4.1]$$

Bigrams can handle relatively straightforward cases, such as when an adjective is immediately negated; trigrams would be required to extend to larger contexts (e.g., *not the worst*). But this approach will not scale to more complex examples like (4.1d) and (4.1e). More sophisticated solutions try to account for the syntactic structure of the sentence (Wilson et al., 2005; Socher et al., 2013b) or apply more complex classifiers such as convolutional neural networks (Kim, 2014), which are described in chapter 3.

4.1.1 Related Problems

Subjectivity Closely related to sentiment analysis is **subjectivity detection**, which requires identifying the parts of a text that express subjective opinions, as well as other nonfactual content such as speculation and hypotheticals (Riloff and Wiebe, 2003). This can be done by treating each sentence as a separate document and then applying a bag-of-words classifier: indeed, Pang and Lee (2004) do exactly this, using a training set consisting of (mostly) subjective sentences gathered from movie reviews and (mostly) objective sentences gathered from plot descriptions. They augment this bag-of-words model with a graph-based algorithm that encourages nearby sentences to have the same subjectivity label.

Stance classification In debates, each participant takes a side: for example, advocating for or against proposals like adopting a vegetarian lifestyle or mandating free college education. The problem of stance classification is to identify the author's position from the text of the argument. In some cases, there is training data available for each position, so that standard document classification techniques can be employed. In other cases, it suffices to classify each document as whether it is in support or opposition of the argument advanced by a previous document (Anand et al., 2011). In the most challenging case, there is no labeled data for any of the stances, so the only possibility is group documents that advocate the same position (Somasundaran and Wiebe, 2009). This is a form of **unsupervised learning**, discussed in chapter 5.

Targeted sentiment analysis The expression of sentiment is often more nuanced than a simple binary label. Consider the following examples:

(4.2) a. The vodka was good, but the meat was rotten.
b. Go to Heaven for the climate, Hell for the company. —*Mark Twain*

These statements display a mixed overall sentiment: positive toward some entities (e.g., *the vodka*) and negative toward others (e.g., *the meat*). **Targeted sentiment analysis** seeks to identify the writer's sentiment toward specific entities (Jiang et al., 2011). This requires identifying the entities in the text and linking them to specific sentiment words—much more than we can do with the classification-based approaches discussed thus far. For example, Kim and Hovy (2006) analyze sentence-internal structure to determine the topic of each sentiment expression.

Aspect-based opinion mining seeks to identify the sentiment of the author of a review toward predefined aspects such as PRICE and SERVICE, or, in the case of (4.2b), CLIMATE and COMPANY (Hu and Liu, 2004). If the aspects are not defined in advance, it may again be necessary to employ unsupervised learning methods to identify them (e.g., Branavan et al., 2009b).

Emotion classification While sentiment analysis is framed in terms of positive and negative categories, psychologists generally regard **emotion** as more multifaceted. For example, Ekman (1992) argues that there are six basic emotions—happiness, surprise, fear, sadness, anger, and contempt—and that they are universal across human cultures. Alm et al. (2005) build a linear classifier for recognizing the emotions expressed in children's stories. The ultimate goal of this work was to improve text-to-speech synthesis, so that stories could be read with intonation that reflected the emotional content. They used bag-of-words features, as well as features capturing the story type (e.g., jokes, folktales), and structural features that reflect the position of each sentence in the story. The task is difficult: even human annotators frequently disagreed with each other, and the best classifiers achieved accuracy between 60% and 70%.

4.1.2 Alternative Approaches to Sentiment Analysis

Regression A more challenging version of sentiment analysis is to determine not just the class of a document, but also its rating on a numerical scale (Pang and Lee, 2005). If the scale is continuous, it is most natural to apply **regression**, identifying a set of weights $\boldsymbol{\theta}$ that minimize the squared error of a predictor $\hat{y} = \boldsymbol{\theta} \cdot \boldsymbol{x} + b$, where b is an offset. This approach is called **linear regression**, and sometimes **least squares**, because the regression coefficients $\boldsymbol{\theta}$ are determined by minimizing the squared error, $(y - \hat{y})^2$. If the weights are regularized using a penalty $\lambda ||\boldsymbol{\theta}||_2^2$, then it is **ridge regression**. Unlike logistic regression, both linear regression and ridge regression can be solved in closed form as a system of linear equations.

Ordinal ranking In many problems, the labels are ordered but discrete: for example, product reviews are often integers on a scale of $1 - 5$, and grades are on a scale of $A - F$. Such problems can be solved by discretizing the score $\boldsymbol{\theta} \cdot \boldsymbol{x}$ into "ranks,"

$$\hat{y} = \underset{r:\ \boldsymbol{\theta} \cdot \boldsymbol{x} \geq b_r}{\operatorname{argmax}}\ r, \tag{4.2}$$

where $\boldsymbol{b} = [b_1 = -\infty, b_2, b_3, \ldots, b_K]$ is a vector of boundaries. It is possible to learn the weights and boundaries simultaneously, using a perceptron-like algorithm (Crammer and Singer, 2001).

Lexicon-based classification Sentiment analysis is one of the only NLP tasks where hand-crafted feature weights are still widely employed. In **lexicon-based classification** (Taboada et al., 2011), the user creates a list of words for each label, and then classifies each document based on how many of the words from each list are present. In our linear classification framework, this is equivalent to choosing the following weights:

$$\theta_{y,j} = \begin{cases} 1, & j \in \mathcal{L}_y \\ 0, & \text{otherwise,} \end{cases} \tag{4.3}$$

where $\mathcal{L}_y$ is the lexicon for label y. Compared to the machine learning classifiers discussed in the previous chapters, lexicon-based classification may seem primitive. However, supervised machine learning relies on large annotated datasets, which are time consuming and expensive to produce. If the goal is to distinguish two or more categories in a new domain, it may be simpler to start by writing down a list of words for each category.

An early lexicon was the *General Inquirer* (Stone, 1966). Today, popular sentiment lexicons include SENTIWORDNET (Esuli and Sebastiani, 2006) and an evolving set of lexicons from Liu (2015). For emotions and more fine-grained analysis, *Linguistic Inquiry and Word Count* (LIWC) provides a set of lexicons (Tausczik and Pennebaker, 2010). The MPQA lexicon indicates the polarity (positive or negative) of 8,221 terms, as well as whether they are strongly or weakly subjective (Wiebe et al., 2005). A comprehensive comparison of sentiment lexicons is offered by Ribeiro et al. (2016). Given an initial **seed lexicon**, it is possible to automatically expand the lexicon by looking for words that frequently co-occur with words in the seed set (Hatzivassiloglou and McKeown, 1997; Qiu et al., 2011).

4.2 Word Sense Disambiguation

Consider the the following headlines:

(4.3) a. Iraqi head seeks arms
b. Prostitutes appeal to Pope
c. Drunk gets nine years in violin case[2]

These headlines are ambiguous because they contain words that have multiple meanings, or **senses**. Word sense disambiguation is the problem of identifying the intended sense of each word token in a document. Word sense disambiguation is part of a larger field of research called **lexical semantics**, which is concerned with meanings of the words.

At a basic level, the problem of word sense disambiguation is to identify the correct sense for each word token in a document. Part-of-speech ambiguity (e.g., noun versus verb) is usually considered to be a different problem, to be solved at an earlier stage. From a linguistic perspective, senses are not properties of words, but of **lemmas**, which are canonical forms that stand in for a set of inflected words. For example, *arm*/N is a lemma that includes the inflected form *arms*/N—the /N indicates that we are referring to the noun, and not its **homonym** *arm*/V, which is another lemma that includes the inflected verbs (*arm*/V, *arms*/V, *armed*/V, *arming*/V). Therefore, word sense disambiguation requires first identifying the correct part of-speech and lemma for each token, and then choosing the correct sense from the inventory associated with the corresponding lemma.[3] (Part-of-speech tagging is discussed in § 8.1.)

4.2.1 How Many Word Senses?

Words sometimes have many more than two senses, as exemplified by the word *serve*:

- [FUNCTION]: *The tree stump served as a table*
- [CONTRIBUTE TO]: *His evasive replies only served to heighten suspicion*
- [PROVIDE]: *We serve only the rawest fish*
- [ENLIST]: *She served in an elite combat unit*
- [JAIL]: *He served six years for a crime he didn't commit*
- [LEGAL]: *They were served with subpoenas*[4]

2. These examples, and many more, can be found at www.ling.upenn.edu/~beatrice/humor/headlines.html.
3. Navigli (2009) provides a survey of approaches for word sense disambiguation.
4. Several of the examples are adapted from WORDNET (Fellbaum, 2017).

These sense distinctions are annotated in **WORDNET** (http://wordnet.princeton.edu), a lexical semantic database for English. WORDNET consists of roughly 100,000 **synsets**, which are groups of lemmas (or phrases) that are synonymous. An example synset is $\{chump^1, fool^2, sucker^1, mark^9\}$, where the superscripts index the sense of each lemma that is included in the synset: for example, there are at least eight other senses of *mark* that have different meanings, and are not part of this synset. A lemma is **polysemous** if it participates in multiple synsets.

WORDNET defines the scope of the word sense disambiguation problem, and, more generally, formalizes lexical semantic knowledge of English. (WordNets have been created for a few dozen other languages, at varying levels of detail.) Some have argued that WordNet's sense granularity is too fine (Ide and Wilks, 2006); more fundamentally, the premise that word senses can be differentiated in a task-neutral way has been criticized as linguistically naïve (Kilgarriff, 1997). One way of testing this question is to ask whether people tend to agree on the appropriate sense for example sentences: according to Mihalcea et al. (2004), people agree on roughly 70% of examples using WordNet senses—far better than chance, but less than agreement on other tasks, such as sentiment annotation (Wilson et al., 2005).

Other lexical semantic relations Besides **synonymy**, WordNet also describes many other lexical semantic relationships, including:

- **antonymy**: x means the opposite of y, for example, FRIEND-ENEMY;
- **hyponymy**: x is a special case of y, for example, RED-COLOR; the inverse relationship is **hypernymy;** and
- **meronymy**: x is a part of y, for example, WHEEL-BICYCLE; the inverse relationship is **holonymy**.

Classification of these relations can be performed by searching for characteristic patterns between pairs of words, for example, *X, such as Y*, which signals hyponymy (Hearst, 1992), or *X but Y*, which signals antonymy (Hatzivassiloglou and McKeown, 1997). Another approach is to analyze each term's **distributional statistics** (the frequency of its neighboring words). Such approaches are described in detail in chapter 14.

4.2.2 Word Sense Disambiguation as Classification

How can we tell living *plants* from manufacturing *plants*? The context is often critical:

(4.4) a. Town officials are hoping to attract new manufacturing plants through weakened environmental regulations.

b. The endangered plants play an important role in the local ecosystem.

It is possible to build a feature vector using the bag-of-words representation, by treating each context as a pseudo-document. The feature function is then

$$f((plant, \textit{The endangered plants play an } \ldots), y) = \{(the, y): 1, (endangered, y): 1, (play, y): 1, (an, y): 1, \ldots\}.$$

As in document classification, many of these features are irrelevant, but a few are very strong predictors. In this example, the context word *endangered* is a strong signal that the intended sense is biology rather than manufacturing. We would therefore expect a learning algorithm to assign high weight to (*endangered*, BIOLOGY), and low weight to (*endangered*, MANUFACTURING).[5]

It may also be helpful to go beyond the bag of words: for example, one might encode the position of each context word with respect to the target,

$$f((bank, \textit{I went to the bank to deposit my paycheck}), y) = \{(i-3, went, y): 1, (i+2, deposit, y): 1, (i+4, paycheck, y): 1\}.$$

These are called **collocation features**, and they give more information about the specific role played by each context word. This idea can be taken further by incorporating additional syntactic information about the grammatical role played by each context feature, such as the **dependency path** (see chapter 11).

Using such features, a classifier can be trained from labeled data. A **semantic concordance** is a corpus in which each open-class word (nouns, verbs, adjectives, and adverbs) is tagged with its word sense from the target dictionary or thesaurus. SemCor is a semantic concordance built from 234K tokens of the Brown corpus (Francis and Kucera, 1982), annotated as part of the WordNet project (Fellbaum, 2017). SemCor annotations look like this:

(4.5) As of Sunday_N^1 night_N^1 there was_V^4 no word_N^2 …,

with the superscripts indicating the annotated sense of each polysemous word, and the subscripts indicating the part of speech.

As always, supervised classification is only possible if enough labeled examples can be accumulated. This is difficult in word sense disambiguation, because each polysemous lemma requires its own training set: having a good classifier for the senses of *serve* is no help toward disambiguating *plant*. For this reason, unsupervised and **semi-supervised** methods are particularly important for word sense disambiguation (e.g., Yarowsky, 1995). These methods will be discussed in chapter 5. Unsupervised methods typically lean on the heuristic of "one sense per discourse," which means that a lemma will usually have a single, consistent sense throughout any given document (Gale et al., 1992). Based on this heuristic, we can propagate information from high-confidence instances to lower-confidence

5. The context bag of words can be also used be used to perform word sense disambiguation without machine learning: the Lesk (1986) algorithm selects the word sense whose dictionary definition best overlaps the local context.

instances in the same document (Yarowsky, 1995). Semi-supervised methods combine labeled and unlabeled data and are discussed in more detail in chapter 5.

4.3 Design Decisions for Text Classification

Text classification involves a number of design decisions. In some cases, the design decision is clear from the mathematics: if you are using regularization, then a regularization weight λ must be chosen. Other decisions are more subtle, arising only in the low-level "plumbing" code that ingests and processes the raw data. Such decisions can be surprisingly consequential for classification accuracy.

4.3.1 What Is a Word?

The bag-of-words representation presupposes that extracting a vector of word counts from text is unambiguous. But text documents are generally represented as a sequences of characters (in an encoding such as ASCII or Unicode), and the conversion to bag of words presupposes a definition of the "words" that are to be counted.

Tokenization The first subtask for constructing a bag-of-words vector is **tokenization**: converting the text from a sequence of characters to a sequence of **word tokens**. A simple approach is to define a subset of characters as whitespace and then split the text on these tokens. However, whitespace-based tokenization is not ideal: we may want to split conjunctions like *isn't* and hyphenated phrases like *prize-winning* and *half-asleep*, and we likely want to separate words from commas and periods that immediately follow them. At the same time, it would be better not to split abbreviations like *U.S.* and *Ph.D.* In languages with Roman scripts, tokenization is typically performed using regular expressions, with modules designed to handle each of these cases. For example, the NLTK package includes a number of tokenizers (Loper and Bird, 2002); the outputs of four of the better-known tokenizers are shown in figure 4.1. Social media researchers have found that emoticons and other forms of orthographic variation pose new challenges for tokenization, leading to the development of special purpose tokenizers to handle these phenomena (O'Connor et al., 2010).

Whitespace	Isn't	Ahab,	Ahab?	;)					
Treebank	Is	n't	Ahab	,	Ahab	?	;	)	
Tweet	Isn't	Ahab	,	Ahab	?	;)			
TokTok (Dehdari, 2014)	Isn	'	t	Ahab	,	Ahab	?	;	)

Figure 4.1
The output of four NLTK tokenizers, applied to the string *Isn't Ahab, Ahab? ;)*.

Tokenization is a language-specific problem, and each language poses unique challenges. For example, Chinese does not include spaces between words, nor any other consistent orthographic markers of word boundaries. A "greedy" approach is to scan the input for character substrings that are in a predefined lexicon. However, Xue (2003) note that this can be ambiguous, because many character sequences could be segmented in multiple ways. Instead, they train a classifier to determine whether each Chinese character, or **hanzi**, is a word boundary. More advanced sequence labeling methods for word segmentation are discussed in § 8.4. Similar problems can occur in languages with alphabetic scripts, such as German, which does not include whitespace in compound nouns, yielding examples such as *Freundschaftsbezeigungen* (demonstration of friendship) and *Dilettantenaufdringlichkeiten* (the importunities of dilettantes). As Twain (1997) argues, "*These things are not words, they are alphabetic processions.*" Social media raises similar problems for English and other languages, with hashtags such as *#TrueLoveInFourWords* requiring decomposition for analysis (Brun and Roux, 2014).

Text normalization After splitting the text into tokens, the next question is which tokens are really distinct. Is it necessary to distinguish *great*, *Great*, and *GREAT*? Sentence-initial capitalization may be irrelevant to the classification task. Going further, the complete elimination of case distinctions will result in a smaller vocabulary, and thus smaller feature vectors. However, case distinctions might be relevant in some situations: for example, *apple* is a delicious pie filling, while *Apple* is a company that specializes in proprietary dongles and power adapters.

For Roman script, case conversion can be performed using Unicode string libraries. Many scripts do not have case distinctions (e.g., the Devanagari script used for South Asian languages, the Thai alphabet, and Japanese kana), and case conversion for all scripts may not be available in every programming environment. (Unicode support is an important distinction between python versions 2 and 3 and is a good reason for migrating to Python 3 if you have not already done so. Compare the output of the code `"\à l\'hôtel".upper()` in the two language versions.)

Case conversion is a type of **text normalization**, which refers to string transformations that remove distinctions that are irrelevant to downstream applications (Sproat et al., 2001). Other forms of normalization include the standardization of numbers (for example *1,000* to *1000*) and dates (e.g., *August 11, 2015* to *2015/11/08*). Depending on the application, it may even be worthwhile to convert all numbers and dates to special tokens, `!NUM` and `!DATE`. In social media, there are additional orthographic phenomena that may be normalized, such as expressive lengthening, for example, *cooooool* (Aw et al., 2006; Yang and Eisenstein, 2013). Similarly, historical texts feature spelling variations that may need to be normalized to a contemporary standard form (Baron and Rayson, 2008).

A more extreme form of normalization is to eliminate **inflectional affixes**, such as the *-ed* and *-s* suffixes in English. On this view, *whale*, *whales*, and *whaling* all refer to the

Original	The	Williams	sisters	are	leaving	this	tennis	centre
Porter stemmer	the	william	sister	are	leav	thi	tenni	centr
Lancaster stemmer	the	william	sist	ar	leav	thi	ten	cent
WordNet lemmatizer	The	Williams	sister	are	leaving	this	tennis	centre

Figure 4.2
Sample outputs of the Porter (Porter, 1980) and Lancaster (Paice, 1990) stemmers, and the WORDNET lemmatizer.

same underlying concept, so they should be grouped into a single feature. A **stemmer** is a program for eliminating affixes, usually by applying a series of regular expression substitutions. Character-based stemming algorithms are necessarily approximate, as shown in figure 4.2: the Lancaster stemmer incorrectly identifies *-ers* as an inflectional suffix of *sisters* (by analogy to *fix/fixers*), and both stemmers incorrectly identify *-s* as a suffix of *this* and *Williams*. Fortunately, even inaccurate stemming can improve bag-of-words classification models, by merging related strings and thereby reducing the vocabulary size.

Accurately handling irregular orthography requires word-specific rules. **Lemmatizers** are systems that identify the underlying lemma of a given wordform. They must avoid the over generalization errors of the stemmers in figure 4.2 and also handle more complex transformations, such as *geese→goose*. The output of the WordNet lemmatizer is shown in the final line of figure 4.2. Both stemming and lemmatization are language specific: an English stemmer or lemmatizer is of little use on a text written in another language. The discipline of **morphology** relates to the study of word-internal structure and is described in more detail in § 9.1.2.

The value of normalization depends on the data and the task. Normalization reduces the size of the feature space, which can help in generalization. However, there is always the risk of merging away linguistically meaningful distinctions. In supervised machine learning, regularization and smoothing can play a similar role to normalization—preventing the learner from overfitting to rare features—while avoiding the language-specific engineering required for accurate normalization. In unsupervised scenarios, such as content-based information retrieval (Manning et al., 2009) and topic modeling (Blei et al., 2003), normalization is more critical.

4.3.2 How Many Words?

Limiting the size of the feature vector reduces the memory footprint of the resulting models and increases the speed of prediction. Normalization can help to play this role, but a more direct approach is simply to limit the vocabulary to the N most frequent words in the dataset. For example, in the MOVIE-REVIEWS dataset provided with NLTK (originally from Pang et al., 2002), there are 39,768 word types and 1.58M tokens. As shown in figure 4.3a, the most frequent 4,000 word types cover 90% of all tokens, offering an order-of-magnitude

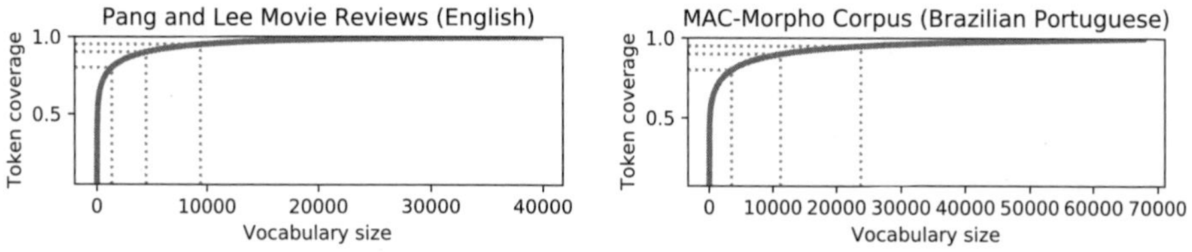

(a) Movie review data in English

(b) News articles in Brazilian Portuguese

Figure 4.3
Tradeoff between token coverage (y-axis) and vocabulary size, on the NLTK movie review dataset, after sorting the vocabulary by decreasing frequency. The dashed lines indicate 80%, 90%, and 95% coverage.

reduction in the model size. Such ratios are language specific for example, in the Brazilian Portuguese Mac-Morpho corpus (Aluísio et al., 2003), attaining 90% coverage requires more than 10,000 word types (figure 4.3b). This reflects the morphological complexity of Portuguese, which includes many more inflectional suffixes than English.

Eliminating rare words is not always advantageous for classification performance: for example, names, which are typically rare, play a large role in distinguishing topics of news articles. Another way to reduce the size of the feature space is to eliminate **stopwords** such as *the*, *to*, and *and*, which may seem to play little role in expressing the topic, sentiment, or stance. This is typically done by creating a **stoplist** (e.g., NLTK.CORPUS.STOPWORDS) and then ignoring all terms that match the list. However, corpus linguists and social psychologists have shown that seemingly inconsequential words can offer surprising insights about the author or nature of the text (Biber, 1991; Chung and Pennebaker, 2007). Furthermore, high-frequency words are unlikely to cause overfitting in discriminative classifiers. As with normalization, stopword filtering is more important for unsupervised problems, such as term-based document retrieval.

Another alternative for controlling model size is **feature hashing** (Weinberger et al., 2009). Each feature is assigned an index using a hash function. If a hash function that permits collisions is chosen (typically by taking the hash output modulo some integer), then the model can be made arbitrarily small, as multiple features share a single weight. Because most features are rare, accuracy is surprisingly robust to such collisions (Ganchev and Dredze, 2008).

4.3.3 Count or Binary?

Finally, we may consider whether we want our feature vector to include the *count* of each word, or its *presence*. This gets at a subtle limitation of linear classification: it's worse to have two *failure*s than one, but is it really twice as bad? Motivated by this intuition, Pang et al. (2002) use binary indicators of presence or absence in the feature vector: $f_j(\boldsymbol{x}, y) \in \{0, 1\}$. They find that classifiers trained on these binary vectors tend to outperform feature vectors based on word counts. One explanation is that words tend to appear in clumps: if a word has appeared once in a document, it is likely to appear again (Church, 2000). These subsequent appearances can be attributed to this tendency toward repetition and thus provide little additional information about the class label of the document.

4.4 Evaluating Classifiers

In any supervised machine learning application, it is critical to reserve a held-out test set. This data should be used for only one purpose: to evaluate the overall accuracy of a single classifier. Using this data more than once would cause the estimated accuracy to be overly optimistic, because the classifier would be customized to this data, and would not perform as well as on unseen data in the future. It is usually necessary to set hyperparameters or perform feature selection, so you may need to construct a **tuning** or **development set** for this purpose, as discussed in § 2.2.5.

There are a number of ways to evaluate classifier performance. The simplest is **accuracy**: the number of correct predictions, divided by the total number of instances:

$$\text{acc}(\boldsymbol{y}, \hat{\boldsymbol{y}}) = \frac{1}{N}\sum_{i}^{N} \delta(y^{(i)} = \hat{y}). \tag{4.4}$$

Exams are usually graded by accuracy. Why are other metrics necessary? The main reason is **class imbalance**. Suppose you are building a classifier to detect whether an electronic health record (EHR) describes symptoms of a rare disease, which appears in only 1% of all documents in the dataset. A classifier that reports $\hat{y} = \text{NEGATIVE}$ for all documents would achieve 99% accuracy, but would be practically useless. We need metrics that are capable of detecting the classifier's ability to discriminate between classes, even when the distribution is skewed.

One solution is to build a **balanced test set**, in which each possible label is equally represented. But in the EHR example, this would mean throwing away 98% of the original dataset! Furthermore, the detection threshold itself might be a design consideration: in health-related applications, we might prefer a very sensitive classifier, which returned a positive prediction if there is even a small chance that $y^{(i)} = \text{POSITIVE}$. In other applications, a positive result might trigger a costly action, so we would prefer a classifier that only makes positive predictions when absolutely certain. We need additional metrics to capture these characteristics.

4.4.1 Precision, Recall, and *F*-MEASURE

For any label (e.g., positive for presence of symptoms of a disease), there are two possible errors:

- **False positive**: the system incorrectly predicts the label.
- **False negative**: the system incorrectly fails to predict the label.

Similarly, for any label, there are two ways to be correct:

- **True positive**: the system correctly predicts the label.
- **True negative**: the system correctly predicts that the label does not apply to this instance.

Classifiers that make a lot of false positives have low **precision**: they predict the label even when it isn't there. Classifiers that make a lot of false negatives have low **recall**: they fail to predict the label, even when it is there. These metrics distinguish these two sources of error, and are defined formally as

$$\text{RECALL}(\boldsymbol{y}, \hat{\boldsymbol{y}}, k) = \frac{\text{TP}}{\text{TP} + \text{FN}} \quad [4.5]$$

$$\text{PRECISION}(\boldsymbol{y}, \hat{\boldsymbol{y}}, k) = \frac{\text{TP}}{\text{TP} + \text{FP}}. \quad [4.6]$$

Recall and precision are both conditional likelihoods of a correct prediction, which is why their numerators are the same. Recall is conditioned on k being the correct label, $y^{(i)} = k$, so the denominator sums over true positives and false negatives. Precision is conditioned on k being the prediction, so the denominator sums over true positives and false positives. Note that true negatives are not considered in either statistic. The classifier that labels every document as "negative" would achieve zero recall; precision would be $\frac{0}{0}$.

Recall and precision are complementary. A high-recall classifier is preferred when false positives are cheaper than false negatives: for example, in a preliminary screening for symptoms of a disease, the cost of a false positive might be an additional test, while a false negative would result in the disease going untreated. Conversely, a high-precision classifier is preferred when false positives are more expensive: for example, in spam detection, a false negative is a relatively minor inconvenience, while a false positive might mean that an important message goes unread.

The F-**MEASURE** combines recall and precision into a single metric, using the harmonic mean:

$$F\text{-MEASURE}(\boldsymbol{y}, \hat{\boldsymbol{y}}, k) = \frac{2rp}{r + p}, \quad [4.7]$$

where r is recall and p is precision.[6]

6. F-MEASURE is sometimes called F_1 and generalizes to $F_\beta = \frac{(1+\beta^2)rp}{\beta^2 p + r}$. The β parameter can be tuned to emphasize recall or precision.

Evaluating multiclass classification Recall, precision, and F-MEASURE are defined with respect to a specific label k. When there are multiple labels of interest (e.g., in word sense disambiguation or emotion classification), it is necessary to combine the F-MEASURE across each class. **Macro F-MEASURE** is the average F-MEASURE across several classes,

$$\text{Macro-}F(\boldsymbol{y}, \hat{\boldsymbol{y}}) = \frac{1}{|\mathcal{K}|} \sum_{k \in \mathcal{K}} F\text{-MEASURE}(\boldsymbol{y}, \hat{\boldsymbol{y}}, k). \quad [4.8]$$

In multiclass problems with unbalanced class distributions, the macro F-MEASURE is a balanced measure of how well the classifier recognizes each class. In **micro F-MEASURE**, we compute true positives, false positives, and false negatives for each class and then add them up to compute a single recall, precision, and F-MEASURE. This metric is balanced across instances rather than classes, so it weights each class in proportion to its frequency—unlike macro F-MEASURE, which weights each class equally.

4.4.2 Threshold-Free Metrics

In binary classification problems, it is possible to trade off between recall and precision by adding a constant "threshold" to the output of the scoring function. This makes it possible to trace out a curve, where each point indicates the performance at a single threshold. In the **receiver operating characteristic (ROC)** curve,[7] the x-axis indicates the **false positive rate**, $\frac{\text{FP}}{\text{FP+TN}}$, and the y-axis indicates the recall, or **true positive rate**. A perfect classifier attains perfect recall without any false positives, tracing a "curve" from the origin (0,0) to the upper-left corner (0,1), and then to (1,1). In expectation, a nondiscriminative classifier traces a diagonal line from the origin (0,0) to the upper-right corner (1,1). Real classifiers tend to fall between these two extremes. Examples are shown in figure 4.4.

The ROC curve can be summarized in a single number by taking its integral, the **area under the curve (AUC)**. The AUC can be interpreted as the probability that a randomly selected positive example will be assigned a higher score by the classifier than a randomly selected negative example. A perfect classifier has AUC $= 1$ (all positive examples score higher than all negative examples); a non-discriminative classifier has AUC $= 0.5$ (given a randomly selected positive and negative example, either could score higher with equal probability); a perfectly wrong classifier would have AUC $= 0$ (all negative examples score higher than all positive examples). One advantage of AUC in comparison to F-MEASURE is that the baseline rate of 0.5 does not depend on the label distribution.

7. The name "receiver operator characteristic" comes from the metric's origin in signal processing (Peterson et al., 1954). Other threshold-free metrics include **precision-recall curves**, **precision-at-k**, and **balanced F-MEASURE**; see Manning et al. (2009) for more details.

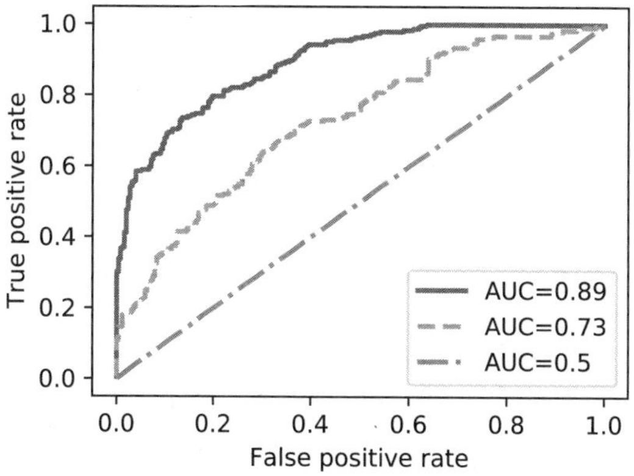

Figure 4.4
ROC curves for three classifiers of varying discriminative power, measured by AUC (area under the curve).

4.4.3 Classifier Comparison and Statistical Significance

Natural language processing research and engineering often involves comparing different classification techniques. In some cases, the comparison is between algorithms, such as logistic regression versus averaged perceptron, or L_2 regularization versus L_1. In other cases, the comparison is between feature sets, such as the bag of words versus positional bag of words (see § 4.2.2). **Ablation testing** involves systematically removing (ablating) various aspects of the classifier, such as feature groups, and testing the **null hypothesis** that the ablated classifier is as good as the full model.

A full treatment of hypothesis testing is beyond the scope of this text, but this section contains a brief summary of the techniques necessary to compare classifiers. The main aim of hypothesis testing is to determine whether the difference between two statistics—for example, the accuracies of two classifiers—is likely to arise by chance. We will be concerned with chance fluctuations that arise due to the finite size of the test set.[8] An improvement of 10% on a test set with 10 instances may reflect a random fluctuation that makes the test set more favorable to classifier c_1 than c_2; on another test set with a different 10 instances, we might find that c_2 does better than c_1. But if we observe the same 10% improvement on a test set with 1,000 instances, this is highly unlikely to be explained by chance. Such a finding is said to be **statistically significant** at a level p, which is the probability of observing an effect of equal or greater magnitude when the null hypothesis is true. The notation $p < .05$ indicates that the likelihood of an equal or greater effect is less than 5%, assuming the null hypothesis is true.[9]

8. Other sources of variance include the initialization of nonconvex classifiers such as neural networks and the ordering of instances in online learning such as stochastic gradient descent and perceptron.

9. Statistical hypothesis testing is useful only to the extent that the existing test set is representative of the instances that will be encountered in the future. If, for example, the test set is constructed from news documents,

The binomial test The statistical significance of a difference in accuracy can be evaluated using classical tests, such as the **binomial test.**[10] Suppose that classifiers c_1 and c_2 disagree on N instances in a test set with binary labels and that c_1 is correct on k of those instances. Under the null hypothesis that the classifiers are equally accurate, we would expect k/N to be roughly equal to $1/2$, and as N increases, k/N should be increasingly close to this expected value. These properties are captured by the **binomial distribution**, which is a probability over counts of binary random variables. We write $k \sim \text{Binom}(\theta, N)$ to indicate that k is drawn from a binomial distribution, with parameter N indicating the number of random "draws," and θ indicating the probability of "success" on each draw. Each draw is an example on which the two classifiers disagree, and a "success" is a case in which c_1 is right and c_2 is wrong. (The label space is assumed to be binary, so if the classifiers disagree, exactly one of them is correct. The test can be generalized to multiclass classification by focusing on the examples in which exactly one classifier is correct.)

The **probability mass function (PMF)** of the binomial distribution is

$$\text{p}_{\text{Binom}}(k; N, \theta) = \binom{N}{k} \theta^k (1-\theta)^{N-k}, \qquad [4.9]$$

with θ^k representing the probability of the k successes and $(1-\theta)^{N-k}$ representing the probability of the $N-k$ unsuccessful draws. The expression $\binom{N}{k} = \frac{N!}{k!(N-k)!}$ is a binomial coefficient, representing the number of possible orderings of events; this ensures that the distribution sums to one over all $k \in \{0, 1, 2, \ldots, N\}$.

Under the null hypothesis, when the classifiers disagree, each classifier is equally likely to be right, so $\theta = \frac{1}{2}$. Now suppose that among N disagreements, c_1 is correct $k < \frac{N}{2}$ times. The probability of c_1 being correct k or fewer times is the **one-tailed** p**-value**, because it is computed from the area under the binomial probability mass function from 0 to k, as shown in the left tail of figure 4.5. This **cumulative probability** is computed as a sum over all values $i \leq k$,

$$\Pr_{\text{Binom}}\left(\text{count}(\hat{y}_2^{(i)} = y^{(i)} \neq \hat{y}_1^{(i)}) \leq k; N, \theta = \frac{1}{2}\right) = \sum_{i=0}^{k} \text{p}_{\text{Binom}}\left(i; N, \theta = \frac{1}{2}\right). \qquad [4.10]$$

The one-tailed p-value applies only to the asymmetric null hypothesis that c_1 is at least as accurate as c_2. To test the **two-tailed** null hypothesis that c_1 and c_2 are equally accurate,

no hypothesis test can predict which classifier will perform best on documents from another domain, such as electronic health records.

10. A well-known alternative to the binomial test is **McNemar's test**, which computes a **test statistic** based on the number of examples that are correctly classified by one system and incorrectly classified by the other. The null hypothesis distribution for this test statistic is known to be drawn from a chi-squared distribution with a single degree of freedom, so a p-value can be computed from the cumulative density function of this distribution (Dietterich, 1998). Both tests give similar results in most circumstances, but the binomial test is easier to understand from first principles.

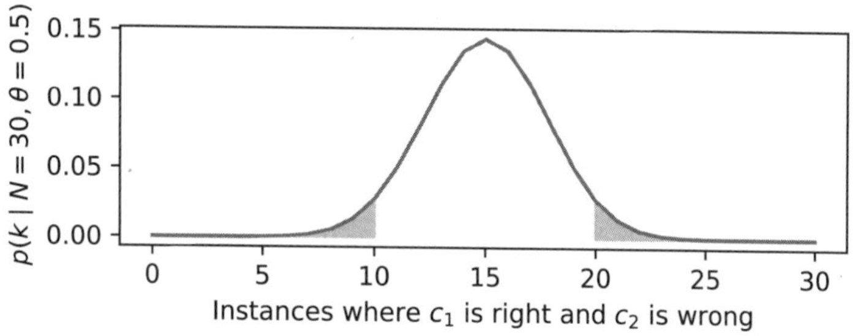

Figure 4.5
Probability mass function for the binomial distribution. The pink highlighted areas represent the cumulative probability for a significance test on an observation of $k = 10$ and $N = 30$.

we would take the sum of one-tailed p-values, where the second term is computed from the right tail of figure 4.5. The binomial distribution is symmetric, so this can be computed by simply doubling the one-tailed p-value.

Two-tailed tests are more stringent, but they are necessary in cases in which there is no prior intuition about whether c_1 or c_2 is better. For example, in comparing logistic regression versus averaged perceptron, a two-tailed test is appropriate. In an ablation test, c_2 may contain a superset of the features available to c_1. If the additional features are thought to be likely to improve performance, then a one-tailed test would be appropriate, if chosen in advance. However, such a test can only prove that c_2 is more accurate than c_1, and not the reverse.

***Randomized testing** The binomial test is appropriate for accuracy, but not for more complex metrics such as F-MEASURE. To compute statistical significance for arbitrary metrics, we can apply randomization. Specifically, draw a set of M **bootstrap samples** (Efron and Tibshirani, 1993) by resampling instances from the original test set with replacement. Each bootstrap sample is itself a test set of size N. Some instances from the original test set will not appear in any given bootstrap sample, while others will appear multiple times; but overall, the sample will be drawn from the same distribution as the original test set. We can then compute any desired evaluation on each bootstrap sample, which gives a distribution over the value of the metric. Algorithm 7 shows how to perform this computation.

To compare the F-MEASURE of two classifiers c_1 and c_2, we set the function $\delta(\cdot)$ to compute the difference in F-MEASURE on the bootstrap sample. If the difference is less than or equal to zero in at least 5% of the samples, then we cannot reject the one-tailed null hypothesis that c_2 is at least as good as c_1 (Berg-Kirkpatrick et al., 2012). We may also be interested in the 95% **confidence interval** around a metric of interest, such as the F-MEASURE of a single classifier. This can be computed by sorting the output of algorithm 7, and then setting the top and bottom of the 95% confidence interval to the values at the 2.5% and 97.5%

Algorithm 7
Bootstrap sampling for classifier evaluation. The original test set is $\{\boldsymbol{x}^{(1:N)}, \boldsymbol{y}^{(1:N)}\}$, the metric is $\delta(\cdot)$, and the number of samples is M.

---

procedure BOOTSTRAP-SAMPLE($\boldsymbol{x}^{(1:N)}, \boldsymbol{y}^{(1:N)}, \delta(\cdot), M$)
  for $t \in \{1, 2, \ldots, M\}$ **do**
    for $i \in \{1, 2, \ldots, N\}$ **do**
      $j \sim \text{UniformInteger}(1, N)$
      $\tilde{\boldsymbol{x}}^{(i)} \leftarrow \boldsymbol{x}^{(j)}$
      $\tilde{\boldsymbol{y}}^{(i)} \leftarrow \boldsymbol{y}^{(j)}$
    $d^{(t)} \leftarrow \delta(\tilde{\boldsymbol{x}}^{(1:N)}, \tilde{\boldsymbol{y}}^{(1:N)})$
  return $\{d^{(t)}\}_{t=1}^{M}$

---

percentiles of the sorted outputs. Alternatively, you can fit a normal distribution to the set of differences across bootstrap samples and compute a Gaussian confidence interval from the mean and variance.

As the number of bootstrap samples goes to infinity, $M \to \infty$, the bootstrap estimate is increasingly accurate. A typical choice for M is 10^4 or 10^5; larger numbers of samples are necessary for smaller p-values. One way to validate your choice of M is to run the test multiple times and ensure that the p-values are similar; if not, increase M by an order of magnitude. This is a heuristic measure of the **variance** of the test, which decreases with the square root $\sqrt{M}$ (Robert and Casella, 2013).

4.4.4 *Multiple Comparisons

Sometimes it is necessary to perform multiple hypothesis tests, such as when comparing the performance of several classifiers on multiple datasets. Suppose you have five datasets, and you compare four versions of your classifier against a baseline system, for a total of 20 comparisons. Even if none of your classifiers is better than the baseline, there will be some chance variation in the results, and in expectation you will get one statistically significant improvement at $p = 0.05 = \frac{1}{20}$. It is therefore necessary to adjust the p-values when reporting the results of multiple comparisons.

One approach is to require a threshold of $\frac{\alpha}{m}$ to report a p-value of $p < \alpha$ when performing m tests. This is known as the **Bonferroni correction**, and it limits the overall probability of incorrectly rejecting the null hypothesis at α. Another approach is to bound the **false discovery rate (FDR)**, which is the fraction of null hypothesis rejections that are incorrect. Benjamini and Hochberg (1995) propose a p-value correction that bounds the fraction of false discoveries at α: sort the p-values of each individual test in ascending order and set the significance threshold equal to largest k such that $p_k \leq \frac{k}{m}\alpha$. If $k > 1$, the FDR adjustment is more permissive than the Bonferroni correction.

4.5 Building Datasets

Sometimes, if you want to build a classifier, you must first build a dataset of your own. This includes selecting a set of documents or instances to annotate and then performing the annotations. The scope of the dataset may be determined by the application: if you want to build a system to classify electronic health records, then you must work with a corpus of records of the type that your classifier will encounter when deployed. In other cases, the goal is to build a system that will work across a broad range of documents. In this case, it is best to have a *balanced* corpus, with contributions from many styles and genres. For example, the Brown corpus draws from texts ranging from government documents to romance novels (Francis, 1964), and the Google Web Treebank includes annotations for five "domains" of web documents: question answers, emails, newsgroups, reviews, and blogs (Petrov and McDonald, 2012).

4.5.1 Metadata as Labels

Annotation is difficult and time consuming, and most people would rather avoid it. It is sometimes possible to exploit existing metadata to obtain labels for training a classifier. For example, reviews are often accompanied by a numerical rating, which can be converted into a classification label (see § 4.1). Similarly, the nationalities of social media users can be estimated from their profiles (Dredze et al., 2013) or even the time zones of their posts (Gouws et al., 2011). More ambitiously, we may try to classify the political affiliations of social media profiles based on their social network connections to politicians and major political parties (Rao et al., 2010).

The convenience of quickly constructing large labeled datasets without manual annotation is appealing. However this approach relies on the assumption that unlabeled instances—for which metadata is unavailable—will be similar to labeled instances. Consider the example of labeling the political affiliation of social media users based on their network ties to politicians. If a classifier attains high accuracy on such a test set, is it safe to assume that it accurately predicts the political affiliation of all social media users? Probably not. Social media users who establish social network ties to politicians may be more likely to mention politics in the text of their messages, as compared to the average user, for whom no political metadata is available. If so, the accuracy on a test set constructed from social network metadata would give an overly optimistic picture of the method's true performance on unlabeled data.

4.5.2 Labeling Data

In many cases, there is no way to get ground truth labels other than manual annotation. An annotation protocol should satisfy several criteria: the annotations should be *expressive* enough to capture the phenomenon of interest; they should be *replicable*, meaning that another annotator or team of annotators would produce very similar annotations if given the same data; and they should be *scalable*, so that they can be produced relatively quickly. Hovy and Lavid (2010) propose a structured procedure for obtaining annotations that meet these criteria, which is summarized below.

1. **Determine what to annotate**. This is usually based on some theory of the underlying phenomenon: for example, if the goal is to produce annotations about the emotional state of a document's author, one should start with a theoretical account of the types or dimensions of emotion (e.g., Mohammad and Turney, 2013). At this stage, the tradeoff between expressiveness and scalability should be considered: a full instantiation of the underlying theory might be too costly to annotate at scale, so reasonable approximations should be considered.

2. Optionally, one may **design or select a software tool to support the annotation effort**. Existing general-purpose annotation tools include BRAT (Stenetorp et al., 2012) and MMAX2 (Müller and Strube, 2006).

3. **Formalize the instructions for the annotation task**. To the extent that the instructions are not explicit, the resulting annotations will depend on the intuitions of the annotators. These intuitions may not be shared by other annotators, or by the users of the annotated data. Therefore explicit instructions are critical to ensuring the annotations are replicable and usable by other researchers.

4. **Perform a pilot annotation** of a small subset of data, with multiple annotators for each instance. This will give a preliminary assessment of both the replicability and scalability of the current annotation instructions. Metrics for computing the rate of agreement are described below. Manual analysis of specific disagreements should help to clarify the instructions and may lead to modifications of the annotation task itself. For example, if two labels are commonly conflated by annotators, it may be best to merge them.

5. **Annotate the data**. After finalizing the annotation protocol and instructions, the main annotation effort can begin. Some, if not all, of the instances should receive multiple annotations, so that inter annotator agreement can be computed. In some annotation projects, instances receive many annotations, which are then aggregated into a "consensus" label (e.g., Danescu-Niculescu-Mizil et al., 2013). However, if the annotations are time consuming or require significant expertise, it may be preferable to maximize scalability by obtaining multiple annotations for only a small subset of examples.

6. **Compute and report interannotator agreement and release the data**. In some cases, the raw text data cannot be released, due to concerns related to copyright or privacy. In these cases, one solution is to publicly release **stand-off annotations**, which contain links to document identifiers. The documents themselves can be released under the terms of a licensing agreement, which can impose conditions on how the data is used. It is important to think through the potential consequences of releasing data: people may make personal data

publicly available without realizing that it could be redistributed in a dataset and publicized far beyond their expectations (boyd and Crawford, 2012).

Measuring interannotator agreement To measure the replicability of annotations, a standard practice is to compute the extent to which annotators agree with each other. If the annotators frequently disagree, this casts doubt on either their reliability or on the annotation system itself. For classification, one can compute the frequency with which the annotators agree; for rating scales, one can compute the average distance between ratings. These raw agreement statistics must then be compared with the rate of agreement by chance—the expected level of agreement that would be obtained between two annotators who ignored the data.

Cohen's Kappa is widely used for quantifying the agreement on discrete labeling tasks (Cohen, 1960; Carletta, 1996),[11]

$$\kappa = \frac{\text{agreement} - E[\text{agreement}]}{1 - E[\text{agreement}]}. \quad [4.11]$$

The numerator is the difference between the observed agreement and the chance agreement, and the denominator is the difference between perfect agreement and chance agreement. Thus, $\kappa = 1$ when the annotators agree in every case, and $\kappa = 0$ when the annotators agree only as often as would happen by chance. Various heuristic scales have been proposed for determining when κ indicates "moderate," "good," or "substantial" agreement; for reference, Lee and Narayanan (2005) report $\kappa \approx 0.45 - 0.47$ for annotations of emotions in spoken dialogues, which they describe as "moderate agreement"; Stolcke et al. (2000) report $\kappa = 0.8$ for annotations of **dialogue acts**, which are labels for the purpose of each turn in a conversation.

When there are two annotators, the expected chance agreement is computed as

$$E[\text{agreement}] = \sum_k \hat{\Pr}(Y = k)^2, \quad [4.12]$$

where k is a sum over labels, and $\hat{\Pr}(Y = k)$ is the empirical probability of label k across all annotations. The formula is derived from the expected number of agreements if the annotations were randomly shuffled. Thus, in a binary labeling task, if one label is applied to 90% of instances, chance agreement is $.9^2 + .1^2 = .82$.

Crowdsourcing Crowdsourcing is often used to rapidly obtain annotations for classification problems. For example, **Amazon Mechanical Turk** makes it possible to define "human

11. For other types of annotations, Krippendorf's alpha is a popular choice (Hayes and Krippendorff, 2007; Artstein and Poesio, 2008).

intelligence tasks (hits)," such as labeling data. The researcher sets a price for each set of annotations and a list of minimal qualifications for annotators, such as their native language and their satisfaction rate on previous tasks. The use of relatively untrained "crowdworkers" contrasts with earlier annotation efforts, which relied on professional linguists (Marcus et al., 1993). However, crowdsourcing has been found to produce reliable annotations for many language-related tasks (Snow et al., 2008). Crowdsourcing is part of the broader field of **human computation** (Law and Ahn, 2011). For a critical examination of ethical issues related to crowdsourcing, see Fort et al. (2011).

Additional Resources

Many of the preprocessing issues discussed in this chapter also arise in information retrieval. See Manning et al. (2009) for discussion of tokenization and related algorithms. For more on hypothesis testing in particular and replicability in general, see Dror et al. (2017, 2018).

Exercises

1. As noted in § 4.3.3, words tend to appear in clumps, with subsequent occurrences of a word being more probable. More concretely, if word j has probability $\phi_{y,j}$ of appearing in a document with label y, then the probability of two appearances ($x_j^{(i)}=2$) is greater than $\phi_{y,j}^2$.

   Suppose you are applying Naïve Bayes to a binary classification. Focus on a word j that is more probable under label $y=1$, so that

   $$\Pr(w=j \mid y=1) > \Pr(w=j \mid y=0). \qquad [4.13]$$

   Now suppose that $x_j^{(i)} > 1$. All else equal, will the classifier overestimate or underestimate the posterior $\Pr(y=1 \mid \boldsymbol{x})$?
2. Prove that F-MEASURE is never greater than the arithmetic mean of recall and precision, $\frac{r+p}{2}$. Your solution should also show that F-MEASURE is equal to $\frac{r+p}{2}$ iff $r=p$.
3. Given a binary classification problem in which the probability of the "positive" label is equal to α, what is the expected F-MEASURE of a random classifier that ignores the data and selects $\hat{y}=+1$ with probability $\frac{1}{2}$? (Assume that $p(\hat{y}) \perp p(y)$.) What is the expected F-MEASURE of a classifier that selects $\hat{y}=+1$ with probability α (also independent of $y^{(i)}$)? Depending on α, which random classifier will score better?
4. Suppose that binary classifiers c_1 and c_2 disagree on $N=30$ cases and that c_1 is correct in $k=10$ of those cases.
   - Write a program that uses primitive functions such as exp and factorial to compute the **two-tailed** p-value—you may use an implementation of the "choose" function if one

is avaiable. Verify your code against the output of a library for computing the binomial test or the binomial CDF, such as `scipy.stats.binom` in Python.

- Then use a randomized test to try to obtain the same p-value. In each sample, draw from a binomial distribution with $N=30$ and $\theta=\frac{1}{2}$. Count the fraction of samples in which $k \leq 10$. This is the one-tailed p-value; double this to compute the two-tailed p-value.
- Try this with varying numbers of bootstrap samples: $M \in \{100, 1000, 5000, 10000\}$. For $M=100$ and $M=1000$, run the test 10 times, and plot the resulting p-values.
- Finally, perform the same tests for $N=70$ and $k=25$.

5. SemCor 3.0 is a labeled dataset for word sense disambiguation. You can download it[12] or access it in `nltk.corpora.semcor`.

   Choose a word that appears at least ten times in SemCor (*find*), and annotate its WordNet senses across 10 randomly selected examples, without looking at the ground truth. Use online WordNet to understand the definition of each of the senses.[13] Have a partner do the same annotations, and compute the raw rate of agreement, expected chance rate of agreement, and Cohen's kappa.

6. Download the Pang and Lee movie review data, currently available from www.cs.cornell.edu/people/pabo/movie-review-data/. Hold out a randomly selected 400 reviews as a test set.

   Download a sentiment lexicon, such as the one currently available from Bing Liu at www.cs.uic.edu/~liub/FBS/sentiment-analysis.html. Tokenize the data, and classify each document as positive iff it has more positive sentiment words than negative sentiment words. Compute the accuracy and F-MEASURE on detecting positive reviews on the test set using this lexicon-based classifier.

   Then train a discriminative classifier (averaged perceptron or logistic regression) on the training set, and compute its accuracy and F-MEASURE on the test set.

   Determine whether the differences are statistically significant, using two-tailed hypothesis tests: binomial for the difference in accuracy, and bootstrap for the difference in macro-F-MEASURE.

The remaining problems will require you to build a classifier and test its properties. Pick a multi class text classification dataset that is not already tokenized. One example is a dataset of headlines and topics from the *New York Times* (Boydstun, 2013).[14]

12. For example, https://github.com/google-research-datasets/word_sense_disambigation_corpora or http://globalwordnet.org/wordnet-annotated-corpora/.

13. http://wordnetweb.princeton.edu/perl/webwn.

14. Available as a CSV file at www.amber-boydstun.com/supplementary-information-for-making-the-news.html. Use the field `Topic_2digit` for this problem.

Divide your data into training (60%), development (20%), and test sets (20%), if no such division already exists. If your dataset is very large, you may want to focus on a few thousand instances at first.

7. Compare various vocabulary sizes of $10^2, 10^3, 10^4,$ *and* 10^5, using the most frequent words in each case (you may use any reasonable tokenizer). Train logistic regression classifiers for each vocabulary size, and apply them to the development set. Plot the accuracy and macro-F-MEASURE with the increasing vocabulary size. For each vocabulary size, tune the regularizer to maximize accuracy on a subset of data that is held out from the training set.
8. Compare the following tokenization algorithms:
   - Whitespace, using a regular expression
   - The Penn Treebank tokenizer from NLTK
   - Splitting the input into nonoverlapping five-character units, regardless of whitespace or punctuation

   Compute the token/type ratio for each tokenizer on the training data, and explain what you find. Train your classifier on each tokenized dataset, tuning the regularizer on a subset of data that is held out from the training data. Tokenize the development set, and report accuracy and macro-F-MEASURE.
9. Apply the Porter and Lancaster stemmers to the training set, using any reasonable tokenizer, and compute the token/type ratios. Train your classifier on the stemmed data, and compute the accuracy and macro-F-MEASURE on stemmed development data, again using a held-out portion of the training data to tune the regularizer.
10. Identify the best combination of vocabulary filtering, tokenization, and stemming from the previous three problems. Apply this preprocessing to the test set, and compute the test set accuracy and macro-F-MEASURE. Compare against a baseline system that applies whitespace tokenization, no vocabulary filtering, and no stemming.

    Use the binomial test to determine whether your best-performing system is significantly more accurate than the baseline.

    Use the bootstrap test with $M = 10^4$ to determine whether your best-performing system achieves a significantly higher macro-F-MEASURE.

5 Learning without Supervision

So far, we have assumed the following setup:

- A **training set** where you get observations $\boldsymbol{x}$ and labels y
- A **test set** where you only get observations $\boldsymbol{x}$

Without labeled data, is it possible to learn anything? This scenario is known as **unsupervised learning**, and we will see that indeed it is possible to learn about the underlying structure of unlabeled observations. This chapter will also explore some related scenarios: **semi-supervised learning**, in which only some instances are labeled, and **domain adaptation**, in which the training data differs from the data on which the trained system will be deployed.

5.1 Unsupervised Learning

To motivate unsupervised learning, consider the problem of word sense disambiguation (§ 4.2). The goal is to classify each instance of a word such as *bank* into a sense:

- `bank#1`: a financial institution
- `bank#2`: the land bordering a river

It is difficult to obtain sufficient training data for word sense disambiguation, because even a large corpus will contain only a few instances of all but the most common words. Is it possible to learn anything about these different senses without labeled data?

Word sense disambiguation is usually performed using feature vectors constructed from the local context of the word to be disambiguated. For example, for the word *bank*, the immediate context might typically include words from one of the following two groups:

1. *Financial, deposits, credit, lending, capital, markets, regulated, reserve, liquid, assets*
2. *Land, water, geography, stream, river, flow, deposits, discharge, channel, ecology*

Now consider a scatterplot, in which each point is a document containing the word *bank*. The location of the document on the x-axis is the count of words in group 1, and the location

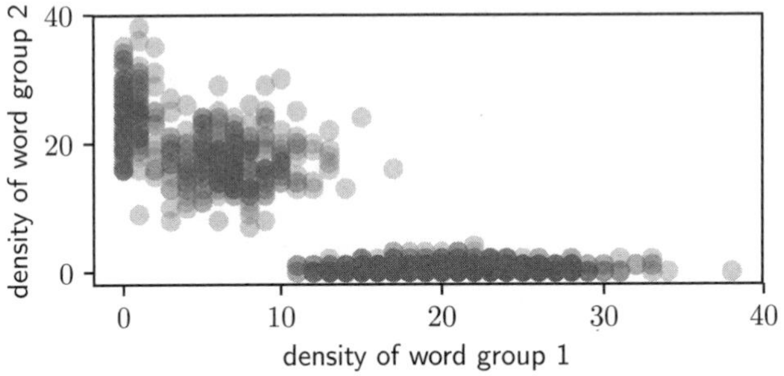

Figure 5.1
Counts of words from two different context groups.

on the y-axis is the count for group 2. In such a plot, shown in figure 5.1, two "blobs" might emerge, and these blobs correspond to the different senses of *bank*.

Here's a related scenario from a different problem. Suppose you download thousands of news articles and make a scatterplot, where each point corresponds to a document: the x-axis is the frequency of the group of words (*hurricane, winds, storm*) and the y-axis is the frequency of the group (*election, voters, vote*). This time, three blobs might emerge: one for documents that are largely about a hurricane, another for documents largely about an election, and a third for documents about neither topic.

These clumps represent the underlying structure of the data. But the two-dimensional scatter plots are based on groupings of context words, and in real scenarios, these word lists are unknown. Unsupervised learning applies the same basic idea but in a high-dimensional space with one dimension for every context word. This space can't be directly visualized, but the goal is the same: try to identify the underlying structure of the observed data, such that there are a few clusters of points, each of which is internally coherent. **Clustering** algorithms are capable of finding such structure automatically.

5.1.1 *K*-Means Clustering

Clustering algorithms assign each data point to a discrete cluster, $z_i \in 1, 2, \ldots K$. One of the best-known clustering algorithms is **K-means**, an iterative algorithm that maintains a cluster assignment for each instance and a central ("mean") location for each cluster. K-means iterates between updates to the assignments and the centers:

1. Each instance is placed in the cluster with the closest center.
2. Each center is recomputed as the average over points in the cluster.

This procedure is formalized in algorithm 8. The term $||\boldsymbol{x}^{(i)} - \boldsymbol{\nu}||^2$ refers to the squared Euclidean norm, $\sum_{j=1}^{V}(x_j^{(i)} - \nu_j)^2$. An important property of K-means is that the converged solution depends on the initialization, and a better clustering can sometimes be found simply by rerunning the algorithm from a different random starting point.

Algorithm 8

K-means clustering algorithm.

---

procedure K-MEANS($\boldsymbol{x}_{1:N}, K$)
    for $i \in 1 \ldots N$ **do** ▷ initialize cluster memberships
        $z^{(i)} \leftarrow \text{RANDOMINT}(1, K)$
    repeat
        for $k \in 1 \ldots K$ **do** ▷ recompute cluster centers
            $\boldsymbol{\nu}_k \leftarrow \frac{1}{\delta(z^{(i)}=k)} \sum_{i=1}^{N} \delta(z^{(i)} = k)\boldsymbol{x}^{(i)}$
        for $i \in 1 \ldots N$ **do** ▷ reassign instances to nearest clusters
            $z^{(i)} \leftarrow \text{argmin}_k \, ||\boldsymbol{x}^{(i)} - \boldsymbol{\nu}_k||^2$
    until converged
    return $\{z^{(i)}\}$ ▷ return cluster assignments

Soft K-means is a particularly relevant variant. Instead of directly assigning each point to a specific cluster, soft K-means assigns to each point a *distribution* over clusters $\boldsymbol{q}^{(i)}$, so that $\sum_{k=1}^{K} q^{(i)}(k) = 1$, and $\forall_k, q^{(i)}(k) \geq 0$. The soft weight $q^{(i)}(k)$ is computed from the distance of $\boldsymbol{x}^{(i)}$ to the cluster center $\boldsymbol{\nu}_k$. In turn, the center of each cluster is computed from a weighted average of the points in the cluster,

$$\boldsymbol{\nu}_k = \frac{1}{\sum_{i=1}^{N} q^{(i)}(k)} \sum_{i=1}^{N} q^{(i)}(k)\boldsymbol{x}^{(i)}. \qquad [5.1]$$

We will now explore a probablistic version of soft K-means clustering, based on **expectation-maximization (EM)**. Because EM clustering can be derived as an approximation to maximum likelihood estimation, it can be extended in a number of useful ways.

5.1.2 Expectation-Maximization (EM)

Expectation-maximization combines the idea of soft K-means with Naïve Bayes classification. To review, Naïve Bayes defines a probability distribution over the data,

$$\log \text{p}(\boldsymbol{x}, \boldsymbol{y}; \boldsymbol{\phi}, \boldsymbol{\mu}) = \sum_{i=1}^{N} \log \left(\text{p}(\boldsymbol{x}^{(i)} \mid y^{(i)}; \boldsymbol{\phi}) \times \text{p}(y^{(i)}; \boldsymbol{\mu}) \right). \qquad [5.2]$$

Now suppose that you never observe the labels. To indicate this, we'll refer to the label of each instance as $z^{(i)}$, rather than $y^{(i)}$, which is usually reserved for observed variables. By marginalizing over the **latent variables** z, we obtain the marginal probability of the observed instances $\boldsymbol{x}$:

$$\log p(\boldsymbol{x}; \boldsymbol{\phi}, \boldsymbol{\mu}) = \sum_{i=1}^{N} \log p(\boldsymbol{x}^{(i)}; \boldsymbol{\phi}, \boldsymbol{\mu}) \tag{5.3}$$

$$= \sum_{i=1}^{N} \log \sum_{z=1}^{K} p(\boldsymbol{x}^{(i)}, z; \boldsymbol{\phi}, \boldsymbol{\mu}) \tag{5.4}$$

$$= \sum_{i=1}^{N} \log \sum_{z=1}^{K} p(\boldsymbol{x}^{(i)} \mid z; \boldsymbol{\phi}) \times p(z; \boldsymbol{\mu}). \tag{5.5}$$

The parameters $\boldsymbol{\phi}$ and $\boldsymbol{\mu}$ can be obtained by maximizing the marginal likelihood in equation 5.5. Why is this the right thing to maximize? Without labels, discriminative learning is impossible—there's nothing to discriminate. So maximum likelihood is all we have.

When the labels are observed, we can estimate the parameters of the Naïve Bayes probability model separately for each label. But marginalizing over the labels couples these parameters, making direct optimization of $\log p(\boldsymbol{x})$ intractable. We will approximate the log-likelihood by introducing an auxiliary variable $\boldsymbol{q}^{(i)}$, which is a distribution over the label set $\mathcal{Z} = \{1, 2, \ldots, K\}$. The optimization procedure will alternate between updates to $\boldsymbol{q}$ and updates to the parameters $(\boldsymbol{\phi}, \boldsymbol{\mu})$. Thus, $\boldsymbol{q}^{(i)}$ plays here as in soft K-means.

To derive the updates for this optimization, multiply the right side of equation 5.5 by the ratio $\frac{q^{(i)}(z)}{q^{(i)}(z)} = 1$,

$$\log p(\boldsymbol{x}; \boldsymbol{\phi}, \boldsymbol{\mu}) = \sum_{i=1}^{N} \log \sum_{z=1}^{K} p(\boldsymbol{x}^{(i)} \mid z; \boldsymbol{\phi}) \times p(z; \boldsymbol{\mu}) \times \frac{q^{(i)}(z)}{q^{(i)}(z)} \tag{5.6}$$

$$= \sum_{i=1}^{N} \log \sum_{z=1}^{K} q^{(i)}(z) \times p(\boldsymbol{x}^{(i)} \mid z; \boldsymbol{\phi}) \times p(z; \boldsymbol{\mu}) \times \frac{1}{q^{(i)}(z)} \tag{5.7}$$

$$= \sum_{i=1}^{N} \log E_{\boldsymbol{q}^{(i)}} \left[\frac{p(\boldsymbol{x}^{(i)} \mid z; \boldsymbol{\phi}) p(z; \boldsymbol{\mu})}{q^{(i)}(z)} \right], \tag{5.8}$$

where $E_{\boldsymbol{q}^{(i)}}[f(z)] = \sum_{z=1}^{K} q^{(i)}(z) \times f(z)$ refers to the expectation of the function f under the distribution $z \sim \boldsymbol{q}^{(i)}$.

Jensen's inequality says that because log is a concave function, we can push it inside the expectation, and obtain a lower bound:

$$\log p(\boldsymbol{x}; \boldsymbol{\phi}, \boldsymbol{\mu}) \geq \sum_{i=1}^{N} E_{\boldsymbol{q}^{(i)}} \left[\log \frac{p(\boldsymbol{x}^{(i)} \mid z; \boldsymbol{\phi}) p(z; \boldsymbol{\mu})}{q^{(i)}(z)} \right] \tag{5.9}$$

$$J \triangleq \sum_{i=1}^{N} E_{\boldsymbol{q}^{(i)}} \left[\log \mathrm{p}(\boldsymbol{x}^{(i)} \mid z; \boldsymbol{\phi}) + \log \mathrm{p}(z; \boldsymbol{\mu}) - \log q^{(i)}(z)\right] \quad [5.10]$$

$$= \sum_{i=1}^{N} E_{\boldsymbol{q}^{(i)}} \left[\log \mathrm{p}(\boldsymbol{x}^{(i)}, z; \boldsymbol{\phi}, \boldsymbol{\mu})\right] + H(\boldsymbol{q}^{(i)}). \quad [5.11]$$

We will focus on equation 5.10, which is the lower bound on the marginal log-likelihood of the observed data, $\log \mathrm{p}(\boldsymbol{x})$. Equation 5.11 shows the connection to the information theoretic concept of **entropy**, $H(\boldsymbol{q}^{(i)}) = -\sum_{z=1}^{K} q^{(i)}(z) \log q^{(i)}(z)$, which measures the average amount of information produced by a draw from the distribution $q^{(i)}$. The lower bound J is a function of two groups of arguments:

- The distributions $\boldsymbol{q}^{(i)}$ for each instance
- The parameters $\boldsymbol{\mu}$ and $\boldsymbol{\phi}$

The expectation-maximization (EM) algorithm maximizes the bound with respect to each of these arguments in turn, while holding the other fixed.

The E-step The step in which we update $\boldsymbol{q}^{(i)}$ is known as the **E-step**, because it updates the distribution under which the expectation is computed. To derive this update, first write out the expectation in the lower bound as a sum,

$$J = \sum_{i=1}^{N} \sum_{z=1}^{K} q^{(i)}(z) \left[\log \mathrm{p}(\boldsymbol{x}^{(i)} \mid z; \boldsymbol{\phi}) + \log \mathrm{p}(z; \boldsymbol{\mu}) - \log q^{(i)}(z)\right]. \quad [5.12]$$

When optimizing this bound, we must also respect a set of "sum-to-one" constraints, $\sum_{z=1}^{K} q^{(i)}(z) = 1$ for all i. Just as in Naïve Bayes, this constraint can be incorporated into a Lagrangian:

$$J_q = \sum_{i=1}^{N} \sum_{z=1}^{K} q^{(i)}(z) \left(\log \mathrm{p}(\boldsymbol{x}^{(i)} \mid z; \boldsymbol{\phi}) + \log \mathrm{p}(z; \mu) - \log q^{(i)}(z)\right) + \lambda^{(i)}(1 - \sum_{z=1}^{K} q^{(i)}(z)), \quad [5.13]$$

where $\lambda^{(i)}$ is the Lagrange multiplier for instance i.

The Lagrangian is maximized by taking the derivative and solving for $q^{(i)}$:

$$\frac{\partial J_q}{\partial q^{(i)}(z)} = \log \mathrm{p}(\boldsymbol{x}^{(i)} \mid z; \boldsymbol{\phi}) + \log \mathrm{p}(z; \boldsymbol{\theta}) - \log q^{(i)}(z) - 1 - \lambda^{(i)} \quad [5.14]$$

$$\log q^{(i)}(z) = \log \mathrm{p}(\boldsymbol{x}^{(i)} \mid z; \boldsymbol{\phi}) + \log \mathrm{p}(z; \mu) - 1 - \lambda^{(i)} \quad [5.15]$$

$$q^{(i)}(z) \propto \mathrm{p}(\boldsymbol{x}^{(i)} \mid z; \boldsymbol{\phi}) \times \mathrm{p}(z; \mu). \quad [5.16]$$

Applying the sum-to-one constraint gives an exact solution,

$$q^{(i)}(z) = \frac{\mathrm{p}(\boldsymbol{x}^{(i)} \mid z; \boldsymbol{\phi}) \times \mathrm{p}(z; \boldsymbol{\mu})}{\sum_{z'=1}^{K} \mathrm{p}(\boldsymbol{x}^{(i)} \mid z'; \boldsymbol{\phi}) \times \mathrm{p}(z'; \boldsymbol{\mu})} \quad [5.17]$$

$$= \mathrm{p}(z \mid \boldsymbol{x}^{(i)}; \boldsymbol{\phi}, \boldsymbol{\mu}). \quad [5.18]$$

After normalizing, each $\boldsymbol{q}^{(i)}$—which is the soft distribution over clusters for data $\boldsymbol{x}^{(i)}$—is set to the posterior probability $\mathrm{p}(z \mid \boldsymbol{x}^{(i)}; \boldsymbol{\phi}, \boldsymbol{\mu})$ under the current parameters. Although the Lagrange multipliers $\lambda^{(i)}$ were introduced as additional parameters, they drop out during normalization.

The M-step Next, we hold fixed the soft assignments $\boldsymbol{q}^{(i)}$ and **m**aximize with respect to the parameters $\boldsymbol{\phi}$ and $\boldsymbol{\mu}$. Let's focus on the parameter $\boldsymbol{\phi}$, which parametrizes the likelihood $\mathrm{p}(\boldsymbol{x} \mid z; \boldsymbol{\phi})$, and leave $\boldsymbol{\mu}$ for an exercise. The parameter $\boldsymbol{\phi}$ is a distribution over words for each cluster, so it is optimized under the constraint that $\sum_{j=1}^{V} \phi_{z,j} = 1$. To incorporate this constraint, we introduce a set of Lagrange multipliers $\{\lambda_z\}_{z=1}^{K}$, and form the Lagrangian,

$$J_\phi = \sum_{i=1}^{N} \sum_{z=1}^{K} q^{(i)}(z) \left(\log \mathrm{p}(\boldsymbol{x}^{(i)} \mid z; \boldsymbol{\phi}) + \log \mathrm{p}(z; \mu) - \log q^{(i)}(z) \right) + \sum_{z=1}^{K} \lambda_z (1 - \sum_{j=1}^{V} \phi_{z,j}). \quad [5.19]$$

The term $\log \mathrm{p}(\boldsymbol{x}^{(i)} \mid z; \boldsymbol{\phi})$ is the conditional log-likelihood for the multinomial, which expands to

$$\log \mathrm{p}(\boldsymbol{x}^{(i)} \mid z, \boldsymbol{\phi}) = C + \sum_{j=1}^{V} x_j \log \phi_{z,j}, \quad [5.20]$$

where C is a constant with respect to $\boldsymbol{\phi}$—see equation 2.12 in § 2.2 for more discussion of this probability function.

Setting the derivative of J_ϕ equal to zero,

$$\frac{\partial J_\phi}{\partial \phi_{z,j}} = \sum_{i=1}^{N} q^{(i)}(z) \times \frac{x_j^{(i)}}{\phi_{z,j}} - \lambda_z \quad [5.21]$$

$$\phi_{z,j} \propto \sum_{i=1}^{N} q^{(i)}(z) \times x_j^{(i)}. \quad [5.22]$$

Because $\boldsymbol{\phi}_z$ is constrained to be a probability distribution, the exact solution is computed as

$$\phi_{z,j} = \frac{\sum_{i=1}^{N} q^{(i)}(z) \times x_j^{(i)}}{\sum_{j'=1}^{V} \sum_{i=1}^{N} q^{(i)}(z) \times x_{j'}^{(i)}} = \frac{E_q\left[\text{count}(z,j)\right]}{\sum_{j'=1}^{V} E_q\left[\text{count}(z,j')\right]}, \tag{5.23}$$

where the counter $j \in \{1, 2, \ldots, V\}$ indexes over base features, such as words.

This update sets $\boldsymbol{\phi}_z$ equal to the relative frequency estimate of the *expected counts* under the distribution $\boldsymbol{q}$. As in supervised Naïve Bayes, we can smooth these counts by adding a constant α. The update for $\boldsymbol{\mu}$ is similar: $\mu_z \propto \sum_{i=1}^{N} q^{(i)}(z) = E_q[\text{count}(z)]$, which is the expected frequency of cluster z. These probabilities can also be smoothed. In sum, the M-step is just like Naïve Bayes, but with expected counts rather than observed counts.

The multinomial likelihood $p(\boldsymbol{x} \mid z)$ can be replaced with other probability distributions: for example, for continuous observations, a Gaussian distribution can be used. In some cases, there is no closed-form update to the parameters of the likelihood. One approach is to run gradient-based optimization at each M-step; another is to simply take a single step along the gradient step and then return to the E-step (Berg-Kirkpatrick et al., 2010).

5.1.3 EM as an Optimization Algorithm

Algorithms that update a global objective by alternating between updates to subsets of the parameters are called **coordinate ascent** algorithms. The objective J (the lower bound on the marginal likelihood of the data) is separately convex in $\boldsymbol{q}$ and $(\boldsymbol{\mu}, \boldsymbol{\phi})$, but it is not jointly convex in all terms; this condition is known as **biconvexity**. Each step of the expectation-maximization algorithm is guaranteed not to decrease the lower bound J, which means that EM will converge toward a solution at which no nearby points yield further improvements. This solution is a **local optimum**—it is as good or better than any of its immediate neighbors but is *not* guaranteed to be optimal among all possible configurations of $(\boldsymbol{q}, \boldsymbol{\mu}, \boldsymbol{\phi})$.

The fact that there is no guarantee of global optimality means that initialization is important: where you start can determine where you finish. To illustrate this point, figure 5.2 shows the objective function for EM with 10 different random initializations: while the

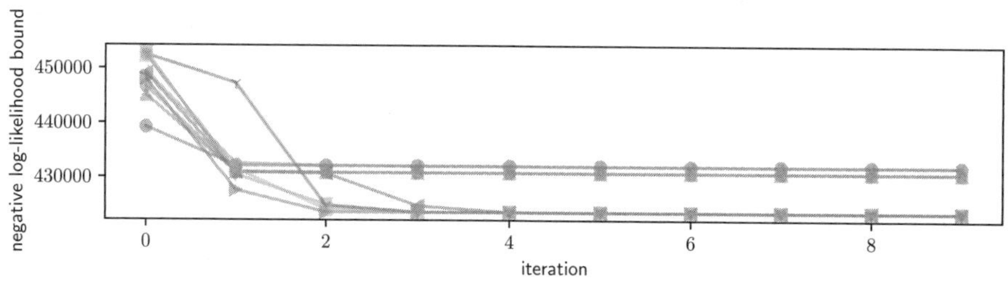

Figure 5.2
Sensitivity of expectation-maximization to initialization. Each line shows the progress of optimization from a different random initialization.

objective function improves monotonically in each run, it converges to several different values.[1] For the convex objectives that we encountered in chapter 2, it was not necessary to worry about initialization, because gradient-based optimization guaranteed to reach the global minimum. But in expectation-maximization—as in the deep neural networks from chapter 3—initialization matters.

In **hard EM**, each $\boldsymbol{q}^{(i)}$ distribution assigns probability of 1 to a single label $\hat{z}^{(i)}$ and zero probability to all others (Neal and Hinton, 1998). This is similar in spirit to K-means clustering and can outperform standard EM in some cases (Spitkovsky et al., 2010). Another variant of expectation-maximization incorporates stochastic gradient descent (SGD): after performing a local E-step at each instance $\boldsymbol{x}^{(i)}$, we immediately make a gradient update to the parameters $(\boldsymbol{\mu}, \boldsymbol{\phi})$. This algorithm has been called **incremental expectation-maximization** (Neal and Hinton, 1998) and **online expectation-maximization** (Sato and Ishii, 2000; Cappé and Moulines, 2009) and is especially useful when there is no closed-form optimum for the likelihood $\mathrm{p}(\boldsymbol{x} \mid z)$, and in online settings where new data is constantly streamed in (see Liang and Klein, 2009, for a comparison of online EM variants).

5.1.4 How Many Clusters?

So far, we have assumed that the number of clusters K is given. In some cases, this assumption is valid. For example, a lexical semantic resource like WORDNET might define the number of senses for a word. In other cases, the number of clusters could be a parameter for the user to tune: some readers want a coarse-grained clustering of news stories into three or four clusters, while others want a fine-grained clustering into 20 or more. But many times there is little extrinsic guidance for how to choose K.

One solution is to choose the number of clusters to maximize a metric of clustering quality. The other parameters $\boldsymbol{\mu}$ and $\boldsymbol{\phi}$ are chosen to maximize the log-likelihood bound J, so this might seem a potential candidate for tuning K. However, J will never decrease with K: if it is possible to obtain a bound of J_K with K clusters, then it is always possible to do at least as well with $K+1$ clusters, by simply ignoring the additional cluster and setting its probability to zero in $\boldsymbol{q}$ and $\boldsymbol{\mu}$. It is therefore necessary to introduce a penalty for model complexity, so that fewer clusters are preferred. For example, the Akaike Information Crition (AIC; Akaike, 1974) is the linear combination of the number of parameters and the log-likelihood,

$$\text{AIC} = 2M - 2J, \qquad [5.24]$$

where M is the number of parameters. In an expectation-maximization clustering algorithm, $M = K \times V + K$. Because the number of parameters increases with the number of

1. The figure shows the upper bound on the *negative* log-likelihood, because optimization is typically framed as minimization rather than maximization.

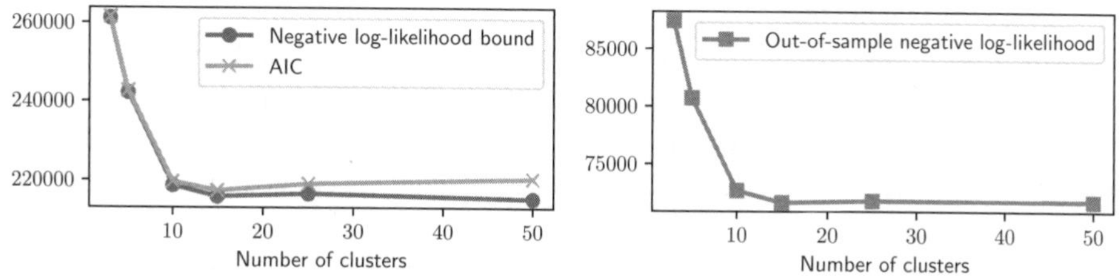

Figure 5.3
The negative log-likelihood and AIC for several runs of expectation-maximization, on synthetic data. Although the data was generated from a model with $K = 10$, the optimal number of clusters is $\hat{K} = 15$, according to AIC and the heldout log-likelihood. The training set log-likelihood continues to improve as K increases.

clusters K, the AIC may prefer more parsimonious models, even if they do not fit the data quite as well.

Another choice is to maximize the **predictive likelihood** on heldout data. This data is not used to estimate the model parameters $\boldsymbol{\phi}$ and $\boldsymbol{\mu}$, and so it is not the case that the likelihood on this data is guaranteed to increase with K. Figure 5.3 shows the negative log-likelihood on training and heldout data, as well as the AIC.

Bayesian nonparametrics An alternative approach is to treat the number of clusters as another latent variable. This requires statistical inference over a set of models with a variable number of clusters. This is not possible within the framework of expectation-maximization, but there are several alternative inference procedures which can be applied, including **Markov Chain Monte Carlo (MCMC)**, which is briefly discussed in § 5.5 (for more details, see chapter 25 of Murphy, 2012). Bayesian nonparametrics have been applied to the problem of unsupervised word sense induction, learning not only the word senses, but also the number of senses, per word (Reisinger and Mooney, 2010).

5.2 Applications of Expectation-Maximization

EM is not really an "algorithm" like, say, quicksort. Rather, it is a framework for learning with missing data. The recipe for using EM on a problem of interest is:

- Introduce latent variables z, such that it is easy to write the probability $P(\boldsymbol{x}, z)$. It should also be easy to estimate the associated parameters, given knowledge of z.
- Derive the E-step updates for $q(z)$, which is typically factored as $q(z) = \prod_{i=1}^{N} q_{z^{(i)}}(z^{(i)})$, where i is an index over instances.
- The M-step updates typically correspond to the soft version of a probabilistic supervised learning algorithm, like Naïve Bayes.

This section discusses a few of the many applications of this general framework.

5.2.1 Word Sense Induction

The chapter began by considering the problem of word sense disambiguation when the senses are not known in advance. Expectation-maximization can be applied to this problem by treating each cluster as a word sense. Each instance represents the use of an ambiguous word, and $\boldsymbol{x}^{(i)}$ is a vector of counts for the other words that appear nearby: Schütze (1998) uses all words within a 50-word window. The probability $\mathrm{p}(\boldsymbol{x}^{(i)} \mid z)$ can be set to the multinomial distribution, as in Naïve Bayes. The EM algorithm can be applied directly to this data, yielding clusters that (hopefully) correspond to the word senses.

Better performance can be obtained by first applying **singular-value decomposition (SVD)** to the matrix of context-counts $\mathbf{C}_{ij} = \text{count}(i,j)$, where $\text{count}(i,j)$ is the count of word j in the context of instance i. **Truncated** singular-value decomposition approximates the matrix $\mathbf{C}$ as a product of three matrices, $\mathbf{U}$, $\mathbf{S}$, and $\mathbf{V}$, under the constraint that $\mathbf{U}$ and $\mathbf{V}$ are orthonormal and $\mathbf{S}$ is diagonal:

$$\begin{aligned}
&\min_{\mathbf{U},\mathbf{S},\mathbf{V}} ||\mathbf{C} - \mathbf{U}\mathbf{S}\mathbf{V}^\top||_F && [5.25]\\
&\quad s.t. \mathbf{U} \in \mathbb{R}^{V \times K}, \mathbf{U}\mathbf{U}^\top = \mathbb{I}\\
&\qquad \mathbf{S} = \text{Diag}(s_1, s_2, \ldots, s_K)\\
&\qquad \mathbf{V}^\top \in \mathbb{R}^{N_p \times K}, \mathbf{V}\mathbf{V}^\top = \mathbb{I},
\end{aligned}$$

where $|| \cdot ||_F$ is the **Frobenius norm**, $||X||_F = \sqrt{\sum_{i,j} X_{i,j}^2}$. The matrix $\mathbf{U}$ contains the left singular vectors of $\mathbf{C}$, and the rows of this matrix can be used as low-dimensional representations of the count vectors $\boldsymbol{c}_i$. EM clustering can be made more robust by setting the instance descriptions $\boldsymbol{x}^{(i)}$ equal to these rows, rather than using raw counts (Schütze, 1998). However, because the instances are now dense vectors of continuous numbers, the probability $\mathrm{p}(\boldsymbol{x}^{(i)} \mid z)$ must be defined as a multivariate Gaussian distribution.

In truncated singular-value decomposition, the hyperparameter K is the truncation limit: when K is equal to the rank of $\mathbf{C}$, the norm of the difference between the original matrix $\mathbf{C}$ and its reconstruction $\mathbf{U}\mathbf{S}\mathbf{V}^\top$ will be zero. Lower values of K increase the reconstruction error, but yield vector representations that are smaller and easier to learn from. Singular-value decomposition is discussed in more detail in chapter 14.

5.2.2 Semi-Supervised Learning

Expectation-maximization can also be applied to the problem of **semi-supervised learning**: learning from both labeled and unlabeled data in a single model. Semi-supervised learning makes use of annotated examples, ensuring that each label y corresponds to the desired concept. By adding unlabeled examples, it is possible to cover a greater fraction of the features than would appear in labeled data alone. Other methods for semi-supervised learning are discussed in § 5.3, but for now, let's approach the problem within the framework of expectation-maximization (Nigam et al., 2000).

Suppose we have labeled data $\{(\boldsymbol{x}^{(i)}, y^{(i)})\}_{i=1}^{N_\ell}$, and unlabeled data $\{\boldsymbol{x}^{(i)}\}_{i=N_\ell+1}^{N_\ell+N_u}$, where N_ℓ is the number of labeled instances and N_u is the number of unlabeled instances. We can learn from the combined data by maximizing a lower bound on the joint log-likelihood,

$$\mathcal{L} = \sum_{i=1}^{N_\ell} \log \mathrm{p}(\boldsymbol{x}^{(i)}, y^{(i)}; \boldsymbol{\mu}, \boldsymbol{\phi}) + \sum_{j=N_\ell+1}^{N_\ell+N_u} \log \mathrm{p}(\boldsymbol{x}^{(j)}; \boldsymbol{\mu}, \boldsymbol{\phi}) \qquad [5.26]$$

$$= \sum_{i=1}^{N_\ell} \left(\log \mathrm{p}(\boldsymbol{x}^{(i)} \mid y^{(i)}; \boldsymbol{\phi}) + \log \mathrm{p}(y^{(i)}; \boldsymbol{\mu}) \right) + \sum_{j=N_\ell+1}^{N_\ell+N_u} \log \sum_{y=1}^{K} \mathrm{p}(\boldsymbol{x}^{(j)}, y; \boldsymbol{\mu}, \boldsymbol{\phi}). \qquad [5.27]$$

The left sum is identical to the objective in Naïve Bayes; the right sum is the marginal log-likelihood for expectation-maximization clustering, from equation 5.5. We can construct a lower bound on this log-likelihood by introducing distributions $\boldsymbol{q}^{(j)}$ for all $j \in \{N_\ell + 1, \ldots, N_\ell + N_u\}$. The E-step updates these distributions; the M-step updates the parameters $\boldsymbol{\phi}$ and $\boldsymbol{\mu}$, using the expected counts from the unlabeled data and the observed counts from the labeled data.

A critical issue in semi-supervised learning is how to balance the impact of the labeled and unlabeled data on the classifier weights, especially when the unlabeled data is much larger than the labeled dataset. The risk is that the unlabeled data will dominate, causing the parameters to drift toward a "natural clustering" of the instances—which may not correspond to a good classifier for the labeled data. One solution is to heuristically reweight the two components of equation 5.26, tuning the weight of the two components on a heldout development set (Nigam et al., 2000).

5.2.3 Multi-component Modeling

As a final application, let's return to fully supervised classification. A classic dataset for text classification is 20 newsgroups, which contains posts to a set of online forums, called newsgroups. One of the newsgroups is `comp.sys.mac.hardware`, which discusses Apple computing hardware. Suppose that within this newsgroup there are two kinds of posts: reviews of new hardware and question-answer posts about hardware problems. The language in these *components* of the `mac.hardware` class might have little in common; if so, it would be better to model these components separately, rather than treating their union as a single class. However, the component responsible for each instance is not directly observed.

Recall that Naïve Bayes is based on a generative process, which provides a stochastic explanation for the observed data. In Naïve Bayes, each label is drawn from a categorical distribution with parameter $\boldsymbol{\mu}$, and each vector of word counts is drawn from a multinomial distribution with parameter $\boldsymbol{\phi}_y$. For multi component modeling, we envision a slightly different generative process, incorporating both the observed label $y^{(i)}$ and the latent component $z^{(i)}$. This generative process is shown in algorithm 9. A new parameter $\boldsymbol{\beta}_{y^{(i)}}$ defines the distribution of components, conditioned on the label $y^{(i)}$. The component, and not the class label, then parametrizes the distribution over words.

Algorithm 9
Generative process for the Naïve Bayes classifier with hidden components.

---

for instance $i \in \{1, 2, \ldots, N\}$ **do**:
  Draw the label $y^{(i)} \sim \text{Categorical}(\boldsymbol{\mu})$;
  Draw the component $z^{(i)} \sim \text{Categorical}(\boldsymbol{\beta}_{y^{(i)}})$;
  Draw the word counts $\boldsymbol{x}^{(i)} \mid y^{(i)}, z^{(i)} \sim \text{Multinomial}(\boldsymbol{\phi}_{z^{(i)}})$.

The labeled data includes $(\boldsymbol{x}^{(i)}, y^{(i)})$, but not $z^{(i)}$, so this is another case of missing data. Again, we sum over the missing data, applying Jensen's inequality to as to obtain a lower bound on the log-likelihood,

$$\log \mathrm{p}(\boldsymbol{x}^{(i)}, y^{(i)}) = \log \sum_{z=1}^{K_z} \mathrm{p}(\boldsymbol{x}^{(i)}, y^{(i)}, z; \boldsymbol{\mu}, \boldsymbol{\phi}, \boldsymbol{\beta}) \qquad [5.28]$$

$$\geq \log \mathrm{p}(y^{(i)}; \boldsymbol{\mu}) + E_{q^{(i)}_{Z|Y}} [\log \mathrm{p}(\boldsymbol{x}^{(i)} \mid z; \boldsymbol{\phi}) + \log \mathrm{p}(z \mid y^{(i)}; \boldsymbol{\beta}) - \log q^{(i)}(z)]. \qquad [5.29]$$

We are now ready to apply expectation-maximization. As usual, the E-step updates the distribution over the missing data, $q^{(i)}_{Z|Y}$. The M-step updates the parameters,

$$\beta_{y,z} = \frac{E_q[\text{count}(y, z)]}{\sum_{z'=1}^{K_z} E_q[\text{count}(y, z')]} \qquad [5.30]$$

$$\phi_{z,j} = \frac{E_q[\text{count}(z, j)]}{\sum_{j'=1}^{V} E_q[\text{count}(z, j')]}. \qquad [5.31]$$

5.3 Semi-Supervised Learning

In semi-supervised learning, the learner makes use of both labeled and unlabeled data. To see how this could help, suppose you want to do sentiment analysis in French. In table 5.1, there are two labeled examples, one positive and one negative. From this data, a learner could conclude that *réussi* is positive and *long* is negative. This isn't much! However, we can propagate this information to the unlabeled data and potentially learn more.

- If we are confident that *réussi* is positive, then we might guess that (5.3) is also positive.
- That suggests that *parfaitement* is also positive.
- We can then propagate this information to (5.5) and learn from the words in this example.

Table 5.1
Labeled and unlabeled reviews of the films *Blade Runner 2049* and *Transformers: The Last Knight*

(5.1)	☺ Villeneuve a bel et bien **réussi** son pari de changer de perspectives tout en assurant une cohérence à la franchise.[2]
(5.2)	☹ Il est également trop **long** et bancal dans sa narration, tiède dans ses intentions, et tiraillé entre deux personnages et directions qui ne parviennent pas à coexister en harmonie.[3]
(5.3)	Denis Villeneuve a **réussi** une suite **parfaitement** maitrisée.[4]
(5.4)	**Long**, **bavard**, hyper design, à peine agité (le comble de l'action : une bagarre dans la flotte), métaphysique et, surtout, ennuyeux jusqu' à la catalepsie.[5]
(5.5)	Une suite d'une écrasante puissance, mêlant **parfaitement** le contemplatif au narratif.[6]
(5.6)	Le film impitoyablement **bavard** finit quand même par se taire quand se lève l'espèce de bouquet final où semble se déchaîner, comme en libre parcours de poulets décapités, l'armée des graphistes numériques griffant nerveusement la palette graphique entre agonie et orgasme.[7]

- Similarly, we can propagate from the labeled data to (5.4), which we guess to be negative because it shares the word *long*. This suggests that *bavard* is also negative, which we propagate to (5.6).

Instances (5.3) and (5.4) were "similar" to the labeled examples for positivity and negativity, respectively. By using these instances to expand the models for each class, it became possible to correctly label instances (5.5) and (5.6), which didn't share any important features with the original labeled data. This requires a key assumption: that similar instances will have similar labels.

In § 5.2.2, we discussed how expectation-maximization can be applied to semi-supervised learning. Using the labeled data, the initial parameters $\boldsymbol{\phi}$ would assign a high weight for *réussi* in the positive class and a high weight for *long* in the negative class. These weights helped to shape the distributions $\boldsymbol{q}$ for instances (5.3) and (5.4) in the E-step. In the next iteration of the M-step, the parameters $\boldsymbol{\phi}$ are updated with counts from these instances, making it possible to correctly label the instances (5.5) and (5.6).

However, expectation-maximization has an important disadvantage: it requires using a generative classification model, which restricts the features that can be used for classification. In this section, we explore nonprobabilistic approaches, which impose fewer restrictions on the classification model.

2. http://www.premiere.fr/Cinema/News-Cinema/Critique-Blade-Runner-2049-est-Le-Parrain-2-de-la-science-fiction.

3. https://www.ecranlarge.com/films/critique/1000531-blade-runner-2049-critique-sans-spoilers.

4. http://www.gqmagazine.fr/pop-culture/cinema/articles/faut-il-aller-voir-blade-runner-2049/56600.

5. http://www.vsd.fr/loisirs/cinema-faut-il-vraiment-aller-voir-blade-runner-2049-22967.

6. http://www.cinemateaser.com/2017/10/71704-blade-runner-2049-chronique.

7. http://next.liberation.fr/cinema/2017/06/27/transformers-the-last-knight-voie-de-garage_1579963.

Table 5.2
Example of multiview learning for named entity classification

	$x^{(1)}$	$x^{(2)}$	y
1.	Peachtree Street	located on	LOC
2.	Dr. Walker	said	PER
3.	Zanzibar	located in	? → LOC
4.	Zanzibar	flew to	? → LOC
5.	Dr. Robert	recommended	? → PER
6.	Oprah	recommended	? → PER

5.3.1 Multiview Learning

EM semi-supervised learning can be viewed as **self-training**: the labeled data guides the initial estimates of the classification parameters; these parameters are used to compute a label distribution over the unlabeled instances, $\boldsymbol{q}^{(i)}$; the label distributions are used to update the parameters. The risk is that self-training drifts away from the original labeled data. This problem can be ameliorated by **multi-view learning**. Here we take the assumption that the features can be decomposed into multiple "views," each of which is conditionally independent, given the label. For example, consider the problem of classifying a name as a person or location: one view is the name itself; another is the context in which it appears. This situation is illustrated in table 5.2.

Co-training is an iterative multiview learning algorithm, in which there are separate classifiers for each view (Blum and Mitchell, 1998). At each iteration of the algorithm, each classifier predicts labels for a subset of the unlabeled instances, using only the features available in its view. These predictions are then used as ground truth to train the classifiers associated with the other views. In the example shown in table 5.2, the classifier on $\boldsymbol{x}^{(1)}$ might correctly label instance #5 as a person, because of the feature *Dr*; this instance would then serve as training data for the classifier on $\boldsymbol{x}^{(2)}$, which would then be able to correctly label instance #6, thanks to the feature *recommended*. If the views are truly independent, this procedure is robust to drift. Furthermore, it imposes no restrictions on the classifiers that can be used for each view.

Word sense disambiguation is particularly suited to multiview learning, thanks to the heuristic of "one sense per discourse": if a polysemous word is used more than once in a given text or conversation, all usages refer to the same sense (Gale et al., 1992). This motivates a multiview learning approach, in which one view corresponds to the local context (the surrounding words) and another view corresponds to the global context at the document level (Yarowsky, 1995). The local context view is first trained on a small seed dataset. We then identify its most confident predictions on unlabeled instances. The global context view is then used to extend these confident predictions to other instances within the same documents. These new instances are added to the training data the local context classifier, which is retrained and then applied to the remaining unlabeled data.

5.3.2 Graph-Based Algorithms

Another family of approaches to semi-supervised learning begins by constructing a graph, in which pairs of instances are linked with symmetric weights $\omega_{i,j}$, e.g.,

$$\omega_{i,j} = \exp(-\alpha \times ||\boldsymbol{x}^{(i)} - \boldsymbol{x}^{(j)}||^2). \quad [5.32]$$

The goal is to use this weighted graph to propagate labels from a small set of labeled instances to a larger set of unlabeled instances.

In **label propagation**, this is done through a series of matrix operations (Zhu et al., 2003). Let $\mathbf{Q}$ be a matrix of size $N \times K$, in which each row $\boldsymbol{q}^{(i)}$ describes the labeling of instance i. When ground truth labels are available, then $\boldsymbol{q}^{(i)}$ is an indicator vector, with $q^{(i)}_{y^{(i)}} = 1$ and $q^{(i)}_{y' \neq y^{(i)}} = 0$. Let us refer to the submatrix of rows containing labeled instances as $\mathbf{Q}_L$ and the remaining rows as $\mathbf{Q}_U$. The rows of $\mathbf{Q}_U$ are initialized to assign equal probabilities to all labels, $q_{i,k} = \frac{1}{K}$.

Now, let $T_{i,j}$ represent the "transition" probability of moving from node j to node i,

$$T_{i,j} \triangleq \Pr(j \rightarrow i) = \frac{\omega_{i,j}}{\sum_{k=1}^{N} \omega_{k,j}}. \quad [5.33]$$

We compute values of $T_{i,j}$ for all instances j and all *unlabeled* instances i, forming a matrix of size $N_U \times N$. If the dataset is large, this matrix may be expensive to store and manipulate; a solution is to sparsify it, by keeping only the κ largest values in each row and setting all other values to zero. We can then "propagate" the label distributions to the unlabeled instances,

$$\tilde{\mathbf{Q}}_U \leftarrow \mathbf{T}\mathbf{Q} \quad [5.34]$$

$$\boldsymbol{s} \leftarrow \tilde{\mathbf{Q}}_U \mathbf{1} \quad [5.35]$$

$$\mathbf{Q}_U \leftarrow \text{Diag}(\boldsymbol{s})^{-1}\tilde{\mathbf{Q}}_U. \quad [5.36]$$

The expression $\tilde{\mathbf{Q}}_U\mathbf{1}$ indicates multiplication of $\tilde{\mathbf{Q}}_U$ by a column vector of ones, which is equivalent to computing the sum of each row of $\tilde{\mathbf{Q}}_U$. The matrix $\text{Diag}(\boldsymbol{s})$ is a diagonal matrix with the elements of $\boldsymbol{s}$ on the diagonals. The product $\text{Diag}(\boldsymbol{s})^{-1}\tilde{\mathbf{Q}}_U$ has the effect of normalizing the rows of $\tilde{\mathbf{Q}}_U$, so that each row of $\mathbf{Q}_U$ is a probability distribution over labels.

5.4 Domain Adaptation

In many practical scenarios, the labeled data differs in some key respects from the data to which the trained model is to be applied. A classic example is in consumer reviews: we may have labeled reviews of movies (the source domain), but we want to predict the reviews of appliances (the target domain). A similar issue arises with genre differences: most linguistically annotated data is news text, but application domains range from social media to electronic health records. In general, there may be several source and target domains, each with their own properties; however, for simplicity, this discussion will focus mainly on the case of a single source and target domain.

The simplest approach is "direct transfer": train a classifier on the source domain and apply it directly to the target domain. The accuracy of this approach depends on the extent to which features are shared across domains. In review text, words like *outstanding* and *disappointing* will apply across both movies and appliances; but others, like *terrifying*, may have meanings that are domain specific. As a result, direct transfer performs poorly: for example, an out-of-domain classifier (trained on book reviews) suffers twice the error rate of an in-domain classifier on reviews of kitchen appliances (Blitzer et al., 2007). **Domain adaptation** algorithms attempt to do better than direct transfer by learning from data in both domains. There are two main families of domain adaptation algorithms, depending on whether any labeled data is available in the target domain.

5.4.1 Supervised Domain Adaptation

In supervised domain adaptation, there is a small amount of labeled data in the target domain and a large amount of data in the source domain. The simplest approach would be to ignore domain differences and simply merge the training data from the source and target domains. There are several other baseline approaches to dealing with this scenario (Daumé III, 2007):

Interpolation Train a classifier for each domain and combine their predictions, for example,

$$\hat{y} = \underset{y}{\operatorname{argmax}}\, \lambda_s \Psi_s(\boldsymbol{x}, y) + (1 - \lambda_s)\Psi_t(\boldsymbol{x}, y), \tag{5.37}$$

where Ψ_s and Ψ_t are the scoring functions from the source and target domain classifiers, respectively, and λ_s is the interpolation weight.

Prediction Train a classifier on the source domain data and use its prediction as an additional feature in a classifier trained on the target domain data,

$$\hat{y}_S = \underset{y}{\operatorname{argmax}}\, \Psi_s(\boldsymbol{x}, y) \tag{5.38}$$

$$\hat{y}_t = \underset{y}{\operatorname{argmax}}\, \Psi_t([\boldsymbol{x}; \hat{y}_S], y). \tag{5.39}$$

Priors Train a classifier on the source domain data and use its weights as a prior distribution on the weights of the classifier for the target domain data. This is equivalent to regularizing the target domain weights toward the weights of the source domain classifier (Chelba and Acero, 2006),

$$\ell(\boldsymbol{\theta}_t) = \sum_{i=1}^{N} \ell^{(i)}(\boldsymbol{x}^{(i)}, y^{(i)}; \boldsymbol{\theta}_t) + \lambda ||\boldsymbol{\theta}_t - \boldsymbol{\theta}_s||_2^2, \tag{5.40}$$

where $\ell^{(i)}$ is the prediction loss on instance i and λ is the regularization weight.

An effective and "frustratingly simple" alternative is EASYADAPT (Daumé III, 2007), which creates copies of each feature: one for each domain and one for the cross-domain setting. For example, a negative review of the film *Wonder Woman* begins, *As boring and flavorless as a three-day-old grilled cheese sandwich ...* [8] The resulting bag-of-words feature vector would be

$$\begin{aligned} \boldsymbol{f}(\boldsymbol{x}, y, d) = \{ & (\textit{boring}, ☹, \text{MOVIE}) : 1, (\textit{boring}, ☹, *) : 1, \\ & (\textit{flavorless}, ☹, \text{MOVIE}) : 1, (\textit{flavorless}, ☹, *) : 1, \\ & (\textit{three-day-old}, ☹, \text{MOVIE}) : 1, (\textit{three-day-old}, ☹, *) : 1, \\ & \ldots \}, \end{aligned}$$

with ($boring$, ☹, MOVIE) indicating the word *boring* appearing in a negative-labeled document in the MOVIE domain and ($boring$, ☹, $*$) indicating the same word in a negative-labeled document in *any* domain. It is up to the learner to allocate weight between the domain-specific and cross-domain features: for words that facilitate prediction in both domains, the learner will use the cross-domain features; for words that are relevant only to a single domain, the domain-specific features will be used. Any discriminative classifier can be used with these augmented features.[9]

5.4.2 Unsupervised Domain Adaptation

In unsupervised domain adaptation, there is no labeled data in the target domain. Unsupervised domain adaptation algorithms cope with this problem by trying to make the data from the source and target domains as similar as possible. This is typically done by learning a **projection function**, which puts the source and target data in a shared space, in which a learner can generalize across domains. This projection is learned from data in both domains and is applied to the base features—for example, the bag of words in text classification. The projected features can then be used both for training and for prediction.

Linear projection In linear projection, the cross-domain representation is constructed by a matrix-vector product,

$$\boldsymbol{g}(\boldsymbol{x}^{(i)}) = \mathbf{U}\boldsymbol{x}^{(i)}. \quad [5.41]$$

The projected vectors $\boldsymbol{g}(\boldsymbol{x}^{(i)})$ can then be used as base features during both training (from the source domain) and prediction (on the target domain).

The projection matrix $\mathbf{U}$ can be learned in a number of different ways, but many approaches focus on compressing and reconstructing the base features (Ando and Zhang,

8. www.colesmithey.com/capsules/2017/06/wonder-woman.HTML. Accessed October 9, 2017.

9. EASYADAPT can be explained as a hierarchical Bayesian model, in which the weights for each domain are drawn from a shared prior (Finkel and Manning, 2009).

2005). For example, we can define a set of **pivot features**, which are typically chosen because they appear in both domains: in the case of review documents, pivot features might include evaluative adjectives like *outstanding* and *disappointing* (Blitzer et al., 2007). For each pivot feature j, we define an auxiliary problem of predicting whether the feature is present in each example, using the remaining base features. Let $\boldsymbol{\phi}_j$ denote the weights of this classifier and us horizontally concatenate the weights for each of the N_p pivot features into a matrix $\Phi = [\boldsymbol{\phi}_1, \boldsymbol{\phi}_2, \ldots, \boldsymbol{\phi}_{N_P}]$.

We then perform truncated singular-value decomposition on Φ, as described in § 5.2.1, obtaining $\Phi \approx \mathbf{USV}^\top$. The rows of the matrix $\mathbf{U}$ summarize information about each base feature: indeed, the truncated singular-value decomposition identifies a low-dimension basis for the weight matrix Φ, which in turn links base features to pivot features. Suppose that the base feature *reliable* occurs only in the target domain of appliance reviews. Nonetheless, it will have a positive weight toward some pivot features (e.g., *outstanding*, *recommended*) and a negative weight toward others (e.g., *worthless*, *unpleasant*). A base feature such as *watchable* might have the same associations with the pivot features, and therefore, $\boldsymbol{u}_{\text{reliable}} \approx \boldsymbol{u}_{\text{watchable}}$. The matrix $\mathbf{U}$ can thus project the base features into a space in which this information is shared.

Nonlinear projection Nonlinear transformations of the base features can be accomplished by implementing the transformation function as a deep neural network, which is trained from an auxiliary objective.

Denoising objectives One possibility is to train a projection function to reconstruct a corrupted version of the original input. The original input can be corrupted in various ways: by the addition of random noise (Glorot et al., 2011; Chen et al., 2012) or by the deletion of features (Chen et al., 2012; Yang and Eisenstein, 2015). Denoising objectives share many properties of the linear projection method described above: they enable the projection function to be trained on large amounts of unlabeled data from the target domain and allow information to be shared across the feature space, thereby reducing sensitivity to rare and domain-specific features.

Adversarial objectives The ultimate goal is for the transformed representations $\boldsymbol{g}(\boldsymbol{x}^{(i)})$ to be domain general. This can be made an explicit optimization criterion by computing the similarity of transformed instances both within and between domains (Tzeng et al., 2015) or by formulating an auxiliary classification task, in which the domain itself is treated as a label (Ganin et al., 2016). This setting is **adversarial**, because we want to learn a representation that makes this classifier perform poorly. At the same time, we want $\boldsymbol{g}(\boldsymbol{x}^{(i)})$ to enable accurate predictions of the labels $y^{(i)}$.

To formalize this idea, let $d^{(i)}$ represent the domain of instance i, and let $\ell_d(\boldsymbol{g}(\boldsymbol{x}^{(i)}), d^{(i)}; \boldsymbol{\theta}_d)$ represent the loss of a classifier (typically a deep neural network) trained

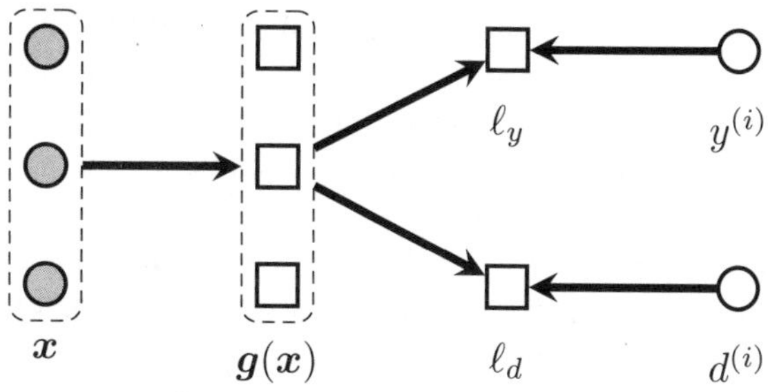

Figure 5.4
A schematic view of adversarial domain adaptation. The loss ℓ_y is computed only for instances from the source domain, where labels $y^{(i)}$ are available.

to predict $d^{(i)}$ from the transformed representation $\boldsymbol{g}(\boldsymbol{x}^{(i)})$, using parameters $\boldsymbol{\theta}_d$. Analogously, let $\ell_y(\boldsymbol{g}(\boldsymbol{x}^{(i)}), y^{(i)}; \boldsymbol{\theta}_y)$ represent the loss of a classifier trained to predict the label $y^{(i)}$ from $\boldsymbol{g}(\boldsymbol{x}^{(i)})$, using parameters $\boldsymbol{\theta}_y$. The transformation $\boldsymbol{g}$ can then be trained from two criteria: it should yield accurate predictions of the labels $y^{(i)}$, while making *inaccurate* predictions of the domains $d^{(i)}$. This can be formulated as a joint optimization problem,

$$\min_{\boldsymbol{\theta}_g, \boldsymbol{\theta}_y, \boldsymbol{\theta}_d} \sum_{i=1}^{N_\ell + N_u} \ell_d(\boldsymbol{g}(\boldsymbol{x}^{(i)}; \boldsymbol{\theta}_g), d^{(i)}; \boldsymbol{\theta}_d) - \sum_{i=1}^{N_\ell} \ell_y(\boldsymbol{g}(\boldsymbol{x}^{(i)}; \boldsymbol{\theta}_g), y^{(i)}; \boldsymbol{\theta}_y), \qquad [5.42]$$

where N_ℓ is the number of labeled instances and N_u is the number of unlabeled instances, with the labeled instances appearing first in the dataset. This setup is shown in figure 5.4. The loss can be optimized by stochastic gradient descent, jointly training the parameters of the nonlinear transformation $\boldsymbol{\theta}_g$ and the parameters of the prediction models $\boldsymbol{\theta}_d$ and $\boldsymbol{\theta}_y$.

5.5 *Other Approaches to Learning With Latent Variables

Expectation-maximization provides a general approach to learning with latent variables, but it has limitations. One is the sensitivity to initialization; in practical applications, considerable attention may need to be devoted to finding a good initialization. A second issue is that EM tends to be easiest to apply in cases where the latent variables have a clear decomposition (in the cases we have considered, they decompose across the instances). For these reasons, it is worth briefly considering some alternatives to EM.

5.5.1 Sampling

In EM clustering, there is a distribution $\boldsymbol{q}^{(i)}$ for the missing data related to each instance. The M-step consists of updating the parameters of this distribution. An alternative is to draw samples of the latent variables. If the sampling distribution is designed correctly, this procedure will eventually converge to drawing samples from the true posterior over the missing data, $\text{p}(\boldsymbol{z}^{(1:N_z)} \mid \boldsymbol{x}^{(1:N_x)})$. For example, in the case of clustering, the missing data $\boldsymbol{z}^{(1:N_z)}$ is the set of cluster memberships, so we draw samples from the posterior distribution over clusterings of the data. If a single clustering is required, we can select the one with the highest conditional likelihood, $\hat{\boldsymbol{z}} = \text{argmax}_{\boldsymbol{z}}\, \text{p}(\boldsymbol{z}^{(1:N_z)} \mid \boldsymbol{x}^{(1:N_x)})$.

This general family of algorithms is called **Markov Chain Monte Carlo (MCMC)**: "Monte Carlo" because it is based on a series of random draws; "Markov Chain" because the sampling procedure must be designed such that each sample depends only on the previous sample, and not on the entire sampling history. **Gibbs sampling** is an MCMC algorithm in which each latent variable is sampled from its posterior distribution,

$$z^{(n)} \mid \boldsymbol{x}, \boldsymbol{z}^{(-n)} \sim \text{p}(z^{(n)} \mid \boldsymbol{x}, \boldsymbol{z}^{(-n)}), \qquad [5.43]$$

where $\boldsymbol{z}^{(-n)}$ indicates $\{\boldsymbol{z} \backslash z^{(n)}\}$, the set of all latent variables except for $z^{(n)}$. Repeatedly drawing samples over all latent variables constructs a Markov chain that is guaranteed to converge to a sequence of samples from $\text{p}(\boldsymbol{z}^{(1:N_z)} \mid \boldsymbol{x}^{(1:N_x)})$. In probabilistic clustering, the sampling distribution has the following form,

$$\text{p}(z^{(i)} \mid \boldsymbol{x}, \boldsymbol{z}^{(-i)}) = \frac{\text{p}(\boldsymbol{x}^{(i)} \mid z^{(i)}; \boldsymbol{\phi}) \times \text{p}(z^{(i)}; \boldsymbol{\mu})}{\sum_{z=1}^{K} \text{p}(\boldsymbol{x}^{(i)} \mid z; \boldsymbol{\phi}) \times \text{p}(z; \boldsymbol{\mu})} \qquad [5.44]$$

$$\propto \text{Multinomial}(\boldsymbol{x}^{(i)}; \boldsymbol{\phi}_{z^{(i)}}) \times \boldsymbol{\mu}_{z^{(i)}}. \qquad [5.45]$$

In this case, the sampling distribution does not depend on the other instances: the posterior distribution over each $z^{(i)}$ can be computed from $\boldsymbol{x}^{(i)}$ and the parameters given the parameters $\boldsymbol{\phi}$ and $\boldsymbol{\mu}$.

In sampling algorithms, there are several choices for how to deal with the parameters. One possibility is to sample them too. To do this, we must add them to the generative story, by introducing a prior distribution. For the multinomial and categorical parameters in the EM clustering model, the **Dirichlet distribution** is a typical choice, because it defines a probability on exactly the set of vectors that can be parameters: vectors that sum to one and include only nonnegative numbers.[10]

10. If $\sum_i^K \theta_i = 1$ and $\theta_i \geq 0$ for all i, then $\boldsymbol{\theta}$ is said to be on the $K-1$ **simplex**. A Dirichlet distribution with parameter $\boldsymbol{\alpha} \in \mathbb{R}_+^K$ has support over the $K-1$ simplex,

$$\text{p}_{\text{Dirichlet}}(\boldsymbol{\theta} \mid \boldsymbol{\alpha}) = \frac{1}{B(\boldsymbol{\alpha})} \prod_{i=1}^{K} \theta_i^{\alpha_i - 1} \qquad [5.46]$$

$$B(\boldsymbol{\alpha}) = \frac{\prod_{i=1}^{K} \Gamma(\alpha_i)}{\Gamma(\sum_{i=1}^{K} \alpha_i)}, \qquad [5.47]$$

with $\Gamma(\cdot)$ indicating the gamma function, a generalization of the factorial function to nonnegative reals.

To incorporate this prior, the generative model must be augmented to indicate that each $\boldsymbol{\phi}_z \sim \text{Dirichlet}(\boldsymbol{\alpha}_\phi)$, and $\boldsymbol{\mu} \sim \text{Dirichlet}(\boldsymbol{\alpha}_\mu)$. The hyperparameters $\boldsymbol{\alpha}$ are typically set to a constant vector $\boldsymbol{\alpha} = [\alpha, \alpha, \ldots, \alpha]$. When α is large, the Dirichlet distribution tends to generate vectors that are nearly uniform; when α is small, it tends to generate vectors that assign most of their probability mass to a few entries. Given prior distributions over $\boldsymbol{\phi}$ and $\boldsymbol{\mu}$, we can now include them in Gibbs sampling, drawing values for these parameters from posterior distributions that are conditioned on the other variables in the model.

Unfortunately, sampling $\boldsymbol{\phi}$ and $\boldsymbol{\mu}$ usually leads to slow "mixing," meaning that adjacent samples tend to be similar, so that a large number of samples is required to explore the space of random variables. The reason is that the sampling distributions for the parameters are tightly constrained by the cluster memberships, which in turn are tightly constrained by the parameters. There are two solutions that are frequently employed:

- **Empirical Bayesian** methods maintain $\boldsymbol{\phi}$ and $\boldsymbol{\mu}$ as parameters rather than latent variables. They still employ sampling in the E-step of the EM algorithm, but they update the parameters using expected counts that are computed from the samples rather than from parametric distributions. This EM-MCMC hybrid is also known as Monte Carlo Expectation Maximization (MCEM; Wei and Tanner, 1990), and is well suited for cases in which it is difficult to compute $\boldsymbol{q}^{(i)}$ directly.
- In **collapsed Gibbs sampling**, we analytically integrate $\boldsymbol{\phi}$ and $\boldsymbol{\mu}$ out of the model. The cluster memberships $y^{(i)}$ are the only remaining latent variable; we sample them from the compound distribution,

$$\begin{aligned}
&\mathrm{p}(y^{(i)} \mid \boldsymbol{x}^{(1:N)}, \boldsymbol{y}^{(-i)}; \alpha_\phi, \alpha_\mu) \\
&= \int_{\boldsymbol{\phi},\boldsymbol{\mu}} \mathrm{p}(\boldsymbol{\phi}, \boldsymbol{\mu} \mid \boldsymbol{y}^{(-i)}, \boldsymbol{x}^{(1:N)}; \alpha_\phi, \alpha_\mu) \mathrm{p}(y^{(i)} \mid \boldsymbol{x}^{(1:N)}, \boldsymbol{y}^{(-i)}, \boldsymbol{\phi}, \boldsymbol{\mu}) d\boldsymbol{\phi} d\boldsymbol{\mu}.
\end{aligned} \quad [5.48]$$

For multinomial and Dirichlet distributions, this integral can be computed in closed form.

MCMC algorithms are guaranteed to converge to the true posterior distribution over the latent variables, but there is no way to know how long this will take. In practice, the rate of convergence depends on initialization, just as expectation-maximization depends on initialization to avoid local optima. Thus, while Gibbs sampling and other MCMC algorithms provide a powerful and flexible array of techniques for statistical inference in latent variable models, they are not a panacea for the problems experienced by EM.

5.5.2 Spectral Learning

Another approach to learning with latent variables is based on the **method of moments**, which makes it possible to avoid the problem of nonconvex log-likelihood. Write $\overline{\boldsymbol{x}}^{(i)}$ for the normalized vector of word counts in document i, so that $\overline{\boldsymbol{x}}^{(i)} = \boldsymbol{x}^{(i)} / \sum_{j=1}^{V} x_j^{(i)}$. Then we can form a matrix of word-word co-occurrence probabilities,

$$\mathbf{C} = \sum_{i=1}^{N} \overline{\boldsymbol{x}}^{(i)} (\overline{\boldsymbol{x}}^{(i)})^\top. \qquad [5.49]$$

The expected value of this matrix under $p(\boldsymbol{x} \mid \boldsymbol{\phi}, \mu)$, is:

$$E[\mathbf{C}] = \sum_{i=1}^{N} \sum_{k=1}^{K} \Pr(Z^{(i)} = k; \boldsymbol{\mu}) \boldsymbol{\phi}_k \boldsymbol{\phi}_k^\top \qquad [5.50]$$

$$= \sum_{k}^{K} N\mu_k \boldsymbol{\phi}_k \boldsymbol{\phi}_k^\top \qquad [5.51]$$

$$= \Phi \text{Diag}(N\mu) \Phi^\top, \qquad [5.52]$$

where Φ is formed by horizontally concatenating $\boldsymbol{\phi}_1 \dots \boldsymbol{\phi}_K$, and $\text{Diag}(N\mu)$ indicates a diagonal matrix with values $N\mu_k$ at position (k, k). Setting $\mathbf{C}$ equal to its expectation gives

$$\mathbf{C} = \Phi \text{Diag}(N\mu) \Phi^\top, \qquad [5.53]$$

which is similar to the eigendecomposition $\mathbf{C} = \mathbf{Q} \Lambda \mathbf{Q}^\top$. This suggests that simply by finding the eigenvectors and eigenvalues of $\mathbf{C}$, we could obtain the parameters $\boldsymbol{\phi}$ and μ, and this is what motivates the name **spectral learning**.

While moment-matching and eigendecomposition are similar in form, they impose different constraints on the solutions: eigendecomposition requires orthonormality, so that $\mathbf{Q}\mathbf{Q}^\top = \mathbb{I}$; in estimating the parameters of a text clustering model, we require that $\boldsymbol{\mu}$ and the columns of Φ are probability vectors. Spectral learning algorithms must therefore include a procedure for converting the solution into vectors that are nonnegative and sum to one. One approach is to replace eigendecomposition (or the related singular-value decomposition) with nonnegative matrix factorization (Xu et al., 2003), which guarantees that the solutions are nonnegative (Arora et al., 2013).

After obtaining the parameters $\boldsymbol{\phi}$ and $\boldsymbol{\mu}$, the distribution over clusters can be computed from Bayes' rule:

$$p(z^{(i)} \mid \boldsymbol{x}^{(i)}; \boldsymbol{\phi}, \boldsymbol{\mu}) \propto p(\boldsymbol{x}^{(i)} \mid z^{(i)}; \boldsymbol{\phi}) \times p(z^{(i)}; \mu). \qquad [5.54]$$

Spectral learning yields provably good solutions without regard to initialization and can be quite fast in practice. However, it is more difficult to apply to a broad family of generative models than EM and Gibbs sampling. For more on applying spectral learning across a range of latent variable models, see Anandkumar et al. (2014).

Additional Resources

There are a number of other learning paradigms that deviate from supervised learning.

- **Active learning**: the learner selects unlabeled instances and requests annotations (Settles, 2012).

- **Multiple instance learning**: labels are applied to bags of instances, with a positive label applied if at least one instance in the bag meets the criterion (Dietterich et al., 1997; Maron and Lozano-Pérez, 1998).
- **Constraint-driven learning**: supervision is provided in the form of explicit constraints on the learner (Chang et al., 2007; Ganchev et al., 2010).
- **Distant supervision**: noisy labels are generated from an external resource (Mintz et al., 2009, also see § 17.2.3).
- **Multitask learning**: the learner induces a representation that can be used to solve multiple classification tasks (Collobert et al., 2011b).
- **Transfer learning**: the learner must solve a classification task that differs from the labeled data (Pan and Yang, 2010).

Expectation-maximization was introduced by Dempster et al. (1977) and is discussed in more detail by Murphy (2012). Like most machine learning treatments, Murphy focuses on continuous observations and Gaussian likelihoods, rather than the discrete observations typically encountered in natural language processing. Murphy (2012) also includes an excellent chapter on MCMC; for a textbook-length treatment, see Robert and Casella (2013). For still more on Bayesian latent variable models, see Barber (2012), and for applications of Bayesian models to natural language processing, see Cohen (2016). Surveys are available for semi-supervised learning (Zhu and Goldberg, 2009) and domain adaptation (Søgaard, 2013), although both predate the current wave of interest in deep learning.

Exercises

1. Derive the expectation-maximization update for the parameter $\boldsymbol{\mu}$ in the EM clustering model.
2. Derive the E-step and M-step updates for the following generative model. You may assume that the labels $y^{(i)}$ are observed, but $z_m^{(i)}$ is not.
   - For each instance i,
     - Draw label $y^{(i)} \sim \text{Categorical}(\boldsymbol{\mu})$
     - For each token $m \in \{1, 2, \ldots, M^{(i)}\}$,
       * Draw $z_m^{(i)} \sim \text{Categorical}(\pi)$
       * If $z_m^{(i)} = 0$, draw the current token from a label-specific distribution, $w_m^{(i)} \sim \boldsymbol{\phi}_{y^{(i)}}$
       * If $z_m^{(i)} = 1$, draw the current token from a document-specific distribution, $w_m^{(i)} \sim \boldsymbol{\nu}^{(i)}$
3. Using the iterative updates in equations 5.34 to 5.36, compute the outcome of the label propagation algorithm for the following examples.

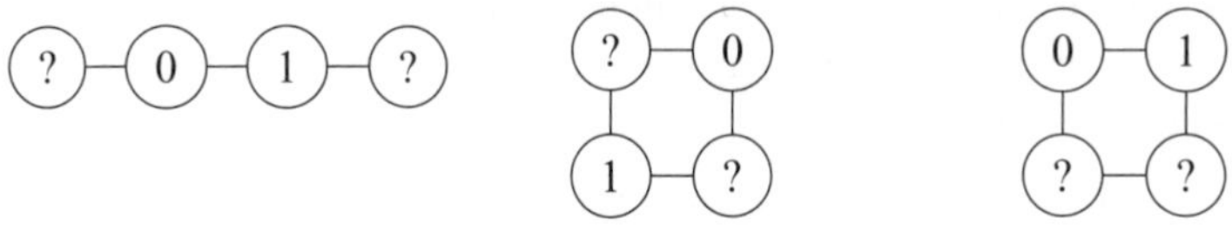

The value inside the node indicates the label, $y^{(i)} \in \{0, 1\}$, with $y^{(i)} =?$ for unlabeled nodes. The presence of an edge between two nodes indicates $w_{i,j} = 1$, and the absence of an edge indicates $w_{i,j} = 0$. For the third example, you need only compute the first three iterations, and then you can guess at the solution in the limit.

4. Use expectation-maximization clustering to train a word sense induction system, applied to the word *say*.
   - Import `nltk`, run `nltk.download()` and select `semcor`. Import `semcor` from `nltk.corpus`.
   - The command `semcor.tagged_sentences(tag='sense')` returns an iterator over sense-tagged sentences in the corpus. Each sentence can be viewed as an iterator over `tree` objects. For `tree` objects that are sense-annotated words, you can access the annotation as `tree.label()` and the word itself with `tree.leaves()`. So `semcor.tagged_sentences(tag='sense')[0][2].label()` would return the sense annotation of the third word in the first sentence.
   - Extract all sentences containing the senses `say.v.01` and `say.v.02`.
   - Build bag-of-words vectors $\boldsymbol{x}^{(i)}$, containing the counts of other words in those sentences, including all words that occur in at least two sentences.
   - Implement and run expectation-maximization clustering on the merged data.
   - Compute the frequency with which each cluster includes instances of `say.v.01` and `say.v.02`.

   In the remaining exercises, you will try out some approaches for semi-supervised learning and domain adaptation. You will need datasets in multiple domains. You can obtain product reviews in multiple domains here: www.cs.jhu.edu/~mdredze/datasets/sentiment/processed_acl.tar.gz. Choose a source and target domain, for example, DVDs and books, and divide the data for the target domain into training and test sets of equal size.

5. First, quantify the cost of cross-domain transfer.
   - Train a logistic regression classifier on the source domain training set, and evaluate it on the target domain test set.
   - Train a logistic regression classifier on the target domain training set, and evaluate it on the target domain test set. This is the “direct transfer” baseline.

Compute the difference in accuracy, which is a measure of the transfer loss across domains.

6. Next, apply the **label propagation** algorithm from § 5.3.2.

   As a baseline, using only 5% of the target domain training set, train a classifier, and compute its accuracy on the target domain test set.

   Next, apply label propagation:

   - Compute the label matrix $\mathbf{Q}_L$ for the labeled data (5% of the target domain training set), with each row equal to an indicator vector for the label (positive or negative).
   - Iterate through the target domain instances, including both test and training data. At each instance i, compute all w_{ij}, using equation 5.32, with $\alpha = 0.01$. Use these values to fill in column i of the transition matrix $\mathbf{T}$, setting all but the 10 largest values to zero for each column i. Be sure to normalize the column so that the remaining values sum to one. You may need to use a sparse matrix for this to fit into memory.
   - Apply the iterative updates from equations 5.34 to 5.36 to compute the outcome of the label propagation algorithm for the unlabeled examples.

   Select the test set instances from $\mathbf{Q}_U$, and compute the accuracy of this method. Compare with the supervised classifier trained only on the 5% sample of the target domain training set.

7. Using only 5% of the target domain training data (and all of the source domain training data), implement one of the supervised domain adaptation baselines in § 5.4.1. See if this improves on the "direct transfer" baseline from the previous problem

8. Implement EASYADAPT (§ 5.4.1), again using 5% of the target domain training data and all of the source domain data.

9. Now try unsupervised domain adaptation, using the "linear projection" method described in § 5.4.2. Specifically:

   - Identify 500 pivot features as the words with the highest frequency in the (complete) training data for the source and target domains. Specifically, let x_i^d be the count of the word i in domain d: choose the 500 words with the largest values of $\min(x_i^{\text{source}}, x_i^{\text{target}})$.
   - Train a classifier to predict each pivot feature from the remaining words in the document.
   - Arrange the features of these classifiers into a matrix Φ, and perform truncated singular-value decomposition, with $k = 20$.
   - Train a classifier from the source domain data, using the combined features $\boldsymbol{x}^{(i)} \oplus \mathbf{U}^\top \boldsymbol{x}^{(i)}$—these include the original bag-of-words features, plus the projected features.
   - Apply this classifier to the target domain test set, and compute the accuracy.

II SEQUENCES AND TREES

6 Language Models

In probabilistic classification, the problem is to compute the probability of a label, conditioned on the text. Let's now consider the inverse problem: computing the probability of text itself. Specifically, we will consider models that assign probability to a sequence of word tokens, $p(w_1, w_2, \ldots, w_M)$, with $w_m \in \mathcal{V}$. The set $\mathcal{V}$ is a discrete vocabulary,

$$\mathcal{V} = \{aardvark, abacus, \ldots, zither\}. \qquad [6.1]$$

Why would you want to compute the probability of a word sequence? In many applications, the goal is to produce word sequences as output:

- In **machine translation** (chapter 18), we convert from text in a source language to text in a target language.
- In **speech recognition**, we convert from audio signal to text.
- In **summarization** (§ 16.3.4; § 19.2), we convert from long texts into short texts.
- In **dialogue systems** (§ 19.3), we convert from the user's input (and perhaps an external knowledge base) into a text response.

In many of the systems for performing these tasks, there is a subcomponent that computes the probability of the output text. The purpose of this component is to generate texts that are more **fluent**. For example, suppose we want to translate a sentence from Spanish to English.

(6.1) El cafe negro me gusta mucho.

Here is a literal word-for-word translation (a **gloss**):

(6.2) The coffee black me pleases much.

A good language model of English will tell us that the probability of this translation is low, in comparison with more grammatical alternatives,

$$p(\textit{The coffee black me pleases much}) < p(\textit{I love dark coffee}). \qquad [6.2]$$

How can we use this fact? Warren Weaver, one of the early leaders in machine translation, viewed it as a problem of breaking a secret code (Weaver, 1955):

> When I look at an article in Russian, I say: 'This is really written in English, but it has been coded in some strange symbols. I will now proceed to decode.'

This observation motivates a generative model (like Naïve Bayes):

- The English sentence $\boldsymbol{w}^{(e)}$ is generated from a **language model**, $\mathrm{p}_e(\boldsymbol{w}^{(e)})$.
- The Spanish sentence $\boldsymbol{w}^{(s)}$ is then generated from a **translation model**, $\mathrm{p}_{s|e}(\boldsymbol{w}^{(s)} \mid \boldsymbol{w}^{(e)})$.

Given these two distributions, translation can be performed by Bayes' rule:

$$\mathrm{p}_{e|s}(\boldsymbol{w}^{(e)} \mid \boldsymbol{w}^{(s)}) \propto \mathrm{p}_{e,s}(\boldsymbol{w}^{(e)}, \boldsymbol{w}^{(s)}) \tag{6.3}$$

$$= \mathrm{p}_{s|e}(\boldsymbol{w}^{(s)} \mid \boldsymbol{w}^{(e)}) \times \mathrm{p}_e(\boldsymbol{w}^{(e)}). \tag{6.4}$$

This is sometimes called the **noisy channel model**, because it envisions English text turning into Spanish by passing through a noisy channel, $\mathrm{p}_{s|e}$. What is the advantage of modeling translation this way, as opposed to modeling $\mathrm{p}_{e|s}$ directly? The crucial point is that the two distributions $\mathrm{p}_{s|e}$ (the translation model) and p_e (the language model) can be estimated from separate data. The translation model requires examples of correct translations, but the language model requires only text in English. Such monolingual data is much more widely available. Furthermore, once estimated, the language model p_e can be reused in any application that involves generating English text, including translation from other languages.

6.1 *N*-Gram Language Models

A simple approach to computing the probability of a sequence of tokens is to use a **relative frequency estimate**. Consider the quote, attributed to Picasso, "*computers are useless, they can only give you answers.*" One way to estimate the probability of this sentence is as follows:

$$\mathrm{p}(\textit{Computers are useless, they can only give you answers})$$

$$= \frac{\mathrm{count}(\textit{Computers are useless, they can only give you answers})}{\mathrm{count}(\text{all sentences ever spoken})}. \tag{6.5}$$

This estimator is **unbiased**: in the theoretical limit of infinite data, the estimate will be correct. But in practice, we are asking for accurate counts over an infinite number of events, because sequences of words can be arbitrarily long. Even with an aggressive upper bound of, say, $M = 20$ tokens in the sequence, the number of possible sequences is V^{20}, where $V = |\mathcal{V}|$. A small vocabularly for English would have $V = 10^5$, so there are 10^{100} possible sequences. Clearly, this estimator is very data hungry and suffers from high variance: even grammatical sentences will have probability zero if they have not occurred in the training data.[1] We therefore need to introduce bias to have a chance of making reliable estimates from finite training data. The language models that follow in this chapter introduce bias in various ways.

We begin with n-gram language models, which compute the probability of a sequence as the product of probabilities of subsequences. The probability of a sequence $\mathrm{p}(\boldsymbol{w}) = \mathrm{p}(w_1, w_2, \ldots, w_M)$ can be refactored using the chain rule (see § A.2):

$$\mathrm{p}(\boldsymbol{w}) = \mathrm{p}(w_1, w_2, \ldots, w_M) \tag{6.6}$$

$$= \mathrm{p}(w_1) \times \mathrm{p}(w_2 \mid w_1) \times \mathrm{p}(w_3 \mid w_2, w_1) \times \cdots \times \mathrm{p}(w_M \mid w_{M-1}, \ldots, w_1). \tag{6.7}$$

Each element in the product is the probability of a word given all its predecessors. We can think of this as a *word prediction* task: given the context *Computers are*, we want to compute a probability over the next token. The relative frequency estimate of the probability of the word *useless* in this context is

$$\mathrm{p}(\textit{useless} \mid \textit{computers are}) = \frac{\mathrm{count}(\textit{computers are useless})}{\sum_{x \in \mathcal{V}} \mathrm{count}(\textit{computers are } x)}$$
$$= \frac{\mathrm{count}(\textit{computers are useless})}{\mathrm{count}(\textit{computers are})}.$$

We haven't made any approximations yet, and we could have just as well applied the chain rule in reverse order,

$$\mathrm{p}(\boldsymbol{w}) = \mathrm{p}(w_M) \times \mathrm{p}(w_{M-1} \mid w_M) \times \cdots \times \mathrm{p}(w_1 \mid w_2, \ldots, w_M), \tag{6.8}$$

or in any other order. But this means that we also haven't really made any progress: to compute the conditional probability $\mathrm{p}(w_M \mid w_{M-1}, w_{M-2}, \ldots, w_1)$, we would need to model V^{M-1} contexts. Such a distribution cannot be estimated from any realistic sample of text.

To solve this problem, n-gram models make a crucial simplifying approximation: they condition on only the past $n-1$ words:

$$\mathrm{p}(w_m \mid w_{m-1} \ldots w_1) \approx \mathrm{p}(w_m \mid w_{m-1}, \ldots, w_{m-n+1}) \tag{6.9}$$

This means that the probability of a sentence $\boldsymbol{w}$ can be approximated as

$$\mathrm{p}(w_1, \ldots, w_M) \approx \prod_{m=1}^{M} \mathrm{p}(w_m \mid w_{m-1}, \ldots, w_{m-n+1}). \tag{6.10}$$

To compute the probability of an entire sentence, it is convenient to pad the beginning and end with special symbols □ and ■. Then the bigram ($n = 2$) approximation to the probability of *I like black coffee* is:

1. Chomsky (1957) famously argued that this is evidence against the very concept of probabilistic language models: no such model could distinguish the grammatical sentence *colorless green ideas sleep furiously* from the ungrammatical permutation *furiously sleep ideas green colorless*.

$$\begin{aligned} \text{p}(I\ like\ black\ coffee) = {} & \text{p}(I \mid \square) \times \text{p}(like \mid I) \times \text{p}(black \mid like) \times \text{p}(coffee \mid black) \\ & \times \text{p}(\blacksquare \mid coffee). \end{aligned} \tag{6.11}$$

This model requires estimating and storing the probability of only V^n events, which is exponential in the order of the n-gram, and not V^M, which is exponential in the length of the sentence. The n-gram probabilities can be computed by relative frequency estimation,

$$\text{p}(w_m \mid w_{m-1}, w_{m-2}) = \frac{\text{count}(w_{m-2}, w_{m-1}, w_m)}{\sum_{w'} \text{count}(w_{m-2}, w_{m-1}, w')}. \tag{6.12}$$

The hyperparameter n controls the size of the context used in each conditional probability. If this is misspecified, the language model will perform poorly. Let's consider the potential problems concretely.

When n is too small. Consider the following sentences:

(6.3) **Gorillas** always like to groom **their** friends.
(6.4) The **computer** that's on the 3rd floor of our office building **crashed**.

In each example, the words written in bold depend on each other: the likelihood of *their* depends on knowing that *gorillas* is plural, and the likelihood of *crashed* depends on knowing that the subject is a *computer*. If the n-grams are not big enough to capture this context, then the resulting language model would offer probabilities that are too low for these sentences, and too high for sentences that fail basic linguistic tests like number agreement.

When n is too big. In this case, it is hard to compute good estimates of the n-gram parameters from our dataset, because of data sparsity. To handle the *gorilla* example, it is necessary to model 6-grams, which means accounting for V^6 events. Under a very small vocabulary of $V = 10^4$, this means estimating the probability of 10^{24} distinct events.

These two problems point to another **bias-variance tradeoff** (see § 2.2.4). A small n-gram size introduces high bias, and a large n-gram size introduces high variance. We can even have both problems at the same time! Language is full of long-range dependencies that we cannot capture because n is too small; at the same time, language datasets are full of rare phenomena, whose probabilities we fail to estimate accurately because n is too large. One solution is to try to keep n large, while still making low-variance estimates of the underlying parameters. To do this, we will introduce a different sort of bias: **smoothing**.

6.2 Smoothing and Discounting

Limited data is a persistent problem in estimating language models. In § 6.1, we presented n-grams as a partial solution. But sparse data can be a problem even for low-order n-grams; at the same time, many linguistic phenomena, like subject-verb agreement, cannot be incorporated into language models without high-order n-grams. It is therefore necessary to add additional inductive biases to n-gram language models. This section covers some of the most intuitive and common approaches, but there are many more (see Chen and Goodman, 1999).

6.2.1 Smoothing

A major concern in language modeling is to avoid the situation $\mathrm{p}(\boldsymbol{w}) = 0$, which could arise as a result of a single unseen n-gram. A similar problem arose in Naïve Bayes, and the solution was **smoothing**: adding imaginary "pseudo" counts. The same idea can be applied to n-gram language models, as shown here in the bigram case:

$$\mathrm{p}_{\text{smooth}}(w_m \mid w_{m-1}) = \frac{\text{count}(w_{m-1}, w_m) + \alpha}{\sum_{w' \in \mathcal{V}} \text{count}(w_{m-1}, w') + V\alpha}. \qquad [6.13]$$

This basic framework is called **Lidstone smoothing**, but special cases have other names:

- **Laplace smoothing** corresponds to the case $\alpha = 1$.
- **Jeffreys-Perks law** corresponds to the case $\alpha = 0.5$, which works well in practice and benefits from some theoretical justification (Manning and Schütze, 1999).

To ensure that the probabilities are properly normalized, anything that we add to the numerator (α) must also appear in the denominator ($V\alpha$). This idea is reflected in the concept of **effective counts**:

$$c_i^* = (c_i + \alpha)\frac{M}{M + V\alpha}, \qquad [6.14]$$

where c_i is the count of event i, c_i^* is the effective count, and $M = \sum_{i=1}^{V} c_i$ is the total number of tokens in the dataset $(w_1, w_2, \ldots, w_M)$. This term ensures that $\sum_{i=1}^{V} c_i^* = \sum_{i=1}^{V} c_i = M$. The **discount** for each n-gram is then computed as

$$d_i = \frac{c_i^*}{c_i} = \frac{(c_i + \alpha)}{c_i} \frac{M}{(M + V\alpha)}.$$

6.2.2 Discounting and Backoff

Discounting "borrows" probability mass from observed n-grams and redistributes it. In Lidstone smoothing, the borrowing is done by increasing the denominator of the relative frequency estimates. The borrowed probability mass is then redistributed by increasing the numerator for all n-grams. Another approach would be to borrow the same amount of probability mass from all observed n-grams, and redistribute it among only the unobserved n-grams. This is called **absolute discounting**. For example, suppose we set an absolute discount $d = 0.1$ in a bigram model, and then redistribute this probability mass equally over the unseen words. The resulting probabilities are shown in table 6.1.

Discounting reserves some probability mass from the observed data, and we need not redistribute this probability mass equally. Instead, we can **backoff** to a lower-order language

Table 6.1
Example of Lidstone smoothing and absolute discounting in a bigram language model, for the context (*alleged*, _), for a toy corpus with a total of 20 counts over the seven words shown. Note that discounting decreases the probability for all but the unseen words, while Lidstone smoothing increases the effective counts and probabilities for *deficiencies* and *outbreak*.

			Lidstone smoothing, $\alpha = 0.1$		Discounting, $d = 0.1$	
	counts	unsmoothed probability	effective counts	smoothed probability	effective counts	smoothed probability
impropriety	8	0.4	7.826	0.391	7.9	0.395
offense	5	0.25	4.928	0.246	4.9	0.245
damage	4	0.2	3.961	0.198	3.9	0.195
deficiencies	2	0.1	2.029	0.101	1.9	0.095
outbreak	1	0.05	1.063	0.053	0.9	0.045
infirmity	0	0	0.097	0.005	0.25	0.013
cephalopods	0	0	0.097	0.005	0.25	0.013

model: if you have trigrams, use trigrams; if you don't have trigrams, use bigrams; if you don't even have bigrams, use unigrams. This is called **Katz backoff**. In the simple case of backing off from bigrams to unigrams, the bigram probabilities are

$$c^*(i,j) = c(i,j) - d \tag{6.15}$$

$$\mathrm{p}_{\mathrm{Katz}}(i \mid j) = \begin{cases} \frac{c^*(i,j)}{c(j)} & \text{if } c(i,j) > 0 \\ \alpha(j) \times \frac{\mathrm{p}_{\mathrm{unigram}}(i)}{\sum_{i' : c(i',j)=0} \mathrm{p}_{\mathrm{unigram}}(i')} & \text{if } c(i,j) = 0. \end{cases} \tag{6.16}$$

The term $\alpha(j)$ indicates the amount of probability mass that has been discounted for context j. This probability mass is then divided across all the unseen events, $\{i' : c(i', j) = 0\}$, proportional to the unigram probability of each word i'. The discount parameter d can be optimized to maximize performance (typically held-out log-likelihood) on a development set.

6.2.3 *Interpolation

Backoff is one way to combine different order n-gram models. An alternative approach is **interpolation**: setting the probability of a word in context to a weighted sum of its probabilities across progressively shorter contexts.

Instead of choosing a single n for the size of the n-gram, we can take the weighted average across several n-gram probabilities. For example, for an interpolated trigram model,

$$\begin{aligned} \mathrm{p}_{\mathrm{Interpolation}}(w_m \mid w_{m-1}, w_{m-2}) = & \lambda_3 \mathrm{p}_3^*(w_m \mid w_{m-1}, w_{m-2}) \\ & + \lambda_2 \mathrm{p}_2^*(w_m \mid w_{m-1}) \\ & + \lambda_1 \mathrm{p}_1^*(w_m). \end{aligned}$$

In this equation, p^*_n is the unsmoothed empirical probability given by an n-gram language model, and λ_n is the weight assigned to this model. To ensure that the interpolated $p(\boldsymbol{w})$ is still a valid probability distribution, the values of λ must obey the constraint, $\sum_{n=1}^{n_{\max}} \lambda_n = 1$. But how to find the specific values?

An elegant solution is **expectation-maximization**. Recall from chapter 5 that we can think about EM as learning with *missing data*: we just need to choose missing data such that learning would be easy if it weren't missing. What's missing in this case? Think of each word w_m as drawn from an n-gram of unknown size, $z_m \in \{1 \ldots n_{\max}\}$. This z_m is the missing data that we are looking for. Therefore, the application of EM to this problem involves the following **generative model**:

for each token $w_m, m = 1, 2, \ldots, M$ **do**:
  draw the n-gram size $z_m \sim \text{Categorical}(\lambda)$;
  draw $w_m \sim p^*_{z_m}(w_m \mid w_{m-1}, \ldots, w_{m-z_m})$.

If the missing data $\{Z_m\}$ were known, then λ could be estimated as the relative frequency,

$$\lambda_z = \frac{\text{count}(Z_m = z)}{M} \quad [6.17]$$

$$\propto \sum_{m=1}^{M} \delta(Z_m = z). \quad [6.18]$$

But since we do not know the values of the latent variables, we impute a distribution q_m in the E-step, which represents the degree of belief that word token w_m was generated from a n-gram of order z_m,

$$q_m(z) \triangleq \Pr(Z_m = z \mid \boldsymbol{w}_{1:m}; \lambda) \quad [6.19]$$

$$= \frac{p(w_m \mid \boldsymbol{w}_{1:m-1}, Z_m = z) \times p(z)}{\sum_{z'} p(w_m \mid \boldsymbol{w}_{1:m-1}, Z_m = z') \times p(z')} \quad [6.20]$$

$$\propto p^*_z(w_m \mid \boldsymbol{w}_{1:m-1}) \times \lambda_z. \quad [6.21]$$

In the M-step, λ is computed by summing the expected counts under q,

$$\lambda_z \propto \sum_{m=1}^{M} q_m(z). \quad [6.22]$$

A solution is obtained by iterating between updates to q and λ. The complete algorithm is shown in algorithm 10.

6.2.4 *Kneser-Ney Smoothing

Kneser-Ney smoothing is based on absolute discounting, but it redistributes the resulting probability mass in a different way from Katz backoff. Empirical evidence points to Kneser-Ney smoothing as the state of the art for n-gram language modeling (Goodman, 2001). To

Algorithm 10
Expectation-maximization for interpolated language modeling.

---

procedure ESTIMATE INTERPOLATED n-GRAM $(\boldsymbol{w}_{1:M}, \{\mathrm{p}_n^*\}_{n \in 1:n_{\max}})$
 for $z \in \{1, 2, \ldots, n_{\max}\}$ **do** ▷ Initialization
  $\lambda_z \leftarrow \frac{1}{n_{\max}}$
 repeat
  for $m \in \{1, 2, \ldots, M\}$ **do** ▷ E-step
   for $z \in \{1, 2, \ldots, n_{\max}\}$ **do**
    $q_m(z) \leftarrow \mathrm{p}_z^*(w_m \mid \boldsymbol{w}_{1:m-}) \times \lambda_z$
   $\boldsymbol{q}_m \leftarrow \text{Normalize}(\boldsymbol{q}_m)$
  for $z \in \{1, 2, \ldots, n_{\max}\}$ **do** ▷ M-step
   $\lambda_z \leftarrow \frac{1}{M} \sum_{m=1}^{M} q_m(z)$
 until tired
 return $\boldsymbol{\lambda}$

---

motivate Kneser-Ney smoothing, consider the example: *I recently visited _*. Which of the following is more likely: *Francisco* or *Duluth*?

Now suppose that both bigrams *visited Duluth* and *visited Francisco* are unobserved in the training data and furthermore that the unigram probability $\mathrm{p}_1^*(\textit{Francisco})$ is greater than $\mathrm{p}_1^*(\textit{Duluth})$. Nonetheless we would still guess that $\mathrm{p}(\textit{visited Duluth}) > \mathrm{p}(\textit{visited Francisco})$, because *Duluth* is a more "versatile" word: it can occur in many contexts, while *Francisco* usually occurs in a single context, following the word *San*. This notion of versatility is the key to Kneser-Ney smoothing.

Writing u for a context of undefined length, and $\text{count}(w, u)$ as the count of word w in context u, we define the Kneser-Ney bigram probability as

$$\mathrm{p}_{KN}(w \mid u) = \begin{cases} \frac{\max(\text{count}(w,u)-d,0)}{\text{count}(u)}, & \text{count}(w,u) > 0 \\ \alpha(u) \times \mathrm{p}_{\text{continuation}}(w), & \text{otherwise} \end{cases} \quad [6.23]$$

$$\mathrm{p}_{\text{continuation}}(w) = \frac{|u : \text{count}(w,u) > 0|}{\sum_{w' \in \mathcal{V}} |u' : \text{count}(w', u') > 0|}. \quad [6.24]$$

Probability mass is conserved using absolute discounting d, which is taken from all unobserved n-grams. The total amount of discounting in context u is $d \times |w : \text{count}(w,u) > 0|$, and we divide this probability mass among the unseen n-grams. To account for versatility, we define the *continuation probability* $\mathrm{p}_{\text{continuation}}(w)$ as proportional to the number of observed contexts in which w appears. The numerator of the continuation probability is the number of contexts u in which w appears; the denominator normalizes the probability by summing the same quantity over all words w'. The coefficient $\alpha(u)$ is set to ensure that the probability distribution $p_{KN}(w \mid u)$ sums to one over the vocabulary w.

The idea of modeling versatility by counting contexts may seem heuristic, but there is an elegant theoretical justification from Bayesian nonparametrics (Teh, 2006). Kneser-Ney smoothing on n-grams was the dominant language modeling technique before the arrival of neural language models.

6.3 Recurrent Neural Network Language Models

N-gram language models have been largely supplanted by neural networks. These models do not make the n-gram assumption of restricted context; indeed, they can incorporate arbitrarily distant contextual information, while remaining computationally and statistically tractable.

The first insight behind neural language models is to treat word prediction as a *discriminative* learning task.[2] The goal is to compute the probability $p(w \mid u)$, where $w \in \mathcal{V}$ is a word, and u is the context, which depends on the previous words. Rather than directly estimating the word probabilities from (smoothed) relative frequencies, we can treat treat language modeling as a machine learning problem and estimate parameters that maximize the log conditional probability of a corpus.

The second insight is to reparametrize the probability distribution $p(w \mid u)$ as a function of two dense K-dimensional numerical vectors, $\boldsymbol{\beta}_w \in \mathbb{R}^K$, and $\boldsymbol{v}_u \in \mathbb{R}^K$,

$$p(w \mid u) = \frac{\exp(\boldsymbol{\beta}_w \cdot \boldsymbol{v}_u)}{\sum_{w' \in \mathcal{V}} \exp(\boldsymbol{\beta}_{w'} \cdot \boldsymbol{v}_u)}, \qquad [6.25]$$

where $\boldsymbol{\beta}_w \cdot \boldsymbol{v}_u$ represents a dot product. As usual, the denominator ensures that the probability distribution is properly normalized. This vector of probabilities is equivalent to applying the **softmax** transformation (see § 3.1) to the vector of dot products,

$$p(\cdot \mid u) = \text{softmax}([\boldsymbol{\beta}_1 \cdot \boldsymbol{v}_u, \boldsymbol{\beta}_2 \cdot \boldsymbol{v}_u, \ldots, \boldsymbol{\beta}_V \cdot \boldsymbol{v}_u]). \qquad [6.26]$$

The word vectors $\boldsymbol{\beta}_w$ are parameters of the model and are estimated directly. The context vectors $\boldsymbol{v}_u$ can be computed in various ways, depending on the model. A simple but effective neural language model can be built from a **recurrent neural network** (RNN; Mikolov et al., 2010). The basic idea is to recurrently update the context vectors while moving through the sequence. Let $\boldsymbol{h}_m$ represent the contextual information at position m in the sequence. RNN language models are defined as

$$\boldsymbol{x}_m \triangleq \boldsymbol{\phi}_{w_m} \qquad [6.27]$$

$$\boldsymbol{h}_m = \text{RNN}(\boldsymbol{x}_m, \boldsymbol{h}_{m-1}) \qquad [6.28]$$

2. This idea predates neural language models (e.g., Rosenfeld, 1996; Roark et al., 2007).

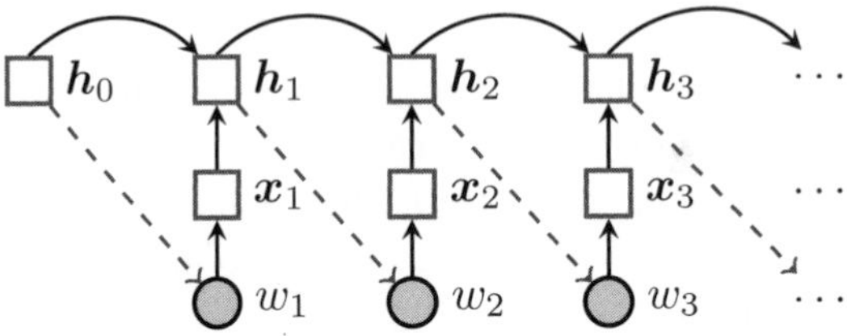

Figure 6.1
The recurrent neural network language model, viewed as an "unrolled" computation graph. Solid lines indicate direct computation, dotted lines indicate probabilistic dependencies, circles indicate random variables, and squares indicate computation nodes.

$$\text{p}(w_{m+1} \mid w_1, w_2, \ldots, w_m) = \frac{\exp(\boldsymbol{\beta}_{w_{m+1}} \cdot \boldsymbol{h}_m)}{\sum_{w' \in \mathcal{V}} \exp(\boldsymbol{\beta}_{w'} \cdot \boldsymbol{h}_m)}, \quad [6.29]$$

where $\boldsymbol{\phi}$ is a matrix of **word embeddings** and $\boldsymbol{x}_m$ denotes the embedding for word w_m. The conversion of w_m to $\boldsymbol{x}_m$ is sometimes known as a **lookup layer**, because we simply look up the embeddings for each word in a table; see § 3.2.4.

The **Elman unit** defines a simple recurrent operation (Elman, 1990),

$$\text{RNN}(\boldsymbol{x}_m, \boldsymbol{h}_{m-1}) \triangleq g(\Theta \boldsymbol{h}_{m-1} + \boldsymbol{x}_m), \quad [6.30]$$

where $\Theta \in \mathbb{R}^{K \times K}$ is the recurrence matrix and g is a nonlinear transformation function, often defined as the elementwise hyperbolic tangent tanh (see § 3.1).[3] The tanh acts as a **squashing function**, ensuring that each element of $\boldsymbol{h}_m$ is constrained to the range $[-1, 1]$.

Although each w_m depends on only the context vector $\boldsymbol{h}_{m-1}$, this vector is in turn influenced by *all* previous tokens, $w_1, w_2, \ldots w_{m-1}$, through the recurrence operation: w_1 affects $\boldsymbol{h}_1$, which affects $\boldsymbol{h}_2$, and so on, until the information is propagated all the way to $\boldsymbol{h}_{m-1}$, and then on to w_m (see figure 6.1). This is an important distinction from n-gram language models, where any information outside the n-word window is ignored. In principle, the RNN language model can handle long-range dependencies, such as number agreement over long spans of text—although it would be difficult to know where exactly in the vector $\boldsymbol{h}_m$ this information is represented. The main limitation is that information is attenuated by repeated application of the squashing function g. **Long short-term memories (LSTMs)**, described below, are a variant of RNNs that address this issue, using memory cells to propagate information through the sequence without applying nonlinearities (Hochreiter and Schmidhuber, 1997).

3. In the original Elman network, the sigmoid function was used in place of tanh. For an illuminating mathematical discussion of the advantages and disadvantages of various nonlinearities in recurrent neural networks, see the lecture notes from Cho (2015).

The denominator in equation 6.29 is a computational bottleneck, because it involves a sum over the entire vocabulary. One solution is to use a **hierarchical softmax** function, which computes the sum more efficiently by organizing the vocabulary into a tree (Mikolov et al., 2011). Another strategy is to optimize an alternative metric, such as **noise-contrastive estimation** (Gutmann and Hyvärinen, 2012), which learns by distinguishing observed instances from artificial instances generated from a noise distribution (Mnih and Teh, 2012). Both of these strategies are described in § 14.5.3.

6.3.1 Backpropagation Through Time

The recurrent neural network language model has the following parameters:

- $\boldsymbol{\phi}_i \in \mathbb{R}^K$, the "input" word vectors (these are sometimes called **word embeddings**, since each word is embedded in a K-dimensional space; see chapter 14);
- $\boldsymbol{\beta}_i \in \mathbb{R}^K$, the "output" word vectors;
- $\Theta \in \mathbb{R}^{K \times K}$, the recurrence operator;
- $\boldsymbol{h}_0$, the initial state.

Each of these parameters can be estimated by formulating an objective function over the training corpus, $L(\boldsymbol{w})$, and then applying backpropagation to obtain gradients on the parameters from a minibatch of training examples (see § 3.3.1). Gradient-based updates can be computed from an online learning algorithm such as stochastic gradient descent (see § 2.6.2).

The application of backpropagation to recurrent neural networks is known as **backpropagation through time**, because the gradients on units at time m depend in turn on the gradients of units at earlier times $n < m$. Let ℓ_{m+1} represent the negative log-likelihood of word $m+1$,

$$\ell_{m+1} = -\log \mathrm{p}(w_{m+1} \mid w_1, w_2, \ldots, w_m). \tag{6.31}$$

We require the gradient of this loss with respect to each parameter, such as $\theta_{k,k'}$, an individual element in the recurrence matrix Θ. Because the loss depends on this parameter only through $\boldsymbol{h}_m$, we can apply the chain rule of differentiation,

$$\frac{\partial \ell_{m+1}}{\partial \theta_{k,k'}} = \frac{\partial \ell_{m+1}}{\partial \boldsymbol{h}_m} \frac{\partial \boldsymbol{h}_m}{\partial \theta_{k,k'}}. \tag{6.32}$$

The vector $\boldsymbol{h}_m$ depends on Θ in several ways. First, $\boldsymbol{h}_m$ is computed by multiplying Θ by the previous state $\boldsymbol{h}_{m-1}$. But the previous state $\boldsymbol{h}_{m-1}$ also depends on Θ:

$$\boldsymbol{h}_m = g(\boldsymbol{x}_m, \boldsymbol{h}_{m-1}) \tag{6.33}$$

$$\frac{\partial h_{m,k}}{\partial \theta_{k,k'}} = g'(x_{m,k} + \boldsymbol{\theta}_k \cdot \boldsymbol{h}_{m-1})(h_{m-1,k'} + \boldsymbol{\theta}_k \cdot \frac{\partial \boldsymbol{h}_{m-1}}{\partial \theta_{k,k'}}), \tag{6.34}$$

where g' is the local derivative of the nonlinear function g. The key point in this equation is that the derivative $\frac{\partial \boldsymbol{h}_m}{\partial \theta_{k,k'}}$ depends on $\frac{\partial \boldsymbol{h}_{m-1}}{\partial \theta_{k,k'}}$, which will depend in turn on $\frac{\partial \boldsymbol{h}_{m-2}}{\partial \theta_{k,k'}}$, and so on, until reaching the initial state $\boldsymbol{h}_0$.

Each derivative $\frac{\partial \boldsymbol{h}_m}{\partial \theta_{k,k'}}$ will be reused many times: it appears in backpropagation from the loss ℓ_m, but also in all subsequent losses $\ell_{n>m}$. Neural network toolkits such as Torch (Collobert et al., 2011a) and DyNet (Neubig et al., 2017b) compute the necessary derivatives automatically and cache them for future use. An important distinction from the feedforward neural networks considered in chapter 3 is that the size of the computation graph is not fixed, but varies with the length of the input.

6.3.2 Hyperparameters

The RNN language model has several hyperparameters that must be tuned to ensure good performance. The model capacity is controlled by the size of the word and context vectors K, which play a role that is somewhat analogous to the size of the n-gram context. For datasets that are large with respect to the vocabulary (i.e., there is a large token-to-type ratio), we can afford to estimate a model with a large K, which enables more subtle distinctions between words and contexts. When the dataset is relatively small, then K must be smaller too, or else the model may "memorize" the training data and fail to generalize. Unfortunately, this general advice has not yet been formalized into any concrete formula for choosing K, and trial and error is still necessary. Overfitting can also be prevented by **dropout**, which involves randomly setting some elements of the computation to zero (Srivastava et al., 2014), forcing the learner not to rely too much on any particular dimension of the word or context vectors. The dropout rate must also be tuned on development data.

6.3.3 Gated Recurrent Neural Networks

In principle, recurrent neural networks can propagate information across infinitely long sequences. But in practice, repeated applications of the nonlinear recurrence function causes this information to be quickly attenuated. The same problem affects learning: backpropagation can lead to **vanishing gradients** that decay to zero, or **exploding gradients** that increase toward infinity (Bengio et al., 1994). The exploding gradient problem can be addressed by clipping gradients at some maximum value (Pascanu et al., 2013). The other issues must be addressed by altering the model itself.

The **long short-term memory** (LSTM; Hochreiter and Schmidhuber, 1997) is a popular variant of RNNs that is more robust to these problems. This model augments the hidden state $\boldsymbol{h}_m$ with a **memory cell** $\boldsymbol{c}_m$. The value of the memory cell at each time m is a gated sum of two quantities: its previous value $\boldsymbol{c}_{m-1}$, and an "update" $\tilde{\boldsymbol{c}}_m$, which is computed from the current input $\boldsymbol{x}_m$ and the previous hidden state $\boldsymbol{h}_{m-1}$. The next state $\boldsymbol{h}_m$ is then

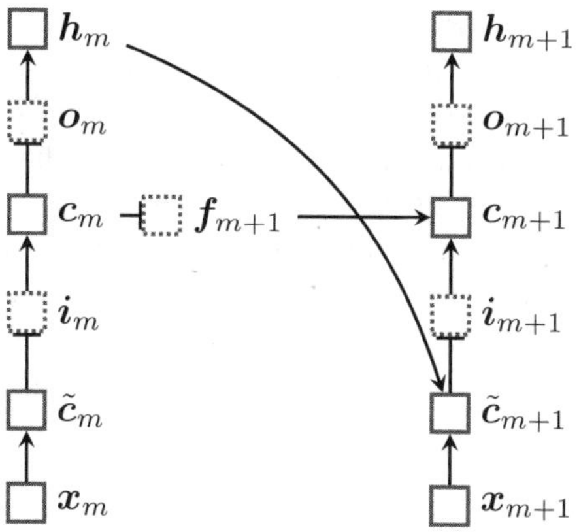

Figure 6.2
The long short-term memory (LSTM) architecture. Gates are shown in boxes with dotted edges. In an LSTM language model, each $\boldsymbol{h}_m$ would be used to predict the next word w_{m+1}.

computed from the memory cell. Because the memory cell is not passed through a nonlinear squashing function during the update, it is possible for information to propagate through the network over long distances.

The gates are functions of the input and previous hidden state. They are computed from elementwise sigmoid activations, $\sigma(x) = (1 + \exp(-x))^{-1}$, ensuring that their values will be in the range [0, 1]. They can therefore be viewed as soft, differentiable logic gates. The LSTM architecture is shown in figure 6.2, and the complete update equations are as follows:

$$\boldsymbol{f}_{m+1} = \sigma(\Theta^{(h\to f)}\boldsymbol{h}_m + \Theta^{(x\to f)}\boldsymbol{x}_{m+1} + \boldsymbol{b}_f) \qquad \text{forget gate} \qquad [6.35]$$

$$\boldsymbol{i}_{m+1} = \sigma(\Theta^{(h\to i)}\boldsymbol{h}_m + \Theta^{(x\to i)}\boldsymbol{x}_{m+1} + \boldsymbol{b}_i) \qquad \text{input gate} \qquad [6.36]$$

$$\tilde{\boldsymbol{c}}_{m+1} = \tanh(\Theta^{(h\to c)}\boldsymbol{h}_m + \Theta^{(w\to c)}\boldsymbol{x}_{m+1}) \qquad \text{update candidate} \qquad [6.37]$$

$$\boldsymbol{c}_{m+1} = \boldsymbol{f}_{m+1} \odot \boldsymbol{c}_m + \boldsymbol{i}_{m+1} \odot \tilde{\boldsymbol{c}}_{m+1} \qquad \text{memory cell update} \qquad [6.38]$$

$$\boldsymbol{o}_{m+1} = \sigma(\Theta^{(h\to o)}\boldsymbol{h}_m + \Theta^{(x\to o)}\boldsymbol{x}_{m+1} + \boldsymbol{b}_o) \qquad \text{output gate} \qquad [6.39]$$

$$\boldsymbol{h}_{m+1} = \boldsymbol{o}_{m+1} \odot \tanh(\boldsymbol{c}_{m+1}) \qquad \text{output.} \qquad [6.40]$$

The operator $\odot$ is an elementwise (Hadamard) product. Each gate is controlled by a vector of weights, which parametrize the previous hidden state (e.g., $\Theta^{(h\to f)}$) and the current input (e.g., $\Theta^{(x\to f)}$), plus a vector offset (e.g., $\boldsymbol{b}_f$). The overall operation can be informally summarized as $(\boldsymbol{h}_m, \boldsymbol{c}_m) = \text{LSTM}(\boldsymbol{x}_m, (\boldsymbol{h}_{m-1}, \boldsymbol{c}_{m-1}))$, with $(\boldsymbol{h}_m, \boldsymbol{c}_m)$ representing the LSTM state after reading token m.

The LSTM outperforms standard recurrent neural networks across a wide range of problems. It was first used for language modeling by Sundermeyer et al. (2012), but can be applied more generally: the vector $\boldsymbol{h}_m$ can be treated as a complete representation of the input sequence up to position m and can be used for any labeling task on a sequence of tokens, as we will see in the next chapter.

There are several LSTM variants, of which the Gated Recurrent Unit (Cho et al., 2014) is one of the more well known. Many software packages implement a variety of RNN architectures, so choosing between them is simple from a user's perspective. Jozefowicz et al. (2015) provide an empirical comparison of various modeling choices circa 2015.

6.4 Evaluating Language Models

Language modeling is not usually an application in itself: language models are typically components of larger systems, and they would ideally be evaluated **extrinisically**. This means evaluating whether the language model improves performance on the application task, such as machine translation or speech recognition. But this is often hard to do, and depends on details of the overall system that may be irrelevant to language modeling. In contrast, **intrinsic evaluation** is task neutral. Better performance on intrinsic metrics may be expected to improve extrinsic metrics across a variety of tasks, but there is always the risk of over-optimizing the intrinsic metric. This section discusses some intrinsic metrics, but keep in mind the importance of performing extrinsic evaluations to ensure that intrinsic performance gains carry over to real applications.

6.4.1 Held-Out Likelihood

The goal of probabilistic language models is to accurately measure the probability of sequences of word tokens. Therefore, an intrinsic evaluation metric is the likelihood that the language model assigns to **held-out data**, which is not used during training. Specifically, we compute

$$\ell(\boldsymbol{w}) = \sum_{m=1}^{M} \log \mathrm{p}(w_m \mid w_{m-1}, \ldots, w_1), \tag{6.41}$$

treating the entire held-out corpus as a single stream of tokens.

Typically, unknown words are mapped to the $\langle\text{UNK}\rangle$ token. This means that we have to estimate some probability for $\langle\text{UNK}\rangle$ on the training data. One way to do this is to fix the vocabulary $\mathcal{V}$ to the $V-1$ words with the highest counts in the training data, and then convert all other tokens to $\langle\text{UNK}\rangle$. Other strategies for dealing with out-of-vocabulary terms are discussed in § 6.5.

6.4.2 Perplexity

Held-out likelihood is usually presented as **perplexity**, which is a deterministic transformation of the log-likelihood into an information-theoretic quantity,

$$\text{Perplex}(\boldsymbol{w}) = 2^{-\frac{\ell(\boldsymbol{w})}{M}}, \qquad [6.42]$$

where M is the total number of tokens in the held-out corpus.

Lower perplexities correspond to higher likelihoods, so lower scores are better on this metric—it is better to be less perplexed. Here are some special cases:

- In the limit of a perfect language model, probability 1 is assigned to the held-out corpus, with $\text{Perplex}(\boldsymbol{w}) = 2^{-\frac{1}{M}\log_2 1} = 2^0 = 1$.
- In the opposite limit, probability zero is assigned to the held-out corpus, which corresponds to an infinite perplexity, $\text{Perplex}(\boldsymbol{w}) = 2^{-\frac{1}{M}\log_2 0} = 2^{\infty} = \infty$.
- Assume a uniform, unigram model in which $\text{p}(w_i) = \frac{1}{V}$ for all words in the vocabulary. Then,

$$\log_2(\boldsymbol{w}) = \sum_{m=1}^{M} \log_2 \frac{1}{V} = -\sum_{m=1}^{M} \log_2 V = -M \log_2 V$$

$$\begin{aligned}\text{Perplex}(\boldsymbol{w}) &= 2^{\frac{1}{M} M \log_2 V} \\ &= 2^{\log_2 V} \\ &= V.\end{aligned}$$

This is the "worst reasonable case" scenario, because you could build such a language model without even looking at the data.

In practice, language models tend to give perplexities in the range between 1 and V. A small benchmark dataset is the **Penn Treebank**, which contains roughly a million tokens; its vocabulary is limited to 10,000 words, with all other tokens mapped a special ⟨UNK⟩ symbol. On this dataset, a well-smoothed 5-gram model achieves a perplexity of 141 (Mikolov and Zweig, [2012]), and an LSTM language model achieves perplexity of roughly 80 (Zaremba et al., [2014]). Various enhancements to the LSTM architecture can bring the perplexity below 60 (Merity et al., 2018). A larger-scale language modeling dataset is the 1B Word Benchmark (Chelba et al., 2013), which contains text from Wikipedia. On this dataset, perplexities of around 25 can be obtained by averaging together multiple LSTM language models (Jozefowicz et al., 2016).

6.5 Out-of-Vocabulary Words

So far, we have assumed a **closed-vocabulary** setting—the vocabulary $\mathcal{V}$ is assumed to be a finite set. In realistic application scenarios, this assumption may not hold. Consider, for example, the problem of translating newspaper articles. The following sentence appeared in a Reuters article on January 6, 2017:[4]

> The report said U.S. intelligence agencies believe Russian military intelligence, the **GRU**, used intermediaries such as **WikiLeaks**, **DCLeaks.com** and the **Guccifer** 2.0 "persona" to release emails. …

Suppose that you trained a language model on the Gigaword corpus,[5] which was released in 2003. The bolded terms either did not exist at this date or were not widely known; they are unlikely to be in the vocabulary. The same problem can occur for a variety of other terms: new technologies, previously unknown individuals, new words (e.g., *hashtag*), and numbers.

One solution is to simply mark all such terms with a special token, $\langle \text{UNK} \rangle$. While training the language model, we decide in advance on the vocabulary (often the K most common terms), and mark all other terms in the training data as $\langle \text{UNK} \rangle$. If we do not want to determine the vocabulary size in advance, an alternative approach is to simply mark the first occurrence of each word type as $\langle \text{UNK} \rangle$.

But is often better to make distinctions about the likelihood of various unknown words. This is particularly important in languages that have rich morphological systems, with many inflections for each word. For example, Portuguese is only moderately complex from a morphological perspective, yet each verb has dozens of inflected forms (see figure 4.3b). In such languages, there will be many word types that we do not encounter in a corpus, which are nonetheless predictable from the morphological rules of the language. To use a somewhat contrived English example, if *transfenestrate* is in the vocabulary, our language model should assign a nonzero probability to the past tense *transfenestrated*, even if it does not appear in the training data.

One way to accomplish this is to supplement word-level language models with **character-level language models**. Such models can use n-grams or RNNs, but with a fixed vocabulary equal to the set of ASCII or Unicode characters. For example, Ling et al. (2015b) propose an LSTM model over characters, and Kim (2014) employs a convolutional neural network. A more linguistically motivated approach is to segment words into meaningful subword units, known as **morphemes** (see chapter 9). For example, Botha and Blunsom (2014) induce vector representations for morphemes, which they build into a log-bilinear language model; Bhatia et al. (2016) incorporate morpheme vectors into an LSTM.

4. Bayoumy, Y., and Strobel, W. (January 6, 2017). U.S. intel report: Putin directed cyber campaign to help Trump. *Reuters*. www.reuters.com/article/us-usa-russia-cyber-idUSKBN14Q1T8. Accessed January 7, 2017.

5. https://catalog.ldc.upenn.edu/LDC2003T05.

Additional Resources

A variety of neural network architectures have been applied to language modeling. Notable earlier nonrecurrent architectures include the neural probabilistic language model (Bengio et al., 2003) and the log-bilinear language model (Mnih and Hinton, 2007). Much more detail on these models can be found in the text by Goodfellow et al. (2016).

Exercises

1. Prove that n-gram language models give valid probabilities if the n-gram probabilities are valid. Specifically, assume that

$$\sum_{w_m}^{\mathcal{V}} \mathrm{p}(w_m \mid w_{m-1}, w_{m-2}, \ldots, w_{m-n+1}) = 1 \quad [6.43]$$

for all contexts $(w_{m-1}, w_{m-2}, \ldots, w_{m-n+1})$. Prove that $\sum_{\boldsymbol{w}} \mathrm{p}_n(\boldsymbol{w}) = 1$ for all $\boldsymbol{w} \in \mathcal{V}^*$, where p_n is the probability under an n-gram language model. Your proof should proceed by induction. You should handle the start-of-string case $\mathrm{p}(w_1 \mid \underbrace{\square, \ldots, \square}_{n-1})$, but you need not handle the end-of-string token.

2. First, show that RNN language models are valid using a similar proof technique to the one in the previous problem.

   Next, let $\mathrm{p}_r(\boldsymbol{w})$ indicate the probability of $\boldsymbol{w}$ under RNN r. An ensemble of RNN language models computes the probability,

$$\mathrm{p}(\boldsymbol{w}) = \frac{1}{R} \sum_{r=1}^{R} \mathrm{p}_r(\boldsymbol{w}). \quad [6.44]$$

   Does an ensemble of RNN language models compute a valid probability?

3. Consider a unigram language model over a vocabulary of size V. Suppose that a word appears m times in a corpus with M tokens in total. With Lidstone smoothing of α, for what values of m is the smoothed probability greater than the unsmoothed probability?

4. Consider a simple language in which each token is drawn from the vocabulary $\mathcal{V}$ with probability $\frac{1}{V}$, independent of all other tokens.

   Given a corpus of size M, what is the expectation of the fraction of all possible bigrams that have zero count? You may assume V is large enough that $\frac{1}{V} \approx \frac{1}{V-1}$.

5. Continuing the previous problem, determine the value of M such that the fraction of bigrams with zero count is at most $\epsilon \in (0, 1)$. As a hint, you may use the approximation $\ln(1 + \alpha) \approx \alpha$ for $\alpha \approx 0$.

6. In real languages, words probabilities are neither uniform nor independent. Assume that word probabilities are independent but not uniform, so that in general $\mathrm{p}(w) \neq \frac{1}{V}$. Prove that the expected fraction of unseen bigrams will be higher than in the IID case.
7. Consider a recurrent neural network with a single hidden unit and a sigmoid activation, $h_m = \sigma(\theta h_{m-1} + x_m)$. Prove that if $|\theta| < 1$, then the gradient $\frac{\partial h_m}{\partial h_{m-k}}$ goes to zero as $k \to \infty$.[6]
8. **Zipf's law** states that if the word types in a corpus are sorted by frequency, then the frequency of the word at rank r is proportional to r^{-s}, where s is a free parameter, usually around 1. (Another way to view Zipf's law is that a plot of log frequency against log rank will be linear.) Solve for s using the counts of the first and second most frequent words, c_1 and c_2.
9. Download the wikitext-2 dataset.[7] Read in the training data and compute word counts. Estimate the Zipf's law coefficient by

$$\hat{s} = \exp\left(\frac{(\log \boldsymbol{r}) \cdot (\log \boldsymbol{c})}{||\log \boldsymbol{r}||_2^2}\right), \qquad [6.45]$$

where $\boldsymbol{r} = [1, 2, 3, \ldots]$ is the vector of ranks of all words in the corpus and $\boldsymbol{c} = [c_1, c_2, c_3, \ldots]$ is the vector of counts of all words in the corpus, sorted in descending order.

   Make a log-log plot of the observed counts, and the expected counts according to Zipf's law. The sum $\sum_{r=1}^{\infty} r^s = \zeta(s)$ is the Riemann zeta function, available in Python's `scipy` library as `scipy.special.zeta`.
10. Using the Pytorch library, train an LSTM language model from the Wikitext training corpus. After each epoch of training, compute its perplexity on the Wikitext validation corpus. Stop training when the perplexity stops improving.

6. This proof generalizes to vector hidden units by considering the largest eigenvector of the matrix Θ (Pascanu et al., 2013).

7. Available at https://github.com/pytorch/examples/tree/master/word_language_model/data/wikitext-2 in September 2018. The dataset is already tokenized and already replaces rare words with ⟨UNK⟩, so no preprocessing is necessary.

7 Sequence Labeling

The goal of sequence labeling is to assign tags to words or, more generally, to assign discrete labels to discrete elements in a sequence. There are many applications of sequence labeling in natural language processing, and chapter 8 presents an overview. For now, we'll focus on the classic problem of **part-of-speech tagging**, which requires tagging each word by its grammatical category. Coarse-grained grammatical categories include **NOUN**s, which describe things, properties, or ideas, and **VERB**s, which describe actions and events. Consider a simple input:

(7.1) They can fish.

A dictionary of coarse-grained part-of-speech tags might include NOUN as the only valid tag for *they*, but both NOUN and VERB as potential tags for *can* and *fish*. An accurate sequence labeling algorithm should select the verb tag for both *can* and *fish* in (7.1), but it should select noun for the same two words in the phrase *can of fish*.

7.1 Sequence Labeling as Classification

One way to solve a tagging problem is to turn it into a classification problem. Let $f((\boldsymbol{w}, m), y)$ indicate the feature function for tag y at position m in the sequence $\boldsymbol{w} = (w_1, w_2, \ldots, w_M)$. A simple tagging model would have a single base feature, the word itself:

$$f((\boldsymbol{w} = \textit{they can fish}, m = 1), \text{N}) = (\textit{they}, \text{N}) \qquad [7.1]$$

$$f((\boldsymbol{w} = \textit{they can fish}, m = 2), \text{V}) = (\textit{can}, \text{V}) \qquad [7.2]$$

$$f((\boldsymbol{w} = \textit{they can fish}, m = 3), \text{V}) = (\textit{fish}, \text{V}). \qquad [7.3]$$

Here the feature function takes three arguments as input: the sentence to be tagged (e.g., *they can fish*), the proposed tag (e.g., N or V), and the index of the token to which this tag is applied. This simple feature function then returns a single feature: a tuple including the word to be tagged and the tag that has been proposed. If the vocabulary size is V and the number of tags is K, then there are $V \times K$ features. Each of these features must be assigned a weight. These weights can be learned from a labeled dataset using a classification algorithm such as perceptron, but this isn't necessary in this case: it would be equivalent to define the classification weights directly, with $\theta_{w,y} = 1$ for the tag y most frequently associated with word w, and $\theta_{w,y} = 0$ for all other tags.

However, it is easy to see that this simple classification approach cannot correctly tag both *they can fish* and *can of fish*, because *can* and *fish* are grammatically ambiguous. To handle both of these cases, the tagger must rely on context, such as the surrounding words. We can build context into the feature set by incorporating the surrounding words as additional features:

$$\begin{aligned} f((\boldsymbol{w} = \textit{they can fish}, 1), \mathrm{N}) = \{&(w_m = \textit{they}, y_m = \mathrm{N}), \\ &(w_{m-1} = \square, y_m = \mathrm{N}), \\ &(w_{m+1} = \textit{can}, y_m = \mathrm{N})\} \end{aligned} \quad [7.4]$$

$$\begin{aligned} f((\boldsymbol{w} = \textit{they can fish}, 2), \mathrm{V}) = \{&(w_m = \textit{can}, y_m = \mathrm{V}), \\ &(w_{m-1} = \textit{they}, y_m = \mathrm{V}), \\ &(w_{m+1} = \textit{fish}, y_m = \mathrm{V})\} \end{aligned} \quad [7.5]$$

$$\begin{aligned} f((\boldsymbol{w} = \textit{they can fish}, 3), \mathrm{V}) = \{&(w_m = \textit{fish}, y_m = \mathrm{V}), \\ &(w_{m-1} = \textit{can}, y_m = \mathrm{V}), \\ &(w_{m+1} = \blacksquare, y_m = \mathrm{V})\}. \end{aligned} \quad [7.6]$$

These features contain enough information that a tagger should be able to choose the right tag for the word *fish*: words that come after *can* are likely to be verbs, so the feature $(w_{m-1} = \textit{can}, y_m = \mathrm{V})$ should have a large positive weight.

However, even with this enhanced feature set, it may be difficult to tag some sequences correctly. One reason is that there are often relationships between the tags themselves. For example, in English it is relatively rare for a verb to follow another verb—particularly if we differentiate **MODAL** verbs like *can* and *should* from more typical verbs, like *give*, *transcend*, and *befuddle*. We would like to incorporate preferences against tag sequences like VERB-VERB, and in favor of tag sequences like NOUN-VERB. The need for such preferences is best illustrated by a **garden path sentence**:

(7.2) The old man the boat.

Grammatically, the word *the* is a **DETERMINER**. When you read the sentence, what part of speech did you first assign to *old*? Typically, this word is an ADJECTIVE—abbreviated as J—which is a class of words that modify nouns. Similarly, *man* is usually a noun. The resulting sequence of tags is D J N D N. But this is a mistaken "garden path" interpretation, which ends up leading nowhere. It is unlikely that a determiner would directly follow a noun,[1] and it is particularly unlikely that the entire sentence would lack a verb. The only

1. The main exception occurs with ditransitive verbs, such as *They gave the winner a trophy.*

possible verb in (7.2) is the word *man*, which can refer to the act of maintaining and piloting something—often boats. But if *man* is tagged as a verb, then *old* is seated between a determiner and a verb, and must be a noun. And indeed, adjectives often have a second interpretation as nouns when used in this way (e.g., *the young*, *the restless*). This reasoning, in which the labeling decisions are intertwined, cannot be applied in a setting where each tag is produced by an independent classification decision.

7.2 Sequence Labeling as Structure Prediction

As an alternative, think of the entire sequence of tags as a label itself. For a given sequence of words $\boldsymbol{w} = (w_1, w_2, \ldots, w_M)$, there is a set of possible taggings $\mathcal{Y}(\boldsymbol{w}) = \mathcal{Y}^M$, where $\mathcal{Y} = \{\text{N}, \text{V}, \text{D}, \ldots\}$ refers to the set of individual tags, and $\mathcal{Y}^M$ refers to the set of tag sequences of length M. We can then treat the sequence labeling problem as a classification problem in the label space $\mathcal{Y}(\boldsymbol{w})$,

$$\hat{\boldsymbol{y}} = \underset{\boldsymbol{y} \in \mathcal{Y}(\boldsymbol{w})}{\operatorname{argmax}}\, \Psi(\boldsymbol{w}, \boldsymbol{y}), \quad [7.7]$$

where $\boldsymbol{y} = (y_1, y_2, \ldots, y_M)$ is a sequence of M tags and Ψ is a scoring function on pairs of sequences, $V^M \times \mathcal{Y}^M \rightarrow \mathbb{R}$. Such a function can include features that capture the relationships between tagging decisions, such as the preference that determiners not follow nouns, or that all sentences have verbs.

Given that the label space is exponentially large in the length of the sequence M, can it ever be practical to perform tagging in this way? The problem of making a series of interconnected labeling decisions is known as **inference**. Because natural language is full of interrelated grammatical structures, inference is a crucial aspect of natural language processing. In English, it is not unusual to have sentences of length $M = 20$; part-of-speech tag sets vary in size from 10 to several hundred. Taking the low end of this range, we have $|\mathcal{Y}(\boldsymbol{w}_{1:M})| \approx 10^{20}$, one hundred billion billion possible tag sequences. Enumerating and scoring each of these sequences would require an amount of work that is exponential in the sequence length, so inference is intractable.

However, the situation changes when we restrict the scoring function. Suppose we choose a function that decomposes into a sum of local parts,

$$\Psi(\boldsymbol{w}, \boldsymbol{y}) = \sum_{m=1}^{M+1} \psi(\boldsymbol{w}, y_m, y_{m-1}, m), \quad [7.8]$$

where each $\psi(\cdot)$ scores a local part of the tag sequence. Note that the sum goes up to $M + 1$, so that we can include a score for a special end-of-sequence tag, $\psi(\boldsymbol{w}_{1:M}, \blacklozenge, y_M, M + 1)$. We also define a special tag to begin the sequence, $y_0 \triangleq \Diamond$.

In a linear model, the local scoring function can be defined as a dot product of weights and features,

$$\psi(\boldsymbol{w}_{1:M}, y_m, y_{m-1}, m) = \boldsymbol{\theta} \cdot \boldsymbol{f}(\boldsymbol{w}, y_m, y_{m-1}, m). \quad [7.9]$$

The feature vector $\boldsymbol{f}$ can consider the entire input $\boldsymbol{w}$ and can look at pairs of adjacent tags. This is a step up from per-token classification: the weights can assign low scores to infelicitous tag pairs, such as noun-determiner, and high scores for frequent tag pairs, such as determiner-noun and noun-verb.

In the example *they can fish*, a minimal feature function would include features for word-tag pairs (sometimes called **emission features**) and tag-tag pairs (sometimes called **transition features**):

$$\boldsymbol{f}(\boldsymbol{w} = \textit{they can fish}, \boldsymbol{y} = \text{N V V}) = \sum_{m=1}^{M+1} \boldsymbol{f}(\boldsymbol{w}, y_m, y_{m-1}, m) \quad [7.10]$$

$$\begin{aligned} &= \boldsymbol{f}(\boldsymbol{w}, \text{N}, \Diamond, 1) \\ &\quad + \boldsymbol{f}(\boldsymbol{w}, \text{V}, \text{N}, 2) \\ &\quad + \boldsymbol{f}(\boldsymbol{w}, \text{V}, \text{V}, 3) \\ &\quad + \boldsymbol{f}(\boldsymbol{w}, \blacklozenge, \text{V}, 4) \end{aligned} \quad [7.11]$$

$$\begin{aligned} &= (w_m = \textit{they}, y_m = \text{N}) + (y_m = \text{N}, y_{m-1} = \Diamond) \\ &\quad + (w_m = \textit{can}, y_m = \text{V}) + (y_m = \text{V}, y_{m-1} = \text{N}) \\ &\quad + (w_m = \textit{fish}, y_m = \text{V}) + (y_m = \text{V}, y_{m-1} = \text{V}) \\ &\quad + (y_m = \blacklozenge, y_{m-1} = \text{V}). \end{aligned} \quad [7.12]$$

There are seven active features for this example: one for each word-tag pair, and one for each tag-tag pair, including a final tag $y_{M+1} = \blacklozenge$. These features capture the two main sources of information for part-of-speech tagging in English: which tags are appropriate for each word, and which tags tend to follow each other in sequence. Given appropriate weights for these features, taggers can achieve high accuracy, even for difficult cases like *the old man the boat.* We will now discuss how this restricted scoring function enables efficient inference, through the **Viterbi algorithm** (Viterbi, 1967).

7.3 The Viterbi Algorithm

By decomposing the scoring function into a sum of local parts, it is possible to rewrite the tagging problem as follows:

$$\hat{\boldsymbol{y}} = \operatorname*{argmax}_{\boldsymbol{y} \in \mathcal{Y}(\boldsymbol{w})} \Psi(\boldsymbol{w}, \boldsymbol{y}) \quad [7.13]$$

$$= \operatorname*{argmax}_{\boldsymbol{y}_{1:M}} \sum_{m=1}^{M+1} \psi(\boldsymbol{w}, y_m, y_{m-1}, m) \quad [7.14]$$

$$= \underset{\boldsymbol{y}_{1:M}}{\operatorname{argmax}} \sum_{m=1}^{M+1} s_m(y_m, y_{m-1}), \tag{7.15}$$

where the final line simplifies the notation with the shorthand,

$$s_m(y_m, y_{m-1}) \triangleq \psi(\boldsymbol{w}_{1:M}, y_m, y_{m-1}, m). \tag{7.16}$$

This inference problem can be solved efficiently using **dynamic programming**, an algorithmic technique for reusing work in recurrent computations. We begin by solving an auxiliary problem: rather than finding the best tag sequence, we compute the *score* of the best tag sequence,

$$\max_{\boldsymbol{y}_{1:M}} \Psi(\boldsymbol{w}, \boldsymbol{y}_{1:M}) = \max_{\boldsymbol{y}_{1:M}} \sum_{m=1}^{M+1} s_m(y_m, y_{m-1}). \tag{7.17}$$

This score involves a maximization over all tag sequences of length M, written $\max_{\boldsymbol{y}_{1:M}}$. This maximization can be broken into two pieces,

$$\max_{\boldsymbol{y}_{1:M}} \Psi(\boldsymbol{w}, \boldsymbol{y}_{1:M}) = \max_{y_M} \max_{\boldsymbol{y}_{1:M-1}} \sum_{m=1}^{M+1} s_m(y_m, y_{m-1}). \tag{7.18}$$

Within the sum, only the final term $s_{M+1}(\blacklozenge, y_M)$ depends on y_M, so we can pull this term out of the second maximization,

$$\max_{\boldsymbol{y}_{1:M}} \Psi(\boldsymbol{w}, \boldsymbol{y}_{1:M}) = \left(\max_{y_M} s_{M+1}(\blacklozenge, y_M)\right) + \left(\max_{\boldsymbol{y}_{1:M-1}} \sum_{m=1}^{M} s_m(y_m, y_{m-1})\right). \tag{7.19}$$

The second term in equation 7.19 has the same form as our original problem, with M replaced by $M-1$. This indicates that the problem can be reformulated as a recurrence. We do this by defining an auxiliary variable called the **Viterbi variable** $v_m(k)$, representing the score of the best sequence terminating in the tag k:

$$v_m(y_m) \triangleq \max_{\boldsymbol{y}_{1:m-1}} \sum_{n=1}^{m} s_n(y_n, y_{n-1}) \tag{7.20}$$

$$= \max_{y_{m-1}} s_m(y_m, y_{m-1}) + \max_{\boldsymbol{y}_{1:m-2}} \sum_{n=1}^{m-1} s_n(y_n, y_{n-1}) \tag{7.21}$$

$$= \max_{y_{m-1}} s_m(y_m, y_{m-1}) + v_{m-1}(y_{m-1}). \tag{7.22}$$

Each set of Viterbi variables is computed from the local score $s_m(y_m, y_{m-1})$ and from the previous set of Viterbi variables. The initial condition of the recurrence is simply the score for the first tag,

Algorithm 11

The Viterbi algorithm. Each $s_m(k, k')$ is a local score for tag $y_m = k$ and $y_{m-1} = k'$.

---

for $k \in \{0, \ldots K\}$ **do**
  $v_1(k) \leftarrow s_1(k, \Diamond)$
for $m \in \{2, \ldots, M\}$ **do**
  for $k \in \{0, \ldots, K\}$ **do**
    $v_m(k) \leftarrow \max_{k'} s_m(k, k') + v_{m-1}(k')$
    $b_m(k) \leftarrow \text{argmax}_{k'} s_m(k, k') + v_{m-1}(k')$
$y_M \leftarrow \text{argmax}_k s_{M+1}(\blacklozenge, k) + v_M(k)$
for $m \in \{M-1, \ldots 1\}$ **do**
  $y_m \leftarrow b_m(y_{m+1})$
return $\boldsymbol{y}_{1:M}$

$$v_1(y_1) \triangleq s_1(y_1, \Diamond). \tag{7.23}$$

The maximum overall score for the sequence is then the final Viterbi variable,

$$\max_{\boldsymbol{y}_{1:M}} \Psi(\boldsymbol{w}_{1:M}, \boldsymbol{y}_{1:M}) = v_{M+1}(\blacklozenge). \tag{7.24}$$

Thus, the score of the best labeling for the sequence can be computed in a single forward sweep: first compute all variables $v_1(\cdot)$ from equation 7.23, and then compute all variables $v_2(\cdot)$ from the recurrence in equation 7.22, continuing until the final variable $v_{M+1}(\blacklozenge)$.

The Viterbi variables can be arranged in a structure known as a **trellis**, shown in figure 7.1. Each column indexes a token m in the sequence, and each row indexes a tag in $\mathcal{Y}$; every $v_{m-1}(k)$ is connected to every $v_m(k')$, indicating that $v_m(k')$ is computed from $v_{m-1}(k)$. Special nodes are set aside for the start and end states.

The original goal was to find the best scoring sequence, not simply to compute its score. But by solving the auxiliary problem, we are almost there. Recall that each $v_m(k)$ represents the score of the best tag sequence ending in that tag k in position m. To compute this, we maximize over possible values of y_{m-1}. By keeping track of the "argmax" tag that maximizes this choice at each step, we can walk backward from the final tag, and recover the optimal tag sequence. This is indicated in figure 7.1 by the thick lines, which we trace back from the final position. These backward pointers are written $b_m(k)$, indicating the optimal tag y_{m-1} on the path to $Y_m = k$.

The complete Viterbi algorithm is shown in algorithm 11. When computing the initial Viterbi variables $v_1(\cdot)$, the special tag $\Diamond$ indicates the start of the sequence. When computing the final tag Y_M, another special tag, $\blacklozenge$, indicates the end of the sequence. These special

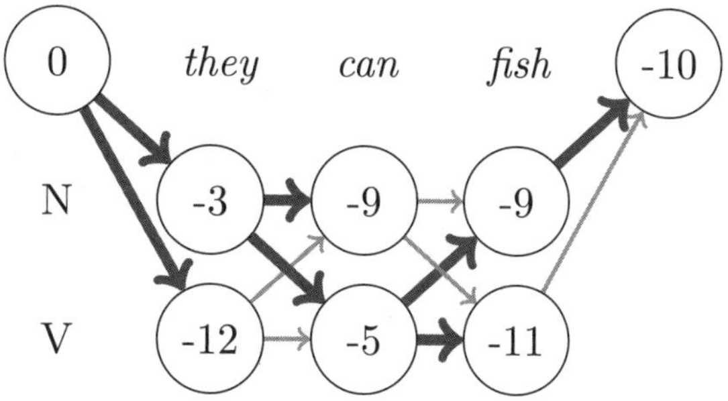

Figure 7.1
The trellis representation of the Viterbi variables, for the example *they can fish*, using the weights shown in table 7.1.

tags enable the use of transition features for the tags that begin and end the sequence: for example, conjunctions are unlikely to end sentences in English, so we would like a low score for $s_{M+1}(\blacklozenge, \text{CC})$; nouns are relatively likely to appear at the beginning of sentences, so we would like a high score for $s_1(\text{N}, \Diamond)$, assuming the noun tag is compatible with the first word token w_1.

Complexity If there are K tags and M positions in the sequence, then there are $M \times K$ Viterbi variables to compute. Computing each variable requires finding a maximum over K possible predecessor tags. The total time complexity of populating the trellis is therefore $\mathcal{O}(MK^2)$, with an additional factor for the number of active features at each position. After completing the trellis, we simply trace the backward pointers to the beginning of the sequence, which takes $\mathcal{O}(M)$ operations.

7.3.1 Example

Consider the minimal tagset {N, V}, corresponding to nouns and verbs. Even in this tagset, there is considerable ambiguity: for example, the words *can* and *fish* can each take both tags. Of the $2 \times 2 \times 2 = 8$ possible taggings for the sentence *they can fish*, four are possible given these possible tags, and two are grammatical.[2]

The values in the trellis in figure 7.1 are computed from the feature weights defined in table 7.1. We begin with $v_1(\text{N})$, which has only one possible predecessor, the start tag $\Diamond$. This score is therefore equal to $s_1(\text{N}, \Diamond) = -2 - 1 = -3$, which is the sum of the scores for the emission and transition features respectively; the backpointer is $b_1(\text{N}) = \Diamond$. The score for $v_1(\text{V})$ is computed in the same way: $s_1(\text{V}, \Diamond) = -10 - 2 = -12$, and again $b_1(\text{V}) = \Diamond$. The backpointers are represented in the figure by thick lines.

2. The tagging *they*/N *can*/V *fish*/N corresponds to the scenario of putting fish into cans, or perhaps of firing them.

Table 7.1
Feature weights for the example trellis shown in figure 7.1. Emission weights from $\lozenge$ and $\blacklozenge$ are implicitly set to $-\infty$.

	they	*can*	*fish*
N	−2	−3	−3
V	−10	−1	−3

(a) Weights for emission features.

	N	V	$\blacklozenge$
$\lozenge$	−1	−2	$-\infty$
N	−3	−1	−1
V	−1	−3	−1

(b) Weights for transition features. The "from" tags are on the columns, and the "to" tags are on the rows.

Things get more interesting at $m=2$. The score $v_2(\text{N})$ is computed by maximizing over the two possible predecessors,

$$v_2(\text{N}) = \max(v_1(\text{N}) + s_2(\text{N}, \text{N}), v_1(\text{V}) + s_2(\text{N}, \text{V})) \quad [7.25]$$

$$= \max(-3 - 3 - 3, \quad -12 - 3 - 1) = -9 \quad [7.26]$$

$$b_2(\text{N}) = \text{N}. \quad [7.27]$$

This continues until reaching $v_4(\blacklozenge)$, which is computed as

$$v_4(\blacklozenge) = \max(v_3(\text{N}) + s_4(\blacklozenge, \text{N}), v_3(\text{V}) + s_4(\blacklozenge, \text{V})) \quad [7.28]$$

$$= \max(-9 + 0 - 1, \quad -11 + 0 - 1) \quad [7.29]$$

$$= -10, \quad [7.30]$$

so $b_4(\blacklozenge) = \text{N}$. As there is no emission w_4, the emission features have scores of zero.

To compute the optimal tag sequence, we walk backward from here, next checking $b_3(\text{N}) = \text{V}$, and then $b_2(\text{V}) = \text{N}$, and finally $b_1(\text{N}) = \lozenge$. This yields $\boldsymbol{y} = (\text{N}, \text{V}, \text{N})$, which corresponds to the linguistic interpretation of the fishes being put into cans.

7.3.2 Higher-Order Features

The Viterbi algorithm was made possible by a restriction of the scoring function to local parts that consider only pairs of adjacent tags. We can think of this as a bigram language model over tags. A natural question is how to generalize Viterbi to tag trigrams, which would involve the following decomposition:

$$\Psi(\boldsymbol{w}, \boldsymbol{y}) = \sum_{m=1}^{M+2} \Psi(\boldsymbol{w}, y_m, y_{m-1}, y_{m-2}, m), \quad [7.31]$$

where $y_{-1} = \lozenge$ and $y_{M+2} = \blacklozenge$.

One solution is to create a new tagset $\mathcal{Y}^{(2)}$ from the Cartesian product of the original tagset with itself, $\mathcal{Y}^{(2)} = \mathcal{Y} \times \mathcal{Y}$. The tags in this product space are ordered pairs, representing adjacent tags at the token level: for example, the tag (N, V) would represent a noun followed by a verb. Transitions between such tags must be consistent: we can have a transition from (N, V) to (V, N) (corresponding to the tag sequence N V N), but not from (N, V) to (N, N), which would not correspond to any coherent tag sequence. This constraint can be enforced in feature weights, with $\theta_{((a,b),(c,d))} = -\infty$ if $b \neq c$. The remaining feature weights can encode preferences for and against various tag trigrams.

In the Cartesian product tag space, there are K^2 tags, suggesting that the time complexity will increase to $\mathcal{O}(MK^4)$. However, it is unnecessary to max over predecessor tag bigrams that are incompatible with the current tag bigram. By exploiting this constraint, it is possible to limit the time complexity to $\mathcal{O}(MK^3)$. The space complexity grows to $\mathcal{O}(MK^2)$, because the trellis must store all possible predecessors of each tag. In general, the time and space complexity of higher-order Viterbi grows exponentially with the order of the tag n-grams that are considered in the feature decomposition.

7.4 Hidden Markov Models

The Viterbi sequence labeling algorithm is built on the scores $s_m(y, y')$. We will now discuss how these scores can be estimated probabilistically. Recall from § 2.2 that the probabilistic Naïve Bayes classifier selects the label y to maximize $\text{p}(y \mid \boldsymbol{x}) \propto \text{p}(y, \boldsymbol{x})$. In probabilistic sequence labeling, our goal is similar: select the tag sequence that maximizes $\text{p}(\boldsymbol{y} \mid \boldsymbol{w}) \propto \text{p}(\boldsymbol{y}, \boldsymbol{w})$. The locality restriction in equation 7.8 can be viewed as a conditional independence assumption on the random variables $\boldsymbol{y}$.

Naïve Bayes was introduced as a **generative model**—a probabilistic story that explains the observed data as well as the hidden label. A similar story can be constructed for probabilistic sequence labeling: first, the tags are drawn from a prior distribution; next, the tokens are drawn from a conditional likelihood. However, for inference to be tractable, additional independence assumptions are required. First, the probability of each token depends only on its tag, and not on any other element in the sequence:

$$\text{p}(\boldsymbol{w} \mid \boldsymbol{y}) = \prod_{m=1}^{M} \text{p}(w_m \mid y_m). \qquad [7.32]$$

Second, each tag y_m depends only on its predecessor,

$$\text{p}(\boldsymbol{y}) = \prod_{m=1}^{M} \text{p}(y_m \mid y_{m-1}), \qquad [7.33]$$

where $y_0 = \Diamond$ in all cases. Due to this **Markov assumption**, probabilistic sequence labeling models are known as **hidden Markov models (HMMs)**.

The generative process for the hidden Markov model is shown in algorithm 12. Given the parameters $\boldsymbol{\lambda}$ and $\boldsymbol{\phi}$, we can compute $\text{p}(\boldsymbol{w}, \boldsymbol{y})$ for any token sequence $\boldsymbol{w}$ and tag sequence $\boldsymbol{y}$.

Algorithm 12

Generative process for the hidden Markov model.

$y_0 \leftarrow \lozenge, \quad m \leftarrow 1$

repeat

  $y_m \sim \text{Categorical}(\boldsymbol{\lambda}_{y_{m-1}})$ ▷ sample the current tag

  $w_m \sim \text{Categorical}(\boldsymbol{\phi}_{y_m})$ ▷ sample the current word

until $y_m = \blacklozenge$ ▷ terminate when the stop symbol is generated

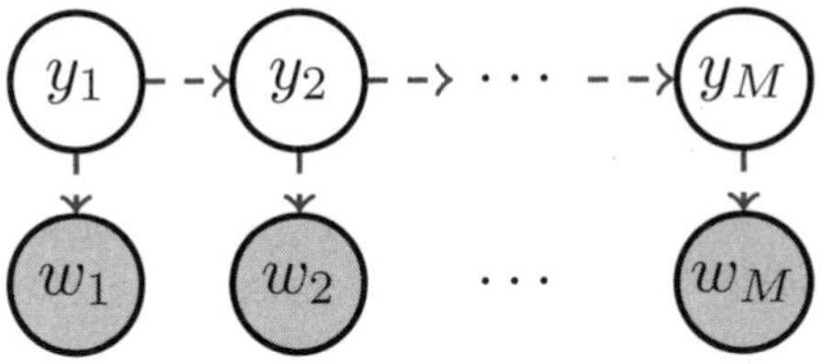

Figure 7.2
Graphical representation of the hidden Markov model. Arrows indicate probabilistic dependencies.

The HMM is often represented as a **graphical model** (Wainwright and Jordan, 2008), as shown in figure 7.2. This representation makes the independence assumptions explicit: if a variable v_1 is probabilistically conditioned on another variable v_2, then there is an arrow $v_2 \rightarrow v_1$ in the diagram. If there are no arrows between v_1 and v_2, they are **conditionally independent**, given each variable's **Markov blanket**. In the hidden Markov model, the Markov blanket for each tag y_m includes the "parent" y_{m-1}, and the "children" y_{m+1} and w_m.[3]

It is important to reflect on the implications of the HMM independence assumptions. A nonadjacent pair of tags y_m and y_n are conditionally independent; if $m < n$ and we are given y_{n-1}, then y_m offers no additional information about y_n. However, if we are not given any information about the tags in a sequence, then all tags are probabilistically coupled.

7.4.1 Estimation

The hidden Markov model has two groups of parameters:

Emission probabilities The probability $p_e(w_m \mid y_m; \phi)$ is the emission probability, because the words are treated as probabilistically "emitted," conditioned on the tags.

3. In general graphical models, a variable's Markov blanket includes its parents, children, and its children's other parents (Murphy, 2012).

Transition probabilities The probability $p_t(y_m \mid y_{m-1}; \lambda)$ is the transition probability, because it assigns probability to each possible tag-to-tag transition.

Both of these groups of parameters are typically computed from smoothed relative frequency estimation on a labeled corpus (see § 6.2 for a review of smoothing). The unsmoothed probabilities are

$$\phi_{k,i} \triangleq \Pr(W_m = i \mid Y_m = k) = \frac{\text{count}(W_m = i, Y_m = k)}{\text{count}(Y_m = k)}$$

$$\lambda_{k,k'} \triangleq \Pr(Y_m = k' \mid Y_{m-1} = k) = \frac{\text{count}(Y_m = k', Y_{m-1} = k)}{\text{count}(Y_{m-1} = k)}.$$

Smoothing is more important for the emission probability than the transition probability, because the vocabulary is much larger than the number of tags.

7.4.2 Inference

The goal of inference in the hidden Markov model is to find the highest probability tag sequence,

$$\hat{\boldsymbol{y}} = \underset{\boldsymbol{y}}{\operatorname{argmax}}\, p(\boldsymbol{y} \mid \boldsymbol{w}). \quad [7.34]$$

As in Naïve Bayes, it is equivalent to find the tag sequence with the highest *log*-probability, because the logarithm is a monotonically increasing function. It is furthermore equivalent to maximize the joint probability $p(\boldsymbol{y}, \boldsymbol{w}) = p(\boldsymbol{y} \mid \boldsymbol{w}) \times p(\boldsymbol{w}) \propto p(\boldsymbol{y} \mid \boldsymbol{w})$, which is proportional to the conditional probability. Putting these observations together, the inference problem can be reformulated as

$$\hat{\boldsymbol{y}} = \underset{\boldsymbol{y}}{\operatorname{argmax}}\, \log p(\boldsymbol{y}, \boldsymbol{w}). \quad [7.35]$$

We can now apply the HMM independence assumptions:

$$\log p(\boldsymbol{y}, \boldsymbol{w}) = \log p(\boldsymbol{y}) + \log p(\boldsymbol{w} \mid \boldsymbol{y}) \quad [7.36]$$

$$= \sum_{m=1}^{M+1} \log p_Y(y_m \mid y_{m-1}) + \log p_{W|Y}(w_m \mid y_m) \quad [7.37]$$

$$= \sum_{m=1}^{M+1} \log \lambda_{y_m, y_{m-1}} + \log \phi_{y_m, w_m} \quad [7.38]$$

$$= \sum_{m=1}^{M+1} s_m(y_m, y_{m-1}), \quad [7.39]$$

where

$$s_m(y_m, y_{m-1}) \triangleq \log \lambda_{y_m, y_{m-1}} + \log \phi_{y_m, w_m}, \quad [7.40]$$

and

$$\phi_{\blacklozenge,w} = \begin{cases} 1, & w = \blacksquare \\ 0, & \text{otherwise}, \end{cases} \qquad [7.41]$$

which ensures that the stop tag $\blacklozenge$ can only be applied to the final token $\blacksquare$.

This derivation shows that HMM inference can be viewed as an application of the Viterbi decoding algorithm, given an appropriately defined scoring function. The local score $s_m(y_m, y_{m-1})$ can be interpreted probabilistically,

$$s_m(y_m, y_{m-1}) = \log \mathrm{p}_y(y_m \mid y_{m-1}) + \log \mathrm{p}_{w|y}(w_m \mid y_m) \qquad [7.42]$$

$$= \log \mathrm{p}(y_m, w_m \mid y_{m-1}). \qquad [7.43]$$

Now recall the definition of the Viterbi variables,

$$v_m(y_m) = \max_{y_{m-1}} s_m(y_m, y_{m-1}) + v_{m-1}(y_{m-1}) \qquad [7.44]$$

$$= \max_{y_{m-1}} \log \mathrm{p}(y_m, w_m \mid y_{m-1}) + v_{m-1}(y_{m-1}). \qquad [7.45]$$

By setting $v_{m-1}(y_{m-1}) = \max_{\boldsymbol{y}_{1:m-2}} \log \mathrm{p}(\boldsymbol{y}_{1:m-1}, \boldsymbol{w}_{1:m-1})$, we obtain the recurrence,

$$v_m(y_m) = \max_{y_{m-1}} \log \mathrm{p}(y_m, w_m \mid y_{m-1}) + \max_{\boldsymbol{y}_{1:m-2}} \log \mathrm{p}(\boldsymbol{y}_{1:m-1}, \boldsymbol{w}_{1:m-1}) \qquad [7.46]$$

$$= \max_{\boldsymbol{y}_{1:m-1}} \log \mathrm{p}(y_m, w_m \mid y_{m-1}) + \log \mathrm{p}(\boldsymbol{y}_{1:m-1}, \boldsymbol{w}_{1:m-1}) \qquad [7.47]$$

$$= \max_{\boldsymbol{y}_{1:m-1}} \log \mathrm{p}(\boldsymbol{y}_{1:m}, \boldsymbol{w}_{1:m}). \qquad [7.48]$$

In words, the Viterbi variable $v_m(y_m)$ is the log-probability of the best tag sequence ending in y_m, joint with the word sequence $\boldsymbol{w}_{1:m}$. The log-probability of the best complete tag sequence is therefore

$$\max_{\boldsymbol{y}_{1:M}} \log \mathrm{p}(\boldsymbol{y}_{1:M+1}, \boldsymbol{w}_{1:M+1}) = v_{M+1}(\blacklozenge). \qquad [7.49]$$

Viterbi as an example of the max-product algorithm The Viterbi algorithm can also be implemented using probabilities, rather than log-probabilities. In this case, each $v_m(y_m)$ is equal to

$$v_m(y_m) = \max_{\boldsymbol{y}_{1:m-1}} \mathrm{p}(\boldsymbol{y}_{1:m-1}, y_m, \boldsymbol{w}_{1:m}) \qquad [7.50]$$

$$= \max_{y_{m-1}} \mathrm{p}(y_m, w_m \mid y_{m-1}) \times \max_{\boldsymbol{y}_{1:m-2}} \mathrm{p}(y_{1:m-2}, y_{m-1}, \boldsymbol{w}_{1:m-1}) \qquad [7.51]$$

$$= \max_{y_{m-1}} \mathrm{p}(y_m, w_m \mid y_{m-1}) \times v_{m-1}(y_{m-1}) \qquad [7.52]$$

$$= \mathrm{p}_{w|y}(w_m \mid y_m) \times \max_{y_{m-1}} \mathrm{p}_y(y_m \mid y_{m-1}) \times v_{m-1}(y_{m-1}). \qquad [7.53]$$

Each Viterbi variable is computed by *maximizing* over a set of *products*. Thus, the Viterbi algorithm is a special case of the **max-product algorithm** for inference in graphical models (Wainwright and Jordan, 2008). However, the product of probabilities tends toward zero over long sequences, so the log-probability version of Viterbi is recommended in practical implementations.

7.5 Discriminative Sequence Labeling with Features

Today, hidden Markov models are rarely used for supervised sequence labeling. This is because HMMs are limited to only two phenomena:

- word-tag compatibility, via the emission probability $p_{W|Y}(w_m \mid y_m)$;
- local context, via the transition probability $p_Y(y_m \mid y_{m-1})$.

The Viterbi algorithm permits the inclusion of richer information in the local scoring function $\psi(\boldsymbol{w}_{1:M}, y_m, y_{m-1}, m)$, which can be defined as a weighted sum of arbitrary local *features*,

$$\psi(\boldsymbol{w}, y_m, y_{m-1}, m) = \boldsymbol{\theta} \cdot \boldsymbol{f}(\boldsymbol{w}, y_m, y_{m-1}, m), \qquad [7.54]$$

where $\boldsymbol{f}$ is a locally defined feature function and $\boldsymbol{\theta}$ is a vector of weights.

The local decomposition of the scoring function Ψ is reflected in a corresponding decomposition of the feature function:

$$\Psi(\boldsymbol{w}, \boldsymbol{y}) = \sum_{m=1}^{M+1} \psi(\boldsymbol{w}, y_m, y_{m-1}, m) \qquad [7.55]$$

$$= \sum_{m=1}^{M+1} \boldsymbol{\theta} \cdot \boldsymbol{f}(\boldsymbol{w}, y_m, y_{m-1}, m) \qquad [7.56]$$

$$= \boldsymbol{\theta} \cdot \sum_{m=1}^{M+1} \boldsymbol{f}(\boldsymbol{w}, y_m, y_{m-1}, m) \qquad [7.57]$$

$$= \boldsymbol{\theta} \cdot \boldsymbol{f}^{(\text{global})}(\boldsymbol{w}, \boldsymbol{y}_{1:M}), \qquad [7.58]$$

where $\boldsymbol{f}^{(\text{global})}(\boldsymbol{w}, \boldsymbol{y})$ is a global feature vector, which is a sum of local feature vectors,

$$\boldsymbol{f}^{(\text{global})}(\boldsymbol{w}, \boldsymbol{y}) = \sum_{m=1}^{M+1} \boldsymbol{f}(\boldsymbol{w}_{1:M}, y_m, y_{m-1}, m), \qquad [7.59]$$

with $y_{M+1} = \blacklozenge$ and $y_0 = \lozenge$ by construction.

Let's now consider what additional information these features might encode.

Word affix features Consider the problem of part-of-speech tagging on the first four lines of the poem *Jabberwocky* (Carroll, 1917):

(7.3) 'Twas brillig, and the slithy toves
Did gyre and gimble in the wabe:
All mimsy were the borogoves,
And the mome raths outgrabe.

Many of these words were made up by the author of the poem, so a corpus would offer no information about their probabilities of being associated with any particular part of speech. Yet it is not so hard to see what their grammatical roles might be in this passage. Context helps: for example, the word *slithy* follows the determiner *the*, so it is probably a noun or adjective. Which do you think is more likely? The suffix *-thy* is found in a number of adjectives, like *frothy, healthy, pithy, worthy*. It is also found in a handful of nouns—for example, *apathy, sympathy*—but nearly all of these have the longer coda *-pathy*, unlike *slithy*. So the suffix gives some evidence that *slithy* is an adjective, and indeed it is: later in the text we find that it is a combination of the adjectives *lithe* and *slimy*.[4]

Fine-grained context The hidden Markov model captures contextual information in the form of part-of-speech tag bigrams. But sometimes, the necessary contextual information is more specific. Consider the noun phrases *this fish* and *these fish*. Many part-of-speech tagsets distinguish between singular and plural nouns, but do not distinguish between singular and plural determiners; for example, the well-known **Penn Treebank** tagset follows these conventions. A hidden Markov model would be unable to correctly label *fish* as singular or plural in both of these cases, because it only has access to two features: the preceding tag (determiner in both cases) and the word (*fish* in both cases). The classification-based tagger discussed in § 7.1 had the ability to use preceding and succeeding words as features, and it can also be incorporated into a Viterbi-based sequence labeler as a local feature.

Example Consider the tagging D J N (determiner, adjective, noun) for the sequence *the slithy toves*, so that

$$\boldsymbol{w} = \textit{the slithy toves}$$

$$\boldsymbol{y} = \text{D J N}.$$

Let's create the feature vector for this example, assuming that we have word-tag features (indicated by W), tag-tag features (indicated by T), and suffix features (indicated by M).

4. **Morphology** is the study of how words are formed from smaller linguistic units. Chapter 9 touches on computational approaches to morphological analysis. See Bender (2013) for an overview of the underlying linguistic principles and Haspelmath and Sims (2013) or Lieber (2015) for a full treatment.

You can assume that you have access to a method for extracting the suffix *-thy* from *slithy*, *-es* from *toves*, and ∅ from *the*, indicating that this word has no suffix.[5] The resulting feature vector is,

$$\begin{aligned}
f(\text{the slithy toves, D J N}) = {} & f(\text{the slithy toves}, \text{D}, \lozenge, 1) \\
& + f(\text{the slithy toves}, \text{J}, \text{D}, 2) \\
& + f(\text{the slithy toves}, \text{N}, \text{J}, 3) \\
& + f(\text{the slithy toves}, \blacklozenge, \text{N}, 4) \\
= {} & \{(T:\lozenge, \text{D}), (W:\text{the}, \text{D}), (M:\varnothing, \text{D}), \\
& (T:\text{D}, \text{J}), (W:\text{slithy}, \text{J}), (M:\text{-thy}, \text{J}), \\
& (T:\text{J}, \text{N}), (W:\text{toves}, \text{N}), (M:\text{-es}, \text{N}) \\
& (T:\text{N}, \blacklozenge)\}.
\end{aligned}$$

These examples show that local features can incorporate information that lies beyond the scope of a hidden Markov model. Because the features are local, it is possible to apply the Viterbi algorithm to identify the optimal sequence of tags. The remaining question is how to estimate the weights on these features. § 2.3 presented three main types of discriminative classifiers: perceptron, support vector machine, and logistic regression. Each of these classifiers has a structured equivalent, enabling it to be trained from labeled sequences rather than individual tokens.

7.5.1 Structured Perceptron

The perceptron classifier is trained by increasing the weights for features that are associated with the correct label and decreasing the weights for features that are associated with incorrectly predicted labels:

$$\hat{y} = \underset{y \in \mathcal{Y}}{\operatorname{argmax}}\, \boldsymbol{\theta} \cdot \boldsymbol{f}(\boldsymbol{x}, y) \quad [7.60]$$

$$\boldsymbol{\theta}^{(t+1)} \leftarrow \boldsymbol{\theta}^{(t)} + \boldsymbol{f}(\boldsymbol{x}, y) - \boldsymbol{f}(\boldsymbol{x}, \hat{y}). \quad [7.61]$$

We can apply exactly the same update in the case of structure prediction,

$$\hat{\boldsymbol{y}} = \underset{\boldsymbol{y} \in \mathcal{Y}(\boldsymbol{w})}{\operatorname{argmax}}\, \boldsymbol{\theta} \cdot \boldsymbol{f}(\boldsymbol{w}, \boldsymbol{y}) \quad [7.62]$$

$$\boldsymbol{\theta}^{(t+1)} \leftarrow \boldsymbol{\theta}^{(t)} + \boldsymbol{f}(\boldsymbol{w}, \boldsymbol{y}) - \boldsymbol{f}(\boldsymbol{w}, \hat{\boldsymbol{y}}). \quad [7.63]$$

5. Such a system is called a **morphological segmenter**. The task of morphological segmentation is briefly described in § 9.1.4; a well-known segmenter is MORFESSOR (Creutz and Lagus, 2007). In real applications, a typical approach is to include features for all orthographic suffixes up to some maximum number of characters: for *slithy*, we would have suffix features for *-y*, *-hy*, and *-thy*.

This learning algorithm is called **structured perceptron**, because it learns to predict the structured output $\boldsymbol{y}$. The only difference is that instead of computing $\hat{\boldsymbol{y}}$ by enumerating the entire set $\mathcal{Y}$, the Viterbi algorithm is used to efficiently search the set of possible taggings, $\mathcal{Y}^M$. Structured perceptron can be applied to other structured outputs as long as efficient inference is possible. As in perceptron classification, weight averaging is crucial to get good performance (see § 2.3.2).

Example For the example *they can fish*, suppose that the reference tag sequence is $\boldsymbol{y}^{(i)} = \text{N V V}$, but the tagger incorrectly returns the tag sequence $\hat{\boldsymbol{y}} = \text{N V N}$. Assuming a model with features for emissions (w_m, y_m) and transitions (y_{m-1}, y_m), the corresponding structured perceptron update is

$$\theta_{(\textit{fish},\text{V})} \leftarrow \theta_{(\textit{fish},\text{V})} + 1, \qquad \theta_{(\textit{fish},\text{N})} \leftarrow \theta_{(\textit{fish},\text{N})} - 1 \tag{7.64}$$

$$\theta_{(\text{V},\text{V})} \leftarrow \theta_{(\text{V},\text{V})} + 1, \qquad \theta_{(\text{V},\text{N})} \leftarrow \theta_{(\text{V},\text{N})} - 1 \tag{7.65}$$

$$\theta_{(\text{V},\blacklozenge)} \leftarrow \theta_{(\text{V},\blacklozenge)} + 1, \qquad \theta_{(\text{N},\blacklozenge)} \leftarrow \theta_{(\text{N},\blacklozenge)} - 1. \tag{7.66}$$

7.5.2 Structured Support Vector Machines

Large-margin classifiers such as the support vector machine improve on the perceptron by pushing the classification boundary away from the training instances. The same idea can be applied to sequence labeling. A support vector machine in which the output is a structured object, such as a sequence, is called a **structured support vector machine** (Tsochantaridis et al., 2004).[6]

In classification, we formalized the large-margin constraint as

$$\forall y \neq y^{(i)}, \boldsymbol{\theta} \cdot \boldsymbol{f}(\boldsymbol{x}, y^{(i)}) - \boldsymbol{\theta} \cdot \boldsymbol{f}(\boldsymbol{x}, y) \geq 1, \tag{7.67}$$

requiring a margin of at least 1 between the scores for all labels y that are not equal to the correct label $y^{(i)}$. The weights $\boldsymbol{\theta}$ are then learned by constrained optimization (see § 2.4.2).

This idea can be applied to sequence labeling by formulating an equivalent set of constraints for all possible labelings $\mathcal{Y}(\boldsymbol{w})$ for an input $\boldsymbol{w}$. However, there are two problems. First, in sequence labeling, some predictions are more wrong than others: we may miss only one tag out of 50, or we may get all 50 wrong. We would like our learning algorithm to be sensitive to this difference. Second, the number of constraints is equal to the number of possible labelings, which is exponentially large in the length of the sequence.

The first problem can be addressed by adjusting the constraint to require larger margins for more serious errors. Let $c(\boldsymbol{y}^{(i)}, \hat{\boldsymbol{y}}) \geq 0$ represent the *cost* of predicting label $\hat{\boldsymbol{y}}$ when the true label is $\boldsymbol{y}^{(i)}$. We can then generalize the margin constraint,

$$\forall \boldsymbol{y}, \boldsymbol{\theta} \cdot \boldsymbol{f}(\boldsymbol{w}^{(i)}, \boldsymbol{y}^{(i)}) - \boldsymbol{\theta} \cdot \boldsymbol{f}(\boldsymbol{w}^{(i)}, \boldsymbol{y}) \geq c(\boldsymbol{y}^{(i)}, \boldsymbol{y}). \tag{7.68}$$

6. This model is also known as a **max-margin Markov network** (Taskar et al., 2003), emphasizing that the scoring function is constructed from a sum of components, which are Markov independent.

This cost-augmented margin constraint specializes to the constraint in equation 7.67 if we choose the delta function $c(\boldsymbol{y}^{(i)}, \boldsymbol{y}) = \delta(\boldsymbol{y}^{(i)} \neq \boldsymbol{y})$. A more expressive cost function is the **Hamming cost**,

$$c(\boldsymbol{y}^{(i)}, \boldsymbol{y}) = \sum_{m=1}^{M} \delta(y_m^{(i)} \neq y_m), \tag{7.69}$$

which computes the number of errors in $\boldsymbol{y}$. By incorporating the cost function as the margin constraint, we require that the true labeling be seperated from the alternatives by a margin that is proportional to the number of incorrect tags in each alternative labeling.

The second problem is that the number of constraints is exponential in the length of the sequence. This can be addressed by focusing on the prediction $\hat{\boldsymbol{y}}$ that *maximally* violates the margin constraint. This prediction can be identified by solving the following **cost-augmented decoding** problem:

$$\hat{\boldsymbol{y}} = \underset{\boldsymbol{y} \neq \boldsymbol{y}^{(i)}}{\operatorname{argmax}} \, \boldsymbol{\theta} \cdot \boldsymbol{f}(\boldsymbol{w}^{(i)}, \boldsymbol{y}) - \boldsymbol{\theta} \cdot \boldsymbol{f}(\boldsymbol{w}^{(i)}, \boldsymbol{y}^{(i)}) + c(\boldsymbol{y}^{(i)}, \boldsymbol{y}) \tag{7.70}$$

$$= \underset{\boldsymbol{y} \neq \boldsymbol{y}^{(i)}}{\operatorname{argmax}} \, \boldsymbol{\theta} \cdot \boldsymbol{f}(\boldsymbol{w}^{(i)}, \boldsymbol{y}) + c(\boldsymbol{y}^{(i)}, \boldsymbol{y}), \tag{7.71}$$

where in the second line we drop the term $\boldsymbol{\theta} \cdot \boldsymbol{f}(\boldsymbol{w}^{(i)}, \boldsymbol{y}^{(i)})$, which is constant in $\boldsymbol{y}$.

We can now reformulate the margin constraint for sequence labeling,

$$\boldsymbol{\theta} \cdot \boldsymbol{f}(\boldsymbol{w}^{(i)}, \boldsymbol{y}^{(i)}) - \max_{\boldsymbol{y} \in \mathcal{Y}(\boldsymbol{w})} \left(\boldsymbol{\theta} \cdot \boldsymbol{f}(\boldsymbol{w}^{(i)}, \boldsymbol{y}) + c(\boldsymbol{y}^{(i)}, \boldsymbol{y}) \right) \geq 0. \tag{7.72}$$

If the score for $\boldsymbol{\theta} \cdot \boldsymbol{f}(\boldsymbol{w}^{(i)}, \boldsymbol{y}^{(i)})$ is greater than the cost-augmented score for all alternatives, then the constraint will be met. The name "cost-augmented decoding" is due to the fact that the objective includes the standard decoding problem, $\max_{\hat{\boldsymbol{y}} \in \mathcal{Y}(\boldsymbol{w})} \boldsymbol{\theta} \cdot \boldsymbol{f}(\boldsymbol{w}, \hat{\boldsymbol{y}})$, plus an additional term for the cost. Essentially, we want to train against predictions that are strong and wrong: they should score highly according to the model, yet incur a large loss with respect to the ground truth. Training adjusts the weights to reduce the score of these predictions.

For cost-augmented decoding to be tractable, the cost function must decompose into local parts, just as the feature function $\boldsymbol{f}(\cdot)$ does. The Hamming cost, defined above, obeys this property. To perform cost-augmented decoding using the Hamming cost, we need only to add features $f_m(y_m) = \delta(y_m \neq y_m^{(i)})$, and assign a constant weight of 1 to these features. Decoding can then be performed using the Viterbi algorithm.[7]

As with large-margin classifiers, it is possible to formulate the learning problem in an unconstrained form, by combining a regularization term on the weights and a Lagrangian for the constraints:

7. Are there cost functions that do not decompose into local parts? Suppose we want to assign a constant loss c to any prediction $\hat{\boldsymbol{y}}$ in which k or more predicted tags are incorrect, and zero loss otherwise. This loss function is combinatorial over the predictions, and thus we cannot decompose it into parts.

$$\min_{\theta} \quad \frac{1}{2}||\theta||_2^2 - C\left(\sum_i \theta \cdot f(w^{(i)}, y^{(i)}) - \max_{y \in \mathcal{Y}(w^{(i)})} \left[\theta \cdot f(w^{(i)}, y) + c(y^{(i)}, y)\right]\right). \quad [7.73]$$

In this formulation, C is a parameter that controls the tradeoff between the regularization term and the margin constraints. A number of optimization algorithms have been proposed for structured support vector machines, some of which are discussed in § 2.4.2. An empirical comparison by Kummerfeld et al. (2015) shows that stochastic subgradient descent—which is essentially a cost-augmented version of the structured perceptron—is highly competitive.

7.5.3 Conditional Random Fields

The **conditional random field** (CRF; Lafferty et al., 2001) is a conditional probabilistic model for sequence labeling; just as structured perceptron is built on the perceptron classifier, conditional random fields are built on the logistic regression classifier.[8] The basic probability model is

$$\mathrm{p}(y \mid w) = \frac{\exp(\Psi(w, y))}{\sum_{y' \in \mathcal{Y}(w)} \exp(\Psi(w, y'))}. \quad [7.74]$$

This is almost identical to logistic regression (§ 2.5), but because the label space is now sequences of tags, we require efficient algorithms for both **decoding** (searching for the best tag sequence given a sequence of words w and a model θ) and for **normalization** (summing over all tag sequences). These algorithms will be based on the usual locality assumption on the scoring function, $\Psi(w, y) = \sum_{m=1}^{M+1} \psi(w, y_m, y_{m-1}, m)$.

Decoding in CRFs Decoding—finding the tag sequence $\hat{y}$ that maximizes $\mathrm{p}(y \mid w)$—is a direct application of the Viterbi algorithm. The key observation is that the decoding problem does not depend on the denominator of $\mathrm{p}(y \mid w)$,

$$\begin{aligned}
\hat{y} &= \operatorname*{argmax}_{y} \log \mathrm{p}(y \mid w) \\
&= \operatorname*{argmax}_{y} \Psi(y, w) - \log \sum_{y' \in \mathcal{Y}(w)} \exp \Psi(y', w) \\
&= \operatorname*{argmax}_{y} \Psi(y, w) = \operatorname*{argmax}_{y} \sum_{m=1}^{M+1} s_m(y_m, y_{m-1}).
\end{aligned}$$

8. The name "conditional random field" is derived from **Markov random fields**, a general class of models in which the probability of a configuration of variables is proportional to a product of scores across pairs (or more generally, cliques) of variables in a **factor graph**. In sequence labeling, the pairs of variables include all adjacent tags (y_m, y_{m-1}). The probability is *conditioned* on the words w, which are always observed, motivating the term "conditional" in the name.

This is identical to the decoding problem for structured perceptron, so the same Viterbi recurrence as defined in equation 7.22 can be used.

Learning in CRFs As with logistic regression, the weights $\boldsymbol{\theta}$ are learned by minimizing the regularized negative log-probability,

$$\ell = \frac{\lambda}{2}||\boldsymbol{\theta}||^2 - \sum_{i=1}^{N} \log \mathrm{p}(\boldsymbol{y}^{(i)} \mid \boldsymbol{w}^{(i)}; \boldsymbol{\theta}) \quad [7.75]$$

$$= \frac{\lambda}{2}||\boldsymbol{\theta}||^2 - \sum_{i=1}^{N} \boldsymbol{\theta} \cdot \boldsymbol{f}(\boldsymbol{w}^{(i)}, \boldsymbol{y}^{(i)}) + \log \sum_{\boldsymbol{y}' \in \mathcal{Y}(\boldsymbol{w}^{(i)})} \exp\left(\boldsymbol{\theta} \cdot \boldsymbol{f}(\boldsymbol{w}^{(i)}, \boldsymbol{y}')\right), \quad [7.76]$$

where λ controls the amount of regularization. The final term in equation 7.76 is a sum over all possible labelings. This term is the log of the denominator in equation 7.74, sometimes known as the **partition function**.[9] There are $|\mathcal{Y}|^M$ possible labelings of an input of size M, so we must again exploit the decomposition of the scoring function to compute this sum efficiently.

The sum $\sum_{\boldsymbol{y} \in \mathcal{Y}_{\boldsymbol{w}^{(i)}}} \exp \Psi(\boldsymbol{y}, \boldsymbol{w})$ can be computed efficiently using the **forward recurrence**, which is closely related to the Viterbi recurrence. We first define a set of **forward variables**, $\alpha_m(y_m)$, which is equal to the sum of the scores of all paths leading to tag y_m at position m:

$$\alpha_m(y_m) \triangleq \sum_{\boldsymbol{y}_{1:m-1}} \exp \sum_{n=1}^{m} s_n(y_n, y_{n-1}) \quad [7.77]$$

$$= \sum_{\boldsymbol{y}_{1:m-1}} \prod_{n=1}^{m} \exp s_n(y_n, y_{n-1}). \quad [7.78]$$

Note the similarity to the definition of the Viterbi variable, $v_m(y_m) = \max_{\boldsymbol{y}_{1:m-1}} \sum_{n=1}^{m} s_n (y_n, y_{n-1})$. In the hidden Markov model, the Viterbi recurrence had an alternative interpretation as the max-product algorithm (see equation 7.53); analogously, the forward recurrence is known as the **sum-product algorithm**, because of the form of [7.78]. The forward variable can also be computed through a recurrence:

$$\alpha_m(y_m) = \sum_{\boldsymbol{y}_{1:m-1}} \prod_{n=1}^{m} \exp s_n(y_n, y_{n-1}) \quad [7.79]$$

$$= \sum_{y_{m-1}} (\exp s_m(y_m, y_{m-1})) \sum_{\boldsymbol{y}_{1:m-2}} \prod_{n=1}^{m-1} \exp s_n(y_n, y_{n-1}) \quad [7.80]$$

9. The terminology of "potentials" and "partition functions" comes from statistical mechanics (Bishop, 2006).

$$= \sum_{y_{m-1}} (\exp s_m(y_m, y_{m-1})) \times \alpha_{m-1}(y_{m-1}). \tag{7.81}$$

Using the forward recurrence, it is possible to compute the denominator of the conditional probability,

$$\sum_{y \in \mathcal{Y}(w)} \Psi(\boldsymbol{w}, \boldsymbol{y}) = \sum_{y_{1:M}} (\exp s_{M+1}(\blacklozenge, y_M)) \prod_{m=1}^{M} \exp s_m(y_m, y_{m-1}) \tag{7.82}$$

$$= \alpha_{M+1}(\blacklozenge). \tag{7.83}$$

The conditional log-likelihood can be rewritten,

$$\ell = \frac{\lambda}{2} ||\boldsymbol{\theta}||^2 - \sum_{i=1}^{N} \boldsymbol{\theta} \cdot \boldsymbol{f}(\boldsymbol{w}^{(i)}, \boldsymbol{y}^{(i)}) + \log \alpha_{M+1}(\blacklozenge). \tag{7.84}$$

Probabilistic programming environments, such as TORCH (Collobert et al., 2011a) and DYNET (Neubig et al., 2017b), can compute the gradient of this objective using automatic differentiation. The programmer need only implement the forward algorithm as a computation graph.

As in logistic regression, the gradient of the likelihood with respect to the parameters is a difference between observed and expected feature counts:

$$\frac{d\ell}{d\theta_j} = \lambda\theta_j + \sum_{i=1}^{N} E[f_j(\boldsymbol{w}^{(i)}, \boldsymbol{y})] - f_j(\boldsymbol{w}^{(i)}, \boldsymbol{y}^{(i)}), \tag{7.85}$$

where $f_j(\boldsymbol{w}^{(i)}, \boldsymbol{y}^{(i)})$ refers to the count of feature j for token sequence $\boldsymbol{w}^{(i)}$ and tag sequence $\boldsymbol{y}^{(i)}$. The expected feature counts are computed "under the hood" when automatic differentiation is applied to equation 7.84 (Eisner, 2016).

Before the widespread use of automatic differentiation, it was common to compute the feature expectations from marginal tag probabilities $p(y_m \mid \boldsymbol{w})$. These marginal probabilities are sometimes useful on their own and can be computed using the **forward-backward algorithm**. This algorithm combines the forward recurrence with an equivalent **backward recurrence**, which traverses the input from w_M back to w_1.

***Forward-backward algorithm** Marginal probabilities over tag bigrams can be written as[10]

$$\Pr(Y_{m-1} = k', Y_m = k \mid \boldsymbol{w}) = \frac{\sum_{\boldsymbol{y}: Y_m = k, Y_{m-1} = k'} \prod_{n=1}^{M} \exp s_n(y_n, y_{n-1})}{\sum_{\boldsymbol{y}'} \prod_{n=1}^{M} \exp s_n(y'_n, y'_{n-1})}. \tag{7.86}$$

10. Recall the notational convention of uppercase letters for random variables, e.g., Y_m, and lowercase letters for specific values, e.g., y_m, so that $Y_m = k$ is interpreted as the event of random variable Y_m taking the value k.

The numerator sums over all tag sequences that include the transition $(Y_{m-1}=k') \rightarrow (Y_m=k)$. Because we are only interested in sequences that include the tag bigram, this sum can be decomposed into three parts: the *prefixes* $\boldsymbol{y}_{1:m-1}$, terminating in $Y_{m-1}=k'$; the transition $(Y_{m-1}=k') \rightarrow (Y_m=k)$; and the *suffixes* $\boldsymbol{y}_{m:M}$, beginning with the tag $Y_m=k$:

$$\sum_{\boldsymbol{y}:Y_m=k,Y_{m-1}=k'} \prod_{n=1}^{M} \exp s_n(y_n, y_{n-1}) = \sum_{\boldsymbol{y}_{1:m-1}:Y_{m-1}=k'} \prod_{n=1}^{m-1} \exp s_n(y_n, y_{n-1}) \times \exp s_m(k,k') \times \sum_{\boldsymbol{y}_{m:M}:Y_m=k} \prod_{n=m+1}^{M+1} \exp s_n(y_n, y_{n-1}). \quad [7.87]$$

The result is product of three terms: a score that sums over all the ways to get to the position $(Y_{m-1}=k')$, a score for the transition from k' to k, and a score that sums over all the ways of finishing the sequence from $(Y_m=k)$. The first term of equation 7.87 is equal to the **forward variable,** $\alpha_{m-1}(k')$. The third term—the sum over ways to finish the sequence—can also be defined recursively, this time moving over the trellis from right to left, which is known as the **backward recurrence**:

$$\beta_m(k) \triangleq \sum_{\boldsymbol{y}_{m:M}:Y_m=k} \prod_{n=m}^{M+1} \exp s_n(y_n, y_{n-1}) \quad [7.88]$$

$$= \sum_{k'\in\mathcal{Y}} \exp s_{m+1}(k',k) \sum_{\boldsymbol{y}_{m+1:M}:Y_m=k'} \prod_{n=m+1}^{M+1} \exp s_n(y_n, y_{n-1}) \quad [7.89]$$

$$= \sum_{k'\in\mathcal{Y}} \exp s_{m+1}(k',k) \times \beta_{m+1}(k'). \quad [7.90]$$

To understand this computation, compare with the forward recurrence in equation 7.81.

In practice, numerical stability demands that we work in the log domain,

$$\log \alpha_m(k) = \log \sum_{k'\in\mathcal{Y}} \exp\left(\log s_m(k,k') + \log \alpha_{m-1}(k')\right) \quad [7.91]$$

$$\log \beta_{m-1}(k) = \log \sum_{k'\in\mathcal{Y}} \exp\left(\log s_m(k',k) + \log \beta_m(k')\right). \quad [7.92]$$

The application of the forward and backward probabilities is shown in figure 7.3. Both the forward and backward recurrences operate on the trellis, which implies a space complexity $\mathcal{O}(MK)$. Because both recurrences require computing a sum over K terms at each node in the trellis, their time complexity is $\mathcal{O}(MK^2)$.

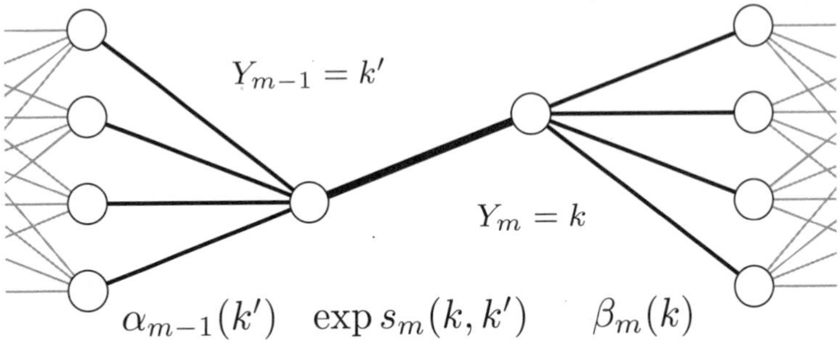

Figure 7.3
A schematic illustration of the computation of the marginal probability $\Pr(Y_{m-1} = k', Y_m = k)$, using the forward score $\alpha_{m-1}(k')$ and the backward score $\beta_m(k)$.

7.6 Neural Sequence Labeling

In neural network approaches to sequence labeling, we construct a vector representation for each tagging decision, based on the word and its context. Neural networks can perform tagging as a per-token classification decision, or they can be combined with the Viterbi algorithm to tag the entire sequence globally.

7.6.1 Recurrent Neural Networks

Recurrent neural networks (RNNs) were introduced in chapter 6 as a language modeling technique, in which the context at token m is summarized by a recurrently updated vector,

$$\boldsymbol{h}_m = g(\boldsymbol{x}_m, \boldsymbol{h}_{m-1}), \quad m = 1, 2, \ldots M,$$

where $\boldsymbol{x}_m$ is the vector **embedding** of the token w_m and the function g defines the recurrence. The starting condition $\boldsymbol{h}_0$ is an additional parameter of the model. The long short-term memory (LSTM) is a more complex recurrence, in which a memory cell is passed through a series of gates, avoiding repeated application of the non-linearity. Despite these bells and whistles, both models share the basic architecture of recurrent updates across a sequence, and both will be referred to as RNNs here.

A straightforward application of RNNs to sequence labeling is to score each tag y_m as a linear function of $\boldsymbol{h}_m$:

$$\psi_m(y) = \boldsymbol{\beta}_y \cdot \boldsymbol{h}_m \quad [7.93]$$

$$\hat{y}_m = \underset{y}{\text{argmax}}\ \psi_m(y). \quad [7.94]$$

The score $\psi_m(y)$ can also be converted into a probability using the usual softmax operation,

$$\text{p}(y \mid \boldsymbol{w}_{1:m}) = \frac{\exp \psi_m(y)}{\sum_{y' \in \mathcal{Y}} \exp \psi_m(y')}. \quad [7.95]$$

Using this transformation, it is possible to train the tagger from the negative log-likelihood of the tags, as in a conditional random field. Alternatively, a hinge loss or margin loss objective can be constructed from the raw scores $\psi_m(y)$.

The hidden state $\boldsymbol{h}_m$ accounts for information in the input leading up to position m, but it ignores the subsequent tokens, which may also be relevant to the tag y_m. This can be addressed by adding a second RNN, in which the input is reversed, running the recurrence from w_M to w_1. This is known as a **bidirectional recurrent neural network** (Graves and Schmidhuber, 2005) and is specified as

$$\overleftarrow{\boldsymbol{h}}_m = g(\boldsymbol{x}_m, \overleftarrow{\boldsymbol{h}}_{m+1}), \quad m = 1, 2, \ldots, M. \tag{7.96}$$

The hidden states of the left-to-right RNN are denoted $\overrightarrow{\boldsymbol{h}}_m$. The left-to-right and right-to-left vectors are concatenated, $\boldsymbol{h}_m = [\overleftarrow{\boldsymbol{h}}_m; \overrightarrow{\boldsymbol{h}}_m]$. The scoring function in equation 7.93 is applied to this concatenated vector.

Bidirectional RNN tagging has several attractive properties. Ideally, the representation $\boldsymbol{h}_m$ summarizes the useful information from the surrounding context, so that it is not necessary to design explicit features to capture this information. If the vector $\boldsymbol{h}_m$ is an adequate summary of this context, then it may not even be necessary to perform the tagging jointly: in general, the gains offered by joint tagging of the entire sequence are diminished as the individual tagging model becomes more powerful. Using backpropagation, the word vectors $\boldsymbol{x}$ can be trained "end to end," so that they capture word properties that are useful for the tagging task. Alternatively, if limited labeled data is available, we can use word embeddings that are pretrained from unlabeled data, using a language modeling objective (as in § 6.3) or a contextualized word embedding technique (see chapter 14). It is even possible to combine both fine-tuned and pre-trained embeddings in a single model.

Neural structure prediction The bidirectional recurrent neural network incorporates information from throughout the input, but each tagging decision is made independently. In some sequence labeling applications, there are very strong dependencies between tags: it may even be impossible for one tag to follow another. In such scenarios, the tagging decision must be made jointly across the entire sequence.

Neural sequence labeling can be combined with the Viterbi algorithm by defining the local scores as

$$s_m(y_m, y_{m-1}) = \boldsymbol{\beta}_{y_m} \cdot \boldsymbol{h}_m + \eta_{y_{m-1}, y_m}, \tag{7.97}$$

where $\boldsymbol{h}_m$ is the RNN hidden state, $\boldsymbol{\beta}_{y_m}$ is a vector associated with tag y_m, and η_{y_{m-1}, y_m} is a scalar parameter for the tag transition (y_{m-1}, y_m). These local scores can then be incorporated into the Viterbi algorithm for inference, and into the forward algorithm for training. This model is shown in figure 7.4. It can be trained from the conditional log-likelihood objective defined in equation 7.76, backpropagating to the tagging parameters $\boldsymbol{\beta}$ and $\boldsymbol{\eta}$, as well as the parameters of the RNN. This model is called the **LSTM-CRF**, due

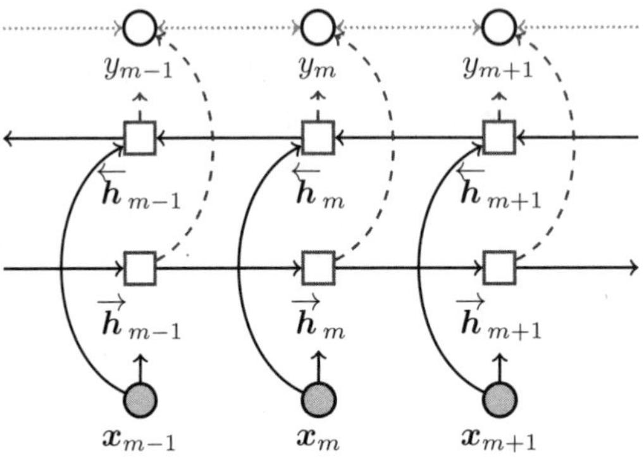

Figure 7.4
Bidirectional LSTM for sequence labeling. The solid lines indicate computation, the dashed lines indicate probabilistic dependency, and the dotted lines indicate the optional additional probabilistic dependencies between labels in the biLSTM-CRF.

to its combination of aspects of the long short-term memory and conditional random field models (Huang et al., 2015).

The LSTM-CRF is especially effective on the task of **named entity recognition** (Lample et al., 2016), a sequence labeling task that is described in detail in § 8.3. This task has strong dependencies between adjacent tags, so structure prediction is especially important.

7.6.2 Character-Level Models

As in language modeling, rare and unseen words are a challenge: if we encounter a word that was not in the training data, then there is no obvious choice for the word embedding $\boldsymbol{x}_m$. One solution is to use a generic **unseen word** embedding for all such words. However, in many cases, properties of unseen words can be guessed from their spellings. For example, *whimsical* does not appear in the Universal Dependencies (UD) English Treebank, yet the suffix *-al* makes it likely to be adjective; by the same logic, *unflinchingly* is likely to be an adverb, and *barnacle* is likely to be a noun.

In feature-based models, these morphological properties were handled by suffix features; in a neural network, they can be incorporated by constructing the embeddings of unseen words from their spellings or morphology. One way to do this is to incorporate an additional layer of bidirectional RNNs, one for each word in the vocabulary (Ling et al., 2015b). For each such character RNN, the inputs are the characters, and the output is the concatenation of the final states of the left-facing and right-facing passes, $\boldsymbol{\phi}_w = [\overrightarrow{\boldsymbol{h}}^{(w)}_{N_w}; \overleftarrow{\boldsymbol{h}}^{(w)}_{0}]$, where $\overrightarrow{\boldsymbol{h}}^{(w)}_{N_w}$ is the final state of the right-facing pass for word w and N_w is the number of characters in the word. The character RNN model is trained by backpropagation from the tagging objective. On the test data, the trained RNN is applied to out-of-vocabulary words (or all words), yielding inputs to the word-level tagging RNN. Other approaches to compositional word embeddings are described in § 14.7.1.

7.6.3 Convolutional Neural Networks for Sequence Labeling

One disadvantage of recurrent neural networks is that the architecture requires iterating through the sequence of inputs and predictions: each hidden vector $\boldsymbol{h}_m$ must be computed from the previous hidden vector $\boldsymbol{h}_{m-1}$, before predicting the tag y_m. These iterative computations are difficult to parallelize and fail to exploit the speedups offered by **graphics processing units (GPUs)** on operations such as matrix multiplication. **Convolutional neural networks** achieve better computational performance by predicting each label y_m from a set of matrix operations on the neighboring word embeddings, $\boldsymbol{x}_{m-k:m+k}$ (Collobert et al., 2011b). Because there is no hidden state to update, the predictions for each y_m can be computed in parallel. For more on convolutional neural networks, see § 3.4. Character-based word embeddings can also be computed using convolutional neural networks (dos Santos and Zadrozny, 2014).

7.7 *Unsupervised Sequence Labeling

In unsupervised sequence labeling, the goal is to induce a hidden Markov model from a corpus of *unannotated* text $(\boldsymbol{w}^{(1)}, \boldsymbol{w}^{(2)}, \ldots, \boldsymbol{w}^{(N)})$, where each $\boldsymbol{w}^{(i)}$ is a sequence of length $M^{(i)}$. This is an example of the general problem of **structure induction**, which is the unsupervised version of structure prediction. The tags that result from unsupervised sequence labeling might be useful for some downstream task, or they might help us to better understand the language's inherent structure. For part-of-speech tagging, it is common to use a tag dictionary that lists the allowed tags for each word, simplifying the problem (Christodoulopoulos et al., 2010).

Unsupervised learning in hidden Markov models can be performed using the **Baum-Welch algorithm**, which combines the forward-backward algorithm (§ 7.5.3) with expectation-maximization (EM; § 5.1.2). In the M-step, the HMM parameters are estimated from expected counts:

$$\Pr(W = i \mid Y = k) = \phi_{k,i} = \frac{E[\text{count}(W = i, Y = k)]}{E[\text{count}(Y = k)]}$$

$$\Pr(Y_m = k \mid Y_{m-1} = k') = \lambda_{k',k} = \frac{E[\text{count}(Y_m = k, Y_{m-1} = k')]}{E[\text{count}(Y_{m-1} = k')]}.$$

The expected counts are computed in the E-step, using the forward and backward recurrences. The local scores follow the usual definition for hidden Markov models,

$$s_m(k, k') = \log \mathrm{p}_E(w_m \mid Y_m = k; \boldsymbol{\phi}) + \log \mathrm{p}_T(Y_m = k \mid Y_{m-1} = k'; \lambda). \quad [7.98]$$

The expected transition counts for a single instance are

$$E[\text{count}(Y_m = k, Y_{m-1} = k') \mid \boldsymbol{w}] = \sum_{m=1}^{M} \Pr(Y_{m-1} = k', Y_m = k \mid \boldsymbol{w}) \quad [7.99]$$

$$= \frac{\sum_{\boldsymbol{y}:Y_m=k,Y_{m-1}=k'} \prod_{n=1}^{M} \exp s_n(y_n, y_{n-1})}{\sum_{\boldsymbol{y}'} \prod_{n=1}^{M} \exp s_n(y'_n, y'_{n-1})}. \quad [7.100]$$

As described in § 7.5.3, these marginal probabilities can be computed from the forward-backward recurrence,

$$\Pr(Y_{m-1}=k', Y_m=k \mid \boldsymbol{w}) = \frac{\alpha_{m-1}(k') \times \exp s_m(k,k') \times \beta_m(k)}{\alpha_{M+1}(\blacklozenge)}. \quad [7.101]$$

In a hidden Markov model, each element of the forward-backward computation has a special interpretation:

$$\alpha_{m-1}(k') = \mathrm{p}(Y_{m-1}=k', \boldsymbol{w}_{1:m-1}) \quad [7.102]$$

$$\exp s_m(k,k') = \mathrm{p}(Y_m=k, w_m \mid Y_{m-1}=k') \quad [7.103]$$

$$\beta_m(k) = \mathrm{p}(\boldsymbol{w}_{m+1:M} \mid Y_m=k). \quad [7.104]$$

Applying the conditional independence assumptions of the hidden Markov model (defined in algorithm 12), the product is equal to the joint probability of the tag bigram and the entire input,

$$\begin{aligned}\alpha_{m-1}(k') \times \exp s_m(k,k') \times \beta_m(k) = {} & \mathrm{p}(Y_{m-1}=k', \boldsymbol{w}_{1:m-1}) \\ & \times \mathrm{p}(Y_m=k, w_m \mid Y_{m-1}=k') \\ & \times \mathrm{p}(\boldsymbol{w}_{m+1:M} \mid Y_m=k) \\ = {} & \mathrm{p}(Y_{m-1}=k', Y_m=k, \boldsymbol{w}_{1:M}). \quad [7.105]\end{aligned}$$

Dividing by $\alpha_{M+1}(\blacklozenge) = \mathrm{p}(\boldsymbol{w}_{1:M})$ gives the desired probability,

$$\begin{aligned}\frac{\alpha_{m-1}(k') \times s_m(k,k') \times \beta_m(k)}{\alpha_{M+1}(\blacklozenge)} = {} & \frac{\mathrm{p}(Y_{m-1}=k', Y_m=k, \boldsymbol{w}_{1:M})}{\mathrm{p}(\boldsymbol{w}_{1:M})} \quad [7.106] \\ = {} & \Pr(Y_{m-1}=k', Y_m=k \mid \boldsymbol{w}_{1:M}). \quad [7.107]\end{aligned}$$

The expected emission counts can be computed in a similar manner, using the product $\alpha_m(k) \times \beta_m(k)$.

7.7.1 Linear Dynamical Systems

The forward-backward algorithm can be viewed as Bayesian state estimation in a discrete state space. In a continuous state space, $\boldsymbol{y}_m \in \mathbb{R}^K$, the equivalent algorithm is the **Kalman smoother**. It also computes marginals $\mathrm{p}(\boldsymbol{y}_m \mid \boldsymbol{x}_{1:M})$, using a similar two-step algorithm of forward and backward passes. Instead of computing a trellis of values at each step, the Kalman smoother computes a probability density function $q_m(\boldsymbol{y}_m; \boldsymbol{\mu}_m, \Sigma_m)$, characterized by a mean $\boldsymbol{\mu}_m$ and a covariance Σ_m around the latent state. Connections between the Kalman smoother and the forward-backward algorithm are elucidated by Minka (1999) and Murphy (2012).

7.7.2 Alternative Unsupervised Learning Methods

As noted in § 5.5, expectation-maximization is just one of many techniques for structure induction. One alternative is to use **Markov Chain Monte Carlo (MCMC)** sampling algorithms, which are briefly described in § 5.5.1. For the specific case of sequence labeling, Gibbs sampling can be applied by iteratively sampling each tag y_m conditioned on all the others (Finkel et al., 2005):

$$\mathrm{p}(y_m \mid \boldsymbol{y}_{-m}, \boldsymbol{w}_{1:M}) \propto \mathrm{p}(w_m \mid y_m)\mathrm{p}(y_m \mid \boldsymbol{y}_{-m}). \qquad [7.108]$$

Gibbs Sampling has been applied to unsupervised part-of-speech tagging by Goldwater and Griffiths (2007). **Beam sampling** is a more sophisticated sampling algorithm, which randomly draws entire sequences $\boldsymbol{y}_{1:M}$, rather than individual tags y_m; this algorithm was applied to unsupervised part-of-speech tagging by Van Gael et al. (2009). Spectral learning (see § 5.5.2) can also be applied to sequence labeling. By factoring matrices of co-occurrence counts of word bigrams and trigrams (Song et al., 2010; Hsu et al., 2012), it is possible to obtain globally optimal estimates of the transition and emission parameters, under mild assumptions.

7.7.3 Semiring Notation and the Generalized Viterbi Algorithm

The Viterbi and forward recurrences can each be performed over probabilities or log-probabilities, yielding a total of four closely related recurrences. These four recurrence scan in fact be expressed as a single recurrence in a more general notation, known as **semiring algebra**. Let the symbols $\oplus$ and $\otimes$ represent generalized addition and multiplication respectively.[11] Given these operators, a generalized Viterbi recurrence is denoted as

$$v_m(k) = \bigoplus_{k' \in \mathcal{Y}} s_m(k, k') \otimes v_{m-1}(k'). \qquad [7.109]$$

Each recurrence that we have seen so far is a special case of this generalized Viterbi recurrence:

- In the max-product Viterbi recurrence over probabilities, the $\oplus$ operation corresponds to maximization, and the $\otimes$ operation corresponds to multiplication.
- In the forward recurrence over probabilities, the $\oplus$ operation corresponds to addition, and the $\otimes$ operation corresponds to multiplication.
- In the max-product Viterbi recurrence over log-probabilities, the $\oplus$ operation corresponds to maximization, and the $\otimes$ operation corresponds to addition.[12]

11. In a semiring, the addition and multiplication operators must both obey associativity, and multiplication must distribute across addition; the addition operator must be commutative; there must be additive and multiplicative identities $\overline{0}$ and $\overline{1}$, such that $a \oplus \overline{0} = a$ and $a \otimes \overline{1} = a$; and there must be a multiplicative annihilator $\overline{0}$, such that $a \otimes \overline{0} = \overline{0}$.

12. This is sometimes called the **tropical semiring**, in honor of the Brazilian mathematician Imre Simon.

- In the forward recurrence over log-probabilities, the $\oplus$ operation corresponds to log-addition, $a \oplus b = \log(e^a + e^b)$. The $\otimes$ operation corresponds to addition.

The mathematical abstraction offered by semiring notation can be applied to the software implementations of these algorithms, yielding concise and modular implementations. For example, in the OPENFST library, generic operations are parametrized by the choice of semiring (Allauzen et al., 2007).

Exercises

1. Extend the example in § 7.3.1 to the sentence *they can can fish*, meaning that "they can put fish into cans." Build the trellis for this example using the weights in table 7.1, and identify the best-scoring tag sequence. If the scores for noun and verb are tied, then you may assume that the back-pointer always goes to noun.
2. Using the tagset $\mathcal{Y} = \{N, V\}$ and the feature set $\boldsymbol{f}(\boldsymbol{w}, y_m, y_{m-1}, m) = \{(w_m, y_m), (y_m, y_{m-1})\}$, show that there is no set of weights that gives the correct tagging for both *they can fish* (N V V) and *they can can fish* (N V V N).
3. Work out what happens if you train a structured perceptron on the two examples mentioned in the previous problem, using the transition and emission features (y_m, y_{m-1}) and (y_m, w_m). Initialize all weights at 0, and assume that the Viterbi algorithm always chooses N when the scores for the two tags are tied, so that the initial prediction for *they can fish* is N N N.
4. Consider the garden path sentence, *The old man the boat.* Given word-tag and tag-tag features, what inequality in the weights must hold for the correct tag sequence to outscore the garden path tag sequence for this example?
5. Using the weights in table 7.1, explicitly compute the log-probabilities for all possible taggings of the input *fish can*. Verify that the forward algorithm recovers the aggregate log-probability.
6. Sketch out an algorithm for a variant of Viterbi that returns the top-n label sequences. What is the time and space complexity of this algorithm?
7. Show how to compute the marginal probability $\Pr(y_{m-2} = k, y_m = k' \mid \boldsymbol{w}_{1:M})$, in terms of the forward and backward variables, and the potentials $s_n(y_n, y_{n-1})$.
8. Suppose you receive a stream of text, where some of tokens have been replaced at random with *NOISE*. For example,

   - Source: *I try all things, I achieve what I can*
   - Message received: *I try NOISE NOISE, I NOISE what I NOISE*

   Assume you have access to a pretrained bigram language model, which gives probabilities $\mathrm{p}(w_m \mid w_{m-1})$. These probabilities can be assumed to be nonzero for all bigrams.

Show how to use the Viterbi algorithm to recover the source by maximizing the bigram language model log-probability. Specifically, set the scores $s_m(y_m, y_{m-1})$ so that the Viterbi algorithm selects a sequence of words that maximizes the bigram language model log-probability, while leaving the nonnoise tokens intact. Your solution should not modify the logic of the Viterbi algorithm, it should only set the scores $s_m(y_m, y_{m-1})$.

9. Let $\alpha(\cdot)$ and $\beta(\cdot)$ indicate the forward and backward variables as defined in § 7.5.3. Prove that $\alpha_{M+1}(\blacklozenge) = \beta_0(\lozenge) = \sum_y \alpha_m(y)\beta_m(y), \forall m \in \{1, 2, \ldots, M\}$.
10. Consider an RNN tagging model with a tanh activation function on the hidden layer, and a hinge loss on the output. (The problem also works for the margin loss and negative log-likelihood.) Suppose you initialize all parameters to zero: this includes the word embeddings that make up $\boldsymbol{x}$, the transition matrix Θ, the output weights $\boldsymbol{\beta}$, and the initial hidden state $\boldsymbol{h}_0$.
    a) Prove that for any data and for any gradient-based learning algorithm, all parameters will be stuck at zero.
    b) Would a sigmoid activation function avoid this problem?

8 Applications of Sequence Labeling

Sequence labeling has applications throughout natural language processing. This chapter focuses on part-of-speech tagging, morpho-syntactic attribute tagging, named entity recognition, and tokenization. It also touches briefly on two applications to interactive settings: dialogue act recognition and the detection of code-switching points between languages.

8.1 Part-of-Speech Tagging

The **syntax** of a language is the set of principles under which sequences of words are judged to be grammatically acceptable by fluent speakers. One of the most basic syntactic concepts is the **part of speech (POS)**, which refers to the syntactic role of each word in a sentence. This concept was used informally in the previous chapter, and you may have some intuitions from your own study of English. For example, in the sentence *We like vegetarian sandwiches*, you may already know that *we* and *sandwiches* are nouns, *like* is a verb, and *vegetarian* is an adjective. These labels depend on the context in which the word appears: in *she eats like a vegetarian*, the word *like* is a preposition, and the word *vegetarian* is a noun.

Parts of speech can help to disentangle or explain various linguistic problems. Recall Chomsky's proposed distinction in chapter 6:

(8.1) a. Colorless green ideas sleep furiously.
b. *Ideas colorless furiously green sleep.

One difference between these two examples is that the first contains part-of-speech transitions that are typical in English: adjective to adjective, adjective to noun, noun to verb, and verb to adverb. The second example contains transitions that are unusual: noun to adjective and adjective to verb. The ambiguity in a headline like

(8.2) Teacher Strikes Idle Children

can also be explained in terms of parts of speech: in the interpretation that was likely intended, *strikes* is a noun and *idle* is a verb; in the alternative explanation, *strikes* is a verb and *idle* is an adjective.

Part-of-speech tagging is often taken as a early step in a natural language processing pipeline. Indeed, parts of speech provide features that can be useful for many of the tasks that we will encounter later, such as parsing (chapter 10), coreference resolution (chapter 15), and relation extraction (chapter 17).

8.1.1 Parts of Speech

The **Universal Dependencies (UD)** project is an effort to create syntactically annotated corpora across many languages, using a single annotation standard (Nivre et al., 2016). As part of this effort, they have designed a part-of-speech **tagset**, which is meant to capture word classes across as many languages as possible.[1] This section describes that inventory, giving rough definitions for each of tags, along with supporting examples.

Part-of-speech tags are **morphosyntactic**, rather than semantic, categories. This means that they describe words in terms of how they pattern together and how they are internally constructed (e.g., what suffixes and prefixes they include). For example, you may think of a noun as referring to objects or concepts, and verbs as referring to actions or events. But events can also be nouns:

(8.3) … the **howling** of the **shrieking** storm.

Here *howling* and *shrieking* are events, but grammatically they act as a noun and adjective, respectively.

The Universal Dependency part-of-speech tagset The UD tagset is broken up into three groups: open class tags, closed class tags, and "others."

Open class tags Nearly all languages contain nouns, verbs, adjectives, and adverbs.[2] These are all **open word classes**, because new words can easily be added to them. The UD tagset includes two other tags that are open classes: proper nouns and interjections.

- **Nouns** (UD tag: NOUN) tend to describe entities and concepts,

(8.4) **Toes** are scarce among veteran **blubber men**.

In English, nouns tend to follow determiners and adjectives and can play the subject role in the sentence. They can be marked for the plural number by an *-s* suffix.

- **Proper nouns** (PROPN) are tokens in names, which uniquely specify a given entity,

(8.5) "**Moby Dick**?" shouted **Ahab**.

1. The UD tagset builds on earlier work from Petrov et al. (2012), in which a set of 12 universal tags was identified by creating mappings from tagsets for individual languages.

2. One prominent exception is Korean, which some linguists argue does not have adjectives (Kim, 2002).

• **Verbs** (VERB), according to the UD guidelines, "typically signal events and actions." But they are also defined grammatically: they "can constitute a minimal predicate in a clause, and govern the number and types of other constituents which may occur in a clause."[3]

(8.6) a. "Moby Dick?" **shouted** Ahab.
b. Shall we **keep chasing** this murderous fish?

English verbs tend to come in between the subject and some number of objects, depending on the verb. They can be marked for **tense** and **aspect** using suffixes such as *-ed* and *-ing*. (These suffixes are an example of **inflectional morphology**, which is discussed in more detail in § 9.1.4.)

• **Adjectives** (ADJ) describe properties of entities,

(8.7) a. Shall we keep chasing this **murderous** fish?
b. Toes are **scarce** among **veteran** blubber men.

In the second example, *scarce* is a predicative adjective, linked to the subject by the **copula verb** *are*. In contrast, *murderous* and *veteran* are attributive adjectives, modifying the noun phrase in which they are embedded.

• **Adverbs** (ADV) describe properties of events and may also modify adjectives or other adverbs:

(8.8) a. It is not down on any map; true places **never** are.
b. ... **treacherously** hidden beneath the loveliest tints of azure
c. Not drowned **entirely**, though.

• **Interjections** (INTJ) are used in exclamations,

(8.9) **Aye aye**! it was that accursed white whale that razed me.

Closed class tags Closed word classes rarely receive new members. They are sometimes referred to as **function words**—as opposed to **content words**—as they have little lexical meaning of their own, but rather, help to organize the components of the sentence.

• **Adpositions** (ADP) describe the relationship between a complement (usually a noun phrase) and another unit in the sentence, typically a noun or verb phrase.

(8.10) a. Toes are scarce **among** veteran blubber men.
b. It is not **down on** any map.
c. Give not thyself **up** then.

3. http://universaldependencies.org/u/pos/VERB.html.

As the examples show, English generally uses prepositions, which are adpositions that appear before their complement. (An exception is *ago*, as in, *we met three days* ***ago***). Postpositions are used in other languages, such as Japanese and Turkish.

• **Auxiliary verbs** (AUX) are a closed class of verbs that add information such as tense, aspect, person, and number.

(8.11) a. **Shall** we keep chasing this murderous fish?
b. What the white whale was to Ahab, **has been** hinted.
c. Ahab **must** use tools.
d. Meditation and water **are** wedded forever.
e. Toes **are** scarce among veteran blubber men.

The final example is a copula verb, which is also tagged as an auxiliary in the UD corpus.

• **Coordinating conjunctions** (CCONJ) express relationships between two words or phrases, which play a parallel role:

(8.12) Meditation **and** water are wedded forever.

• **Subordinating conjunctions** (SCONJ) link two clauses, making one syntactically subordinate to the other:

(8.13) It is the easiest thing in the world for a man to look as **if** he had a great secret in him.

• **Pronouns** (PRON) are words that substitute for nouns or noun phrases.

(8.14) a. Be **it what it** will, **I**'ll go to **it** laughing.
b. **I** try all things, **I** achieve **what I** can.

The example includes the personal pronouns *I* and *it*, as well as the relative pronoun *what*. Other pronouns include *myself*, *somebody*, and *nothing*.

• **Determiners** (DET) provide additional information about the nouns or noun phrases that they modify:

(8.15) a. What **the** white whale was to Ahab, has been hinted.
b. It is not down on **any** map.
c. I try **all** things ...
d. Shall we keep chasing **this** murderous fish?

Determiners include articles (*the*), possessive determiners (*their*), demonstratives (*this murderous fish*), and quantifiers (*any map*).

• **Numerals** (NUM) are an infinite but closed class, which includes integers, fractions, and decimals, regardless of whether spelled out or written in numerical form.

(8.16) a. How then can this **one** small heart beat.
b. I am going to put him down for the **three hundredth**.

- **Particles** (PART) are a catch-all of function words that combine with other words or phrases, but do not meet the conditions of the other tags. In English, this includes the infinitival *to*, the possessive marker, and negation.

(8.17) a. Better **to** sleep with a sober cannibal than a drunk Christian.
b. So man**'s** insanity is heaven**'s** sense
c. It is **not** down on any map

As the second example shows, the possessive marker is not considered part of the same token as the word that it modifies, so that *man's* is split into two tokens. (Tokenization is described in more detail in § 8.4.) A non-English example of a particle is the Japanese question marker *ka*:[4]

(8.18) *Sensei desu ka*
Teacher is ?
Is she a teacher?

Other The remaining UD tags include punctuation (PUN) and symbols (SYM). Punctuation is purely structural—for example, commas, periods, colons—while symbols can carry content of their own. Examples of symbols include dollar and percentage symbols, mathematical operators, emoticons, emojis, and Internet addresses. A final catch-all tag is X, which is used for words that cannot be assigned another part-of-speech category. The X tag is also used in cases of **code switching** (between languages), described in § 8.5.

Other tagsets Prior to the Universal Dependency treebank, part-of-speech tagging was performed using language-specific tagsets. The dominant tagset for English was designed as part of the **Penn Treebank (PTB)**, and it includes 45 tags—more than three times as many as the UD tagset. This granularity is reflected in distinctions between singular and plural nouns, verb tenses and aspects, possessive and nonpossessive pronouns, comparative and superlative adjectives and adverbs (e.g., *faster*, *fastest*), and so on. The Brown corpus includes a tagset that is even more detailed, with 87 tags (Francis, 1964), including special tags for individual auxiliary verbs such as *be*, *do*, and *have*.

Different languages make different distinctions, and so the PTB and Brown tagsets are not appropriate for a language such as Chinese, which does not mark the verb tense (Xia, 2000); nor for Spanish, which marks every combination of person and number in the verb ending; nor for German, which marks the case of each noun phrase. Each of these languages requires more detail than English in some areas of the tagset, and less in other areas. The strategy of the Universal Dependencies corpus is to design a coarse-grained tagset to be used across all languages, and then to additionally annotate language-specific **morphosyntactic**

4. In this notation, the first line is the transliterated Japanese text, the second line is a token-to-token **gloss**, and the third line is the translation.

attributes, such as number, tense, and case. The attribute tagging task is described in more detail in § 8.2.

Social media such as Twitter have been shown to require tagsets of their own (Gimpel et al., 2011). Such corpora contain some tokens that are not equivalent to anything encountered in a typical written corpus: e.g., emoticons, URLs, and hashtags. Social media also includes dialectal words like *gonna*, which can be analyzed either as nonstandard orthography (making tokenization impossible) or as lexical items in their own right. In either case, it is clear that existing tags like NOUN and VERB cannot handle cases like *Ima*, which combine aspects of the noun and verb. Gimpel et al. (2011) therefore propose a new set of tags to deal with these cases.

8.1.2 Accurate Part-of-Speech Tagging

Part-of-speech tagging is the problem of selecting the correct tag for each word in a sentence. Success is typically measured by accuracy on an annotated test set, which is simply the fraction of tokens that were tagged correctly.

Baselines A simple baseline for part-of-speech tagging is to choose the most common tag for each word. For example, in the Universal Dependencies treebank, the word *talk* appears 96 times, and 85 of those times it is labeled as a VERB: therefore, this baseline will always predict VERB for this word. For words that do not appear in the training corpus, the baseline simply guesses the most common tag overall, which is NOUN. In the Penn Treebank, this simple baseline obtains accuracy above 92%. A more rigorous evaluation is the accuracy on **out-of-vocabulary words**, which are not seen in the training data. Tagging these words correctly requires attention to the context and the word's internal structure.

Contemporary approaches Conditional random fields and structured perceptron perform at or near the state of the art for part-of-speech tagging in English. For example, Collins (2002) achieved 97.1% accuracy on the Penn Treebank, using a structured perceptron with the following base features, originally introduced by Ratnaparkhi (1996):

- current word, w_m
- previous words, w_{m-1}, w_{m-2}
- next words, w_{m+1}, w_{m+2}
- previous tag, y_{m-1}
- previous two tags, (y_{m-1}, y_{m-2})
- for rare words:

— first k characters, up to $k = 4$

— last k characters, up to $k = 4$

— whether w_m contains a number, uppercase character, or hyphen.

Similar results for the PTB data have been achieved using conditional random fields (CRFs; Toutanova et al., 2003).

More recent work has demonstrated the power of neural sequence models, such as the **long short-term memory (LSTM)** (§ 7.6). Plank et al. (2016) apply a CRF and a bidirectional LSTM to 22 languages in the UD corpus, achieving an average accuracy of 94.3% for the CRF and 96.5% with the bi-LSTM. Their neural model employs three types of embeddings: fine-tuned word embeddings, which are updated during training; pre-trained word embeddings, which are never updated, but which help to tag out-of-vocabulary words; and character-based embeddings. The character-based embeddings are computed by running an LSTM on the individual characters in each word, thereby capturing common orthographic patterns such as prefixes, suffixes, and capitalization. Extensive evaluations show that these additional embeddings are crucial to their model's success.

8.2 Morphosyntactic Attributes

There is considerably more to say about a word than whether it is a noun or a verb: in English, verbs are distinguish by features such tense and aspect, nouns by number, adjectives by degree, and so on. These features are language specific: other languages distinguish other features, such as **case** (the role of the noun with respect to the action of the sentence, which is marked in languages such as Latin and German[5]) and **evidentiality** (the source of information for the speaker's statement, which is marked in languages such as Turkish). In the UD corpora, these attributes are annotated as feature-value pairs for each token.[6]

An example is shown in figure 8.1. The determiner *the* is marked with two attributes: PRONTYPE=ART, which indicates that it is an **article** (as opposed to another type of determiner or pronominal modifier), and DEFINITE=DEF, which indicates that it is a **definite article** (referring to a specific, known entity). The verbs are each marked with several attributes. The auxiliary verb *was* is third person, singular, past tense, finite (conjugated), and indicative (describing an event that has happened or is currently happenings); the main verb *destroyed* is in participle form (so there is no additional person and number information), past tense, and passive voice. Some, but not all, of these distinctions are reflected in the PTB tags VBD (past-tense verb) and VBN (past participle).

While there are thousands of papers on part-of-speech tagging, there is comparatively little work on automatically labeling morphosyntactic attributes. Faruqui et al. (2016) train a support vector machine classification model, using a minimal feature set that includes

5. Case is marked in English for some personal pronouns, for example, ***She** saw **her***, ***They** saw **them***.

6. The annotation and tagging of morphosyntactic attributes can be traced back to earlier work on Turkish (Oflazer and Kuruöz, 1994) and Czech (Hajič and Hladká, 1998). MULTEXT-East was an early multilingual corpus to include morphosyntactic attributes (Dimitrova et al., 1998).

word	PTB tag	UD tag	UD attributes
The	DT	DET	DEFINITE=DEF PRONTYPE=ART
German	JJ	ADJ	DEGREE=POS
Expressionist	NN	NOUN	NUMBER=SING
movement	NN	NOUN	NUMBER=SING
was	VBD	AUX	MOOD=IND NUMBER=SING PERSON=3 TENSE=PAST VERBFORM=FIN
destroyed	VBN	VERB	TENSE=PAST VERBFORM=PART VOICE=PASS
as	IN	ADP	
a	DT	DET	DEFINITE=IND PRONTYPE=ART
result	NN	NOUN	NUMBER=SING
.	.	PUNCT	

Figure 8.1
UD and PTB part-of-speech tags, and UD morphosyntactic attributes. Example selected from the UD 1.4 English corpus.

the word itself, its prefixes and suffixes, and type-level information listing all possible morphosyntactic attributes for each word and its neighbors. Mueller et al. (2013) use a conditional random field (CRF), in which the tag space consists of all observed combinations of morphosyntactic attributes (e.g., the tag would be DEF+ART for the word *the* in figure 8.1). This massive tag space is managed by decomposing the feature space over individual attributes and pruning paths through the trellis. More recent work has employed bidirectional LSTM sequence models. For example, Pinter et al. (2017) train a bidirectional LSTM sequence model. The input layer and hidden vectors in the LSTM are shared across attributes, but each attribute has its own output layer, culminating in a softmax over all attribute values, for example, $y_t^{\text{NUMBER}} \in \{\text{SING}, \text{PLURAL}, \ldots\}$. They find that character-level information is crucial, especially when the amount of labeled data is limited.

Evaluation is performed by first computing recall and precision for each attribute. These scores can then be averaged at either the type or token level to obtain micro- or macro-F-MEASURE. Pinter et al. (2017) evaluate on 23 languages in the UD treebank, reporting a median micro-F-MEASURE of 0.95. Performance is strongly correlated with the size of the labeled dataset for each language, with a few outliers: for example, Chinese is particularly difficult, because although the dataset is relatively large (10^5 tokens in the UD 1.4 corpus), only 6% of tokens have any attributes, offering few useful labeled instances.

8.3 Named Entity Recognition

A classical problem in information extraction is to recognize and extract mentions of **named entities** in text. In news documents, the core entity types are people, locations, and organizations; more recently, the task has been extended to include amounts of money, percentages, dates, and times. In example (8.20a) (figure 8.2), the named entities include: *The U.S. Army*, an organization; *Atlanta*, a location; and *May 14, 1864*, a date. Named entity recognition is also a key task in **biomedical natural language processing**, with entity types including proteins, DNA, RNA, and cell lines (e.g., Collier et al., 2000; Ohta et al., 2002). Figure 8.2 shows an example from the GENIA corpus of biomedical research abstracts.

A standard approach to tagging named entity spans is to use discriminative sequence labeling methods such as conditional random fields. However, the named entity recognition (NER) task would seem to be fundamentally different from sequence labeling tasks like part-of-speech tagging: rather than tagging each token, the goal in is to recover *spans* of tokens, such as *The United States Army*.

This is accomplished by the **BIO notation**, shown in figure 8.2. Each token at the beginning of a name span is labeled with a B- prefix; each token within a name span is labeled with an I- prefix. These prefixes are followed by a tag for the entity type, for example, B-LOC for the beginning of a location, and I-PROTEIN for the inside of a protein name. Tokens that are not parts of name spans are labeled as O. From this representation, the entity name spans can be recovered unambiguously. This tagging scheme is also advantageous for learning: tokens at the beginning of name spans may have different properties than tokens within the name, and the learner can exploit this. This insight can be taken even further, with special labels for the **l**ast tokens of a name span, and for **u**nique tokens in name spans, such as *Atlanta* in the example in figure 8.2. This is called BILOU notation, and it can yield improvements in supervised named entity recognition (Ratinov and Roth, 2009).

Feature-based sequence labeling Named entity recognition was one of the first applications of conditional random fields (McCallum and Li, 2003). The use of Viterbi decoding restricts the feature function $\boldsymbol{f}(\boldsymbol{w}, \boldsymbol{y})$ to be a sum of local features, $\sum_m \boldsymbol{f}(\boldsymbol{w}, y_m, y_{m-1}, m)$,

(8.20) a. *The U.S. Army captured Atlanta on May 14 , 1864*
B-ORG I-ORG I-ORG O B-LOC O B-DATE I-DATE I-DATE I-DATE

b. *Number of glucocorticoid receptors in lymphocytes and …*
O O B-PROTEIN I-PROTEIN O B-CELLTYPE O …

Figure 8.2
BIO notation for named entity recognition. Example (8.20b) is drawn from the GENIA corpus of biomedical documents (Ohta et al., 2002).

so that each feature can consider only local adjacent tags. Typical features include tag transitions, word features for w_m and its neighbors, character-level features for prefixes and suffixes, and "word shape" features for capitalization and other orthographic properties. As an example, base features for the word *Army* in the example in (8.20a) include

(CURR-WORD:*Army*, PREV-WORD:*U.S.*, NEXT-WORD:*captured*, PREFIX-1:*A-*,

PREFIX-2:*Ar-*, SUFFIX-1:*-y*, SUFFIX-2:*-my*, SHAPE:*Xxxx*).

Features can also be obtained from a **gazetteer**, which is a list of known entity names. For example, the U.S. Social Security Administration provides a list of tens of thousands of given names—more than could be observed in any annotated corpus. Tokens or spans that match an entry in a gazetteer can receive special features; this provides a way to incorporate handcrafted resources such as name lists in a learning-driven framework.

Neural sequence labeling for NER Current research has emphasized neural sequence labeling, using similar LSTM models to those employed in part-of-speech tagging (Hammerton, 2003; Huang et al., 2015; Lample et al., 2016). The bidirectional LSTM-CRF (figure 7.4 in § 7.6) does particularly well on this task, due to its ability to model tag-to-tag dependencies. However, Strubell et al. (2017) show that **convolutional neural networks** can be equally accurate, with significant improvement in speed due to the efficiency of implementing ConvNets on **graphics processing units (GPUs)**. The key innovation in this work was the use of **dilated convolution**, which is described in more detail in § 3.4.

8.4 Tokenization

A basic problem for text analysis, first discussed in § 4.3.1, is to break the text into a sequence of discrete tokens. For alphabetic languages such as English, deterministic scripts usually suffice to achieve accurate tokenization. However, in logographic writing systems such as Chinese script, words are typically composed of a small number of characters, without intervening whitespace. The tokenization must be determined by the reader, with the potential for occasional ambiguity, as shown in figure 8.3. One approach is to match character sequences against a known dictionary (e.g., Sproat et al., 1996), using additional statistical information about word frequency. However, no dictionary is completely comprehensive, and dictionary-based approaches can struggle with out-of-vocabulary words.

Chinese word segmentation has therefore been approached as a supervised sequence labeling problem. Xue (2003) train a logistic regression classifier to make independent segmentation decisions while moving a sliding window across the document. A set of rules is then used to convert these individual classification decisions into an overall tokenization of the input. However, these individual decisions may be globally suboptimal, motivating a structure prediction approach. Peng et al. (2004) train a conditional random field to predict

(1) 日文 章魚 怎麼 說?
Japanese octopus how say
How to say octopus in Japanese?

(2) 日 文章 魚 怎麼 說?
Japan essay fish how say

Figure 8.3
An example of tokenization ambiguity in Chinese (Sproat et al., 1996).

labels of START or NONSTART on each character. More recent work has employed neural network architectures. For example, Chen et al. (2015) use an LSTM-CRF architecture, as described in § 7.6: they construct a trellis, in which each tag is scored according to the hidden state of an LSTM, and tag-tag transitions are scored according to learned transition weights. The best-scoring segmentation is then computed by the Viterbi algorithm.

8.5 Code Switching

Multilingual speakers and writers do not restrict themselves to a single language. **Code switching** is the phenomenon of switching between languages in speech and text (Poplack, 1980; Auer, 2013). Written code switching has become more common in online social media, as in the following extract from the website of Canadian President Justin Trudeau:[7]

(8.21) *Although everything written on this site est disponible en anglais*
is available in English
and in French, my personal videos seront bilingues
will be bilingual

Accurately analyzing such texts requires first determining which languages are being used. Furthermore, quantitative analysis of code switching can provide insights on the languages themselves and their relative social positions.

Code switching can be viewed as a sequence labeling problem, where the goal is to label each token as a candidate switch point. In the example above, the words *est*, *and*, and *seront* would be labeled as switch points. Solorio and Liu (2008) detect English-Spanish switch points using a supervised classifier, with features that include the word, its part of speech in each language (according to a supervised part of speech tagger), and the probabilities of the word and part of speech in each language. Nguyen and Dogruöz (2013) apply a conditional random field to the problem of detecting code switching between Turkish and Dutch.

7. As quoted in http://blogues.lapresse.ca/lagace/2008/09/08/justin-trudeau-really-parfait-bilingue/. Accessed August 21, 2017.

Speaker	Dialogue Act	Utterance
A	YES-NO-QUESTION	*So do you go college right now?*
A	ABANDONED	*Are yo-*
B	YES-ANSWER	*Yeah,*
B	STATEMENT	*It's my last year [laughter].*
A	DECLARATIVE-QUESTION	*You're a, so you're a senior now.*
B	YES-ANSWER	*Yeah,*
B	STATEMENT	*I'm working on my projects trying to graduate [laughter]*
A	APPRECIATION	*Oh, good for you.*
B	BACKCHANNEL	*Yeah.*

Figure 8.4
An example of dialogue act labeling (Stolcke et al., 2000).

Code switching is a special case of the more general problem of word level language identification, which Barman et al. (2014) address in the context of trilingual code switching between Bengali, English, and Hindi. They further observe an even more challenging phenomenon: intra word code switching, such as the use of English suffixes with Bengali roots. They therefore mark each token as either (1) belonging to one of the three languages; (2) a mix of multiple languages; (3) "universal" (e.g., symbols, numbers, emoticons); or (4) undefined.

8.6 Dialogue Acts

The sequence labeling problems that we have discussed so far have been over sequences of word tokens or characters (in the case of tokenization). However, sequence labeling can also be performed over higher-level units, such as **utterances**. **Dialogue acts** are labels over utterances in a dialogue, corresponding roughly to the speaker's intention—the utterance's **illocutionary force** (Austin, 1962). For example, an utterance may state a proposition (*it is not down on any map*), pose a question (*shall we keep chasing this murderous fish?*), or provide a response (*aye aye!*). Stolcke et al. (2000) describe how a set of 42 dialogue acts were annotated for the 1,155 conversations in the Switchboard corpus (Godfrey et al., 1992).[8]

An example is shown in figure 8.4. The annotation is performed over UTTERANCES, with the possibility of multiple utterances per **conversational turn** (in cases such as interruptions, an utterance may split over multiple turns). Some utterances are clauses (e.g., *So do you go to college right now?*), while others are single words (e.g., *yeah*). Stolcke et al. (2000)

8. Dialogue act modeling is not restricted to speech; it is relevant in any interactive conversation. For example, Jeong et al. (2009) annotate a more limited set of **speech acts** in a corpus of emails and online forums.

report that hidden Markov models (HMMs) achieve 96% accuracy on supervised utterance segmentation. The labels themselves reflect the conversational goals of the speaker: the utterance *yeah* functions as an answer in response to the question *you're a senior now*, but in the final line of the excerpt, it is a **backchannel** (demonstrating comprehension).

For task of dialogue act labeling, Stolcke et al. (2000) apply a hidden Markov model. The probability $p(\boldsymbol{w}_m \mid y_m)$ must generate the entire sequence of words in the utterance, and it is modeled as a trigram language model (§ 6.1). Stolcke et al. (2000) also account for acoustic features, which capture the **prosody** of each utterance—for example, tonal and rhythmic properties of speech, which can be used to distinguish dialogue acts such as questions and answers. These features are handled with an additional emission distribution, $p(\boldsymbol{a}_m \mid y_m)$, which is modeled with a probabilistic decision tree (Murphy, 2012). While acoustic features yield small improvements overall, they play an important role in distinguish questions from statements, and agreements from backchannels.

Recurrent neural architectures for dialogue act labeling have been proposed by Kalchbrenner and Blunsom (2013) and Ji et al. (2016), with strong empirical results. Both models are recurrent at the utterance level, so that each complete utterance updates a hidden state. The recurrent-convolutional network of Kalchbrenner and Blunsom (2013) uses convolution to obtain a representation of each individual utterance, while Ji et al. (2016) use a second level of recurrence, over individual words. This enables their method to also function as a language model, giving probabilities over sequences of words in a document.

Exercises

1. Using the Universal Dependencies part-of-speech tags, annotate the following sentences. You may examine the UD tagging guidelines. Tokenization is shown with whitespace. Don't forget about punctuation.

   (8.22) a. I try all things, I achieve what I can.
   b. It was that accursed white whale that razed me.
   c. Better to sleep with a sober cannibal, than a drunk Christian.
   d. Be it what it will, I'll go to it laughing.

2. Select three short sentences from a recent news article, and annotate them for UD part-of-speech tags. Ask a friend to annotate the same three sentences without looking at your annotations. Compute the rate of agreement, using the Kappa metric defined in § 4.5.2. Then work together to resolve any disagreements.

3. Choose one of the following morphosyntactic attributes: MOOD, TENSE, VOICE. Research the definition of this attribute on the universal dependencies website, universal dependencies.org/. Returning to the examples in the first exercise, annotate all verbs for your chosen attribute. It may be helpful to consult examples from an English-language universal dependencies corpus, available at https://github.com/Universal Dependencies/UD_English-EWT/.

4. Download a dataset annotated for universal dependencies, such as the English Treebank at https://github.com/UniversalDependencies/UD_English-EWT/. This corpus is already segmented into training, development, and test data.

   a) First, train a logistic regression or SVM classifier using character suffixes: character n-grams up to length 4. Compute the recall, precision, and F-MEASURE on the development data.

   b) Next, augment your classifier using the same character suffixes of the preceding and succeeding tokens. Again, evaluate your classifier on heldout data.

   c) Optionally, train a Viterbi-based sequence labeling model, using a toolkit such as CRFSuite (www.chokkan.org/software/crfsuite/) or your own Viterbi implementation. This is more likely to be helpful for attributes in which agreement is required between adjacent words. For example, many Romance languages require gender and number agreement for determiners, nouns, and adjectives.

5. Provide BIO-style annotation of the named entities (person, place, organization, date, or product) in the following expressions:

   (8.23) a. The third mate was Flask, a native of Tisbury, in Martha's Vineyard.
   b. Its official Nintendo announced today that they Will release the Nintendo 3DS in north America march 27 (Ritter et al., 2011b).
   c. Jessica Reif, a media analyst at Merrill Lynch & Co., said, "If they can get up and running with exclusive programming within six months, it doesn't set the venture back that far."[9]

6. Run the examples above through the online version of a named entity recognition tagger, such as the Allen NLP system here: http://demo.allennlp.org/named-entity-recognition. Do the predicted tags match your annotations?

7. Build a whitespace tokenizer for English:

   a) Using the NLTK library, download the complete text to the novel *Alice in Wonderland* (Carroll, 1865). Hold out the final 1,000 words as a test set.

   b) Label each alphanumeric character as a segmentation point, $y_m = 1$ if m is the final character of a token. Label every other character as $y_m = 0$. Then concatenate all the tokens in the training and test sets. Make sure that the number of labels $\{y_m\}_{m=1}^{M}$ is identical to the number of characters $\{c_m\}_{m=1}^{M}$ in your concatenated datasets.

   c) Train a logistic regression classifier to predict y_m, using the surrounding characters $\boldsymbol{c}_{m-5:m+5}$ as features. After training the classifier, run it on the test set, using the predicted segmentation points to retokenize the text.

9. From the Message Understanding Conference (MUC-7) dataset (Chinchor and Robinson, 1997).

d) Compute the per-character segmentation accuracy on the test set. You should be able to get at least 88% accuracy.

e) Print out a sample of segmented text from the test set, for example,

```
Thereareno mice in the air , I ' m afraid , but y oumight cat
    chabat , and that ' svery like a mouse , youknow . But
   docatseat bats , I wonder ?'
```

8. Perform the following extensions to your tokenizer in the previous problem.

a) Train a conditional random field sequence labeler, by incorporating the tag bigrams (y_{m-1}, y_m) as additional features. You may use a structured prediction library such as CRFSuite, or you may want to implement Viterbi yourself. Compare the accuracy with your classification-based approach.

b) Compute the token-level performance: treating the original tokenization as ground truth, compute the number of true positives (tokens that are in both the ground truth and predicted tokenization), false positives (tokens that are in the predicted tokenization but not the ground truth), and false negatives (tokens that are in the ground truth but not the predicted tokenization). Compute the F-MEASURE.
Hint: To match predicted and ground truth tokens, add "anchors" for the start character of each token. The number of true positives is then the size of the intersection of the sets of predicted and ground truth tokens.

c) Apply the same methodology in a more practical setting: tokenization of Chinese, which is written without whitespace. You can find annotated datasets at alias-i.com/lingpipe/demos/tutorial/chineseTokens/read-me.html.

9 Formal Language Theory

We have now seen methods for learning to label individual words, vectors of word counts, and sequences of words; we will soon proceed to more complex structural transformations. Most of these techniques could apply to counts or sequences from any discrete vocabulary; there is nothing fundamentally linguistic about, say, a hidden Markov model. This raises a basic question that this text has not yet considered: what is a language?

This chapter will take the perspective of **formal language theory**, in which a language is defined as a set of **strings**, each of which is a sequence of elements from a finite alphabet. For interesting languages, there are an infinite number of strings that are in the language, and an infinite number of strings that are not. For example:

- The set of all even-length sequences from the alphabet $\{a, b\}$, e.g., $\{\varnothing, aa, ab, ba, bb, aaaa, aaab, \ldots\}$.
- The set of all sequences from the alphabet $\{a, b\}$ that contain *aaa* as a substring, for example, $\{aaa, aaaa, baaa, aaab, \ldots\}$.
- The set of all sequences of English words (drawn from a finite dictionary) that contain at least one verb (a finite subset of the dictionary).
- The Python programming language.

Formal language theory defines classes of languages and their computational properties. Of particular interest is the computational complexity of solving the **membership problem**—determining whether a string is in a language. The chapter will focus on three classes of formal languages: regular, context-free, and "mildly" context-sensitive languages.

A key insight of 20th-century linguistics is that formal language theory can be usefully applied to natural languages such as English, by designing formal languages that capture as many properties of the natural language as possible. For many such formalisms, a useful linguistic analysis comes as a byproduct of solving the membership problem. The membership problem can be generalized to the problems of *scoring* strings for their acceptability (as in language modeling), and of **transducing** one string into another (as in translation).

9.1 Regular Languages

If you have written a **regular expression**, then you have defined a **regular language**: a regular language is any language that can be defined by a regular expression. Formally, a regular expression can include the following elements:

- A **literal character** drawn from some finite alphabet Σ.
- The **empty string** ϵ.
- The concatenation of two regular expressions RS, where R and S are both regular expressions. The resulting expression accepts any string that can be decomposed $x = yz$, where y is accepted by R and z is accepted by S.
- The alternation $R \mid S$, where R and S are both regular expressions. The resulting expression accepts a string x if it is accepted by R or it is accepted by S.
- The **Kleene star** R^*, which accepts any string x that can be decomposed into a sequence of strings which are all accepted by R.
- Parenthesization (R), which is used to limit the scope of the concatenation, alternation, and Kleene star operators.

Here are some example regular expressions:

- The set of all even length strings on the alphabet $\{a, b\}$: $((aa)|(ab)|(ba)|(bb))^*$.
- The set of all sequences of the alphabet $\{a, b\}$ that contain aaa as a substring: $(a|b)^*aaa(a|b)^*$.
- The set of all sequences of English words that contain at least one verb: W^*VW^*, where W is an alternation between all words in the dictionary, and V is an alternation between all verbs ($V \subseteq W$).

This list does not include a regular expression for the Python programming language, because this language is not regular—there is no regular expression that can capture its syntax. We will discuss why toward the end of this section.

Regular languages are **closed** under union, intersection, and concatenation. This means that if two languages L_1 and L_2 are regular, then so are the languages $L_1 \cup L_2$, $L_1 \cap L_2$, and the language of strings that can be decomposed as $s = tu$, with $s \in L_1$ and $t \in L_2$. Regular languages are also closed under negation: if L is regular, then so is the language $\overline{L} = \{s \notin L\}$.

9.1.1 Finite State Acceptors

A regular expression defines a regular language, but does not give an algorithm for determining whether a string is in the language that it defines. **Finite state automata** are theoretical models of computation on regular languages, which involve transitions between a finite number of states. The most basic type of finite state automaton is the **finite state acceptor (FSA)**, which describes the computation involved in testing if a string is a member of a language. Formally, a finite state acceptor is a tuple $M = (Q, \Sigma, q_0, F, \delta)$, consisting of:

- a finite alphabet Σ of input symbols;
- a finite set of states $Q = \{q_0, q_1, \ldots, q_n\}$;
- a start state $q_0 \in Q$;
- a set of final states $F \subseteq Q$;
- a transition function $\delta : Q \times (\Sigma \cup \{\epsilon\}) \to 2^Q$.

The transition function maps from a state and an input symbol (or empty string ϵ) to a *set* of possible resulting states.

A **path** in M is a sequence of transitions, $\pi = t_1, t_2, \ldots, t_N$, where each t_i traverses an arc in the transition function δ. The finite state acceptor M accepts a string ω if there is an accepting path, in which the initial transition t_1 begins at the start state q_0, the final transition t_N terminates in a final state in Q, and the entire input ω is consumed.

Example Consider the following FSA, M_1.

$$\Sigma = \{a, b\} \quad [9.1]$$

$$Q = \{q_0, q_1\} \quad [9.2]$$

$$F = \{q_1\} \quad [9.3]$$

$$\delta = \{(q_0, a) \to q_0, \ (q_0, b) \to q_1, \ (q_1, b) \to q_1\}. \quad [9.4]$$

This FSA defines a language over an alphabet of two symbols, a and b. The transition function δ is written as a set of arcs: $(q_0, a) \to q_0$ says that if the machine is in state q_0 and reads symbol a, it stays in q_0. Figure 9.1 provides a graphical representation of M_1. Because each pair of initial state and symbol has at most one resulting state, M_1 is **deterministic**: each string ω induces at most one accepting path. Note that there are no transitions for the symbol a in state q_1; if a is encountered in q_1, then the acceptor is stuck, and the input string is rejected.

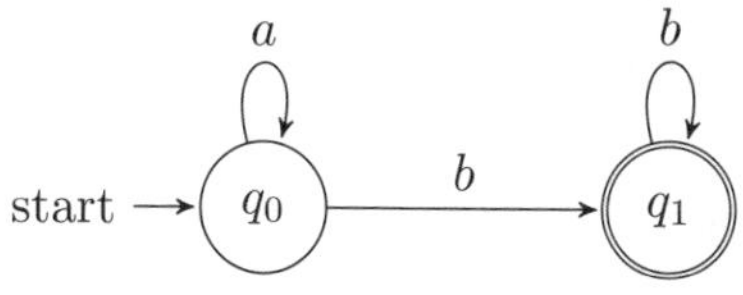

Figure 9.1
State diagram for the finite state acceptor M_1.

What strings does M_1 accept? The start state is q_0, and we have to get to q_1, because this is the only final state. Any number of a symbols can be consumed in q_0, but a b symbol is required to transition to q_1. Once there, any number of b symbols can be consumed, but an a symbol cannot. So the regular expression corresponding to the language defined by M_1 is a^*bb^*.

Computational properties of finite state acceptors The key computational question for finite state acceptors is how fast can we determine whether a string is accepted? For determistic FSAs, this computation can be performed by Dijkstra's algorithm, with time complexity $\mathcal{O}(V \log V + E)$, where V is the number of vertices in the FSA and E is the number of edges (Cormen et al., 2009). Nondeterministic FSAs (NFSAs) can include multiple transitions from a given symbol and state. Any NSFA can be converted into a deterministic FSA, but the resulting automaton may have a number of states that is exponential in the number of size of the original NFSA (Mohri et al., 2002).

9.1.2 Morphology as a Regular Language

Many words have internal structure, such as prefixes and suffixes that shape their meaning. The study of word-internal structure is the domain of **morphology**, of which there are two main types:

- **Derivational morphology** describes the use of affixes to convert a word from one grammatical category to another (e.g., from the noun *grace* to the adjective *graceful*), or to change the meaning of the word (e.g., from *grace* to *disgrace*).
- **Inflectional morphology** describes the addition of details such as gender, number, person, and tense (e.g., the *-ed* suffix for past tense in English).

Morphology is a rich topic in linguistics, deserving of a course in its own right.[1] The focus here will be on the use of finite state automata for morphological analysis. The current section deals with derivational morphology; inflectional morphology is discussed in § 9.1.4.

Suppose that we want to write a program that accepts only those words that are constructed in accordance with the rules of English derivational morphology:

(9.1) a. grace, graceful, gracefully, *gracelyful
b. disgrace, *ungrace, disgraceful, disgracefully
c. allure, *allureful, alluring, alluringly
d. fairness, unfair, *disfair, fairly

1. A good starting point would be a chapter from a linguistics textbook (e.g., Akmajian et al., 2010; Bender, 2013). A key simplification in this chapter is the focus on affixes at the sole method of derivation and inflection. English makes use of affixes, but also incorporates **apophony**, such as the inflection of *foot* to *feet*. Semitic languages like Arabic and Hebrew feature a template-based system of morphology, in which roots are triples of consonants (e.g., *ktb*), and words are created by adding vowels: ***kataba*** (Arabic: he wrote), ***kutub*** (books), ***maktab*** (desk). For more detail on morphology, see texts from Haspelmath and Sims (2013) and Lieber (2015).

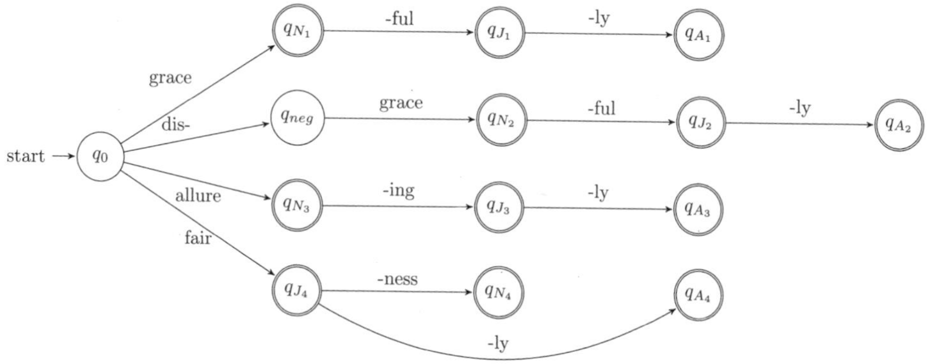

Figure 9.2
A finite state acceptor for a fragment of English derivational morphology. Each path represents possible derivations from a single root form.

(Recall that the asterisk indicates that a linguistic example is judged unacceptable by fluent speakers of a language.) These examples cover only a tiny corner of English derivational morphology, but a number of things stand out. The suffix *-ful* converts the nouns *grace* and *disgrace* into adjectives, and the suffix *-ly* converts adjectives into adverbs. These suffixes must be applied in the correct order, as shown by the unacceptability of **gracelyful*. The *-ful* suffix works for only some words, as shown by the use of *alluring* as the adjectival form of *allure*. Other changes are made with prefixes, such as the derivation of *disgrace* from *grace*, which roughly corresponds to a negation; however, *fair* is negated with the *un-* prefix instead. Finally, while the first three examples suggest that the direction of derivation is noun → adjective → adverb, the example of *fair* suggests that the adjective can also be the base form, with the *-ness* suffix performing the conversion to a noun.

Can we build a computer program that accepts only well-formed English words, and rejects all others? This might at first seem trivial to solve with a brute-force attack: simply make a dictionary of all valid English words. But such an approach fails to account for morphological **productivity**—the applicability of existing morphological rules to new words and names, such as *Trump* to *Trumpy* and *Trumpkin*, and *Clinton* to *Clintonian* and *Clintonite*. We need an approach that represents morphological rules explicitly, and for this we will try a finite state acceptor.

The dictionary approach can be implemented as a finite state acceptor, with the vocabulary Σ equal to the vocabulary of English and a transition from the start state to the accepting state for each word. But this would of course fail to generalize beyond the original vocabulary and would not capture anything about the **morphotactic** rules that govern derivations from new words. The first step toward a more general approach is shown in figure 9.2, which is the state diagram for a finite state acceptor in which the vocabulary consists of **morphemes**, which include **stems** (e.g., *grace, allure*) and **affixes** (e.g., *dis-, -ing, -ly*).

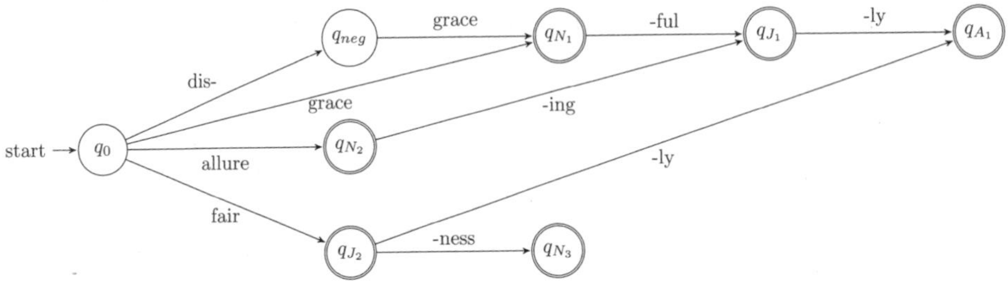

Figure 9.3
Minimization of the finite state acceptor shown in figure 9.2.

This finite state acceptor consists of a set of paths leading away from the start state, with derivational affixes added along the path. Except for q_{neg}, the states on these paths are all final, so the FSA will accept *disgrace*, *disgraceful*, and *disgracefully*, but not *dis-*.

This FSA can be **minimized** to the form shown in figure 9.3, which makes the generality of the finite state approach more apparent. For example, the transition from q_0 to q_{J_2} can be made to accept not only *fair* but any single-morpheme (**monomorphemic**) adjective that takes *-ness* and *-ly* as suffixes. In this way, the finite state acceptor can easily be extended: as new word stems are added to the vocabulary, their derived forms will be accepted automatically. Of course, this FSA would still need to be extended considerably to cover even this small fragment of English morphology. As shown by cases like *music* → *musical*, *athlete* → *athletic*, English includes several classes of nouns, each with its own rules for derivation.

The FSAs shown in figures 9.2 and 9.3 accept *allureing*, not *alluring*. This reflects a distinction between morphology—the question of which morphemes to use, and in what order—and **orthography**—the question of how the morphemes are rendered in written language. Just as orthography requires dropping the *e* preceding the *-ing* suffix, **phonology** imposes a related set of constraints on how words are rendered in speech. As we will see soon, these issues can be handled by **finite state transducers**, which are finite state automata that take inputs and produce outputs.

9.1.3 Weighted Finite State Acceptors

According to the FSA treatment of morphology, every word is either in or out of the language, with no wiggle room. Perhaps you agree that *musicky* and *fishful* are not valid English words; but if forced to choose, you probably find *a fishful stew* or *a musicky tribute* preferable to *behaving disgracelyful*. Rather than asking whether a word is acceptable, we might like to ask how acceptable it is. Aronoff (1976, page 36) puts it another way: "Though many things are possible in morphology, some are more possible than others." But finite state acceptors give no way to express preferences among technically valid choices.

Weighted finite state acceptors (WFSAs) are generalizations of FSAs, in which each accepting path is assigned a score, computed from the transitions, the initial state, and the final state. Formally, a weighted finite state acceptor $M = (Q, \Sigma, \lambda, \rho, \delta)$ consists of

- a finite set of states $Q = \{q_0, q_1, \ldots, q_n\}$;
- a finite alphabet Σ of input symbols;
- an initial weight function, $\lambda : Q \rightarrow \mathbb{R}$;
- a final weight function, $\rho : Q \rightarrow \mathbb{R}$;
- a transition function, $\delta : Q \times \Sigma \times Q \rightarrow \mathbb{R}$.

WFSAs depart from the FSA formalism in three ways: every state can be an initial state, with score $\lambda(q)$; every state can be an accepting state, with score $\rho(q)$; transitions are possible between any pair of states on any input, with a score $\delta(q_i, \omega, q_j)$. Nonetheless, FSAs can be viewed as a special case: for any FSA M, we can build an equivalent WFSA by setting $\lambda(q) = \infty$ for all $q \neq q_0$, $\rho(q) = \infty$ for all $q \notin F$, and $\delta(q_i, \omega, q_j) = \infty$ for all transitions $\{(q_1, \omega) \rightarrow q_2\}$ that are not permitted by the transition function of M.

The total score for any path $\pi = t_1, t_2, \ldots, t_N$ is equal to the sum of these scores,

$$d(\pi) = \lambda(\text{from-state}(t_1)) + \sum_{n}^{N} \delta(t_n) + \rho(\text{to-state}(t_N)). \qquad [9.5]$$

A **shortest-path algorithm** is used to find the minimum-cost path through a WFSA for string ω, with time complexity $\mathcal{O}(E + V \log V)$, where E is the number of edges and V is the number of vertices (Cormen et al., 2009).[2]

N-gram language models as WFSAs In n-gram language models (see § 6.1), the probability of a sequence of tokens $w_1, w_2, \ldots, w_M$ is modeled as

$$\mathrm{p}(w_1, \ldots, w_M) \approx \prod_{m=1}^{M} \mathrm{p}_n(w_m \mid w_{m-1}, \ldots, w_{m-n+1}). \qquad [9.6]$$

The log-probability under an n-gram language model can be modeled in a WFSA. First consider a unigram language model. We need only a single state q_0, with transition scores $\delta(q_0, \omega, q_0) = \log \mathrm{p}_1(\omega)$. The initial and final scores can be set to zero. Then the path score for $w_1, w_2, \ldots, w_M$ is equal to

$$0 + \sum_{m}^{M} \delta(q_0, w_m, q_0) + 0 = \sum_{m}^{M} \log \mathrm{p}_1(w_m). \qquad [9.7]$$

2. Shortest-path algorithms find the path with the minimum cost. In many cases, the path weights are log-probabilities, so we want the path with the maximum score, which can be accomplished by making each local score into a *negative* log-probability.

For an n-gram language model with $n > 1$, we need probabilities that condition on the past history. For example, in a bigram language model, the transition weights must represent $\log p_2(w_m \mid w_{m-1})$. The transition scoring function must somehow "remember" the previous word or words. This can be done by adding more states: to model the bigram probability $p_2(w_m \mid w_{m-1})$, we need a state for every possible w_{m-1}—a total of V states. The construction indexes each state q_i by a context event $w_{m-1} = i$. The weights are then assigned as follows:

$$\delta(q_i, \omega, q_j) = \begin{cases} \log \Pr(w_m = j \mid w_{m-1} = i), & \omega = j \\ -\infty, & \omega \neq j \end{cases}$$

$$\lambda(q_i) = \log \Pr(w_1 = i \mid w_0 = \square)$$

$$\rho(q_i) = \log \Pr(w_{M+1} = \blacksquare \mid w_M = i).$$

The transition function is designed to ensure that the context is recorded accurately: we can move to state j on input ω only if $\omega = j$; otherwise, transitioning to state j is forbidden by the weight of $-\infty$. The initial weight function $\lambda(q_i)$ is the log-probability of receiving i as the first token, and the final weight function $\rho(q_i)$ is the log-probability of receiving an "end-of-string" token after observing $w_M = i$.

***Semiring weighted finite state acceptors** The n-gram language model WFSA is deterministic: each input has exactly one accepting path, for which the WFSA computes a score. In nondeterministic WFSAs, a given input may have multiple accepting paths. In some applications, the score for the input is aggregated across all such paths. Such aggregate scores can be computed by generalizing WFSAs with **semiring notation**, first introduced in § 7.7.3.

Let $d(\pi)$ represent the total score for path $\pi = t_1, t_2, \ldots, t_N$, which is computed as,

$$d(\pi) = \lambda(\text{from-state}(t_1)) \otimes \delta(t_1) \otimes \delta(t_2) \otimes \ldots \otimes \delta(t_N) \otimes \rho(\text{to-state}(t_N)). \quad [9.8]$$

This is a generalization of equation 9.5 to semiring notation, using the semiring multiplication operator $\otimes$ in place of addition.

Now let $s(\omega)$ represent the total score for all paths $\Pi(\omega)$ that consume input ω,

$$s(\omega) = \bigoplus_{\pi \in \Pi(\omega)} d(\pi). \quad [9.9]$$

Here, semiring addition ($\oplus$) is used to combine the scores of multiple paths.

The generalization to semirings covers a number of useful special cases. In the log-probability semiring, multiplication is defined as $\log p(x) \otimes \log p(y) = \log p(x) + \log p(y)$, and addition is defined as $\log p(x) \oplus \log p(y) = \log(p(x) + p(y))$. Thus, $s(\omega)$ represents the log-probability of accepting input ω, marginalizing over all paths $\pi \in \Pi(\omega)$. In the **boolean semiring**, the $\otimes$ operator is logical conjunction, and the $\oplus$ operator is logical disjunction.

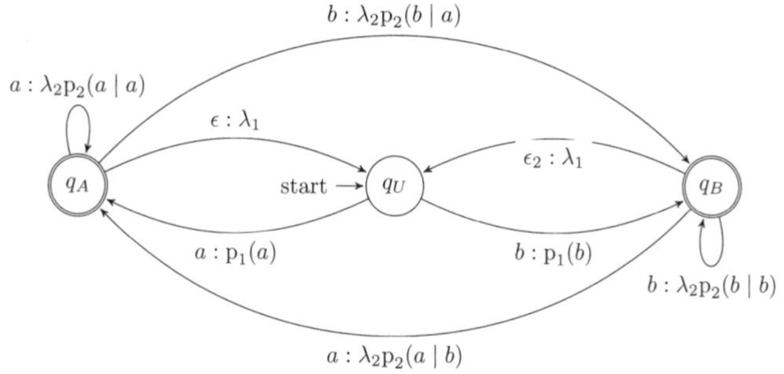

Figure 9.4
WFSA implementing an interpolated bigram/unigram language model, on the alphabet $\Sigma = \{a, b\}$. For simplicity, the WFSA is contrained to force the first token to be generated from the unigram model and does not model the emission of the end-of-sequence token.

This reduces to the special case of unweighted finite state acceptors, where the score $s(\omega)$ is a boolean indicating whether there exists any accepting path for ω. In the **tropical semiring**, the $\oplus$ operator is a maximum, so the resulting score is the score of the best-scoring path through the WFSA. The OPENFST toolkit uses semirings and polymorphism to implement general algorithms for weighted finite state automata (Allauzen et al., 2007).

***Interpolated n-gram language models** Recall from § 6.2.3 that an interpolated n-gram language model combines the probabilities from multiple n-gram models. For example, an interpolated bigram language model computes the probability,

$$\hat{p}(w_m \mid w_{m-1}) = \lambda_1 p_1(w_m) + \lambda_2 p_2(w_m \mid w_{m-1}), \qquad [9.10]$$

with $\hat{p}$ indicating the interpolated probability, p_2 indicating the bigram probability, and p_1 indicating the unigram probability. Setting $\lambda_2 = (1 - \lambda_1)$ ensures that the probabilities sum to one.

Interpolated bigram language models can be implemented using a nondeterministic WFSA (Knight and May, 2009). The basic idea is shown in figure 9.4. In an interpolated bigram language model, there is one state for each element in the vocabulary—in this case, the states q_A and q_B—which capture the contextual conditioning in the bigram probabilities. To model unigram probabilities, there is an additional state q_U, which "forgets" the context. Transitions out of q_U involve unigram probabilities, $p_1(a)$ and $p_2(b)$; transitions into q_U emit the empty symbol ϵ and have probability λ_1, reflecting the interpolation weight for the unigram model. The interpolation weight for the bigram model is included in the weight of the transition $q_A \rightarrow q_B$.

The epsilon transitions into q_U make this WFSA nondeterministic. Consider the score for the sequence (a, b, b). The initial state is q_U, so the symbol a is generated with score

$p_1(a)$[3] Next, we can generate b from the unigram model by taking the transition $q_A \to q_B$, with score $\lambda_2 p_2(b \mid a)$. Alternatively, we can take a transition back to q_U with score λ_1 and then emit b from the unigram model with score $p_1(b)$. To generate the final b token, we face the same choice: emit it directly from the self-transition to q_B or transition to q_U first.

The total score for the sequence (a, b, b) is the semiring sum over all accepting paths,

$$\begin{aligned} s(a,b,b) = & \big(p_1(a) \otimes \lambda_2 p_2(b \mid a) \otimes \lambda_2 p(b \mid b)\big) \\ & \oplus \big(p_1(a) \otimes \lambda_1 \otimes p_1(b) \otimes \lambda_2 p(b \mid b)\big) \\ & \oplus \big(p_1(a) \otimes \lambda_2 p_2(b \mid a) \otimes p_1(b) \otimes p_1(b)\big) \\ & \oplus \big(p_1(a) \otimes \lambda_1 \otimes p_1(b) \otimes p_1(b) \otimes p_1(b)\big). \end{aligned} \quad [9.11]$$

Each line in equation 9.11 represents the probability of a specific path through the WFSA. In the probability semiring, $\otimes$ is multiplication, so that each path is the product of each transition weight, which are themselves probabilities. The $\oplus$ operator is addition, so that the total score is the sum of the scores (probabilities) for each path. This corresponds to the probability under the interpolated bigram language model.

9.1.4 Finite State Transducers

Finite state acceptors can determine whether a string is in a regular language, and weighted finite state acceptors can compute a score for every string over a given alphabet. **Finite state transducers (FSTs)** extend the formalism further, by adding an output symbol to each transition. Formally, a finite state transducer is a tuple $T = (Q, \Sigma, \Omega, \lambda, \rho, \delta)$, with Ω representing an output vocabulary and the transition function $\delta : Q \times (\Sigma \cup \epsilon) \times (\Omega \cup \epsilon) \times Q \to \mathbb{R}$ mapping from states, input symbols, and output symbols to states. The remaining elements $(Q, \Sigma, \lambda, \rho)$ are identical to their definition in weighted finite state acceptors (§ 9.1.3). Thus, each path through the FST T transduces the input string into an output.

String edit distance The **edit distance** between two strings s and t is a measure of how many operations are required to transform one string into another. There are several ways to compute edit distance, but one of the most popular is the Levenshtein edit distance, which counts the minimum number of insertions, deletions, and substitutions. This can be computed by a one-state weighted finite state transducer, in which the input and output alphabets are identical. For simplicity, consider the alphabet $\Sigma = \Omega = \{a, b\}$. The edit distance can be computed by a one-state transducer with the following transitions:

$$\delta(q,a,a,q) = \delta(q,b,b,q) = 0 \quad [9.12]$$

$$\delta(q,a,b,q) = \delta(q,b,a,q) = 1 \quad [9.13]$$

3. We could model the sequence-initial bigram probability $p_2(a \mid \square)$, but for simplicity, the WFSA does not admit this possibility, which would require another state.

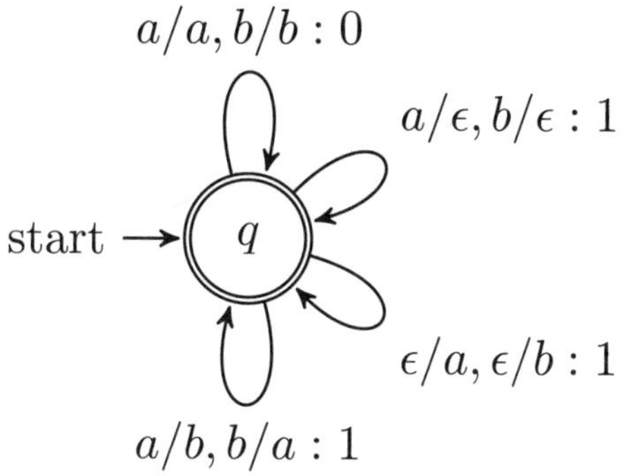

Figure 9.5
State diagram for the Levenshtein edit distance finite state transducer. The label $x/y : c$ indicates a cost of c for a transition with input x and output y.

$$\delta(q, a, \epsilon, q) = \delta(q, b, \epsilon, q) = 1 \quad [9.14]$$

$$\delta(q, \epsilon, a, q) = \delta(q, \epsilon, b, q) = 1. \quad [9.15]$$

The state diagram is shown in figure 9.5.

For a given string pair, there are multiple paths through the transducer: the best-scoring path from *dessert* to *desert* involves a single deletion, for a total score of 1; the worst-scoring path involves seven deletions and six additions, for a score of 13.

The Porter stemmer The Porter (1980) stemming algorithm is a "lexicon-free" algorithm for stripping suffixes from English words, using a sequence of character-level rules. Each rule can be described by an unweighted finite state transducer. The first rule is:

-sses → *-ss*	e.g., *dresses* → *dress*	[9.16]
-ies → *-i*	e.g., *parties* → *parti*	[9.17]
-ss → *-ss*	e.g., *dress* → *dress*	[9.18]
-s → ϵ	e.g., *cats* → *cat*	[9.19]

The final two lines appear to conflict; they are meant to be interpreted as an instruction to remove a terminal *-s* unless it is part of an *-ss* ending. A state diagram to handle just these final two lines is shown in figure 9.6. Make sure you understand how this finite state transducer handles *cats*, *steps*, *bass*, and *basses*.

Inflectional morphology In **inflectional morphology**, word **lemmas** are modified to add grammatical information such as tense, number, and case. For example, many English nouns are pluralized by the suffix *-s*, and many verbs are converted to past tense by the suffix *-ed*. English's inflectional morphology is considerably simpler than many of the world's

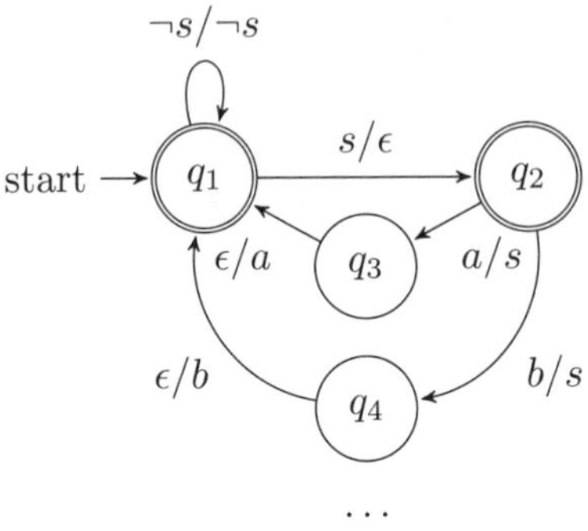

Figure 9.6
State diagram for final two lines of step 1a of the Porter stemming diagram. States q_3 and q_4 "remember" the observations *a* and *b*, respectively; the ellipsis ... represents additional states for each symbol in the input alphabet. The notation $\neg s/\neg s$ is not part of the FST formalism; it is a shorthand to indicate a set of self-transition arcs for every input/output symbol except *s*.

Table 9.1
Spanish verb inflections for the present indicative tense. Each row represents a person and number, and each column is a regular example from a class of verbs, as indicated by the ending of the infinitive form.

infinitive	cantar (to sing)	comer (to eat)	vivir (to live)
yo (1st singular)	canto	como	vivo
tu (2nd singular)	cantas	comes	vives
él, ella, usted (3rd singular)	canta	come	vive
nosotros (1st plural)	cantamos	comemos	vivimos
vosotros (2nd plural, informal)	cantáis	coméis	vivís
ellos, ellas (3rd plural); ustedes (2nd plural)	cantan	comen	viven

languages. For example, Romance languages (derived from Latin) feature complex systems of verb suffixes which must agree with the person and number of the verb, as shown in table 9.1.

The task of morphological analysis is to read a form like *canto*, and output an analysis like CANTAR+VERB+PRESIND+1P+SING, where +PRESIND describes the tense as present indicative, +1P indicates the first person, and +SING indicates the singular number. The task of morphological generation is the reverse, going from CANTAR+VERB+PRESIND+1P+SING to *canto*. Finite state transducers are an attractive solution, because they can solve both problems with a single model (Beesley and Karttunen, 2003). As an example, figure 9.7 shows a fragment of a finite state transducer for Spanish inflectional morphology. The input vocabulary Σ corresponds to the set of letters used in Spanish spelling, and the output vocabulary Ω corresponds to these same letters, plus the vocabulary of morphological features (e.g., +SING, +VERB). In figure 9.7, there are two paths that

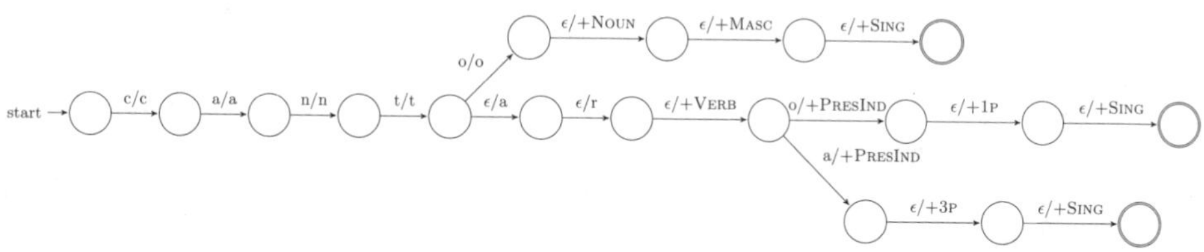

Figure 9.7
Fragment of a finite state transducer for Spanish morphology. There are two accepting paths for the input *canto*: *canto*+NOUN+MASC+SING (masculine singular noun, meaning a song) and *cantar*+VERB+PRESIND+1P+SING (I sing). There is also an accepting path for *canta*, with output *cantar*+VERB+PRESIND+3P+SING (he/she sings).

take *canto* as input, corresponding to the verb and noun meanings; the choice between these paths could be guided by a part-of-speech tagger. By **inversion**, the inputs and outputs for each transition are switched, resulting in a finite state generator, capable of producing the correct **surface form** for any morphological analysis.

Finite state morphological analyzers and other unweighted transducers can be designed by hand. The designer's goal is to avoid **overgeneration**—accepting strings or making transductions that are not valid in the language—as well as **undergeneration**—failing to accept strings or transductions that are valid. For example, a pluralization transducer that does not accept *foot/feet* would undergenerate. Suppose we "fix" the transducer to accept this example, but as a side effect, it now accepts *boot/beet*; the transducer would then be said to overgenerate. If a transducer accepts *foot/foots* but not *foot/feet*, then it simultaneously overgenerates and undergenerates.

Finite state composition Designing finite state transducers to capture the full range of morphological phenomena in any real language is a huge task. Modularization is a classic computer science approach for this situation: decompose a large and unwieldly problem into a set of subproblems, each of which will hopefully have a concise solution. Finite state automata can be modularized through **composition**: feeding the output of one transducer T_1 as the input to another transducer T_2, written $T_2 \circ T_1$. Formally, if there exists some y such that $(x, y) \in T_1$ (meaning that T_1 produces output y on input x), and $(y, z) \in T_2$, then $(x, z) \in (T_2 \circ T_1)$. Because finite state transducers are closed under composition, there is guaranteed to be a single finite state transducer that $T_3 = T_2 \circ T_1$, which can be constructed as a machine with one state for each pair of states in T_1 and T_2 (Mohri et al., 2002).

Example: morphology and orthography In English morphology, the suffix *-ed* is added to signal the past tense for many verbs: *cook*→*cooked*, *want*→*wanted*, etc. However, English **orthography** dictates that this process cannot produce a spelling with consecutive *e*'s, so that *bake*→*baked*, not *bakeed*. A modular solution is to build separate transducers for morphology and orthography. The morphological transducer T_M transduces from *bake*+PAST to *bake*+*ed*, with the + symbol indicating a segment boundary. The input alphabet of T_M

includes the lexicon of words and the set of morphological features; the output alphabet includes the characters *a-z* and the + boundary marker. Next, an orthographic transducer T_O is responsible for the transductions *cook+ed* → *cooked*, and *bake+ed* → *baked*. The input alphabet of T_O must be the same as the output alphabet for T_M, and the output alphabet is simply the characters *a-z*. The composed transducer $(T_O \circ T_M)$ then transduces from *bake*+PAST to the spelling *baked*. The design of T_O is left as an exercise.

Example: hidden Markov models Hidden Markov models (chapter 7) can be viewed as weighted finite state transducers, and they can be constructed by transduction. Recall that a hidden Markov model defines a joint probability over words and tags, $\mathrm{p}(\boldsymbol{w}, \boldsymbol{y})$, which can be computed as a path through a **trellis** structure. This trellis is itself a weighted finite state acceptor, with edges between all adjacent nodes $q_{m-1,i} \rightarrow q_{m,j}$ on input $Y_m = j$. The edge weights are log-probabilities,

$$\delta(q_{m-1,i}, Y_m = j, q_{m,j}) = \log \mathrm{p}(w_m, Y_m = j \mid Y_{m-i} = j) \quad [9.20]$$

$$= \log \mathrm{p}(w_m \mid Y_m = j) + \log \Pr(Y_m = j \mid Y_{m-1} = i). \quad [9.21]$$

Because there is only one possible transition for each tag Y_m, this WFSA is deterministic. The score for any tag sequence $\{y_m\}_{m=1}^{M}$ is the sum of these log-probabilities, corresponding to the total log-probability $\log \mathrm{p}(\boldsymbol{w}, \boldsymbol{y})$. Furthermore, the trellis can be constructed by the composition of simpler FSTs.

- First, construct a "transition" transducer to represent a bigram probability model over tag sequences, T_T. This transducer is almost identical to the n-gram language model acceptor in § 9.1.3: there is one state for each tag, and the edge weights are equal to the transition log-probabilities, $\delta(q_i, j, j, q_j) = \log \Pr(Y_m = j \mid Y_{m-1} = i)$. Note that T_T is a transducer, with identical input and output at each arc; this makes it possible to compose T_T with other transducers.
- Next, construct an "emission" transducer to represent the probability of words given tags, T_E. This transducer has only a single state, with arcs for each word/tag pair, $\delta(q_0, i, j, q_0) = \log \Pr(W_m = j \mid Y_m = i)$. The input vocabulary is the set of all tags, and the output vocabulary is the set of all words.
- The composition $T_E \circ T_T$ is a finite state transducer with one state per tag, as shown in figure 9.8. Each state has $V \times K$ outgoing edges, representing transitions to each of the K other states, with outputs for each of the V words in the vocabulary. The weights for these edges are equal to

$$\delta(q_i, Y_m = j, w_m, q_j) = \log \mathrm{p}(w_m, Y_m = j \mid Y_{m-1} = i). \quad [9.22]$$

- The trellis is a structure with $M \times K$ nodes, for each of the M words to be tagged and each of the K tags in the tagset. It can be built by composition of $(T_E \circ T_T)$ against an unweighted **chain FSA** $M_A(\boldsymbol{w})$ that is specially constructed to accept only a given input $w_1, w_2, \ldots, w_M$,

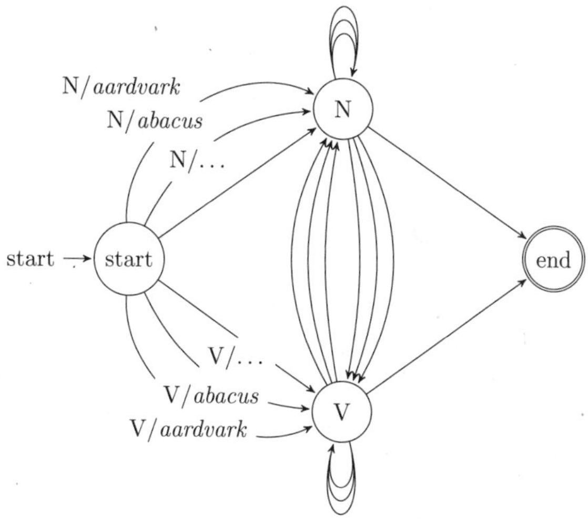

Figure 9.8
Finite state transducer for hidden Markov models, with a small tagset of **n**ouns and **v**erbs. For each pair of tags (including self-loops), there is an edge for every word in the vocabulary. For simplicity, input and output are only shown for the edges from the start state. Weights are also omitted from the diagram; for each edge from q_i to q_j, the weight is equal to $\log \mathrm{p}(w_m, Y_m = j \mid Y_{m-1} = i)$, except for edges to the end state, which are equal to $\log \Pr(Y_m = \blacklozenge \mid Y_{m-1} = i)$.

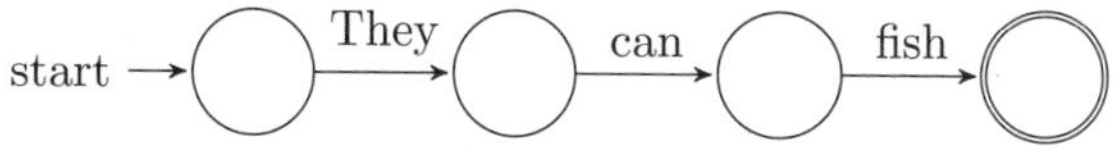

Figure 9.9
Chain finite state acceptor for the input *They can fish*.

shown in figure 9.9. The trellis for input $\boldsymbol{w}$ is built from the composition $M_A(\boldsymbol{w}) \circ (T_E \circ T_T)$. Composing with the unweighted $M_A(\boldsymbol{w})$ does not affect the edge weights from $(T_E \circ T_T)$, but it selects the subset of paths that generate the word sequence $\boldsymbol{w}$.

9.1.5 *Learning Weighted Finite State Automata

In generative models such as n-gram language models and hidden Markov models, the edge weights correspond to log-probabilities, which can be obtained from relative frequency estimation. However, in other cases, we wish to learn the edge weights from input/output pairs. This is difficult in nondeterministic finite state automata, because we do not observe the specific arcs that are traversed in accepting the input, or in transducing from input to output. The path through the automaton is a **latent variable**.

Chapter 5 presented one method for learning with latent variables: expectation-maximization (EM). This involves computing a distribution $q(\cdot)$ over the latent variable and iterating between updates to this distribution and updates to the parameters—in this case, the arc weights. The **forward-backward algorithm** (§ 7.5.3) describes a dynamic program for computing a distribution over arcs in the trellis structure of a hidden Markov model, but this is a special case of the more general problem for finite state automata. Eisner (2002) describes an **expectation semiring**, which enables the expected number of transitions across each arc to be computed through a semiring shortest-path algorithm. Alternative approaches for generative models include Markov Chain Monte Carlo (Chiang et al., 2010) and spectral learning (Balle et al., 2011).

Further afield, we can take a perceptron-style approach, with each arc corresponding to a feature. The classic perceptron update would update the weights by subtracting the difference between the feature vector corresponding to the predicted path and the feature vector corresponding to the correct path. Because the path is not observed, we resort to a **latent variable perceptron**. The model is described formally in § 12.4, but the basic idea is to compute an update from the difference between the features from the predicted path and the features for the best-scoring path that generates the correct output.

9.2 Context-Free Languages

Beyond the class of regular languages lie the context-free languages. An example of a language that is context free but not finite state is the set of arithmetic expressions with balanced parentheses. Intuitively, to accept only strings in this language, an FSA would have to "count" the number of left parentheses, and make sure that they are balanced against the number of right parentheses. An arithmetic expression can be arbitrarily long, yet by definition an FSA has a finite number of states. Thus, for any FSA, there will be a string with too many parentheses to count. More formally, the **pumping lemma** is a proof technique for showing that languages are not regular. It is typically demonstrated for the simpler case $a^n b^n$, the language of strings containing a sequence of a's, and then an equal-length sequence of b's.[4]

There are at least two arguments for the relevance of nonregular formal languages to linguistics. First, there are natural language phenomena that are argued to be isomorphic to $a^n b^n$. For English, the classic example is **center embedding**, shown in figure 9.10. The initial expression *the dog* specifies a single dog. Embedding this expression into *the cat* ___ *chased* specifies a particular cat—the one chased by the dog. This cat can then be embedded again to specify a goat, in the less felicitous but arguably grammatical expression, *the goat the cat the dog chased kissed*, which refers to the goat who was kissed by the cat that was chased by the dog. Chomsky (1957) argues that to be grammatical, a center-embedded construction must be balanced: if it contains n noun phrases (e.g., *the cat*), they

4. Details of the proof can be found in an introductory computer science theory textbook (e.g., Sipser, 2012).

		the dog		
	the cat	the dog	chased	
the goat	the cat	the dog	chased	kissed
		…		

Figure 9.10
Three levels of center embedding.

must be followed by exactly $n-1$ verbs. An FSA that could recognize such expressions would also be capable of recognizing the language $a^n b^n$. Because we can prove that no FSA exists for $a^n b^n$, no FSA can exist for center embedded constructions either. English includes center embedding, and so the argument goes, English grammar as a whole cannot be regular.[5]

A more practical argument for moving beyond regular languages is modularity. Many linguistic phenomena—especially in syntax—involve constraints that apply at long distance. Consider the problem of determiner-noun number agreement in English: we can say *the coffee* and *these coffees*, but not **these coffee*. By itself, this is easy enough to model in an FSA. However, fairly complex modifying expressions can be inserted between the determiner and the noun:

(9.2) a. the burnt coffee
b. the badly-ground coffee
c. the burnt and badly-ground Italian coffee
d. these burnt and badly-ground Italian coffees
e. *these burnt and badly-ground Italian coffee

Again, an FSA can be designed to accept modifying expressions such as *burnt and badly-ground Italian*. Let's call this FSA F_M. To reject the final example, a finite state acceptor must somehow "remember" that the determiner was plural when it reaches the noun *coffee* at the end of the expression. The only way to do this is to make two identical copies of F_M: one for singular determiners, and one for plurals. While this is possible in the finite state framework, it is inconvenient—especially in languages where more than one attribute of the noun is marked by the determiner. **Context-free languages** facilitate modularity across such long-range dependencies.

5. The claim that arbitrarily deep center-embedded expressions are grammatical has drawn skepticism. Corpus evidence shows that embeddings of depth three are exceedingly rare (Karlsson, 2007) and that embeddings of depth greater than three are completely unattested. If center embedding is capped at some finite depth, then it is regular.

9.2.1 Context-Free Grammars

Context-free languages are specified by **context-free grammars (CFGs),** which are tuples (N, Σ, R, S) consisting of:

- a finite set of **nonterminals** N;
- a finite alphabet Σ of **terminal symbols**;
- a set of **production rules** R, each of the form $A \to \beta$, where $A \in N$ and $\beta \in (\Sigma \cup N)^*$;
- a designated start symbol S.

In the production rule $A \to \beta$, the left-hand side (LHS) A must be a nonterminal; the right-hand side (RHS) can be a sequence of terminals or nonterminals, $\{n, \sigma\}^*, n \in N, \sigma \in \Sigma$. A nonterminal can appear on the left-hand side of many production rules. A nonterminal can appear on both the left-hand side and the right-hand side; this is a **recursive production** and is analogous to self-loops in finite state automata. The name "context free" is based on the property that the production rule depends only on the LHS, and not on its ancestors or neighbors; this is analogous to Markov property of finite state automata, in which the behavior at each step depends only on the current state, and not on the path by which that state was reached.

A **derivation** τ is a sequence of steps from the start symbol S to a surface string $\boldsymbol{w} \in \Sigma^*$, which is the **yield** of the derivation. A string $\boldsymbol{w}$ is in a context-free language if there is some derivation from S yielding $\boldsymbol{w}$. **Parsing** is the problem of finding a derivation for a string in a grammar. Algorithms for parsing are described in chapter 10.

Like regular expressions, context-free grammars define the language but not the computation necessary to recognize it. The context-free analogues to finite state acceptors are **pushdown automata**, a theoretical model of computation in which input symbols can be pushed onto a stack with potentially infinite depth. For more details, see Sipser (2012).

Example Figure 9.11 shows a context-free grammar for arithmetic expressions such as $1 + 2 \div 3 - 4$. In this grammar, the terminal symbols include the digits $\{\texttt{1}, \texttt{2}, \ldots, \texttt{9}\}$ and the operators $\{+, -, \times, \div\}$. The rules include the | symbol, a notational convenience that makes

$$\text{S} \to \text{S Op S} \mid \text{Num}$$

$$\text{Op} \to + \mid - \mid \times \mid \div$$

$$\text{Num} \to \text{Num Digit} \mid \text{Digit}$$

$$\text{Digit} \to \texttt{0} \mid \texttt{1} \mid \texttt{2} \mid \ldots \mid \texttt{9}$$

Figure 9.11
A context-free grammar for arithmetic expressions.

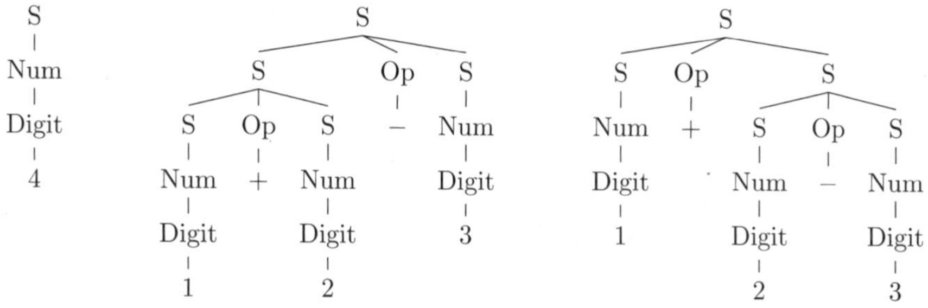

Figure 9.12
Some example derivations from the arithmetic grammar in figure 9.11.

it possible to specify multiple right-hand sides on a single line: the statement $A \rightarrow x \mid y$ defines *two* productions, $A \rightarrow x$ and $A \rightarrow y$. This grammar is recursive: the nonterminals S and NUM can produce themselves.

Derivations are typically shown as trees, with production rules applied from the top to the bottom. The tree on the left in figure 9.12 describes the derivation of a single digit, through the sequence of productions S → NUM → DIGIT → 4 (these are all **unary productions**, because the right-hand side contains a single element). The other two trees in figure 9.12 show alternative derivations of the string $1 + 2 - 3$. The existence of multiple derivations for a string indicates that the grammar is **ambiguous**.

Context-free derivations can also be written out according to the preorder tree traversal.[6] For the two derivations of `1 + 2 - 3` in figure 9.12, the notation is:

(S (S (S (Num (Digit 1))) (Op +) (S (Num (Digit 2)))) (Op −) (S (Num (Digit 3)))) [9.23]

(S (S (Num (Digit 1))) (Op +) (S (Num (Digit 2)) (Op −) (S (Num (Digit 3))))). [9.24]

Grammar equivalence and Chomsky Normal Form A single context-free language can be expressed by more than one context-free grammar. For example, the following two grammars both define the language $a^n b^n$ for $n > 0$:

$S \rightarrow aSb \mid ab$

$S \rightarrow aSb \mid aabb \mid ab$

Two grammars are **weakly equivalent** if they generate the same strings. Two grammars are **strongly equivalent** if they generate the same strings via the same derivations. The grammars above are only weakly equivalent.

6. This is a depth-first, left-to-right search that prints each node the first time it is encountered (Cormen et al., 2009, chapter 12).

In **Chomsky Normal Form (CNF)**, the right-hand side of every production includes either two nonterminals, or a single terminal symbol:

$A \rightarrow BC$

$A \rightarrow a$

Any CFG can be converted into a CNF grammar that is weakly equivalent. To convert a grammar into CNF, we first address productions that have more than two nonterminals on the RHS by creating new "dummy" nonterminals. For example, if we have the production

$$\text{W} \rightarrow \text{X Y Z}, \quad [9.25]$$

it is replaced with two productions,

$$\text{W} \rightarrow \text{X W}\backslash\text{X} \quad [9.26]$$

$$\text{W}\backslash\text{X} \rightarrow \text{Y Z}. \quad [9.27]$$

In these productions, W\X is a new dummy nonterminal. This transformation **binarizes** the grammar, which is critical for efficient bottom-up parsing, as we will see in chapter 10. Productions whose right-hand side contains a mix of terminal and nonterminal symbols can be replaced in a similar fashion.

Unary nonterminal productions $A \rightarrow B$ are replaced as follows: for each production $B \rightarrow \alpha$ in the grammar, add a new production $A \rightarrow \alpha$. For example, in the grammar described in figure 9.11, we would replace NUM → DIGIT with NUM → 1 | 2 | ... | 9. However, we keep the production NUM → NUM DIGIT, which is a valid binary production.

9.2.2 Natural Language Syntax as a Context-Free Language

Context-free grammars can be used to represent **syntax**, which is the set of rules that determine whether an utterance is judged to be grammatical. If this representation were perfectly faithful, then a natural language such as English could be transformed into a formal language, consisting of exactly the (infinite) set of strings that would be judged to be grammatical by a fluent English speaker. We could then build parsing software that would automatically determine if a given utterance were grammatical.[7]

Contemporary theories generally do *not* consider natural languages to be context-free (see § 9.3), yet context-free grammars are widely used in natural language parsing. The reason is that context-free representations strike a good balance: they cover a broad range of syntactic phenomena, and they can be parsed efficiently. This section therefore describes how to handle a core fragment of English syntax in context-free form, following the conventions of the **Penn Treebank** (PTB; Marcus et al., 1993), a large-scale annotation of English language syntax. The generalization to "mildly" context-sensitive languages is discussed in § 9.3.

7. To move beyond this cursory treatment of syntax, consult the short introductory manuscript by Bender (2013), or the longer text by Akmajian et al. (2010).

The Penn Treebank annotation is a **phrase-structure grammar** of English. This means that sentences are broken down into **constituents**, which are contiguous sequences of words that function as coherent units for the purpose of linguistic analysis. Constituents generally have a few key properties:

Movement Constituents can often be moved around sentences as units.

(9.3) a. Abigail gave (her brother) (a fish).
b. Abigail gave (a fish) to (her brother).

In contrast, *gave her* and *brother a* cannot easily be moved while preserving grammaticality.

Substitution Constituents can be substituted by other phrases of the same type.

(9.4) a. Max thanked (his older sister).
b. Max thanked (her).

In contrast, substitution is not possible for other contiguous units like *Max thanked* and *thanked his*.

Coordination Coordinators like *and* and *or* can conjoin constituents.

(9.5) a. (Abigail) and (her younger brother) bought a fish.
b. Abigail (bought a fish) and (gave it to Max).
c. Abigail (bought) and (greedily ate) a fish.

Units like *brother bought* and *bought a* cannot easily be coordinated.

These examples argue for units such as *her brother* and *bought a fish* to be treated as constituents. Other sequences of words in these examples, such as *Abigail gave* and *brother a fish*, cannot be moved, substituted, and coordinated in these ways. In phrase-structure grammar, constituents are nested, so that *the senator from New Jersey* contains the constituent *from New Jersey*, which in turn contains *New Jersey*. The sentence itself is the maximal constituent; each word is a minimal constituent, derived from a unary production from a part-of-speech tag. Between part-of-speech tags and sentences are **phrases**. In phrase-structure grammar, phrases have a type that is usually determined by their **head word**: for example, a **noun phrase** corresponds to a noun and the group of words that modify it, such as *her younger* ***brother***; a **verb phrase** includes the verb and its modifiers, such as ***bought*** *a fish* and *greedily* ***ate*** *it*.

In context-free grammars, each phrase type is a nonterminal, and each constituent is the substring that the nonterminal yields. Grammar design involves choosing the right set of nonterminals. Fine-grained nonterminals make it possible to represent more fine-grained linguistic phenomena. In general, grammar designers must trade off between **overgeneration**—a grammar that permits ungrammatical sentences—and **undergeneration**—a grammar that fails to generate grammatical sentences. Furthermore, if the grammar is to support manual annotation of syntactic structure, it must be simple enough to annotate efficiently.

9.2.3 A Phrase-Structure Grammar for English

To better understand how phrase-structure grammar works, let's consider the specific case of the Penn Treebank grammar of English. The main phrase categories in the Penn Treebank (PTB) are based on the main part-of-speech classes: noun phrase (NP), verb phrase (VP), prepositional phrase (PP), adjectival phrase (ADJP), and adverbial phrase (ADVP). The top-level category is S, which conveniently stands in for both "sentence" and the "start" symbol. **Complement clauses** (e.g., *I take the good old fashioned ground* ***that the whale is a fish***) are represented by the nonterminal SBAR. The terminal symbols in the grammar are individual words, which are generated from unary productions from part-of-speech tags (the PTB tagset is described in § 8.1).

This section describes some of the most common productions from the major phrase-level categories, explaining how to generate individual tag sequences. The production rules are approached in a "theory-driven" manner: first the syntactic properties of each phrase type are described, and then some of the necessary production rules are listed. But it is important to keep in mind that the Penn Treebank was produced in a "data-driven" manner. After the set of nonterminals was specified, annotators were free to analyze each sentence in whatever way seemed most linguistically accurate, subject to some high-level guidelines. The grammar of the Penn Treebank is simply the set of productions that were required to analyze the several million words of the corpus. By design, the grammar overgenerates—it does not exclude ungrammatical sentences. Furthermore, while the productions shown here cover some of the most common cases, they are only a small fraction of the several thousand different types of productions in the Penn Treebank.

Sentences The most common production rule for sentences is

$$\text{S} \rightarrow \text{NP VP}, \quad [9.28]$$

which accounts for simple sentences like *Abigail ate the kimchi*—as we will see, the direct object *the kimchi* is part of the verb phrase. But there are more complex forms of sentences as well:

S → ADVP NP VP	*Unfortunately Abigail ate the kimchi*	[9.29]
S → S Cc S	*Abigail ate the kimchi and Max had a burger*	[9.30]
S → VP	*Eat the kimchi,*	[9.31]

where ADVP is an adverbial phrase (e.g., *unfortunately*, *very unfortunately*) and Cc is a coordinating conjunction (e.g., *and*, *but*).[8]

Noun phrases Noun phrases refer to entities, real or imaginary, physical or abstract: *Asha*, *the steamed dumpling*, *parts and labor*, *nobody*, *the whiteness of the whale*, and *the rise of*

8. Notice that the grammar does not include the recursive production S → ADVP S. It may be helpful to think about why this production would cause the grammar to overgenerate.

revolutionary syndicalism in the early twentieth century. Noun phrase productions include "bare" nouns, which may optionally follow determiners, as well as pronouns:

$$\text{NP} \rightarrow \text{Nn} \mid \text{Nns} \mid \text{Nnp} \mid \text{Prp} \tag{9.32}$$

$$\text{NP} \rightarrow \text{Det Nn} \mid \text{Det Nns} \mid \text{Det Nnp} \tag{9.33}$$

The tags NN, NNS, and NNP refer to singular, plural, and proper nouns; PRP refers to personal pronouns; and DET refers to determiners. The grammar also contains terminal productions from each of these tags, for example, PRP → *I* | *you* | *we* | ….

Noun phrases may be modified by adjectival phrases (ADJP; e.g., *the small Russian dog*) and numbers (CD; e.g., *the five pastries*), each of which may optionally follow a determiner:

$$\text{NP} \rightarrow \text{ADJP Nn} \mid \text{ADJP Nns} \mid \text{Det ADJP Nn} \mid \text{Det ADJP Nns} \tag{9.34}$$

$$\text{NP} \rightarrow \text{Cd Nns} \mid \text{Det Cd Nns} \mid \ldots \tag{9.35}$$

Some noun phrases include multiple nouns, such as *the liberation movement* and *an antelope horn*, necessitating additional productions:

$$\text{NP} \rightarrow \text{Nn Nn} \mid \text{Nn Nns} \mid \text{Det Nn Nn} \mid \ldots \tag{9.36}$$

These multiple noun constructions can be combined with adjectival phrases and cardinal numbers, leading to a large number of additional productions.

Recursive noun phrase productions include coordination, prepositional phrase attachment, subordinate clauses, and verb phrase adjuncts:

NP → NP CC NP	*the red and the black*	[9.37]
NP → NP PP	*the President of the Georgia Institute of Technology*	[9.38]
NP → NP SBAR	*a whale which he had wounded*	[9.39]
NP → NP VP	*a whale taken near Shetland*	[9.40]

These recursive productions are a major source of ambiguity, because the VP and PP nonterminals can also generate NP children. Thus, the *the President of the Georgia Institute of Technology* can be derived in two ways, as can *a whale taken near Shetland in October*.

But aside from these few recursive productions, the noun phrase fragment of the Penn Treebank grammar is relatively flat, containing a large of number of productions that go from NP directly to a sequence of parts of speech. If noun phrases had more internal structure, the grammar would need fewer rules, which, as we will see, would make parsing faster and machine learning easier. Vadas and Curran (2011) propose to add additional structure in the form of a new nonterminal called a **nominal modifier (NML)**, for example,

(9.6) a. (NP (NN crude) (NN oil) (NNS prices)) (PTB analysis);
b. (NP (NML (NN crude) (NN oil)) (NNS prices)) (NML-style analysis).

Another proposal is to treat the determiner as the head of a **determiner phrase** (DP; Abney, 1987). There are linguistic arguments for and against determiner phrases (e.g., Van Eynde, 2006). From the perspective of context-free grammar, DPs enable more structured analyses of some constituents, for example,

(9.7) a. (NP (DT the) (JJ white) (NN whale)) (PTB analysis);
b. (DP (DT the) (NP (JJ white) (NN whale))) (DP-style analysis).

Verb phrases Verb phrases describe actions, events, and states of being. The PTB tagset distinguishes several classes of verb inflections: base form (VB; *she likes to snack*), present-tense, third-person singular (VBZ; *she snacks*), present tense but not third-person singular (VBP; *they snack*), past tense (VBD; *they snacked*), present participle (VBG; *they are snacking*), and past participle (VBN; *they had snacked*).[9] Each of these forms can constitute a verb phrase on its own:

$$\text{VP} \rightarrow \text{VB} \mid \text{VBZ} \mid \text{VBD} \mid \text{VBN} \mid \text{VBG} \mid \text{VBP} \qquad [9.41]$$

More complex verb phrases can be formed by a number of recursive productions, including the use of coordination, modal verbs (MD; *she should snack*), and the infinitive *to* (TO):

VP → MD VP	*She* ***will snack***	[9.42]
VP → VBD VP	*She* ***had snacked***	[9.43]
VP → VBZ VP	*She* ***has been snacking***	[9.44]
VP → VBN VP	*She has* ***been snacking***	[9.45]
VP → TO VP	*She wants* ***to snack***	[9.46]
VP → VP CC VP	*She* ***buys and eats*** *many snacks*	[9.47]

Each of these productions uses recursion, with the VP nonterminal appearing in both the LHS and RHS. This enables the creation of complex verb phrases, such as *She will have wanted to have been snacking.*

Transitive verbs take noun phrases as direct objects, and ditransitive verbs take two direct objects:

VP → VBZ NP	*She* ***teaches algebra***	[9.48]
VP → VBG NP	*She has been* ***teaching algebra***	[9.49]
VP → VBD NP NP	*She* ***taught*** *her brother algebra*	[9.50]

9. This tagset is specific to English: for example, VBP is a meaningful category only because English morphology distinguishes third-person singular from all person-number combinations.

These productions are *not* recursive, so a unique production is required for each verb part of speech. They also do not distinguish transitive from intransitive verbs, so the resulting grammar overgenerates examples like **She sleeps sushi* and **She learns Boyang algebra*. Sentences can also be direct objects:

VP → VBZ S *Hunter* ***wants to eat the kimchi*** [9.51]

VP → VBZ SBAR *Hunter* ***knows that Tristan ate the kimchi*** [9.52]

The first production overgenerates, licensing sentences like **Hunter sees Tristan eats the kimchi*. This problem could be addressed by designing a more specific set of sentence nonterminals, indicating whether the main verb can be conjugated.

Verbs can also be modified by prepositional phrases and adverbial phrases:

VP → VBZ PP *She* ***studies at night*** [9.53]

VP → VBZ ADVP *She* ***studies intensively*** [9.54]

VP → ADVP VBG *She is* ***not studying*** [9.55]

Again, because these productions are not recursive, the grammar must include productions for every verb part of speech.

A special set of verbs, known as **copula**, can take **predicative adjectives** as direct objects:

VP → VBZ ADJP *She* ***is hungry*** [9.56]

VP → VBD ADJP *Success* ***seemed increasingly unlikely*** [9.57]

The PTB does not have a special nonterminal for copular verbs, so this production generates nongrammatical examples such as **She eats tall*.

Particles (PRT as a phrase; RP as a part of speech) help to create phrasal verbs:

VP → VB PRT *She told them to* ***fuck off*** [9.58]

VP → VBD PRT NP *They* ***gave up their ill-gotten gains*** [9.59]

As the second production shows, particle productions are required for all configurations of verb parts of speech and direct objects.

Other contituents The remaining constituents require far fewer productions. **Prepositional phrases** almost always consist of a preposition and a noun phrase,

PP → IN NP *the whiteness* ***of the whale*** [9.60]

PP → TO NP *What the white whale was* ***to Ahab****, has been hinted* [9.61]

Similarly, complement clauses consist of a complementizer (usually a preposition, possibly null) and a sentence:

SBAR → IN S *She said* ***that it was spicy*** [9.62]

SBAR → S *She said* ***it was spicy*** [9.63]

Adverbial phrases are usually bare adverbs (ADVP → RB), with a few exceptions:

ADVP → RB RBR *They went* ***considerably further*** [9.64]

ADVP → ADVP PP *They went* ***considerably further than before*** [9.65]

The tag RBR is a comparative adverb.

Adjectival phrases extend beyond bare adjectives (ADJP → JJ) in a number of ways:

ADJP → RB JJ *very hungry* [9.66]

ADJP → RBR JJ *more hungry* [9.67]

ADJP → JJS JJ *best possible* [9.68]

ADJP → RB JJR *even bigger* [9.69]

ADJP → JJ CC JJ *high and mighty* [9.70]

ADJP → JJ JJ *West German* [9.71]

ADJP → RB VBN *previously reported* [9.72]

The tags JJR and JJS refer to comparative and superlative adjectives, respectively.

All of these phrase types can be coordinated:

PP → PP CC PP *on time and under budget* [9.73]

ADVP → ADVP CC ADVP *now and two years ago* [9.74]

ADJP → ADJP CC ADJP *quaint and rather deceptive* [9.75]

SBAR → SBAR CC SBAR *whether they want control or whether they want exports* [9.76]

9.2.4 Grammatical Ambiguity

Context-free parsing is useful not only because it determines whether a sentence is grammatical, but mainly because the constituents and their relations can be applied to tasks such as information extraction (chapter 17) and sentence compression (Jing, 2000; Clarke and Lapata, 2008). However, the **ambiguity** of wide-coverage natural language grammars poses a serious problem for such potential applications. As an example, figure 9.13 shows two possible analyses for the simple sentence *We eat sushi with chopsticks*, depending on whether the *chopsticks* modify *eat* or *sushi*. Realistic grammars can license thousands or even millions of parses for individual sentences. **Weighted context-free grammars** solve this problem by attaching weights to each production and selecting the derivation with the highest score. This is the focus of chapter 10.

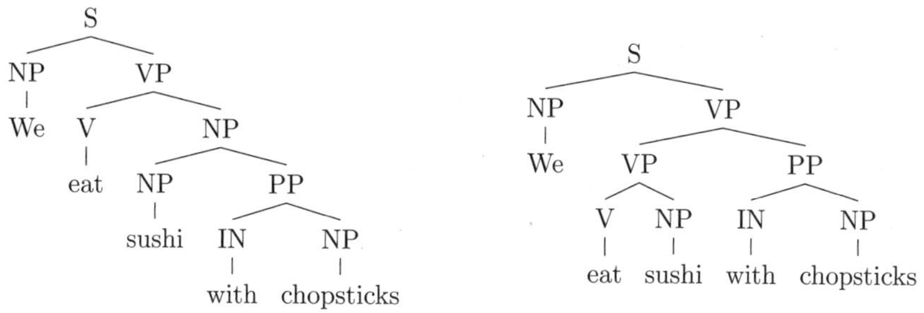

Figure 9.13
Two derivations of the same sentence.

9.3 *Mildly Context-Sensitive Languages

Beyond context-free languages lie **context-sensitive languages**, in which the expansion of a nonterminal depends on its neighbors. In the general class of context-sensitive languages, computation becomes much more challenging: the membership problem for context-sensitive languages is PSPACE-complete. Since PSPACE contains the complexity class NP (problems that can be solved in polynomial time on a nondeterministic Turing machine), PSPACE-complete problems cannot be solved efficiently if P $\neq$ NP. Thus, designing an efficient parsing algorithm for the full class of context-sensitive languages is probably hopeless.[10]

However, Joshi (1985) identifies a set of properties that define **mildly context-sensitive languages**, which are a strict subset of context-sensitive languages. Like context-free languages, mildly context-sensitive languages are parseable in polynomial time. However, the mildly context-sensitive languages include non–context-free languages, such as the "copy language" $\{\boldsymbol{w}\boldsymbol{w} \mid \boldsymbol{w} \in \Sigma^*\}$ and the language $a^m b^n c^m d^n$. Both are characterized by **cross-serial dependencies**, linking symbols at long distance across the string.[11] For example, in the language $a^n b^m c^n d^m$, each a symbol is linked to exactly one c symbol, regardless of the number of intervening b symbols.

9.3.1 Context-Sensitive Phenomena in Natural Language

Such phenomena are occasionally relevant to natural language. A classic example is found in Swiss-German (Shieber, 1985), in which sentences such as *we let the children help Hans paint the house* are realized by listing all nouns before all verbs, which would be

10. If PSPACE $\neq$ NP, then it contains problems that cannot be solved in polynomial time on a nondeterministic Turing machine; equivalently, solutions to these problems cannot even be checked in polynomial time (Arora and Barak, 2009).

11. A further condition of the set of mildly context-sensitive languages is *constant growth*: if the strings in the language are arranged by length, the gap in length between any pair of adjacent strings is bounded by some language-specific constant. This condition excludes languages such as $\{a^{2^n} \mid n \geq 0\}$.

glossed as *we the children Hans the house let help paint*. Furthermore, each noun's determiner is dictated by the noun's **case marking** (the role it plays with respect to the verb). Using an argument that is analogous to the earlier discussion of center-embedding (§ 9.2), Shieber describes these case marking constraints as a set of cross-serial dependencies, homomorphic to $a^m b^n c^m d^n$, and therefore not context-free.

As with the move from regular to context-free languages, mildly context-sensitive languages can also be motivated by expedience. While finite sequences of cross-serial dependencies can in principle be handled in a context-free grammar, it is often more convenient to use a mildly context-sensitive formalism like **tree-adjoining grammar (TAG)** and **combinatory categorial grammar (CCG)**. TAG-inspired parsers have been shown to be particularly effective in parsing the Penn Treebank (Collins, 1997; Carreras et al., 2008), and CCG plays a leading role in research on semantic parsing (Zettlemoyer and Collins, 2005). These two formalisms are weakly equivalent: any language that can be specified in TAG can also be specified in CCG, and vice versa (Joshi et al., 1991). The remainder of the chapter gives a brief overview of CCG, but you are encouraged to consult Joshi and Schabes (1997) and Steedman and Baldridge (2011) for more detail on TAG and CCG, respectively.

9.3.2 Combinatory Categorial Grammar

In combinatory categorial grammar, structural analyses are built up through a small set of generic combinatorial operations, which apply to immediately adjacent substructures. These operations act on the categories of the substructures, producing a new structure with a new category. The basic categories include S (sentence), NP (noun phrase), VP (verb phrase), and N (noun). The goal is to label the entire span of text as a sentence, S.

Complex categories, or types, are constructed from the basic categories, parentheses, and forward and backward slashes: for example, S/NP is a complex type, indicating a sentence that is lacking a noun phrase to its right; $S\backslash NP$ is a sentence lacking a noun phrase to its left. Complex types act as functions, and the most basic combinatory operations are function application to either the right or left neighbor. For example, the type of a verb phrase, such as *talks*, would be $S\backslash NP$. Applying this function to a subject noun phrase to its left results in an analysis of *Abigail talks* as category S, indicating a successful parse.

Transitive verbs must first be applied to the direct object, which in English appears to the right of the verb, before the subject, which appears to the left. They therefore have the more complex type $(S\backslash NP)/NP$. Similarly, the application of a determiner to the noun at its right results in a noun phrase, so determiners have the type NP/N. Figure 9.14 provides an example involving a transitive verb and a determiner. A key point from this example is that it can be trivially transformed into a phrase-structure tree, by treating each function application as a constituent phrase. Indeed, when CCG's only combinatory operators are forward and backward function application, it is equivalent to context-free grammar. However, the location of the "effort" has changed. Rather than designing good productions,

$$\frac{\displaystyle\frac{\text{Abigail}}{NP} \quad \frac{\text{eats}}{(S\backslash NP)/NP} \quad \frac{\displaystyle\frac{\text{the}}{(NP/N)} \quad \frac{\text{kimchi}}{N}}{NP}\!\!{>}}{}$$

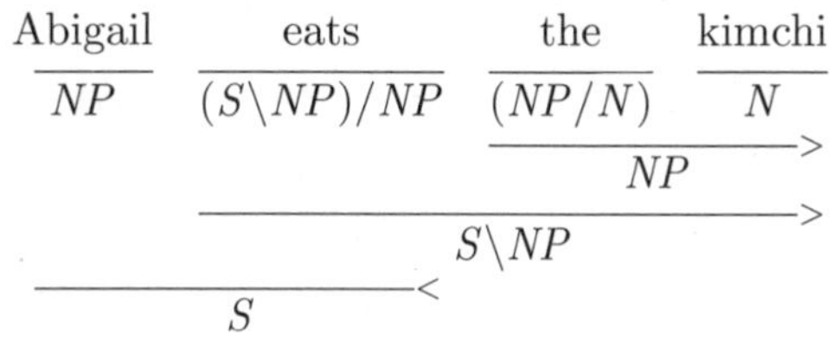

Figure 9.14
A syntactic analysis in CCG involving forward and backward function application.

$$\frac{\displaystyle\frac{\text{Abigail}}{NP} \quad \frac{\displaystyle\frac{\text{might}}{(S\backslash NP)/VP} \quad \frac{\text{learn}}{VP/NP}}{(S\backslash NP)/NP}\!\!{>}_\mathbf{B} \quad \frac{\text{Swahili}}{NP}}{}$$

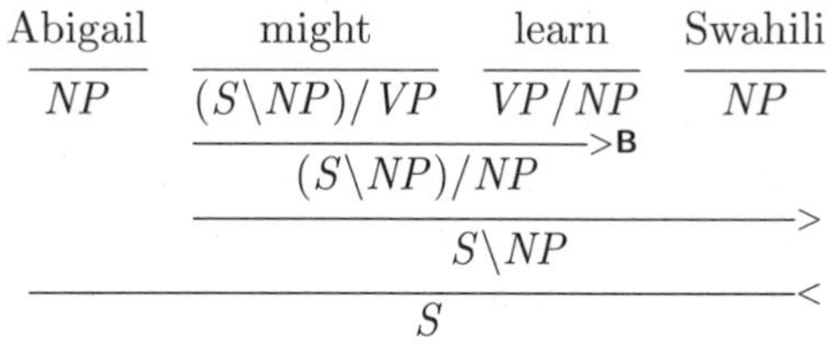

Figure 9.15
A syntactic analysis in CCG involving function composition (example modified from Steedman and Baldridge, 2011).

the grammar designer must focus on the **lexicon**—choosing the right categories for each word. This makes it possible to parse a wide range of sentences using only a few generic combinatory operators.

Things become more interesting with the introduction of two additional operators: **composition** and **type-raising**. Function composition enables the combination of complex types: $X/Y \circ Y/Z \Rightarrow_\mathbf{B} X/Z$ (forward composition) and $Y\backslash Z \circ X\backslash Y \Rightarrow_\mathbf{B} X\backslash Z$ (backward composition).[12] Composition makes it possible to "look inside" complex types and combine two adjacent units if the input for one is the output for the other. Figure 9.15 shows how function composition can be used to handle modal verbs. While this sentence can be parsed using only function application, the composition-based analysis is preferable because the unit *might learn* acts just like a transitive verb, as in the example *Abigail studies Swahili*. This in turn makes it possible to analyze conjunctions such as *Abigail studies and might learn Swahili*, attaching the direct object *Swahili* to the entire conjoined verb phrase *studies and might learn*. The Penn Treebank grammar fragment from § 9.2.3 would be unable to handle this case correctly: the direct object *Swahili* could attach only to the second verb *learn*.

Type-raising converts an element of type X to a more complex type: $X \Rightarrow_T T/(T\backslash X)$ (forward type-raising to type T) and $X \Rightarrow_T T\backslash(T/X)$ (backward type-raising to type T). Type-raising makes it possible to reverse the relationship between a function and its

---

12. The subscript **B** follows notation from Curry and Feys (1958).

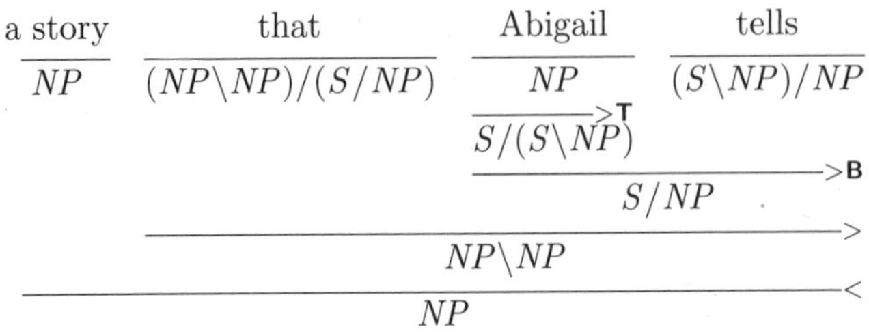
a story
that
Abigail
tells
NP
(NP\NP)/(S/NP)
NP
(S\NP)/NP
>T
S/(S\NP)
>B
S/NP
>
NP\NP
<
NP

Figure 9.16
A syntactic analysis in CCG involving an object relative clause.

argument—by transforming the argument into a function over functions over arguments! An example may help. Figure 9.16 shows how to analyze an object relative clause, *a story that Abigail tells*. The problem is that *tells* is a transitive verb, expecting a direct object to its right. As a result, *Abigail tells* is not a valid constituent. The issue is resolved by raising *Abigail* from NP to the complex type S/(S\NP). This function can then be combined with the transitive verb *tells* by forward composition, resulting in the type (S/NP), which is a sentence lacking a direct object to its right.[13] From here, we need only design the lexical entry for the complementizer *that* to expect a right neighbor of type (S/NP), and the remainder of the derivation can proceed by function application.

Composition and type-raising give CCG considerable power and flexibility, but at a price. The simple sentence *Abigail tells Max* can be parsed in two different ways: by function application (first forming the verb phrase *tells Max*) and by type-raising and composition (first forming the nonconstituent *Abigail tells*). This **derivational ambiguity** does not affect the resulting linguistic analysis, so it is sometimes known as **spurious ambiguity**. Hockenmaier and Steedman (2007) present a translation algorithm for converting the Penn Treebank into CCG derivations, using composition and type-raising only when necessary.

Exercises

1. Sketch out the state diagram for finite-state acceptors for the following languages on the alphabet $\{a, b\}$.
   a) Even-length strings. (Be sure to include 0 as an even number.)
   b) Strings that contain *aaa* as a substring.
   c) Strings containing an even number of *a* and an odd number of *b* symbols.
   d) Strings in which the substring *bbb* must be terminal if it appears—the string need not contain *bbb*, but if it does, nothing can come after it.

13. The missing direct object would be analyzed as a **trace** in CFG-like approaches to syntax, including the Penn Treebank.

2. Levenshtein edit distance is the number of insertions, substitutions, or deletions required to convert one string to another.
   a) Define a finite-state acceptor that accepts all strings with edit distance 1 from the target string, *target*.
   b) Now think about how to generalize your design to accept all strings with edit distance from the target string equal to d. If the target string has length ℓ, what is the minimal number of states required?
3. Construct an FSA in the style of figure 9.3, which handles the following examples:
   - *nation*/N, *national*/ADJ, *nationalize*/V, *nationalizer*/N
   - *America*/N, *American*/ADJ, *Americanize*/V, *Americanizer*/N

   Be sure that your FSA does not accept any further derivations, such as **nationalizeral* and **Americanizern*.
4. Show how to construct a trigram language model in a weighted finite-state acceptor. Make sure that you handle the edge cases at the beginning and end of the input.
5. Extend the FST in figure 9.6 to handle the other two parts of rule 1a of the Porter stemmer: *-sses* → *ss*, and *-ies* → *-i*.
6. § 9.1.4 describes T_O, a transducer that captures English orthography by transducing *cook* + *ed* → *cooked* and *bake* + *ed* → *baked*. Design an unweighted finite-state transducer that captures this property of English orthography.

   Next, augment the transducer to appropriately model the suffix *-s* when applied to words ending in *s*, for example, *kiss*+*s* → *kisses*.
7. Add parenthesization to the grammar in figure 9.11 so that it is no longer ambiguous.
8. Construct three examples—a noun phrase, a verb phrase, and a sentence—which can be derived from the Penn Treebank grammar fragment in § 9.2.3, yet are not grammatical. Avoid reusing examples from the text. Optionally, propose corrections to the grammar to avoid generating these cases.
9. Produce parses for the following sentences, using the Penn Treebank grammar fragment from § 9.2.3.

   (9.8) This aggression will not stand.
   (9.9) I can get you a toe.
   (9.10) Sometimes you eat the bar and sometimes the bar eats you.

   Then produce parses for three short sentences from a news article from this week.
10. *One advantage of CCG is its flexibility in handling coordination:

   (9.11) a. Hunter and Tristan speak Hawaiian
   b. Hunter speaks and Tristan understands Hawaiian

Define the lexical entry for *and* as

$$and := (X/X)\backslash X, \qquad [9.77]$$

where X can refer to any type. Using this lexical entry, show how to parse the two examples above. In the second example, *Hawaiian* should be combined with the coordination *Hunter speaks and Tristan understands*, and not just with the verb *understands*.

10 Context-Free Parsing

Parsing is the task of determining whether a string can be derived from a given context-free grammar, and if so, how. A parser's output is a tree, like the ones shown in figure 9.13. Such trees can answer basic questions of who-did-what-to-whom, and have applications in downstream tasks like semantic analysis (chapters 12 and 13) and information extraction (chapter 17).

For a given input and grammar, how many parse trees are there? Consider a minimal context-free grammar with only one nonterminal, X, and the following productions:

$$\mathrm{X} \rightarrow \mathrm{X}\ \mathrm{X}$$

$$\mathrm{X} \rightarrow \textit{aardvark} \mid \textit{abacus} \mid \ldots \mid \textit{zyther}$$

The second line indicates unary productions to every nonterminal in Σ. In this grammar, the number of possible derivations for a string $\boldsymbol{w}$ is equal to the number of binary bracketings, for example,

$$((((w_1\ w_2)\ w_3)\ w_4)\ w_5), \quad (((w_1\ (w_2\ w_3))\ w_4)\ w_5), \quad ((w_1\ (w_2 (w_3\ w_4)))\ w_5), \quad \ldots.$$

The number of such bracketings is a **Catalan number**, which grows super-exponentially in the length of the sentence, $C_n = \frac{(2n)!}{(n+1)!n!}$. As with sequence labeling, it is only possible to exhaustively search the space of parses by resorting to locality assumptions, which make it possible to search efficiently by reusing shared substructures with dynamic programming. This chapter focuses on a bottom-up dynamic programming algorithm, which enables exhaustive search of the space of possible parses, but imposes strict limitations on the form of scoring function. These limitations can be relaxed by abandoning exhaustive search. Nonexact search methods will be briefly discussed at the end of this chapter, and one of them—**transition-based parsing**—will be the focus of chapter 11.

Table 10.1
A toy example context-free grammar

S	→ NP VP
NP	→ NP PP | *we* | *sushi* | *chopsticks*
PP	→ IN NP
IN	→ *with*
VP	→ V NP | VP PP
V	→ *eat*

10.1 Deterministic Bottom-Up Parsing

The **CKY algorithm**[1] is a bottom-up approach to parsing in a context-free grammar. It efficiently tests whether a string is in a language, without enumerating all possible parses. The algorithm first forms small constituents and then tries to merge them into larger constituents.

To understand the algorithm, consider the input, *We eat sushi with chopsticks*. According to the toy grammar in table 10.1, each terminal symbol can be generated by exactly one unary production, resulting in the sequence NP V NP IN NP. In real examples, there may be many unary productions for each individual token. In any case, the next step is to try to apply binary productions to merge adjacent symbols into larger constituents: for example, V NP can be merged into a verb phrase (VP), and IN NP can be merged into a prepositional phrase (PP). Bottom-up parsing searches for a series of mergers that ultimately results in the start symbol S covering the entire input.

The CKY algorithm systematizes this search by incrementally constructing a table t in which each cell $t[i,j]$ contains the set of nonterminals that can derive the span $\boldsymbol{w}_{i+1:j}$. The algorithm fills in the upper-right triangle of the table; it begins with the diagonal, which corresponds to substrings of length 1, and then computes derivations for progressively larger substrings, until reaching the upper-right corner $t[0,M]$, which corresponds to the entire input, $\boldsymbol{w}_{1:M}$. If the start symbol S is in $t[0,M]$, then the string $\boldsymbol{w}$ is in the language defined by the grammar. This process is detailed in algorithm 13, and the resulting data structure is shown in figure 10.1. Informally, here's how it works:

- Begin by filling in the diagonal: the cells $t[m-1,m]$ for all $m \in \{1,2,\ldots,M\}$. These cells are filled with terminal productions that yield the individual tokens; for the word $w_2 = sushi$, we fill in $t[1,2] = \{\text{NP}\}$, and so on.
- Then fill in the next diagonal, in which each cell corresponds to a subsequence of length two: $t[0,2], t[1,3], \ldots, t[M-2,M]$. These cells are filled in by looking for binary productions capable of producing at least one entry in each of the cells corresponding to left

1. The name is an acronym for Cocke-Kasami-Younger, the inventors of the algorithm. It is a special case of **chart parsing**, because its stores reusable computations in a chart-like data structure.

Algorithm 13

The CKY algorithm for parsing a sequence $w \in \Sigma^*$ in a context-free grammar $G = (N, \Sigma, R, S)$, with nonterminals N, production rules R, and start symbol S. The grammar is assumed to be in Chomsky normal form (§ 9.2.1). The function $\text{PICKFROM}(b[i,j,X])$ selects an element of the set $b[i,j,X]$ arbitrarily. All values of t and b are initialized to $\varnothing$.

1: **procedure** $\text{CKY}(w, G = (N, \Sigma, R, S))$
2:     **for** $m \in \{1 \ldots M\}$ **do**
3:       $t[m-1, m] \leftarrow \{X : (X \to w_m) \in R\}$
4:     **for** $\ell \in \{2, 3, \ldots, M\}$ **do**   ▷ Iterate over constituent lengths
5:       **for** $m \in \{0, 1, \ldots M - \ell\}$ **do**   ▷ Iterate over left endpoints
6:         **for** $k \in \{m+1, m+2, \ldots, m+\ell-1\}$ **do**   ▷ Iterate over split points
7:           **for** $(X \to Y Z) \in R$ **do**   ▷ Iterate over rules
8:             **if** $Y \in t[m, k] \wedge Z \in t[k, m+\ell]$ **then**
9:                $t[m, m+\ell] \leftarrow t[m, m+\ell] \cup X$ ▷ Add nonterminal to table
10:              $b[m, m+\ell, X] \leftarrow b[m, m+\ell, X] \cup (Y, Z, k)$ ▷ Add back-pointers
11:     **if** $S \in t[0, M]$ **then**
12:       **return** $\text{TRACEBACK}(S, 0, M, b)$
13:     **else**
14:       **return** $\varnothing$
15: **procedure** $\text{TRACEBACK}(X, i, j, b)$
16:     **if** $j = i + 1$ **then**
17:       **return** X
18:     **else**
19:       $(Y, Z, k) \leftarrow \text{PICKFROM}(b[i, j, X])$
20:       **return** $X \to (\text{TRACEBACK}(Y, i, k, b), \text{TRACEBACK}(Z, k, j, b))$

---

and right children. For example, VP can be placed in the cell $t[1, 3]$ because the grammar includes the production VP $\to$ V NP, and because the chart contains V $\in t[1, 2]$ and NP $\in t[2, 3]$.

- At the next diagonal, the entries correspond to spans of length three. At this level, there is an additional decision at each cell: where to split the left and right children. The cell $t[i,j]$ corresponds to the subsequence $w_{i+1:j}$, and we must choose some *split point* $i < k < j$, so that the span $w_{i+1:k}$ is the left child, and the span $w_{k+1:j}$ is the right child. We consider all possible k, looking for productions that generate elements in $t[i, k]$ and $t[k, j]$; the left-hand side of all such productions can be added to $t[i,j]$. When it is time to compute $t[i,j]$, the cells $t[i, k]$ and $t[k, j]$ are guaranteed to be complete, because these cells correspond to shorter substrings of the input.

- The process continues until we reach $t[0, M]$.

Figure 10.1 shows the chart that arises from parsing the sentence *We eat sushi with chopsticks* using the grammar defined above.

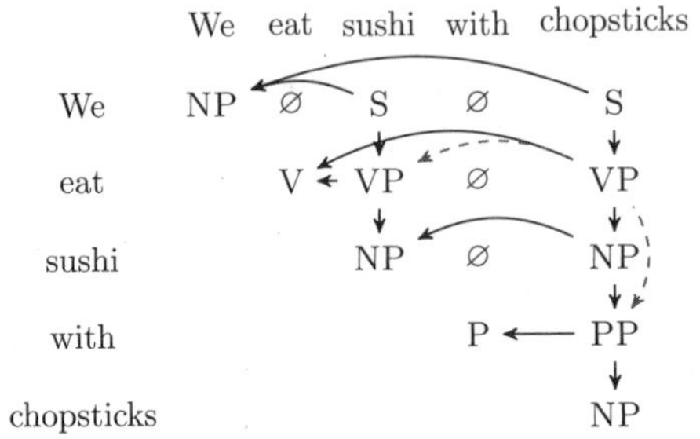

Figure 10.1
An example completed CKY chart. The solid and dashed lines show the back-pointers resulting from the two different derivations of VP in position $t[1, 5]$.

10.1.1 Recovering the Parse Tree

As with the Viterbi algorithm, it is possible to identify a successful parse by storing and traversing an additional table of back-pointers. If we add an entry X to cell $t[i,j]$ by using the production $X \rightarrow YZ$ and the split point k, then we store the back-pointer $b[i,j,X] = (Y, Z, k)$. Once the table is complete, we can recover a parse by tracing this pointers, starting at $b[0, M, \mathrm{S}]$, and stopping when they ground out at terminal productions.

For ambiguous sentences, there will be multiple paths to reach $\mathrm{S} \in t[0, M]$. For example, in figure 10.1, the goal state $\mathrm{S} \in t[0, M]$ is reached through the state $\mathrm{VP} \in t[1, 5]$, and there are two different ways to generate this constituent: one with (*eat sushi*) and (*with chopsticks*) as children, and another with (*eat*) and (*sushi with chopsticks*) as children. The presence of multiple paths indicates that the input can be generated by the grammar in more than one way. In algorithm 13, one of these derivations is selected arbitrarily. As discussed in § 10.3, **weighted context-free grammars** compute a score for all permissible derivations, and a minor modification of CKY allows it to identify the single derivation with the maximum score.

10.1.2 Nonbinary Productions

As presented above, the CKY algorithm assumes that all productions with nonterminals on the right-hand side (RHS) are binary. In real grammars, such as the one considered in chapter 9, there are other types of productions: some have more than two elements on the right-hand side, and others produce a single nonterminal.

- Productions with more than two elements on the right-hand side can be **binarized** by creating additional nonterminals, as described in § 9.2.1. For example, the production $\mathrm{VP} \rightarrow \mathrm{V\ NP\ NP}$ (for ditransitive verbs) can be converted to $\mathrm{VP} \rightarrow \mathrm{VP}_{ditrans}/\mathrm{NP\ NP}$, by adding the nonterminal $\mathrm{VP}_{ditrans}/\mathrm{NP}$ and the production $\mathrm{VP}_{ditrans}/\mathrm{NP} \rightarrow \mathrm{V\ NP}$.
- What about unary productions like $\mathrm{VP} \rightarrow \mathrm{V}$? Although such productions are not a part of Chomsky Normal Form—and can therefore be eliminated in preprocessing the

grammar—in practice, a more typical solution is to modify the CKY algorithm. The algorithm makes a second pass on each diagonal in the table, augmenting each cell $t[i,j]$ with all possible unary productions capable of generating each item already in the cell: formally, $t[i,j]$ is extended to its **unary closure**. Suppose the example grammar in table 10.1 was extended to include the production VP $\rightarrow$ V, enabling sentences with intransitive verb phrases, like *we eat*. Then the cell $t[1,2]$—corresponding to the word *eat*—would first include the set {V} and would be augmented to the set {V, VP} during this second pass.

10.1.3 Complexity

For an input of length M and a grammar with R productions and N nonterminals, the space complexity of the CKY algorithm is $\mathcal{O}(M^2N)$: the number of cells in the chart is $\mathcal{O}(M^2)$, and each cell must hold $\mathcal{O}(N)$ elements. The time complexity is $\mathcal{O}(M^3R)$: each cell is computed by searching over $\mathcal{O}(M)$ split points, with R possible productions for each split point. Both the time and space complexity are considerably worse than the Viterbi algorithm, which is linear in the length of the input.

10.2 Ambiguity

In natural language, there is rarely a single parse for a given sentence. The main culprit is ambiguity, which is endemic to natural language syntax. Here are a few broad categories:

- **Attachment ambiguity**: for example, *We eat sushi with chopsticks*, *I shot an elephant in my pajamas.* In these examples, the prepositions (*with*, *in*) can attach to either the verb or the direct object.
- **Modifier scope**: for example, *southern food store*, *plastic cup holder*. In these examples, the first word could be modifying the subsequent adjective, or the final noun.
- **Particle versus preposition**: for example, *The puppy tore up the staircase.* Phrasal verbs like *tore up* often include particles that could also act as prepositions. This has structural implications: if *up* is a preposition, then *up the staircase* is a prepositional phrase; if *up* is a particle, then *the staircase* is the direct object to the verb.
- **Complement structure**: for example, *The students complained to the professor that they didn't understand.* This is another form of attachment ambiguity, where the complement *that they didn't understand* could attach to the main verb (*complained*), or to the indirect object (*the professor*).
- **Coordination scope**: for example, *"I see," said the blind man, as he picked up the hammer and saw.* In this example, the lexical ambiguity for *saw* enables it to be coordinated either with the noun *hammer* or the verb *picked up*.

These forms of ambiguity can combine, so that seemingly simple headlines like *Fed raises interest rates* have dozens of possible analyses even in a minimal grammar. In a broad coverage grammar, typical sentences can have millions of parses. While careful grammar design can chip away at this ambiguity, a better strategy is combine broad coverage parsers with data-driven strategies for identifying the correct analysis.

10.2.1 Parser Evaluation

Before continuing to parsing algorithms that are able to handle ambiguity, let us stop to consider how to measure parsing performance. Suppose we have a set of *reference parses*—the ground truth—and a set of *system parses* that we would like to score. A simple solution would be per-sentence accuracy: the parser is scored by the proportion of sentences on which the system and reference parses exactly match.[2] But as any student knows, it always nice to get *partial credit*, which we can assign to analyses that correctly match parts of the reference parse. The PARSEval metrics (Grishman et al., 1992) score each system parse via:

Precision: the fraction of constituents in the system parse that match a constituent in the reference parse.

Recall: the fraction of constituents in the reference parse that match a constituent in the system parse.

In **labeled precision** and **recall**, the system must also match the phrase type for each constituent; in **unlabeled precision** and **recall**, it is only required to match the constituent structure. As described in chapter 4, the precision and recall can be combined into an F-MEASURE by their harmonic mean.

Suppose that the left tree of figure 10.2 is the system parse, and that the right tree is the reference parse. Then:

- $\text{S} \rightarrow \boldsymbol{w}_{1:5}$ is *true positive*, because it appears in both trees.
- $\text{VP} \rightarrow \boldsymbol{w}_{2:5}$ is *true positive* as well.
- $\text{NP} \rightarrow \boldsymbol{w}_{3:5}$ is *false positive*, because it appears only in the system output.
- $\text{PP} \rightarrow \boldsymbol{w}_{4:5}$ is *true positive*, because it appears in both trees.
- $\text{VP} \rightarrow \boldsymbol{w}_{2:3}$ is *false negative*, because it appears only in the reference.

The labeled and unlabeled precision of this parse is $\frac{3}{4} = 0.75$, and the recall is $\frac{3}{4} = 0.75$, for an F-MEASURE of 0.75. For an example in which precision and recall are not equal, suppose the reference parse instead included the production $\text{VP} \rightarrow \text{V NP PP}$. In this parse, the reference does not contain the constituent $\boldsymbol{w}_{2:3}$, so the recall would be 1.[3]

2. Most parsing papers do not report results on this metric, but Suzuki et al. (2018) found that a strong parser recovers the exact parse in roughly 50% of all sentences. Performance on short sentences is generally much higher.

3. While the grammar must be binarized before applying the CKY algorithm, evaluation is performed on the original parses. It is therefore necessary to "unbinarize" the output of a CKY-based parser, converting it back to the original grammar.

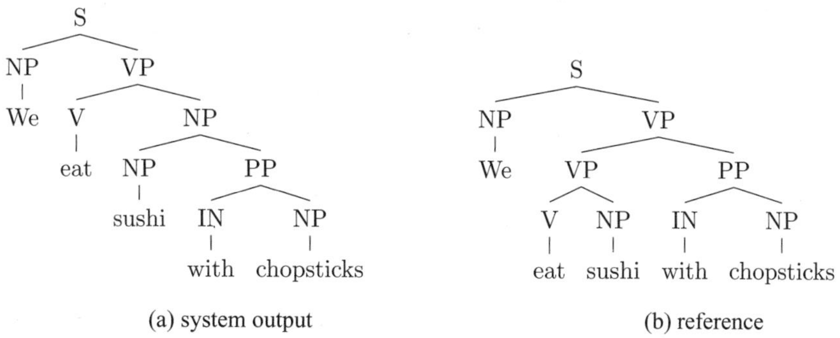

Figure 10.2
Two possible analyses from the grammar in table 10.1.

10.2.2 Local Solutions

Some ambiguity can be resolved locally. Consider the following examples:

(10.1) a. We met the President on Monday.
b. We met the President of Mexico.

Each case ends with a prepositional phrase, which can be attached to the verb *met* or the noun phrase *the president*. If given a labeled corpus, we can compare the likelihood of the observing the preposition alongside each candidate attachment point,

$$\text{p}(\textit{on} \mid \textit{met}) \gtrless \text{p}(\textit{on} \mid \textit{President}) \qquad [10.1]$$

$$\text{p}(\textit{of} \mid \textit{met}) \gtrless \text{p}(\textit{of} \mid \textit{President}). \qquad [10.2]$$

A comparison of these probabilities would successfully resolve this case (Hindle and Rooth, 1993). Other cases, such as *we eat sushi with chopsticks*, require considering the object of the preposition: consider the alternative *we eat sushi with soy sauce*. With sufficient labeled data, some instances of attachment ambiguity can be solved by supervised classification (Ratnaparkhi et al., 1994).

However, there are inherent limitations to local solutions. While toy examples may have just a few ambiguities to resolve, realistic sentences have thousands or millions of possible parses. Furthermore, attachment decisions are interdependent, as shown in this garden path example:

(10.2) Cats scratch people with claws with knives.

We may want to attach *with claws* to *scratch*, as would be correct in the shorter sentence in *cats scratch people with claws*. But this leaves nowhere to attach *with knives*. The correct interpretation can be identified only be considering the attachment decisions jointly. The huge number of potential parses may seem to make exhaustive search impossible. But as with sequence labeling, locality assumptions make it possible to search this space efficiently.

10.3 Weighted Context-Free Grammars

Let us define a derivation τ as a set of **anchored productions**,

$$\tau = \{X \to \alpha, (i,j,k)\}, \qquad [10.3]$$

with X corresponding to the left-hand side nonterminal and α corresponding to the right-hand side. For grammars in Chomsky normal form, α is either a pair of nonterminals or a terminal symbol. The indices i, j, k anchor the production in the input, with X deriving the span $\boldsymbol{w}_{i+1:j}$. For binary productions, $\boldsymbol{w}_{i+1:k}$ indicates the span of the left child, and $\boldsymbol{w}_{k+1:j}$ indicates the span of the right child; for unary productions, k is ignored. For an input $\boldsymbol{w}$, the optimal parse is

$$\hat{\tau} = \underset{\tau \in \mathcal{T}(\boldsymbol{w})}{\operatorname{argmax}}\, \Psi(\tau), \qquad [10.4]$$

where $\mathcal{T}(\boldsymbol{w})$ is the set of derivations that yield the input $\boldsymbol{w}$.

Define a scoring function Ψ that decomposes across anchored productions,

$$\Psi(\tau) = \sum_{(X \to \alpha, (i,j,k)) \in \tau} \psi(X \to \alpha, (i,j,k)). \qquad [10.5]$$

This is a locality assumption, akin to the assumption in Viterbi sequence labeling. In this case, the assumption states that the overall score is a sum over scores of productions, which are computed independently. In a **weighted context-free grammar (WCFG)**, the score of each anchored production $X \to (\alpha, (i,j,k))$ is simply $\psi(X \to \alpha)$, ignoring the anchor (i,j,k). In other parsing models, the anchors can be used to access features of the input, while still permitting efficient bottom-up parsing.

Example Consider the weighted grammar shown in table 10.2, and the analysis in figure 10.2b.

$$\begin{aligned}\Psi(\tau) = {} & \psi(\text{S} \to \text{NP VP}) + \psi(\text{VP} \to \text{VP PP}) + \psi(\text{VP} \to \text{V NP}) + \psi(\text{PP} \to \text{In NP}) \\ & + \psi(\text{NP} \to \textit{We}) + \psi(\text{V} \to \textit{eat}) + \psi(\text{NP} \to \textit{sushi}) + \psi(\text{In} \to \textit{with}) \\ & + \psi(\text{NP} \to \textit{chopsticks}) \qquad [10.6] \\ = {} & 0 - 2 - 1 + 0 - 2 + 0 - 3 + 0 - 3 = -11. \qquad [10.7]\end{aligned}$$

In the alternative parse in figure 10.2a, the production VP $\to$ VP PP (with score -2) is replaced with the production NP $\to$ NP PP (with score -1); all other productions are the same. As a result, the score for this parse is -10. This example hints at a problem with WCFG parsing on nonterminals such as NP, VP, and PP: a WCFG will *always* prefer either VP or NP attachment, regardless of what is being attached! Solutions to this issue are discussed in § 10.5.

Table 10.2
An example weighted context-free grammar (WCFG). The weights are chosen so that $\exp \psi(\cdot)$ sums to one over right-hand sides for each nonterminal; this is required by probabilistic context-free grammars, but not by WCFGs in general.

		$\psi(\cdot)$	$\exp \psi(\cdot)$
S	$\rightarrow$ NP VP	0	1
NP	$\rightarrow$ NP PP	-1	$\frac{1}{2}$
	$\rightarrow$ *we*	-2	$\frac{1}{4}$
	$\rightarrow$ *sushi*	-3	$\frac{1}{8}$
	$\rightarrow$ *chopsticks*	-3	$\frac{1}{8}$
PP	$\rightarrow$ IN NP	0	1
IN	$\rightarrow$ *with*	0	1
VP	$\rightarrow$ V NP	-1	$\frac{1}{2}$
	$\rightarrow$ VP PP	-2	$\frac{1}{4}$
	$\rightarrow$ MD V	-2	$\frac{1}{4}$
V	$\rightarrow$ *eat*	0	1

10.3.1 Parsing With Weighted Context-Free Grammars

The optimization problem in equation 10.4 can be solved by modifying the CKY algorithm. In the deterministic CKY algorithm, each cell $t[i,j]$ stored a set of nonterminals capable of deriving the span $\boldsymbol{w}_{i+1:j}$. We now augment the table so that the cell $t[i,j,X]$ is the *score of the best derivation* of $w_{i+1:j}$ from nonterminal X. This score is computed recursively: for the anchored binary production $(X \rightarrow Y\ Z, (i,j,k))$, we compute:

- the score of the anchored production, $\psi(X \rightarrow Y\ Z, (i,j,k))$;
- the score of the best derivation of the left child, $t[i,k,Y]$;
- the score of the best derivation of the right child, $t[k,j,Z]$.

These scores are combined by addition. As in the unweighted CKY algorithm, the table is constructed by considering spans of increasing length, so the scores for spans $t[i,k,Y]$ and $t[k,j,Z]$ are guaranteed to be available at the time we compute the score $t[i,j,X]$. The value $t[0,M,\mathrm{S}]$ is the score of the best derivation of $\boldsymbol{w}$ from the grammar. Algorithm 14 formalizes this procedure.

As in unweighted CKY, the parse is recovered from the table of back-pointers b, where each $b[i,j,X]$ stores the argmax split point k and production $X \rightarrow Y\ Z$ in the derivation of $\boldsymbol{w}_{i+1:j}$ from X. The top scoring parse can be obtained by tracing these pointers backward from $b[0,M,\mathrm{S}]$, all the way to the terminal symbols. This is analogous to the computation of the best sequence of labels in the Viterbi algorithm by tracing pointers backward from the end of the trellis. Note that we need only store back-pointers for the *best* path to $t[i,j,X]$; this follows from the locality assumption that the global score for a parse is a combination of the local scores of each production in the parse.

Algorithm 14
CKY algorithm for parsing a string $\boldsymbol{w} \in \Sigma^*$ in a weighted context-free grammar (N, Σ, R, S), where N is the set of nonterminals and R is the set of weighted productions. The grammar is assumed to be in Chomsky normal form (§ 9.2.1). The function TRACEBACK is defined in algorithm 13.

---

procedure WCKY($\boldsymbol{w}, G = (N, \Sigma, R, S)$)
  for all i, j, X **do** ▷ Initialization
    $t[i,j,X] \leftarrow 0$
    $b[i,j,X] \leftarrow \varnothing$
  for $m \in \{1, 2, \ldots, M\}$ **do**
    for all $X \in N$ **do**
      $t[m, m+1, X] \leftarrow \psi(X \rightarrow w_m, (m, m+1, m))$
  for $\ell \in \{2, 3, \ldots M\}$ **do**
    for $m \in \{0, 1, \ldots, M - \ell\}$ **do**
      for $k \in \{m+1, m+2, \ldots, m+\ell-1\}$ **do**
        $t[m, m+\ell, X] \leftarrow \max_{k,Y,Z} \psi(X \rightarrow Y\, Z, (m, m+\ell, k)) + t[m, k, Y] + t[k, m+\ell, Z]$
        $b[m, m+\ell, X] \leftarrow \operatorname{argmax}_{k,Y,Z} \psi(X \rightarrow Y\, Z, (m+\ell, k)) + t[m, k, Y] + t[k, m+\ell, Z]$
  return TRACEBACK($S, 0, M, b$)

Example Let's revisit the parsing table in figure 10.1. In a weighted CFG, each cell would include a score for each nonterminal; nonterminals that cannot be generated are assumed to have a score of $-\infty$. The first diagonal contains the scores of unary productions: $t[0,1,\text{NP}] = -2$, $t[1,2,\text{V}] = 0$, and so on. The next diagonal contains the scores for spans of length 2: $t[1,3,\text{VP}] = -1 + 0 - 3 = -4$, $t[3,5,\text{PP}] = 0 + 0 - 3 = -3$, and so on. Things get interesting when we reach the cell $t[1,5,\text{VP}]$, which contains the score for the derivation of the span $\boldsymbol{w}_{2:5}$ from the nonterminal VP. This score is computed as a max over two alternatives,

$$t[1,5,\text{VP}] = \max(\psi(\text{VP} \rightarrow \text{VP PP}, (1,3,5)) + t[1,3,\text{VP}] + t[3,5,\text{PP}],$$

$$\psi(\text{VP} \rightarrow \text{V NP}, (1,2,5)) + t[1,2,\text{V}] + t[2,5,\text{NP}]) \quad [10.8]$$

$$= \max(-2-4-3, -1+0-7) = -8. \quad [10.9]$$

Because the second case is the argmax, we set the back-pointer $b[1,5,\text{VP}] = (\text{V}, \text{NP}, 2)$, enabling the optimal derivation to be recovered.

10.3.2 Probabilistic Context-Free Grammars

Probabilistic context-free grammars (PCFGs) are a special case of weighted context-free grammars that arises when the weights correspond to probabilities. Specifically, the weight $\psi(X \rightarrow \alpha, (i,j,k)) = \log \text{p}(\alpha \mid X)$, where the probability of the right-hand side α is

Algorithm 15
Generative model for derivations from probabilistic context-free grammars in Chomsky Normal Form (CNF).

---

procedure DrawSubtree(X)
  sample $(X \to \alpha) \sim \mathrm{p}(\alpha \mid X)$
  if $\alpha = (Y\ Z)$ **then**
    return DrawSubtree(Y) $\cup$ DrawSubtree(Z)
  else
    return $(X \to \alpha)$ ▷ In CNF, all unary productions yield terminal symbols

---

conditioned on the nonterminal X, and the anchor (i,j,k) is ignored. These probabilities must be normalized over all possible right-hand sides, so that $\sum_\alpha \mathrm{p}(\alpha \mid X) = 1$, for all X. For a given parse τ, the product of the probabilities of the productions is equal to $\mathrm{p}(\tau)$, under the **generative model** $\tau \sim$ DrawSubtree(S), defined in algorithm 15.

The conditional probability of a parse given a string is

$$\mathrm{p}(\tau \mid \boldsymbol{w}) = \frac{\mathrm{p}(\tau)}{\sum_{\tau' \in \mathcal{T}(\boldsymbol{w})} \mathrm{p}(\tau')} = \frac{\exp \Psi(\tau)}{\sum_{\tau' \in \mathcal{T}(\boldsymbol{w})} \exp \Psi(\tau')}, \qquad [10.10]$$

where $\Psi(\tau) = \sum_{X \to \alpha, (i,j,k) \in \tau} \psi(X \to \alpha, (i,j,k))$. Because the probability is monotonic in the score $\Psi(\tau)$, the maximum likelihood parse can be identified by the CKY algorithm without modification. If a normalized probability $\mathrm{p}(\tau \mid \boldsymbol{w})$ is required, the denominator of equation 10.10 can be computed by the **inside recurrence**, described below.

Example The WCFG in table 10.2 is designed so that the weights are log-probabilities, satisfying the constraint $\sum_\alpha \exp \psi(X \to \alpha) = 1$. As noted earlier, there are two parses in $\mathcal{T}$(*we eat sushi with chopsticks*), with scores $\Psi(\tau_1) = \log \mathrm{p}(\tau_1) = -10$ and $\Psi(\tau_2) = \log \mathrm{p}(\tau_2) = -11$. Therefore, the conditional probability $\mathrm{p}(\tau_1 \mid \boldsymbol{w})$ is equal to

$$\mathrm{p}(\tau_1 \mid \boldsymbol{w}) = \frac{\mathrm{p}(\tau_1)}{\mathrm{p}(\tau_1) + \mathrm{p}(\tau_2)} = \frac{\exp \Psi(\tau_1)}{\exp \Psi(\tau_1) + \exp \Psi(\tau_2)} = \frac{2^{-10}}{2^{-10} + 2^{-11}} = \frac{2}{3}. \qquad [10.11]$$

The inside recurrence The denominator of equation 10.10 can be viewed as a language model, summing over all valid derivations of the string $\boldsymbol{w}$,

$$\mathrm{p}(\boldsymbol{w}) = \sum_{\tau' : \mathrm{yield}(\tau') = \boldsymbol{w}} \mathrm{p}(\tau'). \qquad [10.12]$$

Just as the CKY algorithm makes it possible to maximize over all such analyses, with a few modifications it can also compute their sum. Each cell $t[i,j,X]$ must store the log-probability of deriving $\boldsymbol{w}_{i+1:j}$ from nonterminal X. To compute this, we replace the maximization over split points k and productions $X \to Y\ Z$ with a "log-sum-exp" operation, which exponentiates the log-probabilities of the production and the children, sums them in probability space, and then converts back to the log domain:

$$t[i,j,X] = \log \sum_{k,Y,Z} \exp\left(\psi(X \to Y\ Z) + t[i,k,Y] + t[k,j,Z]\right) \quad [10.13]$$

$$= \log \sum_{k,Y,Z} \exp\left(\log p(Y\ Z \mid X) + \log p(Y \to \boldsymbol{w}_{i+1:k}) + \log p(Z \to \boldsymbol{w}_{k+1:j})\right) \quad [10.14]$$

$$= \log \sum_{k,Y,Z} p(Y\ Z \mid X) \times p(Y \to \boldsymbol{w}_{i+1:k}) \times p(Z \to \boldsymbol{w}_{k+1:j}) \quad [10.15]$$

$$= \log \sum_{k,Y,Z} p(Y\ Z, \boldsymbol{w}_{i+1:k}, \boldsymbol{w}_{k+1:j} \mid X) \quad [10.16]$$

$$= \log p(X \rightsquigarrow \boldsymbol{w}_{i+1:j}), \quad [10.17]$$

with $X \rightsquigarrow \boldsymbol{w}_{i+1:j}$ indicating the event that nonterminal X yields the span $w_{i+1}, w_{i+2}, \ldots, w_j$. The recursive computation of $t[i,j,X]$ is called the **inside recurrence**, because it computes the probability of each subtree as a combination of the probabilities of the smaller subtrees that are inside of it. The name implies a corresponding **outside recurrence**, which computes the probability of a nonterminal X spanning $\boldsymbol{w}_{i+1:j}$, joint with the outside context $(\boldsymbol{w}_{1:i}, \boldsymbol{w}_{j+1:M})$. This recurrence is described in § 10.4.3. The inside and outside recurrences are analogous to the forward and backward recurrences in probabilistic sequence labeling (see § 7.5.3). They can be used to compute the marginal probabilities of individual anchored productions, $p(X \to \alpha, (i,j,k) \mid \boldsymbol{w})$, summing over all possible derivations of $\boldsymbol{w}$.

10.3.3 *Semiring Weighted Context-Free Grammars

The weighted and unweighted CKY algorithms can be unified with the inside recurrence using the same semiring notation described in § 7.7.3. The generalized recurrence is

$$t[i,j,X] = \bigoplus_{k,Y,Z} \psi(X \to Y\ Z, (i,j,k)) \otimes t[i,k,Y] \otimes t[k,j,Z]. \quad [10.18]$$

This recurrence subsumes all of the algorithms that have been discussed in this chapter to this point.

Unweighted CKY When $\psi(X \to \alpha, (i,j,k))$ is a *Boolean truth value* $\{\top, \bot\}$, $\otimes$ is logical conjunction, and $\bigoplus$ is logical disjunction, then we derive CKY recurrence for unweighted context-free grammars, discussed in § 10.1 and algorithm 13.

Weighted CKY When $\psi(X \to \alpha, (i,j,k))$ is a scalar, $\otimes$ is addition, and $\bigoplus$ is maximization, then we derive the CKY recurrence for weighted context-free grammars, discussed in § 10.3 and algorithm 14. When $\psi(X \to \alpha, (i,j,k)) = \log p(\alpha \mid X)$, this same setting derives the CKY recurrence for finding the maximum likelihood derivation in a probabilistic context-free grammar.

Inside recurrence When $\psi(X \to \alpha, (i,j,k))$ is a log-probability, $\otimes$ is addition, and $\bigoplus = \log \sum \exp$, then we derive the inside recurrence for probabilistic context-free grammars, discussed in § 10.3.2. It is also possible to set $\psi(X \to \alpha, (i,j,k))$ directly equal to the probability $p(\alpha \mid X)$. In this case, $\otimes$ is multiplication and $\bigoplus$ is addition. While this may seem more intuitive than working with log-probabilities, there is the risk of underflow on long inputs.

Regardless of how the scores are combined, the key point is the locality assumption: the score for a derivation is the combination of the independent scores for each anchored production, and these scores do not depend on any other part of the derivation. For example, if two nonterminals are siblings, the scores of productions from these nonterminals are computed independently. This locality assumption is analogous to the first-order Markov assumption in sequence labeling, where the score for transitions between tags depends only on the previous tag and current tag, and not on the history. As with sequence labeling, this assumption makes it possible to find the optimal parse efficiently; its linguistic limitations are discussed in § 10.5.

10.4 Learning Weighted Context-Free Grammars

Like sequence labeling, context-free parsing is a form of structure prediction. As a result, WCFGs can be learned using the same set of algorithms: generative probabilistic models, structured perceptron, maximum conditional likelihood, and maximum margin learning. In all cases, learning requires a **treebank**, which is a dataset of sentences labeled with context-free parses. Parsing research was catalyzed by the **Penn Treebank** (Marcus et al., 1993), the first large-scale dataset of this type (see § 9.2.2). Phrase structure treebanks exist for roughly two dozen other languages, with coverage mainly restricted to European and East Asian languages, plus Arabic and Urdu.

10.4.1 Probabilistic Context-Free Grammars

Probabilistic context-free grammars are similar to hidden Markov models, in that they are generative models of text. In this case, the parameters of interest correspond to probabilities of productions, conditional on the left-hand side. As with hidden Markov models, these parameters can be estimated by relative frequency:

$$\psi(X \to \alpha) = \log p(X \to \alpha) \qquad [10.19]$$

$$\hat{p}(X \to \alpha) = \frac{\text{count}(X \to \alpha)}{\text{count}(X)}. \qquad [10.20]$$

For example, the probability of the production NP $\rightarrow$ DET NN is the corpus count of this production, divided by the count of the nonterminal NP. This estimator applies to terminal productions as well: the probability of NN $\rightarrow$ *whale* is the count of how often *whale* appears in the corpus as generated from an NN tag, divided by the total count of the NN tag. Even with the largest treebanks—on the order of one million tokens—it is difficult to accurately compute probabilities of even moderately rare events, such as NN $\rightarrow$ *whale*. Therefore, smoothing is critical for making PCFGs effective.

10.4.2 Feature-Based Parsing

The scores for each production can be computed as an inner product of weights and features,

$$\psi(X \rightarrow \alpha, (i,j,k)) = \boldsymbol{\theta} \cdot \boldsymbol{f}(X, \alpha, (i,j,k), \boldsymbol{w}), \tag{10.21}$$

where the feature vector $\boldsymbol{f}$ is a function of the left-hand-side X, the right-hand-side α, the anchor indices (i,j,k), and the input $\boldsymbol{w}$.

The basic feature $\boldsymbol{f}(X, \alpha, (i,j,k)) = \{(X, \alpha)\}$ encodes only the identity of the production itself. Features on anchored productions can include the words that border the span w_i, w_{j+1}, the word at the split point w_{k+1}, the presence of a verb or noun in the left child span $w_{i+1:k}$, and so on (Durrett and Klein, 2015). Scores on anchored productions can be incorporated into CKY parsing without any modification to the algorithm, because it is still possible to compute each element of the table $t[i,j,X]$ recursively from its immediate children.

Other features can be obtained by grouping elements on either the left-hand or right-hand side: for example it can be particularly beneficial to compute additional features by clustering terminal symbols, with features corresponding to groups of words with similar syntactic properties. The clustering can be obtained from unlabeled datasets that are much larger than any treebank, improving coverage. Such methods are described in chapter 14.

Feature-based parsing models can be estimated using the usual array of discriminative learning techniques. For example, a structure perceptron update can be computed as (Carreras et al., 2008)

$$\boldsymbol{f}(\tau, \boldsymbol{w}^{(i)}) = \sum_{(X \rightarrow \alpha, (i,j,k)) \in \tau} \boldsymbol{f}(X, \alpha, (i,j,k), \boldsymbol{w}^{(i)}) \tag{10.22}$$

$$\hat{\tau} = \underset{\tau \in \mathcal{T}(\boldsymbol{w})}{\operatorname{argmax}} \, \boldsymbol{\theta} \cdot \boldsymbol{f}(\tau, \boldsymbol{w}^{(i)}) \tag{10.23}$$

$$\boldsymbol{\theta} \leftarrow \boldsymbol{f}(\tau^{(i)}, \boldsymbol{w}^{(i)}) - \boldsymbol{f}(\hat{\tau}, \boldsymbol{w}^{(i)}). \tag{10.24}$$

A margin-based objective can be optimized by selecting $\hat{\tau}$ through cost-augmented decoding (§ 2.4.2), enforcing a margin of $\Delta(\hat{\tau}, \tau)$ between the hypothesis and the reference parse, where Δ is a nonnegative cost function, such as the Hamming loss (Stern et al., 2017).

It is also possible to train feature-based parsing models by conditional log-likelihood, as described in the next section.

10.4.3 *Conditional Random Field Parsing

The score of a derivation $\Psi(\tau)$ can be converted into a probability by normalizing over all possible derivations,

$$\mathrm{p}(\tau \mid \boldsymbol{w}) = \frac{\exp \Psi(\tau)}{\sum_{\tau' \in \mathcal{T}(\boldsymbol{w})} \exp \Psi(\tau')}. \tag{10.25}$$

Using this probability, a WCFG can be trained by maximizing the conditional log-likelihood of a labeled corpus.

Just as in logistic regression and the conditional random field over sequences, the gradient of the conditional log-likelihood is the difference between the observed and expected counts of each feature. The expectation $E_{\tau \mid \boldsymbol{w}}[\boldsymbol{f}(\tau, \boldsymbol{w}^{(i)}); \boldsymbol{\theta}]$ requires summing over all possible parses and computing the marginal probabilities of anchored productions, $\mathrm{p}(X \rightarrow \alpha, (i,j,k) \mid \boldsymbol{w})$. In CRF sequence labeling, marginal probabilities over tag bigrams are computed by the two-pass **forward-backward algorithm** (§ 7.5.3). The analogue for context-free grammars is the **inside-outside algorithm**, in which marginal probabilities are computed from terms generated by an upward and downward pass over the parsing chart:

- The upward pass is performed by the inside recurrence, which is described in § 10.3.2. Each inside variable $\alpha(i,j,X)$ is the score of deriving $\boldsymbol{w}_{i+1:j}$ from the nonterminal X. In a PCFG, this corresponds to the log-probability $\log \mathrm{p}(\boldsymbol{w}_{i+1:j} \mid X)$. This is computed by the recurrence,

$$\alpha(i,j,X) \triangleq \log \sum_{(X \rightarrow Y\ Z)} \sum_{k=i+1}^{j} \exp\left(\psi(X \rightarrow Y\ Z, (i,j,k)) + \alpha(i,k,Y) + \alpha(k,j,Z)\right). \tag{10.26}$$

The initial condition of this recurrence is $\alpha(m-1, m, X) = \psi(X \rightarrow w_m)$. The denominator $\sum_{\tau \in \mathcal{T}(\boldsymbol{w})} \exp \Psi(\tau)$ is equal to $\exp \alpha(0, M, \mathrm{S})$.

- The downward pass is performed by the **outside recurrence**, which recursively populates the same table structure, starting at the root of the tree. Each outside variable $\beta(i,j,X)$ is the score of having a phrase of type X covering the span $(i+1:j)$, joint with the exterior context $\boldsymbol{w}_{1:i}$ and $\boldsymbol{w}_{j+1:M}$. In a PCFG, this corresponds to the log-probability $\log \mathrm{p}((X, i+1, j), \boldsymbol{w}_{1:i}, \boldsymbol{w}_{j+1:M})$. Each outside variable is computed by the recurrence,

$$\begin{aligned}\exp \beta(i,j,X) \triangleq & \sum_{(Y \rightarrow X\ Z)} \sum_{k=j+1}^{M} \exp\left[\psi(Y \rightarrow X\ Z, (i,k,j)) + \alpha(j,k,Z) + \beta(i,k,Y)\right] \\ & + \sum_{(Y \rightarrow Z\ X)} \sum_{k=0}^{i-1} \exp\left[\psi(Y \rightarrow Z\ X, (k,i,j)) + \alpha(k,i,Z) + \beta(k,j,Y)\right].\end{aligned} \tag{10.27}$$

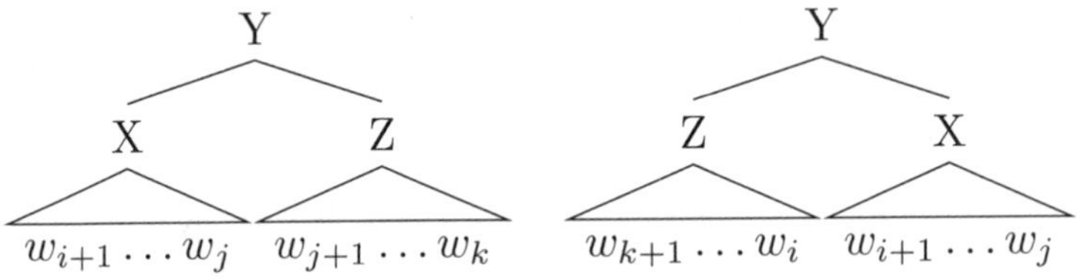

Figure 10.3
The two cases faced by the outside recurrence in the computation of $\beta(i,j,X)$.

The first line of equation 10.27 is the score under the condition that X is a left child of its parent, which spans $\boldsymbol{w}_{i+1:k}$, with $k > j$; the second line is the score under the condition that X is a right child of its parent Y, which spans $\boldsymbol{w}_{k+1:j}$, with $k < i$. The two cases are shown in figure 10.3. In each case, we sum over all possible productions with X on the right-hand side. The parent Y is bounded on one side by either i or j, depending on whether X is a left or right child of Y; we must sum over all possible values for the other boundary. The initial conditions for the outside recurrence are $\beta(0, M, \mathrm{S}) = 0$ and $\beta(0, M, X \neq \mathrm{S}) = -\infty$.

The marginal probability of a nonterminal X over span $\boldsymbol{w}_{i+1:j}$ is written $\mathrm{p}(X \rightsquigarrow \boldsymbol{w}_{i+1:j} \mid \boldsymbol{w})$. This probability can be computed from the inside and outside scores,

$$\mathrm{p}(X \rightsquigarrow \boldsymbol{w}_{i+1:j} \mid \boldsymbol{w}) = \frac{\mathrm{p}(X \rightsquigarrow \boldsymbol{w}_{i+1:j}, \boldsymbol{w})}{\mathrm{p}(\boldsymbol{w})} \tag{10.28}$$

$$= \frac{\mathrm{p}(\boldsymbol{w}_{i+1:j} \mid X) \times \mathrm{p}(X, \boldsymbol{w}_{1:i}, \boldsymbol{x}_{j+1:M})}{\mathrm{p}(\boldsymbol{w})} \tag{10.29}$$

$$= \frac{\exp\left(\alpha(i,j,X) + \beta(i,j,X)\right)}{\exp \alpha(0, M, S)}. \tag{10.30}$$

Marginal probabilities of individual productions can be computed similarly (see exercise 2). These marginal probabilities can be used for training a conditional random field parser, and also for the task of unsupervised **grammar induction**, in which a PCFG is estimated from a dataset of unlabeled text (Lari and Young, 1990; Pereira and Schabes, 1992).

10.4.4 Neural Context-Free Grammars

Neural networks can be applied to parsing by representing each span with a dense numerical vector (Socher et al., 2013a; Durrett and Klein, 2015; Cross and Huang, 2016).[4] For example, the anchor (i,j,k) and sentence $\boldsymbol{w}$ can be associated with a fixed-length column vector,

$$\boldsymbol{v}_{(i,j,k)} = [\boldsymbol{u}_{w_{i-1}}; \boldsymbol{u}_{w_i}; \boldsymbol{u}_{w_{j-1}}; \boldsymbol{u}_{w_j}; \boldsymbol{u}_{w_{k-1}}; \boldsymbol{u}_{w_k}], \tag{10.31}$$

4. Earlier work on neural constituent parsing used transition-based parsing algorithms (§ 10.6.2) rather than CKY-style chart parsing (Henderson, 2004; Titov and Henderson, 2007).

where $\boldsymbol{u}_{w_i}$ is a word embedding associated with the word w_i. The vector $\boldsymbol{v}_{i,j,k}$ can then be passed through a feedforward neural network and used to compute the score of the anchored production. For example, this score can be computed as a bilinear product (Durrett and Klein, 2015),

$$\tilde{\boldsymbol{v}}_{(i,j,k)} = \text{FeedForward}(\boldsymbol{v}_{(i,j,k)}) \quad [10.32]$$

$$\psi(X \rightarrow \alpha, (i,j,k)) = \tilde{\boldsymbol{v}}_{(i,j,k)}^{\top} \Theta \boldsymbol{f}(X \rightarrow \alpha), \quad [10.33]$$

where $\boldsymbol{f}(X \rightarrow \alpha)$ is a vector of features of the production and Θ is a parameter matrix. The matrix Θ and the parameters of the feedforward network can be learned by backpropagating from an objective such as the margin loss or the negative conditional log-likelihood.

10.5 Grammar Refinement

The locality assumptions underlying CFG parsing depend on the granularity of the nonterminals. For the Penn Treebank nonterminals, there are several reasons to believe that these assumptions are too strong (Johnson, 1998):

- The context-free assumption is too strict: for example, the probability of the production NP $\rightarrow$ NP PP is much higher (in the PTB) if the parent of the noun phrase is a verb phrase (indicating that the NP is a direct object) than if the parent is a sentence (indicating that the NP is the subject of the sentence).
- The Penn Treebank nonterminals are too coarse: there are many kinds of noun phrases and verb phrases, and accurate parsing sometimes requires knowing the difference. As we have already seen, when faced with prepositional phrase attachment ambiguity, a weighted CFG will either always choose NP attachment (if $\psi(\text{NP} \rightarrow \text{NP PP}) > \psi(\text{VP} \rightarrow \text{VP PP})$), or it will always choose VP attachment. To get more nuanced behavior, more fine-grained nonterminals are needed.
- More generally, accurate parsing requires some amount of **semantics**—understanding the meaning of the text to be parsed. Consider the example *cats scratch people with claws*: knowledge of about cats, claws, and scratching is necessary to correctly resolve the attachment ambiguity.

An extreme example is shown in figure 10.4. The analysis on the left is preferred because of the conjunction of similar entities *France* and *Italy*. But given the nonterminals shown in the analyses, there is no way to differentiate these two parses, since they include exactly the same productions. What is needed seems to be more precise nonterminals. One possibility would be to rethink the linguistics behind the Penn Treebank and ask the annotators to try again. But the original annotation effort took five years, and there is a little appetite for another annotation effort of this scope. Researchers have therefore turned to automated techniques.

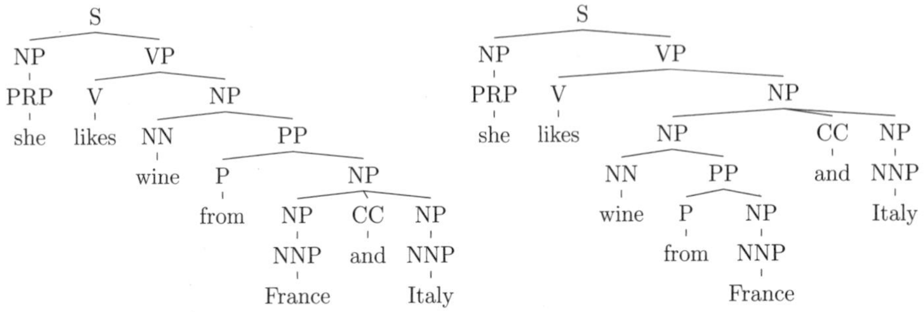

Figure 10.4
The left parse is preferable because of the conjunction of phrases headed by *France* and *Italy*, but these parses cannot be distinguished by a WCFG.

10.5.1 Parent Annotations and Other Tree Transformations

The key assumption underlying context-free parsing is that productions depend only on the identity of the nonterminal on the left-hand side, and not on its ancestors or neighbors. The validity of this assumption is an empirical question, and it depends on the nonterminals themselves: ideally, every noun phrase (and verb phrase, etc.) would be distributionally identical, so the assumption would hold. But in the Penn Treebank, the observed probability of productions often depends on the parent of the left-hand side. For example, noun phrases are more likely to be modified by prepositional phrases when they are in the object position (e.g., *they amused the students from Georgia*) than in the subject position (e.g., *the students from Georgia amused them*). This means that the NP → NP PP production is more likely if the entire constituent is the child of a VP than if it is the child of S. The observed statistics are (Johnson, 1998)

$$\Pr(\text{NP} \rightarrow \text{NP PP}) = 11\% \qquad [10.34]$$

$$\Pr(\text{NP under S} \rightarrow \text{NP PP}) = 9\% \qquad [10.35]$$

$$\Pr(\text{NP under VP} \rightarrow \text{NP PP}) = 23\%. \qquad [10.36]$$

This phenomenon can be captured by **parent annotation** (Johnson, 1998), in which each nonterminal is augmented with the identity of its parent, as shown in figure 10.5. This is sometimes called **vertical Markovization**, because a Markov dependency is introduced between each node and its parent (Klein and Manning, 2003). It is analogous to moving from a bigram to a trigram context in a hidden Markov model. In principle, parent annotation squares the size of the set of nonterminals, which could make parsing considerably less efficient. But in practice, the increase in the number of nonterminals that actually appear in the data is relatively modest (Johnson, 1998).

Parent annotation weakens the WCFG locality assumptions. This improves accuracy by enabling the parser to make more fine-grained distinctions, which better capture real linguistic phenomena. However, each production is more rare, and so careful smoothing or regularization is required to control the variance over production scores.

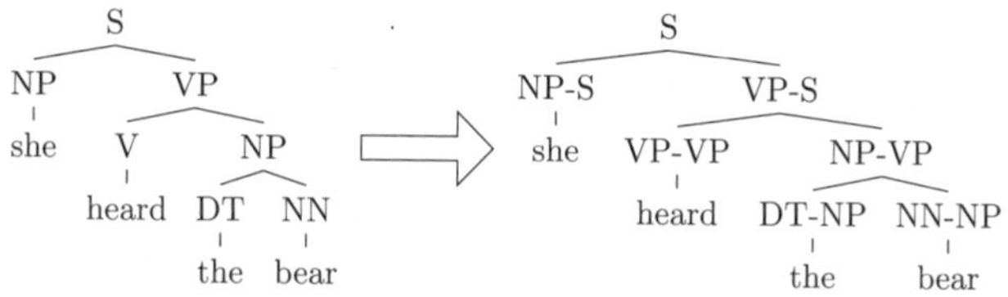

Figure 10.5
Parent annotation in a CFG derivation.

10.5.2 Lexicalized Context-Free Grammars

The examples in § 10.2.2 demonstrate the importance of individual words in resolving parsing ambiguity: the preposition *on* is more likely to attach to *met*, while the preposition *of* is more likely to attachment to *President*. But of all word pairs, which are relevant to attachment decisions? Consider the following variants on the original examples:

(10.3) a. We met the President of Mexico.
b. We met the first female President of Mexico.
c. They had supposedly met the President on Monday.

The underlined words are the **head words** of their respective phrases: *met* heads the verb phrase, and *President* heads the direct object noun phrase. These heads provide useful semantic information. But they break the context-free assumption, which states that the score for a production depends only on the parent and its immediate children, and not the substructure under each child.

The incorporation of head words into context-free parsing is known as **lexicalization** and is implemented in rules of the form:

$$\text{NP}(\textit{President}) \rightarrow \text{NP}(\textit{President})\ \text{PP}(\textit{of}) \tag{10.37}$$

$$\text{NP}(\textit{President}) \rightarrow \text{NP}(\textit{President})\ \text{PP}(\textit{on}). \tag{10.38}$$

Lexicalization was a major step toward accurate PCFG parsing in the 1990s and early 2000s. It requires solving three problems: identifying the heads of all constituents in a treebank; parsing efficiently while keeping track of the heads; and estimating the scores for lexicalized productions.

Identifying head words The head of a constituent is the word that is the most useful for determining how that constituent is integrated into the rest of the sentence.[5] The head word of a constituent is determined recursively: for any nonterminal production, the head of the left-hand side must be the head of one of the children. The head is typically selected according to a set of deterministic rules, sometimes called **head percolation rules**. In many cases, these rules are straightforward: the head of a noun phrase in an NP → DET NN

5. This is a pragmatic definition, befitting our goal of using head words to improve parsing; for a more formal definition, see Bender (2013, chapter 7).

Table 10.3
A fragment of head percolation rules for English (Magerman, 1995; Collins, 1997)

Nonterminal	Direction	Priority
S	right	VP SBAR ADJP UCP NP
VP	left	VBD VBN MD VBZ TO VB VP VBG VBP ADJP NP
NP	right	N* EX $ CD QP PRP ...
PP	left	IN TO FW

production is the head of the noun; the head of a sentence in an S → NP VP production is the head of the verb phrase.

Table 10.3 shows a fragment of the head percolation rules used in many English parsing systems. The meaning of the first rule is that to find the head of an S constituent, first look for the rightmost VP child; if you don't find one, then look for the rightmost SBAR child, and so on down the list. Verb phrases are headed by left verbs (the head of *can plan on walking* is *plan*, because the modal verb *can* is tagged MD); noun phrases are headed by the rightmost noun-like nonterminal (so the head of *the red cat* is *cat*),[6] and prepositional phrases are headed by the preposition (the head of *at Georgia Tech* is *at*). Some of these rules are arbitrary—there's no particular reason why the head of *cats and dogs* should be *dogs*—but the point here is just to get some lexical information that can support parsing, not to make deep claims about syntax. Figure 10.6 shows the application of these rules to two of the running examples.

Parsing lexicalized context-free grammars A naïve application of lexicalization would simply increase the set of nonterminals by taking the cross-product with the set of terminal symbols, so that the nonterminals now include symbols like NP(*President*) and VP(*meet*). Under this approach, the CKY parsing algorithm could be applied directly to the lexicalized production rules. However, the complexity would be cubic in the size of the vocabulary of terminal symbols, which would clearly be intractable.

Another approach is to augment the CKY table with an additional index, keeping track of the head of each constituent. The cell $t[i, j, h, X]$ stores the score of the best derivation in which nonterminal X spans $\boldsymbol{w}_{i+1:j}$ with head word h, where $i < h \leq j$. To compute such a table recursively, we must consider the possibility that each phrase gets its head from either its left or right child. The scores of the best derivations in which the head comes from the left and right child are denoted t_ℓ and t_r, respectively, leading to the following recurrence:

6. The noun phrase nonterminal is sometimes treated as a special case. Collins (1997) used a heuristic that looks for the rightmost child that is a noun-like part of speech (e.g., NN, NNP), a possessive marker, or a superlative adjective (e.g., *the greatest*). If no such child is found, the heuristic then looks for the *leftmost* NP. If there is no child with tag NP, the heuristic then applies another priority list, this time from right to left.

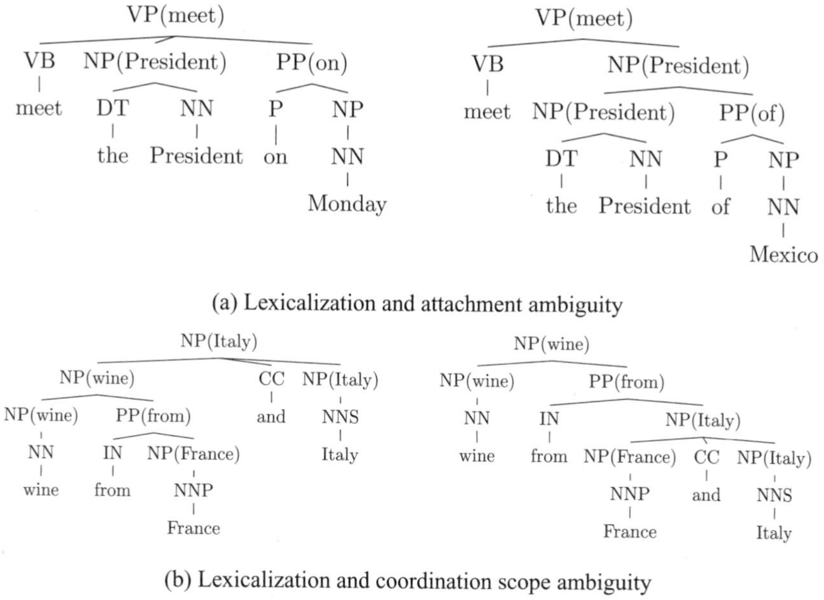

Figure 10.6
Examples of lexicalization.

$$t_\ell[i,j,h,X] = \max_{(X\to YZ)} \max_{k>h} \max_{k<h'\leq j} t[i,k,h,Y] + t[k,j,h',Z] + \psi(X(h) \to Y(h)Z(h')) \quad [10.39]$$

$$t_r[i,j,h,X] = \max_{(X\to YZ)} \max_{k<h} \max_{i<h'\leq k} t[i,k,h',Y] + t[k,j,h,Z] + (\psi(X(h) \to Y(h')Z(h))) \quad [10.40]$$

$$t[i,j,h,X] = \max\left(t_\ell[i,j,h,X], t_r[i,j,h,X]\right). \quad [10.41]$$

To compute t_ℓ, we maximize over all split points $k > h$, because the head word must be in the left child. We then maximize again over possible head words h' for the right child. An analogous computation is performed for t_r. The size of the table is now $\mathcal{O}(M^3N)$, where M is the length of the input and N is the number of nonterminals. Furthermore, each cell is computed by performing $\mathcal{O}(M^2)$ operations, because we maximize over both the split point k and the head h'. The time complexity of the algorithm is therefore $\mathcal{O}(RM^5N)$, where R is the number of rules in the grammar. Fortunately, more efficient solutions are possible. In general, the complexity of parsing can be reduced to $\mathcal{O}(M^4)$ in the length of the input; for a broad class of lexicalized CFGs, the complexity can be made cubic in the length of the input, just as in unlexicalized CFGs (Eisner, 2000).

Estimating lexicalized context-free grammars The final problem for lexicalized parsing is how to estimate weights for lexicalized productions $X(i) \to Y(j)\ Z(k)$. These productions are said to be bilexical, because they involve scores over pairs of words: in the example *meet the President of Mexico*, we hope to choose the correct attachment point by modeling the bilexical affinities of (*meet*, *of*) and (*President*, *of*). The number of such word pairs is quadratic in the size of the vocabulary, making it difficult to estimate the weights of lexicalized production rules directly from data. This is especially true for probabilistic context-free grammars, in which the weights are obtained from smoothed relative frequency. In a treebank with a million tokens, a vanishingly small fraction of the possible lexicalized productions will be observed more than once.[7] The Charniak (1997) and Collins (1997) parsers therefore focus on approximating the probabilities of lexicalized productions, using various smoothing techniques and independence assumptions.

In discriminatively trained weighted context-free grammars, the scores for each production can be computed from a set of features, which can be made progressively more fine grained (Finkel et al., 2008). For example, the score of the lexicalized production NP(*President*) → NP(*President*) PP(*of*) can be computed from the following features:

$$
\begin{aligned}
f(\text{NP}(\textit{President}) \to \text{NP}(\textit{President})\ \text{PP}(\textit{of})) = \{ & \text{NP}(*) \to \text{NP}(*)\ \text{PP}(*), \\
& \text{NP}(\textit{President}) \to \text{NP}(\textit{President})\ \text{PP}(*), \\
& \text{NP}(*) \to \text{NP}(*)\ \text{PP}(\textit{of}), \\
& \text{NP}(\textit{President}) \to \text{NP}(\textit{President})\ \text{PP}(\textit{of})\}.
\end{aligned}
$$

The first feature scores the unlexicalized production NP → NP PP; the next two features lexicalize only one element of the production, thereby scoring the appropriateness of NP attachment for the individual words *President* and *of*; the final feature scores the specific bilexical affinity of *President* and *of*. For bilexical pairs that are encountered frequently in the treebank, this bilexical feature can play an important role in parsing; for pairs that are absent or rare, regularization will drive its weight to zero, forcing the parser to rely on the more coarse-grained features.

In chapter 14, we will encounter techniques for clustering words based on their **distributional** properties—the contexts in which they appear. Such a clustering would group rare and common words, such as *whale, shark, beluga, Leviathan*. Word clusters can be used as features in discriminative lexicalized parsing, striking a middle ground between full lexicalization and nonterminals (Finkel et al., 2008). In this way, labeled examples containing relatively common words like *whale* can help to improve parsing for rare words like *beluga*, as long as those two words are clustered together.

7. The situation may be even more difficult, because nonbinary context-free grammars can involve **trilexical** or higher-order dependencies, between the head of the constituent and several of its children (Carreras et al., 2008).

10.5.3 *Refinement Grammars

Lexicalization improves on context-free parsing by adding detailed information in the form of lexical heads. However, estimating the scores of lexicalized productions is difficult. Klein and Manning (2003) argue that the right level of linguistic detail is somewhere between treebank categories and individual words. Some parts of speech and nonterminals are truly substitutable: for example, *cat*/N and *dog*/N. But others are not: for example, the preposition *of* exclusively attaches to nouns, while the preposition *as* is more likely to modify verb phrases. Klein and Manning (2003) obtained a 2% improvement in F-MEASURE on a parent-annotated PCFG parser by making a single change: splitting the preposition category into six subtypes. They propose a series of linguistically motivated refinements to the Penn Treebank annotations, which in total yield a 40% error reduction.

Nonterminal refinement can be automated by treating the refined categories as **latent variables**. For example, we might split the noun phrase nonterminal into NP1, NP2, NP3, ..., without defining in advance what each refined nonterminal corresponds to. This can be treated as partially supervised learning, similar to the multicomponent document classification model described in § 5.2.3. A latent variable PCFG can be estimated by expectation maximization (Matsuzaki et al., 2005):[8]

- In the E-step, estimate a marginal distribution q over the refinement type of each nonterminal in each derivation. These marginals are constrained by the original annotation: an NP can be reannotated as NP4, but not as VP3. Marginal probabilities over refined productions can be computed from the **inside-outside algorithm**, as described in § 10.4.3, where the E-step enforces the constraints imposed by the original annotations.
- In the M-step, recompute the parameters of the grammar, by summing over the probabilities of anchored productions that were computed in the E-step:

$$E[\text{count}(X \rightarrow Y\, Z)] = \sum_{i=0}^{M} \sum_{j=i}^{M} \sum_{k=i}^{j} \text{p}(X \rightarrow Y\, Z, (i, j, k) \mid \boldsymbol{w}). \qquad [10.42]$$

As usual, this process can be iterated to convergence. To determine the number of refinement types for each tag, Petrov et al. (2006) apply a split-merge heuristic; Liang et al. (2007) and Finkel et al. (2007) apply **Bayesian nonparametrics** (Cohen, 2016).

Some examples of refined nonterminals are shown in table 10.4. The proper nouns differentiate months, first names, middle initials, last names, first names of places, and second names of places; each of these will tend to appear in different parts of grammatical productions. The personal pronouns differentiate grammatical role, with PRP-0 appearing in subject position at the beginning of the sentence (note the capitalization), PRP-1 appearing in subject position but not at the beginning of the sentence, and PRP-2 appearing in object position.

8. Spectral learning, described in § 5.5.2, has also been applied to refinement grammars (Cohen et al., 2014).

Table 10.4
Examples of automatically refined nonterminals and some of the words that they generate (Petrov et al., 2006)

Proper nouns			
NNP-14	*Oct.*	*Nov.*	*Sept.*
NNP-12	*John*	*Robert*	*James*
NNP-2	*J.*	*E.*	*L.*
NNP-1	*Bush*	*Noriega*	*Peters*
NNP-15	*New*	*San*	*Wall*
NNP-3	*York*	*Francisco*	*Street*
Personal Pronouns			
PRP-0	*It*	*He*	*I*
PRP-1	*it*	*he*	*they*
PRP-2	*it*	*them*	*him*

10.6 Beyond Context-Free Parsing

In the context-free setting, the score for a parse is a combination of the scores of individual productions. As we have seen, these models can be improved by using finer-grained nonterminals, via parent-annotation, lexicalization, and automated refinement. However, the inherent limitations to the expressiveness of context-free parsing motivate the consideration of other search strategies. These strategies abandon the optimality guaranteed by bottom-up parsing, in exchange for the freedom to consider arbitrary properties of the proposed parses.

10.6.1 Reranking

A simple way to relax the restrictions of context-free parsing is to perform a two-stage process, in which a context-free parser generates a k-best list of candidates, and a **reranker** then selects the best parse from this list (Charniak and Johnson, 2005; Collins and Koo, 2005). The reranker can be trained from an objective that is similar to multiclass classification: the goal is to learn weights that assign a high score to the reference parse, or to the parse on the k-best list that has the lowest error. In either case, the reranker need only evaluate the k best parses, and so no context-free assumptions are necessary. This opens the door to more expressive scoring functions:

- It is possible to incorporate arbitrary nonlocal features, such as the structural parallelism and right-branching orientation of the parse (Charniak and Johnson, 2005).
- Reranking enables the use of **recursive neural networks**, in which each constituent span $\boldsymbol{w}_{i+1:j}$ receives a vector $\boldsymbol{u}_{i,j}$ which is computed from the vector representations of its children, using a composition function that is linked to the production rule (Socher et al., 2013a), such as,

$$u_{i,j} = f\left(\Theta_{X \to Y\,Z}\begin{bmatrix} u_{i,k} \\ u_{k,j} \end{bmatrix}\right). \quad [10.43]$$

The overall score of the parse can then be computed from the final vector, $\Psi(\tau) = \boldsymbol{\theta} \boldsymbol{u}_{0,M}$.

Reranking can yield substantial improvements in accuracy. The main limitation is that it can only find the best parse among the k best offered by the generator, so it is inherently limited by the ability of the bottom-up parser to find high-quality candidates.

10.6.2 Transition-Based Parsing

Structure prediction can be viewed as a form of search. An alternative to bottom-up parsing is to read the input from left-to-right, gradually building up a parse structure through a series of **transitions**. Transition-based parsing is described in more detail in the next chapter, in the context of dependency parsing. However, it can also be applied to CFG parsing, as briefly described here.

For any context-free grammar, there is an equivalent **pushdown automaton**, a model of computation that accepts exactly those strings that can be derived from the grammar. This computational model consumes the input from left to right, while pushing and popping elements on a stack. This architecture provides a natural transition-based parsing framework for context-free grammars, known as **shift-reduce parsing**.

Shift-reduce parsing is a type of transition-based parsing, in which the parser can take the following actions:

- *shift* the next terminal symbol onto the stack;
- *unary-reduce* the top item on the stack, using a unary production rule in the grammar;
- *binary-reduce* the top two items onto the stack, using a binary production rule in the grammar.

The set of available actions is constrained by the situation: the parser can only shift if there are remaining terminal symbols in the input, and it can only reduce if an applicable production rule exists in the grammar. If the parser arrives at a state where the input has been completely consumed, and the stack contains only the element S, then the input is accepted. If the parser arrives at a nonaccepting state where there are no possible actions, the input is rejected. A parse error occurs if there is some action sequence that would accept an input, but the parser does not find it.

Example Consider the input *we eat sushi* and the grammar in table 10.1. The input can be parsed through the following sequence of actions:

1. **Shift** the first token *we* onto the stack.
2. **Reduce** the top item on the stack to NP, using the production NP $\to$ *we*.

3. **Shift** the next token *eat* onto the stack, and **reduce** it to V with the production V $\to$ *eat*.
4. **Shift** the final token *sushi* onto the stack, and **reduce** it to NP. The input has been completely consumed, and the stack contains [NP, V, NP].
5. **Reduce** the top two items using the production VP $\to$ V NP. The stack now contains [VP, NP].
6. **Reduce** the top two items using the production S $\to$ NP VP. The stack now contains [S]. Because the input is empty, this is an accepting state.

One thing to notice from this example is that the number of shift actions is equal to the length of the input. The number of reduce actions is equal to the number of nonterminals in the analysis, which grows linearly in the length of the input. Thus, the overall time complexity of shift-reduce parsing is linear in the length of the input (assuming the complexity of each individual classification decision is constant in the length of the input). This is far better than the cubic time complexity required by CKY parsing.

Transition-based parsing as inference

In general, it is not possible to guarantee that a transition-based parser will find the optimal parse, $\text{argmax}_\tau\ \Psi(\tau; \boldsymbol{w})$, even under the usual CFG independence assumptions. We could assign a score to each anchored parsing action in each context, with $\psi(a, c)$ indicating the score of performing action a in context c. One might imagine that transition-based parsing could efficiently find the derivation that maximizes the sum of such scores. But this too would require backtracking and searching over an exponentially large number of possible action sequences: if a bad decision is made at the beginning of the derivation, then it may be impossible to recover the optimal action sequence without backtracking to that early mistake. This is known as a **search error**. Transition-based parsers can incorporate arbitrary features, without the restrictive independence assumptions required by chart parsing; search errors are the price that must be paid for this flexibility.

Learning transition-based parsing

Transition-based parsing can be combined with machine learning by training a classifier to select the correct action in each situation. This classifier is free to choose any feature of the input, the state of the parser, and the parse history. However, there is no optimality guarantee: the parser may choose a suboptimal parse, due to a mistake at the beginning of the analysis. Nonetheless, some of the strongest CFG parsers are based on the shift-reduce architecture, rather than CKY. A recent generation of models links shift-reduce parsing with recurrent neural networks, updating a hidden state vector while consuming the input (e.g., Cross and Huang, 2016; Dyer et al., 2016). Learning algorithms for transition-based parsing are discussed in more detail in § 11.3.

Exercises

1. Design a grammar that handles English subject-verb agreement. Specifically, your grammar should handle the examples below correctly:

   (10.4) a. She sings.
   b. We sing.

   (10.5) a. *She sing.
   b. *We sings.

2. Extend your grammar from the previous problem to include the auxiliary verb *can*, so that the following cases are handled:

   (10.6) a. She can sing.
   b. We can sing.

   (10.7) a. *She can sings.
   b. *We can sings.

3. French requires subjects and verbs to agree in person and number, and it requires determiners and nouns to agree in gender and number. Verbs and their objects need not agree. Assuming that French has two genders (feminine and masculine), three persons (first [*me*], second [*you*], third [*her*]), and two numbers (singular and plural), how many productions are required to extend the following simple grammar to handle agreement?

S	$\rightarrow$	NP VP
VP	$\rightarrow$	V | V NP | V NP NP
NP	$\rightarrow$	DET NN

4. Consider the grammar:

S	$\rightarrow$	NP VP
VP	$\rightarrow$	V NP
NP	$\rightarrow$	JJ NP
NP	$\rightarrow$	*fish* (the animal)
V	$\rightarrow$	*fish* (the action of fishing)
JJ	$\rightarrow$	*fish* (a modifier, as in *fish sauce* or *fish stew*)

   Apply the CKY algorithm and identify all possible parses for the sentence *fish fish fish fish*.

5. Choose one of the possible parses for the previous problem, and show how it can be derived by a series of shift-reduce actions.

6. To handle VP coordination, a grammar includes the production VP $\rightarrow$ VP CC VP. To handle adverbs, it also includes the production VP $\rightarrow$ VP ADV. Assume all verbs are generated from a sequence of unary productions, (VP $\rightarrow$ V $\rightarrow$ *eat*).

a) Show how to binarize the production VP → VP CC VP.

b) Use your binarized grammar to parse the sentence *They eat and drink together*, treating *together* as an adverb.

c) Prove that a weighted CFG cannot distinguish the two possible derivations of this sentence. Your explanation should focus on the productions in the original, nonbinary grammar.

d) Explain what condition must hold for a parent-annotated WCFG to prefer the derivation in which *together* modifies the coordination *eat and drink*.

7. Consider the following PCFG:

$$p(X \to X\,X) = \frac{1}{2} \quad [10.44]$$

$$p(X \to Y) = \frac{1}{2} \quad [10.45]$$

$$p(Y \to \sigma) = \frac{1}{|\Sigma|}, \forall \sigma \in \Sigma \quad [10.46]$$

a) Compute the probability $p(\hat{\tau})$ of the maximum probability parse for a string $\boldsymbol{w} \in \Sigma^M$.

b) Compute the conditional probability $p(\hat{\tau} \mid \boldsymbol{w})$.

8. Context-free grammars can be used to parse the internal structure of words. Using the weighted CKY algorithm and the following weighted context-free grammar, identify the best parse for the sequence of morphological segments *in+flame+able*.

S	→	V	0
S	→	N	0
S	→	J	0
V	→	VPref N	-1
J	→	N JSuff	1
J	→	V JSuff	0
J	→	NegPref J	1
VPref	→	*in+*	2
NegPref	→	*in+*	1
N	→	*flame*	0
JSuff	→	*+able*	0

9. Use the inside and outside scores to compute the marginal probability $p(X_{i+1:j} \to Y_{i+1:k}\, Z_{k+1:j} \mid \boldsymbol{w})$, indicating that Y spans $\boldsymbol{w}_{i+1:k}$, Z spans $\boldsymbol{w}_{k+1:j}$, and X is the parent of Y and Z, spanning $\boldsymbol{w}_{i+1:j}$.

10. Suppose that the potentials $\Psi(X \to \alpha)$ are log-probabilities, so that $\sum_\alpha \exp \Psi(X \to \alpha) = 1$ for all X. Verify that the semiring inside recurrence from equation 10.26 generates the log-probability $\log p(\boldsymbol{w}) = \log \sum_{\tau:\text{yield}(\tau)=\boldsymbol{w}} p(\tau)$.

11 Dependency Parsing

The previous chapter discussed algorithms for analyzing sentences in terms of nested constituents, such as noun phrases and verb phrases. However, many of the key sources of ambiguity in phrase-structure analysis relate to questions of **attachment**: where to attach a prepositional phrase or complement clause, how to scope a coordinating conjunction, and so on. These attachment decisions can be represented with a more lightweight structure: a directed graph over the words in the sentence, known as a **dependency parse**. Syntactic annotation has shifted its focus to such dependency structures: at the time of this writing, the **Universal Dependencies** project offers more than 100 dependency treebanks for more than 60 languages.[1] This chapter will describe the linguistic ideas underlying dependency grammar and then discuss exact and transition-based parsing algorithms. The chapter will also discuss research in transition-based structure prediction.

11.1 Dependency Grammar

While **dependency grammar** has a rich history of its own (Tesnière, 1966; Kübler et al., 2009), it can be motivated by extension from the lexicalized context-free grammars that we encountered in previous chapter (§ 10.5.2). Recall that lexicalization augments each nonterminal with a **head word**. The head of a constituent is identified recursively, using a set of **head rules**, as shown in table 10.3. An example of a lexicalized context-free parse is shown in figure 11.1a. In this sentence, the head of the S constituent is the main verb, *scratch*; this nonterminal then produces the noun phrase *the cats*, whose head word is *cats*, and from which we finally derive the word *the*. Thus, the word *scratch* occupies the central position for the sentence, with the word *cats* playing a supporting role. In turn, *cats* occupies the central position for the noun phrase, with the word *the* playing a supporting role.

The relationships between words in a sentence can be formalized in a directed graph, based on the lexicalized phrase-structure parse: create an edge (i,j) iff word i is the head of a phrase whose child is a phrase headed by word j. Thus, in our example, we would have *scratch* $\rightarrow$ *cats* and *cats* $\rightarrow$ *the*. We would not have the edge *scratch* $\rightarrow$ *the*, because

1. universaldependencies.org.

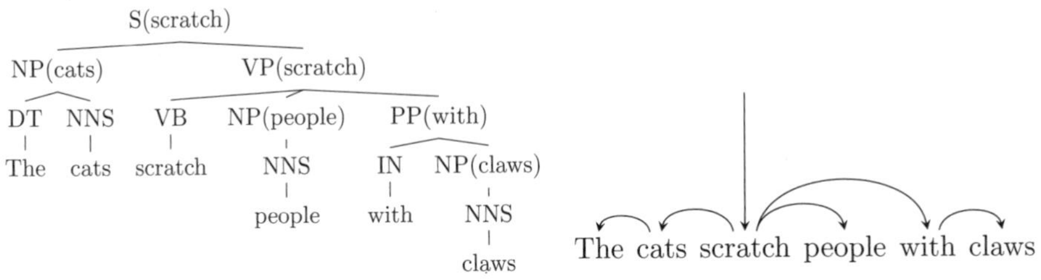

(a) Lexicalized constituency parse (b) Unlabeled dependency tree

Figure 11.1
Dependency grammar is closely linked to lexicalized context-free grammars: each lexical head has a dependency path to every other word in the constituent. (This example is based on the lexicalization rules from § 10.5.2, which make the preposition the head of a prepositional phrase. In the more contemporary Universal Dependencies annotations, the head of *with claws* would be *claws*, so there would be an edge *scratch* $\rightarrow$ *claws*.)

although S(*scratch*) dominates DET(*the*) in the phrase-structure parse tree, it is not its immediate parent. These edges describe **syntactic dependencies**, a bilexical relationship between a **head** and a **dependent**, which is at the heart of dependency grammar.

Continuing to build out this **dependency graph**, we will eventually reach every word in the sentence, as shown in figure 11.1b. In this graph—and in all graphs constructed in this way—every word has exactly one incoming edge, except for the root word, which is indicated by a special incoming arrow from above. Furthermore, the graph is *weakly connected*: if the directed edges were replaced with undirected edges, there would be a path between all pairs of nodes. From these properties, it can be shown that there are no cycles in the graph (or else at least one node would have to have more than one incoming edge), and therefore, the graph is a tree. Because the graph includes all vertices, it is a **spanning tree**.

11.1.1 Heads and Dependents

A dependency edge implies an asymmetric syntactic relationship between the head and dependent words, sometimes called **modifiers**. For a pair like *the cats* or *cats scratch*, how do we decide which is the head? Here are some possible criteria:

- The head sets the syntactic category of the construction: for example, nouns are the heads of noun phrases, and verbs are the heads of verb phrases.
- The modifier may be optional while the head is mandatory: for example, in the sentence *cats scratch people with claws*, the subtrees *cats scratch* and *cats scratch people* are grammatical sentences, but *with claws* is not.
- The head determines the morphological form of the modifier: for example, in languages that require gender agreement, the gender of the noun determines the gender of the adjectives and determiners.
- Edges should first connect content words, and then connect function words.

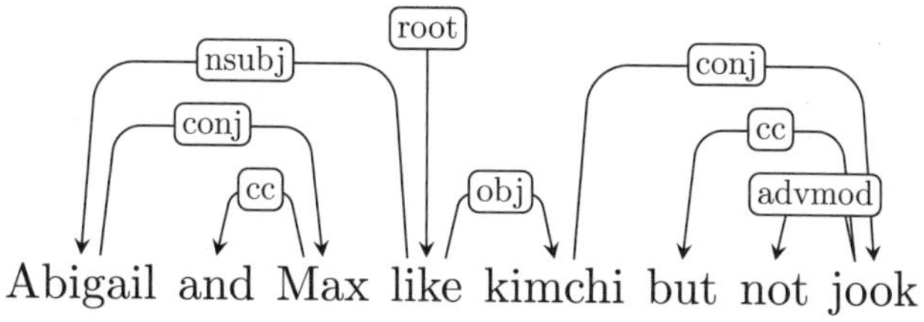

Figure 11.2
In the Universal Dependencies annotation system, the left-most item of a coordination is the head.

These principles are not universally accepted, and they sometimes conflict. The Universal Dependencies (UD) project has attempted to identify a set of principles that can be applied to dozens of different languages (Nivre et al., 2016).[2] These principles are based on the universal part-of-speech tags from chapter 8. They differ somewhat from the head rules described in § 10.5.2: for example, on the principle that dependencies should relate content words, the prepositional phrase *with claws* would be headed by *claws*, resulting in an edge *scratch* → *claws*, and another edge *claws* → *with*.

One objection to dependency grammar is that not all syntactic relations are asymmetric. One such relation is coordination (Popel et al., 2013): in the sentence, *Abigail and Max like kimchi* (figure 11.2), which word is the head of the coordinated noun phrase *Abigail and Max*? Choosing either *Abigail* or *Max* seems arbitrary; fairness argues for making *and* the head, but this seems like the least important word in the noun phrase, and selecting it would violate the principle of linking content words first. The Universal Dependencies annotation system arbitrarily chooses the left-most item as the head—in this case, *Abigail*—and includes edges from this head to both *Max* and the coordinating conjunction *and*. These edges are distinguished by the labels CONJ (for the thing begin conjoined) and CC (for the coordinating conjunction). The labeling system is discussed next.

11.1.2 Labeled Dependencies

Edges may be **labeled** to indicate the nature of the syntactic relation that holds between the two elements. For example, in figure 11.2, the label NSUBJ on the edge from *like* to *Abigail* indicates that the subtree headed by *Abigail* is the noun subject of the verb *like*; similarly, the label OBJ on the edge from *like* to *kimchi* indicates that the subtree headed by *kimchi* is the object.[3] The negation *not* is treated as an adverbial modifier (ADVMOD) on the noun *jook*.

A slightly more complex example is shown in figure 11.3. The multiword expression *New York pizza* is treated as a "flat" unit of text, with the elements linked by the COMPOUND relation. The sentence includes two clauses that are conjoined in the same way that noun

2. The latest and most specific guidelines are available at universaldependencies.org/guidelines.html.

3. Earlier work distinguished direct and indirect objects (De Marneffe and Manning, 2008), but this has been dropped in version 2.0 of the Universal Dependencies annotation system.

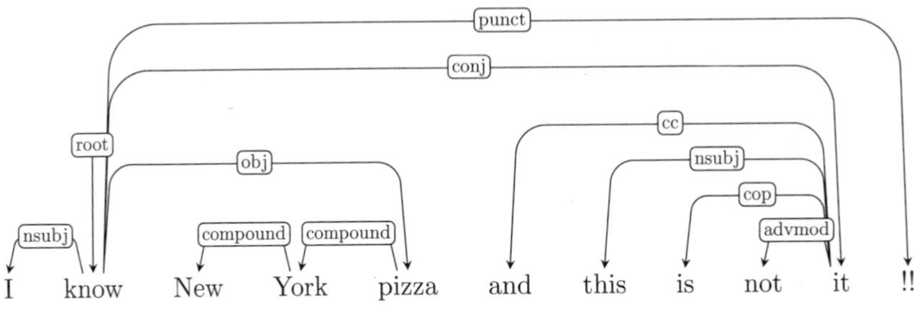

Figure 11.3
A labeled dependency parse from the English UD Treebank (reviews-361348-0006).

phrases are conjoined in figure 11.2. The second clause contains a **copula** verb (see § 8.1.1). For such clauses, we treat the "object" of the verb as the root—in this case, *it*—and label the verb as a dependent, with the COP relation. This example also shows how punctuations are treated, with label PUNCT.

11.1.3 Dependency Subtrees and Constituents

Dependency trees hide information that would be present in a CFG parse. Often what is hidden is in fact irrelevant: for example, figure 11.4 shows three different ways of representing prepositional phrase adjuncts to the verb *ate*. Because there is apparently no meaningful difference between these analyses, the Penn Treebank decides by convention to use the two-level representation (see Johnson, 1998, for a discussion). As shown in figure 11.4d, these three cases all look the same in a dependency parse.

But dependency grammar imposes its own set of annotation decisions, such as the identification of the head of a coordination (§ 11.1.1); without lexicalization, context-free grammar does not require either element in a coordination to be privileged in this way. Dependency parses can be disappointingly flat: for example, in the sentence *Yesterday, Abigail was eagerly feeding Max kimchi*, the root *feeding* is the head of every dependency! The constituent parse arguably offers a more useful structural analysis for such cases.

Projectivity

Thus far, we have defined dependency trees as spanning trees over a graph in which each word is a vertex. As we have seen, one way to construct such trees is by connecting the heads in a lexicalized constituent parse. However, there are spanning trees that cannot be constructed in this way. Syntactic constituents are *contiguous* spans. In a spanning tree constructed from a lexicalized constituent parse, the head h of any constituent that spans the nodes from i to j must have a path to every node in this span. This is property is known as **projectivity**, and projective dependency parses are a restricted class of spanning trees. Informally, projectivity means that "crossing edges" are prohibited. The formal definition follows:

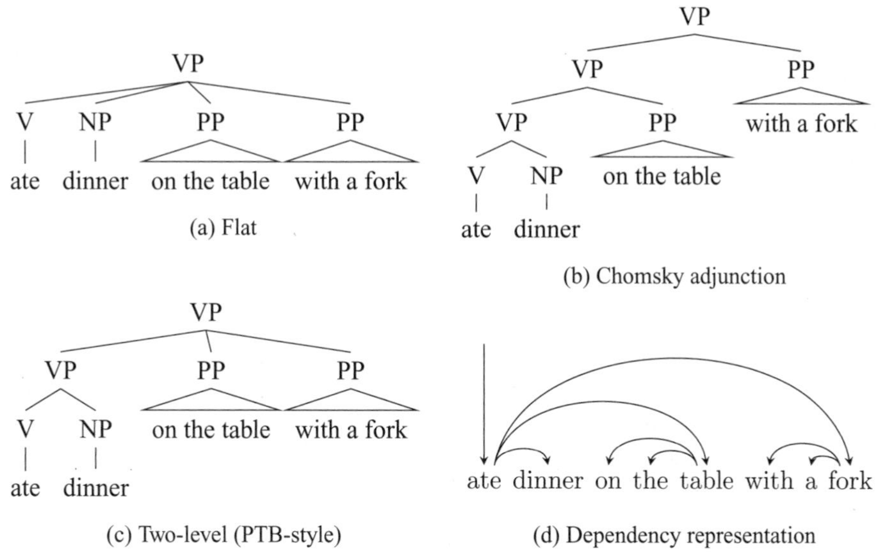

Figure 11.4
The three different CFG analyses of this verb phrase all correspond to a single dependency structure.

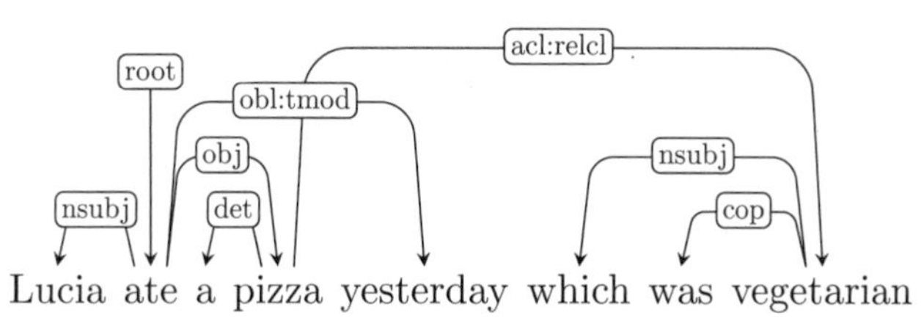

Figure 11.5
An example of a nonprojective dependency parse. The "crossing edge" arises from the relative clause *which was vegetarian* and the oblique temporal modifier *yesterday*.

Definition 2 (Projectivity). *An edge from i to j is projective iff all k between i and j are descendants of i. A dependency parse is projective iff all its edges are projective.*

Figure 11.5 gives an example of a nonprojective dependency graph in English. This dependency graph does not correspond to any constituent parse. As shown in table 11.1, nonprojectivity is more common in languages such as Czech and German. Even though relatively few dependencies are nonprojective in these languages, many sentences have at least one such dependency. As we will soon see, projectivity has important algorithmic consequences.

Table 11.1
Frequency of nonprojective dependencies in three languages (Kuhlmann and Nivre, 2010)

	% nonprojective edges	% nonprojective sentences
Czech	1.86%	22.42%
English	0.39%	7.63%
German	2.33%	28.19%

11.2 Graph-Based Dependency Parsing

Let $\boldsymbol{y} = \{(i \xrightarrow{r} j)\}$ represent a dependency graph, in which each edge is a relation r from head word $i \in \{1, 2, \ldots, M, \text{ROOT}\}$ to modifier $j \in \{1, 2, \ldots, M\}$. The special node ROOT indicates the root of the graph, and M is the length of the input $|\boldsymbol{w}|$. Given a scoring function $\Psi(\boldsymbol{y}, \boldsymbol{w}; \boldsymbol{\theta})$, the optimal parse is

$$\hat{\boldsymbol{y}} = \underset{\boldsymbol{y} \in \mathcal{Y}(\boldsymbol{w})}{\operatorname{argmax}} \Psi(\boldsymbol{y}, \boldsymbol{w}; \boldsymbol{\theta}), \qquad [11.1]$$

where $\mathcal{Y}(\boldsymbol{w})$ is the set of valid dependency parses on the input $\boldsymbol{w}$. As usual, the number of possible labels $|\mathcal{Y}(\boldsymbol{w})|$ is exponential in the length of the input (Wu and Chao, 2004). Algorithms that search over this space of possible graphs are known as **graph-based dependency parsers**.

In sequence labeling and constituent parsing, it was possible to search efficiently over an exponential space by choosing a feature function that decomposes into a sum of local feature vectors. A similar approach is possible for dependency parsing, by requiring the scoring function to decompose across dependency arcs:

$$\Psi(\boldsymbol{y}, \boldsymbol{w}; \boldsymbol{\theta}) = \sum_{i \xrightarrow{r} j \in \boldsymbol{y}} \psi(i \xrightarrow{r} j, \boldsymbol{w}; \boldsymbol{\theta}). \qquad [11.2]$$

Dependency parsers that operate under this assumption are known as **arc factored**, because the score of a graph is a combination of the scores of all arcs.

Higher-order dependency parsing

The arc-factored decomposition can be relaxed to allow higher-order dependencies. In **second-order dependency parsing**, the scoring function may include grandparents and siblings, as shown by the templates in figure 11.6. The scoring function is

$$\Psi(\boldsymbol{y}, \boldsymbol{w}; \boldsymbol{\theta}) = \sum_{i \xrightarrow{r} j \in \boldsymbol{y}} \psi_{\text{parent}}(i \xrightarrow{r} j, \boldsymbol{w}; \boldsymbol{\theta})$$
$$+ \sum_{k \xrightarrow{r'} i \in \boldsymbol{y}} \psi_{\text{grandparent}}(i \xrightarrow{r} j, k, r', \boldsymbol{w}; \boldsymbol{\theta})$$

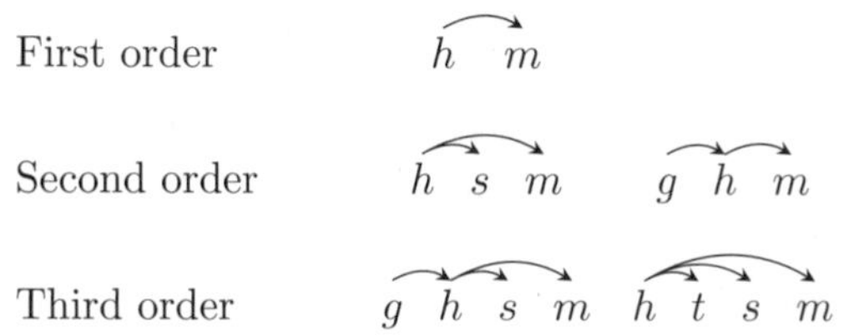

Figure 11.6
Feature templates for higher-order dependency parsing.

$$+ \sum_{\substack{i \xrightarrow{r'} s \in \boldsymbol{y} \\ s \neq j}} \psi_{\text{sibling}}(i \xrightarrow{r} j, s, r', \boldsymbol{w}; \boldsymbol{\theta}). \qquad [11.3]$$

The second line computes a scoring function that includes the grandparent k; the third line computes a scoring function for each sibling s. For projective dependency graphs, there are efficient algorithms for second-order and third-order dependency parsing (Eisner, 1996; McDonald and Pereira, 2006; Koo and Collins, 2010); for nonprojective dependency graphs, second-order dependency parsing is NP-hard (McDonald and Pereira, 2006). The specific algorithms are discussed in the next section.

11.2.1 Graph-Based Parsing Algorithms

The distinction between projective and nonprojective dependency trees (§ 11.1.3) plays a key rôle in the choice of algorithms. Because projective dependency trees are closely related to (and can be derived from) lexicalized constituent trees, lexicalized parsing algorithms can be applied directly. For the more general problem of parsing to arbitrary spanning trees, a different class of algorithms is required. In both cases, arc-factored dependency parsing relies on precomputing the scores $\psi(i \xrightarrow{r} j, \boldsymbol{w}; \boldsymbol{\theta})$ for each potential edge. There are $\mathcal{O}(M^2R)$ such scores, where M is the length of the input and R is the number of dependency relation types, and this is a lower bound on the time and space complexity of any exact algorithm for arc-factored dependency parsing.

Projective dependency parsing Any lexicalized constituency tree can be converted into a projective dependency tree by creating arcs between the heads of constituents and their parents, so any algorithm for lexicalized constituent parsing can be converted into an algorithm for projective dependency parsing, by converting arc scores into scores for lexicalized productions. As noted in § 10.5.2, there are cubic time algorithms for lexicalized constituent parsing, which are extensions of the CKY algorithm. Therefore, arc-factored projective dependency parsing can be performed in cubic time in the length of the input.

Second-order projective dependency parsing can also be performed in cubic time, with minimal modifications to the lexicalized parsing algorithm (Eisner, 1996). It is possible to go even further, to **third-order dependency parsing**, in which the scoring function may consider great-grandparents, grand-siblings, and "tri-siblings," as shown in figure 11.6. Third-order dependency parsing can be performed in $\mathcal{O}(M^4)$ time, which can be made practical through the use of pruning to eliminate unlikely edges (Koo and Collins, 2010).

Nonprojective dependency parsing In nonprojective dependency parsing, the goal is to identify the highest-scoring spanning tree over the words in the sentence. The arc-factored assumption ensures that the score for each spanning tree will be computed as a sum over scores for the edges, which are precomputed. Based on these scores, we build a weighted connected graph. Arc-factored nonprojective dependency parsing is then equivalent to finding the spanning tree that achieves the maximum total score, $\Psi(\boldsymbol{y}, \boldsymbol{w}) = \sum_{i \xrightarrow{r} j \in \boldsymbol{y}} \psi(i \xrightarrow{r} j, \boldsymbol{w})$. The **Chu-Liu-Edmonds algorithm** (Chu and Liu, 1965; Edmonds, 1967) computes this **maximum directed spanning tree** efficiently. It does this by first identifying the best incoming edge $i \xrightarrow{r} j$ for each vertex j. If the resulting graph does not contain cycles, it is the maximum spanning tree. If there is a cycle, it is collapsed into a super-vertex, whose incoming and outgoing edges are based on the edges to the vertices in the cycle. The algorithm is then applied recursively to the resulting graph, and the process repeats until a graph without cycles is obtained.

The time complexity of identifying the best incoming edge for each vertex is $\mathcal{O}(M^2 R)$, where M is the length of the input and R is the number of relations; in the worst case, the number of cycles is $\mathcal{O}(M)$. Therefore, the complexity of the Chu-Liu-Edmonds algorithm is $\mathcal{O}(M^3 R)$. This complexity can be reduced to $\mathcal{O}(M^2 N)$ by storing the edge scores in a Fibonnaci heap (Gabow et al., 1986). For more detail on graph-based parsing algorithms, see Eisner (1997) and Kübler et al. (2009).

Higher-order nonprojective dependency parsing Given the tractability of higher-order projective dependency parsing, you may be surprised to learn that nonprojective second-order dependency parsing is NP-hard. This can be proved by reduction from the vertex cover problem (Neuhaus and Bröker, 1997). A heuristic solution is to do projective parsing first, and then postprocess the projective dependency parse to add nonprojective edges (Nivre and Nilsson, 2005). More recent work has applied techniques for approximate inference in graphical models, including belief propagation (Smith and Eisner, 2008), integer linear programming (Martins et al., 2009), variational inference (Martins et al., 2010), and Markov Chain Monte Carlo (Zhang et al., 2014).

11.2.2 Computing Scores for Dependency Arcs

The arc-factored scoring function $\psi(i \xrightarrow{r} j, \boldsymbol{w}; \boldsymbol{\theta})$ can be defined in several ways:

$$\text{Linear} \qquad \psi(i \xrightarrow{r} j, \boldsymbol{w}; \boldsymbol{\theta}) = \boldsymbol{\theta} \cdot \boldsymbol{f}(i \xrightarrow{r} j, \boldsymbol{w}) \qquad [11.4]$$

$$\text{Neural} \qquad \psi(i \xrightarrow{r} j, \boldsymbol{w}; \boldsymbol{\theta}) = \text{Feedforward}([\boldsymbol{u}_{w_i}; \boldsymbol{u}_{w_j}]; \boldsymbol{\theta}) \qquad [11.5]$$

$$\text{Generative} \qquad \psi(i \xrightarrow{r} j, \boldsymbol{w}; \boldsymbol{\theta}) = \log \mathrm{p}(w_j, r \mid w_i). \qquad [11.6]$$

Linear feature-based arc scores Linear models for dependency parsing incorporate many of the same features used in sequence labeling and discriminative constituent parsing. These include:

- the length and direction of the arc;
- the words w_i and w_j linked by the dependency relation;
- the prefixes, suffixes, and parts of speech of these words;
- the neighbors of the dependency arc, $w_{i-1}, w_{i+1}, w_{j-1}, w_{j+1}$;
- the prefixes, suffixes, and parts of speech of these neighbor words.

Each of these features can be conjoined with the dependency edge label r. Note that features in an arc-factored parser can refer to words other than w_i and w_j. The restriction is that the features consider only a single arc.

Bilexical features (e.g., *sushi* → *chopsticks*) are powerful but rare, so it is useful to augment them with coarse-grained alternatives, by "backing off" to the part of speech or affix. For example, the following features are created by backing off to part-of-speech tags in an unlabeled dependency parser:

$$\begin{aligned} \boldsymbol{f}(3 \rightarrow 5, \textit{we eat sushi with chopsticks}) = \langle & \textit{sushi} \rightarrow \textit{chopsticks}, \\ & \textit{sushi} \rightarrow \text{NNS}, \\ & \text{NN} \rightarrow \textit{chopsticks}, \\ & \text{NNS} \rightarrow \text{NN} \rangle. \end{aligned}$$

Regularized discriminative learning algorithms can then trade off between features at varying levels of detail. McDonald et al. (2005) take this approach as far as *tetralexical* features (e.g., $(w_i, w_{i+1}, w_{j-1}, w_j)$). Such features help to avoid choosing arcs that are unlikely due to the intervening words: for example, there is unlikely to be an edge between two nouns if the intervening span contains a verb. A large list of first- and second-order features is provided by Bohnet (2010), who uses a hashing function to store these features efficiently.

Neural arc scores Given vector representations $\boldsymbol{x}_i$ for each word w_i in the input, a set of arc scores can be computed from a feedforward neural network:

$$\psi(i \xrightarrow{r} j, \boldsymbol{w}; \boldsymbol{\theta}) = \text{FeedForward}([\boldsymbol{x}_i; \boldsymbol{x}_j]; \boldsymbol{\theta}_r), \qquad [11.7]$$

where unique weights $\boldsymbol{\theta}_r$ are available for each arc type (Pei et al., 2015; Kiperwasser and Goldberg, 2016). Kiperwasser and Goldberg (2016) use a feedforward network with a single hidden layer,

$$z = g(\Theta_r[\boldsymbol{x}_i; \boldsymbol{x}_j] + b_r^{(z)}) \quad [11.8]$$

$$\psi(i \xrightarrow{r} j) = \boldsymbol{\beta}_r z + b_r^{(y)}, \quad [11.9]$$

where Θ_r is a matrix, $\boldsymbol{\beta}_r$ is a vector, each b_r is a scalar, and the function g is an elementwise tanh activation function.

The vector $\boldsymbol{x}_i$ can be set equal to the word embedding, which may be pre-trained or learned by backpropagation (Pei et al., 2015). Alternatively, contextual information can be incorporated by applying a bidirectional recurrent neural network across the input, as described in § 7.6. The RNN hidden states at each word can be used as inputs to the arc scoring function (Kiperwasser and Goldberg, 2016).

Feature-based arc scores are computationally expensive, due to the costs of storing and searching a huge table of weights. Neural arc scores can be viewed as a compact solution to this problem. Rather than working in the space of tuples of lexical features, the hidden layers of a feedforward network can be viewed as implicitly computing feature combinations, with each layer of the network evaluating progressively more words. An early paper on neural dependency parsing showed substantial speed improvements at test time, while also providing higher accuracy than feature-based models (Chen and Manning, 2014).

Probabilistic arc scores If each arc score is equal to the log-probability $\log \mathrm{p}(w_j, r \mid w_i)$, then the sum of scores gives the log-probability of the sentence and arc labels, by the chain rule. For example, consider the unlabeled parse of *we eat sushi with rice*:

$$\boldsymbol{y} = \{(\text{ROOT}, 2), (2, 1), (2, 3), (3, 5), (5, 4)\} \quad [11.10]$$

$$\log \mathrm{p}(\boldsymbol{w} \mid \boldsymbol{y}) = \sum_{(i \to j) \in \boldsymbol{y}} \log \mathrm{p}(w_j \mid w_i) \quad [11.11]$$

$$= \log \mathrm{p}(\textit{eat} \mid \text{ROOT}) + \log \mathrm{p}(\textit{we} \mid \textit{eat}) + \log \mathrm{p}(\textit{sushi} \mid \textit{eat})$$
$$+ \log \mathrm{p}(\textit{rice} \mid \textit{sushi}) + \log \mathrm{p}(\textit{with} \mid \textit{rice}). \quad [11.12]$$

Probabilistic generative models are used in combination with expectation-maximization (chapter 5) for unsupervised dependency parsing (Klein and Manning, 2004).

11.2.3 Learning

Having formulated graph-based dependency parsing as a structure prediction problem, we can apply similar learning algorithms to those used in sequence labeling. Given a loss function $\ell(\boldsymbol{\theta}; \boldsymbol{w}^{(i)}, \boldsymbol{y}^{(i)})$, we can compute gradient-based updates to the parameters. For a model with feature-based arc scores and a perceptron loss, we obtain the usual structured perceptron update,

$$\hat{y} = \underset{y' \in \mathcal{Y}(w)}{\operatorname{argmax}}\, \boldsymbol{\theta} \cdot \boldsymbol{f}(\boldsymbol{w}, \boldsymbol{y}') \qquad [11.13]$$

$$\boldsymbol{\theta} = \boldsymbol{\theta} + \boldsymbol{f}(\boldsymbol{w}, \boldsymbol{y}) - \boldsymbol{f}(\boldsymbol{w}, \hat{\boldsymbol{y}}) \qquad [11.14]$$

In this case, the argmax requires a maximization over all dependency trees for the sentence, which can be computed using the algorithms described in § 11.2.1. We can apply all the usual tricks from § 2.3: weight averaging, a large-margin objective, and regularization. McDonald et al. (2005) were the first to treat dependency parsing as a structure prediction problem, using MIRA, an online margin-based learning algorithm. Neural arc scores can be learned in the same way, backpropagating from a margin loss to updates on the feedforward network that computes the score for each edge.

A conditional random field for arc-factored dependency parsing is built on the probability model,

$$\mathrm{p}(\boldsymbol{y} \mid \boldsymbol{w}) = \frac{\exp \sum_{i \xrightarrow{r} j \in \boldsymbol{y}} \psi(i \xrightarrow{r} j, \boldsymbol{w}; \boldsymbol{\theta})}{\sum_{\boldsymbol{y}' \in \mathcal{Y}(\boldsymbol{w})} \exp \sum_{i \xrightarrow{r} j \in \boldsymbol{y}'} \psi(i \xrightarrow{r} j, \boldsymbol{w}; \boldsymbol{\theta})}. \qquad [11.15]$$

Such a model is trained to minimize the negative log conditional-likelihood. Just as in CRF sequence models (§ 7.5.3) and the logistic regression classifier (§ 2.5), the gradients involve marginal probabilities $\mathrm{p}(i \xrightarrow{r} j \mid \boldsymbol{w}; \boldsymbol{\theta})$, which in this case are probabilities over individual dependencies. In arc-factored models, these probabilities can be computed in polynomial time. For projective dependency trees, the marginal probabilities can be computed in cubic time, using a variant of the inside-outside algorithm (Lari and Young, 1990). For non-projective dependency parsing, marginals can also be computed in cubic time, using the **matrix-tree theorem** (Koo et al., 2007; McDonald et al., 2007; Smith and Smith, 2007). Details of these methods are described by Kübler et al. (2009).

11.3 Transition-Based Dependency Parsing

Graph-based dependency parsing offers exact inference, meaning that it is possible to recover the best-scoring parse for any given model. But this comes at a price: the scoring function is required to decompose into local parts—in the case of nonprojective parsing, these parts are restricted to individual arcs. These limitations are felt more keenly in dependency parsing than in sequence labeling, because second-order dependency features are critical to correctly identify some types of attachments. For example, prepositional phrase attachment depends on the attachment point, the object of the preposition, and the preposition itself; arc-factored scores cannot account for all three of these features simultaneously. Graph-based dependency parsing may also be criticized on the basis of intuitions about human language processing: people read and listen to sentences *sequentially*, incrementally building mental models of the sentence structure and meaning before getting to the end (Jurafsky, 1996). This seems hard to reconcile with graph-based algorithms, which perform bottom-up operations on the entire sentence, requiring the parser to keep every word in memory. Finally, from a practical perspective, graph-based dependency parsing is relatively slow, running in cubic time in the length of the input.

Transition-based algorithms address all three of these objections. They work by moving through the sentence sequentially, while performing actions that incrementally update a stored representation of what has been read thus far. As with the shift-reduce parser from § 10.6.2, this representation consists of a stack, onto which parsing substructures can be pushed and popped. In shift-reduce, these substructures were constituents; in the transition systems that follow, they will be projective dependency trees over partial spans of the input.[4] Parsing is complete when the input is consumed and there is only a single structure on the stack. The sequence of actions that led to the parse is known as the **derivation**. One problem with transition-based systems is that there may be multiple derivations for a single parse structure—a phenomenon known as **spurious ambiguity**.

11.3.1 Transition Systems for Dependency Parsing

A **transition system** consists of a representation for describing configurations of the parser, and a set of transition actions, which manipulate the configuration. There are two main transition systems for dependency parsing: **arc-standard**, which is closely related to shift-reduce, and **arc-eager**, which adds an additional action that can simplify derivations (Abney and Johnson, 1991). In both cases, transitions are between **configurations** that are represented as triples, $C = (\sigma, \beta, A)$, where σ is the stack, β is the input buffer, and A is the list of arcs that have been created (Nivre, 2008). In the initial configuration,

$$C_{\text{initial}} = ([\textsc{Root}], \boldsymbol{w}, \varnothing), \qquad [11.16]$$

indicating that the stack contains only the special node ROOT, the entire input is on the buffer, and the set of arcs is empty. An accepting configuration is

$$C_{\text{accept}} = ([\textsc{Root}], \varnothing, A), \qquad [11.17]$$

where the stack contains only ROOT, the buffer is empty, and the arcs A define a spanning tree over the input. The arc-standard and arc-eager systems define a set of transitions between configurations, which are capable of transforming an initial configuration into an accepting configuration. In both of these systems, the number of actions required to parse an input grows linearly in the length of the input, making transition-based parsing considerably more efficient than graph-based methods.

Arc-standard The **arc-standard** transition system is closely related to shift-reduce and to the LR algorithm that is used to parse programming languages (Aho et al., 2006). It includes the following classes of actions:

4. Transition systems also exist for nonprojective dependency parsing (e.g., Nivre, 2008).

Table 11.2
Arc-standard derivation of the unlabeled dependency parse for the input *they like bagels with lox*

	σ	β	action	arc added to $\mathcal{A}$
1.	[ROOT]	*they like bagels with lox*	SHIFT	
2.	[ROOT, *they*]	*like bagels with lox*	ARC-LEFT	(*they* ← *like*)
3.	[ROOT]	*like bagels with lox*	SHIFT	
4.	[ROOT, *like*]	*bagels with lox*	SHIFT	
5.	[ROOT, *like, bagels*]	*with lox*	SHIFT	
6.	[ROOT, *like, bagels, with*]	*lox*	ARC-LEFT	(*with* ← *lox*)
7.	[ROOT, *like, bagels*]	*lox*	ARC-RIGHT	(*bagels* → *lox*)
8.	[ROOT, *like*]	*bagels*	ARC-RIGHT	(*like* → *bagels*)
9.	[ROOT]	*like*	ARC-RIGHT	(ROOT → *like*)
10.	[ROOT]	∅	DONE	

- SHIFT: move the first item from the input buffer on to the top of the stack,

$$(\sigma, i|\beta, A) \Rightarrow (\sigma|i, \beta, A), \qquad [11.18]$$

where we write $i|\beta$ to indicate that i is the leftmost item in the input buffer, and $\sigma|i$ to indicate the result of pushing i on to stack σ.

- ARC-LEFT: create a new left-facing arc of type r between the item on the top of the stack and the first item in the input buffer. The head of this arc is j, which remains at the front of the input buffer. The arc $j \xrightarrow{r} i$ is added to A. Formally,

$$(\sigma|i, j|\beta, A) \Rightarrow (\sigma, j|\beta, A \oplus j \xrightarrow{r} i), \qquad [11.19]$$

where r is the label of the dependency arc and $\oplus$ concatenates the new arc $j \xrightarrow{r} i$ to the list A.

- ARC-RIGHT: creates a new right-facing arc of type r between the item on the top of the stack and the first item in the input buffer. The head of this arc is i, which is "popped" from the stack and pushed to the front of the input buffer. The arc $i \xrightarrow{r} j$ is added to A. Formally,

$$(\sigma|i, j|\beta, A) \Rightarrow (\sigma, i|\beta, A \oplus i \xrightarrow{r} j), \qquad [11.20]$$

where again r is the label of the dependency arc.

Each action has preconditions. The SHIFT action can be performed only when the buffer has at least one element. The ARC-LEFT action cannot be performed when the root node ROOT is on top of the stack, because this node must be the root of the entire tree. The ARC-LEFT and ARC-RIGHT actions remove the modifier words from the stack (in the case of ARC-LEFT) and from the buffer (in the case of ARC-RIGHT), so it is impossible for any word to have more than one parent. Furthermore, the end state can only be reached when every word is removed from the buffer and stack, so the set of arcs is guaranteed to constitute a spanning tree. An example arc-standard derivation is shown in table 11.2.

Arc-eager dependency parsing In the arc-standard transition system, a word is completely removed from the parse once it has been made the modifier in a dependency arc. At this time, any dependents of this word must have already been identified. Right-branching structures are common in English (and many other languages), with words often modified by units such as prepositional phrases to their right. In the arc-standard system, this means that we must first shift all the units of the input onto the stack, and then work backward, creating a series of arcs, as occurs in table 11.2. Note that the decision to shift *bagels* onto the stack guarantees that the prepositional phrase *with lox* will attach to the noun phrase and that this decision must be made before the prepositional phrase is itself parsed. This has been argued to be cognitively implausible (Abney and Johnson, 1991); from a computational perspective, it means that a parser may need to look several steps ahead to make the correct decision.

Arc-eager dependency parsing changes the ARC-RIGHT action so that right dependents can be attached before all of their dependents have been found. Rather than removing the modifier from both the buffer and stack, the ARC-RIGHT action pushes the modifier on to the stack, on top of the head. Because the stack can now contain elements that already have parents in the partial dependency graph, two additional changes are necessary:

- A precondition is required to ensure that the ARC-LEFT action cannot be applied when the top element on the stack already has a parent in A.
- A new REDUCE action is introduced, which can remove elements from the stack if they already have a parent in A:

$$(\sigma | i, \beta, A) \Rightarrow (\sigma, \beta, A). \qquad [11.21]$$

As a result of these changes, it is now possible to create the arc *like* $\rightarrow$ *bagels* before parsing the prepositional phrase *with lox*. Furthermore, this action does not imply a decision about whether the prepositional phrase will attach to the noun or verb. Noun attachment is chosen in the parse in table 11.3, but verb attachment could be achieved by applying the REDUCE action at step 5 or 7.

Projectivity The arc-standard and arc-eager transition systems are guaranteed to produce projective dependency trees, because all arcs are between the word at the top of the stack and the left-most edge of the buffer (Nivre, 2008). Nonprojective transition systems can be constructed by adding actions that create arcs with words that are second or third in the stack (Attardi, 2006), or by adopting an alternative configuration structure, which maintains a list of all words that do not yet have heads (Covington, 2001). In **pseudo-projective dependency parsing**, a projective dependency parse is generated first, and then a set of graph transformation techniques are applied, producing nonprojective edges (Nivre and Nilsson, 2005).

Beam search In "greedy" transition-based parsing, the parser tries to make the best decision at each configuration. This can lead to search errors, when an early decision locks the parser into a poor derivation. For example, in table 11.2, if ARC-RIGHT were chosen at step

Table 11.3
Arc-eager derivation of the unlabeled dependency parse for the input *they like bagels with lox*

	σ	β	action	arc added to $\mathcal{A}$
1.	[ROOT]	*they like bagels with lox*	SHIFT	
2.	[ROOT, *they*]	*like bagels with lox*	ARC-LEFT	(*they* $\leftarrow$ *like*)
3.	[ROOT]	*like bagels with lox*	ARC-RIGHT	(ROOT $\rightarrow$ *like*)
4.	[ROOT, *like*]	*bagels with lox*	ARC-RIGHT	(*like* $\rightarrow$ *bagels*)
5.	[ROOT, *like, bagels*]	*with lox*	SHIFT	
6.	[ROOT, *like, bagels, with*]	*lox*	ARC-LEFT	(*with* $\leftarrow$ *lox*)
7.	[ROOT, *like, bagels*]	*lox*	ARC-RIGHT	(*bagels* $\rightarrow$ *lox*)
8.	[ROOT, *like, bagels, lox*]	$\varnothing$	REDUCE	
9.	[ROOT, *like, bagels*]	$\varnothing$	REDUCE	
10.	[ROOT, *like*]	$\varnothing$	REDUCE	
11.	[ROOT]	$\varnothing$	DONE	

4, then the parser would later be forced to attach the prepositional phrase *with lox* to the verb *likes*. Note that the *likes* $\rightarrow$ *bagels* arc is indeed part of the correct dependency parse, but the arc-standard transition system requires it to be created later in the derivation.

Beam search is a general technique for ameliorating search errors in incremental decoding.[5] While searching, the algorithm maintains a set of partially complete hypotheses, called a beam. At step t of the derivation, there is a set of k hypotheses, each of which includes a score $s_t^{(k)}$ and a set of dependency arcs $A_t^{(k)}$:

$$h_t^{(k)} = (s_t^{(k)}, A_t^{(k)}). \tag{11.22}$$

Each hypothesis is then "expanded" by considering the set of all valid actions from the current configuration $c_t^{(k)}$, written $\mathcal{A}(c_t^{(k)})$. This yields a large set of new hypotheses. For each action $a \in \mathcal{A}(c_t^{(k)})$, we score the new hypothesis $A_t^{(k)} \oplus a$. The top k hypotheses by this scoring metric are kept, and parsing proceeds to the next step (Zhang and Clark, 2008). Note that beam search requires a scoring function for action *sequences*, rather than individual actions. This issue will be revisited in the next section.

Figure 11.7 shows the application of beam search to dependency parsing, with a beam size of $K=2$. For the first transition, the only valid action is SHIFT, so there is only one possible configuration at $t=2$. From this configuration, there are three possible actions. The two best scoring actions are ARC-RIGHT and ARC-LEFT, and so the resulting hypotheses from these actions are on the beam at $t=3$. From these configurations, there are three possible actions each, but the best two are expansions of the bottom hypothesis at $t=3$. Parsing continues until $t=5$, at which point both hypotheses reach an accepting state. The best-scoring hypothesis is then selected as the parse.

5. Beam search is used throughout natural language processing and beyond. In this text, it appears again in coreference resolution (§ 15.2.4) and machine translation (§ 18.4).

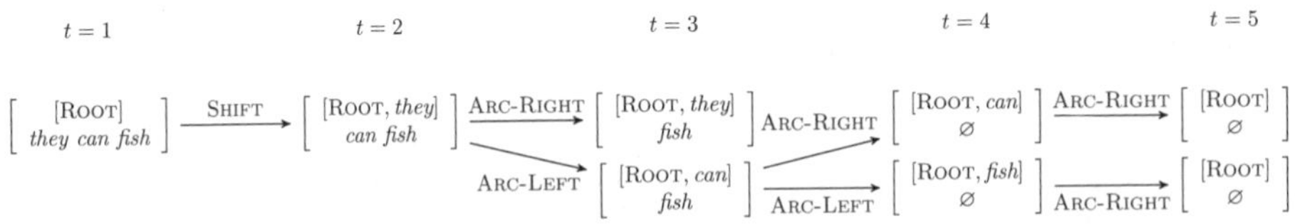

Figure 11.7
Beam search for unlabeled dependency parsing, with beam size $K=2$. The arc lists for each configuration are not shown, but can be computed from the transitions.

11.3.2 Scoring Functions for Transition-Based Parsers

Transition-based parsing requires selecting a series of actions. In greedy transition-based parsing, this can be done by training a classifier,

$$\hat{a} = \underset{a \in \mathcal{A}(c)}{\operatorname{argmax}} \Psi(a, c, \boldsymbol{w}; \boldsymbol{\theta}), \qquad [11.23]$$

where $\mathcal{A}(c)$ is the set of admissible actions in the current configuration c, $\boldsymbol{w}$ is the input, and Ψ is a scoring function with parameters $\boldsymbol{\theta}$ (Yamada and Matsumoto, 2003).

A feature-based score can be computed, $\Psi(a, c, \boldsymbol{w}) = \boldsymbol{\theta} \cdot \boldsymbol{f}(a, c, \boldsymbol{w})$, using features that may consider any aspect of the current configuration and input sequence. Typical features for transition-based dependency parsing include the word and part of speech of the top element on the stack; the word and part of speech of the first, second, and third elements on the input buffer; pairs and triples of words and parts of speech from the top of the stack and the front of the buffer; the distance (in tokens) between the element on the top of the stack and the element in the front of the input buffer; the number of modifiers of each of these elements; and higher-order dependency features as described above in the section on graph-based dependency parsing (see, e.g., Zhang and Nivre, 2011).

Parse actions can also be scored by neural networks. For example, Chen and Manning (2014) build a feedforward network in which the input layer consists of the concatenation of embeddings of several words and tags:

- the top three words on the stack, and the first three words on the buffer;
- the first and second leftmost and rightmost children (dependents) of the top two words on the stack;
- the leftmost and rightmost grandchildren of the top two words on the stack;
- embeddings of the part-of-speech tags of these words.

Let us call this base layer $\boldsymbol{x}(c, \boldsymbol{w})$, defined as,

$$c = (\sigma, \beta, A)$$

$$\boldsymbol{x}(c, \boldsymbol{w}) = [\boldsymbol{v}_{w_{\sigma_1}}, \boldsymbol{v}_{t_{\sigma_1}} \boldsymbol{v}_{w_{\sigma_2}}, \boldsymbol{v}_{t_{\sigma_2}}, \boldsymbol{v}_{w_{\sigma_3}}, \boldsymbol{v}_{t_{\sigma_3}}, \boldsymbol{v}_{w_{\beta_1}}, \boldsymbol{v}_{t_{\beta_1}}, \boldsymbol{v}_{w_{\beta_2}}, \boldsymbol{v}_{t_{\beta_2}}, \ldots],$$

where $\boldsymbol{v}_{w_{\sigma_1}}$ is the embedding of the first word on the stack, $\boldsymbol{v}_{t_{\beta_2}}$ is the embedding of the part-of-speech tag of the second word on the buffer, and so on. Given this base encoding of the parser state, the score for the set of possible actions is computed through a feedforward network,

$$z = g(\Theta^{(x \to z)} \boldsymbol{x}(c, \boldsymbol{w})) \quad [11.24]$$

$$\psi(a, c, \boldsymbol{w}; \boldsymbol{\theta}) = \Theta_a^{(z \to y)} z, \quad [11.25]$$

where the vector z plays the same role as the features $\boldsymbol{f}(a, c, \boldsymbol{w})$, but is a learned representation. Chen and Manning (2014) use a cubic elementwise activation function, $g(x) = x^3$, so that the hidden layer models products across all triples of input features. The learning algorithm updates the embeddings as well as the parameters of the feedforward network.

11.3.3 Learning to Parse

Transition-based dependency parsing suffers from a mismatch between the supervision, which comes in the form of dependency trees, and the classifier's prediction space, which is a set of parsing actions. One solution is to create new training data by converting parse trees into action sequences; another is to derive supervision directly from the parser's performance.

Oracle-based training A transition system can be viewed as a function from action sequences (derivations) to parse trees. The inverse of this function is a mapping from parse trees to derivations, which is called an **oracle**. For the arc-standard and arc-eager parsing system, an oracle can be computed in linear time in the length of the derivation (Kübler et al., 2009, page 32). Both the arc-standard and arc-eager transition systems suffer from spurious ambiguity: there exist dependency parses for which multiple derivations are possible, such as $1 \leftarrow 2 \rightarrow 3$. The oracle must choose between these different derivations. For example, the algorithm described by Kübler et al. (2009) would first create the left arc $(1 \leftarrow 2)$, and then create the right arc, $(1 \leftarrow 2) \rightarrow 3$; another oracle might begin by shifting twice, resulting in the derivation $1 \leftarrow (2 \rightarrow 3)$.

Given such an oracle, a dependency treebank can be converted into a set of oracle action sequences $\{A^{(i)}\}_{i=1}^{N}$. The parser can be trained by stepping through the oracle action sequences and optimizing on an classification-based objective that rewards selecting the oracle action. For transition-based dependency parsing, maximum conditional likelihood is a typical choice (Chen and Manning, 2014; Dyer et al., 2015):

$$\mathrm{p}(a \mid c, \boldsymbol{w}) = \frac{\exp \Psi(a, c, \boldsymbol{w}; \boldsymbol{\theta})}{\sum_{a' \in \mathcal{A}(c)} \exp \Psi(a', c, \boldsymbol{w}; \boldsymbol{\theta})} \quad [11.26]$$

$$\hat{\boldsymbol{\theta}} = \underset{\boldsymbol{\theta}}{\operatorname{argmax}} \sum_{i=1}^{N} \sum_{t=1}^{|A^{(i)}|} \log \mathrm{p}(a_t^{(i)} \mid c_t^{(i)}, \boldsymbol{w}), \quad [11.27]$$

where $|A^{(i)}|$ is the length of the action sequence $A^{(i)}$.

Recall that beam search requires a scoring function for action sequences. Such a score can be obtained by adding the log-likelihoods (or hinge losses) across all actions in the sequence (Chen and Manning, 2014).

Global objectives The objective in equation 11.27 is **locally normalized**: it is the product of normalized probabilities over individual actions. A similar characterization could be made of nonprobabilistic algorithms in which hinge-loss objectives are summed over individual actions. In either case, training on individual actions can be sub-optimal with respect to global performance, due to the **label bias problem** (Lafferty et al., 2001; Andor et al., 2016).

As a stylized example, suppose that a given configuration appears 100 times in the training data, with action a_1 as the oracle action in 51 cases and a_2 as the oracle action in the other 49 cases. However, in cases where a_2 is correct, choosing a_1 results in a cascade of subsequent errors, while in cases where a_1 is correct, choosing a_2 results in only a single error. A classifier that is trained on a local objective function will learn to always choose a_1, but choosing a_2 would minimize the overall number of errors.

This observation motivates a global objective, such as the globally normalized conditional likelihood,

$$\mathrm{p}(A^{(i)} \mid \boldsymbol{w}; \boldsymbol{\theta}) = \frac{\exp \sum_{t=1}^{|A^{(i)}|} \Psi(a_t^{(i)}, c_t^{(i)}, \boldsymbol{w})}{\sum_{A' \in \mathbb{A}(\boldsymbol{w})} \exp \sum_{t=1}^{|A'|} \Psi(a'_t, c'_t, \boldsymbol{w})}, \quad [11.28]$$

where the denominator sums over the set of all possible action sequences, $\mathbb{A}(\boldsymbol{w})$.[6] In the conditional random field model for sequence labeling (§ 7.5.3), it was possible to compute this sum explicitly, using dynamic programming. In transition-based parsing, this is not possible. However, the sum can be approximated using beam search,

$$\sum_{A' \in \mathbb{A}(\boldsymbol{w})} \exp \sum_{t=1}^{|A'|} \Psi(a'_t, c'_t, \boldsymbol{w}) \approx \sum_{k=1}^{K} \exp \sum_{t=1}^{|A^{(k)}|} \Psi(a_t^{(k)}, c_t^{(k)}, \boldsymbol{w}), \quad [11.29]$$

where $A^{(k)}$ is an action sequence on a beam of size K. This gives rise to the following loss function,

$$L(\boldsymbol{\theta}) = -\sum_{t=1}^{|A^{(i)}|} \Psi(a_t^{(i)}, c_t^{(i)}, \boldsymbol{w}) + \log \sum_{k=1}^{K} \exp \sum_{t=1}^{|A^{(k)}|} \Psi(a_t^{(k)}, c_t^{(k)}, \boldsymbol{w}). \quad [11.30]$$

6. Andor et al. (2016) prove that the set of globally normalized conditional distributions is a strict superset of the set of locally normalized conditional distributions and that globally normalized conditional models are therefore strictly more expressive.

The derivatives of this loss involve expectations with respect to a probability distribution over action sequences on the beam.

***Early update and the incremental perceptron** When learning in the context of beam search, the goal is to learn a decision function so that the gold dependency parse is always reachable from at least one of the partial derivations on the beam. (The combination of a transition system, such as beam search, and a scoring function for actions is known as a **policy**.) To achieve this, we can make an **early update** as soon as the oracle action sequence "falls off" the beam, even before a complete analysis is available (Collins and Roark, 2004; Daumé III and Marcu, 2005). The loss can be based on the best-scoring hypothesis on the beam, or the sum of all hypotheses (Huang et al., 2012).

For example, consider the beam search in figure 11.7. In the correct parse, *fish* is the head of dependency arcs to both of the other two words. In the arc-standard system, this can be achieved only by using SHIFT for the first two actions. At $t=3$, the oracle action sequence has fallen off the beam. The parser should therefore stop and update the parameters by the gradient $\frac{\partial}{\partial \boldsymbol{\theta}} L(A^{(i)}_{1:3}, \{A^{(k)}_{1:3}\}; \boldsymbol{\theta})$, where $A^{(i)}_{1:3}$ is the first three actions of the oracle sequence and $\{A^{(k)}_{1:3}\}$ is the beam.

This integration of incremental search and learning was first developed in the **incremental perceptron** (Collins and Roark, 2004). This method updates the parameters with respect to a hinge loss, which compares the top-scoring hypothesis and the gold action sequence, up to the current point t. Several improvements to this basic protocol are possible:

- As noted earlier, the gold dependency parse can be derived by multiple action sequences. Rather than checking for the presence of a single oracle action sequence on the beam, we can check if the gold dependency parse is *reachable* from the current beam, using a **dynamic oracle** (Goldberg and Nivre, 2012).

- By maximizing the score of the gold action sequence, we are training a decision function to find the correct action given the gold context. But in reality, the parser will make errors, and the parser is not trained to find the best action given a context that may not itself be optimal. This issue is addressed by various generalizations of incremental perceptron, known as **learning to search** (Daumé III et al., 2009). Some of these methods are discussed in chapter 15.

11.4 Applications

Dependency parsing is used in many real-world applications: any time you want to know about pairs of words that might not be adjacent, you can use dependency arcs instead of regular expression search patterns. For example, you may want to match strings like *delicious pastries*, *delicious French pastries*, and *the pastries are delicious*.

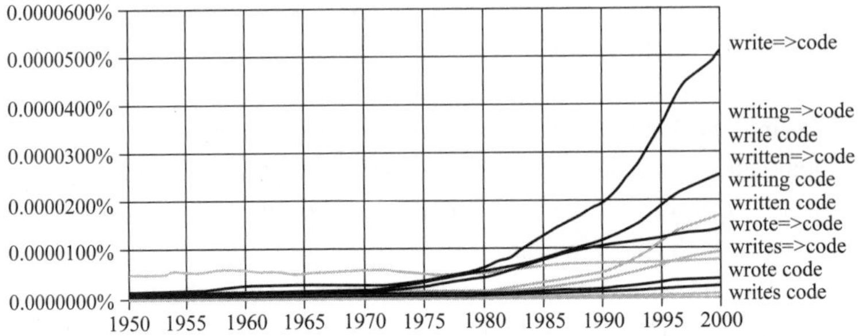

Figure 11.8
Google *n*-gram frequencies results for the bigram *write code* and the dependency arc *write* → *code* (and their morphological variants).

It is possible to search the Google *n*-grams corpus by dependency edges, finding the trend in how often a dependency edge appears over time. For example, we might be interested in knowing when people started talking about *writing code*, but we also want *write some code*, *write good code*, *write all the code*, etc. The result of a search on the dependency edge *write* → *code* is shown in figure 11.8. This capability has been applied to research in digital humanities, such as the analysis of gender in Shakespeare (Muralidharan and Hearst, 2013).

A classic application of dependency parsing is **relation extraction**, which is described in chapter 17. The goal of relation extraction is to identify entity pairs, such as

(MELVILLE, MOBY-DICK)

(TOLSTOY, WAR AND PEACE)

(MARQUÉZ, 100 YEARS OF SOLITUDE)

(SHAKESPEARE, A MIDSUMMER NIGHT'S DREAM),

which stand in some relation to each other (in this case, the relation is authorship). Such entity pairs are often referenced via consistent chains of dependency relations. Therefore, dependency paths are often a useful feature in supervised systems which learn to detect new instances of a relation, based on labeled examples of other instances of the same relation type (Culotta and Sorensen, 2004; Fundel et al., 2007; Mintz et al., 2009).

Cui et al. (2005) show how dependency parsing can improve automated question answering. Suppose you receive the following query:

(11.1) What percentage of the nation's cheese does Wisconsin produce?

The corpus contains this sentence:

(11.2) In Wisconsin, where farmers produce 28% of the nation's cheese, …

The location of *Wisconsin* in the surface form of this string makes it a poor match for the query. However, in the dependency graph, there is an edge from *produce* to *Wisconsin* in both the question and the potential answer, raising the likelihood that this span of text is relevant to the question.

A final example comes from sentiment analysis. As discussed in chapter 4, the polarity of a sentence can be reversed by negation, for example,

(11.3) *There is no reason at all to believe the polluters will suddenly become reasonable.*

By tracking the sentiment polarity through the dependency parse, we can better identify the overall polarity of the sentence, determining when key sentiment words are reversed (Wilson et al., 2005; Nakagawa et al., 2010).

Additional Resources

More details on dependency grammar and parsing algorithms can be found in the manuscript by Kübler et al. (2009). For a comprehensive but whimsical overview of graph-based dependency parsing algorithms, see Eisner (1997). Jurafsky and Martin (2019) describe an **agenda-based** version of beam search, in which the beam contains hypotheses of varying lengths. New hypotheses are added to the beam only if their score is better than the worst item currently on the beam. Another search algorithm for transition-based parsing is **easy-first**, which abandons the left-to-right traversal order and adds the highest-scoring edges first, regardless of where they appear (Goldberg and Elhadad, 2010). Goldberg et al. (2013) note that although transition-based methods can be implemented in linear time in the length of the input, naïve implementations of beam search will require quadratic time, due to the cost of copying each hypothesis when it is expanded on the beam. This issue can be addressed by using a more efficient data structure for the stack.

Exercises

1. The dependency structure $1 \leftarrow 2 \rightarrow 3$, with 2 as the root, can be obtained from more than one set of actions in arc-standard parsing. List both sets of actions that can obtain this parse. Don't forget about the edge $\text{ROOT} \rightarrow 2$.
2. This problem develops the relationship between dependency parsing and lexicalized context-free parsing. Suppose you have a set of unlabeled arc scores $\{\psi(i \rightarrow j)\}_{i,j=1}^{M} \cup \{\psi(\text{ROOT} \rightarrow j)\}_{j=1}^{M}$.
   a) Assuming each word type occurs no more than once in the input $((i \neq j) \Rightarrow (w_i \neq w_j))$, how would you construct a weighted lexicalized context-free grammar so that the

score of *any* projective dependency tree is equal to the score of some equivalent derivation in the lexicalized context-free grammar?

b) Verify that your method works for the example *They fish*.

c) Does your method require the restriction that each word type occur no more than once in the input? If so, why?

d) *If your method required that each word type occur only once in the input, show how to generalize it.

3. In arc-factored dependency parsing of an input of length M, the score of a parse is the sum of M scores, one for each arc. In second-order dependency parsing, the total score is the sum over many more terms. How many terms are the score of the parse for figure 11.2, using a second-order dependency parser with grandparent and sibling features? Assume that a child of ROOT has no grandparent score and that a node with no siblings has no sibling scores.

4. a) In the worst case, how many terms can be involved in the score of an input of length M, assuming second-order dependency parsing? Describe the structure of the worst-case parse. As in the previous problem, assume that there is only one child of ROOT and that it does not have any grandparent scores.

   b) What about third-order dependency parsing?

5. Provide the UD-style unlabeled dependency parse for the sentence *Xi-Lan eats shoots and leaves*, assuming *shoots* is a noun and *leaves* is a verb. Provide arc-standard and arc-eager derivations for this dependency parse.

6. Compute an upper bound on the number of successful derivations in arc-standard shift-reduce parsing for unlabeled dependencies, as a function of the length of the input, M. Hint: a lower bound is the number of projective decision trees, $\frac{1}{M+1}\binom{3M-2}{M-1}$ (Zhang, 2017), where $\binom{a}{b} = \frac{a!}{(a-b)!b!}$.

7. The **label bias problem** arises when a decision is locally correct, yet leads to a cascade of errors in some situations (§ 11.3.3). Design a scenario in which this occurs. Specifically:

   - Assume an arc-standard dependency parser, whose action classifier considers only the words at the top of the stack and at the front of the input buffer.
   - Design two examples, which both involve a decision with identical features.
     - In one example, shift is the correct decision; in the other example, arc-left or arc-right is the correct decision.
     - In one of the two examples, a mistake should lead to at least two attachment errors.
     - In the other example, a mistake should lead only to a single attachment error.

For the following exercises, run a dependency parser, such as Stanford's CoreNLP parser, on a large corpus of text (at least 10^5 tokens), such as `nltk.corpus.webtext`.

8. The dependency relation NMOD:POSS indicates possession. Compute the top 10 words most frequently possessed by each of the following pronouns: *his*, *her*, *our*, *my*, *your*, and *their* (inspired by Muralidharan and Hearst, 2013).
9. Count all pairs of words grouped by the CONJ relation. Select all pairs of words (i,j) for which i and j each participate in CONJ relations at least five times. Compute and sort by the **pointwise mutual information**, which is defined in § 14.3 as

$$\text{PMI}(i,j) = \log \frac{\text{p}(i,j)}{\text{p}(i)\text{p}(j)}. \quad [11.31]$$

Here, $\text{p}(i)$ is the fraction of CONJ relations containing word i (in either position), and $\text{p}(i,j)$ is the fraction of such relations linking i and j (in any order).
10. In § 4.2, we encountered lexical semantic relationships such as **synonymy** (same meaning), **antonymy** (opposite meaning), and **hypernymy** (i is a special case of j). Another relevant relation is **co-hypernymy**, which means that i and j share a hypernym. Of the top 20 pairs identified by PMI in the previous problem, how many participate in synsets that are linked by one of these four relations? Use WORDNET to check for these relations, and count a pair of words if any of their synsets are linked.

III MEANING

12 Logical Semantics

The previous few chapters have focused on building systems that reconstruct the **syntax** of natural language—its structural organization—through tagging and parsing. But some of the most exciting and promising potential applications of language technology involve going beyond syntax to **semantics**—the underlying meaning of the text:

- Answering questions, such as *where is the nearest coffeeshop?* or *what is the middle name of the mother of the 44th President of the United States?*
- Building a robot that can follow natural language instructions to execute tasks.
- Translating a sentence from one language into another, while preserving the underlying meaning.
- Fact-checking an article by searching the web for contradictory evidence.
- Logic-checking an argument by identifying contradictions, ambiguity, and unsupported assertions.

Semantic analysis involves converting natural language into a **meaning representation**. To be useful, a meaning representation must meet several criteria:

- **c1**: It should be unambiguous: unlike natural language, there should be exactly one meaning per statement;
- **c2**: It should provide a way to link language to external knowledge, observations, and actions;
- **c3**: It should support computational **inference**, so that meanings can be combined to derive additional knowledge;
- **c4**: It should be expressive enough to cover the full range of things that people talk about in natural language.

Much more can be said about how best to represent knowledge for computation (e.g., Sowa, 2000), but this chapter will focus on these four criteria.

12.1 Meaning and Denotation

The first criterion for a meaning representation is that statements in the representation should be unambiguous—they should have only one possible interpretation. Natural language does not have this property: as we saw in chapter 10, sentences like *cats scratch people with claws* have multiple interpretations.

What does it mean for a statement to be unambiguous? Programming languages provide a useful example: the output of a program is completely specified by the rules of the language and the properties of the environment in which the program is run. For example, the Python code `5 + 3` will have the output 8, as will the codes `(4*4)-(3*3)+1` and `((8))`. This output is known as the **denotation** of the program, and can be written as

$$[\![\texttt{5+3}]\!] = [\![\texttt{(4*4)-(3*3)+1}]\!] = [\![\texttt{((8))}]\!] = 8. \qquad [12.1]$$

The denotations of these arithmetic expressions are determined by the meaning of the **constants** (e.g., `5`, `3`) and the **relations** (e.g., `+`, `*`, `(`, `)`). Now let's consider another snippet of Python code, `double(4)`. The denotation of this code could be, $[\![\texttt{double(4)}]\!] = \texttt{8}$, or it could be $[\![\texttt{double(4)}]\!] = \texttt{44}$—it depends on the meaning of `double`. This meaning is defined in a **world model** $\mathcal{M}$ as an infinite set of pairs. We write the denotation with respect to model $\mathcal{M}$ as $[\![\cdot]\!]_{\mathcal{M}}$, e.g., $[\![\texttt{double}]\!]_{\mathcal{M}} = \{(\texttt{0},\texttt{0}), (\texttt{1},\texttt{2}), (\texttt{2},\texttt{4}), \ldots\}$. The world model would also define the (infinite) list of constants, for example, $\{\texttt{0},\texttt{1},\texttt{2},\ldots\}$. As long as denotations can be computed unambiguously, the language can be said to be unambiguous.

This approach to meaning is known as **model-theoretic semantics**, and it addresses not only criterion $c1$ (no ambiguity), but also $c2$ (connecting language to external knowledge, observations, and actions). For example, we can connect the meaning of a statement like *the capital of Georgia* with a world model that includes knowledge base of geographical facts, obtaining the denotation `Atlanta`. We might populate a world model by detecting and analyzing the objects in an image and then use this world model to evaluate **propositions** like *a man is riding a moose*. Another desirable property of model-theoretic semantics is that when the facts change, the denotations change too: the meaning representation of *President of the USA* would have a different denotation in the model $\mathcal{M}_{2014}$ as it would in $\mathcal{M}_{2022}$.

12.2 Logical Representations of Meaning

Criterion $c3$ requires that the meaning representation support inference—for example, automatically deducing new facts from known premises. While many representations have been proposed that meet these criteria, the most mature is the language of first-order logic.[1]

1. Alternatives include the "variable-free" representation used in semantic parsing of geographical queries (Zelle and Mooney, 1996) and robotic control (Ge and Mooney, 2005) and dependency-based compositional semantics (Liang et al., 2013).

12.2.1 Propositional Logic

The bare bones of logical meaning representation are Boolean operations on propositions:

Propositional symbols Greek symbols like ϕ and ψ will be used to represent **propositions**, which are statements that are either true or false. For example, ϕ may correspond to the proposition, *bagels are delicious*.

Boolean operators We can build up more complex propositional formulas from Boolean operators. These include:

- Negation $\neg\phi$, which is true when ϕ is false.
- Conjunction, $\phi \wedge \psi$, which is true when both ϕ and ψ are true.
- Disjunction, $\phi \vee \psi$, which is true when at least one of ϕ and ψ is true.
- Implication, $\phi \Rightarrow \psi$, which is true unless ϕ is true and ψ is false. Implication has identical truth conditions to $\neg\phi \vee \psi$.
- Equivalence, $\phi \Leftrightarrow \psi$, which is true when ϕ and ψ are both true or both false. Equivalence has identical truth conditions to $(\phi \Rightarrow \psi) \wedge (\psi \Rightarrow \phi)$.

It is not strictly necessary to have all five Boolean operators: readers familiar with Boolean logic will know that it is possible to construct all other operators from either the NAND (not-and) or NOR (not-or) operators. Nonetheless, it is clearest to use all five operators. From the truth conditions for these operators, it is possible to define a number of "laws" such as

- *Commutativity*: $\phi \wedge \psi = \psi \wedge \phi, \quad \phi \vee \psi = \psi \vee \phi$.
- *Associativity*: $\phi \wedge (\psi \wedge \chi) = (\phi \wedge \psi) \wedge \chi, \quad \phi \vee (\psi \vee \chi) = (\phi \vee \psi) \vee \chi$.
- *Complementation*: $\phi \wedge \neg\phi = \bot, \quad \phi \vee \neg\phi = \top$, where $\top$ indicates a true proposition and $\bot$ indicates a false proposition.

These laws can be combined to derive further equivalences, which can support logical inferences. For example, suppose $\phi =$ *The music is loud* and $\psi =$ *Max can't sleep*. Then if we are given

$\phi \Rightarrow \psi$ *If the music is loud, Max can't sleep.*
ϕ *The music is loud.*

we can derive ψ (*Max can't sleep*) by application of **modus ponens**, which is one of a set of **inference rules** that can be derived from more basic laws and used to manipulate propositional formulas. **Automated theorem provers** are programs that apply inference rules to a set of premises to derive desired propositions (Loveland, 2016).

12.2.2 First-Order Logic

Propositional logic is so named because it treats propositions as its base units. However, the criterion *c*4 states that our meaning representation should be sufficiently expressive. Now consider the sentence pair,

(12.1) If anyone is making noise, then Max can't sleep.
Abigail is making noise.

People are capable of making inferences from this sentence pair, but such inferences require formal tools that are beyond propositional logic. To understand the relationship between the statement *anyone is making noise* and the statement *Abigail is making noise*, our meaning representation requires the additional machinery of **first-order logic (FOL).**

In FOL, logical propositions can be constructed from relationships between entities. Specifically, FOL extends propositional logic with the following classes of terms:

Constants These are elements that name individual entities in the model, such as MAX and ABIGAIL. The denotation of each constant in a model $\mathcal{M}$ is an element in the model, for example, $[\![\text{MAX}]\!] = \texttt{m}$ and $[\![\text{ABIGAIL}]\!] = \texttt{a}$.

Relations Relations can be thought of as sets of entities, or sets of tuples. For example, the relation CAN-SLEEP is defined as the set of entities who can sleep and has the denotation $[\![\text{CAN-SLEEP}]\!] = \{\texttt{a}, \texttt{m}, \ldots\}$. To test the truth value of the proposition CAN-SLEEP(MAX), we ask whether $[\![\text{MAX}]\!] \in [\![\text{CAN-SLEEP}]\!]$. Logical relations that are defined over sets of entities are sometimes called *properties*.

Relations may also be ordered tuples of entities. For example, BROTHER(MAX,ABIGAIL) expresses the proposition that MAX is the brother of ABIGAIL. The denotation of such relations is a set of tuples, $[\![\text{BROTHER}]\!] = \{\texttt{(m, a)}, \texttt{(x, y)}, \ldots\}$. To test the truth value of the proposition BROTHER(MAX,ABIGAIL), we ask whether the tuple $([\![\text{MAX}]\!], [\![\text{ABIGAIL}]\!])$ is in the denotation $[\![\text{BROTHER}]\!]$.

Using constants and relations, it is possible to express statements like *Max can't sleep* and *Max is Abigail's brother*:

$\neg$CAN-SLEEP(MAX)

BROTHER(MAX,ABIGAIL).

These statements can also be combined using Boolean operators, such as

(BROTHER(MAX,ABIGAIL) $\vee$ BROTHER(MAX,STEVE)) $\Rightarrow \neg$CAN-SLEEP(MAX).

This fragment of first-order logic permits only statements about specific entities. To support inferences about statements like *If anyone is making noise, then Max can't sleep*, two more elements must be added to the meaning representation:

Variables Variables are mechanisms for referring to entities that are not locally specified. We can then write CAN-SLEEP(x) or BROTHER(x, ABIGAIL). In these cases, x is a **free variable**, meaning that we have not committed to any particular assignment.

Quantifiers Variables are bound by quantifiers. There are two quantifiers in first-order logic.[2]

2. In first-order logic, it is possible to quantify only over entities. In **second-order logic**, it is possible to quantify over properties. This makes it possible to represent statements like *Butch has every property that a good boxer has* (example from Blackburn and Bos, 2005):

$\forall P \forall x((\text{GOOD-BOXER}(x) \Rightarrow P(x)) \Rightarrow P(\text{BUTCH})).$ [12.2]

- The **existential quantifier** $\exists$, which indicates that there must be at least one entity to which the variable can bind. For example, the statement $\exists x$MAKES-NOISE(X) indicates that there is at least one entity for which MAKES-NOISE is true.
- The **universal quantifier** $\forall$, which indicates that the variable must be able to bind to any entity in the model. For example, the statement

$$\text{MAKES-NOISE}(\text{ABIGAIL}) \Rightarrow (\forall x \neg \text{CAN-SLEEP}(x)) \quad [12.3]$$

asserts that if Abigail makes noise, no one can sleep.

The expressions $\exists x$ and $\forall x$ make x into a **bound variable**. A formula that contains no free variables is a **sentence**.

Functions Functions map from entities to entities, for example, $[\![\text{CAPITAL-OF}]\!]$ $[\![(\text{GEORGIA})]\!] = [\![\text{ATLANTA}]\!]$. With functions, it is convenient to add an equality operator, supporting statements like,

$$\forall x \exists y \text{MOTHER-OF}(x) = \text{DAUGHTER-OF}(y). \quad [12.4]$$

Note that MOTHER-OF is a functional analogue of the relation MOTHER, so that MOTHER-OF$(x) = y$ iff MOTHER(x, y). Any logical formula that uses functions can be rewritten using only relations and quantification. For example,

$$\text{MAKES-NOISE}(\text{MOTHER-OF}(\text{ABIGAIL})) \quad [12.5]$$

can be rewritten as $\exists x \text{MAKES-NOISE}(x) \wedge \text{MOTHER}(x, \text{ABIGAIL})$.

An important property of quantifiers is that the order can matter. Unfortunately, natural language is rarely clear about this! The issue is demonstrated by examples like *everyone speaks a language*, which has the following interpretations:

$$\forall x \exists y \ \text{SPEAKS}(x, y) \quad [12.6]$$

$$\exists y \forall x \ \text{SPEAKS}(x, y). \quad [12.7]$$

In the first case, y may refer to several different languages, while in the second case, there is a single y that is spoken by everyone.

Truth-conditional semantics One way to look at the meaning of an FOL sentence ϕ is as a set of **truth conditions** or models under which ϕ is satisfied. But how to determine whether a sentence is true or false in a given model? We will approach this inductively, starting with a predicate applied to a tuple of constants. The truth of such a sentence depends on whether the tuple of denotations of the constants is in the denotation of the predicate. For example, CAPITAL(GEORGIA,ATLANTA) is true in model $\mathcal{M}$ iff,

$$([\![\text{GEORGIA}]\!]_{\mathcal{M}}, [\![\text{ATLANTA}]\!]_{\mathcal{M}}) \in [\![\text{CAPITAL}]\!]_{\mathcal{M}}. \quad [12.8]$$

The Boolean operators $\wedge, \vee, \ldots$ provide ways to construct more complicated sentences, and the truth of such statements can be assessed based on the truth tables associated with these operators. The statement $\exists x \phi$ is true if there is some assignment of the variable x to an entity in the model such that ϕ is true; the statement $\forall x \phi$ is true if ϕ is true under all possible assignments of x. More formally, we would say that ϕ is **satisfied** under $\mathcal{M}$, written as $\mathcal{M} \models \phi$.

Truth conditional semantics allows us to define several other properties of sentences and pairs of sentences. Suppose that in every $\mathcal{M}$ under which ϕ is satisfied, another formula ψ is also satisfied; then ϕ **entails** ψ, which is also written as $\phi \models \psi$. For example,

$$\text{CAPITAL}(\text{GEORGIA},\text{ATLANTA}) \models \exists x \text{CAPITAL}(\text{GEORGIA}, x). \qquad [12.9]$$

A statement that is satisfied under any model, such as $\phi \vee \neg\phi$, is **valid**, written $\models (\phi \vee \neg\phi)$. A statement that is not satisfied under any model, such as $\phi \wedge \neg\phi$, is **unsatisfiable**, or **inconsistent**. A **model checker** is a program that determines whether a sentence ϕ is satisfied in $\mathcal{M}$. A **model builder** is a program that constructs a model in which ϕ is satisfied. The problems of checking for consistency and validity in first-order logic are **undecidable**, meaning that there is no algorithm that can automatically determine whether an FOL formula is valid or inconsistent.

Inference in first-order logic Our original goal was to support inferences that combine general statements *If anyone is making noise, then Max can't sleep* with specific statements like *Abigail is making noise*. We can now represent such statements in first-order logic, but how are we to perform the inference that *Max can't sleep*? One approach is to use "generalized" versions of propositional inference rules like modus ponens, which can be applied to FOL formulas. By repeatedly applying such inference rules to a knowledge base of facts, it is possible to produce proofs of desired propositions. To find the right sequence of inferences to derive a desired theorem, classical artificial intelligence search algorithms like backward chaining can be applied. Such algorithms are implemented in interpreters for the `prolog` logic programming language (Pereira and Shieber, 2002).

12.3 Semantic Parsing and the Lambda Calculus

The previous section laid out a lot of formal machinery; the remainder of this chapter links these formalisms back to natural language. Given an English sentence like *Alex likes Brit*, how can we obtain the desired first-order logical representation, LIKES(ALEX,BRIT)? This is the task of **semantic parsing**. Just as a syntactic parser is a function from a natural language sentence to a syntactic structure such as a phrase structure tree, a semantic parser is a function from natural language to logical formulas.

As in syntactic analysis, semantic parsing is difficult because the space of inputs and outputs is very large, and their interaction is complex. Our best hope is that, like syntactic parsing, semantic parsing can somehow be decomposed into simpler sub problems. This idea, usually attributed to the German philosopher Gottlob Frege, is called the **principle of compositionality**: the meaning of a complex expression is a function of the meanings of that expression's constituent parts. We will define these "constituent parts" as syntactic constituents: noun phrases and verb phrases. These constituents are combined using function

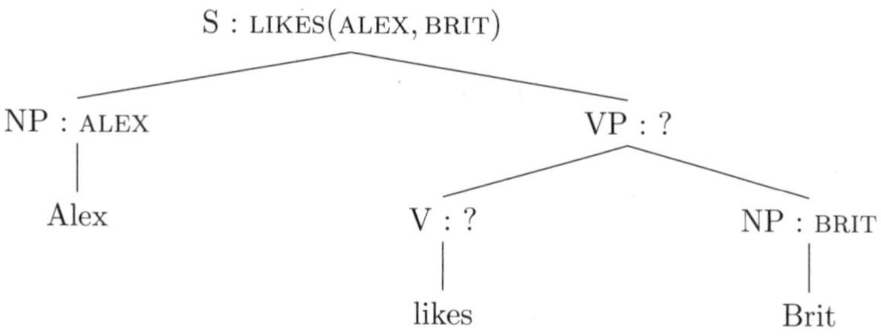

Figure 12.1
The principle of compositionality requires that we identify meanings for the constituents *likes* and *likes Brit* that will make it possible to compute the meaning for the entire sentence.

application: if the syntactic parse contains the production $x \to y\ z$, then the semantics of x, written x.sem, will be computed as a function of the semantics of the constituents, y.sem and z.sem.[3,4]

12.3.1 The Lambda Calculus

Let's see how this works for a simple sentence like *Alex likes Brit*, whose syntactic structure is shown in figure 12.1. Our goal is the formula, LIKES(ALEX,BRIT), and it is clear that the meaning of the constituents *Alex* and *Brit* should be ALEX and BRIT. That leaves two more constituents: the verb *likes* and the verb phrase *likes Brit*. The meanings of these units must be defined in a way that makes it possible to recover the desired meaning for the entire sentence by function application. If the meanings of *Alex* and *Brit* are constants, then the meanings of *likes* and *likes Brit* must be functional expressions, which can be applied to their siblings to produce the desired analyses.

Modeling these partial analyses requires extending the first-order logic meaning representation. We do this by adding **lambda expressions**, which are descriptions of anonymous functions,[5] for example,

$$\lambda x.\text{LIKES}(x, \text{BRIT}). \qquad [12.10]$$

This functional expression is the meaning of the verb phrase *likes Brit*; it takes a single argument and returns the result of substituting that argument for x in the expression

3. § 9.3.2 briefly discusses Combinatory Categorial Grammar (CCG) as an alternative to a phrase-structure analysis of syntax. CCG is argued to be particularly well suited to semantic parsing (Hockenmaier and Steedman, 2007) and is used in much of the contemporary work on machine learning for semantic parsing, summarized in § 12.4.

4. The approach of algorithmically building up meaning representations from a series of operations on the syntactic structure of a sentence is generally attributed to the philosopher Richard Montague, who published a series of influential papers on the topic in the early 1970s (e.g., Montague, 1973).

5. Formally, all first-order logic formulas are lambda expressions; in addition, if ϕ is a lambda expression, then $\lambda x.\phi$ is also a lambda expression. Readers who are familiar with functional programming will recognize lambda expressions from their use in programming languages such as Lisp and Python.

Table 12.1
G_1, a minimal syntactic-semantic context-free grammar

S	$\rightarrow$ NP VP	VP.sem@NP.sem
VP	$\rightarrow$ V_t NP	V_t.sem@NP.sem
VP	$\rightarrow$ V_i	V_i.sem
V_t	$\rightarrow$ *likes*	$\lambda y.\lambda x.\text{LIKES}(x, y)$
V_i	$\rightarrow$ *sleeps*	$\lambda x.\text{SLEEPS}(x)$
NP	$\rightarrow$ *Alex*	ALEX
NP	$\rightarrow$ *Brit*	BRIT

$\text{LIKES}(x, \text{BRIT})$. We write this substitution as

$$(\lambda x.\text{LIKES}(x, \text{BRIT}))@\text{ALEX} = \text{LIKES}(\text{ALEX},\text{BRIT}), \quad [12.11]$$

with the symbol "@" indicating function application. Function application in the lambda calculus is sometimes called **β-reduction** or β-conversion. The expression $\phi@\psi$ indicates a function application to be performed by β-reduction and $\phi(\psi)$ indicates a function or predicate in the final logical form.

Equation 12.11 shows how to obtain the desired semantics for the sentence *Alex likes Brit*: by applying the lambda expression $\lambda x.\text{LIKES}(x, \text{BRIT})$ to the logical constant ALEX. This rule of composition can be specified in a **syntactic-semantic grammar**, in which syntactic productions are paired with semantic operations. For the syntactic production S $\rightarrow$ NP VP, we have the semantic rule VP.sem@NP.sem.

The meaning of the transitive verb phrase *likes Brit* can also be obtained by function application on its syntactic constituents. For the syntactic production VP $\rightarrow$ V NP, we apply the semantic rule,

$$\text{VP.sem} = (\text{V.sem})@\text{NP.sem} \quad [12.12]$$

$$= (\lambda y.\lambda x.\text{LIKES}(x, y))@(\text{BRIT}) \quad [12.13]$$

$$= \lambda x.\text{LIKES}(x, \text{BRIT}). \quad [12.14]$$

Thus, the meaning of the transitive verb *likes* is a lambda expression whose output is *another* lambda expression: it takes y as an argument to fill in one of the slots in the LIKES relation and returns a lambda expression that is ready to take an argument to fill in the other slot.[6]

Table 12.1 shows a minimal syntactic-semantic grammar fragment, G_1. The complete **derivation** of *Alex likes Brit* in G_1 is shown in figure 12.2. In addition to the transitive verb *likes*, the grammar also includes the intransitive verb *sleeps*; it should be clear how to derive the meaning of sentences like *Alex sleeps*. For verbs that can be either transitive

6. This can be written in a few different ways. The notation $\lambda y, x.\text{LIKES}(x, y)$ is a somewhat informal way to indicate a lambda expression that takes two arguments; this would be acceptable in functional programming. Logicians (e.g., Carpenter, 1997) often prefer the more formal notation $\lambda y.\lambda x.\text{LIKES}(x)(y)$, indicating that each lambda expression takes exactly one argument.

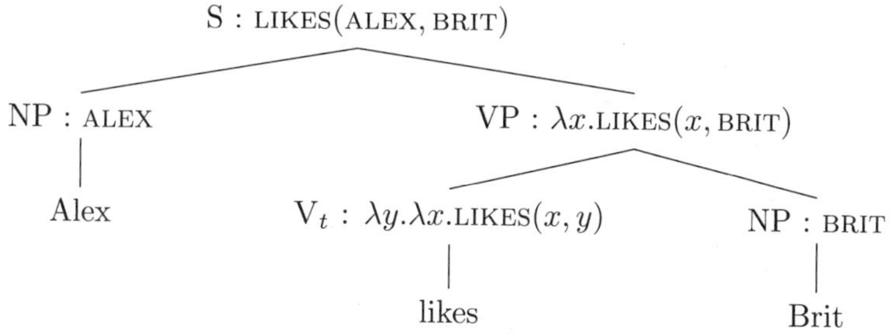

Figure 12.2
Derivation of the semantic representation for *Alex likes Brit* in the grammar G_1.

or intransitive, such as *eats*, we would have two terminal productions, one for each sense (terminal productions are also called the **lexical entries**). Indeed, most of the grammar is in the **lexicon** (the terminal productions), because these productions select the basic units of the semantic interpretation.

12.3.2 Quantification

Things get more complicated when we move from sentences about named entities to sentences that involve other kinds of noun phrases. Let's consider the example, *A dog sleeps*, which has the meaning $\exists x \text{DOG}(x) \wedge \text{SLEEPS}(x)$. Clearly, the DOG relation will be introduced by the word *dog*, and the SLEEP relation will be introduced by the word *sleeps*. The existential quantifier $\exists$ must be introduced by the lexical entry for the determiner *a*.[7] However, this seems problematic for the compositional approach taken in the grammar G_1: If the semantics of the noun phrase *a dog* is an existentially quantified expression, how can it be the argument to the semantics of the verb *sleeps*, which expects an entity? And where does the logical conjunction come from?

There are a few different approaches to handling these issues. We will begin by reversing the semantic relationship between subject NPs and VPs, so that the production S → NP VP has the semantics NP.sem@VP.sem: the meaning of the sentence is now the semantics of the noun phrase applied to the verb phrase. The implications of this change are best illustrated by exploring the derivation of the example, shown in figure 12.3. Let's start with the indefinite article *a*, to which we assign the rather intimidating semantics,

$$\lambda P.\lambda Q.\exists x P(x) \wedge Q(x). \qquad [12.15]$$

7. Conversely, the sentence *Every dog sleeps* would involve a universal quantifier, $\forall x \text{DOG}(x) \Rightarrow \text{SLEEPS}(x)$. The definite article *the* requires more consideration, because *the dog* must refer to some dog that is uniquely identifiable, perhaps from contextual information external to the sentence. Carpenter (1997, pp. 96-100) summarizes some approaches to handling definite descriptions.

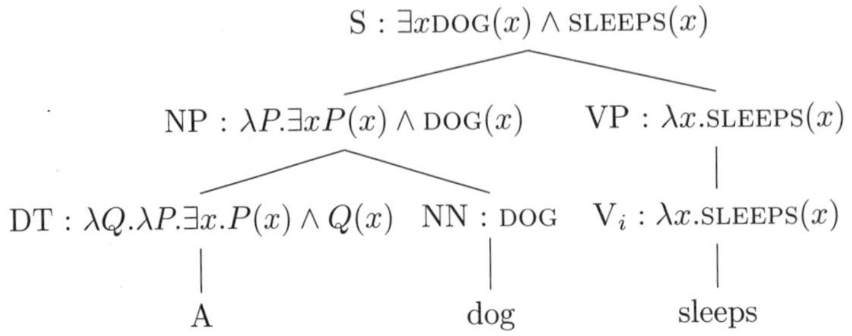

Figure 12.3
Derivation of the semantic representation for *A dog sleeps*, in grammar G_2.

This is a lambda expression that takes two **relations** as arguments, P and Q. The relation P is scoped to the outer lambda expression, so it will be provided by the immediately adjacent noun, which in this case is DOG. Thus, the noun phrase *a dog* has the semantics,

$$\text{NP.sem} = \text{DET.sem@NN.sem} \qquad [12.16]$$

$$= (\lambda P.\lambda Q.\exists x P(x) \wedge Q(x))@(\text{DOG}) \qquad [12.17]$$

$$= \lambda Q.\exists x \text{DOG}(x) \wedge Q(x). \qquad [12.18]$$

This is a lambda expression that is expecting another relation, Q, which will be provided by the verb phrase, SLEEPS. This gives the desired analysis, $\exists x\text{DOG}(x) \wedge \text{SLEEPS}(x)$.[8]

If noun phrases like *a dog* are interpreted as lambda expressions, then proper nouns like *Alex* must be treated in the same way. This is achieved by **type-raising** from constants to lambda expressions, $x \Rightarrow \lambda P.P(x)$. After type-raising, the semantics of *Alex* is $\lambda P.P(\text{ALEX})$—a lambda expression that expects a relation to tell us something about ALEX.[9] Again, make sure you see how the analysis in figure 12.3 can be applied to the sentence *Alex sleeps*.

Direct objects are handled by applying the same type-raising operation to transitive verbs: the meaning of verbs such as *likes* is raised to

$$\lambda P.\lambda x.P(\lambda y.\text{LIKES}(x,y)). \qquad [12.19]$$

8. When applying β-reduction to arguments that are themselves lambda expressions, be sure to use unique variable names to avoid confusion. For example, it is important to distinguish the x in the semantics for *a* from the x in the semantics for *likes*. Variable names are abstractions, and can always be changed—this is known as **α-conversion**. For example, $\lambda x.P(x)$ can be converted to $\lambda y.P(y)$, etc.

9. Compositional semantic analysis is often supported by **type systems**, which make it possible to check whether a given function application is valid. The base types are entities e and truth values t. A property, such as DOG, is a function from entities to truth values, so its type is written $\langle e, t\rangle$. A transitive verb has type $\langle e, \langle e, t\rangle\rangle$: after receiving the first entity (the direct object), it returns a function from entities to truth values, which will be applied to the subject of the sentence. The type-raising operation $x \Rightarrow \lambda P.P(x)$ corresponds to a change in type from e to $\langle\langle e, t\rangle, t\rangle$: it expects a function from entities to truth values and returns a truth value.

Table 12.2
G_2, a syntactic-semantic context-free grammar fragment, which supports quantified noun phrases

S	$\rightarrow$ NP VP	NP.sem@VP.sem
VP	$\rightarrow$ V_t NP	V_t.sem@NP.sem
VP	$\rightarrow$ V_i	V_i.sem
NP	$\rightarrow$ DET NN	DET.sem@NN.sem
NP	$\rightarrow$ NNP	$\lambda P.P(\text{NNP.sem})$
DET	$\rightarrow$ *a*	$\lambda P.\lambda Q.\exists x P(x) \wedge Q(x)$
DET	$\rightarrow$ *every*	$\lambda P.\lambda Q.\forall x(P(x) \Rightarrow Q(x))$
V_t	$\rightarrow$ *likes*	$\lambda P.\lambda x.P(\lambda y.\text{LIKES}(x,y))$
V_i	$\rightarrow$ *sleeps*	$\lambda x.\text{SLEEPS}(x)$
NN	$\rightarrow$ *dog*	DOG
NNP	$\rightarrow$ *Alex*	ALEX
NNP	$\rightarrow$ *Brit*	BRIT

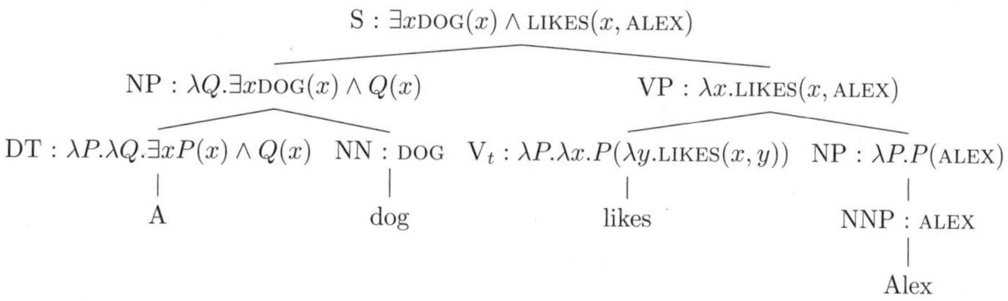

Figure 12.4
Derivation of the semantic representation for *A dog likes Alex*.

As a result, we can keep the verb phrase production VP.sem = V.sem@NP.sem, knowing that the direct object will provide the function P in equation 12.19. To see how this works, let's analyze the verb phrase *likes a dog*. After uniquely relabeling each lambda variable,

$$\begin{aligned}
\text{VP.sem} &= \text{V.sem@NP.sem} \\
&= (\lambda P.\lambda x.P(\lambda y.\text{LIKES}(x,y)))@(\lambda Q.\exists z \text{DOG}(z) \wedge Q(z)) \\
&= \lambda x.(\lambda Q.\exists z \text{DOG}(z) \wedge Q(z))@(\lambda y.\text{LIKES}(x,y)) \\
&= \lambda x.\exists z \text{DOG}(z) \wedge (\lambda y.\text{LIKES}(x,y))@z \\
&= \lambda x.\exists z \text{DOG}(z) \wedge \text{LIKES}(x,z).
\end{aligned}$$

These changes are summarized in the revised grammar G_2, shown in table 12.2. Figure 12.4 shows a derivation that involves a transitive verb, an indefinite noun phrase, and a proper noun.

12.4 Learning Semantic Parsers

As with syntactic parsing, any syntactic-semantic grammar with sufficient coverage risks producing many possible analyses for any given sentence. Machine learning is the dominant approach to selecting a single analysis. We will focus on algorithms that learn to score logical forms by attaching weights to features of their derivations (Zettlemoyer and Collins, 2005). Alternative approaches include transition-based parsing (Zelle and Mooney, 1996; Misra and Artzi, 2016) and methods inspired by machine translation (Wong and Mooney, 2006). Methods also differ in the form of supervision used for learning, which can range from complete derivations to much more limited training signals. We will begin with the case of complete supervision and then consider how learning is still possible even when seemingly key information is missing.

Datasets Early work on semantic parsing focused on natural language expressions of geographical database queries, such as *What states border Texas*. The GeoQuery dataset of Zelle and Mooney (1996) was originally coded in prolog, but has subsequently been expanded and converted into the SQL database query language by Popescu et al. (2003) and into first-order logic with lambda calculus by Zettlemoyer and Collins (2005), providing logical forms like $\lambda x.\text{STATE}(x) \wedge \text{BORDERS}(x, \text{TEXAS})$. Another early dataset consists of instructions for RoboCup robot soccer teams (Kate et al., 2005). More recent work has focused on broader domains, such as the Freebase database (Bollacker et al., 2008), for which queries have been annotated by Krishnamurthy and Mitchell (2012) and Cai and Yates (2013). Other recent datasets include child-directed speech (Kwiatkowski et al., 2012) and elementary school science exams (Krishnamurthy, 2016).

12.4.1 Learning from Derivations

Let $\boldsymbol{w}^{(i)}$ indicate a sequence of text, and let $\boldsymbol{y}^{(i)}$ indicate the desired logical form. For example:

$$\boldsymbol{w}^{(i)} = \text{Alex eats shoots and leaves}$$

$$\boldsymbol{y}^{(i)} = \text{EATS(ALEX,SHOOTS)} \wedge \text{EATS(ALEX,LEAVES)}$$

In the standard supervised learning paradigm that was introduced in § 2.3, we first define a feature function, $\boldsymbol{f}(\boldsymbol{w}, \boldsymbol{y})$ and then learn weights on these features, so that $\boldsymbol{y}^{(i)} = \text{argmax}_{\boldsymbol{y}}\, \boldsymbol{\theta} \cdot \boldsymbol{f}(\boldsymbol{w}, \boldsymbol{y})$. The weight vector $\boldsymbol{\theta}$ is learned by comparing the features of the true label $\boldsymbol{f}(\boldsymbol{w}^{(i)}, \boldsymbol{y}^{(i)})$ against either the features of the predicted label $\boldsymbol{f}(\boldsymbol{w}^{(i)}, \hat{\boldsymbol{y}})$ (perceptron, support vector machine) or the expected feature vector $E_{\boldsymbol{y}|\boldsymbol{w}}[\boldsymbol{f}(\boldsymbol{w}^{(i)}, \boldsymbol{y})]$ (logistic regression).

While this basic framework seems similar to discriminative syntactic parsing, there is a crucial difference. In (context-free) syntactic parsing, the annotation $\boldsymbol{y}^{(i)}$ contains all of the syntactic productions; indeed, the task of identifying the correct set of productions is identical to the task of identifying the syntactic structure. In semantic parsing, this is not

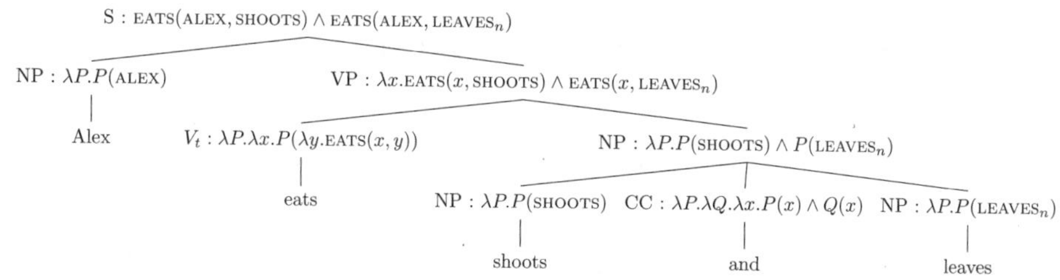

Figure 12.5
Derivation for gold semantic analysis of *Alex eats shoots and leaves*.

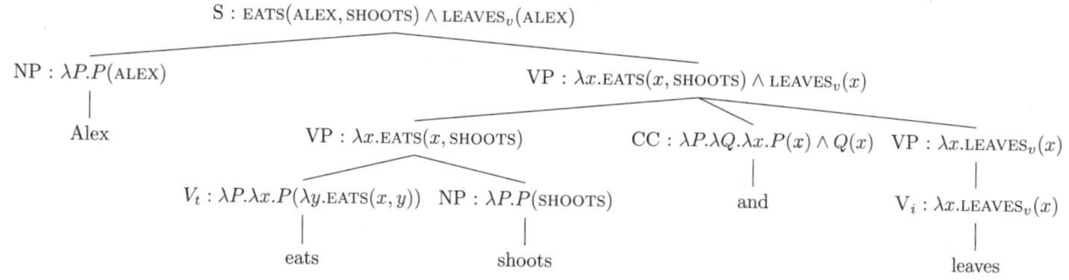

Figure 12.6
Derivation for incorrect semantic analysis of *Alex eats shoots and leaves*.

the case: the logical form EATS(ALEX,SHOOTS) $\wedge$ EATS(ALEX,LEAVES) does not reveal the syntactic-semantic productions that were used to obtain it. Indeed, there may be **spurious ambiguity**, so that a single logical form can be reached by multiple derivations. (We previously encountered spurious ambiguity in transition-based dependency parsing, § 11.3.2.)

These ideas can be formalized by introducing an additional variable z, representing the derivation of the logical form $\boldsymbol{y}$ from the text $\boldsymbol{w}$. Assume that the feature function decomposes across the productions in the derivation, $\boldsymbol{f}(\boldsymbol{w}, z, \boldsymbol{y}) = \sum_{t=1}^{T} \boldsymbol{f}(\boldsymbol{w}, z_t, \boldsymbol{y})$, where z_t indicates a single syntactic-semantic production. For example, we might have a feature for the production S $\rightarrow$ NP VP : NP.sem@VP.sem, as well as for terminal productions like NNP $\rightarrow$ *Alex* : ALEX. Under this decomposition, it is possible to compute scores for each semantically annotated subtree in the analysis of $\boldsymbol{w}$, so that bottom-up parsing algorithms like CKY (§ 10.1) can be applied to find the best-scoring semantic analysis.

Figure 12.5 shows a derivation of the correct semantic analysis of the sentence *Alex eats shoots and leaves*, in a simplified grammar in which the plural noun phrases *shoots* and *leaves* are interpreted as logical constants SHOOTS and LEAVES$_n$. Figure 12.6 shows a derivation of an incorrect analysis. Assuming one feature per production, the perceptron update is shown in table 12.3. From this update, the parser would learn to prefer the noun interpretation of *leaves* over the verb interpretation. It would also learn to prefer noun phrase coordination over verb phrase coordination.

Table 12.3
Perceptron update for analysis in figure 12.5 (gold) and figure 12.6 (predicted)

$\text{NP}_1 \rightarrow \text{NP}_2\ \text{Cc}\ \text{NP}_3$	$(\text{Cc.sem@}(\text{NP}_2.\text{sem}))\text{@}(\text{NP}_3.\text{sem})$	$+1$
$\text{VP}_1 \rightarrow \text{VP}_2\ \text{Cc}\ \text{VP}_3$	$(\text{Cc.sem@}(\text{VP}_2.\text{sem}))\text{@}(\text{VP}_3.\text{sem})$	-1
$\text{NP} \rightarrow$ *leaves*	LEAVES_n	$+1$
$\text{VP} \rightarrow \text{V}_i$	$\text{V}_i.\text{sem}$	-1
$\text{V}_i \rightarrow$ *leaves*	$\lambda x.\text{LEAVES}_v$	-1

Although the update is explained in terms of the perceptron, it would be easy to replace the perceptron with a conditional random field. In this case, the online updates would be based on feature expectations, which can be computed using the inside-outside algorithm (§ 10.6).

12.4.2 Learning From Logical Forms

Complete derivations are expensive to annotate and are rarely available.[10] One solution is to focus on learning from logical forms directly, while treating the derivations as **latent variables** (Zettlemoyer and Collins, 2005). In a conditional probabilistic model over logical forms $\boldsymbol{y}$ and derivations z, we have

$$\text{p}(\boldsymbol{y}, z \mid \boldsymbol{w}) = \frac{\exp(\boldsymbol{\theta} \cdot \boldsymbol{f}(\boldsymbol{w}, z, \boldsymbol{y}))}{\sum_{\boldsymbol{y}', z'} \exp(\boldsymbol{\theta} \cdot \boldsymbol{f}(\boldsymbol{w}, z', \boldsymbol{y}'))}, \quad [12.20]$$

which is the standard log-linear model, applied to the logical form $\boldsymbol{y}$ and the derivation z.

Because the derivation z unambiguously determines the logical form $\boldsymbol{y}$, it may seem silly to model the joint probability over $\boldsymbol{y}$ and z. However, because z is unknown, it can be marginalized out,

$$\text{p}(\boldsymbol{y} \mid \boldsymbol{w}) = \sum_{z} \text{p}(\boldsymbol{y}, z \mid \boldsymbol{w}). \quad [12.21]$$

The semantic parser can then select the logical form with the maximum log marginal probability,

$$\log \sum_{z} \text{p}(\boldsymbol{y}, z \mid \boldsymbol{w}) = \log \sum_{z} \frac{\exp(\boldsymbol{\theta} \cdot \boldsymbol{f}(\boldsymbol{w}, z, \boldsymbol{y}))}{\sum \boldsymbol{y}', z' \exp(\boldsymbol{\theta} \cdot \boldsymbol{f}(\boldsymbol{w}, z', \boldsymbol{y}'))} \quad [12.22]$$

$$\propto \log \sum_{z} \exp(\boldsymbol{\theta} \cdot \boldsymbol{f}(\boldsymbol{w}, z', \boldsymbol{y}')) \quad [12.23]$$

$$\geq \max_{z} \boldsymbol{\theta} \cdot \boldsymbol{f}(\boldsymbol{w}, z, \boldsymbol{y}). \quad [12.24]$$

10. An exception is the work of Ge and Mooney (2005), who annotate the meaning of each syntactic constituents for several hundred sentences.

It is impossible to push the log term inside the sum over z, so our usual linear scoring function does not apply. We can recover this scoring function only in approximation, by taking the max (rather than the sum) over derivations z, which provides a lower bound.

Learning can be performed by maximizing the log marginal likelihood,

$$\ell(\boldsymbol{\theta}) = \sum_{i=1}^{N} \log p(\boldsymbol{y}^{(i)} \mid \boldsymbol{w}^{(i)}; \boldsymbol{\theta}) \tag{12.25}$$

$$= \sum_{i=1}^{N} \log \sum_{z} p(\boldsymbol{y}^{(i)}, z^{(i)} \mid \boldsymbol{w}^{(i)}; \boldsymbol{\theta}). \tag{12.26}$$

This log-likelihood is not **convex** in $\boldsymbol{\theta}$, unlike the log-likelihood of a fully observed conditional random field. This means that learning can give different results depending on the initialization.

The derivative of equation 12.26 is

$$\frac{\partial \ell_i}{\partial \boldsymbol{\theta}} = \sum_{z} p(z \mid \boldsymbol{y}, \boldsymbol{w}; \boldsymbol{\theta}) \boldsymbol{f}(\boldsymbol{w}, z, \boldsymbol{y}) - \sum_{\boldsymbol{y}', z'} p(\boldsymbol{y}', z' \mid \boldsymbol{w}; \boldsymbol{\theta}) \boldsymbol{f}(\boldsymbol{w}, z', \boldsymbol{y}') \tag{12.27}$$

$$= E_{z \mid \boldsymbol{y}, \boldsymbol{w}} \boldsymbol{f}(\boldsymbol{w}, z, \boldsymbol{y}) - E_{\boldsymbol{y}, z \mid \boldsymbol{w}} \boldsymbol{f}(\boldsymbol{w}, z, \boldsymbol{y}). \tag{12.28}$$

Both expectations can be computed via bottom-up algorithms like inside-outside. Alternatively, we can again maximize rather than marginalize over derivations for an approximate solution. In either case, the first term of the gradient requires us to identify derivations z that are compatible with the logical form $\boldsymbol{y}$. This can be done in a bottom-up dynamic programming algorithm, by having each cell in the table $t[i, j, X]$ include the set of all possible logical forms for $X \rightsquigarrow \boldsymbol{w}_{i+1:j}$. The resulting table may therefore be much larger than in syntactic parsing. This can be controlled by using pruning to eliminate intermediate analyses that are incompatible with the final logical form $\boldsymbol{y}$ (Zettlemoyer and Collins, 2005), or by using beam search and restricting the size of each cell to some fixed constant (Liang et al., 2013).

If we replace each expectation in equation 12.28 with argmax and then apply stochastic gradient descent to learn the weights, we obtain the **latent variable perceptron**, a simple and general algorithm for learning with missing data. The algorithm is shown in its most basic form in algorithm 16, but the usual tricks such as averaging and margin loss can be applied (Yu and Joachims, 2009). Aside from semantic parsing, the latent variable perceptron has been used in tasks such as machine translation (Liang et al., 2006) and named entity recognition (Sun et al., 2009). In **latent conditional random fields**, we use the full expectations rather than maximizing over the hidden variable. This model has also been employed in a range of problems beyond semantic parsing, including parse reranking (Koo and Collins, 2005) and gesture recognition (Quattoni et al., 2007).

Algorithm 16
Latent variable perceptron.

---

procedure LATENTVARIABLEPERCEPTRON($\boldsymbol{w}^{(1:N)}, \boldsymbol{y}^{(1:N)}$)
    $\boldsymbol{\theta} \leftarrow \mathbf{0}$
    repeat
        Select an instance i
        $z^{(i)} \leftarrow \text{argmax}_z\, \boldsymbol{\theta} \cdot \boldsymbol{f}(\boldsymbol{w}^{(i)}, z, \boldsymbol{y}^{(i)})$
        $\hat{y}, \hat{z} \leftarrow \text{argmax}_{y', z'}\, \boldsymbol{\theta} \cdot \boldsymbol{f}(\boldsymbol{w}^{(i)}, z', \boldsymbol{y}')$
        $\boldsymbol{\theta} \leftarrow \boldsymbol{\theta} + \boldsymbol{f}(\boldsymbol{w}^{(i)}, z^{(i)}, \boldsymbol{y}^{(i)}) - \boldsymbol{f}(\boldsymbol{w}^{(i)}, \hat{z}, \hat{y})$
    until tired
    return $\boldsymbol{\theta}$

12.4.3 Learning from Denotations

Logical forms are easier to obtain than complete derivations, but the annotation of logical forms still requires considerable expertise. However, it is relatively easy to obtain denotations for many natural language sentences. For example, in the geography domain, the denotation of a question would be its answer (Clarke et al., 2010; Liang et al., 2013):

Text : *What states border Georgia?*

Logical form : $\lambda x.\text{STATE}(x) \wedge \text{BORDER}(x, \text{GEORGIA})$

Denotation : {`Alabama, Florida, North Carolina,`
`South Carolina, Tennessee`}

Similarly, in a robotic control setting, the denotation of a command would be an action or sequence of actions (Artzi and Zettlemoyer, 2013). In both cases, the idea is to reward the semantic parser for choosing an analysis whose denotation is correct: the right answer to the question, or the right action.

Learning from logical forms was made possible by summing or maxing over derivations. This idea can be carried one step further, summing or maxing over all logical forms with the correct denotation. Let $v_i(\boldsymbol{y}) \in \{0, 1\}$ be a **validation function**, which assigns a binary score indicating whether the denotation $[\![\boldsymbol{y}]\!]$ for the text $\boldsymbol{w}^{(i)}$ is correct. We can then learn by maximizing a conditional-likelihood objective,

$$\ell^{(i)}(\boldsymbol{\theta}) = \log \sum_{\boldsymbol{y}} v_i(\boldsymbol{y}) \times \text{p}(\boldsymbol{y} \mid \boldsymbol{w}; \boldsymbol{\theta}) \quad [12.29]$$

$$= \log \sum_{\boldsymbol{y}} v_i(\boldsymbol{y}) \times \sum_{z} \text{p}(\boldsymbol{y}, z \mid \boldsymbol{w}; \boldsymbol{\theta}), \quad [12.30]$$

which sums over all derivations z of all valid logical forms, $\{y : v_i(y) = 1\}$. This corresponds to the log-probability that the semantic parser produces a logical form with a valid denotation.

Differentiating with respect to $\boldsymbol{\theta}$, we obtain

$$\frac{\partial \ell^{(i)}}{\partial \boldsymbol{\theta}} = \sum_{y,z:v_i(y)=1} \mathrm{p}(y, z \mid \boldsymbol{w}) \boldsymbol{f}(\boldsymbol{w}, z, y) - \sum_{y',z'} \mathrm{p}(y', z' \mid \boldsymbol{w}) \boldsymbol{f}(\boldsymbol{w}, z', y'), \qquad [12.31]$$

which is the usual difference in feature expectations. The positive term computes the expected feature expectations conditioned on the denotation being valid, while the second term computes the expected feature expectations according to the current model, without regard to the ground truth. Large-margin learning formulations are also possible for this problem. For example, Artzi and Zettlemoyer (2013) generate a set of valid and invalid derivations and then impose a constraint that all valid derivations should score higher than all invalid derivations. This constraint drives a perceptron-like learning rule.

Additional Resources

A key issue not considered here is how to handle **semantic underspecification**: cases in which there are multiple semantic interpretations for a single syntactic structure. Quantifier scope ambiguity is a classic example. Blackburn and Bos (2005) enumerate a number of approaches to this issue and also provide links between natural language semantics and computational inference techniques. Much of the contemporary research on semantic parsing uses the framework of combinatory categorial grammar (CCG). Carpenter (1997) provides a comprehensive treatment of how CCG can support compositional semantic analysis. Another recent area of research is the semantics of multi sentence texts. This can be handled with models of **dynamic semantics**, such as dynamic predicate logic (Groenendijk and Stokhof, 1991).

Alternative readings on formal semantics include an "informal" reading from Levy and Manning (2009) and a more involved introduction from Briscoe (2011). To learn more about ongoing research on data-driven semantic parsing, readers may consult the survey article by Liang and Potts (2015), tutorial slides and videos by Artzi and Zettlemoyer (2013),[11] and the source code by Yoav Artzi[12] and Percy Liang.[13]

11. Videos are currently available at http://yoavartzi.com/tutorial/.

12. http://yoavartzi.com/spf.

13. https://github.com/percyliang/sempre.

Exercises

1. The **modus ponens** inference rule states that if we know $\phi \Rightarrow \psi$ and ϕ, then ψ must be true. Justify this rule, using the definition of the $\Rightarrow$ operator and some of the laws provided in § 12.2.1, plus one additional identity: $\bot \vee \phi = \phi$.
2. Convert the following examples into first-order logic, using the relations CAN-SLEEP, MAKES-NOISE, and BROTHER.
   - If Abigail makes noise, no one can sleep.
   - If Abigail makes noise, someone cannot sleep.
   - None of Abigail's brothers can sleep.
   - If one of Abigail's brothers makes noise, Abigail cannot sleep.
3. Extend the grammar fragment G_1 to include the ditransitive verb *teaches* and the proper noun *Swahili*. Show how to derive the interpretation for the sentence *Alex teaches Brit Swahili*, which should be TEACHES(ALEX,BRIT,SWAHILI). The grammar need not be in Chomsky Normal Form. For the ditransitive verb, use NP_1 and NP_2 to indicate the two direct objects.
4. Derive the semantic interpretation for the sentence *Alex likes every dog*, using grammar fragment G_2.
5. Extend the grammar fragment G_2 to handle adjectives, so that the meaning of *an angry dog* is $\lambda P.\exists x \text{DOG}(x) \wedge \text{ANGRY}(x) \wedge P(x)$. Specifically, you should supply the lexical entry for the adjective *angry*, and you should specify the syntactic-semantic productions NP $\rightarrow$ DET NOM, NOM $\rightarrow$ JJ NOM, and NOM $\rightarrow$ NN.
6. Extend your answer to the previous question to cover copula constructions with predicative adjectives, such as *Alex is angry*. The interpretation should be ANGRY(ALEX). You should add a verb phrase production VP $\rightarrow$ V_{cop} JJ and a terminal production $\text{V}_{\text{cop}} \rightarrow$ *is*. Show why your grammar extensions result in the correct interpretation.
7. In figure 12.5 and figure 12.6, we treat the plurals *shoots* and *leaves* as entities. Revise G_2 so that the interpretation of *Alex eats leaves* is $\forall x.(\text{LEAF}(x) \Rightarrow \text{EATS}(\text{ALEX}, x))$, and show the resulting perceptron update.
8. Statements like *every student eats a pizza* have two possible interpretations, depending on quantifier scope:

$$\forall x \exists y \text{PIZZA}(y) \wedge (\text{STUDENT}(x) \Rightarrow \text{EATS}(x, y)) \quad [12.32]$$

$$\exists y \forall x \text{PIZZA}(y) \wedge (\text{STUDENT}(x) \Rightarrow \text{EATS}(x, y)) \quad [12.33]$$

   a) Explain why these interpretations really are different.
   b) Which is generated by grammar G_2? Note that you may have to manipulate the logical form to exactly align with the grammar.

9. *Modify G_2 so that produces the second interpretation in the previous problem. **Hint**: One possible solution involves changing the semantics of the sentence production and one other production.
10. In the GeoQuery domain, give a natural language query that has multiple plausible semantic interpretations with the same denotation. List both interpretaions and the denotation.

    Hint: There are many ways to do this, but one approach involves using toponyms (place names) that could plausibly map to several different entities in the model.

13 Predicate-Argument Semantics

This chapter considers more "lightweight" semantic representations, which discard some aspects of first-order logic, while focusing on predicate-argument structures. Let's begin by thinking about the semantics of events, with a simple example:

(13.1) Asha gives Boyang a book.

A first-order logical representation of this sentence is

$$\exists x.\text{BOOK}(x) \wedge \text{GIVE}(\text{ASHA}, \text{BOYANG}, x). \tag{13.1}$$

In this representation, we define variable x for the book, and we link the strings *Asha* and *Boyang* to entities ASHA and BOYANG. Because the action of giving involves a giver, a recipient, and a gift, the predicate GIVE must take three arguments.

Now suppose we have additional information about the event:

(13.2) Yesterday, Asha reluctantly gave Boyang a book.

One possible solution is to extend the predicate GIVE to take additional arguments,

$$\exists x.\text{BOOK}(x) \wedge \text{GIVE}(\text{ASHA}, \text{BOYANG}, x, \text{YESTERDAY}, \text{RELUCTANTLY}). \tag{13.2}$$

But this is clearly unsatisfactory: *yesterday* and *relunctantly* are optional arguments, and we would need a different version of the GIVE predicate for every possible combination of arguments. **Event semantics** solves this problem by **reifying** the event as an existentially quantified variable e,

$$\exists e, x\ \text{GIVE-EVENT}(e) \wedge \text{GIVER}(e, \text{ASHA}) \wedge \text{GIFT}(e, x) \wedge \text{BOOK}(e, x)$$
$$\wedge\ \text{RECIPIENT}(e, \text{BOYANG}) \wedge \text{TIME}(e, \text{YESTERDAY}) \wedge \text{MANNER}(e, \text{RELUCTANTLY}).$$

In this way, each argument of the event—the giver, the recipient, the gift—can be represented with a relation of its own, linking the argument to the event e. The expression $\text{GIVER}(e, \text{ASHA})$ says that ASHA plays the **role** of GIVER in the event. This reformulation handles the problem of optional information such as the time or manner of the event, which are called **adjuncts**. Unlike arguments, adjuncts are not a mandatory part of the relation, but under this representation, they can be expressed with additional logical relations that are conjoined to the semantic interpretation of the sentence.[1]

The event semantic representation can be applied to nested clauses, for example,

(13.3) Chris sees Asha pay Boyang.

This is done by using the event variable as an argument:

$$\exists e_1 \exists e_2 \text{ SEE-EVENT}(e_1) \wedge \text{SEER}(e_1, \text{CHRIS}) \wedge \text{SIGHT}(e_1, e_2) \\ \wedge \text{PAY-EVENT}(e_2) \wedge \text{PAYER}(e_2, \text{ASHA}) \wedge \text{PAYEE}(e_2, \text{BOYANG}). \quad [13.3]$$

As with first-order logic, the goal of event semantics is to provide a representation that generalizes over many surface forms. Consider the following paraphrases of (13.1):

(13.4) a. Asha gives a book to Boyang.
b. A book is given to Boyang by Asha.
c. A book is given by Asha to Boyang.
d. The gift of a book from Asha to Boyang …

All have the same event semantic meaning as equation 13.1, but the ways in which the meaning can be expressed are diverse. The final example does not even include a verb: events are often introduced by verbs, but as shown by (13.4d), the noun *gift* can introduce the same predicate, with the same accompanying arguments.

Semantic role labeling (SRL) is a form of semantic parsing in which each semantic role is filled by a set of tokens from the text itself. It is sometimes called "shallow semantics" because, unlike model-theoretic semantic parsing, role fillers need not be symbolic expressions with denotations in some world model. A semantic role labeling system is required to identify all predicates and then specify the spans of text that fill each role. To give a sense of the task, here is a more complicated example:

(13.5) Boyang wants Asha to give him a linguistics book.

In this example, there are two predicates, expressed by the verbs *want* and *give*. Thus, a semantic role labeler might return the following output:

- (PREDICATE : *wants*, WANTER : *Boyang*, DESIRE : *Asha to give him a linguistics book*)
- (PREDICATE : *give*, GIVER : *Asha*, RECIPIENT : *him*, GIFT : *a linguistics book*)

Boyang and *him* may refer to the same person, but the semantic role labeling is not required to resolve this reference. Other predicate-argument representations, such as **Abstract Meaning Representation (AMR)**, do require reference resolution. We will return to AMR in § 13.3, but first, let us further consider the definition of semantic roles.

1. This representation is often called **Neo-Davidsonian event semantics**. The use of existentially quantified event variables was proposed by Davidson (1967) to handle the issue of optional adjuncts. In Neo-Davidsonian semantics, this treatment of adjuncts is extended to mandatory arguments as well (e.g., Parsons, 1991).

13.1 Semantic Roles

In event semantics, it is necessary to specify a number of additional logical relations to link arguments to events: GIVER, RECIPIENT, SEER, SIGHT, etc. Indeed, every predicate requires a set of logical relations to express its own arguments. In contrast, adjuncts such as TIME and MANNER are shared across many types of events. A natural question is whether it is possible to treat mandatory arguments more like adjuncts, by identifying a set of generic argument types that are shared across many event predicates. This can be further motivated by examples involving related verbs:

(13.6) a. Asha gave Boyang a book.
b. Asha loaned Boyang a book.
c. Asha taught Boyang a lesson.
d. Asha gave Boyang a lesson.

The respective roles of Asha, Boyang, and the book are nearly identical across the first two examples. The third example is slightly different, but the fourth example shows that the roles of GIVER and TEACHER can be viewed as related.

One way to think about the relationship between roles such as GIVER and TEACHER is by enumerating the set of properties that an entity typically possesses when it fulfills these roles: givers and teachers are usually **animate** (they are alive and sentient) and **volitional** (they choose to enter into the action).[2] In contrast, the thing that gets loaned or taught is usually not animate or volitional; furthermore, it is unchanged by the event.

Building on these ideas, **thematic roles** generalize across predicates by leveraging the shared semantic properties of typical role fillers (Fillmore, 1968). For example, in examples (13.6a-13.6d), Asha plays a similar role in all four sentences, which we will call the **agent**. This reflects several shared semantic properties: she is the one who is actively and intentionally performing the action, while Boyang is a more passive participant; the book and the lesson would play a different role, as non animate participants in the event.

Example annotations from three well known systems are shown in figure 13.1. We will now discuss these systems in more detail.

13.1.1 VerbNet

VerbNet (Kipper-Schuler, 2005) is a lexicon of verbs, and it includes 30 "core" thematic roles played by arguments to these verbs. Here are some example roles, accompanied by their definitions from the VerbNet Guidelines.[3]

2. There are always exceptions. For example, in the sentence *The C programming language has taught me a lot about perseverance*, the "teacher" is the *The C programming language*, which is presumably not animate or volitional.

3. http://verbs.colorado.edu/verb-index/VerbNet_Guidelines.pdf.

	Asha	*gave*	*Boyang*	*a book*
VerbNet	AGENT		RECIPIENT	THEME
PropBank	ARG0: giver		ARG2: entity given to	ARG1: thing given
FrameNet	DONOR		RECIPIENT	THEME
	Asha	*taught*	*Boyang*	*algebra*
VerbNet	AGENT		RECIPIENT	TOPIC
PropBank	ARG0: teacher		ARG2: student	ARG1: subject
FrameNet	TEACHER		STUDENT	SUBJECT

Figure 13.1
Example semantic annotations according to VerbNet, PropBank, and FrameNet.

- AGENT: "ACTOR in an event who initiates and carries out the event intentionally or consciously, and who exists independently of the event."
- PATIENT: "UNDERGOER in an event that experiences a change of state, location or condition, that is causally involved or directly affected by other participants, and exists independently of the event."
- RECIPIENT: "DESTINATION that is animate."
- THEME: "UNDERGOER that is central to an event or state that does not have control over the way the event occurs, is not structurally changed by the event, and/or is characterized as being in a certain position or condition throughout the state."
- TOPIC: "THEME characterized by information content transferred to another participant."

VerbNet roles are organized in a hierarchy, so that a TOPIC is a type of THEME, which in turn is a type of UNDERGOER, which is a type of PARTICIPANT, the top-level category.

In addition, VerbNet organizes verb senses into a class hierarchy, in which verb senses that have similar meanings are grouped together. Recall from § 4.2 that multiple meanings of the same word are called **senses** and that WordNet identifies senses for many English words. VerbNet builds on WordNet, so that verb classes are identified by the WordNet senses of the verbs that they contain. For example, the verb class `give-13.1` includes the first WordNet sense of *loan* and the second WordNet sense of *lend*.

Each VerbNet class or subclass takes a set of thematic roles. For example, `give-13.1` takes arguments with the thematic roles of AGENT, THEME, and RECIPIENT;[4] the predicate TEACH takes arguments with the thematic roles AGENT, TOPIC, RECIPIENT, and

4. https://verbs.colorado.edu/verb-index/vn/give-13.1.php.

SOURCE.[5] So according to VerbNet, *Asha* and *Boyang* play the roles of AGENT and RECIPIENT in the following sentences:

(13.7) a. Asha gave Boyang a book.
b. Asha taught Boyang algebra.

The *book* and *algebra* are both THEMES, but *algebra* is a subcategory of THEME—a TOPIC—because it consists of information content that is given to the receiver.

13.1.2 Proto-Roles and PropBank

Detailed thematic role inventories of the sort used in VerbNet are not universally accepted. For example, Dowty (1991, pp. 547) notes that "Linguists have often found it hard to agree on, and to motivate, the location of the boundary between role types." He argues that a solid distinction can be identified between just two **proto-roles**:

Proto-agent. Characterized by volitional involvement in the event or state; sentience and/or perception; causing an event or change of state in another participant; movement; exists independently of the event.

Proto-patient. Undergoes change of state; causally affected by another participant; stationary relative to the movement of another participant; does not exist independently of the event.[6]

In the examples in figure 13.1, Asha has most of the proto-agent properties: in giving the book to Boyang, she is acting volitionally (as opposed to *Boyang got a book from Asha*, in which it is not clear whether Asha gave up the book willingly); she is sentient; she causes a change of state in Boyang; she exists independently of the event. Boyang has some proto-agent properties: he is sentient and exists independently of the event. But he also has some proto-patient properties: he is the one who is causally affected and who undergoes change of state. The book that Asha gives Boyang has even fewer of the proto-agent properties: it is not volitional or sentient, and it has no causal role. But it also lacks many of the proto-patient properties: it does not undergo change of state, exists independently of the event, and is not stationary.

The **Proposition Bank**, or PropBank (Palmer et al., 2005), builds on this basic agent-patient distinction, as a middle ground between generic thematic roles and roles that are specific to each predicate. Each verb is linked to a list of numbered arguments, with ARG0

5. https://verbs.colorado.edu/verb-index/vn/transfer_mesg-37.1.1.php.

6. Reisinger et al. (2015) ask crowd workers to annotate these properties directly, finding that annotators tend to agree on the properties of each argument. They also find that, in English, arguments having more proto-agent properties tend to appear in subject position, while arguments with more proto-patient properties appear in object position.

Table 13.1
PropBank adjuncts (Palmer et al., 2005), sorted by frequency in the corpus

TMP	time	*Boyang ate a bagel* [AM-TMP *yesterday*].
LOC	location	*Asha studies in* [AM-LOC *Stuttgart*]
MOD	modal verb	*Asha* [AM-MOD *will*] *study in Stuttgart*
ADV	general purpose	[AM-ADV *Luckily*], *Asha knew algebra.*
MNR	manner	*Asha ate* [AM-MNR *aggressively*].
DIS	discourse connective	[AM-DIS *However*], *Asha prefers algebra.*
PRP	purpose	*Barry studied* [AM-PRP *to pass the bar*].
DIR	direction	*Workers dumped burlap sacks* [AM-DIR *into a bin*].
NEG	negation	*Asha does* [AM-NEG *not*] *speak Albanian.*
EXT	extent	*Prices increased* [AM-EXT *4%*].
CAU	cause	*Boyang returned the book* [AM-CAU *because it was overdue*].

as the proto-agent and ARG1 as the proto-patient. Additional numbered arguments are verb specific. For example, for the predicate TEACH,[7] the arguments are:

- ARG0: the teacher
- ARG1: the subject
- ARG2: the student(s)

Verbs may have any number of arguments: for example, WANT and GET have five, while EAT has only ARG0 and ARG1. In addition to the verb-specific semantic arguments roughly a dozen general-purpose adjuncts may be used in combination with any verb. These are shown in table 13.1.

PropBank-style semantic role labeling is annotated over the entire Penn Treebank. This annotation includes the sense of each verbal predicate, as well as the argument spans.

13.1.3 FrameNet

Semantic **frames** are descriptions of situations or events. Frames may be *evoked* by one of their **lexical units** (often a verb, but not always), and they include some number of **frame elements**, which are like roles (Fillmore, 1976). For example, the act of teaching is a frame and can be evoked by the verb *taught*; the associated frame elements include the teacher, the student(s), and the subject being taught. Frame semantics has played a significant role in the history of artificial intelligence, in the work of Minsky (1974) and Schank and Abelson (1977). In natural language processing, the theory of frame semantics has been implemented in **FrameNet** (Fillmore and Baker, 2009), which consists of a lexicon of roughly

7. http://verbs.colorado.edu/propbank/framesets-english-aliases/teach.html.

1,000 frames, and a corpus of more than 200,000 "exemplar sentences," in which the frames and their elements are annotated.[8]

Rather than seeking to link semantic roles such as TEACHER and GIVER into thematic roles such as AGENT, FrameNet aggressively groups verbs into frames and links semantically related roles across frames. For example, the following two sentences would be annotated identically in FrameNet:

(13.8) a. Asha taught Boyang algebra.
b. Boyang learned algebra from Asha.

This is because *teach* and *learn* are both lexical units in the EDUCATION_TEACHING frame. Furthermore, roles can be shared even when the frames are distinct, as in the following two examples:

(13.9) a. Asha gave Boyang a book.
b. Boyang got a book from Asha.

The GIVING and GETTING frames both have RECIPIENT and THEME elements, so Boyang and the book would play the same role. Asha's role is different: she is the DONOR in the GIVING frame and the SOURCE in the GETTING frame. FrameNet makes extensive use of inheritance to share information across frames and frame elements: for example, the COMMERCE_SELL and LENDING frames inherit from the GIVING frame.

13.2 Semantic Role Labeling

The task of semantic role labeling is to identify the parts of the sentence comprising the semantic roles. In English, this task is typically performed on the PropBank corpus, with the goal of producing outputs in the following form:

(13.10) [$_{\text{ARG0}}$ Asha][$_{\text{GIVE.01}}$ gave][$_{\text{ARG2}}$ Boyang's mom][$_{\text{ARG1}}$ a book][$_{\text{AM-TMP}}$ yesterday].

Note that a single sentence may have multiple verbs, and therefore a given word may be part of multiple role fillers:

(13.11) [$_{\text{ARG0}}$ Asha] [$_{\text{WANT.01}}$ wanted] [$_{\text{ARG1}}$ Boyang to give her the book].
Asha wanted [$_{\text{ARG0}}$ Boyang] [$_{\text{GIVE.01}}$ to give] [$_{\text{ARG2}}$ her] [$_{\text{ARG1}}$ the book].

13.2.1 Semantic Role Labeling as Classification

PropBank is annotated on the Penn Treebank, and annotators used phrasal constituents (§ 9.2.2) to fill the roles. PropBank semantic role labeling can be viewed as the task of assigning to each phrase a label from the set $\mathcal{R} = \{\varnothing, \text{PRED}, \text{ARG0}, \text{ARG1}, \text{ARG2}, \ldots,$

8. Current details and data can be found at https://framenet.icsi.berkeley.edu/.

AM-LOC, AM-TMP, … } with respect to each predicate. If we treat semantic role labeling as a classification problem, we obtain the following functional form:

$$\hat{y}_{(i,j)} = \underset{y}{\text{argmax}}\ \psi(\boldsymbol{w}, y, i, j, \rho, \tau), \qquad [13.4]$$

where:

- (i,j) indicates the span of a phrasal constituent $(w_{i+1}, w_{i+2}, \ldots, w_j)$;[9]
- $\boldsymbol{w}$ represents the sentence as a sequence of tokens;
- ρ is the index of the predicate verb in $\boldsymbol{w}$;
- τ is the structure of the phrasal constituent parse of $\boldsymbol{w}$.

Early work on semantic role labeling focused on discriminative feature-based models, where $\psi(\boldsymbol{w}, y, i, j, \rho, \tau) = \boldsymbol{\theta} \cdot \boldsymbol{f}(\boldsymbol{w}, y, i, j, \rho, \tau)$. Table 13.2 shows the features used in a seminal paper on FrameNet semantic role labeling (Gildea and Jurafsky, 2002). By 2005 there were several systems for PropBank semantic role labeling, and their approaches and feature sets are summarized by Carreras and Màrquez (2005). Typical features include: the phrase type, head word, part of speech, boundaries, and neighbors of the proposed argument $\boldsymbol{w}_{i+1:j}$; the word, lemma, part of speech, and voice of the verb w_ρ (active or passive), as well as features relating to its frameset; and the distance and path between the verb and the proposed argument. In this way, semantic role labeling systems are high-level "consumers" in the NLP stack, using features produced from lower-level components such as part-of-speech taggers and parsers. More comprehensive feature sets are enumerated by Das et al. (2014) and Täckström et al. (2015).

A particularly powerful class of features relate to the **syntactic path** between the argument and the predicate. These features capture the sequence of moves required to get from the argument to the verb by traversing the phrasal constituent parse of the sentence. The idea of these features is to capture syntactic regularities in how various arguments are realized. Syntactic path features are best illustrated by example, using the parse tree in figure 13.2:

- The path from *Asha* to the verb *taught* is NNP↑NP↑S↓VP↓VBD. The first part of the path, NNP↑NP↑S, means that we must travel up the parse tree from the NNP tag (proper noun) to the S (sentence) constituent. The second part of the path, S↓VP↓VBD, means that we reach the verb by producing a VP (verb phrase) from the S constituent, and then by producing a VBD (past tense verb). This feature is consistent with *Asha* being in subject position, because the path includes the sentence root S.

9. PropBank roles can also be filled by **split constituents**, which are discontinuous spans of text. This situation most frequently in reported speech, for example, [$_{\text{ARG1}}$ *By addressing these problems*], *Mr. Maxwell said,* [$_{\text{ARG1}}$ *the new funds have become extremely attractive.*] (example adapted from Palmer et al., 2005). This issue is typically addressed by defining "continuation arguments," for example, (C-ARG1), which refers to the continuation of ARG1 after the split.

Table 13.2
Features used in semantic role labeling by Gildea and Jurafsky (2002)

Predicate lemma and POS tag	The lemma of the predicate verb and its part-of-speech tag.
Voice	Whether the predicate is in active or passive voice, as determined by a set of syntactic patterns for identifying passive voice constructions.
Phrase type	The constituent phrase type for the proposed argument in the parse tree, e.g. NP, PP.
Headword and POS tag	The head word of the proposed argument and its POS tag, identified using the Collins (1997) rules.
Position	Whether the proposed argument comes before or after the predicate in the sentence.
Syntactic path	The set of steps on the parse tree from the proposed argument to the predicate (described in detail in the text).
Subcategorization	The syntactic production from the first branching node above the predicate. For example, in figure 13.2, the subcategorization feature around *taught* would be VP → VBD NP PP.

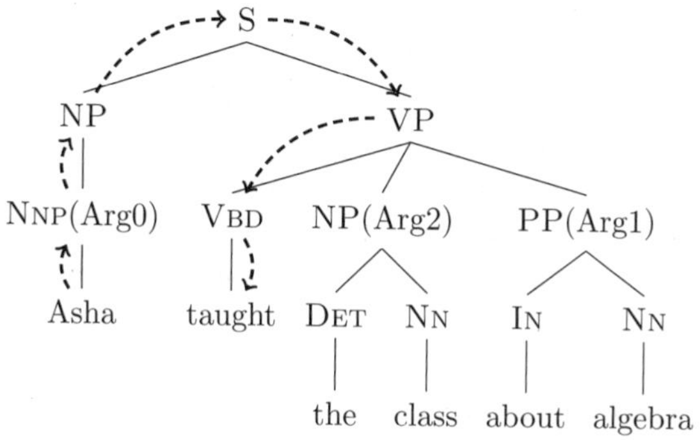

Figure 13.2
Semantic role labeling on the phrase-structure parse tree for a sentence. The dashed line indicates the syntactic path from *Asha* to the predicate verb *taught*.

- The path from *the class* to *taught* is NP↑VP↓VBD. This is consistent with *the class* being in object position, because the path passes through the VP node that dominates the verb *taught*.

Because there are many possible path features, it can also be helpful to look at smaller parts: for example, the upward and downward parts can be treated as separate features; another feature might consider whether S appears anywhere in the path.

Rather than using the constituent parse, it is also possible to build features from the **dependency path** (see § 11.4) between the head word of each argument and the verb (Pradhan et al., 2005). Using the Universal Dependency part-of-speech tagset and dependency relations (Nivre et al., 2016), the dependency path from *Asha* to *taught* is

$\textsc{Propn} \underset{\textsc{Nsubj}}{\leftarrow} \textsc{Verb}$, because *taught* is the head of a relation of type $\underset{\textsc{Nsubj}}{\leftarrow}$ with *Asha*. Similarly, the dependency path from *class* to *taught* is $\textsc{Noun} \underset{\textsc{Dobj}}{\leftarrow} \textsc{Verb}$, because *class* heads the noun phrase that is a direct object of *taught*. A more interesting example is *Asha wanted to teach the class*, where the path from *Asha* to *teach* is $\textsc{Propn} \underset{\textsc{Nsubj}}{\leftarrow} \textsc{Verb} \underset{\textsc{Xcomp}}{\rightarrow} \textsc{Verb}$. The right-facing arrow in second relation indicates that *wanted* is the head of its XCOMP relation with *teach*.

13.2.2 Semantic Role Labeling as Constrained Optimization

A potential problem with treating SRL as a classification problem is that there are a number of sentence-level **constraints**, which a classifier might violate:

- For a given verb, there can be only one argument of each type (ARG0, ARG1, etc.).
- Arguments cannot overlap. This problem arises when we are labeling the phrases in a constituent parse tree, as shown in figure 13.2: if we label the PP *about algebra* as an argument or adjunct, then its children *about* and *algebra* must be labeled as ∅. The same constraint also applies to the syntactic ancestors of this phrase.

These constraints introduce dependencies across labeling decisions. In structure prediction problems such as sequence labeling and parsing, such dependencies are usually handled by defining a scoring function over the entire structure, $\boldsymbol{y}$. Efficient inference requires that the global score decomposes into local parts: for example, in sequence labeling, the scoring function decomposes into scores of pairs of adjacent tags, permitting the application of the Viterbi algorithm for inference. But the constraints that arise in semantic role labeling are less amenable to local decomposition.[10] We therefore consider **constrained optimization** as an alternative solution.

Let the set $\mathcal{C}(\tau)$ refer to all labelings that obey the constraints introduced by the parse τ. The semantic role labeling problem can be reformulated as a constrained optimization over $\boldsymbol{y} \in \mathcal{C}(\tau)$,

$$\max_{\boldsymbol{y}} \quad \sum_{(i,j)\in\tau} \psi(\boldsymbol{w}, y_{i,j}, i, j, \rho, \tau)$$

$$\text{s.t.} \quad \boldsymbol{y} \in \mathcal{C}(\tau). \qquad [13.5]$$

In this formulation, the objective (shown on the first line) is a separable function of each individual labeling decision, but the constraints (shown on the second line) apply to the overall labeling. The sum $\sum_{(i,j)\in\tau}$ indicates that we are summing over all constituent spans in the parse τ. The expression s.t. in the second line means that we maximize the objective *subject to* the constraint $\boldsymbol{y} \in \mathcal{C}(\tau)$.

10. Dynamic programming solutions have been proposed by Tromble and Eisner (2006) and Täckström et al. (2015), but they involve creating a trellis structure whose size is exponential in the number of labels.

A number of practical algorithms exist for restricted forms of constrained optimization. One such restricted form is **integer linear programming**, in which the objective and constraints are linear functions of integer variables. To formulate SRL as an integer linear program, we begin by rewriting the labels as a set of binary variables $z = \{z_{i,j,r}\}$ (Punyakanok et al., 2008),

$$z_{i,j,r} = \begin{cases} 1, & y_{i,j} = r \\ 0, & \text{otherwise}, \end{cases} \quad [13.6]$$

where $r \in \mathcal{R}$ is a label in the set $\{\text{ARG0}, \text{ARG1}, \ldots, \text{AM-LOC}, \ldots, \varnothing\}$. Thus, the variables z are a binarized version of the semantic role labeling $\boldsymbol{y}$.

The objective can then be formulated as a linear function of z:

$$\sum_{(i,j)\in\tau} \psi(\boldsymbol{w}, y_{i,j}, i, j, \rho, \tau) = \sum_{i,j,r} \psi(\boldsymbol{w}, r, i, j, \rho, \tau) \times z_{i,j,r}, \quad [13.7]$$

which is the sum of the scores of all relations, as indicated by $z_{i,j,r}$.

Constraints Integer linear programming permits linear inequality constraints, of the general form $\mathbf{A}z \leq \boldsymbol{b}$, where the parameters $\mathbf{A}$ and $\boldsymbol{b}$ define the constraints. To make this more concrete, let's start with the constraint that each non-null role type can occur only once in a sentence. This constraint can be written as

$$\forall r \neq \varnothing, \quad \sum_{(i,j)\in\tau} z_{i,j,r} \leq 1. \quad [13.8]$$

Recall that $z_{i,j,r} = 1$ iff the span (i,j) has label r; this constraint says that for each possible label $r \neq \varnothing$, there can be at most one (i,j) such that $z_{i,j,r} = 1$. This constraint can be written in the form $\mathbf{A}z \leq \boldsymbol{b}$, as you will find if you complete the exercises at the end of the chapter.

Now consider the constraint that labels cannot overlap. Let's define the convenience function $o((i,j),(i',j')) = 1$ iff (i,j) overlaps (i',j'), and zero otherwise. Thus, o will indicate if a constituent (i',j') is either an ancestor or descendant of (i,j). The constraint is that if two constituents overlap, only one can have a non-null label:

$$\forall (i,j) \in \tau, \quad \sum_{(i',j')\in\tau} \sum_{r\neq\varnothing} o((i,j),(i',j')) \times z_{i',j',r} \leq 1, \quad [13.9]$$

where $o((i,j),(i,j)) = 1$.

In summary, the semantic role labeling problem can thus be rewritten as the following integer linear program:

$$\max_{z\in\{0,1\}^{|\tau|}} \quad \sum_{(i,j)\in\tau} \sum_{r\in\mathcal{R}} z_{i,j,r} \psi_{i,j,r}$$

$$s.t. \quad \forall r \neq \varnothing, \quad \sum_{(i,j) \in \tau} z_{i,j,r} \leq 1.$$
$$\forall (i,j) \in \tau, \quad \sum_{(i',j') \in \tau} \sum_{r \neq \varnothing} o((i,j),(i',j')) \times z_{i',j',r} \leq 1. \qquad [13.10]$$

Learning with constraints Learning can be performed in the context of constrained optimization using the usual perceptron or large-margin classification updates. Because constrained inference is generally more time-consuming, a key question is whether it is necessary to apply the constraints during learning. Chang et al. (2008) find that better performance can be obtained by learning *without* constraints and then applying constraints only when using the trained model to predict semantic roles for unseen data.

How important are the constraints? Das et al. (2014) find that an unconstrained, classification-based method performs nearly as well as constrained optimization for FrameNet parsing: while it commits many violations of the "no-overlap" constraint, the overall F_1 score is less than one point worse than the score at the constrained optimum. Similar results were obtained for PropBank semantic role labeling by Punyakanok et al. (2008). He et al. (2017) find that constrained inference makes a bigger impact if the constraints are based on manually labeled "gold" syntactic parses. This implies that errors from the syntactic parser may limit the effectiveness of the constraints. Punyakanok et al. (2008) hedge against parser error by including constituents from several different parsers; any constituent can be selected from any parse, and additional constraints ensure that overlapping constituents are not selected.

Implementation Integer linear programming solvers such as `glpk`,[11] `cplex`,[12] and `Gurobi`[13] allow inequality constraints to be expressed directly in the problem definition, rather than in the matrix form $\mathbf{A}z \leq \boldsymbol{b}$. The time complexity of integer linear programming is theoretically exponential in the number of variables $|z|$, but in practice these off-the-shelf solvers obtain good solutions efficiently. Using a standard desktop computer, Das et al. (2014) report that the `cplex` solver requires 43 seconds to perform inference on the FrameNet test set, which contains 4,458 predicates.

Many constrained optimization problems in natural language processing can be solved in a highly parallelized fashion, using optimization techniques such as **dual decomposition**, which are capable of exploiting the underlying problem structure (Rush et al., 2010). Das et al. (2014) apply this technique to FrameNet semantic role labeling, obtaining an order-of-magnitude speedup over `cplex`.

11. https://www.gnu.org/software/glpk/.
12. https://www-01.ibm.com/software/commerce/optimization/cplex-optimizer/.
13. http://www.gurobi.com/.

13.2.3 Neural Semantic Role Labeling

Neural network approaches to SRL have tended to treat it as a sequence labeling task, using a labeling scheme such as the **BIO notation**, which we previously saw in named entity recognition (§ 8.3). In this notation, the first token in a span of type ARG1 is labeled B-ARG1; all remaining tokens in the span are *inside* and are therefore labeled I-ARG1. Tokens outside any argument are labeled O. For example:

(13.12)	*Asha*	*taught*	*Boyang*	*'s*	*mom*	*about*	*algebra*
	B-ARG0	PRED	B-ARG2	I-ARG2	I-ARG2	B-ARG1	I-ARG1

Recurrent neural networks (§ 7.6) are a natural approach to this tagging task. For example, Zhou and Xu (2015) apply a deep bidirectional multilayer LSTM (see § 7.6) to PropBank semantic role labeling. In this model, each bidirectional LSTM serves as input for another, higher-level bidirectional LSTM, allowing complex non-linear transformations of the original input embeddings, $\mathbf{X} = [\boldsymbol{x}_1, \boldsymbol{x}_2, \ldots, \boldsymbol{x}_M]$. The hidden state of the final LSTM is $\mathbf{Z}^{(K)} = [\boldsymbol{z}_1^{(K)}, \boldsymbol{z}_2^{(K)}, \ldots, \boldsymbol{z}_M^{(K)}]$. The "emission" score for each tag $Y_m = y$ is equal to the inner product $\boldsymbol{\theta}_y \cdot \boldsymbol{z}_m^{(K)}$, and there is also a transition score for each pair of adjacent tags. The complete model can be written as

$$\mathbf{Z}^{(1)} = \text{BiLSTM}(\mathbf{X}) \tag{13.11}$$

$$\mathbf{Z}^{(i)} = \text{BiLSTM}(\mathbf{Z}^{(i-1)}) \tag{13.12}$$

$$\hat{\boldsymbol{y}} = \underset{\boldsymbol{y}}{\text{argmax}} \sum_{m-1}^{M} \boldsymbol{\theta}_{(y)} \cdot \boldsymbol{z}_m^{(K)} + \psi_{y_{m-1}, y_m}. \tag{13.13}$$

Note that the final step maximizes over the entire labeling $\boldsymbol{y}$ and includes a score for each tag transition ψ_{y_{m-1}, y_m}. This combination of LSTM and pairwise potentials on tags is an example of an **LSTM-CRF**. The maximization over $\boldsymbol{y}$ is performed by the Viterbi algorithm.

This model strongly outperformed alternative approaches at the time, including constrained decoding and convolutional neural networks.[14] More recent work has combined recurrent neural network models with constrained decoding, using the A^* search algorithm to search over labelings that are feasible with respect to the constraints (He et al., 2017). This yields small improvements over the method of Zhou and Xu (2015). He et al. (2017) obtain larger improvements by creating an **ensemble** of SRL systems, each trained on an 80% subsample of the corpus. The average prediction across this ensemble is more robust than any individual model.

14. The successful application of **convolutional neural networks** to semantic role labeling by Collobert and Weston (2008) was an influential early result in the current wave of neural networks in natural language processing.

```
(w / want-01
  :ARG0 (h / whale)
  :ARG1 (p / pursue-02
           :ARG0 (c / captain)
           :ARG1 h))
```

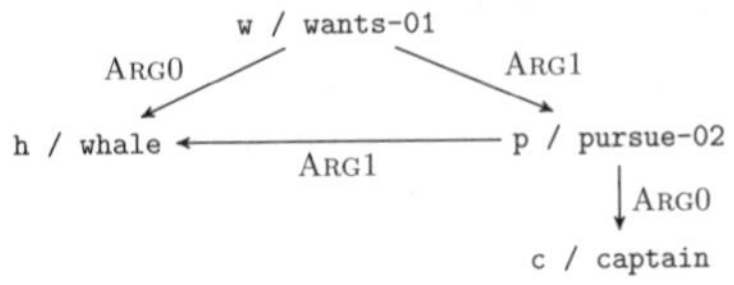

Figure 13.3
Two views of the AMR representation for the sentence *The whale wants the captain to pursue him.*

13.3 Abstract Meaning Representation

Semantic role labeling transforms the task of semantic parsing to a labeling task. Consider this sentence:

(13.13) The whale wants the captain to pursue him.

The PropBank semantic role labeling analysis is:

- (PREDICATE : *wants*, ARG0 : *the whale*, ARG1 : *the captain to pursue him*)
- (PREDICATE : *pursue*, ARG0 : *the captain*, ARG1 : *him*)

The **Abstract Meaning Representation (AMR)** unifies this analysis into a graph structure, in which each node is a **variable**, and each edge indicates a **concept** (Banarescu et al., 2013). This can be written in two ways, as shown in figure 13.3. On the left is the PENMAN notation (Matthiessen and Bateman, 1991), in which each set of parentheses introduces a variable. Each variable is an **instance** of a concept, which is indicated with the slash notation: for example, `w / want-01` indicates that the variable `w` is an instance of the concept `want-01`, which in turn refers to the PropBank frame for the first sense of the verb *want*; `pursue-02` refers to the second sense of *pursue*. Relations are introduced with colons: for example, `:ARG0 (c / captain)` indicates a relation of type ARG0 with the newly introduced variable `c`. Variables can be reused, so that when the variable `h` appears again as an argument to `p`, it is understood to refer to the same whale in both cases. This arrangement is indicated compactly in the graph structure on the right, with edges indicating concepts.

One way in which AMR differs from PropBank-style semantic role labeling is that it reifies each entity as a variable: for example, the *whale* in (13.13) is reified in the variable `h`, which is reused as ARG0 in its relationship with `w / want-01` and as ARG1 in its relationship with `p / pursue-02`. Reifying entities as variables also makes it possible to represent the substructure of noun phrases more explicitly. For example, *Asha borrowed the algebra book* would be represented as follows:

```
(b / borrow-01
   :ARG0 (p / person
            :name (n / name
                     :op1 "Asha"))
   :ARG1 (b2 / book
            :topic (a / algebra)))
```

This indicates that the variable `p` is a person, whose `name` is the variable `n`; that name has one token, the string *Asha*. Similarly, the variable `b2` is a book, and the `topic` of `b2` is a variable `a` whose type is `algebra`. The relations `name` and `topic` are examples of "non-core roles", which are similar to adjunct modifiers in PropBank. However, AMR's inventory is more extensive, including more than 70 non-core roles, such as negation, time, manner, frequency, and location. Lists and sequences—such as the list of tokens in a name—are described using the roles `op1`, `op2`, etc.

Another feature of AMR is that a semantic predicate can be introduced by any syntactic element, as in the following examples from Banarescu et al. (2013):

(13.14) a. The boy destroyed the room.
b. The destruction of the room by the boy ...
c. The boy's destruction of the room ...

All these examples have the same semantics in AMR:

```
(d / destroy-01
   :ARG0 (b / boy)
   :ARG1 (r / room))
```

The noun *destruction* is linked to the verb *destroy*, which is captured by the PropBank frame `destroy-01`. This can happen with adjectives as well: in the phrase *the attractive spy*, the adjective *attractive* is linked to the PropBank frame `attract-01`:

```
(s / spy
   :ARG0-of (a / attract-01))
```

In this example, `ARG0-of` is an **inverse relation**, indicating that `s` is the `ARG0` of the predicate `a`. Inverse relations make it possible for all AMR parses to have a single root concept.

While AMR goes farther than semantic role labeling, it does not link semantically related frames such as `buy/sell` (as FrameNet does). AMR also does not handle quantification (as first-order predicate calculus does), and it makes no attempt to handle noun number and verb tense (as PropBank does).

13.3.1 AMR Parsing

Abstract Meaning Representation is not a labeling of the original text—unlike PropBank semantic role labeling, and most of the other tagging and parsing annotations that we have encountered thus far. The AMR for a given sentence may include multiple concepts for single words in the sentence: as we have seen, the sentence *Asha likes algebra* contains both `person` and `name` concepts for the word *Asha*. Conversely, words in the sentence may not appear in the AMR: in *Boyang made a tour of campus*, the **light verb** *make* would not appear in the AMR, which would instead be rooted on the predicate `tour`. As a result, AMR is difficult to parse, and even evaluating AMR parsing involves considerable algorithmic complexity (Cai and Yates, 2013).

A further complexity is that AMR-labeled datasets do not explicitly show the **alignment** between the AMR annotation and the words in the sentence. For example, the link between the word *wants* and the concept `want-01` is not annotated. To acquire training data, it is therefore necessary to first perform an alignment between the training sentences and their AMR parses. Flanigan et al. (2014) introduce a rule-based parser, which links text to concepts through a series of increasingly high-recall steps.

As with dependency parsing, AMR can be parsed by graph-based methods that explore the space of graph structures or by incremental transition-based algorithms. One approach to graph-based AMR parsing is to first group adjacent tokens into local substructures and then to search the space of graphs over these substructures (Flanigan et al., 2014). The identification of concept subgraphs can be formulated as a sequence labeling problem, and the subsequent graph search can be solved using integer linear programming (§ 13.2.2). Various transition-based parsing algorithms have been proposed. Wang et al. (2015) construct an AMR graph by incrementally modifying the *syntactic* dependency graph. At each step, the parser performs an action: for example, adding an AMR relation label to the current dependency edge, swapping the direction of a syntactic dependency edge or cutting an edge and reattaching the orphaned subtree to a new parent.

Additional Resources

Practical semantic role labeling was first made possible by the PropBank annotations on the Penn Treebank (Palmer et al., 2005). Abend and Rappoport (2017) survey several semantic representation schemes, including semantic role labeling and AMR. Other linguistic features of AMR are summarized in the original paper (Banarescu et al., 2013) and the tutorial slides by Schneider et al. (2015). Recent shared tasks have undertaken semantic dependency parsing, in which the goal is to identify semantic relationships between pairs of words (Oepen et al., 2014); see Ivanova et al. (2012) for an overview of connections between syntactic and semantic dependencies.

Exercises

1. Write out an event semantic representation for the following sentences. You may make up your own predicates.

   (13.15) a. Abigail shares with Max.

(13.16) b. Abigail reluctantly shares a toy with Max.
(13.17) c. Abigail hates to share with Max.

2. Find the PropBank framesets for *share* and *hate* at http://verbs.colorado.edu/propbank/framesets-english-aliases/, and rewrite your answers from the previous question, using the thematic roles ARG0, ARG1, and ARG2.
3. Compute the syntactic path features for Abigail and Max in each of the example sentences (13.15a) and (13.17c) in question 1, with respect to the verb *share*. If you're not sure about the parse, you can try an online parser such as http://nlp.stanford.edu:8080/parser/.
4. Compute the dependency path features for Abigail and Max in each of the example sentences (13.15a) and (13.17c) in question 1, with respect to the verb *share*. Again, if you're not sure about the parse, you can try an online parser. As a hint, the dependency relation between *share* and *Max* is OBL according to the Universal Dependency treebank.
5. PropBank semantic role labeling includes **reference arguments**, such as

   (13.18) [$_{\text{AM-LOC}}$ The bed] on [$_{\text{R-AM-LOC}}$ which] I slept broke.[15]

   The label R-AM-LOC indicates that the word *which* is a reference to *The bed*, which expresses the location of the event. Reference arguments must have referents: the tag R-AM-LOC can appear only when AM-LOC also appears in the sentence. Show how to express this as a linear constraint, specifically for the tag R-AM-LOC. Be sure to correctly handle the case in which neither AM-LOC nor R-AM-LOC appear in the sentence.
6. Explain how to express the constraints on semantic role labeling in equation 13.8 and equation 13.9 in the general form $\mathbf{A}z \geq \boldsymbol{b}$.
7. Produce the AMR annotations for the following examples:

   (13.19) a. The girl likes the boy.
   b. The girl was liked by the boy.
   c. Abigail likes Maxwell Aristotle.
   d. The spy likes the attractive boy.
   e. The girl doesn't like the boy.
   f. The girl likes her dog.

   For (13.19c), recall that multi token names are created using `op1`, `op2`, etc. You will need to consult Banarescu et al. (2013) for (13.19e) and Schneider et al. (2015) for (13.19f). You may assume that *her* refers to *the girl* in this example.
8. In this problem, you will build a FrameNet sense classifier for the verb *can*, which can evoke two frames: POSSIBILITY (can you order a salad with french fries?) and CAPABILITY (can you eat a salad with chopsticks?).

15. Example from 2013 NAACL tutorial slides by Shumin Wu.

To build the dataset, access the FrameNet corpus in NLTK:

```
import nltk
nltk.download('framenet_v17')
from nltk.corpus import framenet as fn
```

Next, find instances in which the lexical unit `can.v` (the verb form of *can*) evokes a frame. Do this by iterating over `fn.docs()`, and then over sentences, and then:

```
for doc in fn.docs():
    if 'sentence' in doc:
        for sent in doc['sentence']:
            for anno_set in sent['annotationSet']:
                if 'luName' in anno_set and anno_set
                              ['luName'] == 'can.v':
                    pass # your code here
```

Use the field `frameName` as a label, and build a set of features from the field `text`. Train a classifier to try to accurately predict the `frameName`, disregarding cases other than CAPABILITY and POSSIBILITY. Treat the first hundred instances as a training set and the remaining instances as the test set. Can you do better than a classifier that simply selects the most common class?

9. *Download the PropBank sample data, using NLTK (www.nltk.org/howto/propbank .html).
   a) Use a deep learning toolkit such as PyTorch to train a BiLSTM sequence labeling model (§ 7.6) to identify words or phrases that are predicates, for example, *we*/O *took*/B-PRED *a*/I-PRED *walk*/I-PRED *together*/O. Your model should compute the tag score from the BiLSTM hidden state $\psi(y_m) = \beta_y \cdot \boldsymbol{h}_m$.
   b) Optionally, implement Viterbi to improve the predictions of the model in the previous section.
   c) Try to identify ARG0 and ARG1 for each predicate. You should again use the BiLSTM and BIO notation, but you may want to include the BiLSTM hidden state at the location of the predicate in your prediction model, for example, $\psi(y_m) = \beta_y \cdot [\boldsymbol{h}_m; \boldsymbol{h}_{\hat{r}}]$, where $\hat{r}$ is the predicted location of the (first word of the) predicate.
10. Using an off-the-shelf PropBank SRL system,[16] build a simplified question answering system in the style of Shen and Lapata (2007). Specifically, your system should do the following:

16. At the time of writing, the following systems are availabe: SENNA (http://ronan.collobert.com/senna/), Illinois Semantic Role Labeler (https://cogcomp.cs.illinois.edu/page/software_view/SRL), and mate-tools (https://code.google.com/archive/p/mate-tools/).

- For each document in a collection, it should apply the semantic role labeler and should store the output as a list of tuples.
- For a question, your system should again apply the semantic role labeler. If any of the roles are filled by a *wh*-pronoun, you should mark that role as the expected answer phrase (EAP).
- To answer the question, search for a stored tuple that matches the question as well as possible (same predicate, no incompatible semantic roles, and as many matching roles as possible). Align the EAP against its role filler in the stored tuple, and return this as the answer.

To evaluate your system, download a set of three news articles on the same topic, and write down five factoid questions that should be answerable from the articles. See if your system can answer these questions correctly. (If this problem is assigned to an entire class, you can build a large-scale test set and compare various approaches.)

14 Distributional and Distributed Semantics

A recurring theme in natural language processing is the complexity of the mapping from words to meaning. In chapter 4, we saw that a single word form, like *bank*, can have multiple meanings; conversely, a single meaning may be created by multiple surface forms, a lexical semantic relationship known as **synonymy**. Despite this complex mapping between words and meaning, natural language processing systems usually rely on words as the basic unit of analysis. This is especially true in semantics: the logical and frame semantic methods from the previous two chapters rely on handcrafted lexicons that map from words to semantic predicates. But how can we analyze texts that contain words that we haven't seen before? This chapter describes methods that learn representations of word meaning by analyzing unlabeled data, vastly improving the generalizability of natural language processing systems. The theory that makes it possible to acquire meaningful representations from unlabeled data is the **distributional hypothesis**.

14.1 The Distributional Hypothesis

Here's a word you may not know: *tezgüino* (the example is from Lin, 1998). If you do not know the meaning of *tezgüino*, then you are in the same situation as a natural language processing system when it encounters a word that did not appear in its training data. Now suppose you see that *tezgüino* is used in the following contexts:

(14.1) A bottle of _____ is on the table.
(14.2) Everybody likes _____.
(14.3) Don't have _____ before you drive.
(14.4) We make _____ out of corn.

What other words fit into these contexts? How about: *loud, motor oil, tortillas, choices, wine*? Each row of table 14.1 is a vector that summarizes the contextual properties for each word, with a value of one for contexts in which the word can appear and a value of zero for contexts in which it cannot. Based on these vectors, we can conclude: *wine* is very similar

Table 14.1
Distributional statistics for *tezgüino* and five related terms

	(14.1)	(14.2)	(14.3)	(14.4)	...
tezgüino	1	1	1	1	
loud	0	0	0	0	
motor oil	1	0	0	1	
tortillas	0	1	0	1	
choices	0	1	0	0	
wine	1	1	1	0	

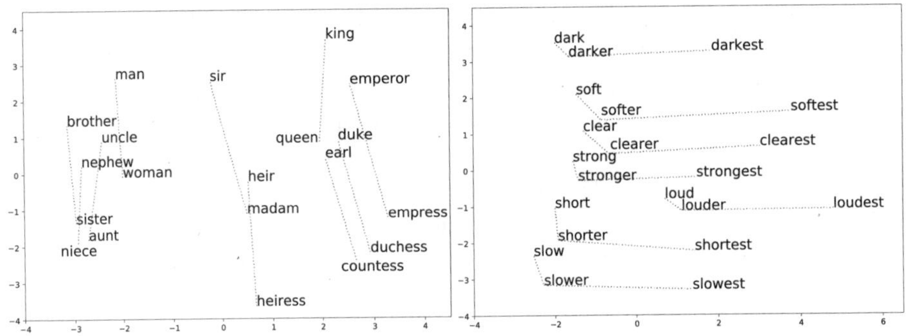

Figure 14.1
Lexical semantic relationships have regular linear structures in two-dimensional projections of distributional statistics (Pennington etal., 2014).

to *tezgüino*; *motor oil* and *tortillas* are fairly similar to *tezgüino*; and *loud* is completely different.

These vectors, which we will call **word representations**, describe the **distributional** properties of each word. Does vector similarity imply semantic similarity? This is the **distributional hypothesis**, stated by Firth (1957) as: "You shall know a word by the company it keeps." The distributional hypothesis has stood the test of time: distributional statistics are a core part of language technology today, because they make it possible to leverage large amounts of unlabeled data to learn about rare words that do not appear in labeled training data.

Distributional statistics have a striking ability to capture lexical semantic relationships such as analogies. Figure 14.1 shows two examples, based on two-dimensional projections of distributional **word embeddings**, discussed later in this chapter. In each case, word-pair relationships correspond to regular linear patterns in this two-dimensional space. No labeled data about the nature of these relationships was required to identify this underlying structure.

Distributional semantics are computed from context statistics. **Distributed** semantics are a related but distinct idea: that meaning can be represented by numerical vectors rather than symbolic structures. Distributed representations are often estimated from distributional statistics, as in latent semantic analysis and WORD2VEC, described later in this chapter. However, distributed representations can also be learned in a supervised fashion from labeled data, as in the neural classification models encountered in chapter 3.

14.2 Design Decisions for Word Representations

There are many approaches for computing word representations, but most can be distinguished on three main dimensions: the nature of the representation, the source of contextual information, and the estimation procedure.

14.2.1 Representation

Today, the dominant word representations are k-dimensional vectors of real numbers, known as **word embeddings**. (The name is due to the fact that each discrete word is embedded in a real vector space.) This representation dates back at least to the late 1980s (Deerwester et al., 1990) and is used in popular techniques such as WORD2VEC (Mikolov et al., 2013a).

Word embeddings are well suited for neural networks, where they can be plugged in as inputs. They can also be applied in linear classifiers and structure prediction models (Turian et al., 2010), although it can be difficult to learn linear models that employ real-valued features (Kummerfeld et al., 2015). A popular alternative is bit-string representations, such as **Brown clusters** (§ 14.4), in which each word is represented by a variable-length sequence of zeros and ones (Brown et al., 1992).

Another representational question is whether to estimate one embedding per surface form (e.g., *bank*) or to estimate distinct embeddings for each word sense or synset. Intuitively, if word representations are to capture the meaning of individual words, then words with multiple meanings should have multiple embeddings. This can be achieved by integrating unsupervised clustering with word embedding estimation (Huang and Yates, 2012; Li and Jurafsky, 2015). However, Arora et al. (2018) argue that it is unnecessary to model distinct word senses explicitly, because the embeddings for each surface form are a linear combination of the embeddings of the underlying senses.

14.2.2 Context

The distributional hypothesis says that word meaning is related to the "contexts" in which the word appears, but context can be defined in many ways. In the *tezgüino* example, contexts are entire sentences, but in practice there are far too many sentences. At the opposite extreme, the context could be defined as the immediately preceding word; this is the context considered in Brown clusters. WORD2VEC takes an intermediate approach, using

Table 14.2
Contexts for the word *learns*, according to various word representations. For dependency context, (*one*, NSUBJ) means that there is a relation of type NSUBJ (nominal subject) to the word *one*, and (*moment*, ACL^{-1}) means that there is a relation of type ACL (adjectival clause) from the word *moment*.

The moment one ***learns*** *English, complications set in* (Alfau, 1999)	
Brown Clusters	{*one*}
WORD2VEC, $h=2$	{*moment, one, English, complications*}
Structured WORD2VEC, $h=2$	{(*moment*, −2), (*one*, −1), (*English*, +1), (*complications*, +2)}
Dependency contexts	{(*one*, NSUBJ), (*English*, DOBJ), (*moment*, ACL^{-1})}

local neighborhoods of words (e.g., $h=5$) as contexts (Mikolov et al., 2013a). Contexts can also be much larger: for example, in **latent semantic analysis**, each word's context vector includes an entry per document, with a value of one if the word appears in the document (Deerwester et al., 1990); in **explicit semantic analysis**, these documents are Wikipedia pages (Gabrilovich and Markovitch, 2007).

In structured WORD2VEC, context words are labeled by their position with respect to the target word w_m (e.g., two words before, one word after), which makes the resulting word representations more sensitive to syntactic differences (Ling et al., 2015a). Another way to incorporate syntax is to perform parsing as a preprocessing step and then form context vectors from the dependency edges (Levy and Goldberg, 2014) or predicate-argument relations (Lin, 1998). The resulting context vectors for several of these methods are shown in table 14.2.

The choice of context has a profound effect on the resulting representations, which can be viewed in terms of word similarity. Applying latent semantic analysis (§ 14.3) to contexts of size $h=2$ and $h=30$ yields the following nearest-neighbors for the word *dog*:[1]

- ($h=2$): *cat, horse, fox, pet, rabbit, pig, animal, mongrel, sheep, pigeon*
- ($h=30$): *kennel, puppy, pet, bitch, terrier, rottweiler, canine, cat, to bark, Alsatian*

Which word list is better? Each word in the $h=2$ list is an animal, reflecting the fact that, locally, the word *dog* tends to appear in the same contexts as other animal types (e.g., *pet the dog, feed the dog*). In the $h=30$ list, nearly everything is dog related, including specific breeds such as *rottweiler* and *Alsatian*. The list also includes words that are not animals (*kennel*) and in one case (*to bark*) a word that is not a noun at all. The two-word context window is more sensitive to syntax, while the 30-word window is more sensitive to topic.

1. The example is from lecture slides by Marco Baroni, Alessandro Lenci, and Stefan Evert, who applied latent semantic analysis to the British National Corpus. You can find an online demo here: http://clic.cimec.unitn.it/infomap-query/.

14.2.3 Estimation

Word embeddings are estimated by optimizing some objective: the likelihood of a set of unlabeled data (or a closely related quantity), or the reconstruction of a matrix of context counts, similar to table 14.1.

Maximum likelihood estimation Likelihood-based optimization is derived from the objective $\log \mathrm{p}(\boldsymbol{w}; \mathbf{U})$, where $\mathbf{U} \in \mathbb{R}^{K \times V}$ is matrix of word embeddings and $\boldsymbol{w} = \{w_m\}_{m=1}^{M}$ is a corpus, represented as a list of M tokens. Recurrent neural network language models (§ 6.3) optimize this objective directly, backpropagating to the input word embeddings through the recurrent structure. However, state-of-the-art word embeddings employ huge corpora with hundreds of billions of tokens, and recurrent architectures are difficult to scale to such data. As a result, likelihood-based word embeddings are usually based on simplified likelihoods or heuristic approximations.

Matrix factorization The matrix $\mathbf{C} = \{\text{count}(i,j)\}$ stores the co-occurrence counts of word i and context j. Word representations can be obtained by approximately factoring this matrix, so that count(i,j) is approximated by a function of a word embedding $\boldsymbol{u}_i$ and a context embedding $\boldsymbol{v}_j$. These embeddings can be obtained by minimizing the norm of the reconstruction error,

$$\min_{\boldsymbol{u},\boldsymbol{v}} ||\mathbf{C} - \tilde{\mathbf{C}}(\boldsymbol{u}, \boldsymbol{v})||_F, \qquad [14.1]$$

where $\tilde{\mathbf{C}}(\boldsymbol{u}, \boldsymbol{v})$ is the approximate reconstruction resulting from the embeddings $\boldsymbol{u}$ and $\boldsymbol{v}$ and $||\mathbf{X}||_F$ indicates the Frobenius norm, $\sqrt{\sum_{i,j} x_{i,j}^2}$. Rather than factoring the matrix of word-context counts directly, it is often helpful to transform these counts using information-theoretic metrics such as **pointwise mutual information (PMI)**, described in the next section.

14.3 Latent Semantic Analysis

Latent semantic analysis (LSA) is one of the oldest approaches to distributed semantics (Deerwester et al., 1990). It induces continuous vector representations of words by factoring a matrix of word and context counts, using **truncated singular-value decomposition (SVD)**,

$$\begin{aligned} \min_{\mathbf{U}\in\mathbb{R}^{V\times K},\mathbf{S}\in\mathbb{R}^{K\times K},\mathbf{V}\in\mathbb{R}^{|\mathcal{C}|\times K}} \quad & ||\mathbf{C} - \mathbf{U}\mathbf{S}\mathbf{V}^\top||_F \qquad [14.2] \\ \text{s.t.} \quad & \mathbf{U}^\top\mathbf{U} = \mathbb{I} \\ & \mathbf{V}^\top\mathbf{V} = \mathbb{I} \\ & \forall i \neq j, \mathbf{S}_{i,j} = 0, \end{aligned}$$

where V is the size of the vocabulary, $|\mathcal{C}|$ is the number of contexts, and K is size of the resulting embeddings, which are set equal to the rows of the matrix $\mathbf{U}$. The matrix $\mathbf{S}$ is constrained to be diagonal (these diagonal elements are called the singular values), and the columns of the product $\mathbf{S}\mathbf{V}^\top$ provide descriptions of the contexts. Each element $c_{i,j}$ is then reconstructed as a **bilinear product**,

$$c_{i,j} \approx \sum_{k=1}^{K} u_{i,k} s_k v_{j,k}. \qquad [14.3]$$

The objective is to minimize the sum of squared approximation errors. The orthonormality constraints $\mathbf{U}^\top\mathbf{U} = \mathbf{V}^\top\mathbf{V} = \mathbb{I}$ ensure that all pairs of dimensions in $\mathbf{U}$ and $\mathbf{V}$ are uncorrelated, so that each dimension conveys unique information. Efficient implementations of truncated singular-value decomposition are available in numerical computing packages such as SCIPY and MATLAB.[2]

Latent semantic analysis is most effective when the count matrix is transformed before the application of SVD. One such transformation is **pointwise mutual information** (**PMI**; Church and Hanks, 1990), which captures the degree of association between word i and context j,

$$\text{PMI}(i,j) = \log \frac{\text{p}(i,j)}{\text{p}(i)\text{p}(j)} = \log \frac{\text{p}(i \mid j)\text{p}(j)}{\text{p}(i)\text{p}(j)} = \log \frac{\text{p}(i \mid j)}{\text{p}(i)} \qquad [14.4]$$

$$= \log \text{count}(i,j) - \log \sum_{i'=1}^{V} \text{count}(i',j)$$

$$- \log \sum_{j' \in \mathcal{C}} \text{count}(i,j') + \log \sum_{i'=1}^{V} \sum_{j' \in \mathcal{C}} \text{count}(i',j'). \qquad [14.5]$$

The pointwise mutual information can be viewed as the logarithm of the ratio of the conditional probability of word i in context j to the marginal probability of word i in all contexts. When word i is statistically associated with context j, the ratio will be greater than one, so $\text{PMI}(i,j) > 0$. The PMI transformation focuses latent semantic analysis on reconstructing strong word-context associations, rather than on reconstructing large counts.

The PMI is negative when a word and context occur together less often than if they were independent, but such negative correlations are unreliable. Furthermore, the PMI is undefined when $\text{count}(i,j) = 0$. One solution to these problems is to use the **Positive PMI (PPMI)**,

2. An important implementation detail is to represent $\mathbf{C}$ as a **sparse matrix**, so that the storage cost is equal to the number of non zero entries, rather than the size $V \times |\mathcal{C}|$.

$$\text{PPMI}(i,j) = \begin{cases} \text{PMI}(i,j), & p(i \mid j) > p(i) \\ 0, & \text{otherwise.} \end{cases} \quad [14.6]$$

Bullinaria and Levy (2007) compare a range of matrix transformations for latent semantic analysis (for more on evaluation, see § 14.6). They find that PPMI-based latent semantic analysis yields strong performance on a battery of tasks related to word meaning: for example, PPMI-based LSA vectors can be used to solve multiple-choice word similarity questions from the Test of English as a Foreign Language (TOEFL), obtaining 85% accuracy.

14.4 Brown Clusters

Learning algorithms like perceptron and conditional random fields often perform better with discrete feature vectors. A simple way to obtain discrete representations from distributional statistics is by clustering (§ 5.1.1), so that words in the same cluster have similar distributional statistics. This can help in downstream tasks, by sharing features between all words in the same cluster. However, there is an obvious tradeoff: if the number of clusters is too small, the words in each cluster will not have much in common; if the number of clusters is too large, then the learner will not see enough examples from each cluster to generalize.

A solution to this problem is **hierarchical clustering**: using the distributional statistics to induce a tree-structured representation. Fragments of **Brown cluster** trees are shown in figure 14.2 and table 14.3. Each word's representation consists of a binary string describing

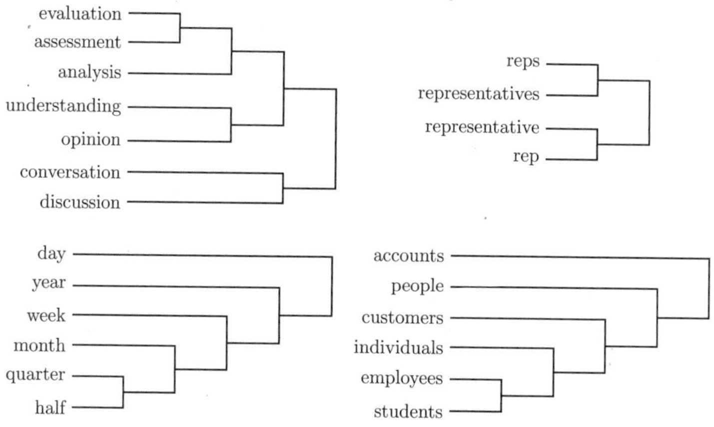

Figure 14.2
Subtrees produced by bottom-up Brown clustering on news text (Miller et al., 2004).

Table 14.3
Fragment of a Brown clustering of Twitter data owoputi et al. Each row is a leaf in the tree, showing the 10 most frequent words. This part of the tree emphasizes verbs of communicating and knowing, especially in the present participle. Each leaf node includes orthographic variants (*thinking, thinkin, thinkn*), semantically related terms (*excited, thankful, grateful*), and some outliers (*5'2, +k*). See www.cs.cmu.edu/~ark/TweetNLP/cluster_viewer.html for more.

bitstring	10 most frequent words
01111010**0111**	*excited thankful grateful stoked pumped anxious hyped psyched exited geeked*
01111010**100**	*talking talkin complaining talkn bitching tlkn tlkin bragging raving +k*
01111010**1010**	*thinking thinkin dreaming worrying thinkn speakin reminiscing dreamin daydreaming fantasizing*
01111010**1011**	*saying sayin suggesting stating sayn jokin talmbout implying insisting 5'2*
01111010**1100**	*wonder dunno wondered duno donno dno dono wonda wounder dunnoe*
01111010**1101**	*wondering wonders debating deciding pondering unsure wonderin debatin woundering wondern*
01111010**1110**	*sure suree suuure suure sure- surre sures shuree*

a path through the tree: `0` for taking the left branch and `1` for taking the right branch. In the subtree in the upper left of the figure, the representation of the word *conversation* is `10`; the representation of the word *assessment* is `0001`. Bitstring prefixes capture similarity at varying levels of specificity, and it is common to use the first eight, 12, 16, and 20 bits as features in tasks such as named entity recognition (Miller et al., 2004) and dependency parsing (Koo et al., 2008).

Hierarchical trees can be induced from a likelihood-based objective, using a discrete latent variable $k_i \in \{1, 2, \ldots, K\}$ to represent the cluster of word i:

$$\log \mathrm{p}(\boldsymbol{w}; \boldsymbol{k}) \approx \sum_{m=1}^{M} \log \mathrm{p}(w_m \mid w_{m-1}; \boldsymbol{k}) \tag{14.7}$$

$$\triangleq \sum_{m=1}^{M} \log \mathrm{p}(w_m \mid k_{w_m}) + \log \mathrm{p}(k_{w_m} \mid k_{w_{m-1}}). \tag{14.8}$$

This is similar to a hidden Markov model, with the crucial difference that each word can be emitted from only a single cluster: $\forall k \neq k_{w_m}, \mathrm{p}(w_m \mid k) = 0$.

Using the objective in equation 14.8, the Brown clustering tree can be constructed from the bottom up: begin with each word in its own cluster, and incrementally merge clusters until only a single cluster remains. At each step, we merge the pair of clusters such that the objective in equation 14.8 is maximized. Although the objective seems to involve a sum over the entire corpus, the score for each merge can be computed from the cluster-to-cluster co-occurrence counts. These counts can be updated incrementally as the clustering proceeds. The optimal merge at each step can be shown to maximize the **average mutual information**,

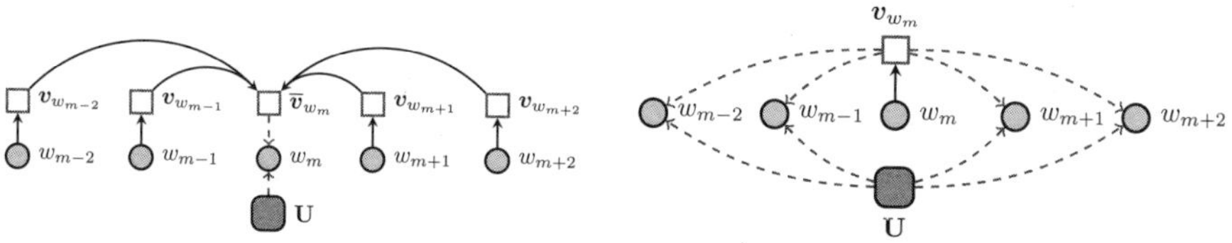
(a) Continuous bag of words (CBOW)
(b) Skipgram

Figure 14.3
The CBOW and skipgram variants of WORD2VEC. The parameter $\mathbf{U}$ is the matrix of word embeddings, and each $\boldsymbol{v}_m$ is the context embedding for word w_m.

$$I(\boldsymbol{k}) = \sum_{k_1=1}^{K} \sum_{k_2=1}^{K} \mathrm{p}(k_1, k_2) \times \mathrm{PMI}(k_1, k_2) \qquad [14.9]$$

$$\mathrm{p}(k_1, k_2) = \frac{\mathrm{count}(k_1, k_2)}{\sum_{k_{1'}=1}^{K} \sum_{k_{2'}=1}^{K} \mathrm{count}(k_{1'}, k_{2'})},$$

where $\mathrm{p}(k_1, k_2)$ is the joint probability of a bigram involving a word in cluster k_1 followed by a word in k_2. This probability and the PMI are both computed from the co-occurrence counts between clusters. After each merge the co-occurrence vectors for the merged clusters are simply added up, so that the next optimal merger can be found efficiently.

This bottom-up procedure requires iterating over the entire vocabulary and evaluating K_t^2 possible merges at each step, where K_t is the current number of clusters at step t of the algorithm. Furthermore, computing the score for each merge involves a sum over K_t^2 clusters. The maximum number of clusters is $K_0 = V$, which occurs when every word is in its own cluster at the beginning of the algorithm. The time complexity is thus $\mathcal{O}(V^5)$.

To avoid this complexity, practical implementations use a heuristic approximation called **exchange clustering**. The K most common words are placed in clusters of their own at the beginning of the process. We then consider the next most common word and merge it with one of the existing clusters. This continues until the entire vocabulary has been incorporated, at which point the K clusters are merged down to a single cluster, forming a tree. The algorithm never considers more than $K + 1$ clusters at any step, and the complexity is $\mathcal{O}(VK + V \log V)$, with the second term representing the cost of sorting the words at the beginning of the algorithm. For more details on the algorithm, see Liang (2005).

14.5 Neural Word Embeddings

Neural word embeddings combine aspects of the previous two methods: like latent semantic analysis, they are a continuous vector representation; like Brown clusters, they are trained from a likelihood-based objective. Let the vector $\boldsymbol{u}_i$ represent the K-dimensional **embedding** for word i, and let $\boldsymbol{v}_j$ represent the K-dimensional embedding for context j.

The inner product $\boldsymbol{u}_i \cdot \boldsymbol{v}_j$ represents the compatibility between word i and context j. By incorporating this inner product into an approximation to the log-likelihood of a corpus, it is possible to estimate both parameters by backpropagation. WORD2VEC (Mikolov et al., 2013a) includes two such approximations: continuous bag of words (CBOW) and skipgrams.

14.5.1 Continuous Bag of Words (CBOW)

In recurrent neural network language models, each word w_m is conditioned on a recurrently updated state vector, which is based on word representations going all the way back to the beginning of the text. The **continuous bag of words (CBOW)** model is a simplification: the local context is computed as an average of embeddings for words in the immediate neighborhood $m-h, m-h+1, \ldots, m+h-1, m+h$,

$$\overline{\boldsymbol{v}}_m = \frac{1}{2h}\sum_{n=1}^{h} \boldsymbol{v}_{w_{m+n}} + \boldsymbol{v}_{w_{m-n}}. \tag{14.10}$$

Thus, CBOW is a bag-of-words model, because the order of the context words does not matter; it is continuous, because rather than conditioning on the words themselves, we condition on a continuous vector constructed from the word embeddings. The parameter h determines the neighborhood size, which Mikolov et al. (2013a) set to $h=4$.

The CBOW model optimizes an approximation to the corpus log-likelihood,

$$\log \mathrm{p}(\boldsymbol{w}) \approx \sum_{m=1}^{M} \log \mathrm{p}(w_m \mid w_{m-h}, w_{m-h+1}, \ldots, w_{m+h-1}, w_{m+h}) \tag{14.11}$$

$$= \sum_{m=1}^{M} \log \frac{\exp\left(\boldsymbol{u}_{w_m} \cdot \overline{\boldsymbol{v}}_m\right)}{\sum_{j=1}^{V} \exp\left(\boldsymbol{u}_j \cdot \overline{\boldsymbol{v}}_m\right)} \tag{14.12}$$

$$= \sum_{m=1}^{M} \boldsymbol{u}_{w_m} \cdot \overline{\boldsymbol{v}}_m - \log \sum_{j=1}^{V} \exp\left(\boldsymbol{u}_j \cdot \overline{\boldsymbol{v}}_m\right). \tag{14.13}$$

14.5.2 Skipgrams

In the CBOW model, words are predicted from their context. In the **skipgram** model, the context is predicted from the word, yielding the objective:[3]

$$\log \mathrm{p}(\boldsymbol{w}) \approx \sum_{m=1}^{M} \sum_{n=1}^{h_m} \log \mathrm{p}(w_{m-n} \mid w_m) + \log \mathrm{p}(w_{m+n} \mid w_m) \tag{14.14}$$

3. As in the CBOW model, $\boldsymbol{v}$ refers to an 'input' embedding (of the thing we condition on) and $\boldsymbol{u}$ refers to an output embedding (of the thing we generate).

$$= \sum_{m=1}^{M} \sum_{n=1}^{h_m} \log \frac{\exp(\boldsymbol{u}_{w_{m-n}} \cdot \boldsymbol{v}_{w_m})}{\sum_{j=1}^{V} \exp(\boldsymbol{u}_j \cdot \boldsymbol{v}_{w_m})} + \log \frac{\exp(\boldsymbol{u}_{w_{m+n}} \cdot \boldsymbol{v}_{w_m})}{\sum_{j=1}^{V} \exp(\boldsymbol{u}_j \cdot \boldsymbol{v}_{w_m})} \quad [14.15]$$

$$= \sum_{m=1}^{M} \sum_{n=1}^{h_m} \boldsymbol{u}_{w_{m-n}} \cdot \boldsymbol{v}_{w_m} + \boldsymbol{u}_{w_{m+n}} \cdot \boldsymbol{v}_{w_m} - 2 \log \sum_{j=1}^{V} \exp\left(\boldsymbol{u}_j \cdot \boldsymbol{v}_{w_m}\right). \quad [14.16]$$

In the skipgram approximation, each word is generated multiple times; each time it is conditioned only on a single word. This makes it possible to avoid averaging the word vectors, as in the CBOW model. The local neighborhood size h_m is randomly sampled from a uniform categorical distribution over the range $\{1, 2, \ldots, h_{\max}\}$; Mikolov et al. (2013a) set $h_{\max} = 10$. Because the neighborhood grows outward with h, this approach has the effect of weighting near neighbors more than distant ones. Skipgram performs better on most evaluations than CBOW (see § 14.6 for details of how to evaluate word representations), but CBOW is faster to train (Mikolov et al., 2013a).

14.5.3 Computational Complexity

The WORD2VEC models can be viewed as an efficient alternative to recurrent neural network language models, which involve a recurrent state update whose time complexity is quadratic in the size of the recurrent state vector. CBOW and skipgram avoid this computation and incur only a linear time complexity in the size of the word and context representations. However, all three models compute a normalized probability over word tokens; a naïve implementation of this probability requires summing over the entire vocabulary. The time complexity of this sum is $\mathcal{O}(V \times K)$, which dominates all other computational costs. There are two solutions: **hierarchical softmax**, a tree-based computation that reduces the cost to a logarithm of the size of the vocabulary, and **negative sampling**, an approximation that eliminates the dependence on vocabulary size. Both methods are also applicable to RNN language models.

Hierarchical softmax In Brown clustering, the vocabulary is organized into a binary tree. Mnih and Hinton (2008) show that the normalized probability over words in the vocabulary can be reparametrized as a probability over paths through such a tree. This hierarchical softmax probability is computed as a product of binary decisions over whether to move left or right through the tree, with each binary decision represented as a sigmoid function of the inner product between the input embedding $\boldsymbol{v}_c$ and an output embedding associated with the node $\boldsymbol{u}_n$,

$$\Pr(\text{left at } n \mid c) = \sigma(\boldsymbol{u}_n \cdot \boldsymbol{v}_c) \quad [14.17]$$

$$\Pr(\text{right at } n \mid c) = 1 - \sigma(\boldsymbol{u}_n \cdot \boldsymbol{v}_c) = \sigma(-\boldsymbol{u}_n \cdot \boldsymbol{v}_c), \quad [14.18]$$

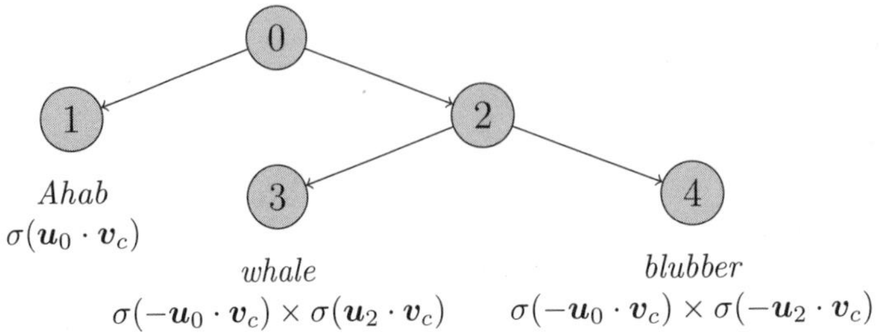

Figure 14.4
A fragment of a hierarchical softmax tree. The probability of each word is computed as a product of probabilities of local branching decisions in the tree.

where σ refers to the sigmoid function, $\sigma(x) = \frac{1}{1+\exp(-x)}$. The range of the sigmoid is the interval (0, 1), and $1 - \sigma(x) = \sigma(-x)$.

As shown in figure 14.4, the probability of generating each word is redefined as the product of the probabilities across its path. The sum of all such path probabilities is guaranteed to be one, for any context vector $\boldsymbol{v}_c \in \mathbb{R}^K$. In a balanced binary tree, the depth is logarithmic in the number of leaf nodes, and thus the number of multiplications is equal to $\mathcal{O}(\log V)$. The number of non leaf nodes is equal to $\mathcal{O}(2V - 1)$, so the number of parameters to be estimated increases by only a small multiple. The tree can be constructed by using an incremental clustering procedure similar to hierarchical Brown clusters (Mnih and Hinton, 2008) or using the Huffman (1952) encoding algorithm for lossless compression.

Negative sampling Likelihood-based methods are computationally intensive because each probability must be normalized over the vocabulary. These probabilities are based on scores for each word in each context, and it is possible to design an alternative objective that is based on these scores more directly: we seek word embeddings that maximize the score for the word-context pairs that were really observed, while minimizing the scores for a set of randomly selected **negative samples**:

$$\psi(i,j) = \log \sigma(\boldsymbol{u}_i \cdot \boldsymbol{v}_j) + \sum_{i' \in \mathcal{W}_{\text{neg}}} \log(1 - \sigma(\boldsymbol{u}_{i'} \cdot \boldsymbol{v}_j)), \qquad [14.19]$$

where $\psi(i,j)$ is the score for generating word i conditioned on word j and $\mathcal{W}_{\text{neg}}$ is the set of negative samples. The skipgram negative sampling objective is to maximize the sum over the corpus, $\sum_{m=1}^{M} \psi(c_m, w_m)$, where w_m is token m and c_m is the associated context.

The set of negative samples $\mathcal{W}_{\text{neg}}$ is obtained by sampling from a unigram language model. Mikolov et al. (2013b) construct this unigram language model by exponentiating the empirical word probabilities, setting $\hat{p}(i) \propto (\text{count}(i))^{\frac{3}{4}}$. This has the effect of redistributing probability mass from common to rare words. The number of negative samples increases the time complexity of training by a constant factor. Mikolov et al. (2013b) report that five to 20 negative samples work for small training sets and that two to five samples suffice for larger corpora.

14.5.4 Word Embeddings as Matrix Factorization

The negative sampling objective in equation 14.19 can be justified as an efficient approximation to the log-likelihood, but it is also closely linked to the matrix factorization objective employed in latent semantic analysis. For a matrix of word-context pairs in which all counts are non zero, negative sampling is equivalent to factorization of the matrix $\mathbf{M}$, where $M_{ij} = \text{PMI}(i,j) - \log k$: each cell in the matrix is equal to the pointwise mutual information of the word and context, shifted by $\log k$, with k equal to the number of negative samples (Levy and Goldberg, 2014). For word-context pairs that are not observed in the data, the pointwise mutual information is $-\infty$, but this can be addressed by considering only PMI values that are greater than $\log k$, resulting in a matrix of **shifted positive pointwise mutual information**,

$$M_{ij} = \max(0, \text{PMI}(i,j) - \log k). \quad [14.20]$$

Word embeddings are obtained by factoring this matrix with truncated singular-value decomposition.

GloVe ("global vectors") are a closely related approach (Pennington et al., 2014), in which the matrix to be factored is constructed from log co-occurrence counts, $M_{ij} = \log \text{count}(i,j)$. The word embeddings are estimated by minimizing the sum of squares,

$$\begin{aligned} \min_{\boldsymbol{u},\boldsymbol{v},b,\tilde{b}} \quad & \sum_{j=1}^{V} \sum_{j \in \mathcal{C}} f(M_{ij}) \left(\widehat{\log M_{ij}} - \log M_{ij} \right)^2 \\ \text{s.t.} \quad & \widehat{\log M_{ij}} = \boldsymbol{u}_i \cdot \boldsymbol{v}_j + b_i + \tilde{b}_j, \end{aligned} \quad [14.21]$$

where b_i and $\tilde{b}_j$ are offsets for word i and context j, which are estimated jointly with the embeddings $\boldsymbol{u}$ and $\boldsymbol{v}$. The weighting function $f(M_{ij})$ is set to be zero at $M_{ij} = 0$, thus avoiding the problem of taking the logarithm of zero counts; it saturates at $M_{ij} = m_{\max}$, thus avoiding the problem of overcounting common word-context pairs. This heuristic turns out to be critical to the method's performance.

The time complexity of sparse matrix reconstruction is determined by the number of non-zero word-context counts. Pennington et al. (2014) show that this number grows sublinearly with the size of the dataset: roughly $\mathcal{O}(N^{0.8})$ for typical English corpora. In contrast, the time complexity of WORD2VEC is linear in the corpus size. Computing the co-occurrence counts also requires linear time in the size of the corpus, but this operation can easily be parallelized using MapReduce-style algorithms (Dean and Ghemawat, 2008).

14.6 Evaluating Word Embeddings

Distributed word representations can be evaluated in two main ways. **Intrinsic** evaluations test whether the representations cohere with our intuitions about word meaning. **Extrinsic** evaluations test whether they are useful for downstream tasks, such as sequence labeling.

14.6.1 Intrinsic Evaluations

A basic question for word embeddings is whether the similarity of words i and j is reflected in the similarity of the vectors $\boldsymbol{v}_i$ and $\boldsymbol{v}_j$. **Cosine similarity** is typically used to compare two word embeddings,

$$\cos(\boldsymbol{v}_i, \boldsymbol{v}_j) = \frac{\boldsymbol{v}_i \cdot \boldsymbol{v}_j}{||\boldsymbol{v}_i||_2 \times ||\boldsymbol{v}_j||_2}. \qquad [14.22]$$

For any embedding method, we can evaluate whether the cosine similarity of word embeddings is correlated with human judgments of word similarity. The WS-353 dataset (Finkelstein et al., 2002) includes similarity scores for 353 word pairs (table 14.4). To test the accuracy of embeddings for rare and morphologically complex words, Luong et al. (2013) introduce a dataset of "rare words." Outside of English, word similarity resources are limited, mainly consisting of translations of WS-353 and the related SimLex-999 dataset (Hill et al., 2015).

Word analogies (e.g., *king:queen :: man:woman*) have also been used to evaluate word embeddings (Mikolov et al., 2013). In this evaluation, the system is provided with the first three parts of the analogy $(i_1 : j_1 :: i_2 :?)$, and the final element is predicted by finding the word embedding most similar to $\boldsymbol{v}_{i_1} - \boldsymbol{v}_{j_1} + \boldsymbol{v}_{i_2}$. Another evaluation tests whether word embeddings are related to broad lexical semantic categories called **supersenses** (Ciaramita and Johnson, 2003): verbs of motion, nouns that describe animals, nouns that describe body parts, and so on. These supersenses are annotated for English synsets in WordNet (Fellbaum, 2017). This evaluation is implemented in the QVEC metric, which tests whether the matrix of supersenses can be reconstructed from the matrix of word embeddings (Tsvetkov et al., 2015).

Table 14.4
Subset of the WS-353 (Finkelstein et al., 2002) dataset of word similarity ratings. Examples are from Faruqui et al. (2016).

word 1	word 2	similarity
love	*sex*	6.77
stock	*jaguar*	0.92
money	*cash*	9.15
development	*issue*	3.97
lad	*brother*	4.46

Levy et al. (2015) compared several dense word representations for English—including latent semantic analysis, WORD2VEC, and GloVe—using six word similarity metrics and two analogy tasks. None of the embeddings outperformed the others on every task, but skipgrams were the most broadly competitive. Hyperparameter tuning played a key role: any method will perform badly if the wrong hyperparameters are used. Relevant hyperparameters include the embedding size, as well as algorithm-specific details such as the neighborhood size and the number of negative samples.

14.6.2 Extrinsic Evaluations

Word representations contribute to downstream tasks like sequence labeling and document classification by enabling generalization across words. The use of distributed representations as features is a form of **semi-supervised learning**, in which performance on a supervised learning problem is augmented by learning distributed representations from unlabeled data (Miller et al., 2004; Koo et al., 2008; Turian et al., 2010). These **pretrained word representations** can be used as features in a linear prediction model, or as the input layer in a neural network, such as a Bi-LSTM tagging model (§ 7.6). Word representations can be evaluated by the performance of the downstream systems that consume them: for example, GloVe embeddings are convincingly better than Latent Semantic Analysis as features in the downstream task of named entity recognition (Pennington et al., 2014). Unfortunately, extrinsic and intrinsic evaluations do not always point in the same direction, and the best word representations for one downstream task may perform poorly on another task (Schnabel et al., 2015).

When word representations are updated from labeled data in the downstream task, they are said to be **fine-tuned**. When labeled data is plentiful, pretraining may be unnecessary; when labeled data is scarce, fine-tuning may lead to overfitting. Various combinations of pretraining and fine-tuning can be employed. Pretrained embeddings can be used as initialization before fine-tuning, and this can substantially improve performance (Lample et al., 2016). Alternatively, both fine-tuned and pretrained embeddings can be used as inputs in a single model (Kim, 2014).

In semi-supervised scenarios, pretrained word embeddings can be replaced by "contextualized" word representations (Peters et al., 2018; Devlin et al., 2018). These contextualized representations can be set to the hidden states of a deep bi directional LSTM, which is trained as a bidirectional language model, motivating the name **ELMo (embeddings from language models)**. By running the language model, we obtain contextualized word representations, which can then be used as the base layer in a supervised neural network for any task. This approach yields significant gains over noncontextual word embeddings on several tasks, presumably because the contextualized embeddings use unlabeled data to learn how to integrate linguistic context into the base layer of the supervised neural network.

14.6.3 Fairness and Bias

Figure 14.1 shows how word embeddings can capture analogies such as *man:woman :: king:queen*. While *king* and *queen* are gender specific by definition, other professions or titles are associated with genders and other groups merely by statistical tendency. This statistical tendency may be a fact about the world (e.g., professional baseball players are usually men) or a fact about the text corpus (e.g., there are professional basketball leagues for both women and men, but the men's basketball is written about far more often).

There is now considerable evidence that word embeddings encode such biases. Bolukbasi et al. (2016) show that the words most aligned with the vector difference *she—he* are stereotypically female professions *homemaker, nurse, receptionist*; in the other direction are *maestro, skipper, protege*. Caliskan et al. (2017) systematize this observation by showing that biases in word embeddings align with well-validated gender stereotypes. Garg et al. (2018) extend these results to ethnic stereotypes of Asian Americans and provide a historical perspective on how stereotypes evolve over 100 years of text data.

Because word embeddings are the input layer for many other natural language processing systems, these findings highlight the risk that natural language processing will replicate and amplify biases in the world, as well as in text. If, for example, word embeddings encode the belief that women are as unlikely to be *programmers* as they are to be *nephews*, then software is unlikely to successfully parse, translate, index, and generate texts in which women do indeed program computers. For example, contemporary NLP systems often fail to properly resolve pronoun references in texts that cut against gender stereotypes (Rudinger et al., 2018; Zhao et al., 2018). (The task of pronoun resolution is described in depth in chapter 15.) Such biases can have profound consequences: for example, search engines are more likely to yield personalized advertisements for public arrest records when queried with names that are statistically associated with African Americans (Sweeney, 2013). There is now an active research literature on "debiasing" machine learning and natural language processing, as evidenced by the growth of annual meetings such as Fairness, Accountability, and Transparency in Machine Learning (FAT/ML). However, given that the ultimate source of these biases is the text itself, it may be too much to hope for a purely algorithmic solution. There is no substitute for critical thought about the inputs to natural language processing systems—and the uses of their outputs.

14.7 Distributed Representations beyond Distributional Statistics

Distributional word representations can be estimated from huge unlabeled datasets, thereby covering many words that do not appear in labeled data: for example, GloVe embeddings are estimated from 800 billion tokens of web data,[4] while the largest labeled datasets for

4. http://commoncrawl.org/.

NLP tasks are on the order of millions of tokens. Nonetheless, even a dataset of hundreds of billions of tokens will not cover every word that may be encountered in the future. Furthermore, many words will appear only a few times, making their embeddings unreliable. Many languages exceed English in morphological complexity and thus have lower token-to-type ratios. When this problem is coupled with small training corpora, it becomes especially important to leverage other sources of information beyond distributional statistics.

14.7.1 Word-Internal Structure

One solution is to incorporate word-internal structure into word embeddings. Purely distributional approaches consider words as atomic units, but in fact, many words have internal structure, so that their meaning can be **composed** from the representations of sub word units. Consider the following terms, all of which are missing from Google's pretrained WORD2VEC embeddings:[5]

millicuries This word has **morphological** structure (see § 9.1.2 for more on morphology): the prefix *milli-* indicates an amount, and the suffix *-s* indicates a plural. (A *millicurie* is an unit of radioactivity.)

caesium This word is a single morpheme, but the characters *-ium* are often associated with chemical elements. (*Caesium* is the British spelling of a chemical element, spelled *cesium* in American English.)

IAEA This term is an acronym, as suggested by the use of capitalization. The prefix *I-* frequently refers to international organizations, and the suffix *-A* often refers to agencies or associations. (*IAEA* is the International Atomic Energy Agency.)

Zhezhgan This term is in title case, suggesting the name of a person or place, and the character bigram *zh* indicates that it is likely a transliteration. (*Zhezhgan* is a mining facility in Kazakhstan.)

How can word-internal structure be incorporated into word representations? One approach is to construct word representations from embeddings of the characters or morphemes. For example, if word i has morphological segments $\mathcal{M}_i$, then its embedding can be constructed by addition (Botha and Blunsom, 2014),

$$\boldsymbol{v}_i = \tilde{\boldsymbol{v}}_i + \sum_{j \in \mathcal{M}_i} \boldsymbol{v}_j^{(M)}, \qquad [14.23]$$

where $\boldsymbol{v}_m^{(M)}$ is a morpheme embedding and $\tilde{\boldsymbol{v}}_i$ is a non compositional embedding of the whole word, which is an additional free parameter of the model (figure 14.5, left side). All embeddings are estimated from a **log-bilinear language model** (Mnih and Hinton, 2007),

5. https://code.google.com/archive/p/word2vec/. Accessed September 20, 2017.

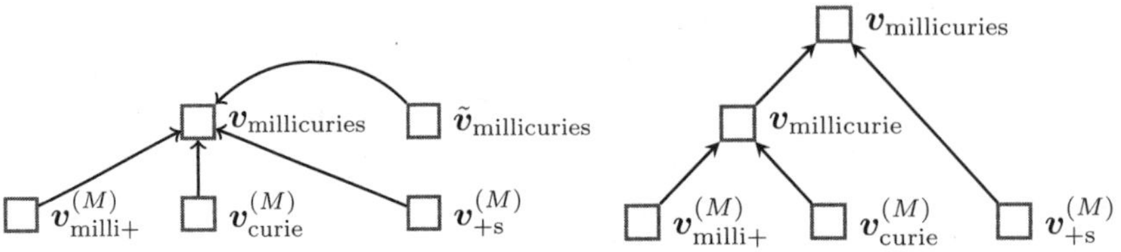

Figure 14.5
Two architectures for building word embeddings from subword units. On the left, morpheme embeddings $v^{(m)}$ are combined by addition with the noncompositional word embedding $\tilde{v}$ (Botha and Blunsom, 2014). On the right, morpheme embeddings are combined in a recursive neural network (Luong et al., 2013).

which is similar to the CBOW model (§ 14.5), but includes only contextual information from preceding words. The morphological segments are obtained using an unsupervised segmenter (Creutz and Lagus, 2007). For words that do not appear in the training data, the embedding can be constructed directly from the morphemes, assuming that each morpheme appears in some other word in the training data. The free parameter $\tilde{\boldsymbol{v}}$ adds flexibility: words with similar morphemes are encouraged to have similar embeddings, but this parameter makes it possible for them to be different.

Word-internal structure can be incorporated into word representations in various other ways. Here are some of the main parameters.

Subword units Examples like *IAEA* and *Zhezhgan* are not based on morphological composition, and a morphological segmenter is unlikely to identify meaningful subword units for these terms. Rather than using morphemes for subword embeddings, one can use characters (dos Santos and Zadrozny, 2014; Ling et al., 2015b; Kim et al., 2016), character *n*-grams (Wieting et al., 2016a; Bojanowski et al., 2017), and **byte-pair encodings**, a compression technique that captures frequent substrings (Gage, 1994; Sennrich et al., 2016).

Composition Combining the subword embeddings by addition does not differentiate between orderings, nor does it identify any particular morpheme as the root. A range of more flexible compositional models has been considered, including recurrence (Ling et al., 2015b), convolution (dos Santos and Zadrozny, 2014; Kim et al., 2016), and **recursive neural networks** (Luong et al., 2013), in which representations of progressively larger units are constructed over a morphological parse, for example, ((*milli+curie*)+*s*), ((*in+flam*)+*able*), and (*in*+(*vis+ible*)). A recursive embedding model is shown in the right panel of figure 14.5.

Estimation Estimating subword embeddings from a full dataset is computationally expensive. An alternative approach is to train a subword model to match pretrained word embeddings (Cotterell et al., 2016; Pinter et al., 2017). To train such a model, it is only necessary to iterate over the vocabulary, and not the corpus.

14.7.2 Lexical Semantic Resources

Resources such as WordNet provide another source of information about word meaning: if we know that *caesium* is a synonym of *cesium*, or that a *millicurie* is a type of *measurement unit*, then this should help to provide embeddings for the unknown words and to smooth embeddings of rare words. One way to do this is to **retrofit** pretrained word embeddings across a network of lexical semantic relationships (Faruqui et al., 2015) by minimizing the following objective,

$$\min_{\mathbf{U}} \sum_{j=1}^{V} ||\boldsymbol{v}_i - \hat{\boldsymbol{v}}_i||_2 + \sum_{(i,j)\in\mathcal{L}} \beta_{ij}||\boldsymbol{v}_i - \boldsymbol{v}_j||_2, \qquad [14.24]$$

where $\hat{\boldsymbol{v}}_i$ is the pretrained embedding of word i and $\mathcal{L} = \{(i,j)\}$ is a lexicon of word relations. The hyperparameter β_{ij} controls the importance of adjacent words having similar embeddings; Faruqui et al. (2015) set it to the inverse of the degree of word i, $\beta_{ij} = |\{j : (i,j) \in \mathcal{L}\}|^{-1}$. Retrofitting improves performance on a range of intrinsic evaluations and gives small improvements on an extrinsic document classification task.

14.8 Distributed Representations of Multiword Units

Can distributed representations extend to phrases, sentences, paragraphs, and beyond? Before exploring this possibility, recall the distinction between distributed and distributional representations. Neural embeddings such as WORD2VEC are both distributed (vector based) and distributional (derived from counts of words in context). As we consider larger units of text, the counts decrease: in the limit, a multi paragraph span of text would never appear twice, except by plagiarism. Thus, the meaning of a large span of text cannot be determined from distributional statistics alone; it must be computed compositionally from smaller spans. But these considerations are orthogonal to the question of whether distributed representations—dense numerical vectors—are sufficiently expressive to capture the meaning of phrases, sentences, and paragraphs.

14.8.1 Purely Distributional Methods

Some multiword phrases are non compositional: the meaning of such phrases is not derived from the meaning of the individual words using typical compositional semantics. This includes proper nouns like *San Francisco* as well as idiomatic expressions like *kick the bucket* (Baldwin and Kim, 2010). For these cases, purely distributional approaches can work. A simple approach is to identify multiword units that appear together frequently and then treat these units as words, learning embeddings using a technique such as WORD2VEC.

The problem of identifying multiword units is sometimes called **collocation extraction**. A good collocation has high **pointwise mutual information** (PMI; see § 14.3). For example,

Naïve Bayes is a good collocation because $p(w_t = \textit{Bayes} \mid w_{t-1} = \textit{naïve})$ is much larger than $p(w_t = \textit{Bayes})$. Collocations of more than two words can be identified by a greedy incremental search: for example, *mutual information* might first be extracted as a collocation and grouped into a single word type *mutual_information*; then *pointwise mutual_information* can be extracted later. After identifying such units, they can be treated as words when estimating skipgram embeddings. Mikolov et al. (2013b) show that the resulting embeddings perform reasonably well on a task of solving phrasal analogies, for example, *New York : New York Times :: Baltimore : Baltimore Sun*.

14.8.2 Distributional-Compositional Hybrids

To move beyond short multiword phrases, composition is necessary. A simple but surprisingly powerful approach is to represent a sentence with the average of its word embeddings (Mitchell and Lapata, 2010). This can be considered a hybrid of the distributional and compositional approaches to semantics: the word embeddings are computed distributionally, and then the sentence representation is computed by composition.

The WORD2VEC approach can be stretched considerably further, embedding entire sentences using a model similar to skipgrams, in the "skip-thought" model of Kiros et al. (2015). Each sentence is *encoded* into a vector using a recurrent neural network: the encoding of sentence t is set to the RNN hidden state at its final token, $\boldsymbol{h}_{M_t}^{(t)}$. This vector is then a parameter in a *decoder* model that is used to generate the previous and subsequent sentences: the decoder is another recurrent neural network, which takes the encoding of the neighboring sentence as an additional parameter in its recurrent update. (This **encoder-decoder model** is discussed at length in chapter 18.) The encoder and decoder are trained simultaneously from a likelihood-based objective, and the trained encoder can be used to compute a distributed representation of any sentence. Skip-thought can also be viewed as a hybrid of distributional and compositional approaches: the vector representation of each sentence is computed compositionally from the representations of the individual words, but the training objective is distributional, based on sentence co-occurrence across a corpus.

Autoencoders are a variant of encoder-decoder models in which the decoder is trained to produce the same text that was originally encoded, using only the distributed encoding vector (Li et al., 2015a). The encoding acts as a bottleneck, so that generalization is necessary if the model is to successfully fit the training data. In **denoising autoencoders**, the input is a corrupted version of the original sentence, and the auto-encoder must reconstruct the uncorrupted original (Vincent et al., 2010; Hill et al., 2016). By interpolating between distributed representations of two sentences, $\alpha \boldsymbol{u}_i + (1 - \alpha)\boldsymbol{u}_j$, it is possible to generate sentences that combine aspects of the two inputs, as shown in figure 14.6 (Bowman et al., 2016).

Autoencoders can also be applied to longer texts, such as paragraphs and documents. This enables applications such as **question answering**, which can be performed by matching the encoding of the question with encodings of candidate answers (Miao et al., 2016).

this was the only way
it was the only way
it was her turn to blink
it was hard to tell
it was time to move on
he had to do it again
they all looked at each other
they all turned to look back
they both turned to face him
they both turned and walked away

Figure 14.6
By interpolating between the distributed representations of two sentences (in bold), it is possible to generate grammatical sentences that combine aspects of both (Bowman et al., 2016).

14.8.3 Supervised Compositional Methods

Given a supervision signal, such as a label describing the sentiment or meaning of a sentence, a wide range of compositional methods can be applied to compute a distributed representation that then predicts the label. The simplest is to average the embeddings of each word in the sentence, and pass this average through a feedforward neural network (Iyyer et al., 2015). Convolutional and recurrent neural networks go further, with the ability to effectively capture multiword phenomena such as negation (Kalchbrenner et al., 2014; Kim, 2014; Li et al., 2015b; Tang et al., 2015). Another approach is to incorporate the syntactic structure of the sentence into a **recursive neural network**, in which the representation for each syntactic constituent is computed from the representations of its children (Socher et al., 2012). However, in many cases, recurrent neural networks perform as well or better than recursive networks (Li et al., 2015b).

Whether convolutional, recurrent, or recursive, a key question is whether supervised sentence representations are task specific, or whether a single supervised sentence representation model can yield useful performance on other tasks. Wieting et al. (2016b) trained a variety of sentence embedding models for the task of labeling pairs of sentences as **paraphrases**. They showed that the resulting sentence embeddings give good performance for sentiment analysis. The **Stanford Natural Language Inference corpus** classifies sentence pairs as **entailments** (the truth of sentence i implies the truth of sentence j), **contradictions** (the truth of sentence i implies the falsity of sentence j), and neutral (i neither entails nor contradicts j). Sentence embeddings trained on this dataset transfer to a wide range of classification tasks (Conneau et al., 2017).

14.8.4 Hybrid Distributed-Symbolic Representations

The power of distributed representations is in their generality: the distributed representation of a unit of text can serve as a summary of its meaning and therefore as the input for downstream tasks such as classification, matching, and retrieval. For example, distributed sentence representations can be used to recognize the paraphrase relationship between closely related sentences like the following:

(14.5) a. Donald thanked Vlad profusely.
b. Donald conveyed to Vlad his profound appreciation.
c. Vlad was showered with gratitude by Donald.

Symbolic representations are relatively brittle to this sort of variation, but are better suited to describe individual entities, the things that they do, and the things that are done to them. In examples (14.5a–c), we not only know that somebody thanked someone else, but also can make a range of inferences about what has happened between the entities named *Donald* and *Vlad*. Because distributed representations do not treat entities symbolically, they lack the ability to reason about the roles played by entities across a sentence or larger discourse.[6] A hybrid between distributed and symbolic representations might give the best of both worlds: robustness to the many different ways of describing the same event, plus the expressiveness to support inferences about entities and the roles that they play.

A "top-down" hybrid approach is to begin with logical semantics (of the sort described in the previous two chapters), but replace the predefined lexicon with a set of distributional word clusters (Poon and Domingos, 2009; Lewis and Steedman, 2013). A "bottom-up" approach is to add minimal symbolic structure to existing distributed representations, such as vector representations for each entity (Ji and Eisenstein, 2015; Wiseman et al., 2016). This has been shown to improve performance on two problems that we will encounter in the following chapters: classification of **discourse relations** between adjacent sentences (chapter 16; Ji and Eisenstein, 2015) and **coreference resolution** of entity mentions (chapter 15; Wiseman et al., 2016; Ji et al., 2017). Research on hybrid semantic representations is still in an early stage, and future representations may deviate more boldly from existing symbolic and distributional approaches.

Additional Resources

Turney and Pantel (2010) survey a number of facets of vector word representations, focusing on matrix factorization methods. Schnabel et al. (2015) highlight problems with similarity-based evaluations of word embeddings and present a novel evaluation that controls for word

6. At a 2014 workshop on semantic parsing, this critique of distributed representations was expressed by Ray Mooney—a leading researcher in computational semantics—in a now well-known quote, "you can't cram the meaning of a whole sentence into a single vector!"

frequency. Baroni et al. (2014) address linguistic issues that arise in attempts to combine distributed and compositional representations.

In bilingual and multilingual distributed representations, embeddings are estimated for translation pairs or tuples, such as (*dog, perro, chien*). These embeddings can improve machine translation (Klementiev et al., 2012; Zou et al., 2013) transfer natural language processing models across languages (Täckström et al., 2012), and make monolingual word embeddings more accurate (Faruqui and Dyer, 2014). A typical approach is to learn a projection that maximizes the correlation of the distributed representations of each element in a translation pair, which can be obtained from a bilingual dictionary. Distributed representations can also be linked to perceptual information, such as image features. Bruni et al. (2014) use textual descriptions of images to obtain visual contextual information for various words, which supplements traditional distributional context. Image features can also be inserted as contextual information in log bilinear language models (Kiros et al., 2014), making it possible to automatically generate text descriptions of images.

Exercises

1. Prove that the sum of probabilities of paths through a hierarchical softmax tree is equal to one.
2. In skipgram word embeddings, the negative sampling objective can be written as

$$\mathcal{L} = \sum_{i \in \mathcal{V}} \sum_{j \in \mathcal{C}} \text{count}(i,j)\, \psi(i,j), \tag{14.25}$$

with $\psi(i,j)$ as defined in equation 14.19.

Suppose we draw the negative samples from the empirical unigram distribution $\hat{\mathrm{p}}(i) = \mathrm{p}_{\text{unigram}}(i)$. First, compute the expectation of $\mathcal{L}$ with respect the negative samples, using this probability.

Next, take the derivative of this expectation with respect to the score of a single word context pair $\sigma(\boldsymbol{u}_i \cdot \boldsymbol{v}_j)$, and solve for the pointwise mutual information $\text{PMI}(i,j)$. You should be able to show that at the optimum, the PMI is a simple function of $\sigma(\boldsymbol{u}_i \cdot \boldsymbol{v}_j)$ and the number of negative samples.

(This exercise is part of a proof that shows that skipgram with negative sampling is closely related to PMI-weighted matrix factorization.)

3. *In Brown clustering, prove that the cluster merge that maximizes the average mutual information (equation 14.9) also maximizes the log-likelihood objective (equation 14.8).
4. A simple way to compute a distributed phrase representation is to add up the distributed representations of the words in the phrase. Consider a sentiment analysis model in which the predicted sentiment is $\psi(\boldsymbol{w}) = \boldsymbol{\theta} \cdot (\sum_{m=1}^{M} \boldsymbol{x}_m)$, where $\boldsymbol{x}_m$ is the vector representation of word m. Prove that, in such a model, the following two inequalities cannot both hold:

$$\psi(\textit{good}) > \psi(\textit{not good}) \quad [14.26]$$

$$\psi(\textit{bad}) < \psi(\textit{not bad}). \quad [14.27]$$

Then construct a similar example pair for the case in which phrase representations are the *average* of the word representations.

5. Now let's consider a slight modification to the prediction model in the previous problem:

$$\psi(\boldsymbol{w}) = \boldsymbol{\theta} \cdot \text{ReLU}(\sum_{m=1}^{M} \boldsymbol{x}_m) \quad [14.28]$$

Show that in this case, it *is* possible to achieve the inequalities above. Your solution should provide the weights $\boldsymbol{\theta}$ and the embeddings $\boldsymbol{x}_{\text{good}}$, $\boldsymbol{x}_{\text{bad}}$, and $\boldsymbol{x}_{\text{not}}$.

For the next two problems, download a set of pre trained word embeddings, such as the WORD2VEC or polyglot embeddings.

6. Use cosine similarity to find the most similar words to: *dog, whale, before, however, fabricate.*
7. Use vector addition and subtraction to compute target vectors for the analogies below. After computing each target vector, find the top three candidates by cosine similarity.
   - *dog:puppy :: cat: ?*
   - *speak:speaker :: sing:?*
   - *France:French :: England:?*
   - *France:wine :: England:?*

   The remaining problems will require you to build a classifier and test its properties. Pick a text classification dataset, such as the Cornell Movie Review data.[7] Divide your data into training (60%), development (20%), and test sets (20%), if no such division already exists.
8. Train a convolutional neural network, with inputs set to pretrained word embeddings from the previous two problems. Use an additional, fine-tuned embedding for out-of-vocabulary words. Train until performance on the development set does not improve. You can also use the development set to tune the model architecture, such as the convolution width and depth. Report F-MEASURE and accuracy, as well as training time.
9. Now modify your model from the previous problem to fine-tune the word embeddings. Report F-MEASURE, accuracy, and training time.
10. Try a simpler approach, in which word embeddings in the document are averaged, and then this average is passed through a feed forward neural network. Again, use the development data to tune the model architecture. How close is the accuracy to the convolutional networks from the previous problems?

7. www.cs.cornell.edu/people/pabo/movie-review-data/.

15 Reference Resolution

References are one of the most noticeable forms of linguistic ambiguity, afflicting not just automated natural language processing systems, but also fluent human readers. Warnings to avoid "ambiguous pronouns" are ubiquitous in manuals and tutorials on writing style. But referential ambiguity is not limited to pronouns, as shown in the text in figure 15.1. Each of the bracketed substrings refers to an entity that is introduced earlier in the passage. These references include the pronouns *he* and *his*, but also the shortened name *Cook*, and **nominals** such as *the firm* and *the firm's biggest growth market*.

Reference resolution subsumes several subtasks. This chapter will focus on **coreference resolution**, which is the task of grouping spans of text that refer to a single underlying entity, or, in some cases, a single event: for example, the spans *Tim Cook*, *he*, and *Cook* are all **coreferent**. These individual spans are called **mentions**, because they mention an entity; the entity is sometimes called the **referent**. Each mention has a set of **antecedents**, which are preceding mentions that are coreferent; for the first mention of an entity, the antecedent set is empty. The task of **pronominal anaphora resolution** requires identifying only the antecedents of pronouns. In **entity linking**, references are resolved not to other spans of text, but to entities in a knowledge base. This task is discussed in chapter 17.

Coreference resolution is a challenging problem for several reasons. Resolving different types of **referring expressions** requires different types of reasoning: the features and methods that are useful for resolving pronouns are different from those that are useful to resolve names and nominals. Coreference resolution involves not only linguistic reasoning, but also world knowledge and pragmatics: you may not have known that China was Apple's biggest growth market, but it is likely that you effortlessly resolved this reference while reading the passage in figure 15.1.[1] A further challenge is that coreference resolution decisions are often entangled: each mention adds information about the entity, which affects other coreference decisions. This means that coreference resolution must be addressed as a structure

1. This interpretation is based in part on the assumption that a **cooperative** author would not use the expression *the firm's biggest growth market* to refer to an entity not yet mentioned in the article (Grice, 1975). **Pragmatics** is the discipline of linguistics concerned with the formalization of such assumptions (Huang, 2015).

(15.1) *[[Apple Inc] Chief Executive Tim Cook] has jetted into [China] for talks with government officials as [he] seeks to clear up a pile of problems in [[the firm] 's biggest growth market] … [Cook] is on [his] first trip to [the country] since taking over …*

Figure 15.1
Running example (Yee and Jones, 2012). Coreferring entity mentions are in brackets.

prediction problem. But as we will see, there is no dynamic program that allows the space of coreference decisions to be searched efficiently.

15.1 Forms of Referring Expressions

There are three main forms of referring expressions—pronouns, names, and nominals.

15.1.1 Pronouns

Pronouns are a closed class of words that are used for references. A natural way to think about pronoun resolution is SMASH (Kehler, 2007):

- **S**earch for candidate antecedents;
- **M**atch against hard agreement constraints;
- **A**nd **S**elect using **H**euristics, which are "soft" constraints such as recency, syntactic prominence, and parallelism.

Search In the search step, candidate antecedents are identified from the preceding text or speech.[2] Any noun phrase can be a candidate antecedent, and pronoun resolution usually requires parsing the text to identify all such noun phrases.[3] Filtering heuristics can help to prune the search space to noun phrases that are likely to be coreferent (Lee et al., 2013; Durrett and Klein, 2013). In nested noun phrases, mentions are generally considered to be

2. Pronouns whose referents come later are known as **cataphora**, as in the opening line from a novel by Márquez (1970):

(15.1) Many years later, as [he] faced the firing squad, [Colonel Aureliano Buendía] was to remember that distant afternoon when [his] father took him to discover ice.

3. In the OntoNotes coreference annotations, verbs can also be antecedents, if they are later referenced by nominals (Pradhan et al., 2011):

(15.1) Sales of passenger cars [grew] 22%. [The strong growth] followed year-to-year increases.

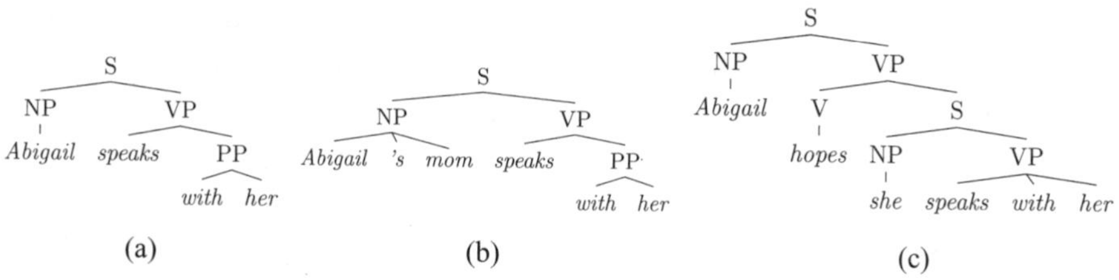

Figure 15.2
In (a), *Abigail* c-commands *her*; in (b), *Abigail* does not c-command *her*, but *Abigail's mom* does; in (c), the scope of *Abigail* is limited by the S nonterminal, so that *she* or *her* can bind to *Abigail*, but not both.

the largest unit with a given **head word** (see § 10.5.2): thus, *Apple Inc. Chief Executive Tim Cook* would be included as a mention, but *Tim Cook* would not, because they share the same head word, *Cook*.

Matching constraints for pronouns References and their antecedents must agree on semantic features such as number, person, gender, and animacy. Consider the pronoun *he* in this passage from the running example:

(15.2) Tim Cook has jetted in for talks with officials as [he] seeks to clear up a pile of problems ...

The pronoun and possible antecedents have the following features:

- *he*: singular, masculine, animate, third person
- *officials*: plural, animate, third person
- *talks*: plural, inanimate, third person
- *Tim Cook*: singular, masculine, animate, third person

The SMASH method searches backward from *he*, discarding *officials* and *talks* because they do not satisfy the agreements constraints.

Another source of constraints comes from syntax—specifically, from the phrase structure trees discussed in chapter 10. Consider a parse tree in which both x and y are phrasal constituents. The constituent x **c-commands** the constituent y iff the first branching node above x also dominates y. For example, in figure 15.2a, *Abigail* c-commands *her*, because the first branching node above *Abigail*, S, also dominates *her*. Now, if x c-commands y, **government and binding theory** (Chomsky, 1982) states that y can refer to x only if it is a **reflexive pronoun** (e.g., *herself*). Furthermore, if y is a reflexive pronoun, then its antecedent must c-command it. Thus, in figure 15.2a, *her* cannot refer to *Abigail*; conversely, if we replace *her* with *herself*, then the reflexive pronoun *must* refer to *Abigail*, because this is the only candidate antecedent that c-commands it.

Now consider the example shown in figure 15.2b. Here, *Abigail* does not c-command *her*, but *Abigail's mom* does. Thus, *her* can refer to *Abigail*—and we cannot use reflexive *herself* in this context, unless we are talking about Abigail's mom. However, *her* does not have to refer to *Abigail*. Finally, figure 15.2c shows how these constraints are limited. In this case, the pronoun *she* can refer to *Abigail*, because the S nonterminal puts *Abigail* outside the domain of *she*. Similarly, *her* can also refer to *Abigail*. But *she* and *her* cannot be coreferent, because *she* c-commands *her*.

Heuristics After applying constraints, heuristics are applied to select among the remaining candidates. Recency is a particularly strong heuristic. All things equal, readers will prefer the more recent referent for a given pronoun, particularly when comparing referents that occur in different sentences. Jurafsky and Martin (2009) offer the following example:

(15.3) The doctor found an old map in the captain's chest. Jim found an even older map hidden on the shelf. [It] described an island.

Readers are expected to prefer the older map as the referent for the pronoun *it*.

However, subjects are often preferred over objects, and this can contradict the preference for recency when two candidate referents are in the same sentence. For example,

(15.4) Abigail loaned Lucia a book on Spanish. [She] is always trying to help people.

Here, we may prefer to link *she* to *Abigail* rather than *Lucia*, because of *Abigail*'s position in the subject role of the preceding sentence. (Arguably, this preference would not be strong enough to select *Abigail* if the second sentence were *She is visiting Valencia next month*.)

A third heuristic is parallelism:

(15.5) Abigail loaned Lucia a book on Spanish. Özlem loaned [her] a book on Portuguese.

Here *Lucia* is preferred as the referent for *her*, contradicting the preference for the subject *Abigail* in the preceding example.

The recency and subject role heuristics can be unified by traversing the document in a syntax-driven fashion (Hobbs, 1978): each preceding sentence is traversed breadth first, left to right (figure 15.3). This heuristic successfully handles (15.4): *Abigail* is preferred as the referent for *she* because the subject NP is visited first. It also handles (15.3): the older map is preferred as the referent for *it* because the more recent sentence is visited first. An alternative unification of recency and syntax is proposed by **centering theory** (Grosz et al., 1995), which is discussed in detail in chapter 16.

In early work on reference resolution, the number of heuristics was small enough that a set of numerical weights could be set by hand (Lappin and Leass, 1994). More recent work uses machine learning to quantify the importance of each of these factors. However,

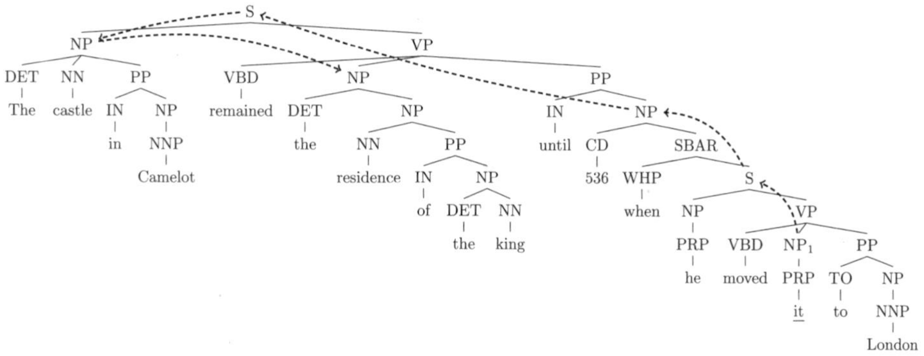

Figure 15.3
Left-to-right, breadth-first tree traversal (Hobbs, 1978), indicating that the search for an antecedent for *it* (NP_1) would proceed in the following order: *536*; *the castle in Camelot*; *the residence of the king*; *Camelot*; *the king*. Hobbs (1978) proposes semantic constraints to eliminate *536* and *the castle in Camelot* as candidates, because they are unlikely to be the direct object of the verb *move*.

pronoun resolution cannot be completely solved by constraints and heuristics alone. This is shown by the classic example pair (Winograd, 1972):

(15.6) The [city council] denied [the protesters] a permit because [they] advocated/feared violence.

Without reasoning about the motivations of the city council and protesters, it is unlikely that any system could correctly resolve both versions of this example.

Nonreferential pronouns While pronouns are generally used for reference, they need not refer to entities. The following examples show how pronouns can refer to propositions, events, and speech acts.

(15.7) a. They told me that I was too ugly for show business, but I didn't believe [it].
b. Elifsu saw Berthold get angry, and I saw [it] too.
c. Emmanuel said he worked in security. I suppose [that]'s one way to put it.

These forms of reference are generally not annotated in large-scale coreference resolution datasets such as OntoNotes (Pradhan et al., 2011).

Pronouns may also have **generic referents**:

(15.8) a. A poor carpenter blames [her] tools.
b. On the moon, [you] have to carry [your] own oxygen.
c. Every farmer who owns a donkey beats [it] (Geach, 1962)

In the OntoNotes dataset, coreference is not annotated for generic referents, even in cases like these examples, in which the same generic entity is mentioned multiple times.

Some pronouns do not refer to anything at all:

(15.9) a. *[It]'s raining.*
[Il] pleut. (Fr)
b. [It] 's money that she's really after.
c. [It] is too bad that we have to work so hard.

How can we automatically distinguish these usages of *it* from referential pronouns? Consider the the difference between the following two examples (Bergsma et al., 2008):

(15.10) a. You can make [it] in advance.
b. You can make [it] in showbiz.

In the second example, the pronoun *it* is nonreferential. One way to see this is by substituting another pronoun, like *them*, into these examples:

(15.11) a. You can make [them] in advance.
b. ? You can make [them] in showbiz.

The questionable grammaticality of the second example suggests that *it* is not referential. Bergsma et al. (2008) operationalize this idea by comparing distributional statistics for the *n*-grams around the word *it*, testing how often other pronouns or nouns appear in the same context. In cases where nouns and other pronouns are infrequent, the *it* is unlikely to be referential.

15.1.2 Proper Nouns

If a proper noun is used as a referring expression, it often corefers with another proper noun, so that the coreference problem is simply to determine whether the two names match. Subsequent proper noun references often use a shortened form, as in the running example (figure 15.1):

(15.12) Apple Inc Chief Executive [Tim Cook] has jetted into China ... [Cook] is on his first business trip to the country ...

A typical solution for proper noun coreference is to match the syntactic head words of the reference with the referent. In § 10.5.2, we saw that the head word of a phrase can be identified by applying head percolation rules to the phrasal parse tree; alternatively, the head can be identified as the root of the dependency subtree covering the name. For sequences of proper nouns, the head word will be the final token.

There are a number of caveats to the practice of matching head words of proper nouns.

- In the European tradition, family names tend to be more specific than given names, and family names usually come last. However, other traditions have other practices: for example, in Chinese names, the family name typically comes first; in Japanese, honorifics come after the name, as in *Nobu-San* (*Mr. Nobu*).

- In organization names, the head word is often not the most informative, as in *Georgia Tech* and *Virginia Tech*. Similarly, *Lebanon* does not refer to the same entity as *Southern Lebanon*, necessitating special rules for the specific case of geographical modifiers (Lee et al., 2011).
- Proper nouns can be nested, as in *[the CEO of [Microsoft]]*, resulting in head word match without coreference.

Despite these difficulties, proper nouns are the easiest category of references to resolve (Stoyanov et al., 2009). In machine learning systems, one solution is to include a range of matching features, including exact match, head match, and string inclusion. In addition to matching features, competitive systems (e.g., Bengtson and Roth, 2008) include large lists, or **gazetteers**, of acronyms (e.g, *the National Basketball Association/NBA*), demonyms (e.g., *the Israelis/Israel*), and other aliases (e.g., *the Georgia Institute of Technology/Georgia Tech*).

15.1.3 Nominals

In coreference resolution, noun phrases that are neither pronouns nor proper nouns are referred to as **nominals**. In the running example (figure 15.1), nominal references include: *the firm* (*Apple Inc*); *the firm's biggest growth market* (*China*); and *the country* (*China*).

Nominals are especially difficult to resolve (Denis and Baldridge, 2007; Durrett and Klein, 2013), and the examples above suggest why this may be the case: world knowledge is required to identify *Apple Inc* as a *firm* and *China* as a *growth market*. Other difficult examples include the use of colloquial expressions, such as coreference between *Clinton campaign officials* and *the Clinton camp* (Soon et al., 2001).

15.2 Algorithms for Coreference Resolution

The ground truth training data for coreference resolution is a set of mention sets, where all mentions within each set refer to a single entity.[4] In the running example from figure 15.1, the ground truth coreference annotation is:

$$c_1 = \{\textit{Apple Inc}_{1:2}, \textit{the firm}_{27:28}\} \quad [15.1]$$

$$c_2 = \{\textit{Apple Inc Chief Executive Tim Cook}_{1:6}, \textit{he}_{17}, \textit{Cook}_{33}, \textit{his}_{36}\} \quad [15.2]$$

$$c_3 = \{\textit{China}_{10}, \textit{the firm 's biggest growth market}_{27:32}, \textit{the country}_{40:41}\}. \quad [15.3]$$

Each row specifies the token spans that mention an entity. ("Singleton" entities, which are mentioned only once [e.g., *talks*, *government officials*], are excluded from the annotations.)

4. In many annotations, the term **markable** is used to refer to spans of text that can *potentially* mention an entity. The set of markables includes nonreferential pronouns, which does not mention any entity. Part of the job of the coreference system is to avoid incorrectly linking these nonreferential markables to any mention chains.

Equivalently, if given a set of M mentions, $\{m_i\}_{i=1}^{M}$, each mention i can be assigned to a cluster z_i, where $z_i = z_j$ if i and j are coreferent. The cluster assignments z are invariant under permutation. The unique clustering associated with the assignment z is written $\boldsymbol{c}(z)$.

Coreference resolution can thus be viewed as a structure prediction problem, involving two subtasks: identifying which spans of text mention entities, and then clustering those spans.

Mention identification The task of identifying mention spans for coreference resolution is often performed by applying a set of heuristics to the phrase structure parse of each sentence. A typical approach is to start with all noun phrases and named entities and then apply filtering rules to remove nested noun phrases with the same head (e.g., *[Apple CEO [Tim Cook]]*), numeric entities (e.g., *[100 miles]*, *[97%]*), nonreferential *it*, etc. (Lee et al., 2013; Durrett and Klein, 2013). In general, these deterministic approaches err in favor of recall, because the mention clustering component can choose to ignore false positive mentions but cannot recover from false negatives. An alternative is to consider all spans (up to some finite length) as candidate mentions, performing mention identification and clustering jointly (Daumé III and Marcu, 2005; Lee et al., 2017).

Mention clustering The subtask of mention clustering will be the focus of the remainder of this chapter. There are two main classes of models. In *mention-based models*, the scoring function for a coreference clustering decomposes over pairs of mentions. These pairwise decisions are then aggregated, using a clustering heuristic. Mention-based clustering can be treated as a fairly direct application of supervised classification or ranking. However, the mention-pair locality assumption can result in incoherent clusters, like {*Hillary Clinton* ← *Clinton* ← *Mr Clinton*}, in which the pairwise links score well, but the overall result is unsatisfactory. *Entity-based models* address this issue by scoring entities holistically. This can make inference more difficult, because the number of possible entity groupings is exponential in the number of mentions.

15.2.1 Mention-Pair Models

In the **mention-pair model**, a binary label $y_{i,j} \in \{0, 1\}$ is assigned to each pair of mentions (i, j), where $i < j$. If i and j corefer ($z_i = z_j$), then $y_{i,j} = 1$; otherwise, $y_{i,j} = 0$. The mention *he* in figure 15.1 is preceded by five other mentions: (1) *Apple Inc*; (2) *Apple Inc Chief Executive Tim Cook*; (3) *China*; (4) *talks*; and (5) *government officials*. The correct mention pair labeling is $y_{2,6} = 1$ and $y_{i \neq 2,6} = 0$ for all other i. If a mention j introduces a new entity, such as mention 3 in the example, then $y_{i,j} = 0$ for all i. The same is true for "mentions" that do not refer to any entity, such as nonreferential pronouns. If mention j refers to an entity that has been mentioned more than once, then $y_{i,j} = 1$ for all $i < j$ that mention the referent.

By transforming coreference into a set of binary labeling problems, the mention-pair model makes it possible to apply an off-the-shelf binary classifier (Soon et al., 2001). This classifier is applied to each mention j independently, searching backward from j until finding an antecedent i that corefers with j with high confidence. After identifying a single **antecedent**, the remaining mention pair labels can be computed by transitivity: if $y_{i,j}=1$ and $y_{j,k}=1$, then $y_{i,k}=1$.

Because the ground truth annotations give entity chains $\boldsymbol{c}$ but not individual mention-pair labels $\mathbf{y}$, an additional heuristic must be employed to convert the labeled data into training examples for classification. A typical approach is to generate at most one positive labeled instance $y_{a_j,j}=1$ for mention j, where a_j is the index of the most recent antecedent, $a_j=\max\{i : i<j \wedge z_i=z_j\}$. Negative labeled instances are generated for all $i \in \{a_j+1, \ldots, j\}$. In the running example, the most recent antecedent of the pronoun *he* is $a_6=2$, so the training data would be $y_{2,6}=1$ and $y_{3,6}=y_{4,6}=y_{5,6}=0$. The variable $y_{1,6}$ is not part of the training data, because the first mention appears before the true antecedent $a_6=2$.

15.2.2 Mention-Ranking Models

In **mention ranking** (Denis and Baldridge, 2007), the classifier learns to identify a single antecedent $a_i \in \{\epsilon, 1, 2, \ldots, i-1\}$ for each referring expression i,

$$\hat{a}_i = \underset{a \in \{\epsilon, 1, 2, \ldots, i-1\}}{\operatorname{argmax}} \psi_M(a, i), \qquad [15.4]$$

where $\psi_M(a, i)$ is a score for the mention pair (a, i). If $a=\epsilon$, then mention i does not refer to any previously introduced entity—it is not **anaphoric**. Mention ranking is similar to the mention-pair model, but all candidates are considered simultaneously, and at most a single antecedent is selected. The mention-ranking model explicitly accounts for the possibility that mention i is not anaphoric, through the score $\psi_M(\epsilon, i)$. The determination of anaphoricity can be made by a special classifier in a preprocessing step, so that non-ϵ antecedents are identified only for spans that are determined to be anaphoric (Denis and Baldridge, 2008).

As a learning problem, ranking can be trained using the same objectives as in discriminative classification. For each mention i, we can define a gold antecedent a_i^*, and an associated loss, such as the hinge loss, $\ell_i=(1-\psi_M(a_i^*, i)+\psi_M(\hat{a}, i))_+$, or the negative log-likelihood, $\ell_i=-\log \mathrm{p}(a_i^* \mid i; \boldsymbol{\theta})$. (For more on learning to rank, see § 17.1.1.) But as with the mention-pair model, there is a mismatch between the labeled data, which comes in the form of mention sets, and the desired supervision, which would indicate the specific antecedent of each mention. The antecedent variables $\{a_i\}_{i=1}^M$ relate to the mention sets in a many-to-one mapping: each set of antecedents induces a single clustering, but a clustering can correspond to many different settings of antecedent variables.

A heuristic solution is to set $a_i^*=\max\{j : j<i \wedge z_j=z_i\}$, the most recent mention in the same cluster as i. But the most recent mention may not be the most informative: in the running example, the most recent antecedent of the mention *Cook* is the pronoun *he*, but a more useful antecedent is the earlier mention *Apple Inc Chief Executive Tim Cook*. Rather than selecting a specific antecedent to train on, the antecedent can be treated as a latent variable, in the manner of the **latent variable perceptron** from § 12.4.2 (Fernandes et al., 2014):

$$\hat{\boldsymbol{a}} = \operatorname*{argmax}_{\boldsymbol{a}} \sum_{i=1}^{M} \psi_M(a_i, i) \tag{15.5}$$

$$\boldsymbol{a}^* = \operatorname*{argmax}_{\boldsymbol{a} \in \mathcal{A}(\boldsymbol{c})} \sum_{i=1}^{M} \psi_M(a_i, i) \tag{15.6}$$

$$\boldsymbol{\theta} \leftarrow \boldsymbol{\theta} + \sum_{i=1}^{M} \frac{\partial L}{\partial \boldsymbol{\theta}} \psi_M(a_i^*, i) - \sum_{i=1}^{M} \frac{\partial L}{\partial \boldsymbol{\theta}} \psi_M(\hat{a}_i, i), \tag{15.7}$$

where $\mathcal{A}(\boldsymbol{c})$ is the set of antecedent structures that is compatible with the ground truth coreference clustering $\boldsymbol{c}$. Another alternative is to sum over all the conditional probabilities of antecedent structures that are compatible with the ground truth clustering (Durrett and Klein, 2013; Lee et al., 2017). For the set of mentions $\boldsymbol{m}$, we compute the following probabilities:

$$\mathrm{p}(\boldsymbol{c} \mid \boldsymbol{m}) = \sum_{\boldsymbol{a} \in \mathcal{A}(\boldsymbol{c})} \mathrm{p}(\boldsymbol{a} \mid \boldsymbol{m}) = \sum_{\boldsymbol{a} \in \mathcal{A}(\boldsymbol{c})} \prod_{i=1}^{M} \mathrm{p}(a_i \mid i, \boldsymbol{m}) \tag{15.8}$$

$$\mathrm{p}(a_i \mid i, \boldsymbol{m}) = \frac{\exp\left(\psi_M(a_i, i)\right)}{\sum_{a' \in \{\epsilon, 1, 2, \ldots, i-1\}} \exp\left(\psi_M(a', i)\right)}. \tag{15.9}$$

This objective rewards models that assign high scores for all valid antecedent structures. In the running example, this would correspond to summing the probabilities of the two valid antecedents for *Cook*, *he* and *Apple Inc Chief Executive Tim Cook*. In one of the exercises, you will compute the number of valid antecedent structures for a given clustering.

15.2.3 Transitive Closure in Mention-Based Models

A problem for mention-based models is that individual mention-level decisions may be incoherent. Consider the following mentions:

$$m_1 = \textit{Hillary Clinton} \tag{15.10}$$

$$m_2 = \textit{Clinton} \tag{15.11}$$

$$m_3 = \textit{Bill Clinton} \tag{15.12}$$

A mention-pair system might predict $\hat{y}_{1,2} = 1, \hat{y}_{2,3} = 1, \hat{y}_{1,3} = 0$. Similarly, a mention-ranking system might choose $\hat{a}_2 = 1$ and $\hat{a}_3 = 2$. Logically, if mentions 1 and 3 are both coreferent with mention 2, then all three mentions must refer to the same entity. This constraint is known as **transitive closure**.

Transitive closure can be applied *post hoc*, revising the independent mention-pair or mention-ranking decisions. However, there are many possible ways to enforce transitive closure: in the example above, we could set $\hat{y}_{1,3} = 1$, or $\hat{y}_{1,2} = 0$, or $\hat{y}_{2,3} = 0$. For documents with many mentions, there may be many violations of transitive closure, and many possible fixes. Transitive closure can be enforced by always adding edges, so that $\hat{y}_{1,3} = 1$ is preferred (e.g., Soon et al., 2001), but this can result in overclustering, with too many mentions grouped into too few entities.

Mention-pair coreference resolution can be viewed as a constrained optimization problem,

$$\max_{y \in \{0,1\}^M} \sum_{j=1}^{M} \sum_{i=1}^{j} \psi_M(i,j) \times y_{i,j}$$

$$\text{s.t.} \quad y_{i,j} + y_{j,k} - 1 \leq y_{i,k}, \quad \forall i < j < k,$$

with the constraint enforcing transitive closure. This constrained optimization problem is equivalent to graph partitioning with positive and negative edge weights: construct a graph where the nodes are mentions, and the edges are the pairwise scores $\psi_M(i,j)$; the goal is to partition the graph so as to maximize the sum of the edge weights between all nodes within the same partition (McCallum and Wellner, 2004). This problem is NP-hard, motivating approximations such as correlation clustering (Bansal et al., 2004) and **integer linear programming** (Klenner, 2007; Finkel and Manning, 2008, also see § 13.2.2).

15.2.4 Entity-Based Models

A weakness of mention-based models is that they treat coreference resolution as a classification or ranking problem, when it is really a clustering problem: the goal is to group the mentions together into clusters that correspond to the underlying entities. Entity-based approaches attempt to identify these clusters directly. Such methods require a scoring function at the entity level, measuring whether each set of mentions is internally consistent. Coreference resolution can then be viewed as the following optimization,

$$\max_{z} \sum_{e=1} \psi_E(\{i : z_i = e\}), \qquad [15.13]$$

where z_i indicates the entity referenced by mention i and $\psi_E(\{i : z_i = e\})$ is a scoring function applied to all mentions i that are assigned to entity e.

Entity-based coreference resolution is conceptually similar to the unsupervised clustering problems encountered in chapter 5: the goal is to obtain clusters of mentions that are internally coherent. The number of possible clusterings of n items is the **Bell number**, which is defined by the following recurrence (Bell, 1934; Luo et al., 2004):

$$B_n = \sum_{k=0}^{n-1} B_k \binom{n-1}{k} B_0 = B_1 = 1. \qquad [15.14]$$

This recurrence is illustrated by the Bell tree, which is applied to a short coreference problem in figure 15.4. The Bell number B_n grows exponentially with n, making exhaustive

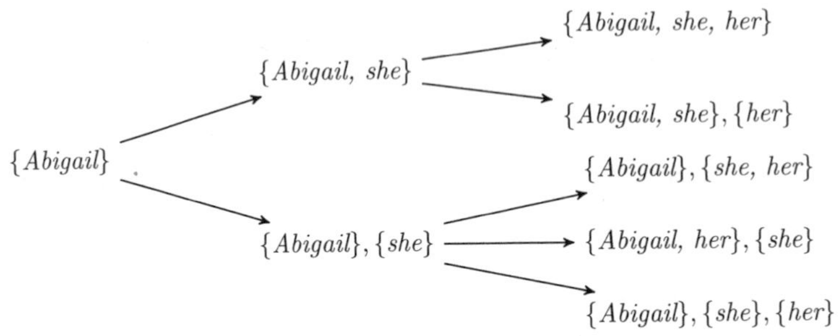

Figure 15.4
The Bell Tree for the sentence *Abigail hopes she speaks with her*. Which paths are excluded by the syntactic constraints mentioned in § 15.1.1?

search of the space of clusterings impossible. For this reason, entity-based coreference resolution typically involves incremental search, in which clustering decisions are based on local evidence, in the hope of approximately optimizing the full objective in equation 15.13. This approach is sometimes called **cluster ranking**, in contrast to mention ranking.

Generative models of coreference Entity-based coreference can be approached through probabilistic **generative models**, in which the mentions in the document are conditioned on a set of latent entities (Haghighi and Klein, 2007, 2010). An advantage of these methods is that they can be learned from unlabeled data (Poon and Domingos, 2008); a disadvantage is that probabilistic inference is required not just for learning, but also for prediction. Furthermore, generative models require independence assumptions that are difficult to apply in coreference resolution, where the diverse and heterogeneous features do not admit an easy decomposition into mutually independent subsets.

Incremental cluster ranking The SMASH method (§ 15.1.1) can be extended to entity-based coreference resolution by building up coreference clusters while moving through the document (Cardie and Wagstaff, 1999). At each mention, the algorithm iterates backward through possible antecedent clusters; but unlike SMASH, a cluster is selected only if *all* members of its cluster are compatible with the current mention. As mentions are added to a cluster, so are their features (e.g., gender, number, animacy). In this way, incoherent chains like {*Hillary Clinton*, *Clinton*, *Bill Clinton*} can be avoided. However, an incorrect assignment early in the document—a **search error**—might lead to a cascade of errors later on.

More sophisticated search strategies can help to ameliorate the risk of search errors. One approach is **beam search** (first discussed in § 11.3), in which a set of hypotheses is maintained throughout search. Each hypothesis represents a path through the Bell tree (figure 15.4). Hypotheses are "expanded" either by adding the next mention to an existing cluster, or by starting a new cluster. Each expansion receives a score, based on equation 15.13, and the top K hypotheses are kept on the beam as the algorithm moves to the next step.

Incremental cluster ranking can be made more accurate by performing multiple passes over the document, applying rules (or "sieves") with increasing recall and decreasing precision at each pass (Lee et al., 2013). In the early passes, coreference links are proposed only between mentions that are highly likely to corefer (e.g., exact string match for full names and nominals). Information can then be shared among these mentions, so that when more permissive matching rules are applied later, agreement is preserved across the entire cluster. For example, in the case of {*Hillary Clinton*, *Clinton*, *she*}, the name-matching sieve would link *Clinton* and *Hillary Clinton*, and the pronoun-matching sieve would then link *she* to the combined cluster. A deterministic multi-pass system won nearly every track of the 2011 CoNLL shared task on coreference resolution (Pradhan et al., 2011). Given the dominance of machine learning in virtually all other areas of natural language processing—and more than 15 years of prior work on machine learning for coreference—this was a surprising result, even if learning-based methods have subsequently regained the upper hand (e.g., Lee et al., 2018, the state of the art at the time of this writing).

Incremental perceptron Incremental coreference resolution can be learned with the **incremental perceptron**, as described in § 11.3.2. At mention i, each hypothesis on the beam corresponds to a clustering of mentions $1 \ldots i-1$, or equivalently, a path through the Bell tree up to position $i-1$. As soon as none of the hypotheses on the beam are compatible with the gold coreference clustering, a perceptron update is made (Daumé III and Marcu, 2005). For concreteness, consider a linear cluster ranking model,

$$\psi_E(\{i : z_i = e\}) = \sum_{i:z_i=e} \boldsymbol{\theta} \cdot \boldsymbol{f}(i, \{j : j < i \wedge z_j = e\}), \qquad [15.15]$$

where the score for each cluster is computed as the sum of scores of all mentions that are linked into the cluster and $\boldsymbol{f}(i, \varnothing)$ is a set of features for the non anaphoric mention that initiates the cluster.

Using figure 15.4 as an example, suppose that the ground truth is

$$\boldsymbol{c}^* = \{\textit{Abigail, her}\}, \{\textit{she}\}, \qquad [15.16]$$

but with a beam of size one, the learner reaches the hypothesis,

$$\hat{\boldsymbol{c}} = \{\textit{Abigail, she}\}. \qquad [15.17]$$

This hypothesis is incompatible with $\boldsymbol{c}^*$, so an update is needed:

$$\boldsymbol{\theta} \leftarrow \boldsymbol{\theta} + \boldsymbol{f}(\boldsymbol{c}^*) - \boldsymbol{f}(\hat{\boldsymbol{c}}) \quad [15.18]$$

$$= \boldsymbol{\theta} + (\boldsymbol{f}(\textit{Abigail}, \varnothing) + \boldsymbol{f}(\textit{she}, \varnothing)) - (\boldsymbol{f}(\textit{Abigail}, \varnothing) + \boldsymbol{f}(\textit{she}, \{\textit{Abigail}\})) \quad [15.19]$$

$$= \boldsymbol{\theta} + \boldsymbol{f}(\textit{she}, \varnothing) - \boldsymbol{f}(\textit{she}, \{\textit{Abigail}\}). \quad [15.20]$$

This style of incremental update can also be applied to a margin loss between the gold clustering and the top clustering on the beam. By backpropagating from this loss, it is also possible to train a more complicated scoring function, such as a neural network in which the score for each entity is a function of embeddings for the entity mentions (Wiseman et al., 2015).

Reinforcement learning **Reinforcement learning** is a topic worthy of a textbook of its own (Sutton and Barto, 2019),[5] so this section will provide only a very brief overview, in the context of coreference resolution. A stochastic **policy** assigns a probability to each possible **action**, conditional on the context. The goal is to learn a policy that achieves a high expected reward, or, equivalently, a low expected cost.

In incremental cluster ranking, a complete clustering on M mentions can be produced by a sequence of M actions, in which the action z_i either merges mention i with an existing cluster or begins a new cluster. We can therefore create a stochastic policy using the cluster scores (Clark and Manning, 2016),

$$\Pr(z_i = e; \boldsymbol{\theta}) = \frac{\exp \psi_E(i \cup \{j : z_j = e\}; \boldsymbol{\theta})}{\sum_{e'} \exp \psi_E(i \cup \{j : z_j = e'\}'; \boldsymbol{\theta})}, \quad [15.21]$$

where $\psi_E(i \cup \{j : z_j = e\}; \boldsymbol{\theta})$ is the score under parameters $\boldsymbol{\theta}$ for assigning mention i to cluster e. This score can be an arbitrary function of the mention i, the cluster e and its (possibly empty) set of mentions; it can also include the history of actions taken thus far.

If a policy assigns probability $\mathrm{p}(\boldsymbol{c}; \boldsymbol{\theta})$ to clustering $\boldsymbol{c}$, then its expected loss is,

$$L(\boldsymbol{\theta}) = \sum_{\boldsymbol{c} \in \mathcal{C}(\boldsymbol{m})} \mathrm{p}_{\boldsymbol{\theta}}(\boldsymbol{c}) \times \ell(\boldsymbol{c}), \quad [15.22]$$

where $\mathcal{C}(\boldsymbol{m})$ is the set of possible clusterings for mentions $\boldsymbol{m}$. The loss $\ell(\boldsymbol{c})$ can be based on any arbitrary scoring function, including the complex evaluation metrics used in coreference resolution (see § 15.4). This is an advantage of reinforcement learning, which can be trained directly on the evaluation metric—unlike traditional supervised learning, which requires a loss function that is differentiable and decomposable across individual decisions.

Rather than summing over the exponentially many possible clusterings, we can approximate the expectation by sampling trajectories of actions, $\boldsymbol{z} = (z_1, z_2, \ldots, z_M)$, from the

5. Reinforcement learning has been used in spoken dialogue systems (Walker, 2000) and text-based game playing (Branavan et al., 2009a) and was applied to coreference resolution by Clark and Manning (2015).

current policy. Each action z_i corresponds to a step in the Bell tree: adding mention m_i to an existing cluster, or forming a new cluster. Each trajectory z corresponds to a single clustering $\boldsymbol{c}$, and so we can write the loss of an action sequence as $\ell(\boldsymbol{c}(z))$. The **policy gradient** algorithm computes the gradient of the expected loss as an expectation over trajectories (Sutton et al., 2000),

$$\frac{\partial}{\partial \boldsymbol{\theta}} L(\boldsymbol{\theta}) = E_{z \sim \mathcal{Z}(\boldsymbol{m})} \ell(\boldsymbol{c}(z)) \sum_{i=1}^{M} \frac{\partial}{\partial \boldsymbol{\theta}} \log \mathrm{p}(z_i \mid z_{1:i-1}, \boldsymbol{m}) \qquad [15.23]$$

$$\approx \frac{1}{K} \sum_{k=1}^{K} \ell(\boldsymbol{c}(z^{(k)})) \sum_{i=1}^{M} \frac{\partial}{\partial \boldsymbol{\theta}} \log \mathrm{p}(z_i^{(k)} \mid z_{1:i-1}^{(k)}, \boldsymbol{m}), \qquad [15.24]$$

where each action sequence $z^{(k)}$ is sampled from the current policy. Unlike the incremental perceptron, an update is not made until the complete action sequence is available.

Learning to search Policy gradient can suffer from high variance: while the average loss over K samples is asymptotically equal to the expected reward of a given policy, this estimate may not be accurate unless K is very large. This can make it difficult to allocate credit and blame to individual actions. In **learning to search**, this problem is addressed through the addition of an **oracle** policy, which is known to receive zero or small loss. The oracle policy can be used in two ways:

- The oracle can be used to generate partial hypotheses that are likely to score well, by generating i actions from the initial state. These partial hypotheses are then used as starting points for the learned policy. This is known as **roll-in**.
- The oracle can be used to compute the minimum possible loss from a given state, by generating $M - i$ actions from the current state until completion. This is known as **roll-out**.

The oracle can be combined with the existing policy during both roll-in and roll-out, sampling actions from each policy (Daumé III et al., 2009). One approach is to gradually decrease the number of actions drawn from the oracle over the course of learning (Ross et al., 2011).

In the context of entity-based coreference resolution, Clark and Manning (2016) use the learned policy for roll-in and the oracle policy for roll-out. Algorithm 17 shows how the gradients on the policy weights are computed in this case. In this application, the oracle is "noisy," because it selects the action that minimizes only the *local* loss—the accuracy of the coreference clustering up to mention i—rather than identifying the action sequence that will lead to the best final coreference clustering on the entire document. When learning from noisy oracles, it can be helpful to mix in actions from the current policy with the oracle during roll-out (Chang et al., 2015).

Algorithm 17
Learning to search for entity-based coreference resolution.

---

procedure COMPUTE-GRADIENT(mentions $\boldsymbol{m}$, loss function ℓ, parameters $\boldsymbol{\theta}$)
  $L(\boldsymbol{\theta}) \leftarrow 0$
  $z \sim \mathrm{p}(z \mid \boldsymbol{m}; \boldsymbol{\theta})$ ▷ Sample a trajectory from the current policy
  for $i \in \{1, 2, \ldots M\}$ **do**
    for action $z \in \mathcal{Z}(z_{1:i-1}, \boldsymbol{m})$ **do** ▷ All possible actions after history $z_{1:i-1}$
      $\boldsymbol{h} \leftarrow z_{1:i-1} \oplus z$ ▷ Concatenate history $z_{1:i-1}$ with action z
      for $j \in \{i+1, i+2, \ldots, M\}$ **do** ▷ Roll-out
        $h_j \leftarrow \mathrm{argmin}_h \, \ell(\boldsymbol{h}_{1:j-1} \oplus h)$ ▷ Oracle selects action with minimum loss
      $L(\boldsymbol{\theta}) \leftarrow L(\boldsymbol{\theta}) + \mathrm{p}(z \mid z_{1:i-1}, \boldsymbol{m}; \boldsymbol{\theta}) \times \ell(\boldsymbol{h})$ ▷ Update expected loss
  return $\frac{\partial}{\partial \boldsymbol{\theta}} L(\boldsymbol{\theta})$

15.3 Representations for Coreference Resolution

Historically, coreference resolution has employed an array of hand-engineered features to capture the linguistic constraints and preferences described in § 15.1 (Soon et al., 2001). Later work has documented the utility of lexical and bilexical features on mention pairs (Björkelund and Nugues, 2011; Durrett and Klein, 2013). The most recent and successful methods replace many (but not all) of these features with distributed representations of mentions and entities (Wiseman et al., 2015; Clark and Manning, 2016; Lee et al., 2017).

15.3.1 Features

Coreference features generally rely on a preprocessing pipeline to provide part-of-speech tags and phrase structure parses. This pipeline makes it possible to design features that capture many of the phenomena from § 15.1 and is also necessary for typical approaches to mention identification. However, the pipeline may introduce errors that propagate to the downstream coreference clustering system. Furthermore, the existence of such a pipeline presupposes resources such as treebanks, which do not exist for many languages.[6]

Mention features Features of individual mentions can help to predict anaphoricity. In systems where mention detection is performed jointly with coreference resolution, these features can also predict whether a span of text is likely to be a mention. For mention i, typical features include:

6. The Universal Dependencies project has produced dependency treebanks for more than 60 languages. However, coreference features and mention detection are generally based on phrase structure trees, which exist for roughly two dozen languages. A list is available here: https://en.wikipedia.org/wiki/Treebank.

• **Mention type:** Each span can be identified as a pronoun, name, or nominal, using the part of speech of the head word of the mention: both the Penn Treebank and Universal Dependencies tagsets (§ 8.1.1) include tags for pronouns and proper nouns, and all other heads can be marked as nominals (Haghighi and Klein, 2009).

• **Mention width:** The number of tokens in a mention is a rough predictor of its anaphoricity, with longer mentions being less likely to refer back to previously defined entities.

• **Lexical features:** The first, last, and head words can help to predict anaphoricity; they are also useful in conjunction with features such as mention type and part of speech, providing a rough measure of agreement (Björkelund and Nugues, 2011). The number of lexical features can be very large, so it can be helpful to select only frequently occurring features (Durrett and Klein, 2013).

• **Morphosyntactic features:** These features include the part of speech, number, gender, and dependency ancestors.

The features for mention i and candidate antecedent a can be conjoined, producing joint features that can help to assess the compatibility of the two mentions. For example, Durrett and Klein (2013) conjoin each feature with the mention types of the anaphora and the antecedent. Coreference resolution corpora such as ACE and OntoNotes contain documents from various genres. By conjoining the genre with other features, it is possible to learn genre-specific feature weights.

Mention-pair features For any pair of mentions i and j, typical features include:

• **Distance:** The number of intervening tokens, mentions, and sentences between i and j can all be used as distance features. These distances can be computed on the surface text, or on a transformed representation reflecting the breadth-first tree traversal (figure 15.3). Rather than using the distances directly, they are typically binned, creating binary features.

• **String match:** A variety of string match features can be employed: exact match, suffix match, head match, and more complex matching rules that disregard irrelevant modifiers (Soon et al., 2001).

• **Compatibility:** Building on the model, features can measure the anaphor and antecedent agree with respect to morphosyntactic attributes such as gender, number, and animacy.

• **Nesting:** If one mention is nested inside another (e.g., *[The President of [France]]*), they generally cannot corefer.

• **Same speaker:** For documents with quotations, such as news articles, personal pronouns can be resolved only by determining the speaker for each mention (Lee et al., 2013). Coreference is also more likely between mentions from the same speaker.

- **Gazetteers:** These features indicate that the anaphor and candidate antecedent appear in a gazetteer of acronyms (e.g., *USA/United States*, *GATech/Georgia Tech*), demonyms (e.g., *Israel/Israeli*), or other aliases (e.g., *Knickerbockers/New York Knicks*).
- **Lexical semantics:** These features use a lexical resource such as WordNet to determine whether the head words of the mentions are related through synonymy, antonymy, and hypernymy (§ 4.2).
- **Dependency paths:** The dependency path between the anaphor and candidate antecedent can help to determine whether the pair can corefer, under the government and binding constraints described in § 15.1.1.

Comprehensive lists of mention-pair features are offered by Bengtson and Roth (2008) and Rahman and Ng (2011). Neural network approaches use far fewer mention-pair features: for example, Lee et al. (2017) include only speaker, genre, distance, and mention width features.

Semantics In many cases, coreference seems to require knowledge and semantic inferences, as in the running example, where we link *China* with a *country* and a *growth market*. Some of this information can be gleaned from WordNet, which defines a graph over **synsets** (see § 4.2). For example, one of the synsets of *China* is an instance of an `Asian_nation#1`, which in turn is a hyponym of `country#2`, a synset that includes *country*.[7] Such paths can be used to measure the similarity between concepts (Pedersen et al., 2004), and this similarity can be incorporated into coreference resolution as a feature (Ponzetto and Strube, 2006). Similar ideas can be applied to knowledge graphs induced from Wikipedia (Ponzetto and Strube, 2007). But while such approaches improve relatively simple classification-based systems, they have proven less useful when added to the current generation of techniques.[8] For example, Durrett and Klein (2013) employ a range of semantics-based features—WordNet synonymy and hypernymy relations on head words, named entity types (e.g., person, organization), and unsupervised clustering over nominal heads—but find that these features give minimal improvement over a baseline system using surface features.

Entity features Many of the features for entity-mention coreference are generated by aggregating mention-pair features over all mentions in the candidate entity (Culotta et al., 2007; Rahman and Ng, 2011). Specifically, for each binary mention-pair feature $f(i,j)$, we compute the following entity-mention features for mention i and entity $e=\{j:j<i \wedge z_j=e\}$.

7. `Teletype font` is used to indicate WordNet synsets, and *italics* are used to indicate strings.

8. This point was made by Michael Strube at a 2015 workshop, noting that as the quality of the machine learning models in coreference has improved, the benefit of including features to capture semantics has become negligible.

- ALL-TRUE: Feature $f(i,j)$ holds for all mentions $j \in e$.
- MOST-TRUE: Feature $f(i,j)$ holds for at least half and fewer than all mentions $j \in e$.
- MOST-FALSE: Feature $f(i,j)$ holds for at least one and fewer than half of all mentions $j \in e$.
- NONE: Feature $f(i,j)$ does not hold for any mention $j \in e$.

For scalar mention-pair features (e.g., distance features), aggregation can be performed by computing the minimum, maximum, and median values across all mentions in the cluster. Additional entity-mention features include the number of mentions currently clustered in the entity, and ALL-X and MOST-X features for each mention type.

15.3.2 Distributed Representations of Mentions and Entities

Recent work has emphasized distributed representations of both mentions and entities. One potential advantage is that pretrained embeddings could help to capture the semantic compatibility underlying nominal coreference, helping with difficult cases like (*Apple*, *the firm*) and (*China*, *the firm's biggest growth market*). Furthermore, a distributed representation of entities can be trained to capture semantic features that are added by each mention.

Mention embeddings Entity mentions can be embedded into a vector space, providing the base layer for neural networks that score coreference decisions (Wiseman et al., 2015).

Constructing the mention embedding Various approaches for embedding multiword units can be applied (see § 14.8). Figure 15.5 shows a recurrent neural network approach, which begins by running a bidirectional LSTM over the entire text, obtaining hidden states from the left-to-right and right-to-left passes, $\boldsymbol{h}_m = [\overleftarrow{\boldsymbol{h}}_m; \overrightarrow{\boldsymbol{h}}_m]$. Each candidate mention span (s, t) is then represented by the vertical concatenation of four vectors:

$$\boldsymbol{u}^{(s,t)} = [\boldsymbol{u}^{(s,t)}_{\text{first}}; \boldsymbol{u}^{(s,t)}_{\text{last}}; \boldsymbol{u}^{(s,t)}_{\text{head}}; \phi^{(s,t)}], \tag{15.25}$$

where $\boldsymbol{u}^{(s,t)}_{\text{first}} = \boldsymbol{h}_{s+1}$ is the embedding of the first word in the span, $\boldsymbol{u}^{(s,t)}_{\text{last}} = \boldsymbol{h}_t$ is the embedding of the last word, $\boldsymbol{u}^{(s,t)}_{\text{head}}$ is the embedding of the "head" word, and $\phi^{(s,t)}$ is a vector of surface features, such as the length of the span (Lee et al., 2017).

Attention over head words Rather than identifying the head word from the output of a parser, it can be computed from a neural **attention mechanism**:

$$\tilde{\alpha}_m = \boldsymbol{\theta}_\alpha \cdot \boldsymbol{h}_m \tag{15.26}$$

$$\boldsymbol{a}^{(s,t)} = \text{softmax}\left([\tilde{\alpha}_{s+1}, \tilde{\alpha}_{s+2}, \ldots, \tilde{\alpha}_t]\right) \tag{15.27}$$

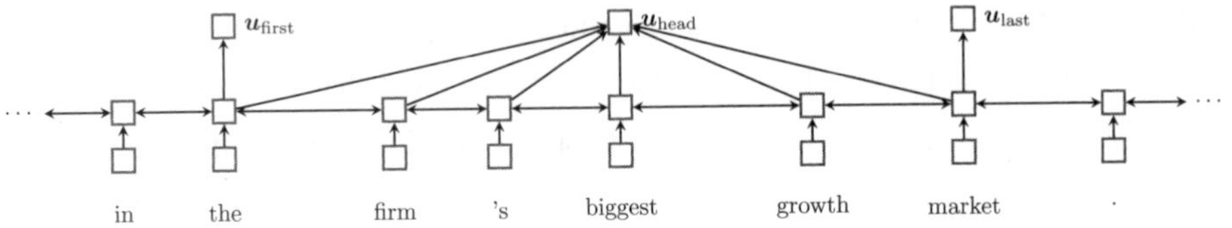

Figure 15.5
A bidirectional recurrent model of mention embeddings. The mention is represented by its first word, its last word, and an estimate of its head word, which is computed from a weighted average (Lee et al., 2017).

$$\boldsymbol{u}_{\text{head}}^{(s,t)} = \sum_{m=s+1}^{t} a_m^{(s,t)} \boldsymbol{h}_m. \qquad [15.28]$$

Each token m gets a scalar score $\tilde{\alpha}_m = \boldsymbol{\theta}_\alpha \cdot \boldsymbol{h}_m$, which is the dot product of the LSTM hidden state $\boldsymbol{h}_m$ and a vector of weights $\boldsymbol{\theta}_\alpha$. The vector of scores for tokens in the span $m \in \{s+1, s+2, \ldots, t\}$ is then passed through a softmax layer, yielding a vector $\boldsymbol{a}^{(s,t)}$ that allocates one unit of attention across the span. This eliminates the need for syntactic parsing to recover the head word; instead, the model learns to identify the most important words in each span. Attention mechanisms were introduced in neural machine translation (Bahdanau et al., 2014) and are described in more detail in § 18.3.1.

Using mention embeddings Given a set of mention embeddings, each mention i and candidate antecedent a is scored as

$$\psi(a,i) = \psi_S(a) + \psi_S(i) + \psi_M(a,i) \qquad [15.29]$$

$$\psi_S(a) = \text{FeedForward}_S(\boldsymbol{u}^{(a)}) \qquad [15.30]$$

$$\psi_S(i) = \text{FeedForward}_S(\boldsymbol{u}^{(i)}) \qquad [15.31]$$

$$\psi_M(a,i) = \text{FeedForward}_M([\boldsymbol{u}^{(a)}; \boldsymbol{u}^{(i)}; \boldsymbol{u}^{(a)} \odot \boldsymbol{u}^{(i)}; \boldsymbol{f}(a,i,\boldsymbol{w})]), \qquad [15.32]$$

where $\boldsymbol{u}^{(a)}$ and $\boldsymbol{u}^{(i)}$ are the embeddings for spans a and i, respectively, as defined in equation 15.25.

- The scores $\psi_S(a)$ quantify whether span a is likely to be a coreferring mention, independent of what it corefers with. This allows the model to learn to identify mentions directly, rather than identifying mentions with a preprocessing step.
- The score $\psi_M(a,i)$ computes the compatibility of spans a and i. Its base layer is a vector that includes the embeddings of spans a and i, their elementwise product $\boldsymbol{u}^{(a)} \odot \boldsymbol{u}^{(i)}$, and a vector of surface features $\boldsymbol{f}(a,i,\boldsymbol{w})$, including distance, speaker, and genre information.

Lee et al. (2017) provide an error analysis that shows how this method can correctly link *a blaze* and *a fire*, while incorrectly linking *pilots* and *fight attendants*. In each case, the coreference decision is based on similarities in the word embeddings.

Rather than embedding individual mentions, Clark and Manning (2016) embed mention pairs. At the base layer, their network takes embeddings of the words in and around each mention, as well as one-hot vectors representing a few surface features, such as the distance and string matching features. This base layer is then passed through a multilayer feedforward network with ReLU nonlinearities, resulting in a representation of the mention pair. The output of the mention pair encoder $\boldsymbol{u}_{i,j}$ is used in the scoring function of a mention-ranking model, $\psi_M(i,j) = \boldsymbol{\theta} \cdot \boldsymbol{u}_{i,j}$. A similar approach is used to score cluster pairs, constructing a cluster-pair encoding by **pooling** over the mention-pair encodings for all pairs of mentions within the two clusters.

Entity embeddings In entity-based coreference resolution, each entity should be represented by properties of its mentions. In a distributed setting, we maintain a set of vector entity embeddings, $\boldsymbol{v}_e$. Each candidate mention receives an embedding $\boldsymbol{u}_i$; Wiseman et al. (2016) compute this embedding by a single-layer neural network, applied to a vector of surface features. The decision of whether to merge mention i with entity e can then be driven by a feedforward network, $\psi_E(i, e) = \text{Feedforward}([\boldsymbol{v}_e; \boldsymbol{u}_i])$. If i is added to entity e, then its representation is updated recurrently, $\boldsymbol{v}_e \leftarrow f(\boldsymbol{v}_e, \boldsymbol{u}_i)$, using a recurrent neural network such as a long short-term memory (LSTM; chapter 6). Alternatively, we can apply a pooling operation, such as max pooling or average pooling (chapter 3), setting $\boldsymbol{v}_e \leftarrow \text{Pool}(\boldsymbol{v}_e, \boldsymbol{u}_i)$. In either case, the update to the representation of entity e can be thought of as adding new information about the entity from mention i.

15.4 Evaluating Coreference Resolution

The state of coreference evaluation is aggravatingly complex. Early attempts at simple evaluation metrics were found to be susceptible to trivial baselines, such as placing each mention in its own cluster, or grouping all mentions into a single cluster. Following Denis and Baldridge (2009), the CoNLL 2011 shared task on coreference (Pradhan et al., 2011) formalized the practice of averaging across three different metrics: MUC (Vilain et al., 1995), B-CUBED (Bagga and Baldwin, 1998a), and CEAF (Luo, 2005). Reference implementations of these metrics are available from Pradhan et al. (2014) at https://github.com/conll/reference-coreference-scorers.

Additional Resources

Ng (2010) surveys coreference resolution through 2010. Early work focused exclusively on pronoun resolution, with rule-based (Lappin and Leass, 1994) and probabilistic methods (Ge et al., 1998). The full coreference resolution problem was popularized in a shared task associated with the sixth Message Understanding Conference, which included coreference annotations for training and test sets of 30 documents each (Grishman and Sundheim, 1996). An influential early paper was the decision tree approach of Soon et al. (2001), who introduced mention ranking. A comprehensive list of surface features for coreference resolution is offered by Bengtson and Roth (2008). Durrett and Klein (2013) improved on prior work by introducing a large lexicalized feature set; subsequent work has emphasized neural representations of entities and mentions (Wiseman et al., 2015).

Exercises

1. Select an article from today's news, and annotate coreference for the first 20 noun phrases and possessive pronouns that appear in the article, include ones that are nested within larger noun phrases. Then specify the mention-pair training data that would result from the first five of these candidate entity mentions.
2. Using your annotations from the preceding problem, compute the following statistics:
   - The number of times new entities are introduced by each of the three types of referring expressions: pronouns, proper nouns, and nominals. Include "singleton" entities that are mentioned only once.
   - For each type of referring expression, compute the fraction of mentions that are anaphoric.
3. Apply a simple heuristic to all pronouns in the article from the previous exercise: link each pronoun to the closest preceding noun phrase that agrees in gender, number, animacy, and person. Compute the following evaluation:
   - True positive: a pronoun that is linked to a noun phrase with which it is coreferent or is labeled as the first mention of an entity when in fact it does not corefer with any preceding mention. In this case, nonreferential pronouns can be true positives if they are marked as having no antecedent.
   - False positive: a pronoun that is linked to a noun phrase with which it is not coreferent. This includes mistakenly linking singleton or nonreferential pronouns.
   - False negative: a pronoun that has at least one antecedent, but is either labeled as not having an antecednet, or is linked to mention with which it does not corefer.

   Compute the F-MEASURE for your method and for a trivial baseline in which every pronoun refers to the immediately preceding entity mention. Are there any additional heuristics that would have improved the performance of this method?
4. Durrett and Klein (2013) compute the probability of the gold coreference clustering by summing over all antecedent structures that are compatible with the clustering. For example, if there are three mentions of a single entity, m_1, m_2, m_3, there are two possible antecedent structures: $a_2 = 1, a_3 = 1$ and $a_2 = 1, a_3 = 2$. Compute the number of antecedent structures for a single entity with K mentions.
5. Suppose that all mentions can be unambiguously divided into C classes, for example by gender and number. Further suppose that mentions from different classes can never

corefer. In a document with M mentions, give upper and lower bounds on the total number of possible coreference clusterings, in terms of the Bell numbers and the parameters M and C. Compute numerical upper and lower bounds for the case $M = 4, C = 2$.

6. Lee et al. (2017) propose a model that considers all contiguous spans in a document as possible mentions.
   a) In a document of length M, how many mention pairs must be evaluated? (All answers can be given in asymptotic, big-O notation.)
   b) To make inference more efficient, Lee et al. (2017) restrict consideration to spans of maximum length $L \ll M$. Under this restriction, how many mention pairs must be evaluated?
   c) To further improve inference, one might evaluate coreference only between pairs of mentions whose endpoints are separated by a maximum of D tokens. Under this additional restriction, how many mention pairs must be evaluated?
7. In Spanish, the subject can be omitted when it is clear from context, for example,

   (15.13) *Las ballenas no son peces. Son mamíferos.*
   The whales no are fish. Are mammals.
   Whales are not fish. They are mammals.

   Resolution of such **null subjects** is facilitated by the Spanish system of verb morphology, which includes distinctive suffixes for most combinations of person and number. For example, the verb form *son* ('are') agrees with the third-person plural pronouns *ellos* (masculine) and *ellas* (feminine), as well as the second-person plural *ustedes*.

   Suppose that you are given the following components:

   - A system that automatically identifies verbs with null subjects.
   - A function $c(j,p) \in \{0, 1\}$ that indicates whether pronoun p is compatible with null subject j, according to the verb morphology.
   - A trained mention-pair model, which computes scores $\psi(w_i, w_j, j-i) \in \mathbb{R}$ for all pairs of mentions i and j, scoring the pair by the antecedent mention w_i, the anaphor w_j, and the distance $j-i$.

   Describe an integer linear program that simultaneously performs two tasks: resolving coreference among all entity mentions and identifying suitable pronouns for all null subjects. In the example above, your program should link the null subject with *las ballenas* ('whales') and identify *ellas* as the correct pronoun. For simplicity, you may assume that null subjects cannot be antecedents, and you need not worry about the transitivity constraint described in § 15.2.3.
8. Use the policy gradient algorithm to compute the gradient for the following scenario, based on the Bell tree in figure 15.4:

- The gold clustering $\boldsymbol{c}^*$ is $\{Abigail, her\}, \{she\}$.
- Drawing a single sequence of actions ($K = 1$) from the current policy, you obtain the following incremental clusterings:

$$\boldsymbol{c}(a_1) = \{Abigail\}$$

$$\boldsymbol{c}(\boldsymbol{a}_{1:2}) = \{Abigail,\ she\}$$

$$\boldsymbol{c}(\boldsymbol{a}_{1:3}) = \{Abigail,\ she\}, \{her\}.$$

- At each mention t, the space of actions $\mathcal{A}_t$ includes merging the mention with each existing cluster or with the empty cluster. The probability of merging m_t with cluster c is proportional to the exponentiated score for the merged cluster,

$$\text{p}(\text{Merge}(m_t, c))) \propto \exp \psi_E(m_t \cup c), \qquad [15.33]$$

where $\psi_E(m_t \cup c)$ is defined in equation 15.15.

Compute the gradient $\frac{\partial}{\partial \boldsymbol{\theta}} L(\boldsymbol{\theta})$ in terms of the loss $\ell(\boldsymbol{c}(\boldsymbol{a}))$ and the features of each (potential) cluster. Explain the differences between the gradient-based update $\boldsymbol{\theta} \leftarrow \boldsymbol{\theta} - \frac{\partial}{\partial \boldsymbol{\theta}} L(\boldsymbol{\theta})$ and the incremental perceptron update from this same example.

9. As discussed in § 15.1.1, some pronouns are not referential. In English, this occurs frequently with the word *it*. Download the text of *Alice in Wonderland* from NLTK, and examine the first 10 appearances of *it*. For each occurrence:

   - First, examine a five-token window around the word. In the first example, this window is as follows:

     ```
     , but it had no
     ```

     Is there another pronoun that could be substituted for *it*? Consider *she*, *they*, and *them*. In this case, both *she* and *they* yield grammatical substitutions. What about the other 10 appearances of *it*?
   - Now, view an 15-word window for each example. Based on this window, mark whether you think the word *it* is referential.

   How often does the substitution test predict whether *it* is referential?

10. Now try to automate the test, using the Google n-grams corpus (Brants and Franz, 2006). Specifically, find the count of each 5-gram containing *it*, and then compute the counts of 5-grams in which *it* is replaced with other third-person pronouns: *he*, *she*, *they*, *her*, *him*, *them*, *herself*, *himself*.

    There are various ways to get these counts. One approach is to download the raw data and search it; another is to construct web queries to https://books.google.com/ngrams.

    Compare the ratio of the counts of the original 5-gram to the summed counts of the 5-grams created by substitution. Is this ratio a good predictor of whether *it* is referential?

16 Discourse

Applications of natural language processing often concern multisentence documents: from paragraph-long restaurant reviews, to 500-word newspaper articles, to 500-page novels. Yet most of the methods that we have discussed thus far are concerned with individual sentences. This chapter discusses theories and methods for handling multisentence linguistic phenomena, known collectively as **discourse**. There are diverse characterizations of discourse structure, and no single structure is ideal for every computational application. This chapter covers some of the most well-studied discourse representations, while highlighting computational models for identifying and exploiting these structures.

16.1 Segments

A document or conversation can be viewed as a sequence of **segments**, each of which is **cohesive** in its content and/or function. In Wikipedia biographies, these segments often pertain to various aspects to the subject's life: early years, major events, impact on others, and so on. This segmentation is organized around **topics**. Alternatively, scientific research articles are often organized by **functional themes**: the introduction, a survey of previous research, experimental setup, and results.

Written texts often mark segments with section headers and related formatting devices. However, such formatting may be too coarse grained to support applications such as the retrieval of specific passages of text that are relevant to a query (Hearst, 1997). Unformatted speech transcripts, such as meetings and lectures, are also an application scenario for segmentation (Carletta, 2007; Glass et al., 2007; Janin et al., 2003).

16.1.1 Topic Segmentation

A cohesive topic segment forms a unified whole, using various linguistic devices: repeated references to an entity or event; the use of conjunctions to create links between related ideas; and the repetition of meaning through lexical choices (Halliday and Hasan, 1976). Each of these cohesive devices can be measured and then used as features for topic segmentation. A classical example is the use of lexical cohesion in the TEXTTILING method for topic

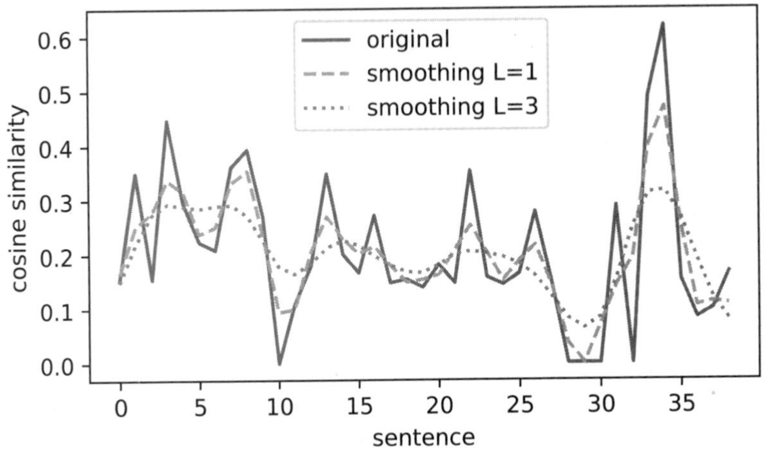

Figure 16.1
Smoothed cosine similarity among adjacent sentences in a news article. Local minima at $m=10$ and $m=29$ indicate likely segmentation points.

segmentation (Hearst, 1997). The basic idea is to compute the textual similarity between each pair of adjacent blocks of text (sentences or fixed-length units), using a formula such as the smoothed **cosine similarity** of their bag-of-words vectors,

$$s_m = \frac{\boldsymbol{x}_m \cdot \boldsymbol{x}_{m+1}}{||\boldsymbol{x}_m||_2 \times ||\boldsymbol{x}_{m+1}||_2} \tag{16.1}$$

$$\bar{s}_m = \sum_{\ell=0}^{L} k_\ell (s_{m+\ell} + s_{m-\ell}), \tag{16.2}$$

with k_ℓ representing the value of a smoothing kernel of size L, for example, $\boldsymbol{k} = [1, 0.5, 0.25]^\top$. Segmentation points are then identified at local minima in the smoothed similarities $\bar{s}$, because these points indicate changes in the overall distribution of words in the text. An example is shown in figure 16.1.

Text segmentation can also be formulated as a probabilistic model, in which each segment has a unique language model that defines the probability over the text in the segment (Utiyama and Isahara, 2001; Eisenstein and Barzilay, 2008; Du et al., 2013).[1] A good segmentation achieves high likelihood by grouping segments with similar word distributions. This probabilistic approach can be extended to **hierarchical topic segmentation**, in which each topic segment is divided into subsegments (Eisenstein, 2009). All of these

1. There is a rich literature on how latent variable models (such as **latent Dirichlet allocation**) can track topics across documents (Blei et al., 2003; Blei, 2012).

approaches are unsupervised. While labeled data can be obtained from well-formatted texts such as textbooks, such annotations may not generalize to speech transcripts in alternative domains. Supervised methods have been tried in cases where in-domain labeled data is available, substantially improving performance by learning weights on multiple types of features (Galley et al., 2003).

16.1.2 Functional Segmentation

In some genres, there is a canonical set of communicative *functions*: for example, in scientific research articles, one such function is to communicate the general background for the article, another is to introduce a new contribution, or to describe the aim of the research (Teufel et al., 1999). A **functional segmentation** divides the document into contiguous segments, sometimes called **rhetorical zones**, in which each sentence has the same function. Teufel and Moens (2002) train a supervised classifier to identify the function of each sentence in a set of scientific research articles, using features that describe the sentence's position in the text, its similarity to the rest of the article and title, tense and voice of the main verb, and the functional role of the previous sentence. Functional segmentation can also be performed without supervision. Noting that some types of Wikipedia articles have very consistent functional segmentations (e.g., articles about cities or chemical elements), Chen et al. (2009) introduce an unsupervised model for functional segmentation, which learns both the language model associated with each function and the typical patterning of functional segments across the article.

16.2 Entities and Reference

Another dimension of discourse relates to which entities are mentioned throughout the text, and how. Consider the examples in figure 16.2: Grosz et al. (1995) argue that the first discourse is more coherent. Do you agree? The examples differ in their choice of **referring**

(16.1) a. John went to his favorite music store to buy a piano.
b. He had frequented the store for many years.
c. He was excited that he could finally buy a piano.
d. He arrived just as the store was closing for the day.

(16.2) a. John went to his favorite music store to buy a piano.
b. It was a store John had frequented for many years.
c. He was excited that he could finally buy a piano.
d. It was closing just as John arrived.

Figure 16.2
Two tellings of the same story (Grosz et al., 1995). The discourse on the left uses referring expressions coherently, while the one on the right does not.

expressions for the protagonist *John* and in the syntactic constructions in sentences (b) and (d). The examples demonstrate the need for theoretical models to explain how referring expressions are chosen and where they are placed within sentences. Such models can then be used to help interpret the overall structure of the discourse, to measure discourse coherence, and to generate discourses in which referring expressions are used coherently.

16.2.1 Centering Theory

Centering theory presents a unified account of the relationship between discourse structure and entity reference (Grosz et al., 1995). According to the theory, every utterance in the discourse is characterized by a set of entities, known as *centers*.

- The **forward-looking centers** in utterance m are all the entities that are mentioned in the utterance, $c_f(\boldsymbol{w}_m) = \{e_1, e_2, \ldots,\}$. The forward-looking centers are partially ordered by their syntactic prominence, favoring subjects over objects, and objects over other positions (Brennan et al., 1987). For example, in example (16.1a), the ordered list of forward-looking centers in the first utterance is John, the music store, and the piano.
- The **backward-looking center** $c_b(\boldsymbol{w}_m)$ is the highest-ranked element in the set of forward-looking centers from the previous utterance $c_f(\boldsymbol{w}_{m-1})$ that is also mentioned in $\boldsymbol{w}_m$. In example (16.1b), the backward-looking center is John.

Given these two definitions, centering theory makes the following predictions about the form and position of referring expressions:

1. If a pronoun appears in the utterance $\boldsymbol{w}_m$, then the backward-looking center $c_b(\boldsymbol{w}_m)$ must also be realized as a pronoun. This rule argues against the use of *it* to refer to the piano store in example (16.2d), because JOHN is the backward-looking center of (16.2d), and he is mentioned by name and not by a pronoun.
2. Sequences of utterances should retain the same backward-looking center if possible, and ideally, the backward-looking center should also be the top-ranked element in the list of forward-looking centers. This rule argues in favor of the preservation of JOHN as the backward-looking center throughout example (16.1).

Centering theory unifies aspects of syntax, discourse, and anaphora resolution. However, it can be difficult to clarify exactly how to rank the elements of each utterance or even how to partition a text or dialog into utterances (Poesio et al., 2004).

16.2.2 The Entity Grid

One way to formalize the ideas of centering theory is to arrange the entities in a text or conversation in an **entity grid**. This is a data structure with one row per sentence and one column per entity (Barzilay and Lapata, 2008). Each cell $c(m, i)$ can take the following values:

	SKYLER	WALTER	DANGER	A GUY	THE DOOR
You don't know who you're talking to,	S	-	-	-	-
so let me clue you in.	O	O	-	-	-
I am not in danger, Skyler.	X	S	X	-	-
I am the danger.	-	S	O	-	-
A guy opens his door and gets shot,	-	-	-	S	O
and you think that of me?	S	X	-	-	-
No. I am the one who knocks!	-	S	-	-	-

Figure 16.3
The entity grid representation for a dialogue from the television show *Breaking Bad*.

$$c(m,i) = \begin{cases} S, & \text{entity } i \text{ is in subject position in sentence } m \\ O, & \text{entity } i \text{ is in object position in sentence } m \\ X, & \text{entity } i \text{ appears in sentence } m, \text{ in neither subject nor object position} \\ -, & \text{entity } i \text{ does not appear in sentence } m. \end{cases} \quad [16.3]$$

To populate the entity grid, syntactic parsing is applied to identify subject and object positions, and coreference resolution is applied to link multiple mentions of a single entity. An example is shown in figure 16.3.

After the grid is constructed, the coherence of a document can be measured by the *transitions* between adjacent cells in each column. For example, the transition $(S \rightarrow S)$ keeps an entity in subject position across adjacent sentences; the transition $(O \rightarrow S)$ promotes an entity from object position to subject position; and the transition $(S \rightarrow -)$ drops the subject of one sentence from the next sentence. The probabilities of each transition can be estimated from labeled data, and an entity grid can then be scored by the sum of the log-probabilities across all columns and all transitions, $\sum_{i=1}^{N_e} \sum_{m=1}^{M} \log p(c(m,i) \mid c(m-1,i))$. The resulting probability can be used as a proxy for the coherence of a text. This has been shown to be useful for a range of tasks: determining which of a pair of articles is more readable (Schwarm and Ostendorf, 2005), correctly ordering the sentences in a scrambled text (Lapata, 2003), and disentangling multiple conversational threads in an online multiparty chat (Elsner and Charniak, 2010).

16.2.3 *Formal Semantics Beyond the Sentence Level

An alternative view of the role of entities in discourse focuses on formal semantics and the construction of meaning representations for multisentence units. Consider the following two sentences (from Bird et al., 2009):

(16.3) a. Angus owns a dog.
b. It bit Irene.

We would like to recover the formal semantic representation,

$$\exists x.\text{DOG}(x) \wedge \text{OWN}(\text{ANGUS}, x) \wedge \text{BITE}(x, \text{IRENE}). \quad [16.4]$$

However, the semantic representations of each individual sentence are

$$\exists x.\text{DOG}(x) \wedge \text{OWN}(\text{ANGUS}, x) \quad [16.5]$$

$$\text{BITE}(y, \text{IRENE}). \quad [16.6]$$

Unifying these two representations into the form of equation 16.4 requires linking the unbound variable y from [16.6] with the quantified variable x in [16.5].[2] Discourse understanding therefore requires the reader to update a set of assignments, from variables to entities. This update would (presumably) link the *dog* in the first sentence of [16.3] with the unbound variable y in the second sentence, thereby licensing the conjunction in [16.4].[3] This basic idea is at the root of **dynamic semantics** (Groenendijk and Stokhof, 1991). **Segmented discourse representation theory** links dynamic semantics with a set of **discourse relations**, which explain how adjacent units of text are rhetorically or conceptually related (Lascarides and Asher, 2007). The next section explores the theory of discourse relations in more detail.

16.3 Relations

In dependency grammar, sentences are characterized by a graph (usually a tree) of syntactic relations between words, such as NSUBJ and DET. A similar idea can be applied at the document level, identifying relations between discourse units, such as clauses, sentences, or paragraphs. The task of **discourse parsing** involves identifying discourse units and the relations that hold between them. These relations can then be applied to tasks such as document classification and summarization, as discussed in § 16.3.4.

16.3.1 Shallow Discourse Relations

The existence of discourse relations is hinted by **discourse connectives**, such as *however*, *moreover*, *meanwhile*, and *if … then*. These connectives explicitly specify the relationship between adjacent units of text: *however* signals a contrastive relationship, *moreover* signals that the subsequent text elaborates or strengthens the point that was made immediately beforehand, *meanwhile* indicates that two events are contemporaneous, and *if … then* sets

2. Groenendijk and Stokhof (1991) treats the y variable in equation 16.6 as unbound. Even if it were bound locally with an existential quantifier ($\exists y \text{BITE}(y, \text{IRENE})$), the variable would still need to be reconciled with the quantified variable in equation 16.5.

3. This linking task is similar to coreference resolution (see chapter 15), but here the connections are between semantic variables, rather than spans of text.

Table 16.1
The hierarchy of discourse relation in the Penn Discourse Treebank annotations Prasad et al., 2008. For example, PRECEDENCE is a subtype of SYNCHRONOUS, which is a type of TEMPORAL relation.

- TEMPORAL
  - Asynchronous
  - Synchronous: precedence, succession
- CONTINGENCY
  - Cause: result, reason
  - Pragmatic cause: justification
  - Condition: hypothetical, general, unreal present, unreal past, real present, real past
  - Pragmatic condition: relevance, implicit assertion
- COMPARISON
  - Contrast: juxtaposition, opposition
  - Pragmatic contrast
  - Concession: expectation, contra-expectation
  - Pragmatic concession
- EXPANSION
  - Conjunction
  - Instantiation
  - Restatement: specification, equivalence, generalization
  - Alternative: conjunctive, disjunctive, chosen alternative
  - Exception
  - List

up a conditional relationship. Discourse connectives can therefore be viewed as a starting point for the analysis of discourse relations.

In **lexicalized tree-adjoining grammar for discourse (D-LTAG)**, each connective anchors a relationship between two units of text (Webber, 2004). This model provides the theoretical basis for the **Penn Discourse Treebank (PDTB)**, the largest corpus of discourse relations in English (Prasad et al., 2008). It includes a hierarchical inventory of discourse relations (shown in table 16.1), which is created by abstracting the meanings implied by the discourse connectives that appear in real texts (Knott, 1996). These relations are then annotated on the same corpus of news text used in the Penn Treebank (see § 9.2.2), adding the following information:

- Each connective is annotated for the discourse relation or relations that it expresses, if any—many discourse connectives have senses in which they do not signal a discourse relation (Pitler and Nenkova, 2009).
- For each discourse relation, the two arguments of the relation are specified as ARG1 and ARG2, where ARG2 is constrained to be adjacent to the connective. These arguments may be sentences, but they may also smaller or larger units of text.
- Adjacent sentences are annotated for **implicit discourse relations**, which are not marked by any connective. When a connective could be inserted between a pair of sentence, the annotator supplies it and also labels its sense (e.g., example 16.5). In some cases, there is no relationship at all between a pair of adjacent sentences; in other cases, the only relation is that the adjacent sentences mention one or more shared entity. These phenomena are annotated as NOREL and ENTREL (entity relation), respectively.

(16.4) *... as this business of whaling has somehow come to be regarded among landsmen as a rather unpoetical and disreputable pursuit*; therefore, **I am all anxiety to convince ye, ye landsmen, of the injustice hereby done to us hunters of whales.**

(16.5) But a few funds have taken other defensive steps. *Some have raised their cash positions to record levels.* Implicit = BECAUSE **High cash positions help buffer a fund when the market falls.**

(16.6) Michelle lives in a hotel room, and although **she drives a canary-colored Porsche,** *she hasn't time to clean or repair it.*

(16.7) *Most oil companies,* when **they set exploration and production budgets for this year,** *forecast revenue of $15 for each barrel of crude produced.*

Figure 16.4
Example annotations of discourse relations. In the style of the Penn Discourse Treebank, the discourse connective is underlined, the first argument is shown in italics, and the second argument is shown in bold. Examples (16.5-16.7) are quoted from Prasad et al. (2008).

Examples of Penn Discourse Treebank annotations are shown in Figure 16.4. In (16.4), the word *therefore* acts as an explicit discourse connective, linking the two adjacent units of text. The Treebank annotations also specify the "sense" of each relation, linking the connective to a relation in the sense inventory shown in table 16.1: in (16.4), the relation is PRAGMATIC CAUSE:JUSTIFICATION because it relates to the author's communicative intentions. The word *therefore* can also signal causes in the external world (e.g., *He was therefore forced to relinquish his plan*). In **discourse sense classification**, the goal is to determine which discourse relation, if any, is expressed by each connective. A related task is the classification of implicit discourse relations, as in (16.5). In this example, the relationship between the adjacent sentences could be expressed by the connective *because*, indicating a CAUSE:REASON relationship.

Classifying explicit discourse relations and their arguments As suggested by the examples above, many connectives can be used to invoke multiple types of discourse relations. Similarly, some connectives have senses that are unrelated to discourse: for example, *and* functions as a discourse connective when it links propositions, but not when it links noun phrases (Lin et al., 2014). Nonetheless, the senses of explicitly marked discourse relations in the Penn Treebank are relatively easy to classify, at least at the coarse-grained level. When classifying the four top-level PDTB relations, 90% accuracy can be obtained simply by selecting the most common relation for each connective (Pitler and Nenkova, 2009). At the more fine-grained levels of the discourse relation hierarchy, connectives are more ambiguous. This fact is reflected both in the accuracy of automatic sense classification (Versley, 2011) and in interannotator agreement, which falls to 80% for level-3 discourse relations (Prasad et al., 2008).

A more challenging task for explicitly marked discourse relations is to identify the scope of the arguments. Discourse connectives need not be adjacent to ARG1, as shown in example (16.6), where ARG1 follows ARG2; furthermore, the arguments need not be contiguous, as shown in (16.7). For these reasons, recovering the arguments of each discourse connective is a challenging subtask. Because intrasentential arguments are often syntactic constituents (see chapter 10), many approaches train a classifier to predict whether each constituent is an appropriate argument for each explicit discourse connective (Lin et al., 2014).

Classifying implicit discourse relations Implicit discourse relations are considerably more difficult to classify and to annotate.[4] Most approaches are based on an encoding of each argument, which is then used as input to a nonlinear classifier:

$$z^{(i)} = \text{Encode}(\boldsymbol{w}^{(i)}) \qquad [16.7]$$

$$z^{(i+1)} = \text{Encode}(\boldsymbol{w}^{(i+1)}) \qquad [16.8]$$

$$\hat{y}_i = \underset{y}{\text{argmax}}\, \Psi(y, z^{(i)}, z^{(i+1)}). \qquad [16.9]$$

This basic framework can be instantiated in several ways, including both feature-based and neural encoders.

Feature-based approaches Each argument can be encoded into a vector of surface features. The encoding typically includes lexical features (all words, or all content words, or a subset of words such as the first three and the main verb), Brown clusters of individual words (§ 14.4), and syntactic features such as terminal productions and dependency arcs (Pitler et al., 2009; Lin et al., 2009; Rutherford and Xue, 2014). The classification function then has two parts. First, it creates a joint feature vector by combining the encodings of each argument, typically by computing the cross-product of all features in each encoding:

$$\boldsymbol{f}(y, z^{(i)}, z^{(i+1)}) = \{(a \times b \times y) : (z_a^{(i)} z_b^{(i+1)})\}. \qquad [16.10]$$

The size of this feature set grows with the square of the size of the vocabulary, so it can be helpful to select a subset of features that are especially useful on the training data (Park and Cardie, 2012). After $\boldsymbol{f}$ is computed, any classifier can be trained to compute the final score, $\Psi(y, z^{(i)}, z^{(i+1)}) = \boldsymbol{\theta} \cdot \boldsymbol{f}(y, z^{(i)}, z^{(i+1)})$.

Neural network approaches In neural network architectures, the encoder is learned jointly with the classifier as an end-to-end model. Each argument can be encoded using a variety of neural architectures (surveyed in § 14.8): recursive (§ 10.6.1; Ji and Eisenstein, 2015),

4. In the dataset for the 2015 shared task on shallow discourse parsing, the interannotator agreement was 91% for explicit discourse relations and 81% for implicit relations, across all levels of detail (Xue et al., 2015).

recurrent (§ 6.3; Ji et al., 2016), and convolutional (§ 3.4; Qin et al., 2017). The classification function can then be implemented as a feedforward neural network on the two encodings (chapter 3; for examples, see Qin et al., 2017; Rutherford et al., 2017), or as a simple bilinear product, $\Psi(y, z^{(i)}, z^{(i+1)}) = (z^{(i)})^\top \Theta_y z^{(i+1)}$ (Ji and Eisenstein, 2015). The encoding model can be trained by backpropagation from the classification objective, such as the margin loss. Rutherford et al. (2017) show that neural architectures outperform feature-based approaches in most settings. While neural approaches require engineering the network architecture (e.g., embedding size, number of hidden units in the classifier), feature-based approaches also require significant engineering to incorporate linguistic resources such as Brown clusters and parse trees and to select a subset of relevant features.

16.3.2 Hierarchical Discourse Relations

In sentence parsing, adjacent phrases combine into larger constituents, ultimately producing a single constituent for the entire sentence. The resulting tree structure enables structured analysis of the sentence, with subtrees that represent syntactically coherent chunks of meaning. **Rhetorical Structure Theory (RST)** extends this style of hierarchical analysis to the discourse level (Mann and Thompson, 1988).

The basic element of RST is the **discourse unit**, which refers to a contiguous span of text. **Elementary discourse units (EDUs)** are the atomic elements in this framework and are typically (but not always) clauses.[5] Each discourse relation combines two or more adjacent discourse units into a larger, composite discourse unit; this process ultimately unites the entire text into a tree-like structure.[6]

Nuclearity In many discourse relations, one argument is primary. For example,

(16.8) [LaShawn loves animals]$_N$
[She has nine dogs and one pig]$_S$.

In this example, the second sentence provides EVIDENCE for the point made in the first sentence. The first sentence is thus the **nucleus** of the discourse relation, and the second sentence is the **satellite**. The notion of nuclearity is similar to the head-modifier structure of dependency parsing (see § 11.1.1). However, in RST, some relations have multiple nuclei. For example, the arguments of the CONTRAST relation are equally important:

5. Details of discourse segmentation can be found in the RST annotation manual (Carlson and Marcu, 2001).

6. While RST analyses are typically trees, this should not be taken as a strong theoretical commitment to the principle that all coherent discourses have a tree structure. Taboada and Mann (2006) write:

> It is simply the case that trees are convenient, easy to represent, and easy to understand. There is, on the other hand, no theoretical reason to assume that trees are the only possible representation of discourse structure and of coherence relations.

The appropriateness of tree structures to discourse has been challenged, for example, by Wolf and Gibson (2005), who propose a more general graph-structured representation.

(16.9) [The clash of ideologies survives this treatment]$_N$
[but the nuance and richness of Gorky's individual characters have vanished in the scuffle]$_N$[7]

Relations that have multiple nuclei are called **coordinating**; relations with a single nucleus are called **subordinating**. Subordinating relations are constrained to have only two arguments, while coordinating relations (such as CONJUNCTION) may have more than two.

RST relations Rhetorical structure theory features a large inventory of discourse relations, which are divided into two high-level groups: subject matter relations and presentational relations. Presentational relations are organized around the intended beliefs of the reader. For example, in (16.8), the second discourse unit provides evidence intended to increase the reader's belief in the proposition expressed by the first discourse unit, that *LaShawn loves animals*. In contrast, subject-matter relations are meant to communicate additional facts about the propositions contained in the discourse units that they relate:

(16.10) [the debt plan was rushed to completion]$_N$
[in order to be announced at the meeting]$_S$[8]

In this example, the satellite describes a world state that is realized by the action described in the nucleus. This relationship is about the world, and not about the author's communicative intentions.

Example Figure 16.5 depicts an RST analysis of a paragraph from a movie review. Asymmetric (subordinating) relations are depicted with an arrow from the satellite to the nucleus; symmetric (coordinating) relations are depicted with lines. The elementary discourse units 1F and 1G are combined into a larger discourse unit with the symmetric CONJUNCTION relation. The resulting discourse unit is then the satellite in a JUSTIFY relation with 1E.

Hierarchical discourse parsing The goal of discourse parsing is to recover a hierarchical structural analysis from a document text, such as the analysis in figure 16.5. For now, let's assume a segmentation of the document into elementary discourse units (EDUs); segmentation algorithms are discussed below. After segmentation, discourse parsing can be viewed as a combination of two components: the discourse relation classification techniques discussed in § 16.3.1 and algorithms for phrase-structure parsing, such as chart parsing and shift-reduce, which were discussed in chapter 10.

Both chart parsing and shift-reduce require encoding composite discourse units, either in a discrete feature vector or a dense neural representation.[9] Some discourse parsers rely on

7. From the RST Treebank (Carlson et al., 2002).

8. From the RST Treebank (Carlson et al., 2002).

9. To use these algorithms, it is also necessary to binarize all discourse relations during parsing and then to "unbinarize" them to reconstruct the desired structure (e.g., Hernault et al., 2010).

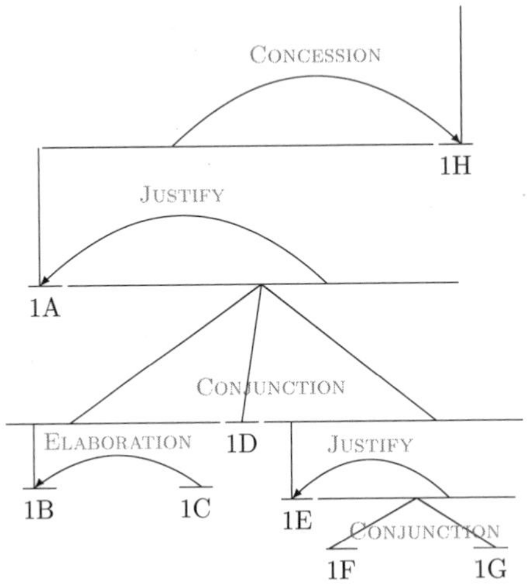

[It could have been a great movie]^{1A} [It does have beautiful scenery,]^{1B} [some of the best since Lord of the Rings.]^{1C} [The acting is well done,]^{1D} [and I really liked the son of the leader of the Samurai.]^{1E} [He was a likable chap,]^{1F} [and I hated to see him die.]^{1G} [But, other than all that, this movie is nothing more than hidden rip-offs.]^{1H}

Figure 16.5
A rhetorical structure theory analysis of a short movie review, adapted from Voll and Taboada (2007). Positive and negative sentiment words are underlined, indicating RST's potential utility in document-level sentiment analysis.

the **strong compositionality criterion** (Marcu, 1996), which states the assumption that a composite discourse unit can be represented by its nucleus. This criterion is used in feature-based discourse parsing to determine the feature vector for a composite discourse unit (Hernault et al., 2010); it is used in neural approaches to setting the vector encoding for a composite discourse unit equal to the encoding of its nucleus (Ji and Eisenstein, 2014). An alternative neural approach is to learn a composition function over the components of a composite discourse unit (Li et al., 2014), using a recursive neural network (see § 14.8.3).

Bottom-up discourse parsing Assume a segmentation of the text into N elementary discourse units with base representations $\{z^{(i)}\}_{i=1}^{N}$, and assume a composition function $\textsc{Compose}\left(z^{(i)}, z^{(j)}, \ell\right)$, which maps two encodings and a discourse relation ℓ into a new encoding. The composition function can follow the strong compositionality criterion and simply select the encoding of the nucleus, or it can do something more complex. We also need a scoring function $\Psi(z^{(i,k)}, z^{(k,j)}, \ell)$, which computes a scalar score for the (binarized) discourse relation ℓ with left child covering the span $i+1:k$ and the right child covering the span $k+1:j$. Given these components, we can construct vector representations for each span, and this is the basic idea underlying **compositional vector grammars** (Socher et al., 2013a).

These same components can also be used in bottom-up parsing, in a manner that is similar to the CKY algorithm for weighted context-free grammars (see § 10.1): compute the score and best analysis for each possible span of increasing lengths, while storing back-pointers that make it possible to recover the optimal parse of the entire input. However, there is an important distinction from CKY parsing: for each labeled span (i,j,ℓ), we must use the composition function to construct a representation $z^{(i,j,\ell)}$. This representation is then used to combine the discourse unit spanning $i+1:j$ in higher-level discourse relations. The representation $z^{(i,j,\ell)}$ depends on the entire substructure of the unit spanning $i+1:j$, and this violates the locality assumption that underlie CKY's optimality guarantee. Bottom-up parsing with recursively constructed span representations is generally not guaranteed to find the best-scoring discourse parse. This problem is explored in an exercise at the end of the chapter.

Transition-based discourse parsing One drawback of bottom-up parsing is its cubic time complexity in the length of the input. For long documents, transition-based parsing is an appealing alternative. The shift-reduce algorithm (see § 10.6.2) can be applied to discourse parsing fairly directly (Sagae, 2009): the stack stores a set of discourse units and their representations, and each action is chosen by a function of these representations. This function could be a linear product of weights and features, or it could be a neural network applied to encodings of the discourse units. The REDUCE action then performs composition on the two discourse units at the top of the stack, yielding a larger composite discourse unit, which goes on top of the stack. All of the techniques for integrating learning and transition-based parsing, described in § 11.3, are applicable to discourse parsing.

Segmenting discourse units In rhetorical structure theory, elementary discourse units do not cross the sentence boundary, so discourse segmentation can be performed within sentences, assuming the sentence segmentation is given. The segmentation of sentences into elementary discourse units is typically performed using features of the syntactic analysis (Braud et al., 2017). One approach is to train a classifier to determine whether each syntactic constituent is an EDU, using features such as the production, tree structure, and head words (Soricut and Marcu, 2003; Hernault et al., 2010). Another approach is to train a sequence labeling model, such as a conditional random field (Sporleder and Lapata, 2005; Xuan Bach et al., 2012; Feng et al., 2014). This is done using the BIO formalism for segmentation by sequence labeling, described in § 8.3.

16.3.3 Argumentation

An alternative view of text-level relational structure focuses on **argumentation** (Stab and Gurevych, 2014b). Each segment (typically a sentence or clause) may support or rebut another segment, creating a graph structure over the text. In the following example (from Peldszus and Stede, 2013), segment $S2$ provides argumentative support for the proposition in the segment $S1$:

(16.11) [We should tear the building down,]$_{S1}$
[because it is full of asbestos]$_{S2}$.

Assertions may also support or rebut proposed links between two other assertions, creating a **hypergraph**, which is a generalization of a graph to the case in which edges can join any number of vertices. This can be seen by introducing another sentence into the example:

(16.12) [In principle it is possible to clean it up,]$_{S3}$
[but according to the mayor that is too expensive.]$_{S4}$

S3 acknowledges the validity of $S2$, but **undercuts** its support of $S1$. This can be represented by introducing a hyperedge, $(S3, S2, S1)_{\text{undercut}}$, indicating that $S3$ undercuts the proposed relationship between $S2$ and $S1$. $S4$ then undercuts the relevance of $S3$.

Argumentation mining is the task of recovering such structures from raw texts. At present, annotations of argumentation structure are relatively small: Stab and Gurevych (2014a) have annotated a collection of 90 persuasive essays, and Peldszus and Stede (2015) have solicited and annotated a set of 112 paragraph-length "microtexts" in German.

16.3.4 Applications of Discourse Relations

The predominant application of discourse parsing is to select content within a document. In rhetorical structure theory, the nucleus is considered the more important element of the relation and is more likely to be part of a summary of the document; it may also be more informative for document classification. The D-LTAG theory that underlies the Penn Discourse Treebank lacks this notion of nuclearity, but arguments may have varying importance, depending on the relation type. For example, the span of text constituting ARG1 of an expansion relation is more likely to appear in a summary, while the sentence constituting ARG2 of an implicit relation is less likely (Louis et al., 2010). Discourse relations may also signal segmentation points in the document structure. Explicit discourse markers have been shown to correlate with changes in subjectivity, and identifying such change points can improve document-level sentiment classification, by helping the classifier to focus on the subjective parts of the text (Trivedi and Eisenstein, 2013; Yang and Cardie, 2014).

Extractive summarization Text **summarization** is the problem of converting a longer text into a shorter one, while still conveying the key facts, events, ideas, and sentiments from the original. In **extractive summarization**, the summary is a subset of the original text; in **abstractive summarization**, the summary is produced *de novo*, by paraphrasing the original, or by first encoding it into a semantic representation (see § 19.2). The main strategy for extractive summarization is to maximize coverage, choosing a subset of the document that best covers the concepts mentioned in the document as a whole; typically, coverage is approximated by bag-of-words overlap (Nenkova and McKeown, 2012). Coverage-based objectives can be supplemented by hierarchical discourse relations, using the principle of nuclearity: in any subordinating discourse relation, the nucleus is more critical to the overall meaning of the text and is therefore more important to include in an extractive summary (Marcu, 1997a).[10] This insight can be generalized from individual relations using the concept of **discourse depth** (Hirao et al., 2013): for each elementary discourse unit e, the discourse depth d_e is the number of relations in which a discourse unit containing e is the satellite.

Both discourse depth and nuclearity can be incorporated into extractive summarization, using constrained optimization. Let $\boldsymbol{x}_n$ be a bag-of-words vector representation of elementary discourse unit n, let $y_n \in \{0, 1\}$ indicate whether n is included in the summary, and let d_n be the depth of unit n. Furthermore, let each discourse unit have a "head" h, which is defined recursively:

- if a discourse unit is produced by a subordinating relation, then its head is the head of the (unique) nucleus;
- if a discourse unit is produced by a coordinating relation, then its head is the head of the left-most nucleus;
- for each elementary discourse unit, its parent $\pi(n) \in \{\varnothing, 1, 2, \ldots, N\}$ is the head of the smallest discourse unit containing n whose head is not n;
- if n is the head of the discourse unit spanning the whole document, then $\pi(n) = \varnothing$.

With these definitions in place, discourse-driven extractive summarization can be formalized as follows (Hirao et al., 2013):

$$\begin{aligned}
\max_{y=\{0,1\}^N} & \sum_{n=1}^{N} y_n \frac{\Psi(\boldsymbol{x}_n, \{\boldsymbol{x}_{1:N}\})}{d_n} \\
\text{s.t.} & \sum_{n=1}^{N} y_n \left(\sum_{j=1}^{V} x_{n,j}\right) \leq L \\
& y_{\pi(n)} \geq y_n, \quad \forall n \text{ s.t. } \pi(n) \neq \varnothing.
\end{aligned} \qquad [16.11]$$

where $\Psi(\boldsymbol{x}_n, \{\boldsymbol{x}_{1:N}\})$ measures the coverage of elementary discourse unit n with respect to the rest of the document and $\sum_{j=1}^{V} x_{n,j}$ is the number of tokens in $\boldsymbol{x}_n$. The first constraint ensures that the number of tokens in the summary has an upper bound L. The second constraint ensures that no elementary discourse unit is included unless its parent is also included. In this way, the discourse structure is used twice: to downweight the contributions of elementary discourse units that are not central to the discourse and to ensure that the resulting structure is a subtree of the original discourse parse. The optimization problem in 16.11 can be solved with **integer linear programming**, described in § 13.2.2.[11]

10. Conversely, the arguments of a multinuclear relation should either both be included in the summary, or both excluded (Durrett et al., 2016).

11. Formally, 16.11 is a special case of the **knapsack problem**, in which the goal is to find a subset of items with maximum value, constrained by some maximum weight (Cormen et al., 2009).

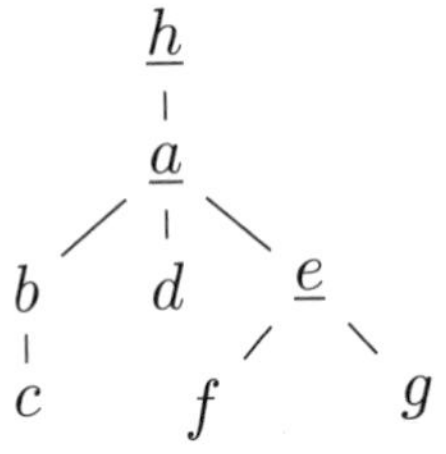

Figure 16.6
A discourse depth tree (Hirao et al., 2013) for the discourse parse from figure 16.5, in which each elementary discourse unit is connected to its parent. The discourse units in one valid summary are underlined.

Figure 16.6 shows a discourse depth tree for the RST analysis from figure 16.5, in which each elementary discourse is connected to (and below) its parent. The underlined discourse units in the figure constitute the following summary:

(16.13) It could have been a great movie, and I really liked the son of the leader of the Samurai. But, other than all that, this movie is nothing more than hidden rip-offs.

Document classification Hierarchical discourse structures lend themselves naturally to text classification: in a subordinating discourse relation, the nucleus should play a stronger role in the classification decision than the satellite. Various implementations of this idea have been proposed.

- Focusing on within-sentence discourse relations and lexicon-based classification (see § 4.1.2), Voll and Taboada (2007) simply ignore the text in the satellites of each discourse relation.
- At the document level, elements of each discourse relation argument can be reweighted, favoring words in the nucleus and disfavoring words in the satellite (Heerschop et al., 2011; Bhatia et al., 2015). This approach can be applied recursively, computing weights across the entire document. The weights can be relation specific, so that the features from the satellites of contrastive relations are discounted or even reversed.
- Alternatively, the hierarchical discourse structure can define the structure of a **recursive neural network** (see § 10.6.1). In this network, the representation of each discourse unit is computed from its arguments and from a parameter corresponding to the discourse relation (Ji and Smith, 2017).

Shallow, nonhierarchical discourse relations have also been applied to document classification. One approach is to impose a set of constraints on the analyses of individual discourse units, so that adjacent units have the same polarity when they are connected by a discourse relation indicating agreement and opposite polarity when connected by a contrastive discourse relation, indicating disagreement (Somasundaran et al., 2009; Zirn et al., 2011). Yang and Cardie (2014) apply explicitly marked relations from the Penn Discourse

Treebank to the problem of sentence-level sentiment polarity classification (see § 4.1). They impose the following soft constraints:

- When a CONTRAST relation appears at the beginning of a sentence, the sentence should have the opposite sentiment polarity as its predecessor.
- When an EXPANSION or CONTINGENCY appears at the beginning of a sentence, it should have the same polarity as its predecessor.
- When a CONTRAST relation appears *within* a sentence, the sentence should have neutral polarity, because it is likely to express both sentiments.

These discourse-driven constraints are shown to improve performance on two datasets of product reviews.

Coherence Just as **grammaticality** is the property shared by well-structured sentences, **coherence** is the property shared by well-structured discourses. One application of discourse processing is to measure (and maximize) the coherence of computer-generated texts like translations and summaries (Kibble and Power, 2004). Coherence assessment is also used to evaluate human-generated texts, such as student essays (e.g., Miltsakaki and Kukich, 2004; Burstein et al., 2013).

Coherence subsumes a range of phenomena, many of which have been highlighted earlier in this chapter: for example, adjacent sentences should be lexically cohesive (Foltz et al., 1998; Ji et al., 2015; Li and Jurafsky, 2017) and entity references should follow the principles of centering theory (Barzilay and Lapata, 2008; Nguyen and Joty, 2017). Discourse relations also bear on the coherence of a text in a variety of ways:

- Hierarchical discourse relations tend to have a "canonical ordering" of the nucleus and satellite (Mann and Thompson, 1988): for example, in the ELABORATION relation from rhetorical structure theory, the nucleus always comes first, while in the JUSTIFICATION relation, the satellite tends to be first (Marcu, 1997b).
- Discourse relations should be signaled by connectives that are appropriate to the semantic or functional relationship between the arguments: for example, a coherent text would be more likely to use *however* to signal a COMPARISON relation than a *temporal* relation (Kibble and Power, 2004).
- Discourse relations tend to be ordered in appear in predictable sequences: for example, COMPARISON relations tend to immediately precede CONTINGENCY relations (Pitler et al., 2008). This observation can be formalized by generalizing the entity grid model (§ 16.2.2), so that each cell (i,j) provides information about the role of the discourse argument containing a mention of entity j in sentence i (Lin et al., 2011). For example, if the first sentence is ARG1 of a comparison relation, then any entity mentions in the sentence would be labeled COMP.ARG1. This approach can also be applied to RST discourse relations (Feng et al., 2014).

Datasets One difficulty with evaluating metrics of discourse coherence is that human-generated texts usually meet some minimal threshold of coherence. For this reason, much of the research on measuring coherence has focused on synthetic data. A typical setting is to permute the sentences of a human-written text and then determine whether the original sentence ordering scores higher according to the proposed coherence measure (Barzilay and Lapata, 2008). There are also small datasets of human evaluations of the coherence of machine summaries: for example, human judgments of the summaries from the participating systems in the 2003 Document Understanding Conference are available online.[12] Researchers from the Educational Testing Service (an organization which administers several national exams in the United States) have studied the relationship between discourse coherence and student essay quality (Burstein et al., 2003, 2010). A public dataset of essays from second-language learners, with quality annotations, has been made available by researchers at Cambridge University (Yannakoudakis et al., 2011). At the other extreme, Louis and Nenkova (2013) analyze the structure of professionally written scientific essays, finding that discourse relation transitions help to distinguish prize-winning essays from other articles in the same genre.

Additional Resources

For a manuscript-length discussion of discourse processing, see Stede (2011). Article-length surveys are offered by Webber et al. (2012) and Webber and Joshi (2012).

Exercises

1. Some discourse connectives tend to occur between their arguments; others can precede both arguments, and a few can follow both arguments. Indicate whether the following connectives can occur between, before, and after their arguments: *however*, *but*, *while* (contrastive, not temporal), *although*, *therefore*, *nonetheless*.
2. This exercise is to be done in pairs. Each participant selects an article from today's news and replaces all mentions of individual people with special tokens like PERSON1, PERSON2, and so on. The other participant should then use the rules of centering theory to guess each type of referring expression: full name (*Captain Ahab*), partial name (e.g., *Ahab*), nominal (e.g., *the ship's captain*), or pronoun. Check whether the predictions match the original text and whether the text conforms to the rules of centering theory.
3. In this exercise, you will produce a figure similar to figure 16.1.
   a) Implement the smoothed cosine similarity metric from equation 16.2, using the smoothing kernel $\boldsymbol{k} = [.5, .3, .15, .05]$.

12. http://homepages.inf.ed.ac.uk/mlap/coherence/.

b) Download the text of a news article with at least 10 paragraphs.

c) Compute and plot the smoothed similarity $\bar{s}$ over the length of the article.

d) Identify *local minima* in $\bar{s}$ as follows: first find all sentences m such that $\bar{s}_m < \bar{s}_{m\pm1}$. Then search among these points to find the five sentences with the lowest $\bar{s}_m$.

e) How often do the five local minima correspond to paragraph boundaries?

- The fraction of local minima that are paragraph boundaries is the **precision-at-k**, where in this case, $k = 5$.
- The fraction of paragraph boundaries which are local minima is the **recall-at-k**.
- Compute precision-at-k and recall-at-k for $k = 3$ and $k = 10$.

4. One way to formulate text segmentation as a probabilistic model is through the **Dirichlet Compound Multinomial (DCM)** distribution, which computes the probability of a bag of words $\text{DCM}(\boldsymbol{x}; \boldsymbol{\alpha})$, where the parameter $\boldsymbol{\alpha}$ is a vector of positive reals. This distribution can be configured to assign high likelihood to bag of words vectors that are internally coherent, such that individual words appear repeatedly: for example, this behavior can be observed for simple parameterizations, such as $\boldsymbol{\alpha} = \alpha\mathbf{1}$ with $\alpha < 1$.

   Let $\psi_\alpha(i,j)$ represent the log-probability of a segment $\boldsymbol{w}_{i+1:j}$ under a DCM distribution with parameter $\boldsymbol{\alpha}$. Give a dynamic program for segmenting a text into a total of K segments maximizing the sum of log-probabilities $\sum_{k=1}^{K} \psi_\alpha(s_{k-1}, s_k)$, where s_k indexes the last token of segment k, and $s_0 = 0$. The time complexity of your dynamic program should not be worse than quadratic in the length of the input and linear in the number of segments.

5. Building on the previous problem, you will now adapt the CKY algorithm to perform hierarchical segmentation. Define a hierarchical segmentation as a set of segmentations $\{\{s_k^{(\ell)}\}_{k=1}^{K^{(\ell)}}\}_{\ell=1}^{L}$, where L is the segmentation depth. To ensure that the segmentation is hierarchically valid, we require that each segmentation point $s_k^{(\ell)}$ at level ℓ is also a segmentation point at level $\ell - 1$, where $\ell > 1$.

   For simplicity, this problem focuses on binary hierarchical segmentation, so that each segment at level $\ell > 1$ has exactly two subsegments. Define the score of a hierarchical segmentation as the sum of the scores of all segments (at all levels), using the the DCM log-probabilities from the previous problem as the segment scores. Give a CKY-like recurrence such that the optimal "parse" of the text is the maximum log-probability binary segmentation with exactly L levels.

6. The entity grid representation of centering theory can be used to compute a score for adjacent sentences, as described in § 16.2.2. Given a set of sentences, these scores can be used to compute an optimal ordering. Show that finding the ordering with the maximum log-probability is NP-complete, by reduction from a well-known problem.

7. In § 16.3.2, it is noted that bottom-up parsing with compositional vector representations of each span is not guaranteed to be optimal. In this exercise, you will construct a minimal example proving this point. Consider a discourse with four units, with base representations $\{z^{(i)}\}_{i=1}^{4}$. Construct a scenario in which the parse selected by bottom-up parsing is not optimal, and give the precise mathematical conditions under which this suboptimal parse is selected. You may ignore the relation labels ℓ for the purpose of this example.

8. As noted in § 16.3.3, arguments can described by hypergraphs, in which a segment may **undercut** a proposed edge between two other segments. Extend the model of extractive summarization described in § 16.3.4 to arguments, adding the follwoing constraint: if segment i undercuts an argumentative relationship between j and k, then i cannot be included in the summary unless both j and k are included. Your solution should take the form of a set of *linear* constraints on an integer linear program—that is, each constraint can only involve addition and subtraction of variables.

In the next two exercises, you will explore the use of discourse connectives in a real corpus. Using NLTK, acquire the Brown corpus, and identify sentences that begin with any of the following connectives: *however, nevertheless, moreover, furthermore, thus*.

9. Both lexical consistency and discourse connectives contribute to the **cohesion** of a text. We might therefore expect adjacent sentences that are joined by explicit discourse connectives to also have higher word overlap. Using the Brown corpus, test this theory by computing the average cosine similarity between adjacent sentences that are connected by one of the connectives mentioned above. Compare this to the average cosine similarity of all other adjacent sentences. If you know how, perform a two-sample t-test to determine whether the observed difference is statistically significant.

10. Group the above connectives into the following three discourse relations:

    - Expansion: *moreover, furthermore*
    - Comparison: *however, nevertheless*
    - Contingency: *thus*

    Focusing on pairs of sentences that are joined by one of these five connectives, build a classifier to predict the discourse relation from the text of the two adjacent sentences—taking care to ignore the connective itself. Use the first 30,000 sentences of the Brown corpus as the training set and the remaining sentences as the test set. Compare the performance of your classifier against simply choosing the most common class. Using a bag-of-words classifier, it is hard to do much better than this baseline, so consider more sophisticated alternatives!

IV APPLICATIONS

17 Information Extraction

Computers offer powerful capabilities for searching and reasoning about structured records and relational data. Some have argued that the most important limitation of artificial intelligence is not inference or learning, but simply having too little knowledge (Lenat et al., 1990). Natural language processing provides an appealing solution: automatically construct a structured **knowledge base** by reading natural language text.

For example, many Wikipedia pages have an "infobox" that provides structured information about an entity or event. An example is shown in figure 17.1a: each row represents one or more properties of the entity IN THE AEROPLANE OVER THE SEA, a record album. The set of properties is determined by a predefined **schema**, which applies to all record albums in Wikipedia. As shown in figure 17.1b, the values for many of these fields are indicated directly in the first few sentences of text on the same Wikipedia page.

The task of automatically constructing (or "populating") an infobox from text is an example of **information extraction**. Much of information extraction can be described in terms of **entities**, **relations**, and **events**.

- **Entities** are uniquely specified objects in the world, such as people (JEFF MANGUM), places (ATHENS, GEORGIA), organizations (MERGE RECORDS), and times (FEBRUARY 10, 1998). Chapter 8 described the task of **named entity recognition**, which labels tokens as parts of entity spans. Now we will see how to go further, **linking** each entity **mention** to an element in a knowledge base.
- **Relations** include a **predicate** and two **arguments**: for example, CAPITAL(GEORGIA, ATLANTA).
- **Events** involve multiple typed arguments. For example, the production and release of the album described in figure 17.1 is described by the event,

$\langle$TITLE : IN THE AEROPLANE OVER THE SEA,

ARTIST : NEUTRAL MILK HOTEL,

RELEASE-DATE : 1998-FEB-10, … $\rangle$.

Studio album by Neutral Milk Hotel	
Released	February 10, 1998
Recorded	July-September 1997
Studio	Pet Sounds Studio, Denver, Colorado
Genre	Indie rock • psychedelic folk • lo-fi
Length	39.55
Label	Merge • Domino
Producer	Robert Schneider

(a) A Wikipedia infobox

(17.1) In the Aeroplane Over the Sea is the second and final studio album by the American indie rock band Neutral Milk Hotel.

(17.2) It was released in the United States on February 10, 1998 on Merge Records and May 1998 on Blue Rose Records in the United Kingdom.

(17.3) Jeff Mangum moved from Athens, Georgia to Denver, Colorado to prepare the bulk of the album's material with producer Robert Schneider, this time at Schneider's newly created Pet Sounds Studio at the home of Jim McIntyre.

(b) The first few sentences of text. Strings that match fields or field names in the info-box are underlined; strings that mention other entities are wavy underlined.

Figure 17.1
From the Wikipedia page for the album "In the Aeroplane Over the Sea," October 26, 2017.

The set of arguments for an event type is defined by a **schema**. Events often refer to time-delimited occurrences: weddings, protests, purchases, terrorist attacks.

Information extraction is similar to semantic role labeling (chapter 13): we may think of predicates as corresponding to events and the arguments as defining slots in the event representation. However, the goals of information extraction are different. Rather than accurately parsing every sentence, information extraction systems often focus on recognizing a few key relation or event types or on the task of identifying all properties of a given entity. Information extraction is often evaluated by the correctness of the resulting knowledge base, and not by how many sentences were accurately parsed. The goal is sometimes described as **macro-reading**, as opposed to **micro-reading**, in which each sentence must be analyzed correctly. Macro-reading systems are not penalized for ignoring difficult sentences, as long as they can recover the same information from other, easier-to-read sources. However, macro-reading systems must resolve apparent inconsistencies (was the album released on MERGE RECORDS or BLUE ROSE RECORDS?), requiring reasoning across the entire dataset.

In addition to the basic tasks of recognizing entities, relations, and events, information extraction systems must handle negation and must be able to distinguish statements of fact from hopes, fears, hunches, and hypotheticals. Finally, information extraction is often paired with the problem of **question answering**, which requires accurately parsing a query, and then selecting or generating a textual answer. Question-answering systems can be built on knowledge bases that are extracted from large text corpora or may attempt to identify answers directly from the source texts.

17.1 Entities

The starting point for information extraction is to identify mentions of entities in text. Consider the following example:

(17.4) The United States Army captured a hill overlooking Atlanta on May 14, 1864.

For this sentence, there are two goals:

1. Identify the spans *United States Army*, *Atlanta*, and *May 14, 1864* as entity mentions. (The hill is not uniquely identified, so it is not a *named* entity.) We may also want to recognize the **named entity types**: organization, location, and date. This is **named entity recognition** and is described in chapter 8.
2. Link these spans to entities in a knowledge base: U.S. ARMY, ATLANTA, and 1864-MAY-14. This task is known as **entity linking**.

The strings to be linked to entities are **mentions**—similar to the use of this term in coreference resolution. In some formulations of the entity linking task, only named entities are candidates for linking. This is sometimes called **named entity linking** (Ling et al., 2015c). In other formulations, such as **Wikification** (Milne and Witten, 2008), any string can be a mention. The set of target entities often corresponds to Wikipedia pages, and Wikipedia is the basis for more comprehensive knowledge bases such as YAGO (Suchanek et al., 2007), DBPedia (Auer et al., 2007), and Freebase (Bollacker et al., 2008). Entity linking may also be performed in more "closed" settings, where a much smaller list of targets is provided in advance. The system must also determine if a mention does not refer to any entity in the knowledge base, sometimes called a **NIL entity** (McNamee and Dang, 2009).

Returning to example 17.4, the three entity mentions may seem unambiguous. But the Wikipedia disambiguation page for the string *Atlanta* says otherwise:[1] there are more than 20 different towns and cities, five United States Navy vessels, a magazine, a television show, a band, and a singer—each prominent enough to have its own Wikipedia page. We now consider how to choose among these dozens of possibilities. In this chapter, we will focus on supervised approaches. Unsupervised entity linking is closely related to the problem of **cross-document coreference resolution**, where the task is to identify pairs of mentions that corefer, across document boundaries (Bagga and Baldwin, 1998b; Singh et al., 2011).

1. https://en.wikipedia.org/wiki/Atlanta_(disambiguation). Accessed November 1, 2017.

17.1.1 Entity Linking by Learning to Rank

Entity linking is often formulated as a **ranking** problem,

$$\hat{y} = \underset{y \in \mathcal{Y}(\boldsymbol{x})}{\text{argmax}}\, \Psi(y, \boldsymbol{x}, \boldsymbol{c}), \qquad [17.1]$$

where y is a target entity, $\boldsymbol{x}$ is a description of the mention, $\mathcal{Y}(\boldsymbol{x})$ is a set of candidate entities, and $\boldsymbol{c}$ is a description of the context—such as the other text in the document, or its metadata. The function Ψ is a scoring function, which could be a linear model, $\Psi(y, \boldsymbol{x}, \boldsymbol{c}) = \boldsymbol{\theta} \cdot \boldsymbol{f}(y, \boldsymbol{x}, \boldsymbol{c})$ or a more complex function such as a neural network. In either case, the scoring function can be learned by minimizing a margin-based **ranking loss**,

$$\ell(\hat{y}, y^{(i)}, \boldsymbol{x}^{(i)}, \boldsymbol{c}^{(i)}) = \left(\Psi(\hat{y}, \boldsymbol{x}^{(i)}, \boldsymbol{c}^{(i)}) - \Psi(y^{(i)}, \boldsymbol{x}^{(i)}, \boldsymbol{c}^{(i)}) + 1\right)_+, \qquad [17.2]$$

where $y^{(i)}$ is the ground truth and $\hat{y} \neq y^{(i)}$ is the predicted target for mention $\boldsymbol{x}^{(i)}$ in context $\boldsymbol{c}^{(i)}$ (Joachims, 2002; Dredze et al., 2010).

Candidate identification For computational tractability, it is helpful to restrict the set of candidates, $\mathcal{Y}(\boldsymbol{x})$. One approach is to use a **name dictionary**, which maps from strings to the entities that they might mention. This mapping is many to many: a string such as *Atlanta* can refer to multiple entities, and conversely, an entity such as ATLANTA can be referenced by multiple strings. A name dictionary can be extracted from Wikipedia, with links between each Wikipedia entity page and the anchor text of all hyperlinks that point to the page (Bunescu and Pasca, 2006; Ratinov et al., 2011). To improve recall, the name dictionary can be augmented by partial and approximate matching (Dredze et al., 2010), but as the set of candidates grows, the risk of false positives increases. For example, the string *Atlanta* is a partial match to *the Atlanta Fed* (a name for the FEDERAL RESERVE BANK OF ATLANTA) and a noisy match (edit distance of one) from *Atalanta* (a heroine in Greek mythology and an Italian soccer team).

Features Feature-based approaches to entity ranking rely on three main types of local information (Dredze et al., 2010):

- The similarity of the mention string to the canonical entity name, as quantified by string similarity. This feature would elevate the city ATLANTA over the basketball team ATLANTA HAWKS for the string *Atlanta*.
- The popularity of the entity, which can be measured by Wikipedia page views or PageRank in the Wikipedia link graph. This feature would elevate ATLANTA, GEORGIA over the unincorporated community of ATLANTA, OHIO.
- The entity type, as output by the named entity recognition system. This feature would elevate the city of ATLANTA over the magazine ATLANTA in contexts where the mention is tagged as a location.

In addition to these local features, the document context can also help. If *Jamaica* is mentioned in a document about the Caribbean, it is likely to refer to the island nation; in the context of New York, it is likely to refer to the neighborhood in Queens; in the context of a menu, it might refer to a hibiscus tea beverage. Such hints can be formalized by computing the similarity between the Wikipedia page describing each candidate entity and the mention context $\boldsymbol{c}^{(i)}$, which may include the bag of words representing the document (Dredze et al., 2010; Hoffart et al., 2011) or a smaller window of text around the mention (Ratinov et al., 2011). For example, we can compute the cosine similarity between bag of words vectors for the context and entity description, typically weighted using **inverse document frequency** to emphasize rare words.[2]

Neural entity linking An alternative approach is to compute the score for each entity candidate using distributed vector representations of the entities, mentions, and context. For example, for the task of entity linking in Twitter, Yang et al. (2016) employ the bilinear scoring function,

$$\Psi(y, \boldsymbol{x}, \boldsymbol{c}) = \boldsymbol{v}_y^\top \Theta^{(y,x)} \boldsymbol{x} + \boldsymbol{v}_y^\top \Theta^{(y,c)} \boldsymbol{c}, \quad [17.3]$$

with $\boldsymbol{v}_y \in \mathbb{R}^{K_y}$ as the vector embedding of entity y, $\boldsymbol{x} \in \mathbb{R}^{K_x}$ as the embedding of the mention, $\boldsymbol{c} \in \mathbb{R}^{K_c}$ as the embedding of the context, and the matrices $\Theta^{(y,x)}$ and $\Theta^{(y,c)}$ as parameters that score the compatibility of each entity with respect to the mention and context. Each of the vector embeddings can be learned from an end-to-end objective, or pretrained on unlabeled data.

- Pretrained **entity embeddings** can be obtained from an existing knowledge base (Bordes et al., 2011, 2013), or by running a word embedding algorithm such as WORD2VEC on the text of Wikipedia, with hyperlinks substituted for the anchor text.[3]
- The embedding of the mention $\boldsymbol{x}$ can be computed by averaging the embeddings of the words in the mention (Yang et al., 2016), or by the compositional techniques described in § 14.8.
- The embedding of the context $\boldsymbol{c}$ can also be computed from the embeddings of the words in the context. A **denoising autoencoder** learns a function from raw text to dense K-dimensional vector encodings by minimizing a reconstruction loss (Vincent et al., 2010),

$$\min_{\boldsymbol{\theta}_g, \boldsymbol{\theta}_h} \sum_{i=1}^{N} ||\boldsymbol{x}^{(i)} - g(h(\tilde{\boldsymbol{x}}^{(i)}; \boldsymbol{\theta}_h); \boldsymbol{\theta}_g)||^2, \quad [17.4]$$

2. The **document frequency** of word j is $\text{DF}(j) = \frac{1}{N}\sum_{i=1}^{N} \delta\left(x_j^{(i)} > 0\right)$, proportional to the number of documents in which the word appears. The contribution of each word to the cosine similarity of two bag-of-words vectors can be weighted by the **inverse document frequency** $\frac{1}{\text{DF}(j)}$ or $\log \frac{1}{\text{DF}(j)}$, to emphasize rare words (Spärck Jones, 1972).

3. Pretrained entity embeddings can be downloaded from code.google.com/archive/p/word2vec/.

where $\tilde{\boldsymbol{x}}^{(i)}$ is a noisy version of the bag-of-words counts $\boldsymbol{x}^{(i)}$, which is produced by randomly setting some counts to zero; $h : \mathbb{R}^V \rightarrow \mathbb{R}^K$ is an encoder with parameters $\boldsymbol{\theta}_h$; and $g : \mathbb{R}^K \rightarrow \mathbb{R}^V$ is a decoder with parameters $\boldsymbol{\theta}_g$. The encoder and decoder functions are typically implemented as feedforward neural networks. To apply this model to entity linking, each entity and context are initially represented by the encoding of their bag-of-words vectors, $h(\boldsymbol{e})$ and $h(\boldsymbol{c})$, and these encodings are then fine-tuned from labeled data (He et al., 2013). The context vector $\boldsymbol{c}$ can also be obtained by convolution (§ 3.4) on the embeddings of words in the document (Sun et al., 2015) or by examining metadata such as the author's social network (Yang et al., 2016).

The remaining parameters $\Theta^{(y,x)}$ and $\Theta^{(y,c)}$ can be trained by backpropagation from the margin loss in equation 17.2.

17.1.2 Collective Entity Linking

Entity linking can be more accurate when it is performed jointly across a document. To see why, consider the following lists:

(17.5) a. California, Oregon, Washington
b. Baltimore, Washington, Philadelphia
c. Washington, Adams, Jefferson

In each case, the term *Washington* refers to a different entity, and this reference is strongly suggested by the other entries on the list. In the last list, all three names are highly ambiguous—there are dozens of other *Adams* and *Jefferson* entities in Wikipedia. But a preference for coherence motivates **collectively** linking these references to the first three U.S. presidents.

A general approach to collective entity linking is to introduce a compatibility score $\psi_c(\boldsymbol{y})$. Collective entity linking is then performed by optimizing the global objective,

$$\hat{\boldsymbol{y}} = \underset{\boldsymbol{y} \in \mathbb{Y}(\boldsymbol{x})}{\operatorname{argmax}} \Psi_c(\boldsymbol{y}) + \sum_{i=1}^{N} \Psi_\ell(y^{(i)}, \boldsymbol{x}^{(i)}, \boldsymbol{c}^{(i)}), \qquad [17.5]$$

where $\mathbb{Y}(\boldsymbol{x})$ is the set of all possible collective entity assignments for the mentions in $\boldsymbol{x}$ and Ψ_e is the local scoring function for each entity i. The compatibility function is typically decomposed into a sum of pairwise scores, $\Psi_c(\boldsymbol{y}) = \sum_{i=1}^{N} \sum_{j \neq i}^{N} \Psi_c(y^{(i)}, y^{(j)})$. These scores can be computed in a number of different ways:

- Wikipedia defines high-level categories for entities (e.g., *living people*, *Presidents of the United States*, *States of the United States*), and Ψ_c can reward entity pairs for the number of categories that they have in common (Cucerzan, 2007).
- Compatibility can be measured by the number of incoming hyperlinks shared by the Wikipedia pages for the two entities (Milne and Witten, 2008).

- In a neural architecture, the compatibility of two entities can be set equal to the inner product of their embeddings, $\Psi_c(y^{(i)}, y^{(j)}) = \boldsymbol{v}_{y^{(i)}} \cdot \boldsymbol{v}_{y^{(j)}}$.
- A nonpairwise compatibility score can be defined using a type of latent variable model known as a **probabilistic topic model** (Blei et al., 2003; Blei, 2012). In this framework, each latent topic is a probability distribution over entities, and each document has a probability distribution over topics. Each entity helps to determine the document's distribution over topics, and in turn these topics help to resolve ambiguous entity mentions (Newman et al., 2006). Inference can be performed using the sampling techniques described in chapter 5.

Unfortunately, collective entity linking is **NP-hard** even for pairwise compatibility functions, so exact optimization is almost certainly intractable. Various approximate inference techniques have been proposed, including **integer linear programming** (Cheng and Roth, 2013), **Gibbs sampling** (Han and Sun, 2012), and graph-based algorithms (Hoffart et al., 2011; Han et al., 2011).

17.1.3 *Pairwise Ranking Loss Functions

The loss function defined in equation 17.2 considers only the highest-scoring prediction $\hat{y}$, but in fact, the true entity $y^{(i)}$ should outscore *all* other entities. A loss function based on this idea would give a gradient against the features or representations of several entities, not just the top-scoring prediction. Usunier et al. (2009) define a general ranking error function,

$$L_{\text{rank}}(k) = \sum_{j=1}^{k} \alpha_j, \quad \text{with } \alpha_1 \geq \alpha_2 \geq \cdots \geq 0, \qquad [17.6]$$

where k is equal to the number of labels ranked higher than the correct label $y^{(i)}$. This function defines a class of ranking errors: if $\alpha_j = 1$ for all j, then the ranking error is equal to the rank of the correct entity; if $\alpha_1 = 1$ and $\alpha_{j>1} = 0$, then the ranking error is one whenever the correct entity is not ranked first; if α_j decreases smoothly with j, as in $\alpha_j = \frac{1}{j}$, then the error is between these two extremes.

This ranking error can be integrated into a margin objective. Remember that large-margin classification requires not only the correct label, but also that the correct label outscores other labels by a substantial margin. A similar principle applies to ranking: we want a high rank for the correct entity, and we want it to be separated from other entities by a substantial margin. We therefore define the margin-augmented rank,

$$r(y^{(i)}, \boldsymbol{x}^{(i)}) \triangleq \sum_{y \in \mathcal{Y}(\boldsymbol{x}^{(i)}) \setminus y^{(i)}} \delta\left(1 + \psi(y, \boldsymbol{x}^{(i)}) \geq \psi(y^{(i)}, \boldsymbol{x}^{(i)})\right), \qquad [17.7]$$

where $\delta(\cdot)$ is a delta function and $\mathcal{Y}(\boldsymbol{x}^{(i)}) \setminus y^{(i)}$ is the set of all entity candidates minus the true entity $y^{(i)}$. The margin-augmented rank is the rank of the true entity, after augmenting

Algorithm 18
WARP approximate ranking loss.

---

procedure WARP($y^{(i)}, \boldsymbol{x}^{(i)}$)
  $N \leftarrow 0$
  repeat
    Randomly sample $y \sim \mathcal{Y}(\boldsymbol{x}^{(i)})$
    $N \leftarrow N+1$
    if $\psi(y, \boldsymbol{x}^{(i)}) + 1 > \psi(y^{(i)}, \boldsymbol{x}^{(i)})$ **then** ▷ check for margin violation
      $r \leftarrow \lfloor |\mathcal{Y}(\boldsymbol{x}^{(i)})|/N \rfloor$ ▷ compute approximate rank
      return $L_{\text{rank}}(r) \times (\psi(y, \boldsymbol{x}^{(i)}) + 1 - \psi(y^{(i)}, \boldsymbol{x}^{(i)}))$
  until $N \geq |\mathcal{Y}(\boldsymbol{x}^{(i)})| - 1$ ▷ no violation found
  return 0 ▷ return zero loss

---

every other candidate with a margin of one, under the current scoring function ψ. (The context $\boldsymbol{c}$ is omitted for clarity and can be considered part of $\boldsymbol{x}$.)

For each instance, a hinge loss is computed from the ranking error associated with this margin-augmented rank, and the violation of the margin constraint,

$$\ell(y^{(i)}, \boldsymbol{x}^{(i)}) = \frac{L_{\text{rank}}(r(y^{(i)}, \boldsymbol{x}^{(i)}))}{r(y^{(i)}, \boldsymbol{x}^{(i)})} \sum_{y \in \mathcal{Y}(\boldsymbol{x}) \setminus y^{(i)}} \left(\psi(y, \boldsymbol{x}^{(i)}) - \psi(y^{(i)}, \boldsymbol{x}^{(i)}) + 1\right)_+. \quad [17.8]$$

The sum in equation 17.8 includes nonzero values for every label that is ranked at least as high as the true entity, after applying the margin augmentation. Dividing by the margin-augmented rank of the true entity thus gives the average violation.

The objective in equation 17.8 is expensive to optimize when the label space is large, as is usually the case for entity linking against large knowledge bases. This motivates a randomized approximation called **WARP** (Weston et al., 2011), shown in algorithm 18. In this procedure, we sample random entities until one violates the pairwise margin constraint, $\psi(y, \boldsymbol{x}^{(i)}) + 1 \geq \psi(y^{(i)}, \boldsymbol{x}^{(i)})$. The number of samples N required to find such a violation yields an approximation of the margin-augmented rank of the true entity, $r(y^{(i)}, \boldsymbol{x}^{(i)}) \approx \left\lfloor \frac{|\mathcal{Y}(\boldsymbol{x})|}{N} \right\rfloor$. If a violation is found immediately, $N = 1$, the correct entity probably ranks below many others, $r \approx |\mathcal{Y}(\boldsymbol{x})|$. If many samples are required before a violation is found, $N \rightarrow |\mathcal{Y}(\boldsymbol{x})|$, then the correct entity is probably highly ranked, $r \rightarrow 1$. A computational advantage of WARP is that it is not necessary to find the highest-scoring label, which can impose a nontrivial computational cost when $\mathcal{Y}(\boldsymbol{x}^{(i)})$ is large. The objective is conceptually similar to the **negative sampling** objective in WORD2VEC (chapter 14), which compares the observed word against randomly sampled alternatives.

17.2 Relations

After identifying the entities that are mentioned in a text, the next step is to determine how they are related. Consider the following example:

(17.6) George Bush traveled to France on Thursday for a summit.

This sentence introduces a relation between the entities referenced by *George Bush* and *France*. In the Automatic Content Extraction (ACE) ontology (Linguistic Data Consortium, 2005), the type of this relation is PHYSICAL, and the subtype is LOCATED. This relation would be written as follows:

$$\text{PHYSICAL.LOCATED}(\text{GEORGE BUSH}, \text{FRANCE}). \quad [17.9]$$

Relations take exactly two arguments, and the order of the arguments matters.

In the ACE datasets, relations are annotated between entity mentions, as in the example above. Relations can also hold between nominals, as in the following example from the SemEval-2010 shared task (Hendrickx et al., 2009):

(17.7) The cup contained tea from dried ginseng.

This sentence describes a relation of type ENTITY-ORIGIN between *tea* and *ginseng*. Nominal relation extraction is closely related to **semantic role labeling** (chapter 13). The main difference is that relation extraction is restricted to a relatively small number of relation types; for example, table 17.1 shows the 10 relation types from SemEval-2010.

17.2.1 Pattern-Based Relation Extraction

Early work on relation extraction focused on hand crafted patterns (Hearst, 1992). For example, the appositive *Starbuck, a native of Nantucket* signals the relation ENTITY-ORIGIN between *Starbuck* and *Nantucket*. This pattern can be written as

$$\text{PERSON}\textit{, a native of}\ \text{LOCATION} \Rightarrow \text{ENTITY-ORIGIN}(\text{PERSON}, \text{LOCATION}). \quad [17.10]$$

This pattern will be "triggered" whenever the literal string *, a native of* occurs between an entity of type PERSON and an entity of type LOCATION. Such patterns can be generalized

Table 17.1
Relations and example sentences from the SemEval-2010 dataset (Hendrickx et al., 2009)

CAUSE-EFFECT	*those cancers were caused by radiation exposures*
INSTRUMENT-AGENCY	*phone operator*
PRODUCT-PRODUCER	*a factory manufactures suits*
CONTENT-CONTAINER	*a bottle of honey was weighed*
ENTITY-ORIGIN	*letters from foreign countries*
ENTITY-DESTINATION	*the boy went to bed*
COMPONENT-WHOLE	*my apartment has a large kitchen*
MEMBER-COLLECTION	*there are many trees in the forest*
COMMUNICATION-TOPIC	*the lecture was about semantics*

beyond literal matches using techniques such as lemmatization, which would enable the words (*buy*, *buys*, *buying*) to trigger the same patterns (see § 4.3.1). A more aggressive strategy would be to group all words in a WordNet synset (§ 4.2), so that, for example, *buy* and *purchase* trigger the same patterns.

Relation extraction patterns can be implemented in finite-state automata (§ 9.1). If the named entity recognizer is also a finite-state machine, then the systems can be combined by finite-state transduction (Hobbs et al., 1997). This makes it possible to propagate uncertainty through the finite-state cascade and disambiguate from higher-level context. For example, suppose the entity recognizer cannot decide whether *Starbuck* refers to either a PERSON or a LOCATION; in the composed transducer, the relation extractor would be free to select the PERSON annotation when it appears in the context of an appropriate pattern.

17.2.2 Relation Extraction as a Classification Task

Relation extraction can be formulated as a classification problem,

$$\hat{r}_{(i,j),(m,n)} = \underset{r \in \mathcal{R}}{\operatorname{argmax}}\, \Psi(r, (i,j), (m,n), \boldsymbol{w}), \tag{17.11}$$

where $r \in \mathcal{R}$ is a relation type (possibly NIL), $\boldsymbol{w}_{i+1:j}$ is the span of the first argument, and $\boldsymbol{w}_{m+1:n}$ is the span of the second argument. The argument $\boldsymbol{w}_{m+1:n}$ may appear before or after $\boldsymbol{w}_{i+1:j}$ in the text, or they may overlap; we stipulate only that $\boldsymbol{w}_{i+1:j}$ is the first argument of the relation. We now consider three alternatives for computing the scoring function.

Feature-based classification In a feature-based classifier, the scoring function is defined as

$$\Psi(r, (i,j), (m,n), \boldsymbol{w}) = \boldsymbol{\theta} \cdot \boldsymbol{f}(r, (i,j), (m,n), \boldsymbol{w}), \tag{17.12}$$

with $\boldsymbol{\theta}$ representing a vector of weights and $\boldsymbol{f}(\cdot)$ a vector of features. The pattern-based methods described in § 17.2.1 suggest several features:

- Local features of $\boldsymbol{w}_{i+1:j}$ and $\boldsymbol{w}_{m+1:n}$, including: the strings themselves; whether they are recognized as entities, and if so, which type; whether the strings are present in a **gazetteer** of entity names; and each string's syntactic head (§ 9.2.2).
- Features of the span between the two arguments, $\boldsymbol{w}_{j+1:m}$ or $\boldsymbol{w}_{n+1:i}$ (depending on which argument appears first): the length of the span; the specific words that appear in the span, either as a literal sequence or a bag of words; and the WordNet synsets (§ 4.2) that appear in the span between the arguments.
- Features of the syntactic relationship between the two arguments, typically the **dependency path** between the arguments (§ 13.2.1). Example dependency paths are shown in table 17.2.

Table 17.2
Candidates instances for the PHYSICAL.LOCATED relation and their dependency paths

1. ***George Bush*** *traveled to* ***France***	*George Bush* $\xleftarrow[\text{NSUBJ}]{}$ *traveled* $\xrightarrow[\text{OBL}]{}$ *France*
2. ***Ahab*** *traveled to* ***Nantucket***	*Ahab* $\xleftarrow[\text{NSUBJ}]{}$ *traveled* $\xrightarrow[\text{OBL}]{}$ *Nantucket*
3. ***George Bush*** *will travel to* ***France***	*George Bush* $\xleftarrow[\text{NSUBJ}]{}$ *travel* $\xrightarrow[\text{OBL}]{}$ *France*
4. ***George Bush*** *wants to travel to* ***France***	*George Bush* $\xleftarrow[\text{NSUBJ}]{}$ *wants* $\xrightarrow[\text{XCOMP}]{}$ *travel* $\xrightarrow[\text{OBL}]{}$ *France*
5. ***Ahab*** *traveled to a city in* ***France***	*Ahab* $\xleftarrow[\text{NSUBJ}]{}$ *traveled* $\xrightarrow[\text{OBL}]{}$ *city* $\xrightarrow[\text{NMOD}]{}$ *France*
6. *We await* ***Ahab*** *'s visit to France*	*Ahab* $\xleftarrow[\text{NMOD:POSS}]{}$ *visit* $\xrightarrow[\text{NMOD}]{}$ *France*

Kernels Suppose that the first line of table 17.2 is a labeled example, and the remaining lines are instances to be classified. A feature-based approach would have to decompose the dependency paths into features that capture individual edges, with or without their labels, and then learn weights for each of these features: for example, the second line contains identical dependencies, but different arguments; the third line contains a different inflection of the word *travel*; the fourth and fifth lines each contain an additional edge on the dependency path; and the sixth example uses an entirely different path. Rather than attempting to create local features that capture all of the ways in which these dependencies paths are similar and different, we can instead define a similarity function κ, which computes a score for any pair of instances, $\kappa : \mathcal{X} \times \mathcal{X} \to \mathbb{R}_+$. The score for any pair of instances (i,j) is $\kappa(\boldsymbol{x}^{(i)}, \boldsymbol{x}^{(j)}) \geq 0$, with $\kappa(i,j)$ being large when instances $\boldsymbol{x}^{(i)}$ and $\boldsymbol{x}^{(j)}$ are similar. If the function κ has a few key properties, it is a valid **kernel function**.[4]

Given a valid kernel function, we can build a nonlinear classifier without explicitly defining a feature vector or neural network architecture. For a binary classification problem $y \in \{-1, 1\}$, we have the decision function,

$$\hat{y} = \text{Sign}(b + \sum_{i=1}^{N} y^{(i)} \alpha^{(i)} \kappa(\boldsymbol{x}^{(i)}, \boldsymbol{x})), \tag{17.13}$$

where b and $\{\alpha^{(i)}\}_{i=1}^{N}$ are parameters that must be learned from the training set, under the constraint $\forall_i, \alpha^{(i)} \geq 0$. Intuitively, each α_i specifies the importance of the instance $\boldsymbol{x}^{(i)}$ toward the classification rule. Kernel-based classification can be viewed as a weighted form of the **nearest-neighbor** classifier (Hastie et al., 2009), in which test instances are assigned the most common label among their near neighbors in the training set. This results in a nonlinear classification boundary. The parameters are typically learned from a margin-based objective (see § 2.4), leading to the **kernel support vector machine**. To generalize to

4. The **Gram matrix K** arises from computing the kernel function between all pairs in a set of instances. For a valid kernel, the Gram matrix must be symmetric ($\mathbf{K} = \mathbf{K}^\top$) and positive semi-definite ($\forall \boldsymbol{a}, \boldsymbol{a}^\top \mathbf{K} \boldsymbol{a} \geq 0$). For more on kernel-based classification, see chapter 14 of Murphy (2012).

multiclass classification, we can train separate binary classifiers for each label (sometimes called **one-versus-all**), or train binary classifiers for each pair of possible labels (**one-versus-one**).

Dependency kernels are particularly effective for relation extraction, due to their ability to capture syntactic properties of the path between the two candidate arguments. One class of dependency tree kernels is defined recursively, with the score for a pair of trees equal to the similarity of the root nodes and the sum of similarities of matched pairs of child subtrees (Zelenko et al., 2003; Culotta and Sorensen, 2004). Alternatively, Bunescu and Mooney (2005) define a kernel function over sequences of unlabeled dependency edges, in which the score is computed as a product of scores for each pair of words in the sequence: identical words receive a high score, words that share a synset or part of speech receive a small non-zero score (e.g., *travel / visit*), and unrelated words receive a score of zero.

Neural relation extraction **Convolutional neural networks** (§ 3.4) were an early neural architecture for relation extraction (Zeng et al., 2014; dos Santos et al., 2015). For the sentence $(w_1, w_2, \ldots, w_M)$, obtain a matrix of word embeddings $\mathbf{X}$, where $\boldsymbol{x}_m \in \mathbb{R}^K$ is the embedding of w_m. Now, suppose the candidate arguments appear at positions a_1 and a_2; then for each word in the sentence, its position with respect to each argument is $m - a_1$ and $m - a_2$. (Following Zeng et al. (2014), this is a restricted version of the relation extraction task in which the arguments are single tokens.) To capture any information conveyed by these positions, the word embeddings are concatenated with vector encodings of the positional offsets, $\boldsymbol{x}^{(p)}_{m-a_1}$ and $\boldsymbol{x}^{(p)}_{m-a_2}$. (For more on **positional encodings**, see § 18.3.2.) The complete base representation of the sentence is

$$\mathbf{X}(a_1, a_2) = \begin{pmatrix} \boldsymbol{x}_1 & \boldsymbol{x}_2 & \cdots & \boldsymbol{x}_M \\ \boldsymbol{x}^{(p)}_{1-a_1} & \boldsymbol{x}^{(p)}_{2-a_1} & \cdots & \boldsymbol{x}^{(p)}_{M-a_1} \\ \boldsymbol{x}^{(p)}_{1-a_2} & \boldsymbol{x}^{(p)}_{2-a_2} & \cdots & \boldsymbol{x}^{(p)}_{M-a_2} \end{pmatrix}, \quad [17.14]$$

where each column is a vertical concatenation of a word embedding, represented by the column vector $\boldsymbol{x}_m$, and two positional encodings, specifying the position with respect to a_1 and a_2. The matrix $\mathbf{X}(a_1, a_2)$ is then taken as input to a convolutional layer (see § 3.4), and max pooling is applied to obtain a vector. The final scoring function is then

$$\Psi(r, i, j, \mathbf{X}) = \boldsymbol{\theta}_r \cdot \text{MaxPool}(\text{ConvNet}(\mathbf{X}(i, j); \boldsymbol{\phi})), \quad [17.15]$$

where $\boldsymbol{\phi}$ defines the parameters of the convolutional operator and the $\boldsymbol{\theta}_r$ defines a set of weights for relation r. The model can be trained using a margin objective,

$$\hat{r} = \underset{r}{\text{argmax}}\, \Psi(r, i, j, \mathbf{X}) \quad [17.16]$$

$$\ell = (\delta(r \neq \hat{r}) + \psi(\hat{r}, i, j, \mathbf{X}) - \psi(r, i, j, \mathbf{X}))_+. \quad [17.17]$$

Recurrent neural networks (§ 6.3) have also been applied to relation extraction, using a network such as a bidirectional LSTM to encode the words or dependency path between the two arguments. Xu et al. (2015) segment each dependency path into left and right subpaths: the path $\textit{Bush} \underset{\textsc{Nsubj}}{\leftarrow} \textit{wants} \underset{\textsc{Xcomp}}{\rightarrow} \textit{travel} \underset{\textsc{Obl}}{\rightarrow} \textit{France}$ is segmented into the subpaths, $\textit{Bush} \underset{\textsc{Nsubj}}{\leftarrow} \textit{wants}$ and $\textit{wants} \underset{\textsc{Xcomp}}{\rightarrow} \textit{travel} \underset{\textsc{Obl}}{\rightarrow} \textit{France}$. In each path, a recurrent neural network is run from the argument to the root word (in this case, *wants*). The final representation is obtained by max pooling (§ 3.4) across all the recurrent states along each path. This process can be applied across separate "channels," in which the inputs consist of embeddings for the words, parts of speech, dependency relations, and WordNet hypernyms (e.g., *France-nation*; see § 4.2). To define the model formally, let $s(m)$ define the successor of word m in either the left or right subpath (in a dependency path, each word can have a successor in at most one subpath). Let $\boldsymbol{x}_m^{(c)}$ indicate the embedding of word (or relation) m in channel c, and let $\overleftarrow{\boldsymbol{h}}_m^{(c)}$ and $\overrightarrow{\boldsymbol{h}}_m^{(c)}$ indicate the associated recurrent states in the left and right subtrees, respectively. Then the complete model is specified as follows:

$$\boldsymbol{h}_{s(m)}^{(c)} = \text{RNN}(\boldsymbol{x}_{s(m)}^{(c)}, \boldsymbol{h}_m^{(c)}) \quad [17.18]$$

$$z^{(c)} = \text{MaxPool}\left(\overleftarrow{\boldsymbol{h}}_i^{(c)}, \overleftarrow{\boldsymbol{h}}_{s(i)}^{(c)}, \ldots, \overleftarrow{\boldsymbol{h}}_{\text{root}}^{(c)}, \overrightarrow{\boldsymbol{h}}_j^{(c)}, \overrightarrow{\boldsymbol{h}}_{s(j)}^{(c)}, \ldots, \overrightarrow{\boldsymbol{h}}_{\text{root}}^{(c)}\right) \quad [17.19]$$

$$\Psi(r,i,j) = \boldsymbol{\theta} \cdot \left[z^{(\text{word})}; z^{(\text{POS})}; z^{(\text{dependency})}; z^{(\text{hypernym})}\right]. \quad [17.20]$$

Note that z is computed by applying max pooling to the *matrix* of horizontally concatenated vectors $\boldsymbol{h}$, while Ψ is computed from the *vector* of vertically concatenated vectors z. Xu et al. (2015) pass the score Ψ through a **softmax** layer to obtain a probability $\text{p}(r \mid i, j, \boldsymbol{w})$ and train the model by regularized **cross-entropy**. Miwa and Bansal (2016) show that a related model can solve the more challenging "end-to-end" relation extraction task, in which the model must simultaneously detect entities and then extract their relations.

17.2.3 Knowledge Base Population

In many applications, what matters is not what fraction of sentences are analyzed correctly, but how much accurate knowledge can be extracted. **Knowledge base population (KBP)** refers to the task of filling in Wikipedia-style infoboxes, as shown in figure 17.1a. Knowledge base population can be decomposed into two subtasks: **entity linking** (described in § 17.1) and **slot filling** (Ji and Grishman, 2011). Slot filling has two key differences from the formulation of relation extraction presented above: the relations hold between entities rather than spans of text, and the performance is evaluated at the *type level* (on entity pairs), rather than on the *token level* (on individual sentences).

From a practical standpoint, there are three other important differences between slot filling and per-sentence relation extraction.

- KBP tasks are often formulated from the perspective of identifying attributes of a few "query" entities. As a result, these systems often start with an **information retrieval** phase, in which relevant passages of text are obtained by search.
- For many entity pairs, there will be multiple passages of text that provide evidence. Slot filling systems must aggregate this evidence to predict a single relation type (or set of relations).
- Labeled data is usually available in the form of pairs of related entities, rather than annotated passages of text. Training from such type-level annotations is a challenge: two entities may be linked by several relations, or they may appear together in a passage of text that nonetheless does not describe their relation to each other.

Information retrieval is beyond the scope of this text (see Manning et al., 2009). The remainder of this section describes approaches to information fusion and learning from type-level annotations.

Information fusion In knowledge base population, there will often be multiple pieces of evidence for (and sometimes against) a single relation. For example, a search for the entity MAYNARD JACKSON, JR. may return several passages that reference the entity ATLANTA:[5]

(17.8) a. Elected mayor of **Atlanta** in 1973, **Maynard Jackson** was the first African American to serve as mayor of a major southern city.
b. **Atlanta**'s airport will be renamed to honor **Maynard Jackson**, the city's first Black mayor.
c. Born in Dallas, Texas in 1938, **Maynard Holbrook Jackson, Jr.** moved to **Atlanta** when he was 8.
d. **Maynard Jackson** has gone from one of the worst high schools in **Atlanta** to one of the best.

The first and second examples provide evidence for the relation MAYOR holding between the entities ATLANTA and MAYNARD JACKSON, JR. The third example provides evidence for a different relation between these same entities, LIVED-IN. The fourth example poses an entity linking problem, referring to MAYNARD JACKSON HIGH SCHOOL. Knowledge base population requires aggregating this sort of textual evidence and predicting the relations that are most likely to hold.

One approach is to run a single-document relation extraction system (using the techniques described in § 17.2.2) and then aggregate the results (Li et al., 2011). Relations

5. First three examples from: www.georgiaencyclopedia.org/articles/government-politics/maynard-jackson-1938-2003; JET magazine, November 10, 2003; www.todayingeorgiahistory.org/content/maynard-jackson-elected.

that are detected with high confidence in multiple documents are more likely to be valid, motivating the heuristic,

$$\psi(r, e_1, e_2) = \sum_{i=1}^{N} (\mathrm{p}(r(e_1, e_2) \mid \boldsymbol{w}^{(i)}))^{\alpha}, \qquad [17.21]$$

where $\mathrm{p}(r(e_1, e_2) \mid \boldsymbol{w}^{(i)})$ is the probability of relation r between entities e_1 and e_2 conditioned on the text $\boldsymbol{w}^{(i)}$, and $\alpha \gg 1$ is a tunable hyperparameter. Using this heuristic, it is possible to rank all candidate relations and trace out a **precision-recall curve** as more relations are extracted.[6] Alternatively, features can be aggregated across multiple passages of text, feeding a single type-level relation extraction system (Wolfe et al., 2017).

Precision can be improved by introducing constraints across multiple relations. For example, if we are certain of the relation PARENT(e_1, e_2), then it cannot also be the case that PARENT(e_2, e_1). Integer linear programming makes it possible to incorporate such constraints into a global optimization (Li et al., 2011). Other pairs of relations have positive correlations, such MAYOR(e_1, e_2) and LIVED-IN(e_1, e_2). Compatibility across relation types can be incorporated into probabilistic graphical models (e.g., Riedel et al., 2010).

Distant supervision Relation extraction is "annotation hungry," because each relation requires its own labeled data. Rather than relying on annotations of individual documents, it would be preferable to use existing knowledge resources—such as the many facts that are already captured in knowledge bases like DBPedia. However, such annotations raise the inverse of the information fusion problem considered above: the existence of the relation MAYOR(MAYNARD JACKSON JR., ATLANTA) provides only **distant supervision** for the example texts in which this entity pair is mentioned.

One approach is to treat the entity pair as the instance, rather than the text itself (Mintz et al., 2009). Features are then aggregated across all sentences in which both entities are mentioned, and labels correspond to the relation (if any) between the entities in a knowledge base, such as Freebase. Negative instances are constructed from entity pairs that are not related in the knowledge base. In some cases, two entities are related, but the knowledge base is missing the relation; however, because the number of possible entity pairs is huge, these missing relations are presumed to be relatively rare. This approach is shown in figure 17.2.

In **multiple-instance learning**, labels are assigned to *sets* of instances, of which only an unknown subset are actually relevant (Dietterich et al., 1997; Maron and Lozano-Pérez, 1998). This formalizes the framework of distant supervision: the relation REL(A, B) acts as a label for the entire set of sentences mentioning entities A and B, even when only a subset

6. The precision-recall curve is similar to the ROC curve shown in figure 4.4, but it includes the precision $\frac{\mathrm{TP}}{\mathrm{TP}+\mathrm{FP}}$ rather than the false positive rate $\frac{\mathrm{FP}}{\mathrm{FP}+\mathrm{TN}}$.

- **Label** : MAYOR(ATLANTA, MAYNARD JACKSON)
  - Elected mayor of **Atlanta** in 1973, **Maynard Jackson** ...
  - **Atlanta**'s airport will be renamed to honor **Maynard Jackson**, the city's first Black mayor
  - Born in Dallas, Texas in 1938, **Maynard Holbrook Jackson, Jr.** moved to **Atlanta** when he was 8.
- **Label** : MAYOR(NEW YORK, FIORELLO LA GUARDIA)
  - **Fiorello La Guardia** was Mayor of **New York** for three terms ...
  - **Fiorello La Guardia**, then serving on the **New York** City Board of Aldermen ...
- **Label** : BORN-IN(DALLAS, MAYNARD JACKSON)
  - Born in **Dallas**, Texas in 1938, **Maynard Holbrook Jackson, Jr.** moved to Atlanta when he was 8.
  - **Maynard Jackson** was raised in **Dallas** ...
- **Label** : NIL(NEW YORK, MAYNARD JACKSON)
  - **Jackson** married Valerie Richardson, whom he had met in **New York** ...
  - **Jackson** was a member of the Georgia and **New York** bars ...

Figure 17.2
Four training instances for relation classification using **distant supervision** (Mintz et al. 2009). The first two instances are positive for the MAYOR relation, and the third instance is positive for the BORN-IN relation. The fourth instance is a negative example, constructed from a pair of entities (NEW YORK, MAYNARD JACKSON) that do not appear in any Freebase relation. Each instance's features are computed by aggregating across all sentences in which the two entities are mentioned.

of these sentences actually describes the relation. One approach to multi-instance learning is to introduce a binary **latent variable** for each sentence, indicating whether the sentence expresses the labeled relation (Riedel et al., 2010). A variety of inference techniques have been employed for this probabilistic model of relation extraction: Surdeanu et al. (2012) use expectation-maximization, Riedel et al. (2010) use sampling, and Hoffmann et al. (2011) use a custom graph-based algorithm. Expectation-maximization and sampling are surveyed in chapter 5 and are covered in more detail by Murphy (2012); graph-based methods are surveyed by Mihalcea and Radev (2011).

17.2.4 Open Information Extraction

In classical relation extraction, the set of relations is defined in advance, using a **schema**. The relation for any pair of entities can then be predicted using multi-class classification. In **open information extraction (OpenIE)**, a relation can be any triple of text. The example sentence (17.8a) instantiates several "relations" of this sort, for example,

- (*mayor of, Maynard Jackson, Atlanta*),
- (*elected, Maynard Jackson, mayor of Atlanta*),
- (*elected in, Maynard Jackson, 1973*).

Table 17.3
Various relation extraction tasks and their properties. VerbNet and FrameNet are described in chapter 13. ACE (Linguistic Data Consortium, 2005), TAC (McNamee and Dang, 2009), and SemEval (Hendrickx et al., 2009) refer to shared tasks, each of which involves an ontology of relation types.

Task	Relation ontology	Supervision
PropBank semantic role labeling	VerbNet	sentence
FrameNet semantic role labeling	FrameNet	sentence
Relation extraction	ACE, TAC, SemEval, etc	sentence
Slot filling	ACE, TAC, SemEval, etc	relation
Open Information Extraction	open	seed relations or patterns

Extracting such tuples can be viewed as a lightweight version of **semantic role labeling** (chapter 13), with only two argument types: first slot and second slot. The task is generally evaluated on the relation level, rather than on the level of sentences: precision is measured by the number of extracted relations that are accurate, and recall is measured by the number of true relations that were successfully extracted. OpenIE systems are trained from distant supervision or bootstrapping, rather than from labeled sentences.

An early example is the TEXTRUNNER system (Banko et al., 2007), which identifies relations with a set of handcrafted syntactic rules. The examples that are acquired from the handcrafted rules are then used to train a classification model that uses part-of-speech patterns as features. Finally, the relations that are extracted by the classifier are aggregated, removing redundant relations and computing the number of times that each relation is mentioned in the corpus. TEXTRUNNER was the first in a series of systems that performed increasingly accurate open relation extraction by incorporating more precise linguistic features (Etzioni et al., 2011), distant supervision from Wikipedia infoboxes (Wu and Weld, 2010), and better learning algorithms (Zhu et al., 2009).

17.3 Events

Relations link pairs of entities, but many real-world situations involve more than two entities. Consider again the example sentence (17.8a), which describes the event of an election, with four properties: the office (MAYOR), the district (ATLANTA), the date (1973), and the person elected (MAYNARD JACKSON, JR.). In **event detection**, a schema is provided for each event type (e.g., an election, a terrorist attack, or a chemical reaction), indicating all the possible properties of the event. The system is then required to fill in as many of these properties as possible (Doddington et al., 2004).

Event detection systems generally involve a retrieval component (finding relevant documents and passages of text) and an extraction component (determining the properties of the event based on the retrieved texts). Early approaches focused on finite-state patterns for identify event properties (Hobbs et al., 1997); such patterns can be automatically induced by searching for patterns that are especially likely to appear in documents that match the event query (Riloff, 1996). Contemporary approaches employ techniques that are similar to FrameNet semantic role labeling (§ 13.2), such as structured prediction over local and global features (Li et al., 2013) and bidirectional recurrent neural networks (Feng et al., 2016). These methods detect whether an event is described in a sentence and, if so, what are its properties.

Event coreference Because multiple sentences may describe unique properties of a single event, **event coreference** is required to link event mentions across a single passage of text, or between passages (Humphreys et al., 1997). Bejan and Harabagiu (2014) define event coreference as the task of identifying event mentions that share the same event participants (i.e., the slot-filling entities) and the same event properties (e.g., the time and location), within or across documents. Event coreference resolution can be performed using supervised learning techniques in a similar way to entity coreference, as described in chapter 15: move left to right through the document, and use a classifier to decide whether to link each event reference to an existing cluster of coreferent events, or to create a new cluster (Ahn, 2006). Each clustering decision is based on the compatibility of features describing the participants and properties of the event. Due to the difficulty of annotating large amounts of data for entity coreference, unsupervised approaches are especially desirable (Chen and Ji, 2009; Bejan and Harabagiu, 2014).

Relations between events Just as entities are related to other entities, events may be related to other events: for example, the event of winning an election both *precedes* and *causes* the event of serving as mayor; moving to Atlanta *precedes* and *enables* the event of becoming mayor of Atlanta; and moving from Dallas to Atlanta *prevents* the event of later becoming mayor of Dallas. As these examples show, events may be related both temporally and causally. The **TimeML** annotation scheme specifies a set of six temporal relations between events (Pustejovsky et al., 2005), derived in part from **interval algebra** (Allen, 1984). The TimeBank corpus provides TimeML annotations for 186 documents (Pustejovsky et al., 2003). Methods for detecting these temporal relations combine supervised machine learning with temporal constraints, such as transitivity (e.g. Mani et al., 2006; Chambers and Jurafsky, 2008).

More recent annotation schemes and datasets combine temporal and causal relations (Mirza et al., 2014; Dunietz et al., 2017): for example, the CaTeRS dataset includes annotations of 320 five-sentence short stories (Mostafazadeh et al., 2016). Abstracting still further, **processes** are networks of causal relations between multiple events. A small dataset of biological processes is annotated in the ProcessBank dataset (Berant et al., 2014), with the goal of supporting automatic question answering on scientific textbooks.

Table 17.4
Table of factuality values from the FactBank corpus (Saurí and Pustejovsky, 2009). The entry (NA) indicates that this combination is not annotated.

	Positive (+)	Negative (−)	Underspecified (u)
Certain (CT)	Fact: CT+	Counterfact: CT−	Certain, but unknown: CTU
Probable (PR)	Probable: PR+	Not probable: PR−	(NA)
Possible (PS)	Possible: PS+	Not possible: PS−	(NA)
Underspecified (U)	(NA)	(NA)	Unknown or uncommitted: UU

17.4 Hedges, Denials, and Hypotheticals

The methods described thus far apply to **propositions** about the way things are in the real world. But natural language can also describe events and relations that are likely or unlikely, possible or impossible, desired or feared. The following examples hint at the scope of the problem (Prabhakaran et al., 2010):

(17.9) a. GM will lay off workers.
b. A spokesman for GM said GM will lay off workers.
c. GM may lay off workers.
d. The politician claimed that GM will lay off workers.
e. Some wish GM would lay off workers.
f. Will GM lay off workers?
g. Many wonder whether GM will lay off workers.

Accurate information extraction requires handling these **extra-propositional** aspects of meaning, which are sometimes summarized under the terms **modality** and **negation**.[7] Modality refers to expressions of the speaker's attitude toward her own statements, including "degree of certainty, reliability, subjectivity, sources of information, and perspective" (Morante and Sporleder, 2012). Various systematizations of modality have been proposed (e.g., Palmer, 2001), including categories such as future, interrogative, imperative, conditional, and subjective. Information extraction is particularly concerned with negation and certainty. For example, Saurí and Pustejovsky (2009) link negation with a modal calculus of certainty, likelihood, and possibility, creating the two-dimensional schema shown in table 17.4. This is the basis for the FactBank corpus, with annotations of the **factuality** of all sentences in 208 documents of news text.

7. The classification of negation as extra-propositional is controversial: Packard et al. (2014) argue that negation is a "core part of compositionally constructed logical-form representations." Negation is an element of the semantic parsing tasks discussed in chapters 12 and 13—for example, negation markers are treated as adjuncts in PropBank semantic role labeling. However, many of the relation extraction methods mentioned in this chapter do not handle negation directly. A further consideration is that negation interacts closely with aspects of modality that are generally not considered in propositional semantics, such as certainty and subjectivity.

A related concept is **hedging**, in which speakers limit their commitment to a proposition (Lakoff, 1973):

(17.10) a. These results **suggest** that expression of c-jun, jun B, and jun D genes **might** be involved in terminal granulocyte differentiation ... (Morante and Daelemans, 2009).

b. A whale is **technically** a mammal (Lakoff, 1973).

In the first example, the hedges *suggest* and *might* communicate uncertainty; in the second example, there is no uncertainty, but the hedge *technically* indicates that the evidence for the proposition will not fully meet the reader's expectations. Hedging has been studied extensively in scientific texts (Medlock and Briscoe, 2007; Morante and Daelemans, 2009), where the goal of large-scale extraction of scientific facts is obstructed by hedges and speculation. Still another related aspect of modality is **evidentiality**, in which speakers mark the source of their information. In many languages, it is obligatory to mark evidentiality through affixes or particles (Aikhenvald, 2004); while evidentiality is not grammaticalized in English, authors are expected to express this information in contexts such as journalism (Kovach and Rosenstiel, 2014) and Wikipedia.[8]

Methods for handling negation and modality generally include two phases:

1. detecting negated or uncertain events;
2. identifying **scope** of the negation or modal operator.

A considerable body of work on negation has employed rule-based techniques such as regular expressions (Chapman et al., 2001) to detect negated events. Such techniques match lexical cues (e.g., *Norwood was* ***not*** *elected Mayor*), while avoiding "double negatives" (e.g., *surely all this is* ***not without*** *meaning*). Supervised techniques involve classifiers over lexical and syntactic features (Uzuner et al., 2009) and sequence labeling (Prabhakaran et al., 2010).

The scope refers to the elements of the text whose propositional meaning is negated or modulated (Huddleston and Pullum, 2005), as elucidated in the following example from Morante and Sporleder (2012):

(17.11) [After his habit he <u>said</u>] **nothing**, and after mine I asked no questions.
After his habit he said nothing, and [after mine I <u>asked</u>] **no** [questions].

In this sentence, there are two negation cues (*nothing* and *no*). Each negates an event, indicated by the underlined verbs *said* and *asked*, and each occurs within a scope: *after his habit he said* and *after mine I asked* _____ *questions*. Scope identification is typically formalized as a sequence labeling problem, with each word token labeled as beginning, inside, or outside of a cue, focus, or scope span (see § 8.3). Conventional sequence labeling approaches

8. https://en.wikipedia.org/wiki/Wikipedia:Verifiability.

can then be applied, using surface features as well as syntax (Velldal et al., 2012) and semantic analysis (Packard et al., 2014). Labeled datasets include the BioScope corpus of biomedical texts (Vincze et al., 2008) and a shared task dataset of detective stories by Arthur Conan Doyle (Morante and Blanco, 2012).

17.5 Question Answering and Machine Reading

The victory of the Watson question-answering system against three top human players on the game show *Jeopardy!* was a landmark moment for natural language processing (Ferrucci et al., 2010). Game show questions are usually answered by **factoids**: entity names and short phrases.[9] The task of factoid question answering is therefore closely related to information extraction, with the additional problem of accurately parsing the question.

17.5.1 Formal Semantics

Semantic parsing is an effective method for answering questions in restricted domains such as questions about geography and airline reservations (Zettlemoyer and Collins, 2005) and has also been applied in "open-domain" settings such as question answering on Freebase (Berant et al., 2013) and biomedical research abstracts (Poon and Domingos, 2009). One approach is to convert the question into a lambda calculus expression that returns a boolean value: for example, the question *who is the mayor of the capital of Georgia?* would be converted to

$$\lambda x . \exists y \ \textsc{capital}(\textsc{Georgia}, y) \wedge \textsc{mayor}(y, x). \qquad [17.22]$$

This lambda expression can then be used to query an existing knowledge base, returning "true" for all entities that satisfy it.

17.5.2 Machine Reading

Recent work has focused on answering questions about specific textual passages, similar to the reading comprehension examinations for young students (Hirschman et al., 1999). This task has come to be known as **machine reading**.

Datasets The machine reading problem can be formulated in a number of different ways. The most important distinction is what form the answer should take.

- **Multiple-choice question answering**, as in the MCTest dataset of stories (Richardson et al., 2013) and the New York Regents Science Exams (Clark, 2015). In MCTest, the answer is deducible from the text alone, while in the science exams, the system must make

9. The broader landscape of question answering includes "why" questions (*Why did Ahab continue to pursue the white whale?*), "how questions" (*How did Queequeg die?*), and requests for summaries (*What was Ishmael's attitude toward organized religion?*). For more, see Hirschman and Gaizauskas (2001).

inferences using an existing model of the underlying scientific phenomena. Here is an example from MCTest:

(17.12) James the turtle was always getting into trouble. Sometimes he'd reach into the freezer and empty out all the food …

Q: What is the name of the trouble making turtle?
(a) Fries
(b) Pudding
(c) James
(d) Jane

- **Cloze**-style "fill-in-the-blank" questions, as in the CNN/Daily Mail comprehension task (Hermann et al., 2015), the Children's Book Test (Hill et al., 2016), and the Who-did-What dataset (Onishi et al., 2016). In these tasks, the system must guess which word or entity completes a sentence, based on reading a passage of text. Here is an example from Who-did-What:

(17.13) Q: Tottenham manager Juande Ramos has hinted he will allow _____ to leave if the Bulgaria striker makes it clear he is unhappy (Onishi et al., 2016).

The query sentence may be selected either from the story itself or from an external summary. In either case, datasets can be created automatically by processing large quantities existing documents. An additional constraint is that that missing element from the cloze must appear in the main passage of text: for example, in Who-did-What, the candidates include all entities mentioned in the main passage. In the CNN/Daily Mail dataset, each entity name is replaced by a unique identifier, for example, ENTITY37. This ensures that correct answers can only be obtained by accurately reading the text and not from external knowledge about the entities.

- **Extractive** question answering, in which the answer is drawn from the original text. In WikiQA, answers are sentences (Yang et al., 2015). In the Stanford Question Answering Dataset (SQuAD), answers are words or short phrases (Rajpurkar et al., 2016):

(17.14) In metereology, precipitation is any product of the condensation of atmospheric water vapor that falls under gravity.

Q: What causes precipitation to fall? A: gravity

In both WikiQA and SQuAD, the original texts are Wikipedia articles, and the questions are generated by crowdworkers.

Methods A baseline method is to search the text for sentences or short passages that overlap with both the query and the candidate answer (Richardson et al., 2013). In example (17.12), this baseline would select the correct answer, because *James* appears in a sentence that includes the query terms *trouble* and *turtle*.

This baseline can be implemented as a neural architecture, using an **attention mechanism** (see § 18.3.1), which scores the similarity of the query to each part of the source text (Chen et al., 2016). The first step is to encode the passage $\boldsymbol{w}^{(p)}$ and the query $\boldsymbol{w}^{(q)}$, using two bidirectional LSTMs (§ 7.6):

$$\boldsymbol{h}^{(q)} = \text{BiLSTM}(\boldsymbol{w}^{(q)}; \Theta^{(q)}) \quad [17.23]$$

$$\boldsymbol{h}^{(p)} = \text{BiLSTM}(\boldsymbol{w}^{(p)}; \Theta^{(p)}). \quad [17.24]$$

The query is represented by vertically concatenating the final states of the left-to-right and right-to-left passes:

$$\boldsymbol{u} = [\overrightarrow{\boldsymbol{h}^{(q)}}_{M_q}; \overleftarrow{\boldsymbol{h}^{(q)}}_0]. \quad [17.25]$$

The attention vector is computed as a softmax over a vector of bilinear products, and the expected representation is computed by summing over attention values,

$$\tilde{\alpha}_m = (\boldsymbol{u}^{(q)})^\top \mathbf{W}_a \boldsymbol{h}_m^{(p)} \quad [17.26]$$

$$\boldsymbol{\alpha} = \text{SoftMax}(\tilde{\boldsymbol{\alpha}}) \quad [17.27]$$

$$\boldsymbol{o} = \sum_{m=1}^{M} \alpha_m \boldsymbol{h}_m^{(p)}. \quad [17.28]$$

Each candidate answer c is represented by a vector $\boldsymbol{x}_c$. Assuming the candidate answers are spans from the original text, these vectors can be set equal to the corresponding element in $\boldsymbol{h}^{(p)}$. The score for each candidate answer a is computed by the inner product,

$$\hat{c} = \operatorname*{argmax}_c \boldsymbol{o} \cdot \boldsymbol{x}_c. \quad [17.29]$$

This architecture can be trained end to end from a loss based on the log-likelihood of the correct answer. A number of related architectures have been proposed (e.g., Hermann et al., 2015; Kadlec et al., 2016; Cui et al., 2017; Dhingra et al., 2017), and these methods are surveyed by Wang et al. (2017).

Additional Resources

The field of information extraction is surveyed in course notes by Grishman (2012) and more recently in a short survey paper (Grishman, 2015). Shen et al. (2015) survey the task of entity linking, and Ji and Grishman (2011) survey work on knowledge base population. This chapter's discussion of nonpropositional meaning was strongly influenced by Morante and Sporleder (2012), who introduced a special issue of the journal *Computational Linguistics* dedicated to modality and negation.

Exercises

1. Go to the Wikipedia page for your favorite movie. For each record in the info box (e.g., *Screenplay by: Stanley Kubrick*), report whether there is a sentence in the article containing both the field and value (e.g., *The screenplay was written by Stanley Kubrick*). If not, is there is a sentence in the article containing just the value? (For records with more than one value, just use the first value.)
2. Building on your answer in the previous question, report the dependency path between the head words of the field and value for at least three records.
3. Consider the following heuristic for entity linking:
   - Among all entities that have the same type as the mention (e.g., LOC, PER), choose the one whose name has the lowest edit distance from the mention.
   - If more than one entity has the right type and the lowest edit distance from the mention, choose the most popular one.
   - If no candidate entity has the right type, choose NIL.

   Now suppose you have the following feature function:

   $\boldsymbol{f}(y, \boldsymbol{x}) = [\text{edit-dist}(\text{name}(y), \boldsymbol{x}), \text{same-type}(y, \boldsymbol{x}), \text{popularity}(y), \delta(y = \text{NIL})]$

   Design a set of ranking weights $\boldsymbol{\theta}$ that match the heuristic. You may assume that edit distance and popularity are always in the range $[0, 100]$ and that the NIL entity has values of zero for all features except $\delta(y = \text{NIL})$.
4. Now consider another heuristic:
   - Among all candidate entities that have edit distance zero from the mention, and are the right type, choose the most popular one.
   - If no entity has edit distance zero from the mention, choose the one with the right type that is most popular, regardless of edit distance.
   - If no entity has the right type, choose NIL.

   Using the same features and assumptions from the previous problem, prove that there is no set of weights that could implement this heuristic. Then show that the heuristic can be implemented by adding a single feature. Your new feature should consider only the edit distance.
5. Download the Reuters corpus in NLTK, and iterate over the tokens in the corpus:

```
import nltk
nltk.corpus.download('reuters')
from nltk.corpus import reuters
for word in reuters.words():
  #your code here
```

a) Apply the pattern _____, *such as* _____ to obtain candidates for the IS-A relation, for example, IS-A(ROMANIA, COUNTRY). What are three pairs that this method identifies correctly? What are three different pairs that it gets wrong?

b) Design a pattern for the PRESIDENT relation, for example, PRESIDENT(PHILIPPINES, CORAZON AQUINO). In this case, you may want to augment your pattern matcher with the ability to match multiple token wildcards, perhaps using case information to detect proper names. Again, list three correct and incorrect outputs.

c) Preprocess the Reuters data by running a named entity recognizer, replacing tokens with named entity spans when applicable—for example, your pattern can now match on *the United States* if the NER system tags it. Apply your PRESIDENT matcher to this preprocessed data. Does the accuracy improve? Compare 20 randomly selected pairs from this pattern and the one you designed in the previous part.

6. Using the same NLTK Reuters corpus, apply distant supervision to build a training set for detecting the relation between nations and their capitals. Start with the following known relations: (JAPAN, TOKYO), (FRANCE, PARIS), (ITALY, ROME). How many positive and negative examples are you able to extract?

7. Represent the dependency path $\boldsymbol{x}^{(i)}$ as a sequence of words and dependency arcs of length M_i, ignoring the endpoints of the path. In example 1 of table 17.2, the dependency path is

$$\boldsymbol{x}^{(1)} = (\underset{\text{NSUBJ}}{\leftarrow}, \textit{traveled}, \underset{\text{OBL}}{\rightarrow}). \quad [17.30]$$

If $x_m^{(i)}$ is a word, then let $\text{pos}(x_m^{(i)})$ be its part of speech, using the tagset defined in chapter 8.

We can define the following kernel function over pairs of dependency paths (Bunescu and Mooney, 2005):

$$\kappa(\boldsymbol{x}^{(i)}, \boldsymbol{x}^{(j)}) = \begin{cases} 0, & M_i \neq M_j \\ \prod_{m=1}^{M_i} c(x_m^{(i)}, x_m^{(j)}), & M_i = M_j \end{cases}$$

$$c(x_m^{(i)}, x_m^{(j)}) = \begin{cases} 2, & x_m^{(i)} = x_m^{(j)} \\ 1, & x_m^{(i)} \neq x_m^{(j)} \text{ and } \text{pos}(x_m^{(i)}) = \text{pos}(x_m^{(j)}) \\ 0, & \text{otherwise} \end{cases}$$

Using this kernel function, compute the kernel similarities of example 1 from table 17.2 with the other five examples.

8. Continuing from the previous problem, suppose that the instances have the following labels:

$$y_2 = 1, y_3 = -1, y_4 = -1, y_5 = 1, y_6 = 1 \quad [17.31]$$

Equation 17.13 defines a kernel-based classification in terms of parameters α and b. Using the above labels for $y_2, \ldots, y_6$, identify the values of α and b under which $\hat{y}_1 = 1$. Remember the constraint that $\alpha_i \geq 0$ for all i.

9. Consider the neural QA system described in § 17.5.2, but restrict the set of candidate answers to words in the passage, and set each candidate answer embedding $\boldsymbol{x}$ equal to the vector $\boldsymbol{h}_m^{(p)}$, representing token m in the passage, so that $\hat{m} = \text{argmax}_m\, \boldsymbol{o} \cdot \boldsymbol{h}_m^{(p)}$. Suppose the system selects answer $\hat{m}$, but the correct answer is m^*. Consider the gradient of the margin loss with respect to the attention:
   a) Prove that $\frac{\partial \ell}{\partial \alpha_{\hat{m}}} \geq \frac{\partial \ell}{\partial \alpha_{m*}}$.
   b) Assuming that $||\boldsymbol{h}_{\hat{m}}|| = ||\boldsymbol{h}_{m^*}||$, prove that $\frac{\partial \ell}{\partial \alpha_{\hat{m}}} \geq 0$ and $\frac{\partial \ell}{\partial \alpha_{m^*}} \leq 0$. Explain in words what this means about how the attention is expected to change after a gradient-based update.

18 Machine Translation

Machine translation (MT) is one of the "holy grail" problems in artificial intelligence, with the potential to facilitate communication between people anywhere in the world. As a result, MT has received significant attention and funding since the early 1950s. However, it has proved remarkably challenging, and while there has been substantial progress toward usable MT systems—especially for high-resource language pairs like English-French—we are still far from translation systems that match the nuance and depth of human translations.

18.1 Machine Translation as a Task

Machine translation can be formulated as an optimization problem:

$$\hat{\boldsymbol{w}}^{(t)} = \underset{\boldsymbol{w}^{(t)}}{\operatorname{argmax}}\, \Psi(\boldsymbol{w}^{(s)}, \boldsymbol{w}^{(t)}), \tag{18.1}$$

where $\boldsymbol{w}^{(s)}$ is a sentence in a **source** language, $\boldsymbol{w}^{(t)}$ is a sentence in the **target language**, and Ψ is a scoring function. As usual, this formalism requires two components: a decoding algorithm for computing $\hat{\boldsymbol{w}}^{(t)}$ and a learning algorithm for estimating the parameters of the scoring function Ψ.

Decoding is difficult for machine translation because of the huge space of possible translations. We have faced large label spaces before: for example, in sequence labeling, the set of possible label sequences is exponential in the length of the input. In these cases, it was possible to search the space quickly by introducing locality assumptions: for example, that each tag depends only on its predecessor, or that each production depends only on its parent. In machine translation, no such locality assumptions seem possible: human translators reword, reorder, and rearrange words; they replace single words with multiword phrases, and vice versa. This flexibility means that in even relatively simple translation models, decoding is NP-hard (Knight, 1999). Approaches for dealing with this complexity are described in § 18.4.

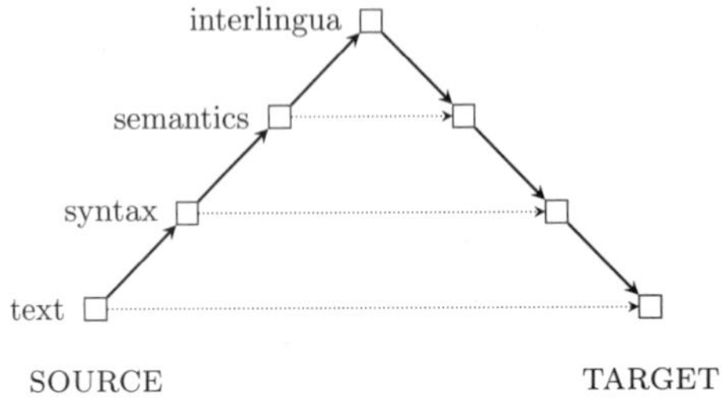

Figure 18.1
The Vauquois Pyramid.

Estimating translation models is difficult as well. Labeled translation data usually comes in the form parallel sentences, like the following Spanish sentence and its English translation:

$\boldsymbol{w}^{(s)} = $ *A Vinay le gusta las manzanas.*

$\boldsymbol{w}^{(t)} = $ *Vinay likes apples.*

A useful feature function would note the translation pairs (*gusta, likes*), (*manzanas, apples*), and even (*Vinay, Vinay*). But this word-to-word **alignment** is not given in the data. One solution is to treat this alignment as a **latent variable**; this is the approach taken by classical **statistical machine translation (SMT)** systems, described in § 18.2. Another solution is to model the relationship between $\boldsymbol{w}^{(t)}$ and $\boldsymbol{w}^{(s)}$ through a more complex and expressive function; this is the approach taken by **neural machine translation (NMT)** systems, described in § 18.3.

The **Vauquois Pyramid** is a theory of how translation should be done. At the lowest level, the translation system operates on individual words, but the horizontal distance at this level is large, because languages express ideas differently. If we can move up the pyramid to syntactic structure, the distance for translation is reduced; we then need only produce target-language text from the syntactic representation, which can be as simple as reading off a tree. Further up the pyramid lies semantics; translating between semantic representations should be easier still, but mapping between semantics and surface text is a difficult, unsolved problem. At the top of the pyramid is **interlingua**, a semantic representation that is so generic that it is identical across all human languages. Philosophers debate whether such a thing as interlingua is really possible (e.g., Derrida, 1985). While the first-order logic representations discussed in chapter 12 might be thought to be language independent, they are built on an inventory of predicates that are suspiciously similar to English words (Nirenburg and Wilks, 2001). Nonetheless, the idea of linking translation and semantic understanding may still be a promising path, if the resulting translations better preserve the meaning of the original text.

Table 18.1
Adequacy and fluency for translations of the Spanish sentence *A Vinay le gusta Python*

	Adequate?	Fluent?
To Vinay it like Python	yes	no
Vinay debugs memory leaks	no	yes
Vinay likes Python	yes	yes

18.1.1 Evaluating Translations

There are two main criteria for a translation, summarized in table 18.1.

- **Adequacy**: The translation $\boldsymbol{w}^{(t)}$ should adequately reflect the content of $\boldsymbol{w}^{(s)}$. For example, if $\boldsymbol{w}^{(s)} =$ *A Vinay le gusta Python*, the reference translation is $\boldsymbol{w}^{(t)} =$ *Vinay likes Python*. However, the **gloss**, or word-for-word translation $\boldsymbol{w}^{(t)} =$ *To Vinay it like Python,* is also considered adequate because it contains all the relevant content. The output $\boldsymbol{w}^{(t)} =$ *Vinay debugs memory leaks* is not adequate.
- **Fluency**: The translation $\boldsymbol{w}^{(t)}$ should read like fluent text in the target language. By this criterion, the gloss $\boldsymbol{w}^{(t)} =$ *To Vinay it like Python* will score poorly, and $\boldsymbol{w}^{(t)} =$ *Vinay debugs memory leaks* will be preferred.

Automated evaluations of machine translations typically merge both of these criteria, by comparing the system translation with one or more **reference translations**, produced by professional human translators. The most popular quantitative metric is **BLEU** (bilingual evaluation understudy; Papineni et al., 2002), which is based on n-gram precision: what fraction of n-grams in the system translation appear in the reference? Specifically, for each n-gram length, the precision is defined as

$$p_n = \frac{\text{number of } n\text{-grams appearing in both reference and hypothesis translations}}{\text{number of } n\text{-grams appearing in the hypothesis translation}}. \qquad [18.2]$$

The n-gram precisions for three hypothesis translations are shown in figure 18.2.

The BLEU score is then based on the average, $\exp \frac{1}{N} \sum_{n=1}^{N} \log p_n$. Two modifications of equation 18.2 are necessary: (1) to avoid computing $\log 0$, all precisions are smoothed to ensure that they are positive and (2) each n-gram in the reference can be used at most once, so that *to to to to to to* does not achieve $p_1 = 1$ against the reference *to be or not to be*. Furthermore, precision-based metrics are biased in favor of short translations, which can achieve high scores by minimizing the denominator in [18.2]. To avoid this issue, a **brevity penalty** is applied to translations that are shorter than the reference. This penalty is indicated as "BP" in figure 18.2.

Automated metrics like BLEU have been validated by correlation with human judgments of translation quality. Nonetheless, it is not difficult to construct examples in which the BLEU score is high, yet the translation is disfluent or carries a completely different

	Translation	p_1	p_2	p_3	p_4	BP	BLEU
Reference	*Vinay likes programming in Python*						
Sys1	*To Vinay it like to program Python*	$\frac{2}{7}$	0	0	0	1	.21
Sys2	*Vinay likes Python*	$\frac{3}{3}$	$\frac{1}{2}$	0	0	.51	.33
Sys3	*Vinay likes programming in his pajamas*	$\frac{4}{6}$	$\frac{3}{5}$	$\frac{2}{4}$	$\frac{1}{3}$	1	.76

Figure 18.2
A reference translation and three system outputs. For each output, p_n indicates the precision at each n-gram, and BP indicates the brevity penalty.

meaning from the original. To give just one example, consider the problem of translating pronouns. Because pronouns refer to specific entities, a single incorrect pronoun can obliterate the semantics of the original sentence. Existing state-of-the-art systems generally do not attempt the reasoning necessary to correctly resolve pronominal anaphora (Hardmeier, 2012). Despite the importance of pronouns for semantics, they have a marginal impact on BLEU, which may help to explain why existing systems do not make a greater effort to translate them correctly.

Fairness and bias The problem of pronoun translation intersects with issues of fairness and bias. In many languages, such as Turkish, the third-person singular pronoun is gender neutral. Today's state-of-the-art systems produce the following Turkish-English translations (Caliskan et al., 2017):

(18.1) *O bir doktor.*
He is a doctor.

(18.2) *O bir hemşire.*
She is a nurse.

The same problem arises for other professions that have stereotypical genders, such as engineers, soldiers, and teachers and for other languages that have gender-neutral pronouns. This bias was not directly programmed into the translation model; it arises from statistical tendencies in existing datasets. This highlights a general problem with data-driven approaches, which can perpetuate biases that negatively impact disadvantaged groups. Worse, machine learning can *amplify* biases in data (Bolukbasi et al., 2016): if a dataset has even a slight tendency toward men as doctors, the resulting translation model may produce translations in which doctors are always *he* and nurses are always *she*.

Other metrics A range of other automated metrics have been proposed for machine translation. One potential weakness of BLEU is that it only measures precision; **METEOR** is a weighted F-MEASURE, which is a combination of recall and precision (see § 4.4.1). **Translation Error Rate (TER)** computes the string **edit distance** (see § 9.1.4) between the reference and the hypothesis (Snover et al., 2006). For language pairs like English and Japanese, there are substantial differences in word order, and word order errors are not sufficiently captured by n-gram-based metrics. The **RIBES** metric applies rank correlation to measure the similarity in word order between the system and reference translations (Isozaki et al., 2010).

18.1.2 Data

Data-driven approaches to machine translation rely primarily on **parallel corpora**, which are translations at the sentence level. Early work focused on government records, in which fine-grained official translations are often required. For example, the IBM translation systems were based on the proceedings of the Canadian Parliament, called **Hansards**, which are recorded in English and French (Brown et al., 1990). The growth of the European Union led to the development of the **EuroParl corpus**, which spans 21 European languages (Koehn, 2005). While these datasets helped to launch the field of statistical machine translation, they are restricted to narrow domains and a formal speaking style, limiting their applicability to other types of text. As more resources are committed to machine translation, new translation datasets have been commissioned. This has broadened the scope of available data to news,[1] movie subtitles,[2] social media (Ling et al., 2013), dialogues (Fordyce, 2007), TED talks (Paul et al., 2010), and scientific research articles (Nakazawa et al., 2016).

Despite this growing set of resources, the main bottleneck in machine translation data is the need for parallel corpora that are aligned at the sentence level. Many languages have sizable parallel corpora with some high-resource language, but not with each other. The high-resource language can then be used as a "pivot" or "bridge" (Boitet, 1988; Utiyama and Isahara, 2007): for example, De Gispert and Marino (2006) use Spanish as a bridge for translation between Catalan and English. For most of the 6,000 languages spoken today, the only source of translation data remains the Judeo-Christian Bible (Resnik et al., 1999). While relatively small, at less than a million tokens, the Bible has been translated into more than 2,000 languages, far outpacing any other corpus. Some research has explored the possibility of automatically identifying parallel sentence pairs from unaligned parallel texts, such as web pages and Wikipedia articles (Kilgarriff and Grefenstette, 2003; Resnik and Smith, 2003; Adafre and De Rijke, 2006). Another approach is to create large parallel corpora through crowdsourcing (Zaidan and Callison-Burch, 2011).

1. https://catalog.ldc.upenn.edu/LDC2010T10, http://www.statmt.org/wmt15/translation-task.html.
2. http://opus.nlpl.eu/.

18.2 Statistical Machine Translation

The previous section introduced adequacy and fluency as the two main criteria for machine translation. A natural modeling approach is to represent them with separate scores,

$$\Psi(\boldsymbol{w}^{(s)}, \boldsymbol{w}^{(t)}) = \Psi_A(\boldsymbol{w}^{(s)}, \boldsymbol{w}^{(t)}) + \Psi_F(\boldsymbol{w}^{(t)}). \tag{18.3}$$

The fluency score Ψ_F need not even consider the source sentence; it only judges $\boldsymbol{w}^{(t)}$ on whether it is fluent in the target language. This decomposition is advantageous because it makes it possible to estimate the two scoring functions on separate data. While the adequacy model must be estimated from aligned sentences—which are relatively expensive and rare—the fluency model can be estimated from monolingual text in the target language. Large monolingual corpora are now available in many languages, thanks to resources such as Wikipedia.

An elegant justification of the decomposition in equation 18.3 is provided by the **noisy channel model**, in which each scoring function is a log-probability:

$$\Psi_A(\boldsymbol{w}^{(s)}, \boldsymbol{w}^{(t)}) \triangleq \log \mathrm{p}_{S|T}(\boldsymbol{w}^{(s)} \mid \boldsymbol{w}^{(t)}) \tag{18.4}$$

$$\Psi_F(\boldsymbol{w}^{(t)}) \triangleq \log \mathrm{p}_T(\boldsymbol{w}^{(t)}) \tag{18.5}$$

$$\Psi(\boldsymbol{w}^{(s)}, \boldsymbol{w}^{(t)}) = \log \mathrm{p}_{S|T}(\boldsymbol{w}^{(s)} \mid \boldsymbol{w}^{(t)}) + \log \mathrm{p}_T(\boldsymbol{w}^{(t)}) = \log \mathrm{p}_{S,T}(\boldsymbol{w}^{(s)}, \boldsymbol{w}^{(t)}). \tag{18.6}$$

By setting the scoring functions equal to the logarithms of the prior and likelihood, their sum is equal to $\log \mathrm{p}_{S,T}$, which is the logarithm of the joint probability of the source and target. The sentence $\hat{\boldsymbol{w}}^{(t)}$ that maximizes this joint probability is also the maximizer of the conditional probability $\mathrm{p}_{T|S}$, making it the most likely target language sentence, conditioned on the source.

The noisy channel model can be justified by a generative story. The target text is originally generated from a probability model p_T. It is then encoded in a "noisy channel" $\mathrm{p}_{S|T}$, which converts it to a string in the source language. In decoding, we apply Bayes' rule to recover the string $\boldsymbol{w}^{(t)}$ that is maximally likely under the conditional probability $\mathrm{p}_{T|S}$. Under this interpretation, the target probability p_T is just a language model and can be estimated using any of the techniques from chapter 6. The only remaining learning problem is to estimate the translation model $\mathrm{p}_{S|T}$.

18.2.1 Statistical Translation Modeling

The simplest decomposition of the translation model is word to word: each word in the source should be aligned to a word in the translation. This approach presupposes an **alignment** $\mathcal{A}(\boldsymbol{w}^{(s)}, \boldsymbol{w}^{(t)})$, which contains a list of pairs of source and target tokens. For example, given $\boldsymbol{w}^{(s)} =$ *A Vinay le gusta Python* and $\boldsymbol{w}^{(t)} =$ *Vinay likes Python*, one possible word-to-word alignment is

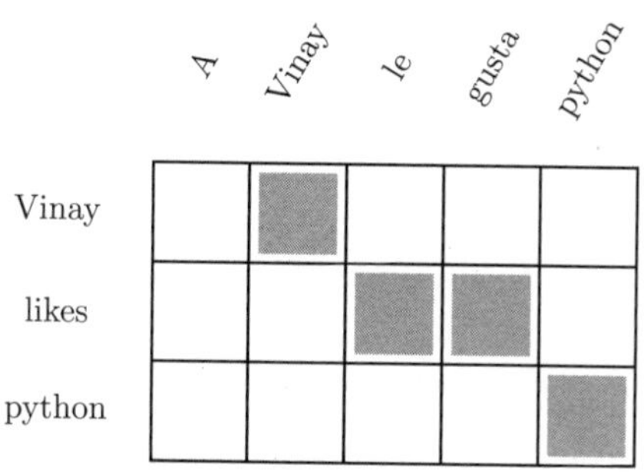

Figure 18.3
An example word-to-word alignment.

$$\mathcal{A}(\boldsymbol{w}^{(s)}, \boldsymbol{w}^{(t)}) = \{(A, \varnothing), (\textit{Vinay, Vinay}), (\textit{le, likes}), (\textit{gusta, likes}), (\textit{Python, Python})\}. \quad [18.7]$$

This alignment is shown in figure 18.3. Another, less promising, alignment is

$$\mathcal{A}(\boldsymbol{w}^{(s)}, \boldsymbol{w}^{(t)}) = \{(\textit{A, Vinay}), (\textit{Vinay, likes}), (\textit{le, Python}), (\textit{gusta}, \varnothing), (\textit{Python}, \varnothing)\}. \quad [18.8]$$

Each alignment contains exactly one tuple for each word in the *source*, which serves to explain how the source word could be translated from the target, as required by the translation probability $p_{S|T}$. If no appropriate word in the target can be identified for a source word, it is aligned to ∅—as is the case for the Spanish function word *a* in the example, which glosses to the English word *to*. Words in the target can align with multiple words in the source, so that the target word *likes* can align to both *le* and *gusta* in the source.

The joint probability of the alignment and the translation can be defined conveniently as

$$p(\boldsymbol{w}^{(s)}, \mathcal{A} \mid \boldsymbol{w}^{(t)}) = \prod_{m=1}^{M^{(s)}} p(w_m^{(s)}, a_m \mid w_{a_m}^{(t)}, m, M^{(s)}, M^{(t)}) \quad [18.9]$$

$$= \prod_{m=1}^{M^{(s)}} p(a_m \mid m, M^{(s)}, M^{(t)}) \times p(w_m^{(s)} \mid w_{a_m}^{(t)}). \quad [18.10]$$

This probability model makes two key assumptions:

- The alignment probability factors across tokens,

$$p(\mathcal{A} \mid \boldsymbol{w}^{(s)}, \boldsymbol{w}^{(t)}) = \prod_{m=1}^{M^{(s)}} p(a_m \mid m, M^{(s)}, M^{(t)}). \quad [18.11]$$

This means that each alignment decision is independent of the others and depends only on the index m and the sentence lengths $M^{(s)}$ and $M^{(t)}$.

- The translation probability also factors across tokens,

$$p(\boldsymbol{w}^{(s)} \mid \boldsymbol{w}^{(t)}, \mathcal{A}) = \prod_{m=1}^{M^{(s)}} p(w_m^{(s)} \mid w_{a_m}^{(t)}), \tag{18.12}$$

so that each word in $\boldsymbol{w}^{(s)}$ depends only on its aligned word in $\boldsymbol{w}^{(t)}$. This means that translation is word to word, ignoring context. The hope is that the target language model $p(\boldsymbol{w}^{(t)})$ will correct any disfluencies that arise from word-to-word translation.

To translate with such a model, we could sum or max over all possible alignments,

$$p(\boldsymbol{w}^{(s)}, \boldsymbol{w}^{(t)}) = \sum_{\mathcal{A}} p(\boldsymbol{w}^{(s)}, \boldsymbol{w}^{(t)}, \mathcal{A}) \tag{18.13}$$

$$= p(\boldsymbol{w}^{(t)}) \sum_{\mathcal{A}} p(\mathcal{A}) \times p(\boldsymbol{w}^{(s)} \mid \boldsymbol{w}^{(t)}, \mathcal{A}) \tag{18.14}$$

$$\geq p(\boldsymbol{w}^{(t)}) \max_{\mathcal{A}} p(\mathcal{A}) \times p(\boldsymbol{w}^{(s)} \mid \boldsymbol{w}^{(t)}, \mathcal{A}). \tag{18.15}$$

The term $p(\mathcal{A})$ defines the prior probability over alignments. A series of alignment models with increasingly relaxed independence assumptions was developed by researchers at IBM in the 1980s and 1990s, known as IBM Models 1-6 (Och and Ney, 2003). IBM Model 1 makes the strongest independence assumption:

$$p(a_m \mid m, M^{(s)}, M^{(t)}) = \frac{1}{M^{(t)}}. \tag{18.16}$$

In this model, every alignment is equally likely. This is almost surely wrong, but it results in a convex learning objective, yielding a good initialization for the more complex alignment models (Brown et al., 1993; Koehn, 2009).

18.2.2 Estimation

Let us define the parameter $\theta_{u \to v}$ as the probability of translating target word u to source word v. If word-to-word alignments were annotated, these probabilities could be computed from relative frequencies,

$$\hat{\theta}_{u \to v} = \frac{\text{count}(u, v)}{\text{count}(u)}, \tag{18.17}$$

where $\text{count}(u, v)$ is the count of instances in which word v was aligned to word u in the training set and $\text{count}(u)$ is the total count of the target word u. The smoothing techniques in chapter 6 can help to reduce the variance of these probability estimates.

Conversely, if we had an accurate translation model, we could estimate the likelihood of each alignment decision,

$$q_m(a_m \mid \boldsymbol{w}^{(s)}, \boldsymbol{w}^{(t)}) \propto \mathrm{p}(a_m \mid m, M^{(s)}, M^{(t)}) \times \mathrm{p}(w_m^{(s)} \mid w_{a_m}^{(t)}), \qquad [18.18]$$

where $q_m(a_m \mid \boldsymbol{w}^{(s)}, \boldsymbol{w}^{(t)})$ is a measure of our confidence in aligning source word $w_m^{(s)}$ to target word $w_{a_m}^{(t)}$. The relative frequencies could then be computed from the *expected counts*,

$$\hat{\theta}_{u \to v} = \frac{E_q\,[\mathrm{count}(u, v)]}{\mathrm{count}(u)} \qquad [18.19]$$

$$E_q\,[\mathrm{count}(u, v)] = \sum_m q_m(a_m \mid \boldsymbol{w}^{(s)}, \boldsymbol{w}^{(t)}) \times \delta(w_m^{(s)} = v) \times \delta(w_{a_m}^{(t)} = u). \qquad [18.20]$$

The **expectation-maximization (EM)** algorithm proceeds by iteratively updating q_m and $\hat{\Theta}$. The algorithm is described in general form in chapter 5. For statistical machine translation, the steps of the algorithm are:

1. **E-step**: Update beliefs about word alignment using equation 18.18.
2. **M-step**: Update the translation model using equations 18.19 and 18.20.

As discussed in chapter 5, the expectation-maximization algorithm is guaranteed to converge, but not to a global optimum. However, for IBM Model 1, it can be shown that EM optimizes a convex objective, and global optimality is guaranteed. For this reason, IBM Model 1 is often used as an initialization for more complex alignment models. For more detail, see Koehn (2009).

18.2.3 Phrase-Based Translation

Real translations are not word-to-word substitutions. One reason is that many multiword expressions are not translated literally, as shown in this example from French:

(18.3) *Nous allons prendre un verre*
We will take a glass
We'll have a drink

The line *we will take a glass* is the word-for-word gloss of the French sentence; the translation *we'll have a drink* is shown on the third line. Such examples are difficult for word-to-word translation models, because they require translating *prendre* to *have* and *verre* to *drink*. These translations are only correct in the context of these specific phrases.

Phrase-based translation generalizes on word-based models by building translation tables and alignments between multiword spans. (These "phrases" are not necessarily syntactic constituents like the noun phrases and verb phrases described in chapters 9 and 10.) The generalization from word-based translation is surprisingly straightforward: the translation tables can now condition on multiword units and can assign probabilities to multiword units; alignments are mappings from spans to spans, $((i,j), (k,\ell))$, so that

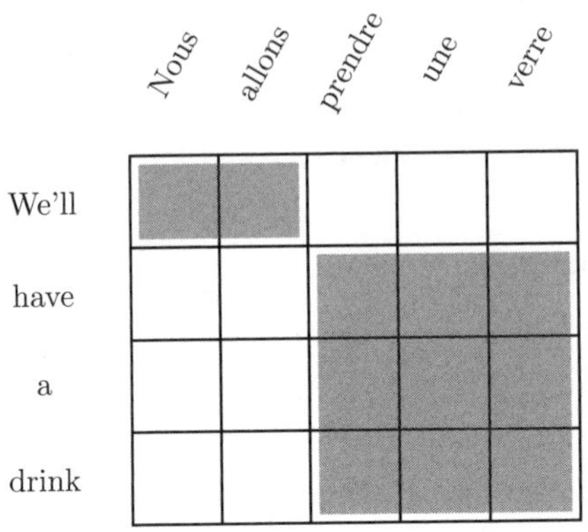

Figure 18.4
A phrase-based alignment between French and English, corresponding to example (18.3).

$$p(\boldsymbol{w}^{(s)} \mid \boldsymbol{w}^{(t)}, \mathcal{A}) = \prod_{((i,j),(k,\ell)) \in \mathcal{A}} p_{w^{(s)}|w^{(t)}}(\{w_{i+1}^{(s)}, w_{i+2}^{(s)}, \ldots, w_j^{(s)}\} \mid \{w_{k+1}^{(t)}, w_{k+2}^{(t)}, \ldots, w_\ell^{(t)}\}). \quad [18.21]$$

The phrase alignment $((i,j), (k,\ell))$ indicates that the span $\boldsymbol{w}_{i+1:j}^{(s)}$ is the translation of the span $\boldsymbol{w}_{k+1:\ell}^{(t)}$. An example phrasal alignment is shown in figure 18.4. Note that the alignment set $\mathcal{A}$ is required to cover all of the tokens in the source, just as in word-based translation. The probability model $p_{w^{(s)}|w^{(t)}}$ must now include translations for all phrase pairs, which can be learned from expectation-maximization just as in word-based statistical machine translation.

18.2.4 *Syntax-Based Translation

The Vauquois Pyramid (figure 18.1) suggests that translation might be easier if we take a higher-level view. One possibility is to incorporate the syntactic structure of the source, the target, or both. This is particularly promising for language pairs that have consistent syntactic differences. For example, English adjectives almost always precede the nouns that they modify, while in Romance languages such as French and Spanish, the adjective often follows the noun: thus, *angry fish* would translate to *pez (fish) enojado (angry)* in Spanish. In word-to-word translation, these reorderings cause the alignment model to be overly permissive. It is not that the order of *any* pair of English words can be reversed when translating into Spanish, but only adjectives and nouns within a noun phrase. Similar issues arise when translating between verb-final languages such as Japanese (in which verbs usually follow the subject and object), verb-initial languages like Tagalog and classical Arabic, and verb-medial languages such as English.

An elegant solution is to link parsing and translation in a **synchronous context-free grammar** (SCFG; Chiang, 2007).[3] An SCFG is a set of productions of the form $X \to (\alpha, \beta, \sim)$, where X is a nonterminal, α and β are sequences of terminals or nonterminals, and $\sim$ is a one-to-one alignment of items in α with items in β. English-Spanish adjective-noun ordering can be handled by a set of synchronous productions, for example,

$$\text{NP} \to (\text{DET}_1\ \text{NN}_2\ \text{JJ}_3, \quad \text{DET}_1\ \text{JJ}_3\ \text{NN}_2), \qquad [18.22]$$

with subscripts indicating the alignment between the Spanish (left) and English (right) parts of the right-hand side. Terminal productions yield translation pairs,

$$\text{JJ} \to (enojado_1, \quad angry_1). \qquad [18.23]$$

A synchronous derivation begins with the start symbol S and derives a pair of sequences of terminal symbols.

Given an SCFG in which each production yields at most two symbols in each language (Chomsky Normal Form; see § 9.2.1), a sentence can be parsed using only the CKY algorithm (chapter 10). The resulting derivation also includes productions in the other language, all the way down to the surface form. Therefore, SCFGs make translation very similar to parsing. In a weighted SCFG, the log-probability $\log \text{p}_{S|T}$ can be computed from the sum of the log-probabilities of the productions. However, combining SCFGs with a target language model is computationally expensive, necessitating approximate search algorithms (Huang and Chiang, 2007).

Synchronous context-free grammars are an example of **tree-to-tree translation**, because they model the syntactic structure of both the target and source language. In **string-to-tree translation**, string elements are translated into constituent tree fragments, which are then assembled into a translation (Yamada and Knight, 2001; Galley et al., 2004); in **tree-to-string translation**, the source side is parsed, and then transformed into a string on the target side (Liu et al., 2006). A key question for syntax-based translation is the extent to which phrasal constituents align across translations (Fox, 2002), because this governs the extent to which we can rely on monolingual parsers and treebanks. For more on syntax-based machine translation, see the monograph by Williams et al. (2016).

18.3 Neural Machine Translation

Neural network models for machine translation are based on the **encoder-decoder** architecture (Cho et al., 2014). The encoder network converts the source language sentence into a vector or matrix representation; the decoder network then converts the encoding into a sentence in the target language:

3. Earlier approaches to syntactic machine translation includes syntax-driven transduction (Lewis II and Stearns, 1968) and stochastic inversion transduction grammars (Wu, 1997).

$$z = \text{Encode}(\boldsymbol{w}^{(s)}) \tag{18.24}$$

$$\boldsymbol{w}^{(t)} \mid \boldsymbol{w}^{(s)} \sim \text{Decode}(z), \tag{18.25}$$

where the second line means that the function $\text{Decode}(z)$ defines the conditional probability $\text{p}(\boldsymbol{w}^{(t)} \mid \boldsymbol{w}^{(s)})$.

The decoder is typically a recurrent neural network, which generates the target language sentence one word at a time, while recurrently updating a hidden state. The encoder and decoder networks are trained end to end from parallel sentences. If the output layer of the decoder is a logistic function, then the entire architecture can be trained to maximize the conditional log-likelihood,

$$\log \text{p}(\boldsymbol{w}^{(t)} \mid \boldsymbol{w}^{(s)}) = \sum_{m=1}^{M^{(t)}} \text{p}(w_m^{(t)} \mid \boldsymbol{w}_{1:m-1}^{(t)}, z) \tag{18.26}$$

$$\text{p}(w_m^{(t)} \mid \boldsymbol{w}_{1:m-1}^{(t)}, \boldsymbol{w}^{(s)}) \propto \exp\left(\boldsymbol{\beta}_{w_m^{(t)}} \cdot \boldsymbol{h}_{m-1}^{(t)}\right), \tag{18.27}$$

where the hidden state $\boldsymbol{h}_{m-1}^{(t)}$ is a recurrent function of the previously generated text $\boldsymbol{w}_{1:m-1}^{(t)}$ and the encoding z, and $\boldsymbol{\beta} \in \mathbb{R}^{(V^{(t)} \times K)}$ is the matrix of output word vectors for the $V^{(t)}$ words in the target language vocabulary.

A simple encoder-decoder architecture is the **sequence-to-sequence model** (Sutskever et al., 2014). In this model, the encoder is set to the final hidden state of a **long short-term memory (LSTM)** (see § 6.3.3) on the source sentence:

$$\boldsymbol{h}_m^{(s)} = \text{LSTM}(\boldsymbol{x}_m^{(s)}, \boldsymbol{h}_{m-1}^{(s)}) \tag{18.28}$$

$$z \triangleq \boldsymbol{h}_{M^{(s)}}^{(s)}, \tag{18.29}$$

where $\boldsymbol{x}_m^{(s)}$ is the embedding of source language word $w_m^{(s)}$. The encoding then provides the initial hidden state for the decoder LSTM:

$$\boldsymbol{h}_0^{(t)} = z \tag{18.30}$$

$$\boldsymbol{h}_m^{(t)} = \text{LSTM}(\boldsymbol{x}_m^{(t)}, \boldsymbol{h}_{m-1}^{(t)}), \tag{18.31}$$

where $\boldsymbol{x}_m^{(t)}$ is the embedding of the target language word $w_m^{(t)}$.

Sequence-to-sequence translation is nothing more than wiring together two LSTMs: one to read the source and another to generate the target. To make the model work well, some additional tweaks are needed:

- Most notably, the model works much better if the source sentence is reversed, reading from the end of the sentence back to the beginning. In this way, the words at the beginning of the source have the greatest impact on the encoding z, and therefore impact the words at the beginning of the target sentence. Later work on more advanced encoding models,

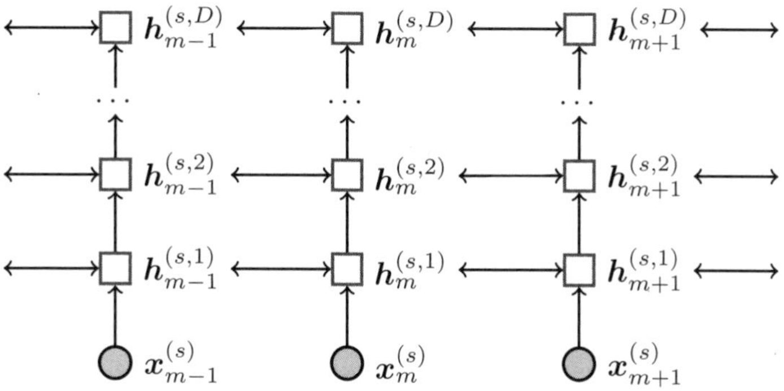

Figure 18.5
A deep bidirectional LSTM encoder.

such as **neural attention** (see § 18.3.1), has eliminated the need for reversing the source sentence.

- The encoder and decoder can be implemented as **deep LSTMs**, with multiple layers of hidden states. As shown in figure 18.5, each hidden state $\boldsymbol{h}_m^{(s,i)}$ at layer i is treated as the input to an LSTM at layer $i+1$:

$$\boldsymbol{h}_m^{(s,1)} = \text{LSTM}(\boldsymbol{x}_m^{(s)}, \boldsymbol{h}_{m-1}^{(s)}) \tag{18.32}$$

$$\boldsymbol{h}_m^{(s,i+1)} = \text{LSTM}(\boldsymbol{h}_m^{(s,i)}, \boldsymbol{h}_{m-1}^{(s,i+1)}), \quad \forall i \geq 1. \tag{18.33}$$

The original work on sequence-to-sequence translation used four layers; in 2016, Google's commercial machine translation system used eight layers (Wu et al., 2016).[4]

- Significant improvements can be obtained by creating an **ensemble** of translation models, each trained from a different random initialization. For an ensemble of size N, the per-token decoding probability is set equal to

$$\text{p}(w^{(t)} \mid \boldsymbol{z}, \boldsymbol{w}_{1:m-1}^{(t)}) = \frac{1}{N} \sum_{i=1}^{N} \text{p}_i(w^{(t)} \mid \boldsymbol{z}, \boldsymbol{w}_{1:m-1}^{(t)}), \tag{18.34}$$

where p_i is the decoding probability for model i. Each translation model in the ensemble includes its own encoder and decoder networks.

- The original sequence-to-sequence model used a fairly standard training setup: stochastic gradient descent with an exponentially decreasing learning rate after the first five epochs; minibatches of 128 sentences, chosen to have similar length so that each sentence

4. Google reports that this system took six days to train for English-French translation, using 96 NVIDIA K80 GPUs, which would have cost roughly half a million dollars at the time.

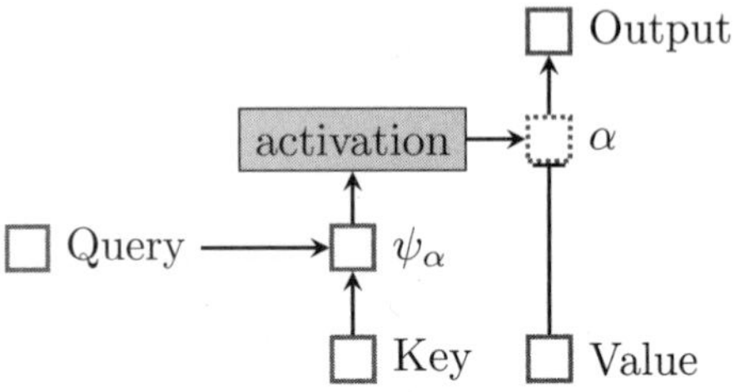

Figure 18.6
A general view of neural attention. The dotted box indicates that each $\alpha_{m\to n}$ can be viewed as a **gate** on value n.

on the batch will take roughly the same amount of time to process; and gradient clipping (see § 3.3.4) to ensure that the norm of the gradient never exceeds some predefined value.

18.3.1 Neural Attention

The sequence-to-sequence model discussed in the previous section was a radical departure from statistical machine translation, in which each word or phrase in the target language is conditioned on a single word or phrase in the source language. Both approaches have advantages. Statistical translation leverages the idea of compositionality—translations of large units should be based on the translations of their component parts—and this seems crucial if we are to scale translation to longer units of text. But the translation of each word or phrase often depends on the larger context, and encoder-decoder models capture this context at the sentence level.

Is it possible for translation to be both contextualized and compositional? One approach is to augment neural translation with an **attention mechanism**. The idea of neural attention was described in § 17.5, but its application to translation bears further discussion. In general, attention can be thought of as using a query to select from a memory of key-value pairs. However, the query, keys, and values are all vectors, and the entire operation is differentiable. For each key n in the memory, we compute a score $\psi_\alpha(m, n)$ with respect to the query m. That score is a function of the compatibility of the key and the query and can be computed using a small feedforward neural network. The vector of scores is passed through an activation function, such as softmax. The output of this activation function is a vector of nonnegative numbers $[\alpha_{m\to 1}, \alpha_{m\to 2}, \ldots, \alpha_{m\to N}]^\top$, with length N equal to the size of the memory. Each value in the memory $\boldsymbol{v}_n$ is multiplied by the attention $\alpha_{m\to n}$; the sum of these scaled values is the output. This process is shown in figure 18.6. In the extreme case that $\alpha_{m\to n} = 1$ and $\alpha_{m\to n'} = 0$ for all other n', then the attention mechanism simply selects the value $\boldsymbol{v}_n$ from the memory.

Neural attention makes it possible to integrate alignment into the encoder-decoder architecture. Rather than encoding the entire source sentence into a fixed-length vector $\boldsymbol{z}$, it can be encoded into a matrix $\mathbf{Z} \in \mathbb{R}^{K \times M^{(S)}}$, where K is the dimension of the hidden state and $M^{(S)}$ is the number of tokens in the source input. Each column of $\mathbf{Z}$ represents the state of a recurrent neural network over the source sentence. These vectors are constructed from a **bidirectional LSTM** (see § 7.6), which can be a deep network as shown in figure 18.5. These columns are both the keys and the values in the attention mechanism.

At each step m in decoding, the attentional state is computed by executing a query, which is equal to the state of the decoder, $\boldsymbol{h}_m^{(t)}$. The resulting compatibility scores are

$$\psi_\alpha(m,n) = \boldsymbol{v}_\alpha \cdot \tanh(\Theta_\alpha[\boldsymbol{h}_m^{(t)}; \boldsymbol{h}_n^{(s)}]). \quad [18.35]$$

The function ψ is thus a two-layer feedforward neural network, with weights $\boldsymbol{v}_\alpha$ on the output layer and weights Θ_α on the input layer. To convert these scores into attention weights, we apply an activation function, which can be vector-wise softmax or an element-wise sigmoid:

Softmax attention

$$\alpha_{m \to n} = \frac{\exp \psi_\alpha(m,n)}{\sum_{n'=1}^{M^{(s)}} \exp \psi_\alpha(m,n')} \quad [18.36]$$

Sigmoid attention

$$\alpha_{m \to n} = \sigma\left(\psi_\alpha(m,n)\right) \quad [18.37]$$

The attention $\boldsymbol{\alpha}$ is then used to compute a context vector $\boldsymbol{c}_m$ by taking a weighted sum over the columns of $\mathbf{Z}$,

$$\boldsymbol{c}_m = \sum_{n=1}^{M^{(s)}} \alpha_{m \to n} \boldsymbol{z}_n, \quad [18.38]$$

where $\alpha_{m \to n} \in [0,1]$ is the amount of attention from word m of the target to word n of the source. The context vector can be incorporated into the decoder's word output probability model, by adding another layer to the decoder (Luong et al., 2015a):

$$\tilde{\boldsymbol{h}}_m^{(t)} = \tanh\left(\Theta_c[\boldsymbol{h}_m^{(t)}; \boldsymbol{c}_m]\right) \quad [18.39]$$

$$\mathrm{p}(w_{m+1}^{(t)} \mid \boldsymbol{w}_{1:m}^{(t)}, \boldsymbol{w}^{(s)}) \propto \exp\left(\boldsymbol{\beta}_{w_{m+1}^{(t)}} \cdot \tilde{\boldsymbol{h}}_m^{(t)}\right). \quad [18.40]$$

Here the decoder state $\boldsymbol{h}_m^{(t)}$ is concatenated with the context vector, forming the input to compute a final output vector $\tilde{\boldsymbol{h}}_m^{(t)}$. The context vector can be incorporated into the decoder recurrence in a similar manner (Bahdanau et al., 2014).

18.3.2 *Neural Machine Translation without Recurrence

In the encoder-decoder model, attention's "keys and values" are the hidden state representations in the encoder network, z, and the "queries" are state representations in the decoder network $\boldsymbol{h}^{(t)}$. It is also possible to completely eliminate recurrence from neural translation, by applying **self-attention** (Kim et al., 2017; Lin et al., 2017) within the encoder and decoder, as in the **transformer architecture** (Vaswani et al., 2017). For level i, the basic equations of the encoder side of the transformer are

$$z_m^{(i)} = \sum_{n=1}^{M^{(s)}} \alpha_{m\to n}^{(i)} (\Theta_v \boldsymbol{h}_n^{(i-1)}) \quad [18.41]$$

$$\boldsymbol{h}_m^{(i)} = \Theta_2 \, \text{ReLU}\left(\Theta_1 z_m^{(i)} + \boldsymbol{b}_1\right) + \boldsymbol{b}_2. \quad [18.42]$$

For each token m at level i, we compute self-attention over the entire source sentence. The keys, values, and queries are all projections of the vector $\boldsymbol{h}^{(i-1)}$: for example, in equation 18.41, the value $\boldsymbol{v}_n$ is the projection $\Theta_v \boldsymbol{h}_n^{(i-1)}$. The attention scores $\alpha_{m\to n}^{(i)}$ are computed using a scaled form of softmax attention,

$$\alpha_{m\to n} \propto \exp(\psi_\alpha(m,n)/M), \quad [18.43]$$

where M is the length of the input. This encourages the attention to be more evenly dispersed across the input. Self-attention is applied across multiple "heads," each using different projections of $\boldsymbol{h}^{(i-1)}$ to form the keys, values, and queries. This architecture is shown in figure 18.7. The output of the self-attentional layer is the representation $z_m^{(i)}$, which is then passed through a two-layer feedforward network, yielding the input to the next layer, $\boldsymbol{h}^{(i)}$. This self-attentional architecture can be applied in the decoder as well, but this requires that there is zero attention to future words: $\alpha_{m\to n} = 0$ for all $n > m$.

To ensure that information about word order in the source is integrated into the model, the encoder augments the base layer of the network with **positional encodings** of the indices of each word in the source. These encodings are vectors for each position $m \in \{1, 2, \ldots, M\}$. The transformer sets these encodings equal to a set of sinusoidal functions of m,

$$e_{2i-1}(m) = \sin(m/(10000^{\frac{2i}{K_e}})) \quad [18.44]$$

$$e_{2i}(m) = \cos(m/(10000^{\frac{2i}{K_e}})), \quad \forall i \in \{1, 2, \ldots, K_e/2\}, \quad [18.45]$$

where $e_{2i}(m)$ is the value at element $2i$ of the encoding for index m. As we progress through the encoding, the sinusoidal functions have progressively narrower bandwidths. This enables the model to learn to attend by relative positions of words. The positional encodings are concatenated with the word embeddings $\boldsymbol{x}_m$ at the base layer of the model.[5]

5. The transformer architecture relies on several additional tricks, including **layer normalization** (see § 3.3.4), residual connections around the nonlinear activations (see § 3.2.2), and a non-monotonic learning rate schedule.

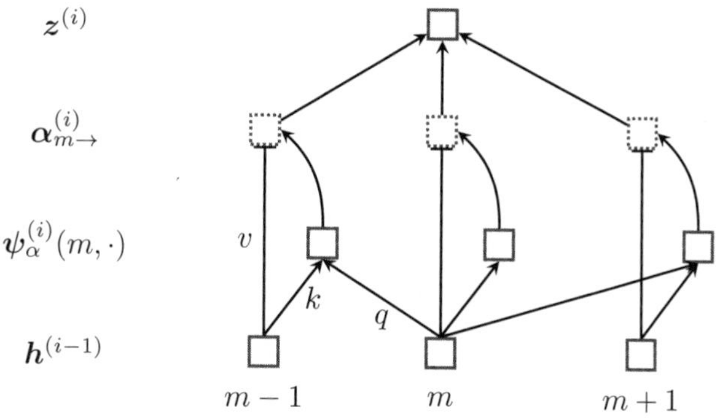

Figure 18.7

The transformer encoder's computation of $z_m^{(i)}$ from $h^{(i-1)}$. The **k**ey, **v**alue, and **q**uery are shown for token $m-1$. For example, $\psi_\alpha^{(i)}(m, m-1)$ is computed from the key $\Theta_k h_{m-1}^{(i-1)}$ and the query $\Theta_q h_m^{(i-1)}$, and the gate $\alpha_{m\to m-1}^{(i)}$ operates on the value $\Theta_v h_{m-1}^{(i-1)}$. The figure shows a minimal version of the architecture, with a single attention head. With multiple heads, it is possible to attend to different properties of multiple words.

Convolutional neural networks (see § 3.4) have also been applied as encoders in neural machine translation (Gehring et al., 2017). For each word $w_m^{(s)}$, a convolutional network computes a representation $h_m^{(s)}$ from the embeddings of the word and its neighbors. This procedure is applied several times, creating a deep convolutional network. The recurrent decoder then computes a set of attention weights over these convolutional representations, using the decoder's hidden state $h^{(t)}$ as the queries. This attention vector is used to compute a weighted average over the outputs of *another* convolutional neural network of the source, yielding an averaged representation c_m, which is then fed into the decoder. As with the transformer, speed is the main advantage over recurrent encoding models; another similarity is that word order information is approximated through the use of positional encodings.[6]

18.3.3 Out-of-Vocabulary Words

Thus far, we have treated translation as a problem at the level of words or phrases. For words that do not appear in the training data, all such models will struggle. There are two main reasons for the presence of out-of-vocabulary (OOV) words:

- New proper nouns, such as family names or organizations, are constantly arising—particularly in the news domain. The same is true, to a lesser extent, for technical terminology. This issue is shown in figure 18.8.

6. A recent evaluation found that best performance was obtained by using a recurrent network for the decoder and a transformer for the encoder (Chen et al., 2018). The transformer was also found to significantly outperform a convolutional neural network.

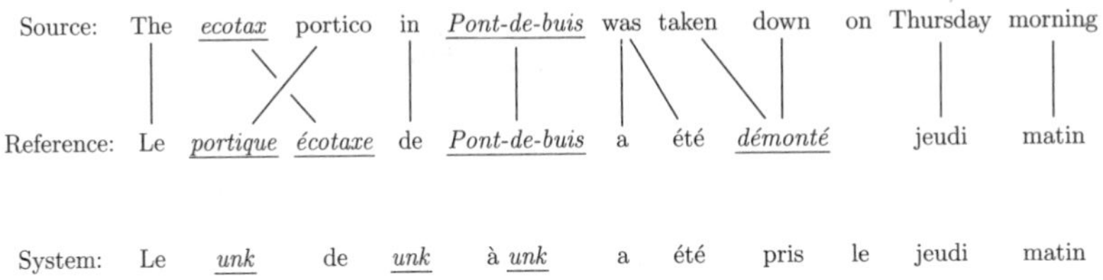

Figure 18.8
Translation with *unknown words*. The system outputs *unk* to indicate words that are outside its vocabulary. Figure adapted from Luong et al. (2015b).

- In many languages, words have complex internal structure, known as **morphology**. An example is German, which uses compounding to form nouns like *Abwasserbehandlungsanlage* (*sewage water treatment plant*; example from Sennrich et al. (2016)). While compounds could in principle be addressed by better tokenization (see § 8.4), other morphological processes involve more complex transformations of subword units.

Names and technical terms can be handled in a postprocessing step: after first identifying alignments between unknown words in the source and target, we can look up each aligned source word in a dictionary and choose a replacement (Luong et al., 2015b). If the word does not appear in the dictionary, it is likely to be a proper noun and can be copied directly from the source to the target. This approach can also be integrated directly into the translation model, rather than applying it as a postprocessing step (Jean et al., 2015).

Words with complex internal structure can be handled by translating subword units rather than entire words. A popular technique for identifying subword units is **byte-pair encoding** (BPE; Gage, 1994; Sennrich et al., 2016). The initial vocabulary is defined as the set of characters used in the text. The most common character bigram is then merged into a new symbol, the vocabulary is updated, and the merging operation is applied again. For example, given the dictionary {*fish, fished, want, wanted, bike, biked*}, we would first form the subword unit *ed*, because this character bigram appears in three of the six words. Next, there are several bigrams that each appear in a pair of words: *fi*, *is*, *sh*, *wa*, *an*, etc. These can be merged in any order. By iterating this process, we eventually reach the segmentation, {*fish*, *fish+ed*, *want*, *want+ed*, *bik+e*, *bik+ed*}. At this point, there are no bigrams that appear more than once. In real applications, merging is performed until the number of subword units reaches some predefined threshold, such as 10^4.

Each subword unit is treated as a token for translation, in both the encoder (source side) and decoder (target side). BPE can be applied jointly to the union of the source and target vocabularies, identifying subword units that appear in both languages. For languages that have different scripts, such as English and Russian, **transliteration** between the scripts should be applied first.[7]

18.4 Decoding

Given a trained translation model, the decoding task is

$$\hat{\boldsymbol{w}}^{(t)} = \underset{\boldsymbol{w} \in \mathcal{V}^*}{\operatorname{argmax}}\, \Psi(\boldsymbol{w}, \boldsymbol{w}^{(s)}), \qquad [18.46]$$

where $\hat{w}^{(t)}$ is a sequence of tokens from the target vocabulary $\mathcal{V}$. It is not possible to efficiently obtain exact solutions to the decoding problem, for even minimally effective models in either statistical or neural machine translation. Today's state-of-the-art translation systems use **beam search** (see § 11.3.1), which is an incremental decoding algorithm that maintains a small constant number of competitive hypotheses. Such greedy approximations are reasonably effective in practice, and this may be in part because the decoding objective is only loosely correlated with measures of translation quality, so that exact optimization of [18.46] may not greatly improve the resulting translations.

Decoding in neural machine translation is simpler than in phrase-based statistical machine translation.[8] The scoring function Ψ is defined as

$$\Psi(\boldsymbol{w}^{(t)}, \boldsymbol{w}^{(s)}) = \sum_{m=1}^{M^{(t)}} \psi(w_m^{(t)}; \boldsymbol{w}_{1:m-1}^{(t)}, z) \qquad [18.47]$$

$$\psi(w^{(t)}; \boldsymbol{w}_{1:m-1}^{(t)}, z) = \beta_{w_m^{(t)}} \cdot \boldsymbol{h}_m^{(t)} - \log \sum_{w \in \mathcal{V}} \exp\left(\beta_w \cdot \boldsymbol{h}_m^{(t)}\right), \qquad [18.48]$$

where z is the encoding of the source sentence $\boldsymbol{w}^{(s)}$ and $\boldsymbol{h}_m^{(t)}$ is a function of the encoding z and the decoding history $\boldsymbol{w}_{1:m-1}^{(t)}$. This formulation subsumes the attentional translation model, where z is a matrix encoding of the source.

Now consider the incremental decoding algorithm:

$$\hat{w}_m^{(t)} = \underset{w \in \mathcal{V}}{\operatorname{argmax}}\, \psi(w; \hat{\boldsymbol{w}}_{1:m-1}^{(t)}, z), \quad m = 1, 2, \ldots \qquad [18.49]$$

This algorithm selects the best target language word at position m, assuming that it has already generated the sequence $\hat{\boldsymbol{w}}_{1:m-1}^{(t)}$. (Termination can be handled by augmenting the vocabulary $\mathcal{V}$ with a special end-of-sequence token, ■.) The incremental algorithm is likely to produce a suboptimal solution to the optimization problem defined in equation 18.46, because selecting the highest-scoring word at position m can set the decoder on a "garden

7. Transliteration is crucial for converting names and other foreign words between languages that do not share a single script, such as English and Japanese. It is typically approached using the finite-state methods discussed in chapter 9 (Knight and Graehl, 1998).

8. For more on decoding in phrase-based statistical models, see Koehn (2009).

path," in which there are no good choices at some later position $n > m$. We might hope for some dynamic programming solution, as in sequence labeling (§ 7.3). But the Viterbi algorithm and its relatives rely on a Markov decomposition of the objective function into a sum of local scores: for example, scores can consider locally adjacent tags (y_m, y_{m-1}), but not the entire tagging history $\boldsymbol{y}_{1:m}$. This decomposition is not applicable to recurrent neural networks, because the hidden state $\boldsymbol{h}_m^{(t)}$ is impacted by the entire history $\boldsymbol{w}_{1:m}^{(t)}$; this sensitivity to long-range context is precisely what makes recurrent neural networks so effective.[9] In fact, it can be shown that decoding from any recurrent neural network is NP-complete (Siegelmann and Sontag, 1995; Chen et al., 2018).

Beam search **Beam search** is a general technique for avoiding search errors when exhaustive search is impossible; it was discussed in more detail in § 11.3.1. Beam search can be seen as a variant of the incremental decoding algorithm sketched in equation 18.49, but at each step m, a set of K different hypotheses are kept on the beam. For each hypothesis $k \in \{1, 2, \ldots, K\}$, we compute both the current score $\sum_{m=1}^{M^{(t)}} \psi(w_{k,m}^{(t)}; \boldsymbol{w}_{k,1:m-1}^{(t)}, \boldsymbol{z})$ as well as the current hidden state $\boldsymbol{h}_k^{(t)}$. At each step in the beam search, the K top-scoring children of each hypothesis currently on the beam are "expanded," and the beam is updated. For a detailed description of beam search for RNN decoding, see Graves (2012).

Learning and search Conventionally, the learning algorithm is trained to predict the next token in the translation, conditioned on the translation history being correct. But if decoding must be approximate, then we might do better by modifying the learning algorithm to be robust to errors in the translation history. **Scheduled sampling** does this by training on histories that sometimes come from the ground truth and sometimes come from the model's own output (Bengio et al., 2015).[10] As training proceeds, the training wheels come off: we increase the fraction of tokens that come from the model rather than the ground truth. Another approach is to train on an objective that relates directly to beam search performance (Wiseman et al., 2016). **Reinforcement learning** has also been applied to decoding of RNN-based translation models, making it possible to directly optimize translation metrics such as BLEU (Ranzato et al., 2016).

18.5 Training toward the Evaluation Metric

In likelihood-based training, the objective is the maximize the probability of a parallel corpus. However, translations are not evaluated in terms of likelihood: metrics like BLEU consider only the correctness of a single output translation and not the range of

9. Note that this problem does not impact RNN-based sequence labeling models (see § 7.6). This is because the tags produced by these models do not affect the recurrent state.

10. Scheduled sampling builds on earlier work on learning to search (Daumé III et al., 2009; Ross et al., 2011), which are also described in § 15.2.4.

probabilities that the model assigns. It might therefore be better to train translation models to achieve the highest BLEU score possible—to the extent that we believe BLEU measures translation quality. Unfortunately, BLEU and related metrics are not friendly for optimization: they are discontinuous, nondifferentiable functions of the parameters of the translation model.

Consider an error function $\Delta(\hat{\boldsymbol{w}}^{(t)}, \boldsymbol{w}^{(t)})$, which measures the discrepancy between the system translation $\hat{\boldsymbol{w}}^{(t)}$ and the reference translation $\boldsymbol{w}^{(t)}$; this function could be based on BLEU or any other metric on translation quality. One possible criterion would be to select the parameters $\boldsymbol{\theta}$ that minimize the error of the system's preferred translation,

$$\hat{\boldsymbol{w}}^{(t)} = \underset{\boldsymbol{w}^{(t)}}{\operatorname{argmax}}\ \Psi(\boldsymbol{w}^{(t)}, \boldsymbol{w}^{(s)}; \boldsymbol{\theta}) \qquad [18.50]$$

$$\hat{\boldsymbol{\theta}} = \underset{\boldsymbol{\theta}}{\operatorname{argmin}}\ \Delta(\hat{\boldsymbol{w}}^{(t)}, \boldsymbol{w}^{(s)}). \qquad [18.51]$$

However, identifying the top-scoring translation $\hat{\boldsymbol{w}}^{(t)}$ is usually intractable, as described in the previous section. In **minimum error-rate training (MERT)**, $\hat{\boldsymbol{w}}^{(t)}$ is selected from a set of candidate translations $\mathcal{Y}(\boldsymbol{w}^{(s)})$; this is typically a strict subset of all possible translations, so that it is only possible to optimize an approximation to the true error rate (Och and Ney, 2003).

A further issue is that the objective function in equation 18.51 is discontinuous and nondifferentiable, due to the argmax over translations: an infinitesimal change in the parameters $\boldsymbol{\theta}$ could cause another translation to be selected, with a completely different error. To address this issue, we can instead minimize the **risk**, which is defined as the expected error rate,

$$R(\boldsymbol{\theta}) = E_{\hat{\boldsymbol{w}}^{(t)} \mid \boldsymbol{w}^{(s)}; \boldsymbol{\theta}}[\Delta(\hat{\boldsymbol{w}}^{(t)}, \boldsymbol{w}^{(t)})] \qquad [18.52]$$

$$= \sum_{\hat{\boldsymbol{w}}^{(t)} \in \mathcal{Y}(\boldsymbol{w}^{(s)})} \mathrm{p}(\hat{\boldsymbol{w}}^{(t)} \mid \boldsymbol{w}^{(s)}) \times \Delta(\hat{\boldsymbol{w}}^{(t)}, \boldsymbol{w}^{(t)}), \qquad [18.53]$$

Minimum risk training minimizes the sum of $R(\boldsymbol{\theta})$ across all instances in the training set.

The risk can be generalized by exponentiating the translation probabilities,

$$\tilde{p}(\boldsymbol{w}^{(t)}; \boldsymbol{\theta}, \alpha) \propto \left(\mathrm{p}(\boldsymbol{w}^{(t)} \mid \boldsymbol{w}^{(s)}; \boldsymbol{\theta})\right)^{\alpha} \qquad [18.54]$$

$$\tilde{R}(\boldsymbol{\theta}) = \sum_{\hat{\boldsymbol{w}}^{(t)} \in \mathcal{Y}(\boldsymbol{w}^{(s)})} \tilde{p}(\hat{\boldsymbol{w}}^{(t)} \mid \boldsymbol{w}^{(s)}; \alpha, \boldsymbol{\theta}) \times \Delta(\hat{\boldsymbol{w}}^{(t)}, \boldsymbol{w}^{(t)}), \qquad [18.55]$$

where $\mathcal{Y}(\boldsymbol{w}^{(s)})$ is now the set of *all* possible translations for $\boldsymbol{w}^{(s)}$. Exponentiating the probabilities in this way is known as **annealing** (Smith and Eisner, 2006). When $\alpha = 1$, then $\tilde{R}(\boldsymbol{\theta}) = R(\boldsymbol{\theta})$; when $\alpha = \infty$, then $\tilde{R}(\boldsymbol{\theta})$ is equivalent to the sum of the errors of the maximum probability translations for each sentence in the dataset.

Clearly the set of candidate translations $\mathcal{Y}(\boldsymbol{w}^{(s)})$ is too large to explicitly sum over. Because the error function Δ generally does not decompose into smaller parts, there is no efficient dynamic programming solution to sum over this set. We can approximate the sum $\sum_{\hat{\boldsymbol{w}}^{(t)} \in \mathcal{Y}(\boldsymbol{w}^{(s)})}$ with a sum over a finite number of samples, $\{\boldsymbol{w}_1^{(t)}, \boldsymbol{w}_2^{(t)}, \ldots, \boldsymbol{w}_K^{(t)}\}$. If these samples were drawn uniformly at random, then the (annealed) risk would be approximated as follows (Shen et al., 2016):

$$\tilde{R}(\boldsymbol{\theta}) \approx \frac{1}{Z} \sum_{k=1}^{K} \tilde{p}(\boldsymbol{w}_k^{(t)} \mid \boldsymbol{w}^{(s)}; \boldsymbol{\theta}, \alpha) \times \Delta(\boldsymbol{w}_k^{(t)}, \boldsymbol{w}^{(t)}) \tag{18.56}$$

$$Z = \sum_{k=1}^{K} \tilde{p}(\boldsymbol{w}_k^{(t)} \mid \boldsymbol{w}^{(s)}; \boldsymbol{\theta}, \alpha). \tag{18.57}$$

Shen et al. (2016) report that performance plateaus at $K = 100$ for minimum risk training of neural machine translation.

Uniform sampling over the set of all possible translations is undesirable, because most translations have very low probability. A solution from Monte Carlo estimation is **importance sampling**, in which we draw samples from a **proposal distribution** $q(\boldsymbol{w}^{(s)})$. This distribution can be set equal to the current translation model $\mathrm{p}(\boldsymbol{w}^{(t)} \mid \boldsymbol{w}^{(s)}; \boldsymbol{\theta})$. Each sample is then weighted by an **importance score**, $\omega_k = \frac{\tilde{p}(\boldsymbol{w}_k^{(t)} \mid \boldsymbol{w}^{(s)})}{q(\boldsymbol{w}_k^{(t)}; \boldsymbol{w}^{(s)})}$. The effect of this weighting is to correct for any mismatch between the proposal distribution q and the true distribution $\tilde{p}$. The risk can then be approximated as

$$\boldsymbol{w}_k^{(t)} \sim q(\boldsymbol{w}^{(s)}) \tag{18.58}$$

$$\omega_k = \frac{\tilde{p}(\boldsymbol{w}_k^{(t)} \mid \boldsymbol{w}^{(s)})}{q(\boldsymbol{w}_k^{(t)}; \boldsymbol{w}^{(s)})} \tag{18.59}$$

$$\tilde{R}(\boldsymbol{\theta}) \approx \frac{1}{\sum_{k=1}^{K} \omega_k} \sum_{k=1}^{K} \omega_k \times \Delta(\boldsymbol{w}_k^{(t)}, \boldsymbol{w}^{(t)}). \tag{18.60}$$

Importance sampling will generally give a more accurate approximation than uniform sampling. The only formal requirement is that the proposal assigns nonzero probability to every $\boldsymbol{w}^{(t)} \in \mathcal{Y}(\boldsymbol{w}^{(s)})$. For more on importance sampling and related methods, see Robert and Casella (2013).

Additional Resources

A complete textbook on machine translation is available from Koehn (2009). While this book precedes recent work on neural translation, a more recent draft chapter on neural translation models is also available (Koehn, 2017). Neubig (2017) provides a comprehensive tutorial on neural machine translation, starting from first principles. The course notes from Cho (2015) are also useful. Several neural machine translation libraries are available: LAMTRAM is an implementation of neural machine translation in DYNET (Neubig et al., 2017b); OPENNMT (Klein et al., 2017) and FAIRSEQ are available in PYTORCH and TENSOR2TENSOR is an implementation of several of the Google translation models in TENSORFLOW (Abadi et al., 2016).

Literary translation is especially challenging, even for expert human translators. Messud (2014) describes some of these issues in her review of an English translation of *L'étranger*, the 1942 French novel by Albert Camus.[11] She compares the new translation by Sandra Smith against earlier translations by Stuart Gilbert and Matthew Ward, focusing on the difficulties presented by a single word in the first sentence:

> Then, too, Smith has reconsidered the book's famous opening. Camus's original is deceptively simple: "*Aujourd'hui, maman est morte.*" Gilbert influenced generations by offering us "Mother died today"—inscribing in Meursault [the narrator] from the outset a formality that could be construed as heartlessness. But *maman*, after all, is intimate and affectionate, a child's name for his mother. Matthew Ward concluded that it was essentially untranslatable ("mom" or "mummy" being not quite apt), and left it in the original French: "Maman died today." There is a clear logic in this choice; but as Smith has explained, in an interview in *The Guardian*, *maman* "didn't really tell the reader anything about the connotation." She, instead, has translated the sentence as "My mother died today."
>
>> I chose "My mother" because I thought about how someone would tell another person that his mother had died. Meursault is speaking to the reader directly. "My mother died today" seemed to me the way it would work, and also implied the closeness of "maman" you get in the French.
>
> Elsewhere in the book, she has translated *maman* as "mama"—again, striving to come as close as possible to an actual, colloquial word that will carry the same connotations as *maman* does in French.

The passage is a reminder that while the quality of machine translation has improved dramatically in recent years, expert human translations draw on considerations that are beyond the ken of any contemporary computational approach.

Exercises

1. Using Google translate or another online service, translate the following example into two different languages of your choice:

   (18.4) It is not down on any map; true places never are.

   Then translate each result back into English. Which is closer to the original? Can you explain the differences?

11. The book review is currently available online at www.nybooks.com/articles/2014/06/05/camus-new-letranger/.

2. Compute the unsmoothed n-gram precisions $p_1 \dots p_4$ for the two back translations in the previous problem, using the original source as the reference. Your n-grams should include punctuation, and you should segment conjunctions like *it's* into two tokens.
3. You are given the following dataset of translations from "simple" to "difficult" English:

   (18.5) a. *Kids like cats.*
   Children adore felines.

   b. *Cats hats.*
   Felines fedoras.

   Estimate a word-to-word statistical translation model from simple English (source) to difficult English (target), using the expectation-maximization as described in § 18.2.2. Compute two iterations of the algorithm by hand, starting from a uniform translation model, and using the simple alignment model $\text{p}(a_m \mid m, M^{(s)}, M^{(t)}) = \frac{1}{M^{(t)}}$. Hint: in the final M-step, you will want to switch from fractions to decimals.
4. Building on the previous problem, what will be the converged translation probability table? Can you state a general condition about the data, under which this translation model will fail in the way that it fails here?
5. Propose a simple alignment model that would make it possible to recover the correct translation probabilities from the toy dataset in the previous two problems.
6. Let $\ell^{(t)}_{m+1}$ represent the loss at word $m+1$ of the target, and let $\boldsymbol{h}^{(s)}_n$ represent the hidden state at word n of the source. Write the expression for the derivative $\frac{\partial \ell^{(t)}_{m+1}}{\partial \boldsymbol{h}^{(s)}_n}$ in the sequence-to-sequence translation model expressed in equations [18.28-18.31]. You may assume that both the encoder and decoder are one-layer LSTMs. In general, how many terms are on the shortest backpropagation path from $\ell^{(t)}_{m+1}$ to $\boldsymbol{h}^{(s)}_n$?
7. Now consider the neural attentional model from § 18.3.1, with sigmoid attention. The derivative $\frac{\partial \ell^{(t)}_{m+1}}{\partial z_n}$ is the sum of many paths through the computation graph; identify the shortest such path. You may assume that the initial state of the decoder recurrence $\boldsymbol{h}^{(t)}_0$ is *not* tied to the final state of the encoder recurrence $\boldsymbol{h}^{(s)}_{M^{(s)}}$.
8. Apply byte-pair encoding for the vocabulary *it*, *unit*, *unite*, until no bigram appears more than once.
9. This problem relates to the complexity of machine translation. Suppose you have an oracle that returns the list of words to include in the translation, so that your only task is to order the words. Furthermore, suppose that the scoring function over orderings is a sum over bigrams, $\sum_{m=1}^{M} \psi(\boldsymbol{w}^{(t)}_m, \boldsymbol{w}^{(t)}_{m-1})$. Show that the problem of finding the optimal translation is NP-complete, by reduction from a well-known problem.
10. Hand-design an attentional recurrent translation model that simply copies the input from the source to the target. You may assume an arbitrarily large hidden state, and

you may assume that there is a finite maximum input length M. Specify all the weights such that the maximum probability translation of any source is the source itself. Hint: it is simplest to use the Elman recurrence $\boldsymbol{h}_m = f(\Theta \boldsymbol{h}_{m-1} + \boldsymbol{x}_m)$ rather than an LSTM.

11. Give a synchronized derivation (§ 18.2.4) for this Spanish-English translation:

    (18.6) *El pez enojado atacado.*
    The fish angry attacked.
    The angry fish attacked.

    As above, the second line shows a word-for-word gloss, and the third line shows the desired translation. Use the synchronized production rule in [18.22], and design the other production rules necessary to derive this sentence pair. You may derive (*atacado, attacked*) directly from VP.

19 Text Generation

In many of the most interesting problems in natural language processing, language is the output. The previous chapter described the specific case of machine translation, but there are many other applications, from summarization of research articles, to automated journalism, to dialogue systems. This chapter emphasizes three main scenarios: data to text, in which text is generated to explain or describe a structured record or unstructured perceptual input; text to text, which typically involves fusing information from multiple linguistic sources into a single coherent summary; and dialogue, in which text is generated as part of an interactive conversation with one or more human participants.

19.1 Data-to-Text Generation

In data-to-text generation, the input ranges from structured records, such as the description of an weather forecast (as shown in figure 19.1), to unstructured perceptual data, such as a raw image or video; the output may be a single sentence, such as an image caption, or a multi paragraph argument. Despite this diversity of conditions, all data-to-text systems share some of the same challenges (Reiter and Dale, 2000):

- determining what parts of the data to describe;
- planning a presentation of this information;
- **lexicalizing** the data into words and phrases;
- organizing words and phrases into well-formed sentences and paragraphs.

The earlier stages of this process are sometimes called **content selection** and **text planning**; the later stages are often called **surface realization**.

Early systems for data-to-text generation were modular, with separate software components for each task. Artificial intelligence **planning** algorithms can be applied to both the high-level information structure and the organization of individual sentences, ensuring that communicative goals are met (McKeown, 1992; Moore and Paris, 1993). Surface realization can be performed by grammars or templates, which link specific types of data

Temperature			
time	*min*	*mean*	*max*
06:00-21:00	9	15	21

Cloud sky cover	
time	*percent (%)*
06:00-09:00	25-50
09:00-12:00	50-75

Wind speed			
time	*min*	*mean*	*max*
06:00-21:00	15	20	30

Wind direction	
time	*mode*
06:00-21:00	S

Cloudy, with temperatures between 10 and 20 degrees. South wind around 20 mph.

Figure 19.1
An example input-output pair for the task of generating text descriptions of weather forecasts (adapted from Konstas and Lapata, 2013).

to candidate words and phrases. A simple example template is offered by Wiseman et al. (2017), for generating descriptions of basketball games:

(19.1) The <team1> (<wins1>-losses1) defeated the <team2> (<wins2>-<losses2>), <pts1>-<pts2>.
The New York Knicks (45-5) defeated the Boston Celtics (11-38), 115-79.

For more complex cases, it may be necessary to apply morphological inflections such as pluralization and tense marking—even in the simple example above, languages such as Russian would require case marking suffixes for the team names. Such inflections can be applied as a postprocessing step. Another difficult challenge for surface realization is the generation of varied **referring expressions** (e.g., *The Knicks*, *New York*, *they*), which is critical to avoid repetition. As discussed in § 16.2.1, the form of referring expressions is constrained by the discourse and information structure.

An example at the intersection of rule-based and statistical techniques is the NITROGEN system (Langkilde and Knight, 1998). The input to NITROGEN is an abstract meaning representation (AMR; see § 13.3) of semantic content to be expressed in a single sentence. In data-to-text scenarios, the abstract meaning representation is the output of a higher-level text planning stage. A set of rules then converts the abstract meaning representation into various sentence plans, which may differ in both the high-level structure (e.g., active versus passive voice) as well as the low-level details (e.g., word and phrase choice). Some examples are shown in figure 19.2. To control the combinatorial explosion in the number of possible realizations for any given meaning, the sentence plans are unified into a single finite-state acceptor, in which word tokens are represented by arcs (see § 9.1.1). A bigram language model is then used to compute weights on the arcs, so that the shortest path is also the surface realization with the highest bigram language model probability.

More recent systems are unified models that are trained end to end using backpropagation. Data-to-text generation shares many properties with machine translation, including

```
(a / admire-01
  :ARG0 (v / visitor
        :ARG1-of (c / arrive-01
                 :ARG4 (j / Japan)))
  :ARG1 (m / "Mount Fuji"))
```

- Visitors who came to Japan admire Mount Fuji.
- Visitors who came in Japan admire Mount Fuji.
- Mount Fuji is admired by the visitor who came in Japan.

Figure 19.2
Abstract meaning representation and candidate surface realizations from the NITROGEN system. Example adapted from Langkilde and Knight (1998).

a problem of **alignment**: labeled examples provide the data and the text, but they do not specify which parts of the text correspond to which parts of the data. For example, to learn from figure 19.1, the system must align the word *cloudy* to records in CLOUD SKY COVER, the phrases *10* and *20 degrees* to the MIN and MAX fields in TEMPERATURE, and so on. As in machine translation, both latent variables and neural attention have been proposed as solutions.

19.1.1 Latent Data-to-Text Alignment

Given a dataset of texts and associated records $\{(\boldsymbol{w}^{(i)}, \boldsymbol{y}^{(i)})\}_{i=1}^{N}$, our goal is to learn a model Ψ, so that

$$\hat{\boldsymbol{w}} = \underset{\boldsymbol{w} \in \mathcal{V}^*}{\operatorname{argmax}}\ \Psi(\boldsymbol{w}, \boldsymbol{y}; \boldsymbol{\theta}), \quad [19.1]$$

where $\mathcal{V}^*$ is the set of strings over a discrete vocabulary and $\boldsymbol{\theta}$ is a vector of parameters. The relationship between $\boldsymbol{w}$ and $\boldsymbol{y}$ is complex: the data $\boldsymbol{y}$ may contain dozens of records and $\boldsymbol{w}$ may extend to several sentences. To facilitate learning and inference, it would be helpful to decompose the scoring function Ψ into subcomponents. This would be possible if given an **alignment**, specifying which element of $\boldsymbol{y}$ is expressed in each part of $\boldsymbol{w}$. Specifically, let z_m indicates the record aligned to word m. In figure 19.1, z_1 might specify that the word *cloudy* is aligned to the record `cloud-sky-cover:percent`. The score for this alignment would then be given by the weight on features such as

$$(\textit{cloudy}, \texttt{cloud-sky-cover:percent}). \quad [19.2]$$

In general, given an observed set of alignments, the score for a generated text can be written as sum of local scores (Angeli et al., 2010):

$$\Psi(\boldsymbol{w}, \boldsymbol{y}; \boldsymbol{\theta}) = \sum_{m=1}^{M} \psi_{w,y}(\boldsymbol{w}_m, \boldsymbol{y}_{z_m}) + \psi_w(w_m, w_{m-1}) + \psi_z(z_m, z_{m-1}), \quad [19.3]$$

where ψ_w represents a bigram language model and ψ_z can be tuned to reward coherence, such as the use of related records in nearby words.[1] The parameters of this model could

1. More expressive decompositions of Ψ are possible. For example, Wong and Mooney (2007) use a synchronous context-free grammar (see § 18.2.4) to "translate" between a meaning representation and natural language text.

be learned from labeled data $\{(\boldsymbol{w}^{(i)}, \boldsymbol{y}^{(i)}, \boldsymbol{z}^{(i)})\}_{i=1}^{N}$. However, while several datasets include structured records and natural language text (Barzilay and McKeown, 2005; Chen and Mooney, 2008; Liang and Klein, 2009), the alignments between text and records are usually not available.[2] One solution is to model the problem probabilistically, treating the alignment as a latent variable (Liang et al., 2009; Konstas and Lapata, 2013). The model can then be estimated using expectation-maximization or sampling (see chapter 5).

19.1.2 Neural Data-to-Text Generation

The **encoder-decoder model** and **neural attention** were introduced in § 18.3 as methods for neural machine translation. They can also be applied to data-to-text generation, with the data acting as the source language (Mei et al., 2016). In neural machine translation, the attention mechanism linked words in the source to words in the target; in data-to-text generation, the attention mechanism can link each part of the generated text back to a record in the data. The biggest departure from translation is in the encoder, which depends on the form of the data.

Data encoders In some types of structured records, all values are drawn from discrete sets. For example, the birthplace of an individual is drawn from a discrete set of possible locations; the diagnosis and treatment of a patient are drawn from an exhaustive list of clinical codes (Johnson et al., 2016). In such cases, vector embeddings can be estimated for each field and possible value: for example, a vector embedding for the field BIRTHPLACE and another embedding for the value BERKELEY_CALIFORNIA (Bordes et al., 2011). The table of such embeddings serves as the encoding of a structured record (He et al., 2017). It is also possible to compress the entire table into a single vector representation, by **pooling** across the embeddings of each field and value (Lebret et al., 2016).

Sequences Some types of structured records have a natural ordering, such as events in a game (Chen and Mooney, 2008) and steps in a recipe (Tutin and Kittredge, 1992). For example, the following records describe a sequence of events in a robot soccer match (Mei et al., 2016):

PASS(arg1 = PURPLE6, arg2 = PURPLE3)

KICK(arg1 = PURPLE3)

BADPASS(arg1 = PURPLE3, arg2 = PINK9).

Each event is a single record and can be encoded by a concatenation of vector representations for the event type (e.g., PASS), the field (e.g., arg1), and the values (e.g., PURPLE3),

2. An exception is a dataset of records and summaries from American football games, containing annotations of alignments between sentences and records (Snyder and Barzilay, 2007).

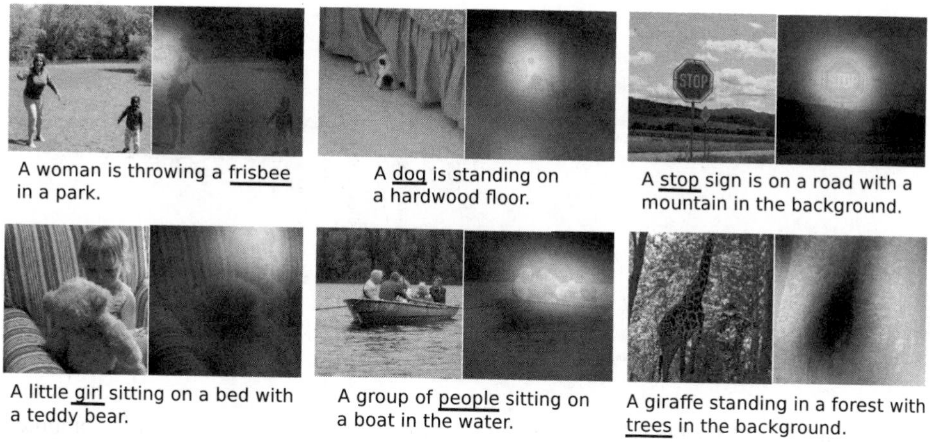

A woman is throwing a frisbee in a park.
A dog is standing on a hardwood floor.
A stop sign is on a road with a mountain in the background.
A little girl sitting on a bed with a teddy bear.
A group of people sitting on a boat in the water.
A giraffe standing in a forest with trees in the background.

Figure 19.3
Examples of the image captioning task, with attention masks shown for each of the underlined words (Xu et al., 2015).

for example,

$$\mathbf{X} = \left[\boldsymbol{u}_{\text{PASS}}, \boldsymbol{u}_{\text{arg1}}, \boldsymbol{u}_{\text{PURPLE6}}, \boldsymbol{u}_{\text{arg2}}, \boldsymbol{u}_{\text{PURPLE3}}\right]. \tag{19.4}$$

This encoding can then act as the input layer for a recurrent neural network, yielding a sequence of vector representations $\{z_r\}_{r=1}^{R}$, where r indexes over records. Interestingly, this sequence-based approach can work even in cases where there is no natural ordering over the records, such as the weather data in figure 19.1 (Mei et al., 2016).

Images Another flavor of data-to-text generation is the generation of text captions for images. Examples from this task are shown in figure 19.3. Images are naturally represented as tensors: a color image of 320×240 pixels would be stored as a tensor with $320 \times 240 \times 3$ intensity values. The dominant approach to image classification is to encode images as vectors using a combination of convolution and pooling (Krizhevsky et al., 2012). Chapter 3 explains how to use convolutional networks for text; for images, convolution is applied across the vertical, horizontal, and color dimensions. By pooling the results of successive convolutions, the image is converted to a vector representation, which can then be fed directly into the decoder as the initial state (Vinyals et al., 2015), just as in the sequence-to-sequence translation model (see § 18.3). Alternatively, one can apply a set of convolutional networks, yielding vector representations for different parts of the image, which can then be combined using neural attention (Xu et al., 2015).

Attention Given a set of embeddings of the data $\{z_r\}_{r=1}^{R}$ and a decoder state $\boldsymbol{h}_m$, an attention vector over the data can be computed using the same techniques as in machine

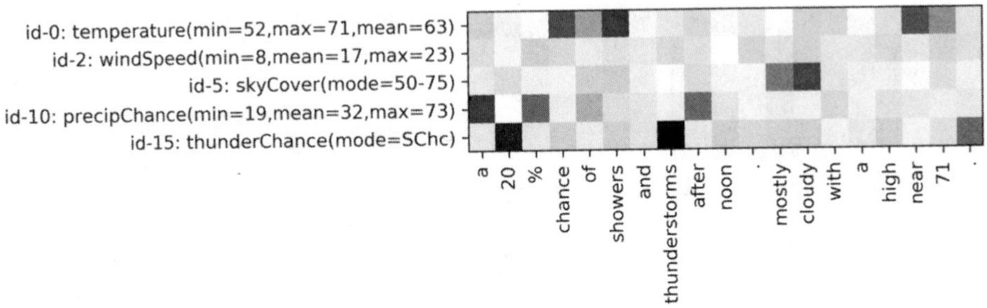

Figure 19.4
Neural attention in text generation. Figure adapted from Mei et al. (2016).

translation (see § 18.3.1). When generating word m of the output, attention is computed over the records,

$$\psi_\alpha(m, r) = \boldsymbol{\beta}_\alpha \cdot f(\Theta_\alpha[\boldsymbol{h}_m; z_r]) \qquad [19.5]$$

$$\boldsymbol{\alpha}_m = g\left([\psi_\alpha(m, 1), \psi_\alpha(m, 2), \ldots, \psi_\alpha(m, R)]\right) \qquad [19.6]$$

$$\boldsymbol{c}_m = \sum_{r=1}^{R} \alpha_{m\to r} z_r, \qquad [19.7]$$

where f is an elementwise nonlinearity such as tanh or ReLU and g is the softmax or elementwise sigmoid function. The weighted sum $\boldsymbol{c}_m$ can then be included in the recurrent update to the decoder state, or in the emission probabilities, as described in § 18.3.1. Figure 19.4 shows the attention to components of a weather record, while generating the text shown on the x-axis.

Adapting this architecture to image captioning is straightforward. A convolutional neural networks is applied to a set of image locations, and the output at each location ℓ is represented with a vector z_ℓ. Attention can then be computed over the image locations, as shown in the right panels of each pair of images in figure 19.3.

Various modifications to this basic mechanism have been proposed. In **coarse-to-fine attention** (Mei et al., 2016), each record receives a global attention $a_r \in [0, 1]$, which is independent of the decoder state. This global attention, which represents the overall importance of the record, is multiplied with the decoder-based attention scores, before computing the final normalized attentions. In **structured attention**, the attention vector $\boldsymbol{\alpha}_{m\to\cdot}$ can include structural biases, which can favor assigning higher attention values to contiguous segments or to dependency subtrees (Kim et al., 2017). Structured attention vectors can be computed by running the forward-backward algorithm to obtain marginal attention probabilities (see § 7.5.3). Because each step in the forward-backward algorithm is differentiable, it can be encoded in a computation graph, and end-to-end learning can be performed by backpropagation.

Decoder Given the encoding, the decoder can function just as in neural machine translation (see § 18.3.1), using the attention-weighted encoder representation in the decoder recurrence and/or output computation. As in machine translation, beam search can help to avoid search errors (Lebret et al., 2016).

Many applications require generating words that do not appear in the training vocabulary. For example, a weather record may contain a previously unseen city name; a sports record may contain a previously unseen player name. Such tokens can be generated in the text by copying them over from the input (e.g., Gulcehre et al., 2016).[3] First introduce an additional variable $s_m \in \{\text{gen}, \text{copy}\}$, indicating whether token $w_m^{(t)}$ should be generated or copied. The decoder probability is then

$$p(w^{(t)} \mid \boldsymbol{w}_{1:m-1}^{(t)}, \mathbf{Z}, s_m) = \begin{cases} \text{softmax}(\boldsymbol{\beta}_{w^{(t)}} \cdot \boldsymbol{h}_{m-1}^{(t)}), & s_m = \text{gen} \\ \sum_{r=1}^{R} \delta\left(w_r^{(s)} = w^{(t)}\right) \times \alpha_{m \to r}, & s_m = \text{copy}, \end{cases} \quad [19.8]$$

where $\delta(w_r^{(s)} = w^{(t)})$ is an indicator function, taking the value 1 iff the text of the record $w_r^{(s)}$ is identical to the target word $w^{(t)}$. The probability of copying record r from the source is $\delta\left(s_m = \text{copy}\right) \times \alpha_{m \to r}$, the product of the copy probability by the local attention. Note that in this model, the attention weights $\boldsymbol{\alpha}_m$ are computed from the *previous* decoder state $\boldsymbol{h}_{m-1}$. The computation graph therefore remains a feedforward network, with recurrent paths such as $\boldsymbol{h}_{m-1}^{(t)} \to \boldsymbol{\alpha}_m \to w_m^{(t)} \to \boldsymbol{h}_m^{(t)}$.

To facilitate end-to-end training, the switching variable s_m can be represented by a gate π_m, which is computed from a two-layer feedforward network, whose input consists of the concatenation of the decoder state $\boldsymbol{h}_{m-1}^{(t)}$ and the attention-weighted representation of the data, $\boldsymbol{c}_m = \sum_{r=1}^{R} \alpha_{m \to r} \boldsymbol{z}_r$,

$$\pi_m = \sigma(\Theta^{(2)} f(\Theta^{(1)}[\boldsymbol{h}_{m-1}^{(t)}; \boldsymbol{c}_m])). \quad [19.9]$$

The full generative probability at token m is then

$$p(w^{(t)} \mid \boldsymbol{w}_{1:m}^{(t)}, \mathbf{Z}) = \pi_m \times \underbrace{\frac{\exp \boldsymbol{\beta}_{w^{(t)}} \cdot \boldsymbol{h}_{m-1}^{(t)}}{\sum_{j=1}^{V} \exp \boldsymbol{\beta}_j \cdot \boldsymbol{h}_{m-1}^{(t)}}}_{\text{generate}} + (1 - \pi_m) \times \underbrace{\sum_{r=1}^{R} \delta(w_r^{(s)} = w^{(t)}) \times \alpha_{m \to r}}_{\text{copy}}. \quad [19.10]$$

19.2 Text-to-Text Generation

In text-to-text generation, text is both the input and output. The goal is usually related to summarization and simplification. For example:

3. A number of variants of this strategy have been proposed (e.g., Gu et al., 2016; Merity et al., 2017). See Wiseman et al. (2017) for an overview.

- reading a novel and outputting a paragraph-long summary of the plot;
- reading a set of blog posts about politics, and outputting a bullet list of the various issues and perspectives;
- reading a technical research article about the long-term health consequences of drinking kombucha, and outputting a summary of the article in language that non-experts can understand.

Of particular interest is abstractive summarization, in which the summary can include words that do not appear in the original text. This generalizes the extractive summarization methods described in § 16.3.4. We will now explore two computational methods for text-to-text generation: (1) the encoder-decoder architecture; (2) direct manipulation of the input text.

19.2.1 Neural Abstractive Summarization

To contrast abstractive and extractive summarization, let's focus on the subtask of sentence summarization: shortening a sentence while preserving its meaning. Consider the following examples (Knight and Marcu, 2000; Rush et al., 2015):

(19.2) a. The documentation is typical of Epson quality: excellent.
Documentation is excellent.

b. Russian defense minister Ivanov called sunday for the creation of a joint front for combating global terrorism.
Russia calls for joint front against terrorism.

In (19.2a), the summary is extractive: it can be produced by deleting tokens from the input. This form of summarization is also known as sentence compression (Clarke and Lapata, 2008). In (19.2b), the summary introduces new words, such as *against,* which replaces the phrase *for combating*. This is an example of abstractive summarization.

Sentence summarization can be treated as a machine translation problem, using the attentional encoder-decoder translation model discussed in § 18.3.1 (Rush et al., 2015). The longer sentence is encoded into a sequence of vectors, one for each token. The decoder then computes attention over these vectors when updating its own recurrent state. As with data-to-text generation, it can be useful to augment the encoder-decoder model with the ability to copy words directly from the source. Rush et al. (2015) train this model by building four million sentence pairs from news articles. In each pair, the longer sentence is the first sentence of the article, and the summary is the article headline. Sentence summarization can also be trained in a semi-supervised fashion, using a probabilistic formulation of the encoder-decoder model called a **variational autoencoder** (Miao and Blunsom, 2016, also see § 14.8.2).

When summarizing longer documents, an additional concern is that the summary not be repetitive: each part of the summary should cover new ground. This can be addressed by maintaining a vector of the sum total of all attention values thus far, $\boldsymbol{t}_m = \sum_{n=1}^{m} \boldsymbol{\alpha}_n$. This total can be used as an additional input to the computation of the attention weights,

$$\alpha_{m \to n} \propto \exp\left(\boldsymbol{v}_\alpha \cdot \tanh(\Theta_\alpha[\boldsymbol{h}_m^{(t)}; \boldsymbol{h}_n^{(s)}; \boldsymbol{t}_m])\right), \qquad [19.11]$$

which enables the model to learn to prefer parts of the source that have not been attended to yet (Tu et al., 2016). To further encourage diversity in the generated summary, See et al. (2017) introduce a **coverage loss** to the objective function,

$$\ell_m = \sum_{n=1}^{M^{(s)}} \min(\alpha_{m \to n}, t_{m \to n}). \qquad [19.12]$$

This loss will be low if $\boldsymbol{\alpha}_m$ assigns little attention to words that already have large values in $\boldsymbol{t}_m$. Coverage loss is similar to the concept of **marginal relevance**, in which the reward for adding new content is proportional to the extent to which it increases the overall amount of information conveyed by the summary (Carbonell and Goldstein, 1998).

19.2.2 Sentence Fusion for Multidocument Summarization

In **multidocument summarization**, the goal is to produce a summary that covers the content of several documents (McKeown et al., 2002). One approach to this challenging problem is to identify sentences across multiple documents that relate to a single theme and then to fuse them into a single sentence (Barzilay and McKeown, 2005). As an example, consider the following two sentences (McKeown et al., 2010):

(19.3) a. Palin actually turned against the bridge project only after it became a national symbol of wasteful spending.
b. Ms. Palin supported the bridge project while running for governor, and abandoned it after it became a national scandal.

An *intersection* preserves only the content that is present in both sentences:

(19.4) Palin turned against the bridge project after it became a national scandal.

A *union* includes information from both sentences:

(19.5) Ms. Palin supported the bridge project while running for governor, but turned against it when it became a national scandal and a symbol of wasteful spending.

Dependency parsing is often used as a technique for sentence fusion. After parsing each sentence, the resulting dependency trees can be aggregated into a lattice (Barzilay and McKeown, 2005) or a graph structure (Filippova and Strube, 2008), in which identical or closely related words (e.g., *Palin, bridge, national*) are fused into a single node. The resulting graph can then be pruned back to a tree by solving an **integer linear program** (see § 13.2.2),

$$\max_{\boldsymbol{y}} \quad \sum_{i,j,r} \psi(i \xrightarrow{r} j, \boldsymbol{w}; \boldsymbol{\theta}) \times y_{i,j,r} \qquad [19.13]$$

$$\text{s.t.} \quad \boldsymbol{y} \in \mathcal{C}, \qquad [19.14]$$

where the variable $y_{i,j,r} \in \{0, 1\}$ indicates whether there is an edge from i to j of type r, the score of this edge is $\psi(i \xrightarrow{r} j, \boldsymbol{w}; \boldsymbol{\theta})$, and $\mathcal{C}$ is a set of constraints, which ensures that $\boldsymbol{y}$ forms a valid dependency graph. As usual, $\boldsymbol{w}$ is the list of words in the graph, and $\boldsymbol{\theta}$ is a vector of parameters. The score $\psi(i \xrightarrow{r} j, \boldsymbol{w}; \boldsymbol{\theta})$ reflects the "importance" of the modifier j to the overall meaning: in intersective fusion, this score indicates the extent to which the content in this edge is expressed in all sentences; in union fusion, the score indicates whether the content in the edge is expressed in any sentence. The constraint set $\mathcal{C}$ can impose additional linguistic constraints: for example, ensuring that coordinated nouns are sufficiently similar. The resulting tree must then be **linearized** into a sentence. Linearization is like the inverse of dependency parsing: instead of parsing from a sequence of tokens into a tree, we must convert the tree back into a sequence of tokens. This is typically done by generating a set of candidate linearizations and choosing the one with the highest score under a language model (Langkilde and Knight, 1998; Song et al., 2016).

19.3 Dialogue

Dialogue systems are capable of conversing with a human interlocutor, often to perform some task (Grosz, 1979), but sometimes just to chat (Weizenbaum, 1966). While research on dialogue systems goes back several decades (Carbonell, 1970; Winograd, 1972), commercial systems such as Alexa and Siri have recently brought this technology into widespread use. Nonetheless, there is a significant gap between research and practice: many practical dialogue systems remain scripted and inflexible, while research systems emphasize abstractive text generation, "on-the-fly" decision-making, and probabilistic reasoning about the user's intentions.

19.3.1 Finite-State and Agenda-Based Dialogue Systems

Finite-state automata were introduced in chapter 9 as a formal model of computation, in which string inputs and outputs are linked to transitions between a finite number of discrete states. This model naturally fits simple task-oriented dialogues, such as the one shown in the left panel of figure 19.5. This (somewhat frustrating) dialogue can be represented with a finite-state transducer, as shown in the right panel of the figure. The accepting state is reached only when the two needed pieces of information are provided, and the human user confirms that the order is correct. In this simple scenario, the TOPPING and ADDRESS are the two **slots** associated with the activity of ordering a pizza, which is called a **frame**. Frame representations can be hierarchical: for example, an ADDRESS could have slots of its own, such as STREET and CITY.

In the example dialogue in figure 19.5, the user provides the precise inputs that are needed in each turn (e.g., *anchovies*; *the College of Computing building*). Some users may prefer to communicate more naturally, with phrases like *I'd, uh, like some anchovies please*. One approach to handling such utterances is to design a custom grammar, with nonterminals

(19.6) A: I want to order a pizza.
B: What toppings?
A: Anchovies.
B: Ok, what address?
A: The College of Computing building.
B: Please confirm: one pizza with artichokes, to be delivered to the College of Computing building.
A: No.
B: What toppings?
...

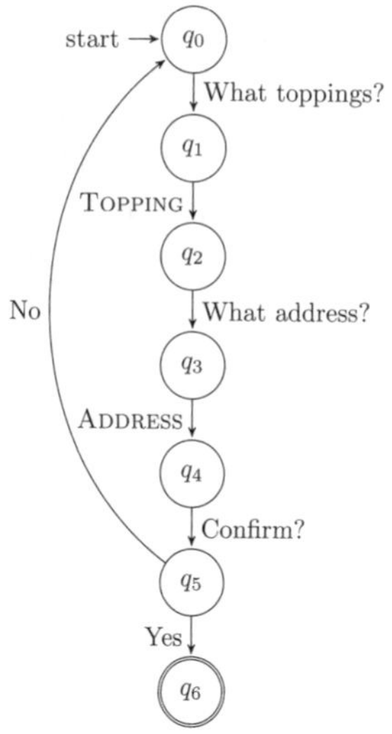

Figure 19.5
An example dialogue and the associated finite-state model. In the finite-state model, SMALL CAPS indicates that the user must provide information of this type in their answer.

for slots such as TOPPING and LOCATION. However, context-free parsing of unconstrained speech input is challenging. A more lightweight alternative is BIO-style sequence labeling (see § 8.3), for example,

(19.7) *I'd like anchovies , and please bring it to the College of*
O O B-TOPPING O O O O O O B-ADDR I-ADDR I-ADDR
Computing Building .
I-ADDR I-ADDR O

The tagger can be driven by a bidirectional recurrent neural network, similar to recurrent approaches to semantic role labeling described in § 13.2.3.

The input in (19.7) could not be handled by the finite-state system from figure 19.5, which forces the user to provide the topping first and then the location, in separate turns. In this sense, the "initiative" is driven completely by the system. **Agenda-based dialogue systems** extend finite-state architectures by attempting to recognize all slots that are filled by the user's reply, thereby handling these more complex examples. Agenda-based systems dynamically pose additional questions until the frame is complete (Bobrow et al., 1977; Allen et al., 1995; Rudnicky and Xu, 1999). Such systems are said to be **mixed-initiative**, because both the user and the system can drive the direction of the dialogue.

19.3.2 Markov Decision Processes

The task of dynamically selecting the next move in a conversation is known as **dialogue management**. This problem can be framed as a **Markov decision process**, which is a theoretical model that includes a discrete set of states, a discrete set of actions, a function that computes the probability of transitions between states, and a function that computes the cost or reward of action-state pairs. Let's see how each of these elements pertains to the pizza ordering dialogue system.

- Each state is a tuple of information about whether the topping and address are known and whether the order has been confirmed. For example,

$$(\textsc{Known Topping}, \textsc{Unknown Address}, \textsc{Not confirmed}) \quad [19.15]$$

is a possible state. Any state in which the pizza order is confirmed is a terminal state, and the Markov decision process stops after entering such a state.

- The set of actions includes querying for the topping, querying for the address, and requesting confirmation. Each action induces a probability distribution over states, $\text{p}(s_t \mid a_t, s_{t-1})$. For example, requesting confirmation of the order is not likely to result in a transition to the terminal state if the topping is not yet known. This probability distribution over state transitions may be learned from data, or it may be specified in advance.

- Each state-action-state tuple earns a reward, $r_a(s_t, s_{t+1})$. In the context of the pizza ordering system, a simple reward function would be

$$r_a(s_t, s_{t-1}) = \begin{cases} 0, & a = \textsc{Confirm}, s_t = (*, *, \textsc{Confirmed}) \\ -10, & a = \textsc{Confirm}, s_t = (*, *, \textsc{Not Confirmed}). \\ -1, & a \neq \textsc{Confirm} \end{cases} \quad [19.16]$$

This function assigns zero reward for successful transitions to the terminal state, a large negative reward to a rejected request for confirmation, and a small negative reward for every other type of action. The system is therefore rewarded for reaching the terminal state in few steps and penalized for prematurely requesting confirmation.

In a Markov decision process, a **policy** is a function $\pi : \mathcal{S} \rightarrow \mathcal{A}$ that maps from states to actions (see § 15.2.4). The value of a policy is the expected sum of discounted rewards, $E_\pi[\sum_{t=1}^{T} \gamma^t r_{a_t}(s_t, s_{t+1})]$, where γ is the discount factor, $\gamma \in [0, 1)$. Discounting has the effect of emphasizing rewards that can be obtained immediately over less certain rewards in the distant future.

An optimal policy can be obtained by dynamic programming, by iteratively updating the **value function** $V(s)$, which is the expectation of the cumulative reward from s under the optimal action a,

$$V(s) \leftarrow \max_{a \in \mathcal{A}} \sum_{s' \in \mathcal{S}} \text{p}(s' \mid s, a)[r_a(s, s') + \gamma V(s')]. \quad [19.17]$$

The value function $V(s)$ is computed in terms of $V(s')$ for all states $s' \in \mathcal{S}$. A series of iterative updates to the value function will eventually converge to a stationary point. This algorithm is known as **value iteration**. Given the converged value function $V(s)$, the optimal action at each state is the argmax,

$$\pi(s) = \underset{a \in \mathcal{A}}{\text{argmax}} \sum_{s' \in \mathcal{S}} p(s' \mid s, a)[r_a(s, s') + \gamma V(s')]. \quad [19.18]$$

Value iteration and related algorithms are described in detail by Sutton and Barto (2019). For applications to dialogue systems, see Levin et al. (1998) and Walker (2000).

The Markov decision process framework assumes that the current state of the dialogue is known. In reality, the system may misinterpret the user's statements—for example, believing that a specification of the delivery location (PEACHTREE) is in fact a specification of the topping (PEACHES). In a **partially observable Markov decision process (POMDP)**, the system receives an *observation* o, which is probabilistically conditioned on the state, $p(o \mid s)$. It must therefore maintain a distribution of beliefs about which state it is in, with $q_t(s)$ indicating the degree of belief that the dialogue is in state s at time t. The POMDP formulation can help to make dialogue systems more robust to errors, particularly in the context of spoken language dialogues, where the speech itself may be misrecognized (Roy et al., 2000; Williams and Young, 2007). However, finding the optimal policy in a POMDP is computationally intractable, requiring additional approximations.

19.3.3 Neural Chatbots

It's easier to talk when you don't need to get anything done. **Chatbots** are systems that parry the user's input with a response that keeps the conversation going. They can be built from the encoder-decoder architecture discussed in § 18.3 and § 19.1.2: the encoder converts the user's input into a vector, and the decoder produces a sequence of words as a response. For example, Shang et al. (2015) apply the attentional encoder-decoder translation model, training on a dataset of posts and responses from the Chinese microblogging platform Sina Weibo.[4] This approach is capable of generating replies that relate thematically to the input, as shown in the following examples (translated from Chinese by Shang et al., 2015).

(19.8) a. A: High fever attacks me every New Year's day.
B: Get well soon and stay healthy!
b. A: I gain one more year. Grateful to my group, so happy.
B: Getting old now. Time has no mercy.

While encoder-decoder models can generate responses that make sense in the context of the immediately preceding turn, they struggle to maintain coherence over longer

4. Twitter is also frequently used for construction of dialogue datasets (Ritter et al., 2011a; Sordoni et al., 2015). Another source is technical support chat logs from the Ubuntu linux distribution (Uthus and Aha, 2013; Lowe et al., 2015).

conversations. One solution is to model the dialogue context recurrently. This creates a **hierarchical recurrent network**, including both word-level and turn-level recurrences. The turn-level hidden state is then used as additional context in the decoder (Serban et al., 2016).

An open question is how to integrate the encoder-decoder architecture into task-oriented dialogue systems. Neural chatbots can be trained end-to-end: the user's turn is analyzed by the encoder, and the system output is generated by the decoder. This architecture can be trained by log-likelihood using backpropagation (e.g., Sordoni et al., 2015; Serban et al., 2016), or by more elaborate objectives, using reinforcement learning (Li et al., 2016). In contrast, the task-oriented dialogue systems described in § 19.3.1 typically involve a set of specialized modules: one for recognizing the user input, another for deciding what action to take, and a third for arranging the text of the system output.

Recurrent neural network decoders can be integrated into Markov decision process dialogue systems, by conditioning the decoder on a representation of the information that is to be expressed in each turn (Wen et al., 2015). Specifically, the long short-term memory (LSTM; § 6.3) architecture is augmented so that the memory cell at turn m takes an additional input $\boldsymbol{d}_m$, which is a representation of the slots and values to be expressed in the next turn. However, this approach still relies on additional modules to recognize the user's utterance and to plan the overall arc of the dialogue.

Another promising direction is to create embeddings for the elements in the domain: for example, the slots in a record and the entities that can fill them. The encoder then encodes not only the words of the user's input, but also the embeddings of the elements that the user mentions. Similarly, the decoder is endowed with the ability to refer to specific elements in the knowledge base. He et al. (2017) show that such a method can learn to play a collaborative dialogue game, in which both players are given a list of entities and their properties, and the goal is to find an entity that is on both players' lists.

Additional Resources

Gatt and Krahmer (2018) provide a comprehensive recent survey on text generation. For a book-length treatment of earlier work, see Reiter and Dale (2000). For a survey on image captioning, see Bernardi et al. (2016); for a survey of pre-neural approaches to dialogue systems, see Rieser and Lemon (2011). **Dialogue acts** were introduced in § 8.6 as a labeling scheme for human-human dialogues; they also play a critical in task-based dialogue systems (e.g., Allen et al., 1996). The incorporation of theoretical models of dialogue into computational systems is reviewed by Jurafsky and Martin (2009, chapter 24).

While this chapter has focused on the informative dimension of text generation, another line of research aims to generate text with configurable stylistic properties (Walker et al., 1997; Mairesse and Walker, 2011; Ficler and Goldberg, 2017; Hu et al., 2017). This chapter also does not address the generation of creative text such as narratives (Riedl and Young,

2010), jokes (Ritchie, 2001), poems (Colton et al., 2012), and song lyrics (Gonçalo Oliveira et al., 2007).

Exercises

1. Find an article about a professional basketball game, with an associated "box score" of statistics. Which are the first three elements in the box score that are expressed in the article? Can you identify template-based patterns that express these elements of the record? Now find a second article about a different basketball game. Does it mention the same first three elements of the box score? Do your templates capture how these elements are expressed in the text?
2. This exercise is to be done by a pair of students. One student should choose an article from the news or from Wikipedia and manually perform semantic role labeling (SRL) on three short sentences or clauses. (See chapter 13 for a review of SRL.) Identify the main semantic relation and its arguments and adjuncts. Pass this structured record—but not the original sentence—to the other student, whose job is to generate a sentence expressing the semantics. Then reverse roles, and try to regenerate three sentences from another article, based on the predicate-argument semantics.
3. Compute the BLEU scores (see § 18.1.1) for the generated sentences in the previous problem, using the original article text as the reference.
4. Align each token in the text of figure 19.1 to a specific single record in the database, or to the null record ∅. For example, the tokens *south wind* would align to the record `wind direction: 06:00-21:00: mode=S`. How often is each token aligned to the same record as the previous token? How many transitions are there? How might a system learn to output *10 degrees* for the record `min=9`?
5. In sentence compression and fusion, we may wish to preserve contiguous sequences of tokens (n-grams) and/or dependency edges. Find five short news articles with headlines. For each headline, compute the fraction of bigrams that appear in the main text of the article. Then do a manual depenency parse of the headline. For each dependency edge, count how often it appears as a dependency edge in the main text. You may use an automatic dependency parser to assist with this exercise, but check the output, and focus on UD 2.0 dependency grammar, as described in chapter 11.
6. § 19.2.2 presents the idea of generating text from dependency trees, which requires **linearization**. Sometimes there are multiple ways that a dependency tree can be linearized. For example:

(19.9) a. The sick kids stayed at home in bed.
b. The sick kids stayed in bed at home.

Both sentences have an identical dependency parse: both *home* and *bed* are (oblique) dependents of *stayed*.

Identify two more English dependency trees that can each be linearized in more than one way, and try to use a different pattern of variation in each tree. As usual, specify your trees in the Universal Dependencies 2 style, which is described in chapter 11.

7. In § 19.3.2, we considered a pizza delivery service. Let's simplify the problem to take-out, where it is only necessary to determine the topping and confirm the order. The state is a tuple in which the first element is T if the topping is specified and ? otherwise, and the second element is either YES or NO, depending on whether the order has been confirmed. The actions are TOPPING? (request information about the topping) and CONFIRM? (request confirmation). The state transition function is

$$p(s_t \mid s_{t-1} = (?, \textsc{No}), a = \textsc{Topping?}) = \begin{cases} 0.9, & s_t = (\mathrm{T}, \textsc{No}) \\ 0.1, & s_t = (?, \textsc{No}). \end{cases} \quad [19.19]$$

$$p(s_t \mid s_{t-1} = (?, \textsc{No}), a = \textsc{Confirm?}) = \begin{cases} 1, & s_t = (?, \textsc{No}). \end{cases} \quad [19.20]$$

$$p(s_t \mid s_{t-1} = (\mathrm{T}, \textsc{No}), a = \textsc{Topping?}) = \begin{cases} 1, & s_t = (\mathrm{T}, \textsc{No}). \end{cases} \quad [19.21]$$

$$p(s_t \mid s_{t-1} = (\mathrm{T}, \textsc{No}), a = \textsc{Confirm?}) = \begin{cases} 0.9, & s_t = (\mathrm{T}, \textsc{Yes}) \\ 0.1, & s_t = (\mathrm{T}, \textsc{No}). \end{cases} \quad [19.22]$$

Using the reward function defined in equation 19.16, the discount $\gamma = 0.9$, and the initialization $V(s) = 0$, execute three iterations of equation 19.17. After these three iterations, compute the optimal action in each state. You can assume that for the terminal states, $V(*, \textsc{Yes}) = 0$, so you only need to compute the values for nonterminal states, $V(?, \textsc{No})$ and $V(\mathrm{T}, \textsc{No})$.

8. There are several toolkits that allow you to train encoder-decoder translation models "out of the box," such as FAIRSEQ (Gehring et al., 2017), XNMT (Neubig et al., 2018), TENSOR2TENSOR (Vaswani et al., 2018), and OPENNMT (Klein et al., 2017).[5] Use one of these toolkits to train a chatbot dialogue system, using either the NPS dialogue corpus that comes with NLTK (Forsyth and Martell, 2007) or, if you are feeling more ambitious, the Ubuntu dialogue corpus (Lowe et al., 2015).

5. https://github.com/facebookresearch/fairseq; https://github.com/neulab/xnmt; https://github.com/tensorflow/tensor2tensor; and http://opennmt.net/.

Appendix A: Probability

Probability theory provides a way to reason about random events. The sorts of random events that are typically used to explain probability theory include coin flips, card draws, and the weather. It may seem odd to think about the choice of a word as akin to the flip of a coin, particularly if you are the type of person to choose words carefully. But random or not, language has proven to be extremely difficult to model deterministically. Probability offers a powerful tool for modeling and manipulating linguistic data.

Probability can be thought of in terms of **random outcomes**: for example, a single coin flip has two possible outcomes, heads or tails. The set of possible outcomes is the **sample space** and a subset of the **sample space** is an **event**. For a sequence of two coin flips, there are four possible outcomes, $\{HH, HT, TH, TT\}$, representing the ordered sequences heads-head, heads-tails, tails-heads, and tails-tails. The event of getting exactly one head includes two outcomes: $\{HT, TH\}$.

Formally, a probability is a function from events to the interval between zero and one: $\Pr : \mathcal{F} \rightarrow [0, 1]$, where $\mathcal{F}$ is the set of possible events. An event that is certain has probability one; an event that is impossible has probability zero. For example, the probability of getting fewer than three heads on two coin flips is one. Each outcome is also an event (a set with exactly one element), and for two flips of a fair coin, the probability of each outcome is

$$\Pr(\{HH\}) = \Pr(\{HT\}) = \Pr(\{TH\}) = \Pr(\{TT\}) = \frac{1}{4}. \qquad [A.1]$$

A.1 Probabilities of Event Combinations

Because events are sets of outcomes, we can use set-theoretic operations such as complement, intersection, and union to reason about the probabilities of events and their combinations.

For any event A, there is a **complement** $\neg A$, such that:

- The probability of the union $A \cup \neg A$ is $\Pr(A \cup \neg A) = 1$;
- The intersection $A \cap \neg A = \varnothing$ is the empty set, and $\Pr(A \cap \neg A) = 0$.

In the coin flip example, the event of obtaining a single head on two flips corresponds to the set of outcomes $\{HT, TH\}$; the complement event is the set consisting of the other two outcomes, $\{TT, HH\}$.

A.1.1 Probabilities of Disjoint Events

When two events have an empty intersection, $A \cap B = \varnothing$, they are **disjoint**. The probability of the union of two disjoint events is equal to the sum of their probabilities,

$$A \cap B = \varnothing \quad \Rightarrow \quad \Pr(A \cup B) = \Pr(A) + \Pr(B). \qquad \text{[A.2]}$$

This is the **third axiom of probability**, and it can be generalized to any countable sequence of disjoint events.

In the coin flip example, this axiom can derive the probability of the event of getting a single head on two flips. This event is the set of outcomes $\{HT, TH\}$, which is the union of two simpler events, $\{HT, TH\} = \{HT\} \cup \{TH\}$. The events $\{HT\}$ and $\{TH\}$ are disjoint. Therefore,

$$\Pr(\{HT, TH\}) = \Pr(\{HT\} \cup \{TH\}) = \Pr(\{HT\}) + \Pr(\{TH\}) \qquad \text{[A.3]}$$

$$= \frac{1}{4} + \frac{1}{4} = \frac{1}{2}. \qquad \text{[A.4]}$$

In the general, the probability of the union of two events is

$$\Pr(A \cup B) = \Pr(A) + \Pr(B) - \Pr(A \cap B). \qquad \text{[A.5]}$$

This can be seen visually in figure A.1, and it can be derived from the third axiom of probability. Consider an event that includes all outcomes in B that are not in A, denoted as $B - (A \cap B)$. By construction, this event is disjoint from A. We can therefore apply the

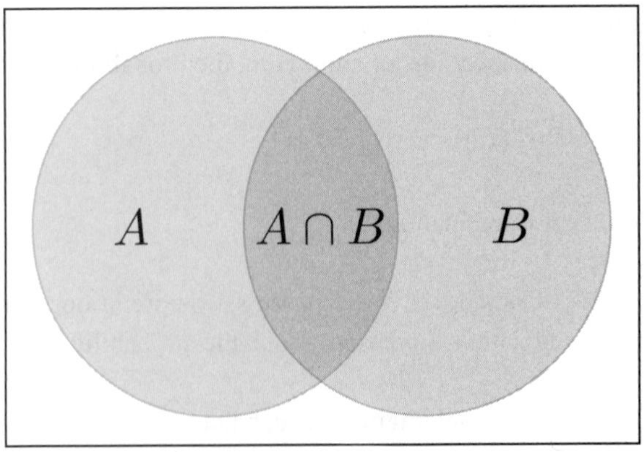

Figure A.1
A visualization of the probability of nondisjoint events A and B.

additive rule,

$$\Pr(A \cup B) = \Pr(A) + \Pr(B - (A \cap B)). \quad [A.6]$$

Furthermore, the event B is the union of two disjoint events, $A \cap B$ and $B - (A \cap B)$:

$$\Pr(B) = \Pr(B - (A \cap B)) + \Pr(A \cap B). \quad [A.7]$$

Reorganizing and substituting into equation A.6 gives the desired result:

$$\Pr(B - (A \cap B)) = \Pr(B) - \Pr(A \cap B) \quad [A.8]$$

$$\Pr(A \cup B) = \Pr(A) + \Pr(B) - \Pr(A \cap B). \quad [A.9]$$

A.1.2 Law of Total Probability

A set of events $\mathcal{B} = \{B_1, B_2, \ldots, B_N\}$ is a **partition** of the sample space iff each pair of events is disjoint ($B_i \cap B_j = \varnothing$), and the union of the events is the entire sample space. The law of total probability states that we can **marginalize** over these events as follows:

$$\Pr(A) = \sum_{B_n \in \mathcal{B}} \Pr(A \cap B_n). \quad [A.10]$$

For any event B, the union $B \cup \neg B$ is a partition of the sample space. Therefore, a special case of the law of total probability is

$$\Pr(A) = \Pr(A \cap B) + \Pr(A \cap \neg B). \quad [A.11]$$

A.2 Conditional Probability and Bayes' Rule

A **conditional probability** is an expression like $\Pr(A \mid B)$, which is the probability of the event A, assuming that event B happens too. For example, we may be interested in the probability of a randomly selected person answering the phone by saying *hello*, conditioned on that person being a speaker of English. Conditional probability is defined as the ratio,

$$\Pr(A \mid B) = \frac{\Pr(A \cap B)}{\Pr(B)}. \quad [A.12]$$

The **chain rule of probability** states that $\Pr(A \cap B) = \Pr(A \mid B) \times \Pr(B)$, which is just a rearrangement of terms from equation A.12. The chain rule can be applied repeatedly:

$$\begin{aligned}\Pr(A \cap B \cap C) &= \Pr(A \mid B \cap C) \times \Pr(B \cap C) \\ &= \Pr(A \mid B \cap C) \times \Pr(B \mid C) \times \Pr(C).\end{aligned}$$

Bayes' rule (sometimes called Bayes' law or Bayes' theorem) gives us a way to convert between $\Pr(A \mid B)$ and $\Pr(B \mid A)$. It follows from the definition of conditional probability and the chain rule:

$$\Pr(A \mid B) = \frac{\Pr(A \cap B)}{\Pr(B)} = \frac{\Pr(B \mid A) \times \Pr(A)}{\Pr(B)}. \quad [A.13]$$

Each term in Bayes' rule has a name, which we will occasionally use:

- $\Pr(A)$ is the **prior**, the probability of event A without knowledge about whether B happens or not.
- $\Pr(B \mid A)$ is the **likelihood**, the probability of event B given that event A has occurred.
- $\Pr(A \mid B)$ is the **posterior**, the probability of event A with knowledge that B has occurred.

Example The classic examples for Bayes' rule involve tests for rare diseases, but Manning and Schütze (1999) reframe this example in a linguistic setting. Suppose that you are interested in a rare syntactic construction, such as *parasitic gaps*, which occur on average once in 100,000 sentences. Here is an example of a parasitic gap:

(A.1) Which class did you attend __ without registering for __?

Lana Linguist has developed a complicated pattern matcher that attempts to identify sentences with parasitic gaps. It's pretty good, but it's not perfect:

- If a sentence has a parasitic gap, the pattern matcher will find it with probability 0.95. (This is the **recall**, which is one minus the **false negative rate**.)
- If the sentence doesn't have a parasitic gap, the pattern matcher will wrongly say it does with probability 0.005. (This is the **false positive rate**, which is one minus the **precision**.)

Suppose that Lana's pattern matcher says that a sentence contains a parasitic gap. What is the probability that this is true?

Let G be the event of a sentence having a parasitic gap, and T be the event of the test being positive. We are interested in the probability of a sentence having a parasitic gap given that the test is positive. This is the conditional probability $\Pr(G \mid T)$, and it can be computed by Bayes' rule:

$$\Pr(G \mid T) = \frac{\Pr(T \mid G) \times \Pr(G)}{\Pr(T)}. \qquad [A.14]$$

We already know both terms in the numerator: $\Pr(T \mid G)$ is the recall, which is 0.95; $\Pr(G)$ is the prior, which is 10^{-5}.

We are not given the denominator, but it can be computed using tools developed earlier in this section. First apply the law of total probability, using the partition $\{G, \neg G\}$:

$$\Pr(T) = \Pr(T \cap G) + \Pr(T \cap \neg G). \qquad [A.15]$$

This says that the probability of the test being positive is the sum of the probability of a **true positive** ($T \cap G$) and the probability of a **false positive** ($T \cap \neg G$). The probability of each of these events can be computed using the chain rule:

$$\Pr(T \cap G) = \Pr(T \mid G) \times \Pr(G) = 0.95 \times 10^{-5} \qquad [A.16]$$

$$\Pr(T \cap \neg G) = \Pr(T \mid \neg G) \times \Pr(\neg G) = 0.005 \times (1 - 10^{-5}) \approx 0.005 \quad \text{[A.17]}$$

$$\Pr(T) = \Pr(T \cap G) + \Pr(T \cap \neg G) \quad \text{[A.18]}$$

$$= 0.95 \times 10^{-5} + 0.005. \quad \text{[A.19]}$$

Plugging these terms into Bayes' rule gives the desired posterior probability,

$$\Pr(G \mid T) = \frac{\Pr(T \mid G)\Pr(G)}{\Pr(T)} \quad \text{[A.20]}$$

$$= \frac{0.95 \times 10^{-5}}{0.95 \times 10^{-5} + 0.005 \times (1 - 10^{-5})} \quad \text{[A.21]}$$

$$\approx 0.002. \quad \text{[A.22]}$$

Lana's pattern matcher seems accurate, with false positive and false negative rates below 5%. Yet the extreme rarity of the phenomenon means that a positive result from the detector is most likely to be wrong.

A.3 Independence

Two events are independent if the probability of their intersection is equal to the product of their probabilities: $\Pr(A \cap B) = \Pr(A) \times \Pr(B)$. For example, for two flips of a fair coin, the probability of getting heads on the first flip is independent of the probability of getting heads on the second flip:

$$\Pr(\{HT, HH\}) = \Pr(HT) + \Pr(HH) = \frac{1}{4} + \frac{1}{4} = \frac{1}{2} \quad \text{[A.23]}$$

$$\Pr(\{HH, TH\}) = \Pr(HH) + \Pr(TH) = \frac{1}{4} + \frac{1}{4} = \frac{1}{2} \quad \text{[A.24]}$$

$$\Pr(\{HT, HH\}) \times \Pr(\{HH, TH\}) = \frac{1}{2} \times \frac{1}{2} = \frac{1}{4} \quad \text{[A.25]}$$

$$\Pr(\{HT, HH\} \cap \{HH, TH\}) = \Pr(HH) = \frac{1}{4} \quad \text{[A.26]}$$

$$= \Pr(\{HT, HH\}) \times \Pr(\{HH, TH\}). \quad \text{[A.27]}$$

If $\Pr(A \cap B \mid C) = \Pr(A \mid C) \times \Pr(B \mid C)$, then the events A and B are **conditionally independent**, written $A \perp B \mid C$. Conditional independence plays a important role in probabilistic models such as Naïve Bayes (chapter 2).

A.4 Random Variables

Random variables are functions from events to $\mathbb{R}^n$, where $\mathbb{R}$ is the set of real numbers. This subsumes several useful special cases:

- An **indicator random variable** is a function from events to the set $\{0, 1\}$. In the coin flip example, we can define Y as an indicator random variable, taking the value 1 when the coin has come up heads on at least one flip. This would include the outcomes $\{HH, HT, TH\}$. The probability $\Pr(Y = 1)$ is the sum of the probabilities of these outcomes, $\Pr(Y = 1) = \frac{1}{4} + \frac{1}{4} + \frac{1}{4} = \frac{3}{4}$.
- A **discrete random variable** is a function from events to a discrete subset of $\mathbb{R}$. Consider the coin flip example: the number of heads on two flips, X, can be viewed as a discrete random variable, $X \in 0, 1, 2$. The event probability $\Pr(X = 1)$ can again be computed as the sum of the probabilities of the events in which there is one head, $\{HT, TH\}$, giving $\Pr(X = 1) = \frac{1}{4} + \frac{1}{4} = \frac{1}{2}$.

Each possible value of a random variable is associated with a subset of the sample space. In the coin flip example, $X = 0$ is associated with the event $\{TT\}$, $X = 1$ is associated with the event $\{HT, TH\}$, and $X = 2$ is associated with the event $\{HH\}$. Assuming a fair coin, the probabilities of these events are, respectively, 1/4, 1/2, and 1/4. This list of numbers represents the **probability distribution** over X, written p_X, which maps from the possible values of X to the nonnegative reals. For a specific value x, we write $\mathrm{p}_X(x)$, which is equal to the event probability $\Pr(X = x)$.[1] The function p_X is called a probability **mass** function (pmf) if X is discrete; it is called a probability **density** function (pdf) if X is continuous. In either case, the function must sum to one, and all values must be nonnegative:

$$\int_x \mathrm{p}_X(x)dx = 1 \qquad \text{[A.28]}$$

$$\forall x, \mathrm{p}_X(x) \geq 0. \qquad \text{[A.29]}$$

Probabilities over multiple random variables can written as **joint probabilities**, e.g., $\mathrm{p}_{A,B}(a, b) = \Pr(A = a \cap B = b)$. Several properties of event probabilities carry over to probability distributions over random variables:

- The **marginal probability distribution** is $\mathrm{p}_A(a) = \sum_b \mathrm{p}_{A,B}(a, b)$.
- The **conditional probability distribution** is $\mathrm{p}_{A|B}(a \mid b) = \frac{\mathrm{p}_{A,B}(a,b)}{\mathrm{p}_B(b)}$.
- Random variables A and B are independent iff $\mathrm{p}_{A,B}(a, b) = \mathrm{p}_A(a) \times \mathrm{p}_B(b)$.

A.5 Expectations

Sometimes we want the **expectation** of a function, such as $E[g(x)] = \sum_{x \in \mathcal{X}} g(x)\mathrm{p}(x)$. Expectations are easiest to think about in terms of probability distributions over discrete events:

1. In general, capital letters (e.g., X) refer to random variables, and lowercase letters (e.g., x) refer to specific values. When the distribution is clear from context, I will simply write $\mathrm{p}(x)$.

- If it is sunny, Lucia will eat three ice creams.
- If it is rainy, she will eat only one ice cream.
- There's a 80% chance it will be sunny.
- The expected number of ice creams she will eat is $0.8 \times 3 + 0.2 \times 1 = 2.6$.

If the random variable X is continuous, the expectation is an integral:

$$E[g(x)] = \int_{\mathcal{X}} g(x)\mathrm{p}(x)dx. \quad [A.30]$$

For example, a fast food restaurant in Quebec has a special offer for cold days: they give a 1% discount on poutine for every degree below zero. Assuming a thermometer with infinite precision, the expected price would be an integral over all possible temperatures,

$$E[\text{price}(x)] = \int_{\mathcal{X}} \min(1, 1 + x/100) \times \text{original-price} \times \mathrm{p}(x)dx. \quad [A.31]$$

A.6 Modeling and Estimation

Probabilistic models provide a principled way to reason about random events and random variables. Let's consider the coin toss example. Each toss can be modeled as a random event, with probability θ of the event H and probability $1 - \theta$ of the complementary event T. If we define a random variable X as the total number of heads on three coin flips, then the distribution of X depends on θ. In this case, X is distributed as a **binomial random variable**, meaning that it is drawn from a binomial distribution, with **parameters** $(\theta, N = 3)$. This is written

$$X \sim \text{Binomial}(\theta, N = 3). \quad [A.32]$$

The properties of the binomial distribution enable us to make statements about X, such as its expected value and the likelihood that its value will fall within some interval.

Now suppose that θ is unknown, but we have run an experiment, in which we executed N trials, and obtained x heads. We can **estimate** θ by the principle of **maximum likelihood**:

$$\hat{\theta} = \underset{\theta}{\operatorname{argmax}}\, \mathrm{p}_X(x; \theta, N). \quad [A.33]$$

This says that the estimate $\hat{\theta}$ should be the value that maximizes the likelihood of the data. The semicolon indicates that θ and N are parameters of the probability function. The likelihood $\mathrm{p}_X(x; \theta, N)$ can be computed from the binomial distribution,

$$\mathrm{p}_X(x; \theta, N) = \frac{N!}{x!(N-x)!}\theta^x(1-\theta)^{N-x}. \quad [A.34]$$

This likelihood is proportional to the product of the probability of individual outcomes: for example, the sequence T, H, H, T, H would have probability $\theta^3(1-\theta)^2$. The term

$\frac{N!}{x!(N-x)!}$ arises from the many possible orderings by which we could obtain x heads on N trials. This term does not depend on θ, so it can be ignored during estimation.

In practice, we maximize the log-likelihood, which is a monotonic function of the likelihood. Under the binomial distribution, the log-likelihood is a **convex** function of θ (see § 2.4), so it can be maximized by taking the derivative and setting it equal to zero:

$$\ell(\theta) = x \log \theta + (N - x)\log(1 - \theta) \quad \text{[A.35]}$$

$$\frac{\partial \ell(\theta)}{\partial \theta} = \frac{x}{\theta} - \frac{N - x}{1 - \theta} \quad \text{[A.36]}$$

$$\frac{N - x}{1 - \theta} = \frac{x}{\theta} \quad \text{[A.37]}$$

$$\frac{N - x}{x} = \frac{1 - \theta}{\theta} \quad \text{[A.38]}$$

$$\frac{N}{x} - 1 = \frac{1}{\theta} - 1 \quad \text{[A.39]}$$

$$\hat{\theta} = \frac{x}{N}. \quad \text{[A.40]}$$

In this case, the maximum likelihood estimate is equal to $\frac{x}{N}$, the fraction of trials that came up heads. This intuitive solution is also known as the **relative frequency estimate**, because it is equal to the relative frequency of the outcome.

Is maximum likelihood estimation always the right choice? Suppose you conduct one trial and get heads. Would you conclude that $\theta = 1$, meaning that the coin is guaranteed to come up heads? If not, then you must have some **prior expectation** about θ. To incorporate this prior information, we can treat θ as a random variable, and use Bayes' rule:

$$\mathrm{p}(\theta \mid x; N) = \frac{\mathrm{p}(x \mid \theta) \times \mathrm{p}(\theta)}{\mathrm{p}(x)} \quad \text{[A.41]}$$

$$\propto \mathrm{p}(x \mid \theta) \times \mathrm{p}(\theta) \quad \text{[A.42]}$$

$$\hat{\theta} = \underset{\theta}{\operatorname{argmax}}\, \mathrm{p}(x \mid \theta) \times \mathrm{p}(\theta). \quad \text{[A.43]}$$

This it the **maximum a posteriori** (MAP) estimate. Given a form for $\mathrm{p}(\theta)$, you can derive the MAP estimate using the same approach that was used to derive the maximum likelihood estimate.

Additional Resources

A good introduction to probability theory is offered by Manning and Schütze (1999), which helped to motivate this section. For more detail, Sharon Goldwater provides another useful reference, http://homepages.inf.ed.ac.uk/sgwater/teaching/general/probability.pdf. A historical and philosophical perspective on probability is offered by Diaconis and Skyrms (2017).

Appendix B: Numerical Optimization

Unconstrained numerical optimization involves solving problems of the form,

$$\min_{\boldsymbol{x} \in \mathbb{R}^D} f(\boldsymbol{x}), \qquad \text{[B.1]}$$

where $\boldsymbol{x} \in \mathbb{R}^D$ is a vector of D real numbers.

Differentiation is fundamental to numerical optimization. Suppose that at some $\boldsymbol{x}^*$, every partial derivative of f is equal to 0: formally, $\left.\frac{\partial f}{\partial x_i}\right|_{\boldsymbol{x}^*} = 0$. Then $\boldsymbol{x}^*$ is said to be a **critical point** of f. If f is a **convex** function (defined in § 2.4), then the value of $f(\boldsymbol{x}^*)$ is equal to the global minimum of f iff $\boldsymbol{x}^*$ is a critical point of f.

As an example, consider the convex function $f(x) = (x-2)^2 + 3$, shown in figure B.1a. The derivative is $\frac{\partial f}{\partial x} = 2x - 4$. A unique minimum can be obtained by setting the derivative equal to zero and solving for x, obtaining $x^* = 2$. Now consider the multivariate convex function $f(\boldsymbol{x}) = \frac{1}{2}||\boldsymbol{x} - [2, 1]^\top||^2$, where $||\boldsymbol{x}||^2$ is the squared Euclidean norm. The partial derivatives are

$$\frac{\partial d}{\partial x_1} = x_1 - 2 \qquad \text{[B.2]}$$

$$\frac{\partial d}{\partial x_2} = x_2 - 1. \qquad \text{[B.3]}$$

The unique minimum is $\boldsymbol{x}^* = [2, 1]^\top$.

For nonconvex functions, critical points are not necessarily global minima. A **local minimum** $\boldsymbol{x}^*$ is a point at which the function takes a smaller value than at all nearby neighbors: formally, $\boldsymbol{x}^*$ is a local minimum if there is some positive ϵ such that $f(\boldsymbol{x}^*) \leq f(\boldsymbol{x})$ for all $\boldsymbol{x}$ within distance ϵ of $\boldsymbol{x}^*$. Figure B.1b shows the function $f(x) = |x| - 2\cos(x)$, which has many local minima, as well as a unique global minimum at $x = 0$. A critical point may also be the local or global maximum of the function; it may be a **saddle point**, which is a minimum with respect to at least one coordinate, and a maximum with respect at least one other coordinate; it may be an **inflection point**, which is neither or a minimum nor maximum. When available, the second derivative of f can help to distinguish these cases.

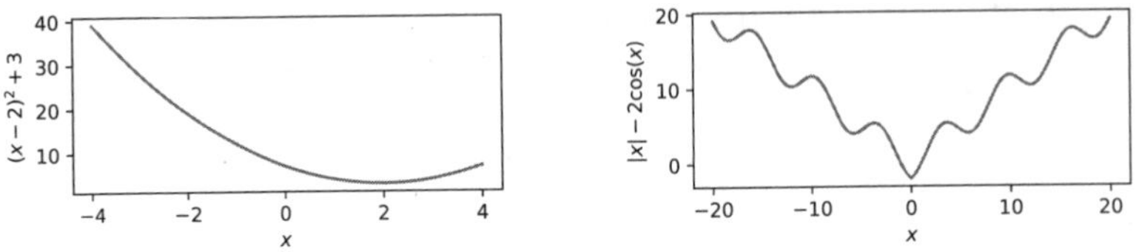

(a) The function $f(x) = (x - 2)^2 + 3$

(b) The function $f(x) = |x| - 2\cos(x)$

Figure B.1
Two functions with unique global minima.

B.1 Gradient Descent

For many convex functions, it is not possible to solve for $\boldsymbol{x}^*$ in closed form. In gradient descent, we compute a series of solutions, $\boldsymbol{x}^{(0)}, \boldsymbol{x}^{(1)}, \ldots$ by taking steps along the local gradient $\nabla_{\boldsymbol{x}^{(t)}} f$, which is the vector of partial derivatives of the function f, evaluated at the point $\boldsymbol{x}^{(t)}$. Each solution $\boldsymbol{x}^{(t+1)}$ is computed

$$\boldsymbol{x}^{(t+1)} \leftarrow \boldsymbol{x}^{(t)} - \eta^{(t)} \nabla_{\boldsymbol{x}^{(t)}} f, \qquad \text{[B.4]}$$

where $\eta^{(t)} > 0$ is a **step size**. If the step size is chosen appropriately, this procedure will find the global minimum of a differentiable convex function. For nonconvex functions, gradient descent will find a local minimum. The extension to nondifferentiable convex functions is discussed in § 2.4.

B.2 Constrained Optimization

Optimization must often be performed under constraints: for example, when optimizing the parameters of a probability distribution, the probabilities of all events must sum to one. Constrained optimization problems can be written

$$\min_{\boldsymbol{x}} f(\boldsymbol{x}) \qquad \text{[B.5]}$$

$$\text{s.t. } g_c(\boldsymbol{x}) \leq 0, \quad \forall c = 1, 2, \ldots, C, \qquad \text{[B.6]}$$

where each $g_c(\boldsymbol{x})$ is a scalar function of $\boldsymbol{x}$. For example, suppose that $\boldsymbol{x}$ must be nonnegative and that its sum cannot exceed a budget b. Then there are $D+1$ inequality constraints,

$$g_i(\boldsymbol{x}) = -x_i, \quad \forall i = 1, 2, \ldots, D \qquad \text{[B.7]}$$

$$g_{D+1}(\boldsymbol{x}) = -b + \sum_{i=1}^{D} x_i. \qquad \text{[B.8]}$$

Inequality constraints can be combined with the original objective function f by forming a **Lagrangian**,

$$L(\boldsymbol{x}, \boldsymbol{\lambda}) = f(\boldsymbol{x}) + \sum_{c=1}^{C} \lambda_c g_c(\boldsymbol{x}), \quad \text{[B.9]}$$

where λ_c is a **Lagrange multiplier**. For any Lagrangian, there is a corresponding dual form, which is a function of $\boldsymbol{\lambda}$:

$$D(\boldsymbol{\lambda}) = \min_{\boldsymbol{x}} L(\boldsymbol{x}, \boldsymbol{\lambda}). \quad \text{[B.10]}$$

The Lagrangian L can be referred to as the **primal form**.

B.3 Example: Passive-Aggressive Online Learning

Sometimes it is possible to solve a constrained optimization problem by manipulating the Lagrangian. One example is maximum likelihood estimation of a Naïve Bayes probability model, as described in § 2.2.3. In that case, it is unnecessary to explicitly compute the Lagrange multiplier. Another example is illustrated by the **passive-aggressive** algorithm for online learning (Crammer et al., 2006). This algorithm is similar to the perceptron, but the goal at each step is to make the most conservative update that gives zero margin loss on the current example.[1] Each update can be formulated as a constrained optimization over the weights $\boldsymbol{\theta}$:

$$\min_{\boldsymbol{\theta}} \frac{1}{2}||\boldsymbol{\theta} - \boldsymbol{\theta}^{(i-1)}||^2 \quad \text{[B.11]}$$

$$\text{s.t. } \ell^{(i)}(\boldsymbol{\theta}) = 0, \quad \text{[B.12]}$$

where $\boldsymbol{\theta}^{(i-1)}$ is the previous set of weights and $\ell^{(i)}(\boldsymbol{\theta})$ is the margin loss on instance i. As in § 2.4.1, this loss is defined as

$$\ell^{(i)}(\boldsymbol{\theta}) = 1 - \boldsymbol{\theta} \cdot \boldsymbol{f}(\boldsymbol{x}^{(i)}, y^{(i)}) + \max_{y \neq y^{(i)}} \boldsymbol{\theta} \cdot \boldsymbol{f}(\boldsymbol{x}^{(i)}, y). \quad \text{[B.13]}$$

When the margin loss is zero for $\boldsymbol{\theta}^{(i-1)}$, the optimal solution is $\boldsymbol{\theta}^* = \boldsymbol{\theta}^{(i-1)}$, so we will focus on the case where $\ell^{(i)}(\boldsymbol{\theta}^{(i-1)}) > 0$. The Lagrangian for this problem is

$$L(\boldsymbol{\theta}, \lambda) = \frac{1}{2}||\boldsymbol{\theta} - \boldsymbol{\theta}^{(i-1)}||^2 + \lambda \ell^{(i)}(\boldsymbol{\theta}). \quad \text{[B.14]}$$

Holding λ constant, we can solve for $\boldsymbol{\theta}$ by differentiating,

$$\nabla_{\boldsymbol{\theta}} L = \boldsymbol{\theta} - \boldsymbol{\theta}^{(i-1)} + \lambda \frac{\partial}{\partial \boldsymbol{\theta}} \ell^{(i)}(\boldsymbol{\theta}) \quad \text{[B.15]}$$

1. This is the basis for the name of the algorithm: it is passive when the loss is zero, but it aggressively moves to make the loss zero when necessary.

$$\boldsymbol{\theta}^* = \boldsymbol{\theta}^{(i-1)} + \lambda \boldsymbol{\delta}, \tag{B.16}$$

where $\boldsymbol{\delta} = \boldsymbol{f}(\boldsymbol{x}^{(i)}, y^{(i)}) - \boldsymbol{f}(\boldsymbol{x}^{(i)}, \hat{y})$ and $\hat{y} = \text{argmax}_{y \neq y^{(i)}} \boldsymbol{\theta} \cdot \boldsymbol{f}(\boldsymbol{x}^{(i)}, y)$.

The Lagrange multiplier λ acts as the learning rate in a perceptron-style update to $\boldsymbol{\theta}$. We can solve for λ by plugging $\boldsymbol{\theta}^*$ back into the Lagrangian, obtaining the dual function,

$$D(\lambda) = \frac{1}{2}||\boldsymbol{\theta}^{(i-1)} + \lambda\boldsymbol{\delta} - \boldsymbol{\theta}^{(i-1)}||^2 + \lambda(1 - (\boldsymbol{\theta}^{(i-1)} + \lambda\boldsymbol{\delta}) \cdot \boldsymbol{\delta}) \tag{B.17}$$

$$= \frac{\lambda^2}{2}||\boldsymbol{\delta}||^2 - \lambda^2||\boldsymbol{\delta}||^2 + \lambda(1 - \boldsymbol{\theta}^{(i-1)} \cdot \boldsymbol{\delta}) \tag{B.18}$$

$$= -\frac{\lambda^2}{2}||\boldsymbol{\delta}||^2 + \lambda\ell^{(i)}(\boldsymbol{\theta}^{(i-1)}). \tag{B.19}$$

Differentiating and solving for λ,

$$\frac{\partial D}{\partial \lambda} = -\lambda||\boldsymbol{\delta}||^2 + \ell^{(i)}(\boldsymbol{\theta}^{(i-1)}) \tag{B.20}$$

$$\lambda^* = \frac{\ell^{(i)}(\boldsymbol{\theta}^{(i-1)})}{||\boldsymbol{\delta}||^2}. \tag{B.21}$$

The complete update equation is therefore

$$\boldsymbol{\theta}^* = \boldsymbol{\theta}^{(i-1)} + \frac{\ell^{(i)}(\boldsymbol{\theta}^{(i-1)})}{||\boldsymbol{f}(\boldsymbol{x}^{(i)}, y^{(i)}) - \boldsymbol{f}(\boldsymbol{x}^{(i)}, \hat{y})||^2}(\boldsymbol{f}(\boldsymbol{x}^{(i)}, y^{(i)}) - \boldsymbol{f}(\boldsymbol{x}^{(i)}, \hat{y})). \tag{B.22}$$

This learning rate makes intuitive sense. The numerator grows with the loss; the denominator grows with the norm of the difference between the feature vectors associated with the correct and predicted label. If this norm is large, then the step with respect to each feature should be small, and vice versa.

Bibliography

Abadi, M., A. Agarwal, P. Barham, E. Brevdo, Z. Chen, C. Citro, G. S. Corrado, A. Davis, J. Dean, M. Devin, S. Ghemawat, I. J. Goodfellow, A. Harp, G. Irving, M. Isard, Y. Jia, R. Józefowicz, L. Kaiser, M. Kudlur, J. Levenberg, D. Mané, R. Monga, S. Moore, D. G. Murray, C. Olah, M. Schuster, J. Shlens, B. Steiner, I. Sutskever, K. Talwar, P. A. Tucker, V. Vanhoucke, V. Vasudevan, F. B. Viégas, O. Vinyals, P. Warden, M. Wattenberg, M. Wicke, Y. Yu, and X. Zheng. 2016. Tensorflow: Large-scale machine learning on heterogeneous distributed systems. *CoRR* abs/1603.04467. http://arxiv.org/abs/1603.04467.

Abend, O., and A. Rappoport. 2017. The state of the art in semantic representation. In *Proceedings of the Association for Computational Linguistics (ACL)*.

Abney, S., R. E. Schapire, and Y. Singer. 1999. Boosting applied to tagging and PP attachment. In *Proceedings of Empirical Methods for Natural Language Processing (EMNLP)*.

Abney, S. P. 1987. The English noun phrase in its sentential aspect. PhD diss, Massachusetts Institute of Technology.

Abney, S. P., and M. Johnson. 1991. Memory requirements and local ambiguities of parsing strategies. *Journal of Psycholinguistic Research* 20 (3): 233–250.

Adafre, S. F., and M. De Rijke. 2006. Finding similar sentences across multiple languages in wikipedia. In *Proceedings of the Workshop on NEW TEXT Wikis and Blogs and Other Dynamic Text Sources*.

Ahn, D. 2006. The stages of event extraction. In *Proceedings of the Workshop on Annotating and Reasoning About Time and Events*.

Aho, A. V., M. S. Lam, R. Sethi, and J. D. Ullman. 2006. *Compilers: Principles, Techniques, & Tools*, 2nd edn. Reading, MA: Addison-Wesley Publishing Company.

Aikhenvald, A. Y. 2004. *Evidentiality*. Oxford, UK: Oxford University Press.

Akaike, H. 1974. A new look at the statistical model identification. *IEEE Transactions on Automatic Control* 19 (6): 716–723.

Akmajian, A., R. A. Demers, A. K. Farmer, and R. M. Harnish. 2010. *Linguistics: An Introduction to Language and Communication*, 6th edn. Cambridge, MA: MIT Press.

Alfano, M., D. Hovy, M. Mitchell, and M. Strube. 2018. *Proceedings of the Second ACL Workshop on Ethics in Natural Language Processing*.

Alfau, F. 1999. *Chromos*. Champaign, IL: Dalkey Archive Press.

Allauzen, C., M. Riley, J. Schalkwyk, W. Skut, and M. Mohri. 2007. OpenFst: A general and efficient weighted finite-state transducer library. In *International Conference on Implementation and Application of Automata*.

Allen, J. F. 1984. Towards a general theory of action and time. *Artificial Intelligence* 23 (2): 123–154.

Allen, J. F., B. W. Miller, E. K. Ringger, and T. Sikorski. 1996. A robust system for natural spoken dialogue. In *Proceedings of the Association for Computational Linguistics (ACL)*.

Allen, J. F., L. K. Schubert, G. Ferguson, P. Heeman, C. H. Hwang, T. Kato, M. Light, N. Martin, B. Miller, M. Poesio, and D. Traum. 1995. The TRAINS project: A case study in building a conversational planning agent. *Journal of Experimental & Theoretical Artificial Intelligence* 7 (1): 7–48.

Alm, C. O., D. Roth, and R. Sproat. 2005. Emotions from text: Machine learning for text-based emotion prediction. In *Proceedings of Empirical Methods for Natural Language Processing (EMNLP)*.

Aluísio, S., J. Pelizzoni, A. Marchi, L. de Oliveira, R. Manenti, and V. Marquiafável. 2003. An account of the challenge of tagging a reference corpus for Brazilian Portuguese. In *Proceedings of Computational Processing of the Portuguese Language (PROPOR)*.

Anand, P., M. Walker, R. Abbott, J. E. Fox Tree, R. Bowmani, and M. Minor. 2011. Cats rule and dogs drool!: Classifying stance in online debate. In *Proceedings of the 2nd Workshop on Computational Approaches to Subjectivity and Sentiment Analysis*.

Anandkumar, A., and R. Ge. 2016. Efficient approaches for escaping higher order saddle points in non-convex optimization. In *Proceedings of the Conference on Learning Theory (COLT)*.

Anandkumar, A., R. Ge, D. Hsu, S. M. Kakade, and M. Telgarsky. 2014. Tensor decompositions for learning latent variable models. *The Journal of Machine Learning Research* 15 (1): 2773–2832.

Ando, R. K., and T. Zhang. 2005. A framework for learning predictive structures from multiple tasks and unlabeled data. *The Journal of Machine Learning Research* 6: 1817–1853.

Andor, D., C. Alberti, D. Weiss, A. Severyn, A. Presta, K. Ganchev, S. Petrov, and M. Collins. 2016. Globally normalized transition-based neural networks. In *Proceedings of the Association for Computational Linguistics (ACL)*.

Angeli, G., P. Liang, and D. Klein. 2010. A simple domain-independent probabilistic approach to generation. In *Proceedings of Empirical Methods for Natural Language Processing (EMNLP)*.

Antol, S., A. Agrawal, J. Lu, M. Mitchell, D. Batra, L. Zitnick, and D. Parikh. 2015. VQA: Visual question answering. In *Proceedings of the International Conference on Computer Vision (ICCV)*.

Aronoff, M. 1976. *Word Formation in Generative Grammar*. Cambridge, MA: MIT Press.

Arora, S., and B. Barak. 2009. *Computational Complexity: A Modern Approach*. Cambridge, UK: Cambridge University Press.

Arora, S., R. Ge, Y. Halpern, D. Mimno, A. Moitra, D. Sontag, Y. Wu, and M. Zhu. 2013. A practical algorithm for topic modeling with provable guarantees. In *Proceedings of the International Conference on Machine Learning (ICML)*.

Arora, S., Y. Li, Y. Liang, T. Ma, and A. Risteski. 2018. Linear algebraic structure of word senses, with applications to polysemy. *Transactions of the Association of Computational Linguistics* 6: 483–495.

Artstein, R., and M. Poesio. 2008. Inter-coder agreement for computational linguistics. *Computational Linguistics* 34 (4): 555–596.

Artzi, Y., and L. Zettlemoyer. 2013. Weakly supervised learning of semantic parsers for mapping instructions to actions. *Transactions of the Association for Computational Linguistics* 1: 49–62.

Attardi, G. 2006. Experiments with a multilanguage non-projective dependency parser. In *Proceedings of the Conference on Natural Language Learning (CoNLL)*.

Auer, P., ed. 2013. *Code-Switching in Conversation: Language, Interaction and Identity*. London, UK: Routledge.

Auer, S., C. Bizer, G. Kobilarov, J. Lehmann, R. Cyganiak, and Z. Ives. 2007. DBpedia: A nucleus for a web of open data. In *Proceedings of the International Semantic Web Conference*.

Austin, J. L. 1962. *How to Do Things with Words*. Oxford, UK: Oxford University Press.

Aw, A., M. Zhang, J. Xiao, and J. Su. 2006. A phrase-based statistical model for SMS text normalization. In *Proceedings of the Association for Computational Linguistics (ACL)*.

Ba, J. L., J. R. Kiros, and G. E. Hinton. 2016. Layer normalization. *arXiv preprint arXiv:1607.06450*.

Bagga, A., and B. Baldwin. 1998a. Algorithms for scoring coreference chains. In *Proceedings of the Language Resources and Evaluation Conference (LREC)*.

Bagga, A., and B. Baldwin. 1998b. Entity-based cross-document coreferencing using the vector space model. In *Proceedings of the International Conference on Computational Linguistics (COLING)*.

Bahdanau, D., K. Cho, and Y. Bengio. 2014. Neural machine translation by jointly learning to align and translate. In *Neural Information Processing Systems (NeurIPS)*.

Baldwin, T., and S. N. Kim. 2010. Multiword expressions. In *Handbook of Natural Language Processing*, Vol. 2, 267–292. Boca Raton, FL: CRC Press.

Balle, B., A. Quattoni, and X. Carreras. 2011. A spectral learning algorithm for finite state transducers. In *Proceedings of the European Conference on Machine Learning and Principles and Practice of Knowledge Discovery in Databases (ECML)*.

Banarescu, L., C. Bonial, S. Cai, M. Georgescu, K. Griffitt, U. Hermjakob, K. Knight, P. Koehn, M. Palmer, and N. Schneider. 2013. Abstract meaning representation for sembanking. In *Proceedings of the Linguistic Annotation Workshop (LAW)*.

Banko, M., M. J. Cafarella, S. Soderland, M. Broadhead, and O. Etzioni. 2007. Open information extraction from the web. In *Proceedings of the International Joint Conference on Artificial Intelligence (IJCAI)*.

Bansal, N., A. Blum, and S. Chawla. 2004. Correlation clustering. *Machine Learning* 56: 89–113.

Barber, D. 2012. *Bayesian Reasoning and Machine Learning*. Cambridge University Press.

Barman, U., A. Das, J. Wagner, and J. Foster. 2014. Code mixing: A challenge for language identification in the language of social media. In *Proceedings of the First Workshop on Computational Approaches to Code Switching*.

Baron, A., and P. Rayson. 2008. Vard2: A tool for dealing with spelling variation in historical corpora. In *Postgraduate Conference in Corpus Linguistics*.

Baroni, M., R. Bernardi, and R. Zamparelli. 2014. Frege in space: A program for compositional distributional semantics. *Linguistic Issues in Language Technologies* 9: 241–346.

Barzilay, R., and M. Lapata. 2008. Modeling local coherence: An entity-based approach. *Computational Linguistics* 34 (1): 1–34.

Barzilay, R., and K. R. McKeown. 2005. Sentence fusion for multidocument news summarization. *Computational Linguistics* 31 (3): 297–328.

Beesley, K. R., and L. Karttunen. 2003. *Finite-State Morphology*. Stanford, CA: Center for the Study of Language and Information.

Bejan, C. A., and S. Harabagiu. 2014. Unsupervised event coreference resolution. *Computational Linguistics* 40 (2): 311–347.

Bell, E. T. 1934. Exponential numbers. *The American Mathematical Monthly* 41 (7): 411–419.

Bender, E. M. 2013. *Linguistic Fundamentals for Natural Language Processing: 100 Essentials from Morphology and Syntax*. San Rafael, CA: Morgan & Claypool.

Bengio, S., O. Vinyals, N. Jaitly, and N. Shazeer. 2015. Scheduled sampling for sequence prediction with recurrent neural networks. In *Neural Information Processing Systems (NeurIPS)*.

Bengio, Y., P. Simard, and P. Frasconi. 1994. Learning long-term dependencies with gradient descent is difficult. *IEEE Transactions on Neural Networks* 5 (2): 157–166.

Bengio, Y., R. Ducharme, P. Vincent, and C. Janvin. 2003. A neural probabilistic language model. *The Journal of Machine Learning Research* 3: 1137–1155.

Bengtson, E., and D. Roth. 2008. Understanding the value of features for coreference resolution. In *Proceedings of Empirical Methods for Natural Language Processing (EMNLP)*.

Benjamini, Y., and Y. Hochberg. 1995. Controlling the false discovery rate: A practical and powerful approach to multiple testing. *Journal of the Royal Statistical Society. Series B (Methodological)*.

Berant, J., A. Chou, R. Frostig, and P. Liang. 2013. Semantic parsing on freebase from question-answer pairs. In *Proceedings of Empirical Methods for Natural Language Processing (EMNLP)*.

Berant, J., V. Srikumar, P.-C. Chen, A. Vander Linden, B. Harding, B. Huang, P. Clark, and C. D. Manning. 2014. Modeling biological processes for reading comprehension. In *Proceedings of Empirical Methods for Natural Language Processing (EMNLP)*.

Berger, A. L., V. J. D. Pietra, and S. A. D. Pietra. 1996. A maximum entropy approach to natural language processing. *Computational Linguistics* 22 (1): 39–71.

Berg-Kirkpatrick, T., D. Burkett, and D. Klein. 2012. An empirical investigation of statistical significance in NLP. In *Proceedings of Empirical Methods for Natural Language Processing (EMNLP)*.

Berg-Kirkpatrick, T., A. Bouchard-Côté, J. DeNero, and D. Klein. 2010. Painless unsupervised learning with features. In *Proceedings of the North American Chapter of the Association for Computational Linguistics (NAACL)*.

Bergsma, S., D. Lin, and R. Goebel. 2008. Distributional identification of non-referential pronouns. In *Proceedings of the Association for Computational Linguistics (ACL)*.

Bernardi, R., R. Cakici, D. Elliott, A. Erdem, E. Erdem, N. Ikizler-Cinbis, F. Keller, A. Muscat, and B. Plank. 2016. Automatic description generation from images: A survey of models, datasets, and evaluation measures. *Journal of Artificial Intelligence Research* 55: 409–442.

Bertsekas, D. P. 2012. Incremental gradient, subgradient, and proximal methods for convex optimization: A survey. In *Optimization for Machine Learning*, eds. S. Sra, S. Nowozin, and S. J. Wright. Cambridge, MA: MIT Press.

Bhatia, P., R. Guthrie, and J. Eisenstein. 2016. Morphological priors for probabilistic neural word embeddings. In *Proceedings of Empirical Methods for Natural Language Processing (EMNLP)*.

Bhatia, P., Y. Ji, and J. Eisenstein. 2015. Better document-level sentiment analysis from RST discourse parsing. In *Proceedings of Empirical Methods for Natural Language Processing (EMNLP)*.

Biber, D. 1991. *Variation Across Speech and Writing*. Cambridge, UK: Cambridge University Press.

Bird, S., E. Klein, and E. Loper. 2009. *Natural Language Processing with Python*. Sebastopol, CA: O'Reilly Media.

Bishop, C. M. 2006. *Pattern Recognition and Machine Learning*. New York, NY: Springer.

Björkelund, A., and P. Nugues. 2011. Exploring lexicalized features for coreference resolution. In *Proceedings of the Conference on Natural Language Learning (CoNLL)*. http://www.aclweb.org/anthology/W11-1905.

Blackburn, P., and J. Bos. 2005. *Representation and Inference for Natural Language: A First Course in Computational Semantics*. Stanford, CA: Center for the Study of Language and Information.

Blei, D. M. 2012. Probabilistic topic models. *Communications of the ACM* 55 (4): 77–84.

Blei, D. M. 2014. Build, compute, critique, repeat: Data analysis with latent variable models. *Annual Review of Statistics and Its Application* 1: 203–232.

Blei, D. M., A. Y. Ng, and M. I. Jordan. 2003. Latent dirichlet allocation. *The Journal of Machine Learning Research* 3: 993–1022.

Blitzer, J., M. Dredze, and F. Pereira. 2007. Biographies, bollywood, boom-boxes and blenders: Domain adaptation for sentiment classification. In *Proceedings of the Association for Computational Linguistics (ACL)*.

Blum, A., and T. Mitchell. 1998. Combining labeled and unlabeled data with co-training. In *Proceedings of the Conference on Learning Theory (COLT)*.

Bobrow, D. G., R. M. Kaplan, M. Kay, D. A. Norman, H. Thompson, and T. Winograd. 1977. GUS, a frame-driven dialog system. *Artificial Intelligence* 8 (2): 155–173.

Bohnet, B. 2010. Very high accuracy and fast dependency parsing is not a contradiction. In *Proceedings of the International Conference on Computational Linguistics (COLING)*.

Boitet, C. 1988. Pros and cons of the pivot and transfer approaches in multilingual machine translation. In *Readings in Machine Translation*, eds. S. Nirenburg, H. L. Somers, and Y. Wilks, 273–279. Cambridge, MA: MIT Press.

Bojanowski, P., E. Grave, A. Joulin, and T. Mikolov. 2017. Enriching word vectors with subword information. *Transactions of the Association for Computational Linguistics* 5: 135–146.

Bollacker, K., C. Evans, P. Paritosh, T. Sturge, and J. Taylor. 2008. Freebase: A collaboratively created graph database for structuring human knowledge. In *Proceedings of the ACM International Conference on Management of Data (SIGMOD)*.

Bolukbasi, T., K.-W. Chang, J. Y. Zou, V. Saligrama, and A. T. Kalai. 2016. Man is to computer programmer as woman is to homemaker? Debiasing word embeddings. In *Neural Information Processing Systems (NeurIPS)*.

Bordes, A., J. Weston, R. Collobert, and Y. Bengio. 2011. Learning structured embeddings of knowledge bases. In *Proceedings of the National Conference on Artificial Intelligence (AAAI)*.

Bordes, A., N. Usunier, A. Garcia-Duran, J. Weston, and O. Yakhnenko. 2013. Translating embeddings for modeling multi-relational data. In *Neural Information Processing Systems (NeurIPS)*.

Borges, J. L. 1993. *Other Inquisitions 1937–1952*. Austin, TX: University of Texas Press. Translated by Ruth L. C. Simms.

Botha, J. A., and P. Blunsom. 2014. Compositional morphology for word representations and language modelling. In *Proceedings of the International Conference on Machine Learning (ICML)*.

Bottou, L. 2012. Stochastic gradient descent tricks. In *Neural Networks: Tricks of the Trade*, eds. G. Montavon, G. B. Orr, and K.-R. Müller, 421–436. New York, NY: Springer.

Bottou, L., F. E. Curtis, and J. Nocedal. 2018. Optimization methods for large-scale machine learning. *SIAM Review* 60 (2): 223–311.

Bowman, S. R., L. Vilnis, O. Vinyals, A. Dai, R. Jozefowicz, and S. Bengio. 2016. Generating sentences from a continuous space. In *Proceedings of the Conference on Natural Language Learning (CoNLL)*.

boyd, d., and K. Crawford. 2012. Critical questions for big data. *Information, Communication & Society* 15 (5): 662–679.

Boyd, S., and L. Vandenberghe. 2004. *Convex Optimization*. Cambridge, UK: Cambridge University Press.

Boydstun, A. E. 2013. *Making the News: Politics, the Media, and Agenda Setting*. Chicago, IL: University of Chicago Press.

Branavan, S. R., H. Chen, L. S. Zettlemoyer, and R. Barzilay. 2009a. Reinforcement learning for mapping instructions to actions. In *Proceedings of the Association for Computational Linguistics (ACL)*.

Branavan, S., H. Chen, J. Eisenstein, and R. Barzilay. 2009b. Learning document-level semantic properties from free-text annotations. *Journal of Artificial Intelligence Research* 34 (2): 569–603.

Brants, T., and A. Franz. 2006. The Google 1T 5-gram Corpus. LDC2006T13.

Braud, C., O. Lacroix, and A. Søgaard. 2017. Does syntax help discourse segmentation? Not so much. In *Proceedings of Empirical Methods for Natural Language Processing (EMNLP)*.

Brennan, S. E., M. W. Friedman, and C. J. Pollard. 1987. A centering approach to pronouns. In *Proceedings of the Association for Computational Linguistics (ACL)*.

Briscoe, T. 2011 (accessed February 6, 2019). Introduction to Formal Semantics for Natural Language. www.cl.cam.ac.uk/teaching/1011/L107/semantics.pdf.

Brown, P. F., J. Cocke, S. A. D. Pietra, V. J. D. Pietra, F. Jelinek, J. D. Lafferty, R. L. Mercer, and P. S. Roossin. 1990. A statistical approach to machine translation. *Computational Linguistics* 16 (2): 79–85.

Brown, P. F., P. V. Desouza, R. L. Mercer, V. J. D. Pietra, and J. C. Lai. 1992. Class-based n-gram models of natural language. *Computational Linguistics* 18 (4): 467–479.

Brown, P. F., V. J. D. Pietra, S. A. D. Pietra, and R. L. Mercer. 1993. The mathematics of statistical machine translation: Parameter estimation. *Computational Linguistics* 19 (2): 263–311.

Brun, C., and C. Roux. 2014. Décomposition des "hash tags" pour l'amélioration de la classification en polarité des "tweets". In *Proceedings of Traitement Automatique des Langues Naturelles (TAL)*.

Bruni, E., N.-K. Tran, and M. Baroni. 2014. Multimodal distributional semantics. *Journal of Artificial Intelligence Research* 49 (2014): 1–47.

Brutzkus, A., A. Globerson, E. Malach, and S. Shalev-Shwartz. 2018. SGD learns over-parameterized networks that provably generalize on linearly separable data. In *Proceedings of the International Conference on Learning Representations (ICLR)*.

Bullinaria, J. A., and J. P. Levy. 2007. Extracting semantic representations from word co-occurrence statistics: A computational study. *Behavior Research Methods* 39 (3): 510–526.

Bunescu, R. C., and R. J. Mooney. 2005. A shortest path dependency kernel for relation extraction. In *Proceedings of Empirical Methods for Natural Language Processing (EMNLP)*.

Bunescu, R. C., and M. Pasca. 2006. Using encyclopedic knowledge for named entity disambiguation. In *Proceedings of the European Chapter of the Association for Computational Linguistics (EACL)*.

Burstein, J., D. Marcu, and K. Knight. 2003. Finding the WRITE stuff: Automatic identification of discourse structure in student essays. *IEEE Intelligent Systems* 18 (1): 32–39.

Burstein, J., J. Tetreault, and S. Andreyev. 2010. Using entity-based features to model coherence in student essays. In *Proceedings of the North American Chapter of the Association for Computational Linguistics (NAACL)*.

Burstein, J., J. Tetreault, and M. Chodorow. 2013. Holistic discourse coherence annotation for noisy essay writing. *Dialogue & Discourse* 4 (2): 34–52.

Cai, Q., and A. Yates. 2013. Large-scale semantic parsing via schema matching and lexicon extension. In *Proceedings of the Association for Computational Linguistics (ACL)*.

Caliskan, A., J. J. Bryson, and A. Narayanan. 2017. Semantics derived automatically from language corpora contain human-like biases. *Science* 356 (6334): 183–186.

Canny, J. 1986. A computational approach to edge detection. *IEEE Transactions on Pattern Analysis and Machine Intelligence (PAMI)*.

Cappé, O., and E. Moulines. 2009. On-line expectation–maximization algorithm for latent data models. *Journal of the Royal Statistical Society: Series B (Statistical Methodology)* 71 (3): 593–613.

Carbonell, J., and J. Goldstein. 1998. The use of MMR, diversity-based reranking for reordering documents and producing summaries. In *Proceedings of the ACM SIGIR Conference on Research and Development in Information Retrieval*.

Carbonell, J. R. 1970. Mixed-initiative man-computer instructional dialogues., Technical report, Bolt Beranek and Newman.

Cardie, C., and K. Wagstaff. 1999. Noun phrase coreference as clustering. In *Proceedings of Empirical Methods for Natural Language Processing (EMNLP)*.

Carletta, J. 1996. Assessing agreement on classification tasks: the kappa statistic. *Computational Linguistics* 22 (2): 249–254.

Carletta, J. 2007. Unleashing the killer corpus: Experiences in creating the multi-everything AMI meeting corpus. *Language Resources and Evaluation* 41 (2): 181–190.

Carlson, L., and D. Marcu. 2001. Discourse tagging reference manual, Technical Report ISI-TR-545, Information Sciences Institute.

Carlson, L., M. E. Okurowski, and D. Marcu. 2002. RST discourse treebank. Linguistic Data Consortium, University of Pennsylvania.

Carpenter, B. 1997. *Type-Logical Semantics*. Cambridge, MA: MIT Press.

Carreras, X., and L. Màrquez. 2005. Introduction to the CoNLL-2005 shared task: Semantic role labeling. In *Proceedings of the Conference on Natural Language Learning (CoNLL)*.

Carreras, X., M. Collins, and T. Koo. 2008. Tag, dynamic programming, and the perceptron for efficient, feature-rich parsing. In *Proceedings of the Conference on Natural Language Learning (CoNLL)*.

Carroll, L. 1865. *Alice's Adventures in Wonderland*. London: Macmillan.

Carroll, L. 1917. *Through the Looking Glass: And What Alice Found There*. Chicago: Rand McNally.

Chambers, N., and D. Jurafsky. 2008. Jointly combining implicit constraints improves temporal ordering. In *Proceedings of Empirical Methods for Natural Language Processing (EMNLP)*.

Chang, K.-W., A. Krishnamurthy, A. Agarwal, H. Daume III, and J. Langford. 2015. Learning to search better than your teacher. In *Proceedings of the International Conference on Machine Learning (ICML)*.

Chang, M.-W., L. Ratinov, and D. Roth. 2007. Guiding semi-supervision with constraint-driven learning. In *Proceedings of the Association for Computational Linguistics (ACL)*.

Chang, M.-W., L.-A. Ratinov, N. Rizzolo, and D. Roth. 2008. Learning and inference with constraints. In *Proceedings of the National Conference on Artificial Intelligence (AAAI)*.

Chapman, W. W., W. Bridewell, P. Hanbury, G. F. Cooper, and B. G. Buchanan. 2001. A simple algorithm for identifying negated findings and diseases in discharge summaries. *Journal of Biomedical Informatics* 34 (5): 301–310.

Charniak, E. 1997. Statistical techniques for natural language parsing. *AI Magazine* 18 (4): 33–43.

Charniak, E., and M. Johnson. 2005. Coarse-to-fine n-best parsing and maxent discriminative reranking. In *Proceedings of the Association for Computational Linguistics (ACL)*.

Chelba, C., and A. Acero. 2006. Adaptation of maximum entropy capitalizer: Little data can help a lot. *Computer Speech & Language* 20 (4): 382–399.

Chelba, C., T. Mikolov, M. Schuster, Q. Ge, T. Brants, P. Koehn, and T. Robinson. 2013. One billion word benchmark for measuring progress in statistical language modeling. *arXiv preprint arXiv:1312.3005*.

Chen, D., and C. D. Manning. 2014. A fast and accurate dependency parser using neural networks. In *Proceedings of Empirical Methods for Natural Language Processing (EMNLP)*.

Chen, D., J. Bolton, and C. D. Manning. 2016. A thorough examination of the CNN/Daily Mail reading comprehension task. In *Proceedings of the Association for Computational Linguistics (ACL)*.

Chen, D. L., and R. J. Mooney. 2008. Learning to sportscast: A test of grounded language acquisition. In *Proceedings of the International Conference on Machine Learning (ICML)*.

Chen, H., S. Branavan, R. Barzilay, and D. R. Karger. 2009. Content modeling using latent permutations. *Journal of Artificial Intelligence Research* 36 (1): 129–163.

Chen, M., Z. Xu, K. Weinberger, and F. Sha. 2012. Marginalized denoising autoencoders for domain adaptation. In *Proceedings of the International Conference on Machine Learning (ICML)*.

Chen, M. X., O. Firat, A. Bapna, M. Johnson, W. Macherey, G. Foster, L. Jones, N. Parmar, M. Schuster, Z. Chen, Y. Wu, and M. Hughes. 2018. The best of both worlds: Combining recent advances in neural machine translation. In *Proceedings of the Association for Computational Linguistics (ACL)*.

Chen, S. F., and J. Goodman. 1999. An empirical study of smoothing techniques for language modeling. *Computer Speech & Language* 13 (4): 359–393.

Chen, T., and C. Guestrin. 2016. XGBoost: A scalable tree boosting system. In *Proceedings of Knowledge Discovery and Data Mining (KDD)*.

Chen, X., X. Qiu, C. Zhu, P. Liu, and X. Huang. 2015. Long short-term memory neural networks for chinese word segmentation. In *Proceedings of Empirical Methods for Natural Language Processing (EMNLP)*.

Chen, Y., S. Gilroy, A. Malletti, K. Knight, and J. May. 2018. Recurrent neural networks as weighted language recognizers. In *Proceedings of the North American Chapter of the Association for Computational Linguistics (NAACL)*.

Chen, Z., and H. Ji. 2009. Graph-based event coreference resolution. In *Proceedings of the Workshop on Graph-Based Methods for Natural Language Processing*.

Cheng, X., and D. Roth. 2013. Relational inference for wikification. In *Proceedings of Empirical Methods for Natural Language Processing (EMNLP)*.

Chiang, D. 2007. Hierarchical phrase-based translation. *Computational Linguistics* 33 (2): 201–228.

Chiang, D., J. Graehl, K. Knight, A. Pauls, and S. Ravi. 2010. Bayesian inference for finite-state transducers. In *Proceedings of the North American Chapter of the Association for Computational Linguistics (NAACL)*.

Chinchor, N., and P. Robinson. 1997. MUC-7 named entity task definition. In *Proceedings of the 7th Conference on Message Understanding (MUC)*.

Cho, K. 2015. Natural language understanding with distributed representation. *CoRR* abs/1511.07916.

Cho, K., B. Van Merriënboer, C. Gulcehre, D. Bahdanau, F. Bougares, H. Schwenk, and Y. Bengio. 2014. Learning phrase representations using rnn encoder-decoder for statistical machine translation. In *Proceedings of Empirical Methods for Natural Language Processing (EMNLP)*.

Chomsky, N. 1957. *Syntactic Structures*. The Hague: Mouton & Co.

Chomsky, N. 1982. *Some Concepts and Consequences of the Theory of Government and Binding*. Cambridge, MA: MIT Press.

Choromanska, A., M. Henaff, M. Mathieu, G. B. Arous, and Y. LeCun. 2015. The loss surfaces of multilayer networks. In *Proceedings of Artificial Intelligence and Statistics (AISTATS)*.

Christodoulopoulos, C., S. Goldwater, and M. Steedman. 2010. Two decades of unsupervised pos induction: How far have we come? In *Proceedings of Empirical Methods for Natural Language Processing (EMNLP)*.

Chu, Y.-J., and T.-H. Liu. 1965. On shortest arborescence of a directed graph. *Scientia Sinica* 14 (10): 1396–1400.

Chung, C., and J. W. Pennebaker. 2007. The psychological functions of function words. In *Social Communication*, ed. K. Fiedler, 343–359. New York and Hove: Psychology Press.

Church, K. 2011. A pendulum swung too far. *Linguistic Issues in Language Technology* 6 (5): 1–27.

Church, K. W. 2000. Empirical estimates of adaptation: The chance of two Noriegas is closer to $p/2$ than p^2. In *Proceedings of the International Conference on Computational Linguistics (COLING)*.

Church, K. W., and P. Hanks. 1990. Word association norms, mutual information, and lexicography. *Computational Linguistics* 16 (1): 22–29.

Ciaramita, M., and M. Johnson. 2003. Supersense tagging of unknown nouns in WordNet. In *Proceedings of Empirical Methods for Natural Language Processing (EMNLP)*.

Clark, K., and C. D. Manning. 2015. Entity-centric coreference resolution with model stacking. In *Proceedings of the Association for Computational Linguistics (ACL)*.

Clark, K., and C. D. Manning. 2016. Improving coreference resolution by learning entity-level distributed representations. In *Proceedings of the Association for Computational Linguistics (ACL)*.

Clark, P. 2015. Elementary school science and math tests as a driver for AI: Take the Aristo challenge! In *Proceedings of the National Conference on Artificial Intelligence (AAAI)*.

Clarke, J., and M. Lapata. 2008. Global inference for sentence compression: An integer linear programming approach. *Journal of Artificial Intelligence Research* 31: 399–429.

Clarke, J., D. Goldwasser, M.-W. Chang, and D. Roth. 2010. Driving semantic parsing from the world's response. In *Proceedings of the Conference on Natural Language Learning (CoNLL)*.

Cohen, J. 1960. A coefficient of agreement for nominal scales. *Educational and Psychological Measurement* 20 (1): 37–46.

Cohen, S. 2016. *Bayesian Analysis in Natural Language Processing*. Vol. 9 of *Synthesis Lectures on Human Language Technologies*. San Rafael, CA: Morgan & Claypool.

Cohen, S. B., K. Stratos, M. Collins, D. P. Foster, and L. Ungar. 2014. Spectral learning of latent-variable PCFGs: Algorithms and sample complexity. *Journal of Machine Learning Research* 15: 2399–2449.

Collier, N., C. Nobata, and J.-i. Tsujii. 2000. Extracting the names of genes and gene products with a hidden Markov model. In *Proceedings of the International Conference on Computational Linguistics (COLING)*.

Collins, M. 1997. Three generative, lexicalised models for statistical parsing. In *Proceedings of the Association for Computational Linguistics (ACL)*.

Collins, M. 2002. Discriminative training methods for hidden Markov models: Theory and experiments with perceptron algorithms. In *Proceedings of Empirical Methods for Natural Language Processing (EMNLP)*.

Collins, M., and T. Koo. 2005. Discriminative reranking for natural language parsing. *Computational Linguistics* 31 (1): 25–70.

Collins, M., and B. Roark. 2004. Incremental parsing with the perceptron algorithm. In *Proceedings of the Association for Computational Linguistics (ACL)*.

Collobert, R., and J. Weston. 2008. A unified architecture for natural language processing: Deep neural networks with multitask learning. In *Proceedings of the International Conference on Machine Learning (ICML)*.

Collobert, R., K. Kavukcuoglu, and C. Farabet. 2011a. Torch7: A matlab-like environment for machine learning, Technical Report EPFL-CONF-192376, EPFL.

Collobert, R., J. Weston, L. Bottou, M. Karlen, K. Kavukcuoglu, and P. Kuksa. 2011b. Natural language processing (almost) from scratch. *Journal of Machine Learning Research* 12: 2493–2537.

Colton, S., J. Goodwin, and T. Veale. 2012. Full-face poetry generation. In *Proceedings of the International Conference on Computational Creativity*.

Conneau, A., D. Kiela, H. Schwenk, L. Barrault, and A. Bordes. 2017. Supervised learning of universal sentence representations from natural language inference data. In *Proceedings of Empirical Methods for Natural Language Processing (EMNLP)*.

Cormen, T. H., C. E. Leiserson, R. L. Rivest, and C. Stein. 2009. *Introduction to Algorithms*, 3rd edn. Cambridge, MA: MIT Press.

Cotterell, R., H. Schütze, and J. Eisner. 2016. Morphological smoothing and extrapolation of word embeddings. In *Proceedings of the Association for Computational Linguistics (ACL)*.

Coviello, L., Y. Sohn, A. D. Kramer, C. Marlow, M. Franceschetti, N. A. Christakis, and J. H. Fowler. 2014. Detecting emotional contagion in massive social networks. *PloS One* 9 (3): 90315.

Covington, M. A. 2001. A fundamental algorithm for dependency parsing. In *Proceedings of the 39th Annual ACM Southeast Conference*.

Crammer, K., and Y. Singer. 2001. Pranking with ranking. In *Neural Information Processing Systems (NeurIPS)*.

Crammer, K., and Y. Singer. 2003. Ultraconservative online algorithms for multiclass problems. *The Journal of Machine Learning Research* 3: 951–991.

Crammer, K., O. Dekel, J. Keshet, S. Shalev-Shwartz, and Y. Singer. 2006. Online passive-aggressive algorithms. *The Journal of Machine Learning Research* 7: 551–585.

Creutz, M., and K. Lagus. 2007. Unsupervised models for morpheme segmentation and morphology learning. *ACM Transactions on Speech and Language Processing (TSLP)* 4 (1): 3.

Cross, J., and L. Huang. 2016. Span-based constituency parsing with a structure-label system and provably optimal dynamic oracles. In *Proceedings of Empirical Methods for Natural Language Processing (EMNLP)*.

Cucerzan, S. 2007. Large-scale named entity disambiguation based on Wikipedia data. In *Proceedings of Empirical Methods for Natural Language Processing (EMNLP)*.

Cui, H., R. Sun, K. Li, M.-Y. Kan, and T.-S. Chua. 2005. Question answering passage retrieval using dependency relations. In *Proceedings of the ACM SIGIR Conference on Research and Development in Information Retrieval*.

Cui, Y., Z. Chen, S. Wei, S. Wang, T. Liu, and G. Hu. 2017. Attention-over-attention neural networks for reading comprehension. In *Proceedings of the Association for Computational Linguistics (ACL)*.

Culotta, A., and J. Sorensen. 2004. Dependency tree kernels for relation extraction. In *Proceedings of the Association for Computational Linguistics (ACL)*.

Culotta, A., M. Wick, and A. McCallum. 2007. First-order probabilistic models for coreference resolution. In *Proceedings of the North American Chapter of the Association for Computational Linguistics (NAACL)*.

Curry, H. B., and R. Feys. 1958. *Combinatory Logic*, Vol. I. Amsterdam: North Holland.

Danescu-Niculescu-Mizil, C., M. Sudhof, D. Jurafsky, J. Leskovec, and C. Potts. 2013. A computational approach to politeness with application to social factors. In *Proceedings of the Association for Computational Linguistics (ACL)*.

Das, D., D. Chen, A. F. Martins, N. Schneider, and N. A. Smith. 2014. Frame-semantic parsing. *Computational Linguistics* 40 (1): 9–56.

Daumé III, H. 2007. Frustratingly easy domain adaptation. In *Proceedings of the Association for Computational Linguistics (ACL)*.

Daumé III, H., and D. Marcu. 2005. A large-scale exploration of effective global features for a joint entity detection and tracking model. In *Proceedings of Empirical Methods for Natural Language Processing (EMNLP)*.

Daumé III, H., J. Langford, and D. Marcu. 2009. Search-based structured prediction. *Machine Learning* 75 (3): 297–325.

Dauphin, Y. N., R. Pascanu, C. Gulcehre, K. Cho, S. Ganguli, and Y. Bengio. 2014. Identifying and attacking the saddle point problem in high-dimensional non-convex optimization. In *Neural Information Processing Systems (NeurIPS)*.

Davidson, D. 1967. The logical form of action sentences. In *The Logic of Decision and Action*, ed. N. Rescher. Pittsburgh, PA: University of Pittsburgh Press.

Dean, J., and S. Ghemawat. 2008. MapReduce: Simplified data processing on large clusters. *Communications of the ACM* 51 (1): 107–113.

Deerwester, S. C., S. T. Dumais, T. K. Landauer, G. W. Furnas, and R. A. Harshman. 1990. Indexing by latent semantic analysis. *Journal of the American Society for Information Science* 41 (6): 391–407.

De Gispert, A., and J. B. Marino. 2006. Catalan-English statistical machine translation without parallel corpus: Bridging through Spanish. In *Proceedings of the Language Resources and Evaluation Conference (LREC)*.

Dehdari, J. 2014. A neurophysiologically-inspired statistical language model. PhD diss, The Ohio State University.

Deisenroth, M. P., A. A. Faisal, and C. S. Ong. 2018. *Mathematics for Machine Learning*. Cambridge, UK: Cambridge University Press.

De Marneffe, M.-C., and C. D. Manning. 2008. The Stanford typed dependencies representation. In *Proceedings of the Workshop on Cross-Framework and Cross-Domain Parser Evaluation*.

Dempster, A. P., N. M. Laird, and D. B. Rubin. 1977. Maximum likelihood from incomplete data via the EM algorithm. *Journal of the Royal Statistical Society. Series B (Methodological)*.

Denis, P., and J. Baldridge. 2007. A ranking approach to pronoun resolution. In *Proceedings of the International Joint Conference on Artificial Intelligence (IJCAI)*.

Denis, P., and J. Baldridge. 2008. Specialized models and ranking for coreference resolution. In *Proceedings of Empirical Methods for Natural Language Processing (EMNLP)*.

Denis, P., and J. Baldridge. 2009. Global joint models for coreference resolution and named entity classification. *Procesamiento del Lenguaje Natural* 42: 87–96.

Derrida, J. 1985. Des tours de babel. In *Difference in Translation*, ed. J. Graham. Ithaca, NY: Cornell University Press.

Devlin, J., M. q. W. Chang, K. Lee, and K. Toutanova. 2018. BERT: Pre-training of deep bidirectional transformers for language understanding. *CoRR* abs/1810.04805.

Dhingra, B., H. Liu, Z. Yang, W. W. Cohen, and R. Salakhutdinov. 2017. Gated-attention readers for text comprehension. In *Proceedings of the Association for Computational Linguistics (ACL)*.

Diaconis, P., and B. Skyrms. 2017. *Ten Great Ideas About Chance*. Princeton, NJ: Princeton University Press.

Dietterich, T. G. 1998. Approximate statistical tests for comparing supervised classification learning algorithms. *Neural Computation* 10 (7): 1895–1923.

Dietterich, T. G., R. H. Lathrop, and T. Lozano-Pérez. 1997. Solving the multiple instance problem with axis-parallel rectangles. *Artificial Intelligence* 89 (1): 31–71.

Dimitrova, L., N. Ide, V. Petkevic, T. Erjavec, H. J. Kaalep, and D. Tufis. 1998. Multext-east: Parallel and comparable corpora and lexicons for six central and eastern European languages. In *Proceedings of the International Conference on Computational Linguistics (COLING)*.

Doddington, G. R., A. Mitchell, M. A. Przybocki, L. A. Ramshaw, S. Strassel, and R. M. Weischedel. 2004. The automatic content extraction (ACE) program-tasks, data, and evaluation. In *Proceedings of the Language Resources and Evaluation Conference (LREC)*.

dos Santos, C., and B. Zadrozny. 2014. Learning character-level representations for part-of-speech tagging. In *Proceedings of the International Conference on Machine Learning (ICML)*.

dos Santos, C., B. Xiang, and B. Zhou. 2015. Classifying relations by ranking with convolutional neural networks. In *Proceedings of the Association for Computational Linguistics (ACL)*.

Dowty, D. 1991. Thematic proto-roles and argument selection. *Language* 67 (3): 547–619.

Dredze, M., P. McNamee, D. Rao, A. Gerber, and T. Finin. 2010. Entity disambiguation for knowledge base population. In *Proceedings of the International Conference on Computational Linguistics (COLING)*.

Dredze, M., M. J. Paul, S. Bergsma, and H. Tran. 2013. Carmen: A Twitter geolocation system with applications to public health. In *AAAI Workshop on Expanding the Boundaries of Health Informatics Using AI (HIAI)*.

Dreyfus, H. L. 1992. *What Computers Still Can't Do: A Critique of Artificial Reason*. Cambridge, MA: MIT Press.

Dror, R., G. Baumer, M. Bogomolov, and R. Reichart. 2017. Replicability analysis for natural language processing: Testing significance with multiple datasets. *Transactions of the Association for Computational Linguistics* 5: 471–486.

Dror, R., G. Baumer, S. Shlomov, and R. Reichart. 2018. The hitchhiker's guide to testing statistical significance in natural language processing. In *Proceedings of the Association for Computational Linguistics (ACL)*.

Du, L., W. Buntine, and M. Johnson. 2013. Topic segmentation with a structured topic model. In *Proceedings of the North American Chapter of the Association for Computational Linguistics (NAACL)*.

Duchi, J., E. Hazan, and Y. Singer. 2011. Adaptive subgradient methods for online learning and stochastic optimization. *The Journal of Machine Learning Research* 12: 2121–2159.

Dunietz, J., L. Levin, and J. Carbonell. 2017. The because corpus 2.0: Annotating causality and overlapping relations. In *Proceedings of the Linguistic Annotation Workshop*.

Durrett, G., and D. Klein. 2013. Easy victories and uphill battles in coreference resolution. In *Proceedings of Empirical Methods for Natural Language Processing (EMNLP)*.

Durrett, G., and D. Klein. 2015. Neural CRF parsing. In *Proceedings of the Association for Computational Linguistics (ACL)*.

Durrett, G., T. Berg-Kirkpatrick, and D. Klein. 2016. Learning-based single-document summarization with compression and anaphoricity constraints. In *Proceedings of the Association for Computational Linguistics (ACL)*.

Dyer, C., M. Ballesteros, W. Ling, A. Matthews, and N. A. Smith. 2015. Transition-based dependency parsing with stack long short-term memory. In *Proceedings of the Association for Computational Linguistics (ACL)*.

Dyer, C., A. Kuncoro, M. Ballesteros, and N. A. Smith. 2016. Recurrent neural network grammars. In *Proceedings of the North American Chapter of the Association for Computational Linguistics (NAACL)*.

Edmonds, J. 1967. Optimum branchings. *Journal of Research of the National Bureau of Standards B* 71 (4): 233–240.

Efron, B., and R. J. Tibshirani. 1993. *An Introduction to the Bootstrap. Monographs on Statistics and Applied Probability*. New York and London: Chapman and Hall/CRC.

Eisenstein, J. 2009. Hierarchical text segmentation from multi-scale lexical cohesion. In *Proceedings of the North American Chapter of the Association for Computational Linguistics (NAACL)*.

Eisenstein, J., and R. Barzilay. 2008. Bayesian unsupervised topic segmentation. In *Proceedings of Empirical Methods for Natural Language Processing (EMNLP)*.

Eisner, J. 1997 (accessed February 6, 2019). State-of-the-art algorithms for minimum spanning trees: A tutorial discussion. www.cs.jhu.edu/~jason/papers/eisner.mst-tutorial.pdf.

Eisner, J. 2000. Bilexical grammars and their cubic-time parsing algorithms. In *Advances in Probabilistic and Other Parsing Technologies*, eds. H. Bunt and A. Nijholt, 29–61. New York, NY: Springer.

Eisner, J. 2002. Parameter estimation for probabilistic finite-state transducers. In *Proceedings of the Association for Computational Linguistics (ACL)*.

Eisner, J. 2016. Inside-outside and forward-backward algorithms are just backprop. In *Proceedings of the Workshop on Structured Prediction for NLP*.

Eisner, J. M. 1996. Three new probabilistic models for dependency parsing: An exploration. In *Proceedings of the International Conference on Computational Linguistics (COLING)*.

Ekman, P. 1992. Are there basic emotions? *Psychological Review* 99 (3): 550–553.

Elman, J. L. 1990. Finding structure in time. *Cognitive Science* 14 (2): 179–211.

Elman, J. L., E. A. Bates, M. H. Johnson, A. Karmiloff-Smith, D. Parisi, and K. Plunkett. 1998. *Rethinking Innateness: A Connectionist Perspective on Development*, Vol. 10. Cambridge, MA: MIT Press.

Elsner, M., and E. Charniak. 2010. Disentangling chat. *Computational Linguistics* 36 (3): 389–409.

Esuli, A., and F. Sebastiani. 2006. SentiWordNet: A publicly available lexical resource for opinion mining. In *Proceedings of the Language Resources and Evaluation Conference (LREC)*.

Etzioni, O., A. Fader, J. Christensen, S. Soderland, and M. Mausam. 2011. Open information extraction: The second generation. In *Proceedings of the International Joint Conference on Artificial Intelligence (IJCAI)*.

Faruqui, M., and C. Dyer. 2014. Improving vector space word representations using multilingual correlation. In *Proceedings of the European Chapter of the Association for Computational Linguistics (EACL)*.

Faruqui, M., R. McDonald, and R. Soricut. 2016. Morpho-syntactic lexicon generation using graph-based semi-supervised learning. *Transactions of the Association for Computational Linguistics* 4: 1–16.

Faruqui, M., J. Dodge, S. K. Jauhar, C. Dyer, E. Hovy, and N. A. Smith. 2015. Retrofitting word vectors to semantic lexicons. In *Proceedings of the North American Chapter of the Association for Computational Linguistics (NAACL)*.

Faruqui, M., Y. Tsvetkov, P. Rastogi, and C. Dyer. 2016. Problems with evaluation of word embeddings using word similarity tasks. In *Proceedings of the 1st Workshop on Evaluating Vector-Space Representations for NLP*.

Fellbaum, C. 2017. WordNet: An electronic lexical resource for English. In *The Oxford Handbook of Cognitive Science*, ed. S. Chipman, 301–313. Oxford, UK: Oxford University Press.

Feng, V. W., Z. Lin, and G. Hirst. 2014. The impact of deep hierarchical discourse structures in the evaluation of text coherence. In *Proceedings of the International Conference on Computational Linguistics (COLING)*.

Feng, X., L. Huang, D. Tang, H. Ji, B. Qin, and T. Liu. 2016. A language-independent neural network for event detection. In *Proceedings of the Association for Computational Linguistics (ACL)*.

Fernandes, E. R., C. N. dos Santos, and R. L. Milidiú. 2014. Latent trees for coreference resolution. *Computational Linguistics* 40 (4): 801–835.

Ferrucci, D., E. Brown, J. Chu-Carroll, J. Fan, D. Gondek, A. A. Kalyanpur, A. Lally, J. W. Murdock, E. Nyberg, J. Prager, et al.. 2010. Building Watson: An overview of the DeepQA project. *AI Magazine* 31 (3): 59–79.

Ficler, J., and Y. Goldberg. 2017. Controlling linguistic style aspects in neural language generation. In *Proceedings of the Workshop on Stylistic Variation*.

Filippova, K., and M. Strube. 2008. Sentence fusion via dependency graph compression. In *Proceedings of Empirical Methods for Natural Language Processing (EMNLP)*.

Fillmore, C. J. 1968. The case for case. In *Universals in Linguistic Theory*, eds. E. Bach and R. Harms. New York, NY: Holt, Rinehart, and Winston.

Fillmore, C. J. 1976. Frame semantics and the nature of language. *Annals of the New York Academy of Sciences* 280 (1): 20–32.

Fillmore, C. J., and C. Baker. 2009. A frames approach to semantic analysis. In *The Oxford Handbook of Linguistic Analysis*. Oxford, UK: Oxford University Press.

Finkel, J. R., and C. Manning. 2009. Hierarchical Bayesian domain adaptation. In *Proceedings of the North American Chapter of the Association for Computational Linguistics (NAACL)*.

Finkel, J. R., and C. D. Manning. 2008. Enforcing transitivity in coreference resolution. In *Proceedings of the Association for Computational Linguistics (ACL)*.

Finkel, J. R., T. Grenager, and C. Manning. 2005. Incorporating non-local information into information extraction systems by gibbs sampling. In *Proceedings of the Association for Computational Linguistics (ACL)*.

Finkel, J. R., T. Grenager, and C. D. Manning. 2007. The infinite tree. In *Proceedings of the Association for Computational Linguistics (ACL)*.

Finkel, J. R., A. Kleeman, and C. D. Manning. 2008. Efficient, feature-based, conditional random field parsing. In *Proceedings of the Association for Computational Linguistics (ACL)*.

Finkelstein, L., E. Gabrilovich, Y. Matias, E. Rivlin, Z. Solan, G. Wolfman, and E. Ruppin. 2002. Placing search in context: The concept revisited. *ACM Transactions on Information Systems* 20 (1): 116–131.

Firth, J. R. 1957. *Papers in linguistics 1934-1951*. Oxford, UK: Oxford University Press.

Flanigan, J., S. Thomson, J. Carbonell, C. Dyer, and N. A. Smith. 2014. A discriminative graph-based parser for the abstract meaning representation. In *Proceedings of the Association for Computational Linguistics (ACL)*.

Foltz, P. W., W. Kintsch, and T. K. Landauer. 1998. The measurement of textual coherence with latent semantic analysis. *Discourse Processes* 25 (2-3): 285–307.

Fordyce, C. 2007. Overview of the IWSLT 2007 evaluation campaign. In *Proceedings of the International Workshop on Spoken Language Translation (IWSLT)*.

Forsyth, E. N., and C. H. Martell. 2007. Lexical and discourse analysis of online chat dialog. In *Proceedings of the International Conference on Semantic Computing*.

Fort, K., G. Adda, and K. B. Cohen. 2011. Amazon mechanical turk: Gold mine or coal mine? *Computational Linguistics* 37 (2): 413–420.

Fox, H. 2002. Phrasal cohesion and statistical machine translation. In *Proceedings of Empirical Methods for Natural Language Processing (EMNLP)*.

Francis, W., and H. Kucera. 1982. *Frequency Analysis of English Usage*. Boston, MA: Houghton Mifflin Company.

Francis, W. N. 1964. A standard sample of present-day English for use with digital computers. Report to the U.S Office of Education on Cooperative Research Project No. E-007.

Freund, Y., and R. E. Schapire. 1999. Large margin classification using the perceptron algorithm. *Machine Learning* 37 (3): 277–296.

Fromkin, V., R. Rodman, and N. Hyams. 2013. *An Introduction to Language*, 10th edn. Boston, MA: Cengage Learning.

Fundel, K., R. Küffner, and R. Zimmer. 2007. Relex – relation extraction using dependency parse trees. *Bioinformatics* 23 (3): 365–371.

Gabow, H. N., Z. Galil, T. Spencer, and R. E. Tarjan. 1986. Efficient algorithms for finding minimum spanning trees in undirected and directed graphs. *Combinatorica* 6 (2): 109–122.

Gabrilovich, E., and S. Markovitch. 2007. Computing semantic relatedness using Wikipedia-based explicit semantic analysis. In *Proceedings of the International Joint Conference on Artificial Intelligence (IJCAI)*, Vol. 7.

Gage, P. 1994. A new algorithm for data compression. *The C Users Journal* 12 (2): 23–38.

Gale, W. A., K. W. Church, and D. Yarowsky. 1992. One sense per discourse. In *Proceedings of the Workshop on Speech and Natural Language*.

Galley, M., K. R. McKeown, E. Fosler-Lussier, and H. Jing. 2003. Discourse segmentation of multi-party conversation. In *Proceedings of the Association for Computational Linguistics (ACL)*.

Galley, M., M. Hopkins, K. Knight, and D. Marcu. 2004. What's in a translation rule? In *Proceedings of the North American Chapter of the Association for Computational Linguistics (NAACL)*.

Ganchev, K., and M. Dredze. 2008. Small statistical models by random feature mixing. In *Proceedings of Workshop on Mobile Language Processing*.

Ganchev, K., J. Graça, J. Gillenwater, and B. Taskar. 2010. Posterior regularization for structured latent variable models. *The Journal of Machine Learning Research* 11: 2001–2049.

Ganin, Y., E. Ustinova, H. Ajakan, P. Germain, H. Larochelle, F. Laviolette, M. Marchand, and V. Lempitsky. 2016. Domain-adversarial training of neural networks. *The Journal of Machine Learning Research* 17 (59): 1–35.

Gao, J., G. Andrew, M. Johnson, and K. Toutanova. 2007. A comparative study of parameter estimation methods for statistical natural language processing. In *Proceedings of the Association for Computational Linguistics (ACL)*.

Garg, N., L. Schiebinger, D. Jurafsky, and J. Zou. 2018. Word embeddings quantify 100 years of gender and ethnic stereotypes. *Proceedings of the National Academy of Sciences* 115 (16): 3635–3644.

Gatt, A., and E. Krahmer. 2018. Survey of the state of the art in natural language generation: Core tasks, applications and evaluation. *Journal of Artificial Intelligence Research* 61: 65–170.

Ge, D., X. Jiang, and Y. Ye. 2011. A note on the complexity of l_p minimization. *Mathematical Programming* 129 (2): 285–299.

Ge, N., J. Hale, and E. Charniak. 1998. A statistical approach to anaphora resolution. In *Proceedings of the Sixth Workshop on Very Large Corpora*.

Ge, R., and R. J. Mooney. 2005. A statistical semantic parser that integrates syntax and semantics. In *Proceedings of the Conference on Natural Language Learning (CoNLL)*.

Ge, R., F. Huang, C. Jin, and Y. Yuan. 2015. Escaping from saddle points—online stochastic gradient for tensor decomposition. In *Proceedings of the Conference on Learning Theory (COLT)*, eds. P. Grünwald, E. Hazan, and S. Kale.

Geach, P. T. 1962. *Reference and Generality: An Examination of Some Medieval and Modern Theories*. Ithaca, NY: Cornell University Press.

Gehring, J., M. Auli, D. Grangier, D. Yarats, and Y. N. Dauphin. 2017. Convolutional sequence to sequence learning. In *Proceedings of the International Conference on Machine Learning (ICML)*.

Gildea, D., and D. Jurafsky. 2002. Automatic labeling of semantic roles. *Computational Linguistics* 28 (3): 245–288.

Gimpel, K., N. Schneider, B. O'Connor, D. Das, D. Mills, J. Eisenstein, M. Heilman, D. Yogatama, J. Flanigan, and N. A. Smith. 2011. Part-of-speech tagging for Twitter: Annotation, features, and experiments. In *Proceedings of the Association for Computational Linguistics (ACL)*.

Glass, J., T. J. Hazen, S. Cyphers, I. Malioutov, D. Huynh, and R. Barzilay. 2007. Recent progress in the MIT spoken lecture processing project. In *Proceedings of the International Speech Communication Association*.

Glorot, X., and Y. Bengio. 2010. Understanding the difficulty of training deep feedforward neural networks. In *Proceedings of Artificial Intelligence and Statistics (AISTATS)*.

Glorot, X., A. Bordes, and Y. Bengio. 2011. Deep sparse rectifier networks. In *Proceedings of Artificial Intelligence and Statistics (AISTATS)*.

Godfrey, J. J., E. C. Holliman, and J. McDaniel. 1992. Switchboard: Telephone speech corpus for research and development. In *Proceedings of the International Conference on Acoustics, Speech, and Signal Processing (ICASSP)*.

Goldberg, Y. 2017. *Neural Network Methods for Natural Language Processing. Synthesis Lectures on Human Language Technologies*. San Rafael, CA: Morgan & Claypool.

Goldberg, Y. 2017 (accessed February 6, 2019). An Adversarial Review of "Adversarial Generation of Natural Language." medium.com/@yoav.goldberg/an-adversarial-review-of-adversarial-generation-of-natural-language-409ac3378bd7.

Goldberg, Y., and M. Elhadad. 2010. An efficient algorithm for easy-first non-directional dependency parsing. In *Proceedings of the North American Chapter of the Association for Computational Linguistics (NAACL)*.

Goldberg, Y., and J. Nivre. 2012. A dynamic oracle for arc-eager dependency parsing. In *Proceedings of the International Conference on Computational Linguistics (COLING)*.

Goldberg, Y., K. Zhao, and L. Huang. 2013. Efficient implementation of beam-search incremental parsers. In *Proceedings of the Association for Computational Linguistics (ACL)*.

Goldwater, S., and T. Griffiths. 2007. A fully Bayesian approach to unsupervised part-of-speech tagging. In *Proceedings of the Association for Computational Linguistics (ACL)*.

Gonçalo Oliveira, H. R., F. A. Cardoso, and F. C. Pereira. 2007. Tra-la-lyrics: An approach to generate text based on rhythm. In *Proceedings of the International Joint Workshop on Computational Creativity*.

Goodfellow, I., Y. Bengio, and A. Courville. 2016. *Deep Learning*. Cambridge, MA: MIT Press.

Goodman, J. T. 2001. A bit of progress in language modeling. *Computer Speech & Language* 15 (4): 403–434.

Gouws, S., D. Metzler, C. Cai, and E. Hovy. 2011. Contextual bearing on linguistic variation in social media. In *Proceedings of the Workshop on Language and Social Media*.

Goyal, A., H. Daumé III, and S. Venkatasubramanian. 2009. Streaming for large scale NLP: Language modeling. In *Proceedings of the North American Chapter of the Association for Computational Linguistics (NAACL)*.

Graves, A. 2012. Sequence transduction with recurrent neural networks. In *Proceedings of the International Conference on Machine Learning (ICML)*.

Graves, A., and N. Jaitly. 2014. Towards end-to-end speech recognition with recurrent neural networks. In *Proceedings of the International Conference on Machine Learning (ICML)*.

Graves, A., and J. Schmidhuber. 2005. Framewise phoneme classification with bidirectional LSTM and other neural network architectures. *Neural Networks* 18 (5): 602–610.

Grice, H. P. 1975. Logic and conversation. In *Syntax and Semantics Volume 3: Speech Acts*, eds. P. Cole and J. L. Morgan, 41–58. New York, NY: Academic Press.

Grishman, R. 2012. Information Extraction: Capabilities and Challenges. Notes prepared for the 2012 International Winter School in Language and Speech Technologies, Rovira i Virgili University, Tarragona, Spain.

Grishman, R. 2015. Information extraction. *IEEE Intelligent Systems* 30 (5): 8–15.

Grishman, R., and B. Sundheim. 1996. Message understanding conference-6: A brief history. In *Proceedings of the International Conference on Computational Linguistics (COLING)*.

Grishman, R., C. Macleod, and J. Sterling. 1992. Evaluating parsing strategies using standardized parse files. In *Proceedings of the Third Conference on Applied Natural Language Processing*.

Groenendijk, J., and M. Stokhof. 1991. Dynamic predicate logic. *Linguistics and Philosophy* 14 (1): 39–100.

Grosz, B. J. 1979. Focusing and description in natural language dialogues, Technical report, SRI International.

Grosz, B. J., S. Weinstein, and A. K. Joshi. 1995. Centering: A framework for modeling the local coherence of discourse. *Computational Linguistics* 21 (2): 203–225.

Gu, J., Z. Lu, H. Li, and V. O. Li. 2016. Incorporating copying mechanism in sequence-to-sequence learning. In *Proceedings of the Association for Computational Linguistics (ACL)*.

Gulcehre, C., S. Ahn, R. Nallapati, B. Zhou, and Y. Bengio. 2016. Pointing the unknown words. In *Proceedings of the Association for Computational Linguistics (ACL)*.

Gutmann, M. U., and A. Hyvärinen. 2012. Noise-contrastive estimation of unnormalized statistical models, with applications to natural image statistics. *The Journal of Machine Learning Research* 13 (1): 307–361.

Haghighi, A., and D. Klein. 2007. Unsupervised coreference resolution in a nonparametric Bayesian model. In *Proceedings of the Association for Computational Linguistics (ACL)*.

Haghighi, A., and D. Klein. 2009. Simple coreference resolution with rich syntactic and semantic features. In *Proceedings of Empirical Methods for Natural Language Processing (EMNLP)*.

Haghighi, A., and D. Klein. 2010. Coreference resolution in a modular, entity-centered model. In *Proceedings of the North American Chapter of the Association for Computational Linguistics (NAACL)*.

Hajič, J., and B. Hladká. 1998. Tagging inflective languages: Prediction of morphological categories for a rich, structured tagset. In *Proceedings of the Association for Computational Linguistics (ACL)*.

Halliday, M., and R. Hasan. 1976. *Cohesion in English*. London: Longman.

Hammerton, J. 2003. Named entity recognition with long short-term memory. In *Proceedings of the Conference on Natural Language Learning (CoNLL)*.

Han, X., and L. Sun. 2012. An entity-topic model for entity linking. In *Proceedings of Empirical Methods for Natural Language Processing (EMNLP)*.

Han, X., L. Sun, and J. Zhao. 2011. Collective entity linking in web text: A graph-based method. In *Proceedings of the ACM SIGIR Conference on Research and Development in Information Retrieval*.

Hannak, A., E. Anderson, L. F. Barrett, S. Lehmann, A. Mislove, and M. Riedewald. 2012. Tweetin'in the rain: Exploring societal-scale effects of weather on mood. In *Proceedings of the International Conference on Web and Social Media (ICWSM)*.

Hardmeier, C. 2012. Discourse in statistical machine translation: A survey and a case study. *Discours*.

Haspelmath, M., and A. Sims. 2013. *Understanding Morphology*. London, UK: Routledge.

Hastie, T., R. Tibshirani, and J. Friedman. 2009. *The Elements of Statistical Learning*, 2nd edn. New York, NY: Springer.

Hatzivassiloglou, V., and K. R. McKeown. 1997. Predicting the semantic orientation of adjectives. In *Proceedings of the Association for Computational Linguistics (ACL)*.

Hayes, A. F., and K. Krippendorff. 2007. Answering the call for a standard reliability measure for coding data. *Communication Methods and Measures* 1 (1): 77–89.

He, H., A. Balakrishnan, M. Eric, and P. Liang. 2017. Learning symmetric collaborative dialogue agents with dynamic knowledge graph embeddings. In *Proceedings of the Association for Computational Linguistics (ACL)*.

He, K., X. Zhang, S. Ren, and J. Sun. 2015. Delving deep into rectifiers: Surpassing human-level performance on imagenet classification. In *Proceedings of the International Conference on Computer Vision (ICCV)*.

He, K., X. Zhang, S. Ren, and J. Sun. 2016. Deep residual learning for image recognition. In *Proceedings of the International Conference on Computer Vision (ICCV)*.

He, L., K. Lee, M. Lewis, and L. Zettlemoyer. 2017. Deep semantic role labeling: What works and what's next. In *Proceedings of the Association for Computational Linguistics (ACL)*.

He, Z., S. Liu, M. Li, M. Zhou, L. Zhang, and H. Wang. 2013. Learning entity representation for entity disambiguation. In *Proceedings of the Association for Computational Linguistics (ACL)*.

Hearst, M. A. 1992. Automatic acquisition of hyponyms from large text corpora. In *Proceedings of the International Conference on Computational Linguistics (COLING)*.

Hearst, M. A. 1997. TextTiling: Segmenting text into multi-paragraph subtopic passages. *Computational Linguistics* 23 (1): 33–64.

Heerschop, B., F. Goossen, A. Hogenboom, F. Frasincar, U. Kaymak, and F. de Jong. 2011. Polarity analysis of texts using discourse structure. In *Proceedings of the International Conference on Information and Knowledge Management (CIKM)*.

Henderson, J. 2004. Discriminative training of a neural network statistical parser. In *Proceedings of the Association for Computational Linguistics (ACL)*.

Hendrickx, I., S. N. Kim, Z. Kozareva, P. Nakov, D. Ó Séaghdha, S. Padó, M. Pennacchiotti, L. Romano, and S. Szpakowicz. 2009. Semeval-2010 task 8: Multi-way classification of semantic relations between pairs of nominals. In *Proceedings of the Workshop on Semantic Evaluations: Recent Achievements and Future Directions*.

Hermann, K. M., T. Kocisky, E. Grefenstette, L. Espeholt, W. Kay, M. Suleyman, and P. Blunsom. 2015. Teaching machines to read and comprehend. In *Neural Information Processing Systems (NeurIPS)*.

Hernault, H., H. Prendinger, D. A. duVerle, and M. Ishizuka. 2010. HILDA: A discourse parser using support vector machine classification. *Dialogue and Discourse* 1 (3): 1–33.

Hill, F., K. Cho, and A. Korhonen. 2016. Learning distributed representations of sentences from unlabelled data. In *Proceedings of the North American Chapter of the Association for Computational Linguistics (NAACL)*.

Hill, F., R. Reichart, and A. Korhonen. 2015. Simlex-999: Evaluating semantic models with (genuine) similarity estimation. *Computational Linguistics* 41 (4): 665–695.

Hill, F., A. Bordes, S. Chopra, and J. Weston. 2016. The goldilocks principle: Reading children's books with explicit memory representations. In *Proceedings of the International Conference on Learning Representations (ICLR)*.

Hindle, D., and M. Rooth. 1993. Structural ambiguity and lexical relations. *Computational Linguistics* 19 (1): 103–120.

Hirao, T., Y. Yoshida, M. Nishino, N. Yasuda, and M. Nagata. 2013. Single-document summarization as a tree knapsack problem. In *Proceedings of Empirical Methods for Natural Language Processing (EMNLP)*.

Hirschman, L., and R. Gaizauskas. 2001. Natural language question answering: The view from here. *Natural Language Engineering* 7 (4): 275–300.

Hirschman, L., M. Light, E. Breck, and J. D. Burger. 1999. Deep read: A reading comprehension system. In *Proceedings of the Association for Computational Linguistics (ACL)*.

Hobbs, J. R. 1978. Resolving pronoun references. *Lingua* 44 (4): 311–338.

Hobbs, J. R., D. Appelt, J. Bear, D. Israel, M. Kameyama, M. Stickel, and M. Tyson. 1997. FASTUS: A cascaded finite-state transducer for extracting information from natural-language text. In *Finite-state Language Processing*, eds. E. Roche and Y. Schabes, 383–406. Cambridge, MA: MIT Press.

Hochreiter, S., and J. Schmidhuber. 1997. Long short-term memory. *Neural Computation* 9 (8): 1735–1780.

Hockenmaier, J., and M. Steedman. 2007. CCGbank: A corpus of CCG derivations and dependency structures extracted from the Penn Treebank. *Computational Linguistics* 33 (3): 355–396.

Hoffart, J., M. A. Yosef, I. Bordino, H. Fürstenau, M. Pinkal, M. Spaniol, B. Taneva, S. Thater, and G. Weikum. 2011. Robust disambiguation of named entities in text. In *Proceedings of Empirical Methods for Natural Language Processing (EMNLP)*.

Hoffmann, R., C. Zhang, X. Ling, L. Zettlemoyer, and D. S. Weld. 2011. Knowledge-based weak supervision for information extraction of overlapping relations. In *Proceedings of the Association for Computational Linguistics (ACL)*.

Holmstrom, L., and P. Koistinen. 1992. Using additive noise in back-propagation training. *IEEE Transactions on Neural Networks* 3 (1): 24–38.

Hovy, D., S. Spruit, M. Mitchell, E. M. Bender, M. Strube, and H. Wallach, eds. 2017. Proceedings of the First ACL Workshop on Ethics in Natural Language Processing.

Hovy, E., and J. Lavid. 2010. Towards a "science" of corpus annotation: A new methodological challenge for corpus linguistics. *International Journal of Translation* 22 (1): 13–36.

Hsu, D., S. M. Kakade, and T. Zhang. 2012. A spectral algorithm for learning hidden Markov models. *Journal of Computer and System Sciences* 78 (5): 1460–1480.

Hu, M., and B. Liu. 2004. Mining and summarizing customer reviews. In *Proceedings of Knowledge Discovery and Data Mining (KDD)*.

Hu, Z., Z. Yang, X. Liang, R. Salakhutdinov, and E. P. Xing. 2017. Toward controlled generation of text. In *Proceedings of the International Conference on Machine Learning (ICML)*.

Huang, F., and A. Yates. 2012. Biased representation learning for domain adaptation. In *Proceedings of Empirical Methods for Natural Language Processing (EMNLP)*.

Huang, L., and D. Chiang. 2007. Forest rescoring: Faster decoding with integrated language models. In *Proceedings of the Association for Computational Linguistics (ACL)*.

Huang, L., S. Fayong, and Y. Guo. 2012. Structured perceptron with inexact search. In *Proceedings of the North American Chapter of the Association for Computational Linguistics (NAACL)*.

Huang, Y. 2015. *Pragmatics*, 2nd edn. *Oxford textbooks in linguistics*. Oxford, UK: Oxford University Press.

Huang, Z., W. Xu, and K. Yu. 2015. Bidirectional LSTM-CRF models for sequence tagging. *arXiv preprint arXiv:1508.01991*.

Huddleston, R., and G. K. Pullum. 2005. *A Student's Introduction to English Grammar*. Cambridge, UK: Cambridge University Press.

Huffman, D. A. 1952. A method for the construction of minimum-redundancy codes. *Proceedings of the IRE* 40 (9): 1098–1101.

Humphreys, K., R. Gaizauskas, and S. Azzam. 1997. Event coreference for information extraction. In *Proceedings of a Workshop on Operational Factors in Practical, Robust Anaphora Resolution for Unrestricted Texts*.

Ide, N., and Y. Wilks. 2006. Making sense about sense. In *Word Sense Disambiguation*, eds. E. Agirre and P. Edmonds, 47–73. New York, NY: Springer.

Ioffe, S., and C. Szegedy. 2015. Batch normalization: Accelerating deep network training by reducing internal covariate shift. In *Proceedings of the International Conference on Machine Learning (ICML)*.

Isozaki, H., T. Hirao, K. Duh, K. Sudoh, and H. Tsukada. 2010. Automatic evaluation of translation quality for distant language pairs. In *Proceedings of Empirical Methods for Natural Language Processing (EMNLP)*.

Ivanova, A., S. Oepen, L. Øvrelid, and D. Flickinger. 2012. Who did what to whom? A contrastive study of syntacto-semantic dependencies. In *Proceedings of the Sixth Linguistic Annotation Workshop*.

Iyyer, M., V. Manjunatha, J. Boyd-Graber, and H. Daumé III. 2015. Deep unordered composition rivals syntactic methods for text classification. In *Proceedings of the Association for Computational Linguistics (ACL)*.

James, G., D. Witten, T. Hastie, and R. Tibshirani. 2013. *An Introduction to Statistical Learning*. New York, NY: Springer.

Janin, A., D. Baron, J. Edwards, D. Ellis, D. Gelbart, N. Morgan, B. Peskin, T. Pfau, E. Shriberg, A. Stolcke, et al.. 2003. The ICSI meeting corpus. In *Proceedings of the International Conference on Acoustics, Speech, and Signal Processing (ICASSP)*.

Jean, S., K. Cho, R. Memisevic, and Y. Bengio. 2015. On using very large target vocabulary for neural machine translation. In *Proceedings of the Association for Computational Linguistics (ACL)*.

Jeong, M., C.-Y. Lin, and G. G. Lee. 2009. Semi-supervised speech act recognition in emails and forums. In *Proceedings of Empirical Methods for Natural Language Processing (EMNLP)*.

Ji, H., and R. Grishman. 2011. Knowledge base population: Successful approaches and challenges. In *Proceedings of the Association for Computational Linguistics (ACL)*.

Ji, Y., and J. Eisenstein. 2014. Representation learning for text-level discourse parsing. In *Proceedings of the Association for Computational Linguistics (ACL)*.

Ji, Y., and J. Eisenstein. 2015. One vector is not enough: Entity-augmented distributional semantics for discourse relations. *Transactions of the Association for Computational Linguistics (TACL)* 3: 329–344.

Ji, Y., and N. A. Smith. 2017. Neural discourse structure for text categorization. In *Proceedings of the Association for Computational Linguistics (ACL)*.

Ji, Y., G. Haffari, and J. Eisenstein. 2016. A latent variable recurrent neural network for discourse relation language models. In *Proceedings of the North American Chapter of the Association for Computational Linguistics (NAACL)*.

Ji, Y., T. Cohn, L. Kong, C. Dyer, and J. Eisenstein. 2015. Document context language models. In *International Conference on Learning Representations, workshop track*, Vol. abs/1511.03962.

Ji, Y., C. Tan, S. Martschat, Y. Choi, and N. A. Smith. 2017. Dynamic entity representations in neural language models. In *Proceedings of Empirical Methods for Natural Language Processing (EMNLP)*.

Jiang, L., M. Yu, M. Zhou, X. Liu, and T. Zhao. 2011. Target-dependent Twitter sentiment classification. In *Proceedings of the Association for Computational Linguistics (ACL)*.

Jing, H. 2000. Sentence reduction for automatic text summarization. In *Proceedings of Applied Natural Language Processing*.

Joachims, T. 2002. Optimizing search engines using clickthrough data. In *Proceedings of Knowledge Discovery and Data Mining (KDD)*.

Jockers, M. L. 2015 (accessed February 9, 2019). Revealing Sentiment and Plot Arcs with the Syuzhet Package. www.matthewjockers.net/2015/02/02/syuzhet/.

Johnson, A. E., T. J. Pollard, L. Shen, H. L. Li-wei, M. Feng, M. Ghassemi, B. Moody, P. Szolovits, L. A. Celi, and R. G. Mark. 2016. MIMIC-III, a freely accessible critical care database. *Scientific Data* 3: 160035.

Johnson, M. 1998. PCFG models of linguistic tree representations. *Computational Linguistics* 24 (4): 613–632.

Johnson, R., and T. Zhang. 2017. Deep pyramid convolutional neural networks for text categorization. In *Proceedings of the Association for Computational Linguistics (ACL)*.

Joshi, A. K. 1985. Tree adjoining grammars: How much context-sensitivity is required to provide reasonable structural descriptions? In *Natural Language Processing: Theoretical, Computational and Psychological Perspectives*, eds. D. Dowty, L. Karttunen, and A. Zwicky. Cambridge, UK: Cambridge University Press.

Joshi, A. K., and Y. Schabes. 1997. Tree-adjoining grammars. In *Handbook of Formal Languages*, 69–123. New York, NY: Springer.

Joshi, A. K., K. V. Shanker, and D. Weir. 1991. The convergence of mildly context-sensitive grammar formalisms. In *Foundational Issues in Natural Language Processing*. Cambridge, MA: MIT Press.

Jozefowicz, R., W. Zaremba, and I. Sutskever. 2015. An empirical exploration of recurrent network architectures. In *Proceedings of the International Conference on Machine Learning (ICML)*.

Jozefowicz, R., O. Vinyals, M. Schuster, N. Shazeer, and Y. Wu. 2016. Exploring the limits of language modeling. *arXiv preprint arXiv:1602.02410*.

Jurafsky, D. 1996. A probabilistic model of lexical and syntactic access and disambiguation. *Cognitive Science* 20 (2): 137–194.

Jurafsky, D., and J. H. Martin. 2009. *Speech and Language Processing*, 2nd edn. Upper Saddle River, NJ: Prentice Hall.

Jurafsky, D., and J. H. Martin. 2019. *Speech and Language Processing*, 3rd edn. Upper Saddle River, NJ: Prentice Hall.

Kadlec, R., M. Schmid, O. Bajgar, and J. Kleindienst. 2016. Text understanding with the attention sum reader network. In *Proceedings of the Association for Computational Linguistics (ACL)*.

Kalchbrenner, N., and P. Blunsom. 2013. Recurrent convolutional neural networks for discourse compositionality. In *Proceedings of the Workshop on Continuous Vector Space Models and their Compositionality*.

Kalchbrenner, N., E. Grefenstette, and P. Blunsom. 2014. A convolutional neural network for modelling sentences. In *Proceedings of the Association for Computational Linguistics (ACL)*.

Kalchbrenner, N., L. Espeholt, K. Simonyan, A. v. d. Oord, A. Graves, and K. Kavukcuoglu. 2016. Neural machine translation in linear time. *arXiv preprint arXiv:1610.10099*.

Karlsson, F. 2007. Constraints on multiple center-embedding of clauses. *Journal of Linguistics* 43 (2): 365–392.

Kate, R. J., Y. W. Wong, and R. J. Mooney. 2005. Learning to transform natural to formal languages. In *Proceedings of the National Conference on Artificial Intelligence (AAAI)*.

Kawaguchi, K., L. P. Kaelbling, and Y. Bengio. 2017. Generalization in deep learning. *arXiv preprint arXiv:1710.05468*.

Kehler, A. 2007. Rethinking the SMASH approach to pronoun interpretation. In *Interdisciplinary Perspectives on Reference Processing*, eds. J. Gundel and N. Hedberg. *New Directions in Cognitive Science Series*, 95–122. Oxford, UK: Oxford University Press.

Kibble, R., and R. Power. 2004. Optimizing referential coherence in text generation. *Computational Linguistics* 30 (4): 401–416.

Kilgarriff, A. 1997. I don't believe in word senses. *Computers and the Humanities* 31 (2): 91–113.

Kilgarriff, A., and G. Grefenstette. 2003. Introduction to the special issue on the web as corpus. *Computational Linguistics* 29 (3): 333–347.

Kim, M.-J. 2002. Does Korean have adjectives? *MIT Working Papers in Linguistics* 43: 71–89.

Kim, S.-M., and E. Hovy. 2006. Extracting opinions, opinion holders, and topics expressed in online news media text. In *Proceedings of the Workshop on Sentiment and Subjectivity in Text*.

Kim, Y. 2014. Convolutional neural networks for sentence classification. In *Proceedings of Empirical Methods for Natural Language Processing (EMNLP)*.

Kim, Y., Y. Jernite, D. Sontag, and A. M. Rush. 2016. Character-aware neural language models. In *Proceedings of the National Conference on Artificial Intelligence (AAAI)*.

Kim, Y., C. Denton, L. Hoang, and A. M. Rush. 2017. Structured attention networks. In *Proceedings of the International Conference on Learning Representations (ICLR)*.

Kingma, D., and J. Ba. 2014. Adam: A method for stochastic optimization. *arXiv preprint arXiv:1412.6980*.

Kiperwasser, E., and Y. Goldberg. 2016. Simple and accurate dependency parsing using bidirectional LSTM feature representations. *Transactions of the Association for Computational Linguistics* 4: 313–327.

Kipper-Schuler, K. 2005. VerbNet: A broad-coverage, comprehensive verb lexicon. PhD diss, Computer and Information Science, University of Pennsylvania.

Kiros, R., R. Salakhutdinov, and R. Zemel. 2014. Multimodal neural language models. In *Proceedings of the International Conference on Machine Learning (ICML)*.

Kiros, R., Y. Zhu, R. Salakhudinov, R. S. Zemel, A. Torralba, R. Urtasun, and S. Fidler. 2015. Skip-thought vectors. In *Neural Information Processing Systems (NeurIPS)*.

Klein, D., and C. D. Manning. 2003. Accurate unlexicalized parsing. In *Proceedings of the Association for Computational Linguistics (ACL)*.

Klein, D., and C. D. Manning. 2004. Corpus-based induction of syntactic structure: Models of dependency and constituency. In *Proceedings of the Association for Computational Linguistics (ACL)*.

Klein, G., Y. Kim, Y. Deng, J. Senellart, and A. M. Rush. 2017. OpenNMT: Open-source toolkit for neural machine translation. *arXiv preprint arXiv:1701.02810*.

Klementiev, A., I. Titov, and B. Bhattarai. 2012. Inducing crosslingual distributed representations of words. In *Proceedings of the International Conference on Computational Linguistics (COLING)*.

Klenner, M. 2007. Enforcing consistency on coreference sets. In *Recent Advances in Natural Language Processing (RANLP)*.

Knight, K. 1999. Decoding complexity in word-replacement translation models. *Computational Linguistics* 25 (4): 607–615.

Knight, K., and J. Graehl. 1998. Machine transliteration. *Computational Linguistics* 24 (4): 599–612.

Knight, K., and D. Marcu. 2000. Statistics-based summarization—step one: Sentence compression. In *Proceedings of the National Conference on Artificial Intelligence (AAAI)*.

Knight, K., and J. May. 2009. Applications of weighted automata in natural language processing. In *Handbook of Weighted Automata*, 571–596. New York, NY: Springer.

Knott, A. 1996. A data-driven methodology for motivating a set of coherence relations. PhD diss, The University of Edinburgh.

Koehn, P. 2005. Europarl: A parallel corpus for statistical machine translation. In *MT Summit*, Vol. 5.

Koehn, P. 2009. *Statistical Machine Translation*. Cambridge, UK: Cambridge University Press.

Koehn, P. 2017. Neural machine translation. *arXiv preprint arXiv:1709.07809*.

Konstas, I., and M. Lapata. 2013. A global model for concept-to-text generation. *Journal of Artificial Intelligence Research* 48: 305–346.

Koo, T., and M. Collins. 2005. Hidden-variable models for discriminative reranking. In *Proceedings of Empirical Methods for Natural Language Processing (EMNLP)*.

Koo, T., and M. Collins. 2010. Efficient third-order dependency parsers. In *Proceedings of the Association for Computational Linguistics (ACL)*.

Koo, T., X. Carreras, and M. Collins. 2008. Simple semi-supervised dependency parsing. In *Proceedings of the Association for Computational Linguistics (ACL)*.

Koo, T., A. Globerson, X. Carreras, and M. Collins. 2007. Structured prediction models via the matrix-tree theorem. In *Proceedings of Empirical Methods for Natural Language Processing (EMNLP)*.

Kovach, B., and T. Rosenstiel. 2014. *The Elements of Journalism: What Newspeople Should Know and the Public Should Expect*. New York, NY: Three Rivers Press.

Krishnamurthy, J. 2016. Probabilistic models for learning a semantic parser lexicon. In *Proceedings of the North American Chapter of the Association for Computational Linguistics (NAACL)*.

Krishnamurthy, J., and T. M. Mitchell. 2012. Weakly supervised training of semantic parsers. In *Proceedings of Empirical Methods for Natural Language Processing (EMNLP)*.

Krizhevsky, A., I. Sutskever, and G. E. Hinton. 2012. Imagenet classification with deep convolutional neural networks. In *Neural Information Processing Systems (NeurIPS)*.

Kübler, S., R. McDonald, and J. Nivre. 2009. Dependency parsing. *Synthesis Lectures on Human Language Technologies* 1 (1): 1–127.

Kuhlmann, M., and J. Nivre. 2010. Transition-based techniques for non-projective dependency parsing. *Northern European Journal of Language Technology (NEJLT)* 2 (1): 1–19.

Kummerfeld, J. K., T. Berg-Kirkpatrick, and D. Klein. 2015. An empirical analysis of optimization for max-margin NLP. In *Proceedings of Empirical Methods for Natural Language Processing (EMNLP)*.

Kwiatkowski, T., S. Goldwater, L. Zettlemoyer, and M. Steedman. 2012. A probabilistic model of syntactic and semantic acquisition from child-directed utterances and their meanings. In *Proceedings of the European Chapter of the Association for Computational Linguistics (EACL)*.

Lafferty, J., A. McCallum, and F. Pereira. 2001. Conditional random fields: Probabilistic models for segmenting and labeling sequence data. In *Proceedings of the International Conference on Machine Learning (ICML)*.

Lakoff, G. 1973. Hedges: A study in meaning criteria and the logic of fuzzy concepts. *Journal of Philosophical Logic* 2 (4): 458–508.

Lample, G., M. Ballesteros, S. Subramanian, K. Kawakami, and C. Dyer. 2016. Neural architectures for named entity recognition. In *Proceedings of the North American Chapter of the Association for Computational Linguistics (NAACL)*.

Langkilde, I., and K. Knight. 1998. Generation that exploits corpus-based statistical knowledge. In *Proceedings of the Association for Computational Linguistics (ACL)*.

Lapata, M. 2003. Probabilistic text structuring: Experiments with sentence ordering. In *Proceedings of the Association for Computational Linguistics (ACL)*.

Lappin, S., and H. J. Leass. 1994. An algorithm for pronominal anaphora resolution. *Computational Linguistics* 20 (4): 535–561.

Lari, K., and S. J. Young. 1990. The estimation of stochastic context-free grammars using the inside-outside algorithm. *Computer Speech & Language* 4 (1): 35–56.

Lascarides, A., and N. Asher. 2007. Segmented discourse representation theory: Dynamic semantics with discourse structure. In *Computing Meaning*, eds. H. Bunt and R. Muskens, Vol. 3, 87–124. New York, NY: Springer.

Law, E., and L. v. Ahn. 2011. *Human Computation*. Vol. 5 of *Synthesis lectures on artificial intelligence and machine learning*. San Rafael, CA: Morgan & Claypool.

Lebret, R., D. Grangier, and M. Auli. 2016. Neural text generation from structured data with application to the biography domain. In *Proceedings of Empirical Methods for Natural Language Processing (EMNLP)*.

LeCun, Y., L. Bottou, G. B. Orr, and K.-R. Müller. 2012. Efficient backprop. In *Neural Networks: Tricks of the Trade*, eds. G. Montavon, G. B. Orr, and K.-R. Müller, 9–50. New York, NY: Springer.

Lee, C. M., and S. S. Narayanan. 2005. Toward detecting emotions in spoken dialogs. *IEEE Transactions on Speech and Audio Processing* 13 (2): 293–303.

Lee, H., Y. Peirsman, A. Chang, N. Chambers, M. Surdeanu, and D. Jurafsky. 2011. Stanford's multi-pass sieve coreference resolution system at the conll-2011 shared task. In *Proceedings of the Conference on Natural Language Learning (CoNLL)*.

Lee, H., A. Chang, Y. Peirsman, N. Chambers, M. Surdeanu, and D. Jurafsky. 2013. Deterministic coreference resolution based on entity-centric, precision-ranked rules. *Computational Linguistics* 39 (4): 885–916.

Lee, K., L. He, and L. Zettlemoyer. 2018. Higher-order coreference resolution with coarse-to-fine inference. In *Proceedings of the North American Chapter of the Association for Computational Linguistics (NAACL)*.

Lee, K., L. He, M. Lewis, and L. Zettlemoyer. 2017. End-to-end neural coreference resolution. In *Proceedings of Empirical Methods for Natural Language Processing (EMNLP)*.

Lenat, D. B., R. V. Guha, K. Pittman, D. Pratt, and M. Shepherd. 1990. Cyc: Toward programs with common sense. *Communications of the ACM* 33 (8): 30–49.

Lesk, M. 1986. Automatic sense disambiguation using machine readable dictionaries: How to tell a pine cone from an ice cream cone. In *Proceedings of the 5th Annual International Conference on Systems Documentation*.

Levesque, H. J., E. Davis, and L. Morgenstern. 2011. The Winograd schema challenge. In *AAAI Spring Symposium: Logical Formalizations of Commonsense Reasoning*.

Levin, E., R. Pieraccini, and W. Eckert. 1998. Using Markov decision process for learning dialogue strategies. In *Proceedings of the International Conference on Acoustics, Speech and Signal Processing*, Vol. 1.

Levy, O., and Y. Goldberg. 2014. Dependency-based word embeddings. In *Proceedings of the Association for Computational Linguistics (ACL)*.

Levy, O., Y. Goldberg, and I. Dagan. 2015. Improving distributional similarity with lessons learned from word embeddings. *Transactions of the Association for Computational Linguistics* 3: 211–225.

Levy, R., and C. Manning. 2009 (accessed February 9, 2019). An Informal Introduction to Computational Semantics. idiom.ucsd.edu/~rlevy/teaching/winter2009/ligncse256/lectures/lecture_14_compositional_semantics.pdf.

Lewis II, P. M., and R. E. Stearns. 1968. Syntax-directed transduction. *Journal of the ACM* 15 (3): 465–488.

Lewis, M., and M. Steedman. 2013. Combined distributional and logical semantics. *Transactions of the Association for Computational Linguistics* 1: 179–192.

Li, J., and D. Jurafsky. 2015. Do multi-sense embeddings improve natural language understanding? In *Proceedings of Empirical Methods for Natural Language Processing (EMNLP)*. http://aclweb.org/anthology/D15-1200.

Li, J., and D. Jurafsky. 2017. Neural net models of open-domain discourse coherence. In *Proceedings of Empirical Methods for Natural Language Processing (EMNLP)*.

Li, J., R. Li, and E. Hovy. 2014. Recursive deep models for discourse parsing. In *Proceedings of Empirical Methods for Natural Language Processing (EMNLP)*.

Li, J., M.-T. Luong, and D. Jurafsky. 2015a. A hierarchical neural autoencoder for paragraphs and documents. In *Proceedings of Empirical Methods for Natural Language Processing (EMNLP)*.

Li, J., T. Luong, D. Jurafsky, and E. Hovy. 2015b. When are tree structures necessary for deep learning of representations? In *Proceedings of Empirical Methods for Natural Language Processing (EMNLP)*.

Li, J., W. Monroe, A. Ritter, D. Jurafsky, M. Galley, and J. Gao. 2016. Deep reinforcement learning for dialogue generation. In *Proceedings of Empirical Methods for Natural Language Processing (EMNLP)*.

Li, Q., H. Ji, and L. Huang. 2013. Joint event extraction via structured prediction with global features. In *Proceedings of the Association for Computational Linguistics (ACL)*.

Li, Q., S. Anzaroot, W.-P. Lin, X. Li, and H. Ji. 2011. Joint inference for cross-document information extraction. In *Proceedings of the International Conference on Information and Knowledge Management (CIKM)*.

Liang, P. 2005. Semi-supervised learning for natural language. Master's thesis, Massachusetts Institute of Technology.

Liang, P., and D. Klein. 2009. Online EM for unsupervised models. In *Proceedings of the North American Chapter of the Association for Computational Linguistics (NAACL)*.

Liang, P., and C. Potts. 2015. Bringing machine learning and compositional semantics together. *Annual Review of Linguistics* 1 (1): 355–376.

Liang, P., M. Jordan, and D. Klein. 2009. Learning semantic correspondences with less supervision. In *Proceedings of the Association for Computational Linguistics (ACL)*.

Liang, P., M. I. Jordan, and D. Klein. 2013. Learning dependency-based compositional semantics. *Computational Linguistics* 39 (2): 389–446.

Liang, P., A. Bouchard-Côté, D. Klein, and B. Taskar. 2006. An end-to-end discriminative approach to machine translation. In *Proceedings of the Association for Computational Linguistics (ACL)*.

Liang, P., S. Petrov, M. I. Jordan, and D. Klein. 2007. The infinite PCFG using hierarchical Dirichlet processes. In *Proceedings of Empirical Methods for Natural Language Processing (EMNLP)*.

Lieber, R. 2015. *Introducing Morphology*. Cambridge, UK: Cambridge University Press.

Lin, D. 1998. Automatic retrieval and clustering of similar words. In *Proceedings of the International Conference on Computational Linguistics (COLING)*.

Lin, J., and C. Dyer. 2010. Data-intensive text processing with mapreduce. *Synthesis Lectures on Human Language Technologies* 3 (1): 1–177.

Lin, Z., M.-Y. Kan, and H. T. Ng. 2009. Recognizing implicit discourse relations in the Penn Discourse Treebank. In *Proceedings of Empirical Methods for Natural Language Processing (EMNLP)*.

Lin, Z., H. T. Ng, and M.-Y. Kan. 2011. Automatically evaluating text coherence using discourse relations. In *Proceedings of the Association for Computational Linguistics (ACL)*.

Lin, Z., H. T. Ng, and M.-Y. Kan. 2014. A PDTB-styled end-to-end discourse parser. *Natural Language Engineering* 20 (2): 151–184.

Lin, Z., M. Feng, C. N. d. Santos, M. Yu, B. Xiang, B. Zhou, and Y. Bengio. 2017. A structured self-attentive sentence embedding. In *Proceedings of the International Conference on Learning Representations (ICLR)*.

Ling, W., G. Xiang, C. Dyer, A. Black, and I. Trancoso. 2013. Microblogs as parallel corpora. In *Proceedings of the Association for Computational Linguistics (ACL)*.

Ling, W., C. Dyer, A. Black, and I. Trancoso. 2015a. Two/too simple adaptations of word2vec for syntax problems. In *Proceedings of the North American Chapter of the Association for Computational Linguistics (NAACL)*.

Ling, W., T. Luís, L. Marujo, R. F. Astudillo, S. Amir, C. Dyer, A. W. Black, and I. Trancoso. 2015b. Finding function in form: Compositional character models for open vocabulary word representation. In *Proceedings of Empirical Methods for Natural Language Processing (EMNLP)*.

Ling, X., S. Singh, and D. S. Weld. 2015c. Design challenges for entity linking. *Transactions of the Association for Computational Linguistics* 3: 315–328.

Linguistic Data Consortium. 2005. ACE (automatic content extraction) English annotation guidelines for relations, Technical Report 5.8.3, Linguistic Data Consortium.

Liu, B. 2015. *Sentiment Analysis: Mining Opinions, Sentiments, and Emotions*. Cambridge, UK: Cambridge University Press.

Liu, D. C., and J. Nocedal. 1989. On the limited memory BFGS method for large scale optimization. *Mathematical Programming* 45 (1-3): 503–528.

Liu, Y., Q. Liu, and S. Lin. 2006. Tree-to-string alignment template for statistical machine translation. In *Proceedings of the Association for Computational Linguistics (ACL)*.

Loper, E., and S. Bird. 2002. NLTK: The natural language toolkit. In *Proceedings of the Workshop on Effective Tools and Methodologies for Teaching Natural Language Processing and Computational Linguistics*.

Louis, A., and A. Nenkova. 2013. What makes writing great? first experiments on article quality prediction in the science journalism domain. *Transactions of the Association for Computational Linguistics* 1: 341–352.

Louis, A., A. Joshi, and A. Nenkova. 2010. Discourse indicators for content selection in summarization. In *Proceedings of the Special Interest Group on Discourse and Dialogue (SIGDIAL)*.

Loveland, D. W. 2016. *Automated Theorem Proving: A Logical Basis*. New York, NY: Elsevier.

Lowe, R., N. Pow, I. V. Serban, and J. Pineau. 2015. The Ubuntu Dialogue Corpus: A large dataset for research in unstructured multi-turn dialogue systems. In *Proceedings of the Special Interest Group on Discourse and Dialogue (SIGDIAL)*.

Luo, X. 2005. On coreference resolution performance metrics. In *Proceedings of Empirical Methods for Natural Language Processing (EMNLP)*.

Luo, X., A. Ittycheriah, H. Jing, N. Kambhatla, and S. Roukos. 2004. A mention-synchronous coreference resolution algorithm based on the bell tree. In *Proceedings of the Association for Computational Linguistics (ACL)*.

Luong, M.-T., R. Socher, and C. D. Manning. 2013. Better word representations with recursive neural networks for morphology. In *Proceedings of the Conference on Natural Language Learning (CoNLL)*.

Luong, T., H. Pham, and C. D. Manning. 2015a. Effective approaches to attention-based neural machine translation. In *Proceedings of Empirical Methods for Natural Language Processing (EMNLP)*.

Luong, T., I. Sutskever, Q. Le, O. Vinyals, and W. Zaremba. 2015b. Addressing the rare word problem in neural machine translation. In *Proceedings of the Association for Computational Linguistics (ACL)*.

Maas, A. L., A. Y. Hannun, and A. Y. Ng. 2013. Rectifier nonlinearities improve neural network acoustic models. In *Proceedings of the International Conference on Machine Learning (ICML)*.

Magerman, D. M. 1995. Statistical decision-tree models for parsing. In *Proceedings of the Association for Computational Linguistics (ACL)*.

Mairesse, F., and M. A. Walker. 2011. Controlling user perceptions of linguistic style: Trainable generation of personality traits. *Computational Linguistics* 37 (3): 455–488.

Mani, I., M. Verhagen, B. Wellner, C. M. Lee, and J. Pustejovsky. 2006. Machine learning of temporal relations. In *Proceedings of the Association for Computational Linguistics (ACL)*.

Mann, W. C., and S. A. Thompson. 1988. Rhetorical structure theory: Toward a functional theory of text organization. *Text* 8 (3): 243–281.

Manning, C. D. 2015. Last words: Computational linguistics and deep learning. *Computational Linguistics* 41 (4): 701–707.

Manning, C. D., and H. Schütze. 1999. *Foundations of Statistical Natural Language Processing*. Cambridge, MA: MIT Press.

Manning, C. D., P. Raghavan, and H. Schütze. 2009. *An Introduction to Information Retrieval*. Cambridge, UK: Cambridge University Press.

Marcu, D. 1996. Building up rhetorical structure trees. In *Proceedings of the National Conference on Artificial Intelligence*.

Marcu, D. 1997a. From discourse structures to text summaries. In *Proceedings of the Workshop on Intelligent Scalable Text Summarization*.

Marcu, D. 1997b. From local to global coherence: A bottom-up approach to text planning. In *Proceedings of the National Conference on Artificial Intelligence (AAAI)*.

Marcus, M. P., M. A. Marcinkiewicz, and B. Santorini. 1993. Building a large annotated corpus of English: The Penn Treebank. *Computational Linguistics* 19 (2): 313–330.

Maron, O., and T. Lozano-Pérez. 1998. A framework for multiple-instance learning. In *Neural Information Processing Systems (NeurIPS)*.

Márquez, G. G. 1970. *One Hundred Years of Solitude*. New York, NY: Harper & Row. English translation by Gregory Rabassa.

Martins, A. F. T., N. A. Smith, and E. P. Xing. 2009. Concise integer linear programming formulations for dependency parsing. In *Proceedings of the Association for Computational Linguistics (ACL)*.

Martins, A. F. T., N. A. Smith, E. P. Xing, P. M. Q. Aguiar, and M. A. T. Figueiredo. 2010. Turbo parsers: Dependency parsing by approximate variational inference. In *Proceedings of Empirical Methods for Natural Language Processing (EMNLP)*.

Matsuzaki, T., Y. Miyao, and J. Tsujii. 2005. Probabilistic CFG with latent annotations. In *Proceedings of the Association for Computational Linguistics (ACL)*.

Matthiessen, C., and J. A. Bateman. 1991. *Text Generation and Systemic-Functional Linguistics: Experiences from English and Japanese*. London, UK: Pinter Publishers.

McCallum, A., and W. Li. 2003. Early results for named entity recognition with conditional random fields, feature induction and web-enhanced lexicons. In *Proceedings of the North American Chapter of the Association for Computational Linguistics (NAACL)*.

McCallum, A., and B. Wellner. 2004. Conditional models of identity uncertainty with application to noun coreference. In *Neural Information Processing Systems (NeurIPS)*.

McDonald, R., and F. Pereira. 2006. Online learning of approximate dependency parsing algorithms. In *Proceedings of the European Chapter of the Association for Computational Linguistics (EACL)*.

McDonald, R., K. Crammer, and F. Pereira. 2005. Online large-margin training of dependency parsers. In *Proceedings of the Association for Computational Linguistics (ACL)*.

McDonald, R., K. Hannan, T. Neylon, M. Wells, and J. Reynar. 2007. Structured models for fine-to-coarse sentiment analysis. In *Proceedings of the Association for Computational Linguistics (ACL)*.

McKeown, K. 1992. *Text Generation*. Cambridge, UK: Cambridge University Press.

McKeown, K. R., R. Barzilay, D. Evans, V. Hatzivassiloglou, J. L. Klavans, A. Nenkova, C. Sable, B. Schiffman, and S. Sigelman. 2002. Tracking and summarizing news on a daily basis with Columbia's Newsblaster. In *Proceedings of the International Conference on Human Language Technology Research (HLT)*.

McKeown, K., S. Rosenthal, K. Thadani, and C. Moore. 2010. Time-efficient creation of an accurate sentence fusion corpus. In *Proceedings of the North American Chapter of the Association for Computational Linguistics (NAACL)*.

McNamee, P., and H. T. Dang. 2009. Overview of the TAC 2009 knowledge base population track. In *Proceedings of the Text Analysis Conference (TAC)*.

Medlock, B., and T. Briscoe. 2007. Weakly supervised learning for hedge classification in scientific literature. In *Proceedings of the Association for Computational Linguistics (ACL)*.

Mei, H., M. Bansal, and M. R. Walter. 2016. What to talk about and how? Selective generation using LSTMs with coarse-to-fine alignment. In *Proceedings of the North American Chapter of the Association for Computational Linguistics (NAACL)*.

Merity, S., N. S. Keskar, and R. Socher. 2018. Regularizing and optimizing LSTM language models. In *Proceedings of the International Conference on Learning Representations (ICLR)*.

Merity, S., C. Xiong, J. Bradbury, and R. Socher. 2017. Pointer sentinel mixture models. In *Proceedings of the International Conference on Learning Representations (ICLR)*.

Messud, C. 2014. A new 'l'étranger'. *New York Review of Books*. June 5.

Miao, Y., and P. Blunsom. 2016. Language as a latent variable: Discrete generative models for sentence compression. In *Proceedings of Empirical Methods for Natural Language Processing (EMNLP)*.

Miao, Y., L. Yu, and P. Blunsom. 2016. Neural variational inference for text processing. In *Proceedings of the International Conference on Machine Learning (ICML)*.

Mihalcea, R., and D. Radev. 2011. *Graph-Based Natural Language Processing and Information Retrieval*. Cambridge, UK: Cambridge University Press.

Mihalcea, R., T. A. Chklovski, and A. Kilgarriff. 2004. The SENSEVAL-3 English lexical sample task. In *Proceedings of SENSEVAL-3*.

Mikolov, T., and G. Zweig. 2012. Context dependent recurrent neural network language model. In *Proceedings of the International Workshop on Spoken Language Translation (IWSLT)*.

Mikolov, T., W.-t. Yih, and G. Zweig. 2013. Linguistic regularities in continuous space word representations. In *Proceedings of the North American Chapter of the Association for Computational Linguistics (NAACL)*.

Mikolov, T., M. Karafiát, L. Burget, J. Cernockỳ, and S. Khudanpur. 2010. Recurrent neural network based language model. In *Proceedings of the International Speech Communication Association (INTERSPEECH)*.

Mikolov, T., A. Deoras, D. Povey, L. Burget, and J. Cernocky. 2011. Strategies for training large scale neural network language models. In *Proceedings of the Workshop on Automatic Speech Recognition and Understanding (ASRU)*.

Mikolov, T., K. Chen, G. Corrado, and J. Dean. 2013a. Efficient estimation of word representations in vector space. In *Proceedings of the International Conference on Learning Representations (ICLR)*.

Mikolov, T., I. Sutskever, K. Chen, G. S. Corrado, and J. Dean. 2013b. Distributed representations of words and phrases and their compositionality. In *Neural Information Processing Systems (NeurIPS)*.

Miller, G. A., G. A. Heise, and W. Lichten. 1951. The intelligibility of speech as a function of the context of the test materials. *Journal of Experimental Psychology* 41 (5): 329.

Miller, M., C. Sathi, D. Wiesenthal, J. Leskovec, and C. Potts. 2011. Sentiment flow through hyperlink networks. In *Proceedings of the International Conference on Web and Social Media (ICWSM)*.

Miller, S., J. Guinness, and A. Zamanian. 2004. Name tagging with word clusters and discriminative training. In *Proceedings of the North American Chapter of the Association for Computational Linguistics (NAACL)*.

Milne, D., and I. H. Witten. 2008. Learning to link with Wikipedia. In *Proceedings of the International Conference on Information and Knowledge Management (CIKM)*.

Miltsakaki, E., and K. Kukich. 2004. Evaluation of text coherence for electronic essay scoring systems. *Natural Language Engineering* 10 (1): 25–55.

Minka, T. P. 1999. From hidden Markov models to linear dynamical systems, Technical Report 531, Vision and Modeling Group of Media Lab, MIT.

Minsky, M. 1974. A framework for representing knowledge, Technical Report 306, MIT AI Laboratory.

Minsky, M., and S. Papert. 1969. *Perceptrons*. Cambridge, MA: MIT Press.

Mintz, M., S. Bills, R. Snow, and D. Jurafsky. 2009. Distant supervision for relation extraction without labeled data. In *Proceedings of the Association for Computational Linguistics (ACL)*.

Mirza, P., R. Sprugnoli, S. Tonelli, and M. Speranza. 2014. Annotating causality in the TempEval-3 corpus. In *Proceedings of Workshop on Computational Approaches to Causality in Language (CAtoCL)*.

Misra, D. K., and Y. Artzi. 2016. Neural shift-reduce CCG semantic parsing. In *Proceedings of Empirical Methods for Natural Language Processing (EMNLP)*.

Mitchell, J., and M. Lapata. 2010. Composition in distributional models of semantics. *Cognitive Science* 34 (8): 1388–1429.

Miwa, M., and M. Bansal. 2016. End-to-end relation extraction using LSTMs on sequences and tree structures. In *Proceedings of the Association for Computational Linguistics (ACL)*.

Mnih, A., and G. Hinton. 2007. Three new graphical models for statistical language modelling. In *Proceedings of the International Conference on Machine Learning (ICML)*.

Mnih, A., and G. E. Hinton. 2008. A scalable hierarchical distributed language model. In *Neural Information Processing Systems (NeurIPS)*.

Mnih, A., and Y. W. Teh. 2012. A fast and simple algorithm for training neural probabilistic language models. In *Proceedings of the International Conference on Machine Learning (ICML)*.

Mohammad, S. M., and P. D. Turney. 2013. Crowdsourcing a word–emotion association lexicon. *Computational Intelligence* 29 (3): 436–465.

Mohri, M., F. Pereira, and M. Riley. 2002. Weighted finite-state transducers in speech recognition. *Computer Speech & Language* 16 (1): 69–88.

Mohri, M., A. Rostamizadeh, and A. Talwalkar. 2012. *Foundations of Machine Learning*. Cambridge, MA: MIT Press.

Montague, R. 1973. The proper treatment of quantification in ordinary English. In *Approaches to Natural Language*, eds. J. Hintikka, J. Moravcsik, and P. Suppes, 221–242. New York, NY: Springer.

Moore, J. D., and C. L. Paris. 1993. Planning text for advisory dialogues: Capturing intentional and rhetorical information. *Computational Linguistics* 19 (4): 651–694.

Morante, R., and E. Blanco. 2012. *SEM 2012 shared task: Resolving the scope and focus of negation. In *Proceedings of the First Joint Conference on Lexical and Computational Semantics*.

Morante, R., and W. Daelemans. 2009. Learning the scope of hedge cues in biomedical texts. In *Proceedings of the Workshop on Current Trends in Biomedical Natural Language Processing*.

Morante, R., and C. Sporleder. 2012. Modality and negation: An introduction to the special issue. *Computational Linguistics* 38 (2): 223–260.

Mostafazadeh, N., A. Grealish, N. Chambers, J. Allen, and L. Vanderwende. 2016. CaTeRS: Causal and temporal relation scheme for semantic annotation of event structures. In *Proceedings of the Fourth Workshop on Events*.

Mueller, T., H. Schmid, and H. Schütze. 2013. Efficient higher-order CRFs for morphological tagging. In *Proceedings of Empirical Methods for Natural Language Processing (EMNLP)*.

Müller, C., and M. Strube. 2006. Multi-level annotation of linguistic data with MMAX2. In *Corpus Technology and Language Pedagogy: New Resources, New Tools, New Methods*, eds. S. Braun, K. Kohn, and J. Mukherjee, 197–214. Frankfurt: Peter Lang Publishing.

Muralidharan, A., and M. A. Hearst. 2013. Supporting exploratory text analysis in literature study. *Literary and Linguististic Computing* 28 (2): 283–295.

Murphy, K. P. 2012. *Machine Learning: A Probabilistic Perspective*. Cambridge, MA: MIT Press.

Nakagawa, T., K. Inui, and S. Kurohashi. 2010. Dependency tree-based sentiment classification using CRFs with hidden variables. In *Proceedings of the North American Chapter of the Association for Computational Linguistics (NAACL)*.

Nakazawa, T., M. Yaguchi, K. Uchimoto, M. Utiyama, E. Sumita, S. Kurohashi, and H. Isahara. 2016. ASPEC: Asian scientific paper excerpt corpus. In *Proceedings of the Language Resources and Evaluation Conference (LREC)*.

Navigli, R. 2009. Word sense disambiguation: A survey. *ACM Computing Surveys* 41 (2): 10.

Neal, R. M., and G. E. Hinton. 1998. A view of the EM algorithm that justifies incremental, sparse, and other variants. In *Learning in Graphical Models*, ed. M. I. Jordan, 355–368. New York, NY: Springer.

Nenkova, A., and K. McKeown. 2012. A survey of text summarization techniques. In *Mining Text Data*, eds. C. Aggarwal and C. Zhai, 43–76. Boston, MA: Springer.

Neubig, G. 2017. Neural machine translation and sequence-to-sequence models: A tutorial. *arXiv preprint arXiv:1703.01619*.

Neubig, G., Y. Goldberg, and C. Dyer. 2017a. On-the-fly operation batching in dynamic computation graphs. In *Neural Information Processing Systems (NeurIPS)*.

Neubig, G., C. Dyer, Y. Goldberg, A. Matthews, W. Ammar, A. Anastasopoulos, M. Ballesteros, D. Chiang, D. Clothiaux, T. Cohn, K. Duh, M. Faruqui, C. Gan, D. Garrette, Y. Ji, L. Kong, A. Kuncoro, G. Kumar, C. Malaviya, P. Michel, Y. Oda, M. Richardson, N. Saphra, S. Swayamdipta, and P. Yin. 2017b. Dynet: The dynamic neural network toolkit. *arXiv:1701.03980*.

Neubig, G., M. Sperber, X. Wang, M. Felix, A. Matthews, S. Padmanabhan, Y. Qi, D. S. Sachan, P. Arthur, P. Godard, J. Hewitt, R. Riad, and L. Wang. 2018. XNMT: The extensible neural machine translation toolkit. In *Proceedings of the Association for Machine Translation in the Americas (AMTA)*.

Neuhaus, P., and N. Bröker. 1997. The complexity of recognition of linguistically adequate dependency grammars. In *Proceedings of the European Chapter of the Association for Computational Linguistics (EACL)*.

Newman, D., C. Chemudugunta, and P. Smyth. 2006. Statistical entity-topic models. In *Proceedings of Knowledge Discovery and Data Mining (KDD)*.

Ng, V. 2010. Supervised noun phrase coreference research: The first fifteen years. In *Proceedings of the Association for Computational Linguistics (ACL)*.

Nguyen, D., and A. S. Dogruöz. 2013. Word level language identification in online multilingual communication. In *Proceedings of Empirical Methods for Natural Language Processing (EMNLP)*.

Nguyen, D. T., and S. Joty. 2017. A neural local coherence model. In *Proceedings of the Association for Computational Linguistics (ACL)*.

Nigam, K., A. K. McCallum, S. Thrun, and T. Mitchell. 2000. Text classification from labeled and unlabeled documents using em. *Machine Learning* 39 (2-3): 103–134.

Nirenburg, S., and Y. Wilks. 2001. What's in a symbol: Ontology, representation and language. *Journal of Experimental & Theoretical Artificial Intelligence* 13 (1): 9–23.

Nivre, J. 2008. Algorithms for deterministic incremental dependency parsing. *Computational Linguistics* 34 (4): 513–553.

Nivre, J., and J. Nilsson. 2005. Pseudo-projective dependency parsing. In *Proceedings of the Association for Computational Linguistics (ACL)*.

Nivre, J., M.-C. de Marneffe, F. Ginter, Y. Goldberg, J. Hajič, C. D. Manning, R. McDonald, S. Petrov, S. Pyysalo, N. Silveira, R. Tsarfaty, and D. Zeman. 2016. Universal dependencies v1: A multilingual treebank collection. In *Proceedings of the Language Resources and Evaluation Conference (LREC)*.

Novikoff, A. B. J. 1962. On convergence proofs on perceptrons. In *Proceedings of the Symposium on the Mathematical Theory of Automata*, Vol. 12.

Och, F. J., and H. Ney. 2003. A systematic comparison of various statistical alignment models. *Computational Linguistics* 29 (1): 19–51.

O'Connor, B., M. Krieger, and D. Ahn. 2010. Tweetmotif: Exploratory search and topic summarization for Twitter. In *Proceedings of the International Conference on Web and Social Media (ICWSM)*.

Oepen, S., M. Kuhlmann, Y. Miyao, D. Zeman, D. Flickinger, J. Hajic, A. Ivanova, and Y. Zhang. 2014. SemEval 2014 task 8: Broad-coverage semantic dependency parsing. In *Proceedings of the 8th International Workshop on Semantic Evaluation (SemEval 2014)*.

Oflazer, K., and İ. Kuruöz. 1994. Tagging and morphological disambiguation of Turkish text. In *Proceedings of the Conference on Applied Natural Language Processing*.

Ohta, T., Y. Tateisi, and J.-D. Kim. 2002. The GENIA corpus: An annotated research abstract corpus in molecular biology domain. In *Proceedings of the International Conference on Human Language Technology Research (HLT)*.

Onishi, T., H. Wang, M. Bansal, K. Gimpel, and D. McAllester. 2016. Who did what: A large-scale person-centered cloze dataset. In *Proceedings of Empirical Methods for Natural Language Processing (EMNLP)*.

Owoputi, O., B. O'Connor, C. Dyer, K. Gimpel, N. Schneider, and N. A. Smith. 2013. Improved part-of-speech tagging for online conversational text with word clusters. In *Proceedings of the North American Chapter of the Association for Computational Linguistics (NAACL)*.

Packard, W., E. M. Bender, J. Read, S. Oepen, and R. Dridan. 2014. Simple negation scope resolution through deep parsing: A semantic solution to a semantic problem. In *Proceedings of the Association for Computational Linguistics (ACL)*.

Paice, C. D. 1990. Another stemmer. In *ACM SIGIR Forum*, Vol. 24.

Pak, A., and P. Paroubek. 2010. Twitter as a corpus for sentiment analysis and opinion mining. In *Proceedings of the Language Resources and Evaluation Conference (LREC)*.

Palmer, F. R. 2001. *Mood and Modality*. Cambridge, UK: Cambridge University Press.

Palmer, M., D. Gildea, and P. Kingsbury. 2005. The Proposition Bank: An annotated corpus of semantic roles. *Computational Linguistics* 31 (1): 71–106.

Pan, S. J., and Q. Yang. 2010. A survey on transfer learning. *IEEE Transactions on Knowledge and Data Engineering* 22 (10): 1345–1359.

Pang, B., and L. Lee. 2004. A sentimental education: Sentiment analysis using subjectivity summarization based on minimum cuts. In *Proceedings of the Association for Computational Linguistics (ACL)*.

Pang, B., and L. Lee. 2005. Seeing stars: Exploiting class relationships for sentiment categorization with respect to rating scales. In *Proceedings of the Association for Computational Linguistics (ACL)*.

Pang, B., and L. Lee. 2008. Opinion mining and sentiment analysis. *Foundations and Trends in Information Retrieval* 2 (1-2): 1–135.

Pang, B., L. Lee, and S. Vaithyanathan. 2002. Thumbs up? Sentiment classification using machine learning techniques. In *Proceedings of Empirical Methods for Natural Language Processing (EMNLP)*.

Papineni, K., S. Roukos, T. Ward, and W.-J. Zhu. 2002. BLEU: A method for automatic evaluation of machine translation. In *Proceedings of the Association for Computational Linguistics (ACL)*.

Park, J., and C. Cardie. 2012. Improving implicit discourse relation recognition through feature set optimization. In *Proceedings of the Special Interest Group on Discourse and Dialogue (SIGDIAL)*.

Parsons, T. 1991. *Events in the Semantics of English*. Cambridge, MA: MIT Press.

Pascanu, R., T. Mikolov, and Y. Bengio. 2013. On the difficulty of training recurrent neural networks. In *Proceedings of the International Conference on Machine Learning (ICML)*.

Paul, M., M. Federico, and S. Stüker. 2010. Overview of the IWSLT 2010 evaluation campaign. In *Proceedings of the International Workshop on Spoken Language Translation (IWSLT)*.

Pedersen, T., S. Patwardhan, and J. Michelizzi. 2004. WordNet::Similarity – measuring the relatedness of concepts. In *Proceedings of the North American Chapter of the Association for Computational Linguistics (NAACL)*.

Pedregosa, F., G. Varoquaux, A. Gramfort, V. Michel, B. Thirion, O. Grisel, M. Blondel, P. Prettenhofer, R. Weiss, V. Dubourg, J. Vanderplas, A. Passos, D. Cournapeau, M. Brucher, M. Perrot, and E. Duchesnay. 2011. Scikit-learn: Machine learning in Python. *Journal of Machine Learning Research* 12: 2825–2830.

Pei, W., T. Ge, and B. Chang. 2015. An effective neural network model for graph-based dependency parsing. In *Proceedings of the Association for Computational Linguistics (ACL)*.

Peldszus, A., and M. Stede. 2013. From argument diagrams to argumentation mining in texts: A survey. *International Journal of Cognitive Informatics and Natural Intelligence (IJCINI)* 7 (1): 1–31.

Peldszus, A., and M. Stede. 2015. An annotated corpus of argumentative microtexts. In *Proceedings of the First Conference on Argumentation*.

Peng, F., F. Feng, and A. McCallum. 2004. Chinese segmentation and new word detection using conditional random fields. In *Proceedings of the International Conference on Computational Linguistics (COLING)*.

Pennington, J., R. Socher, and C. Manning. 2014. Glove: Global vectors for word representation. In *Proceedings of Empirical Methods for Natural Language Processing (EMNLP)*.

Pereira, F., and Y. Schabes. 1992. Inside-outside reestimation from partially bracketed corpora. In *Proceedings of the Association for Computational Linguistics (ACL)*.

Pereira, F. C. N., and S. M. Shieber. 2002. *Prolog and Natural-Language Analysis*. Brookline, MA: Microtome Publishing.

Peters, M. E., M. Neumann, M. Iyyer, M. Gardner, C. Clark, K. Lee, and L. Zettlemoyer. 2018. Deep contextualized word representations. In *Proceedings of the North American Chapter of the Association for Computational Linguistics (NAACL)*.

Peterson, W. W., T. G. Birdsall, and W. C. Fox. 1954. The theory of signal detectability. *Transactions of the IRE Professional Group on Information Theory* 4 (4): 171–212.

Petrov, S., and R. McDonald. 2012. Overview of the 2012 shared task on parsing the web. In *Notes of the First Workshop on Syntactic Analysis of Non-Canonical Language (SANCL)*.

Petrov, S., D. Das, and R. McDonald. 2012. A universal part-of-speech tagset. In *Proceedings of the Language Resources and Evaluation Conference (LREC)*.

Petrov, S., L. Barrett, R. Thibaux, and D. Klein. 2006. Learning accurate, compact, and interpretable tree annotation. In *Proceedings of the Association for Computational Linguistics (ACL)*.

Pinker, S. 2003. *The Language Instinct: How the Mind Creates Language*. New York, NY: William Morrow & Company.

Pinter, Y., R. Guthrie, and J. Eisenstein. 2017. Mimicking word embeddings using subword RNNs. In *Proceedings of Empirical Methods for Natural Language Processing (EMNLP)*.

Pitler, E., and A. Nenkova. 2009. Using syntax to disambiguate explicit discourse connectives in text. In *Proceedings of the Association for Computational Linguistics (ACL)*.

Pitler, E., A. Louis, and A. Nenkova. 2009. Automatic sense prediction for implicit discourse relations in text. In *Proceedings of the Association for Computational Linguistics (ACL)*.

Pitler, E., M. Raghupathy, H. Mehta, A. Nenkova, A. Lee, and A. Joshi. 2008. Easily identifiable discourse relations. In *Proceedings of the International Conference on Computational Linguistics (COLING)*.

Plank, B., A. Søgaard, and Y. Goldberg. 2016. Multilingual part-of-speech tagging with bidirectional long short-term memory models and auxiliary loss. In *Proceedings of the Association for Computational Linguistics (ACL)*.

Poesio, M., R. Stevenson, B. Di Eugenio, and J. Hitzeman. 2004. Centering: A parametric theory and its instantiations. *Computational Linguistics* 30 (3): 309–363.

Polanyi, L., and A. Zaenen. 2006. Contextual valence shifters. In *Computing Attitude and Affect in Text: Theory and Applications*, eds. J. G. Shanahan, Y. Qu, and J. Wiebe. New York, NY: Springer.

Ponzetto, S. P., and M. Strube. 2006. Exploiting semantic role labeling, WordNet and Wikipedia for coreference resolution. In *Proceedings of the North American Chapter of the Association for Computational Linguistics (NAACL)*.

Ponzetto, S. P., and M. Strube. 2007. Knowledge derived from Wikipedia for computing semantic relatedness. *Journal of Artificial Intelligence Research* 30: 181–212.

Poon, H., and P. Domingos. 2008. Joint unsupervised coreference resolution with Markov logic. In *Proceedings of Empirical Methods for Natural Language Processing (EMNLP)*.

Poon, H., and P. Domingos. 2009. Unsupervised semantic parsing. In *Proceedings of Empirical Methods for Natural Language Processing (EMNLP)*.

Popel, M., D. Marecek, J. Stepánek, D. Zeman, and Z. Zabokrtský. 2013. Coordination structures in dependency treebanks. In *Proceedings of the Association for Computational Linguistics (ACL)*.

Popescu, A.-M., O. Etzioni, and H. Kautz. 2003. Towards a theory of natural language interfaces to databases. In *Proceedings of Intelligent User Interfaces (IUI)*.

Poplack, S. 1980. Sometimes I'll start a sentence in Spanish y termino en Español: Toward a typology of code-switching. *Linguistics* 18 (7-8): 581–618.

Porter, M. F. 1980. An algorithm for suffix stripping. *Program* 14 (3): 130–137.

Prabhakaran, V., O. Rambow, and M. Diab. 2010. Automatic committed belief tagging. In *Proceedings of the International Conference on Computational Linguistics (COLING)*.

Pradhan, S., W. Ward, K. Hacioglu, J. H. Martin, and D. Jurafsky. 2005. Semantic role labeling using different syntactic views. In *Proceedings of the Association for Computational Linguistics (ACL)*.

Pradhan, S., L. Ramshaw, M. Marcus, M. Palmer, R. Weischedel, and N. Xue. 2011. CoNLL-2011 shared task: Modeling unrestricted coreference in OntoNotes. In *Proceedings of the Conference on Natural Language Learning (CoNLL)*.

Pradhan, S., X. Luo, M. Recasens, E. Hovy, V. Ng, and M. Strube. 2014. Scoring coreference partitions of predicted mentions: A reference implementation. In *Proceedings of the Association for Computational Linguistics (ACL)*.

Prasad, R., N. Dinesh, A. Lee, E. Miltsakaki, L. Robaldo, A. Joshi, and B. Webber. 2008. The Penn Discourse Treebank 2.0. In *Proceedings of the Language Resources and Evaluation Conference (LREC)*.

Punyakanok, V., D. Roth, and W.-t. Yih. 2008. The importance of syntactic parsing and inference in semantic role labeling. *Computational Linguistics* 34 (2): 257–287.

Pustejovsky, J., P. Hanks, R. Saurí, A. See, R. Gaizauskas, A. Setzer, D. Radev, B. Sundheim, D. Day, L. Ferro, and M. Lazo. 2003. The TIMEBANK corpus. In *Proceedings of the Conference on Corpus Linguistics*.

Pustejovsky, J., B. Ingria, R. Sauri, J. Castano, J. Littman, R. Gaizauskas, A. Setzer, G. Katz, and I. Mani. 2005. The specification language TimeML. In *The Language of Time: A Reader*, 545–557. Oxford, UK: Oxford University Press.

Qin, L., Z. Zhang, H. Zhao, Z. Hu, and E. Xing. 2017. Adversarial connective-exploiting networks for implicit discourse relation classification. In *Proceedings of the Association for Computational Linguistics (ACL)*.

Qiu, G., B. Liu, J. Bu, and C. Chen. 2011. Opinion word expansion and target extraction through double propagation. *Computational Linguistics* 37 (1): 9–27.

Quattoni, A., S. Wang, L.-P. Morency, M. Collins, and T. Darrell. 2007. Hidden conditional random fields. *IEEE Transactions on Pattern Analysis and Machine Intelligence* 29 (10): 1848–1852.

Rahman, A., and V. Ng. 2011. Narrowing the modeling gap: A cluster-ranking approach to coreference resolution. *Journal of Artificial Intelligence Research* 40: 469–521.

Rajpurkar, P., J. Zhang, K. Lopyrev, and P. Liang. 2016. SQuAD: 100,000+ questions for machine comprehension of text. In *Proceedings of Empirical Methods for Natural Language Processing (EMNLP)*.

Ranzato, M., S. Chopra, M. Auli, and W. Zaremba. 2016. Sequence level training with recurrent neural networks. In *Proceedings of the International Conference on Learning Representations (ICLR)*.

Rao, D., D. Yarowsky, A. Shreevats, and M. Gupta. 2010. Classifying latent user attributes in Twitter. In *Proceedings of Workshop on Search and Mining User-Generated Contents*.

Ratinov, L., and D. Roth. 2009. Design challenges and misconceptions in named entity recognition. In *Proceedings of the Conference on Natural Language Learning (CoNLL)*.

Ratinov, L., D. Roth, D. Downey, and M. Anderson. 2011. Local and global algorithms for disambiguation to wikipedia. In *Proceedings of the Association for Computational Linguistics (ACL)*.

Ratliff, N. D., J. A. Bagnell, and M. Zinkevich. 2007. (Approximate) subgradient methods for structured prediction. In *Proceedings of Artificial Intelligence and Statistics (AISTATS)*.

Ratnaparkhi, A. 1996. A maximum entropy model for part-of-speech tagging. In *Proceedings of Empirical Methods for Natural Language Processing (EMNLP)*.

Ratnaparkhi, A., J. Reynar, and S. Roukos. 1994. A maximum entropy model for prepositional phrase attachment. In *Proceedings of the International Conference on Human Language Technology Research (HLT)*.

Read, J. 2005. Using emoticons to reduce dependency in machine learning techniques for sentiment classification. In *Proceedings of the ACL Student Research Workshop*.

Reisinger, D., R. Rudinger, F. Ferraro, C. Harman, K. Rawlins, and B. V. Durme. 2015. Semantic proto-roles. *Transactions of the Association for Computational Linguistics* 3: 475–488.

Reisinger, J., and R. J. Mooney. 2010. Multi-prototype vector-space models of word meaning. In *Proceedings of the North American Chapter of the Association for Computational Linguistics (NAACL)*.

Reiter, E., and R. Dale. 2000. *Building Natural Language Generation Systems*. Cambridge, UK: Cambridge University Press.

Resnik, P., and N. A. Smith. 2003. The web as a parallel corpus. *Computational Linguistics* 29 (3): 349–380.

Resnik, P., M. B. Olsen, and M. Diab. 1999. The bible as a parallel corpus: Annotating the "Book of 2000 Tongues." *Computers and the Humanities* 33 (1–2): 129–153.

Ribeiro, F. N., M. Araújo, P. Gonçalves, M. A. Gonçalves, and F. Benevenuto. 2016. Sentibench—a benchmark comparison of state-of-the-practice sentiment analysis methods. *EPJ Data Science* 5 (1): 1–29.

Richardson, M., C. J. Burges, and E. Renshaw. 2013. MCTest: A challenge dataset for the open-domain machine comprehension of text. In *Proceedings of Empirical Methods for Natural Language Processing (EMNLP)*.

Riedel, S., L. Yao, and A. McCallum. 2010. Modeling relations and their mentions without labeled text. In *Proceedings of the European Conference on Machine Learning and Principles and Practice of Knowledge Discovery in Databases (ECML)*.

Riedl, M. O., and R. M. Young. 2010. Narrative planning: Balancing plot and character. *Journal of Artificial Intelligence Research* 39: 217–268.

Rieser, V., and O. Lemon. 2011. *Reinforcement Learning for Adaptive Dialogue Systems: A Data-Driven Methodology for Dialogue Management and Natural Language Generation*. New York, NY: Springer.

Riloff, E. 1996. Automatically generating extraction patterns from untagged text. In *Proceedings of the National Conference on Artificial Intelligence (AAAI)*.

Riloff, E., and J. Wiebe. 2003. Learning extraction patterns for subjective expressions. In *Proceedings of Empirical Methods for Natural Language Processing (EMNLP)*.

Ritchie, G. 2001. Current directions in computational humour. *Artificial Intelligence Review* 16 (2): 119–135.

Ritter, A., C. Cherry, and W. B. Dolan. 2011a. Data-driven response generation in social media. In *Proceedings of Empirical Methods for Natural Language Processing (EMNLP)*.

Ritter, A., S. Clark, Mausam, and O. Etzioni. 2011b. Named entity recognition in tweets: An experimental study. In *Proceedings of Empirical Methods for Natural Language Processing (EMNLP)*.

Roark, B., M. Saraclar, and M. Collins. 2007. Discriminative *n*-gram language modeling. *Computer Speech & Language* 21 (2): 373–392.

Robert, C., and G. Casella. 2013. *Monte Carlo Statistical Methods*. New York, NY: Springer.

Rosenfeld, R. 1996. A maximum entropy approach to adaptive statistical language modelling. *Computer Speech & Language* 10 (3): 187–228.

Ross, S., G. Gordon, and D. Bagnell. 2011. A reduction of imitation learning and structured prediction to no-regret online learning. In *Proceedings of Artificial Intelligence and Statistics (AISTATS)*.

Roy, N., J. Pineau, and S. Thrun. 2000. Spoken dialogue management using probabilistic reasoning. In *Proceedings of the Association for Computational Linguistics (ACL)*.

Rudinger, R., J. Naradowsky, B. Leonard, and B. Van Durme. 2018. Gender bias in coreference resolution. In *Proceedings of the North American Chapter of the Association for Computational Linguistics (NAACL)*.

Rudnicky, A., and W. Xu. 1999. An agenda-based dialog management architecture for spoken language systems. In *Proceedings of the IEEE Automatic Speech Recognition and Understanding Workshop*.

Rush, A. M., S. Chopra, and J. Weston. 2015. A neural attention model for abstractive sentence summarization. In *Proceedings of Empirical Methods for Natural Language Processing (EMNLP)*.

Rush, A. M., D. Sontag, M. Collins, and T. Jaakkola. 2010. On dual decomposition and linear programming relaxations for natural language processing. In *Proceedings of Empirical Methods for Natural Language Processing (EMNLP)*.

Russell, S. J., and P. Norvig. 2009. *Artificial Intelligence: A Modern Approach*, 3rd edn. Upper Saddle River, NJ: Prentice Hall.

Rutherford, A., and N. Xue. 2014. Discovering implicit discourse relations through brown cluster pair representation and coreference patterns. In *Proceedings of the European Chapter of the Association for Computational Linguistics (EACL)*.

Rutherford, A., V. Demberg, and N. Xue. 2017. A systematic study of neural discourse models for implicit discourse relation. In *Proceedings of the European Chapter of the Association for Computational Linguistics (EACL)*.

Sag, I. A., T. Baldwin, F. Bond, A. Copestake, and D. Flickinger. 2002. Multiword expressions: A pain in the neck for NLP. In *Proceedings of the International Conference on Intelligent Text Processing and Computational Linguistics*.

Sagae, K. 2009. Analysis of discourse structure with syntactic dependencies and data-driven shift-reduce parsing. In *Proceedings of the 11th International Conference on Parsing Technologies*.

Sato, M.-A., and S. Ishii. 2000. On-line EM algorithm for the normalized Gaussian network. *Neural Computation* 12 (2): 407–432.

Saurí, R., and J. Pustejovsky. 2009. FactBank: A corpus annotated with event factuality. *Language Resources and Evaluation* 43 (3): 227.

Saxe, A. M., J. L. McClelland, and S. Ganguli. 2014. Exact solutions to the nonlinear dynamics of learning in deep linear neural networks. In *Proceedings of the International Conference on Learning Representations (ICLR)*.

Schank, R. C., and R. Abelson. 1977. *Scripts, Goals, Plans, and Understanding*. Hillsdale, NJ: Erlbaum.

Schapire, R. E., and Y. Singer. 2000. BoosTexter: A boosting-based system for text categorization. *Machine Learning* 39 (2-3): 135–168.

Schaul, T., S. Zhang, and Y. LeCun. 2013. No more pesky learning rates. In *Proceedings of the International Conference on Machine Learning (ICML)*.

Schnabel, T., I. Labutov, D. Mimno, and T. Joachims. 2015. Evaluation methods for unsupervised word embeddings. In *Proceedings of Empirical Methods for Natural Language Processing (EMNLP)*.

Schneider, N., J. Flanigan, and T. O'Gorman. 2015. The logic of AMR: Practical, unified, graph-based sentence semantics for NLP. In *Proceedings of the North American Chapter of the Association for Computational Linguistics (NAACL)*.

Schütze, H. 1998. Automatic word sense discrimination. *Computational Linguistics* 24 (1): 97–123.

Schwarm, S. E., and M. Ostendorf. 2005. Reading level assessment using support vector machines and statistical language models. In *Proceedings of the Association for Computational Linguistics (ACL)*.

See, A., P. J. Liu, and C. D. Manning. 2017. Get to the point: Summarization with pointer-generator networks. In *Proceedings of the Association for Computational Linguistics (ACL)*.

Sennrich, R., B. Haddow, and A. Birch. 2016. Neural machine translation of rare words with subword units. In *Proceedings of the Association for Computational Linguistics (ACL)*.

Serban, I. V., A. Sordoni, Y. Bengio, A. C. Courville, and J. Pineau. 2016. Building end-to-end dialogue systems using generative hierarchical neural network models. In *Proceedings of the National Conference on Artificial Intelligence (AAAI)*.

Settles, B. 2012. Active learning. *Synthesis Lectures on Artificial Intelligence and Machine Learning* 6 (1): 1–114.

Shang, L., Z. Lu, and H. Li. 2015. Neural responding machine for short-text conversation. In *Proceedings of the Association for Computational Linguistics (ACL)*.

Shen, D., and M. Lapata. 2007. Using semantic roles to improve question answering. In *Proceedings of Empirical Methods for Natural Language Processing (EMNLP)*.

Shen, S., Y. Cheng, Z. He, W. He, H. Wu, M. Sun, and Y. Liu. 2016. Minimum risk training for neural machine translation. In *Proceedings of the Association for Computational Linguistics (ACL)*.

Shen, W., J. Wang, and J. Han. 2015. Entity linking with a knowledge base: Issues, techniques, and solutions. *IEEE Transactions on Knowledge and Data Engineering* 27 (2): 443–460.

Shieber, S. M. 1985. Evidence against the context-freeness of natural language. *Linguistics and Philosophy* 8 (3): 333–343.

Siegelmann, H. T., and E. D. Sontag. 1995. On the computational power of neural nets. *Journal of Computer and System Sciences* 50 (1): 132–150.

Singh, S., A. Subramanya, F. Pereira, and A. McCallum. 2011. Large-scale cross-document coreference using distributed inference and hierarchical models. In *Proceedings of the Association for Computational Linguistics (ACL)*.

Sipser, M. 2012. *Introduction to the Theory of Computation*. Boston, MA: Cengage Learning.

Smith, D. A., and J. Eisner. 2006. Minimum risk annealing for training log-linear models. In *Proceedings of the Association for Computational Linguistics (ACL)*.

Smith, D. A., and J. Eisner. 2008. Dependency parsing by belief propagation. In *Proceedings of Empirical Methods for Natural Language Processing (EMNLP)*.

Smith, D. A., and N. A. Smith. 2007. Probabilistic models of nonprojective dependency trees. In *Proceedings of Empirical Methods for Natural Language Processing (EMNLP)*.

Smith, N. A. 2011. Linguistic structure prediction. *Synthesis Lectures on Human Language Technologies* 4 (2): 1–274.

Snover, M., B. Dorr, R. Schwartz, L. Micciulla, and J. Makhoul. 2006. A study of translation edit rate with targeted human annotation. In *Proceedings of the Association for Machine Translation in the Americas (AMTA)*.

Snow, R., B. O'Connor, D. Jurafsky, and A. Y. Ng. 2008. Cheap and fast—but is it good? Evaluating non-expert annotations for natural language tasks. In *Proceedings of Empirical Methods for Natural Language Processing (EMNLP)*.

Snyder, B., and R. Barzilay. 2007. Database-text alignment via structured multilabel classification. In *Proceedings of the International Joint Conference on Artificial Intelligence (IJCAI)*.

Socher, R., B. Huval, C. D. Manning, and A. Y. Ng. 2012. Semantic compositionality through recursive matrix-vector spaces. In *Proceedings of Empirical Methods for Natural Language Processing (EMNLP)*.

Socher, R., J. Bauer, C. D. Manning, and A. Y. Ng. 2013a. Parsing with compositional vector grammars. In *Proceedings of the Association for Computational Linguistics (ACL)*.

Socher, R., A. Perelygin, J. Y. Wu, J. Chuang, C. D. Manning, A. Y. Ng, and C. Potts. 2013b. Recursive deep models for semantic compositionality over a sentiment treebank. In *Proceedings of Empirical Methods for Natural Language Processing (EMNLP)*.

Søgaard, A. 2013. Semi-supervised learning and domain adaptation in natural language processing. *Synthesis Lectures on Human Language Technologies* 6 (2): 1–103.

Solorio, T., and Y. Liu. 2008. Learning to predict code-switching points. In *Proceedings of Empirical Methods for Natural Language Processing (EMNLP)*.

Somasundaran, S., and J. Wiebe. 2009. Recognizing stances in online debates. In *Proceedings of the Association for Computational Linguistics (ACL)*.

Somasundaran, S., G. Namata, J. Wiebe, and L. Getoor. 2009. Supervised and unsupervised methods in employing discourse relations for improving opinion polarity classification. In *Proceedings of Empirical Methods for Natural Language Processing (EMNLP)*.

Song, L., B. Boots, S. M. Siddiqi, G. J. Gordon, and A. J. Smola. 2010. Hilbert space embeddings of hidden Markov models. In *Proceedings of the International Conference on Machine Learning (ICML)*.

Song, L., Y. Zhang, X. Peng, Z. Wang, and D. Gildea. 2016. AMR-to-text generation as a traveling salesman problem. In *Proceedings of Empirical Methods for Natural Language Processing (EMNLP)*.

Soon, W. M., H. T. Ng, and D. C. Y. Lim. 2001. A machine learning approach to coreference resolution of noun phrases. *Computational Linguistics* 27 (4): 521–544.

Sordoni, A., M. Galley, M. Auli, C. Brockett, Y. Ji, M. Mitchell, J.-Y. Nie, J. Gao, and B. Dolan. 2015. A neural network approach to context-sensitive generation of conversational responses. In *Proceedings of the North American Chapter of the Association for Computational Linguistics (NAACL)*.

Soricut, R., and D. Marcu. 2003. Sentence level discourse parsing using syntactic and lexical information. In *Proceedings of the North American Chapter of the Association for Computational Linguistics (NAACL)*.

Sowa, J. F. 2000. *Knowledge Representation: Logical, Philosophical, and Computational Foundations*. Pacific Grove, CA: Brooks/Cole.

Spärck Jones, K. 1972. A statistical interpretation of term specificity and its application in retrieval. *Journal of Documentation* 28 (1): 11–21.

Spitkovsky, V. I., H. Alshawi, D. Jurafsky, and C. D. Manning. 2010. Viterbi training improves unsupervised dependency parsing. In *Proceedings of the Conference on Natural Language Learning (CoNLL)*.

Sporleder, C., and M. Lapata. 2005. Discourse chunking and its application to sentence compression. In *Proceedings of Empirical Methods for Natural Language Processing (EMNLP)*.

Sproat, R., W. Gale, C. Shih, and N. Chang. 1996. A stochastic finite-state word-segmentation algorithm for Chinese. *Computational Linguistics* 22 (3): 377–404.

Sproat, R., A. W. Black, S. Chen, S. Kumar, M. Ostendorf, and C. Richards. 2001. Normalization of non-standard words. *Computer Speech & Language* 15 (3): 287–333.

Sra, S., S. Nowozin, and S. J. Wright. 2012. *Optimization for Machine Learning*. Cambridge, MA: MIT Press.

Srivastava, N., G. Hinton, A. Krizhevsky, I. Sutskever, and R. Salakhutdinov. 2014. Dropout: A simple way to prevent neural networks from overfitting. *The Journal of Machine Learning Research* 15 (1): 1929–1958.

Srivastava, R. K., K. Greff, and J. Schmidhuber. 2015. Training very deep networks. In *Neural Information Processing Systems (NeurIPS)*.

Stab, C., and I. Gurevych. 2014a. Annotating argument components and relations in persuasive essays. In *Proceedings of the International Conference on Computational Linguistics (COLING)*.

Stab, C., and I. Gurevych. 2014b. Identifying argumentative discourse structures in persuasive essays. In *Proceedings of Empirical Methods for Natural Language Processing (EMNLP)*.

Stede, M. 2011. *Discourse Processing*. Vol. 4 of *Synthesis Lectures on Human Language Technologies*. San Rafael, CA: Morgan & Claypool.

Steedman, M., and J. Baldridge. 2011. Combinatory categorial grammar. In *Non-Transformational Syntax: Formal and Explicit Models of Grammar*, eds. K. Börjars and R. D. Borsley. Hoboken, NJ: Wiley-Blackwell.

Stenetorp, P., S. Pyysalo, G. Topić, T. Ohta, S. Ananiadou, and J. Tsujii. 2012. BRAT: A web-based tool for NLP-assisted text annotation. In *Proceedings of the European Chapter of the Association for Computational Linguistics (EACL)*.

Stern, M., J. Andreas, and D. Klein. 2017. A minimal span-based neural constituency parser. In *Proceedings of the Association for Computational Linguistics (ACL)*.

Stolcke, A., K. Ries, N. Coccaro, E. Shriberg, R. Bates, D. Jurafsky, P. Taylor, R. Martin, C. Van Ess-Dykema, and M. Meteer. 2000. Dialogue act modeling for automatic tagging and recognition of conversational speech. *Computational Linguistics* 26 (3): 339–373.

Stone, P. J. 1966. *The General Inquirer: A Computer Approach to Content Analysis*. Cambridge, MA: MIT Press.

Stoyanov, V., N. Gilbert, C. Cardie, and E. Riloff. 2009. Conundrums in noun phrase coreference resolution: Making sense of the state-of-the-art. In *Proceedings of the Association for Computational Linguistics (ACL)*.

Strang, G. 2016. *Introduction to Linear Algebra*, 5th edn. Wellesley, MA: Wellesley-Cambridge Press.

Strubell, E., P. Verga, D. Belanger, and A. McCallum. 2017. Fast and accurate entity recognition with iterated dilated convolutions. In *Proceedings of Empirical Methods for Natural Language Processing (EMNLP)*.

Suchanek, F. M., G. Kasneci, and G. Weikum. 2007. Yago: A core of semantic knowledge. In *Proceedings of the Conference on World-Wide Web (WWW)*.

Sun, X., T. Matsuzaki, D. Okanohara, and J. Tsujii. 2009. Latent variable perceptron algorithm for structured classification. In *Proceedings of the International Joint Conference on Artificial Intelligence (IJCAI)*.

Sun, Y., L. Lin, D. Tang, N. Yang, Z. Ji, and X. Wang. 2015. Modeling mention, context and entity with neural networks for entity disambiguation. In *Proceedings of the International Joint Conference on Artificial Intelligence (IJCAI)*.

Sundermeyer, M., R. Schlüter, and H. Ney. 2012. LSTM neural networks for language modeling. In *Proceedings of the International Speech Communication Association (INTERSPEECH)*.

Surdeanu, M., J. Tibshirani, R. Nallapati, and C. D. Manning. 2012. Multi-instance multi-label learning for relation extraction. In *Proceedings of Empirical Methods for Natural Language Processing (EMNLP)*.

Sutskever, I., O. Vinyals, and Q. V. Le. 2014. Sequence to sequence learning with neural networks. In *Neural Information Processing Systems (NeurIPS)*.

Sutton, R. S., and A. G. Barto. 2019. *Reinforcement Learning: An Introduction*, 2nd edn. Cambridge, MA: MIT Press.

Sutton, R. S., D. A. McAllester, S. P. Singh, and Y. Mansour. 2000. Policy gradient methods for reinforcement learning with function approximation. In *Neural Information Processing Systems (NeurIPS)*.

Suzuki, J., S. Takase, H. Kamigaito, M. Morishita, and M. Nagata. 2018. An empirical study of building a strong baseline for constituency parsing. In *Proceedings of the Association for Computational Linguistics (ACL)*.

Sweeney, L. 2013. Discrimination in online ad delivery. *Queue* 11 (3): 10.

Taboada, M., and W. C. Mann. 2006. Rhetorical structure theory: Looking back and moving ahead. *Discourse Studies* 8 (3): 423–459.

Taboada, M., J. Brooke, M. Tofiloski, K. Voll, and M. Stede. 2011. Lexicon-based methods for sentiment analysis. *Computational Linguistics* 37 (2): 267–307.

Täckström, O., K. Ganchev, and D. Das. 2015. Efficient inference and structured learning for semantic role labeling. *Transactions of the Association for Computational Linguistics* 3: 29–41.

Täckström, O., R. McDonald, and J. Uszkoreit. 2012. Cross-lingual word clusters for direct transfer of linguistic structure. In *Proceedings of the North American Chapter of the Association for Computational Linguistics (NAACL)*.

Tang, D., B. Qin, and T. Liu. 2015. Document modeling with gated recurrent neural network for sentiment classification. In *Proceedings of Empirical Methods for Natural Language Processing (EMNLP)*.

Taskar, B., C. Guestrin, and D. Koller. 2003. Max-margin Markov networks. In *Neural Information Processing Systems (NeurIPS)*.

Tausczik, Y. R., and J. W. Pennebaker. 2010. The psychological meaning of words: LIWC and computerized text analysis methods. *Journal of Language and Social Psychology* 29 (1): 24–54.

Teh, Y. W. 2006. A hierarchical Bayesian language model based on Pitman-Yor processes. In *Proceedings of the Association for Computational Linguistics (ACL)*.

Tesnière, L. 1966. *Éléments de Syntaxe Structurale*, 2nd edn. Paris: Klincksieck.

Teufel, S., and M. Moens. 2002. Summarizing scientific articles: experiments with relevance and rhetorical status. *Computational Linguistics* 28 (4): 409–445.

Teufel, S., J. Carletta, and M. Moens. 1999. An annotation scheme for discourse-level argumentation in research articles. In *Proceedings of the European Chapter of the Association for Computational Linguistics (EACL)*.

Thomas, M., B. Pang, and L. Lee. 2006. Get out the vote: Determining support or opposition from Congressional floor-debate transcripts. In *Proceedings of Empirical Methods for Natural Language Processing (EMNLP)*.

Tibshirani, R. 1996. Regression shrinkage and selection via the lasso. *Journal of the Royal Statistical Society. Series B (Methodological)*.

Titov, I., and J. Henderson. 2007. Constituent parsing with incremental sigmoid belief networks. In *Proceedings of the Association for Computational Linguistics (ACL)*.

Toutanova, K., D. Klein, C. D. Manning, and Y. Singer. 2003. Feature-rich part-of-speech tagging with a cyclic dependency network. In *Proceedings of the North American Chapter of the Association for Computational Linguistics (NAACL)*.

Trivedi, R., and J. Eisenstein. 2013. Discourse connectors for latent subjectivity in sentiment analysis. In *Proceedings of the North American Chapter of the Association for Computational Linguistics (NAACL)*.

Tromble, R. W., and J. Eisner. 2006. A fast finite-state relaxation method for enforcing global constraints on sequence decoding. In *Proceedings of the North American Chapter of the Association for Computational Linguistics (NAACL)*.

Tsochantaridis, I., T. Hofmann, T. Joachims, and Y. Altun. 2004. Support vector machine learning for interdependent and structured output spaces. In *Proceedings of the International Conference on Machine Learning (ICML)*.

Tsvetkov, Y., M. Faruqui, W. Ling, G. Lample, and C. Dyer. 2015. Evaluation of word vector representations by subspace alignment. In *Proceedings of Empirical Methods for Natural Language Processing (EMNLP)*.

Tu, Z., Z. Lu, Y. Liu, X. Liu, and H. Li. 2016. Modeling coverage for neural machine translation. In *Proceedings of the Association for Computational Linguistics (ACL)*.

Turian, J., L. Ratinov, and Y. Bengio. 2010. Word representations: A simple and general method for semi-supervised learning. In *Proceedings of the Association for Computational Linguistics (ACL)*.

Turing, A. M. 2009. Computing machinery and intelligence. In *Parsing the Turing Test*, eds. R. Epstein, G. Roberts, and G. Beber, 23–65. New York, NY: Springer.

Turney, P. D., and P. Pantel. 2010. From frequency to meaning: Vector space models of semantics. *Journal of Artificial Intelligence Research* 37: 141–188.

Tutin, A., and R. Kittredge. 1992. Lexical choice in context: Generating procedural texts. In *Proceedings of the International Conference on Computational Linguistics (COLING)*.

Twain, M. 1997. *A Tramp Abroad*. New York: Penguin.

Tzeng, E., J. Hoffman, T. Darrell, and K. Saenko. 2015. Simultaneous deep transfer across domains and tasks. In *Proceedings of the International Conference on Computer Vision (ICCV)*.

Usunier, N., D. Buffoni, and P. Gallinari. 2009. Ranking with ordered weighted pairwise classification. In *Proceedings of the International Conference on Machine Learning (ICML)*.

Uthus, D. C., and D. W. Aha. 2013. The Ubuntu chat corpus for multiparticipant chat analysis. In *AAAI Spring Symposium: Analyzing Microtext*.

Utiyama, M., and H. Isahara. 2001. A statistical model for domain-independent text segmentation. In *Proceedings of the Association for Computational Linguistics (ACL)*.

Utiyama, M., and H. Isahara. 2007. A comparison of pivot methods for phrase-based statistical machine translation. In *Proceedings of the North American Chapter of the Association for Computational Linguistics (NAACL)*.

Uzuner, Ö., X. Zhang, and T. Sibanda. 2009. Machine learning and rule-based approaches to assertion classification. *Journal of the American Medical Informatics Association* 16 (1): 109–115.

Vadas, D., and J. R. Curran. 2011. Parsing noun phrases in the Penn Treebank. *Computational Linguistics* 37 (4): 753–809.

Van Eynde, F. 2006. NP-internal agreement and the structure of the noun phrase. *Journal of Linguistics* 42 (1): 139–186.

Van Gael, J., A. Vlachos, and Z. Ghahramani. 2009. The infinite HMM for unsupervised PoS tagging. In *Proceedings of Empirical Methods for Natural Language Processing (EMNLP)*.

Vaswani, A., N. Shazeer, N. Parmar, J. Uszkoreit, L. Jones, A. N. Gomez, Ł. Kaiser, and I. Polosukhin. 2017. Attention is all you need. In *Neural Information Processing Systems (NeurIPS)*.

Vaswani, A., S. Bengio, E. Brevdo, F. Chollet, A. N. Gomez, S. Gouws, L. Jones, L. Kaiser, N. Kalchbrenner, N. Parmar, R. Sepassi, N. Shazeer, and J. Uszkoreit. 2018. Tensor2tensor for neural machine translation. *CoRR* abs/1803.07416.

Velldal, E., L. Øvrelid, J. Read, and S. Oepen. 2012. Speculation and negation: Rules, rankers, and the role of syntax. *Computational Linguistics* 38 (2): 369–410.

Versley, Y. 2011. Towards finer-grained tagging of discourse connectives. In *Proceedings of the Workshop Beyond Semantics: Corpus-Based Investigations of Pragmatic and Discourse Phenomena.*

Vilain, M., J. Burger, J. Aberdeen, D. Connolly, and L. Hirschman. 1995. A model-theoretic coreference scoring scheme. In *Proceedings of the 6th Conference on Message Understanding.*

Vincent, P., H. Larochelle, I. Lajoie, Y. Bengio, and P.-A. Manzagol. 2010. Stacked denoising autoencoders: Learning useful representations in a deep network with a local denoising criterion. *The Journal of Machine Learning Research* 11: 3371–3408.

Vincze, V., G. Szarvas, R. Farkas, G. Móra, and J. Csirik. 2008. The BioScope corpus: Biomedical texts annotated for uncertainty, negation and their scopes. *BMC Bioinformatics* 9 (11): 9.

Vinyals, O., A. Toshev, S. Bengio, and D. Erhan. 2015. Show and tell: A neural image caption generator. In *Proceedings of Computer Vision and Pattern Recognition (CVPR).*

Viterbi, A. 1967. Error bounds for convolutional codes and an asymptotically optimum decoding algorithm. *IEEE Transactions on Information Theory* 13 (2): 260–269.

Voll, K., and M. Taboada. 2007. Not all words are created equal: Extracting semantic orientation as a function of adjective relevance. In *Proceedings of Australian Conference on Artificial Intelligence.*

Wager, S., S. Wang, and P. S. Liang. 2013. Dropout training as adaptive regularization. In *Neural Information Processing Systems (NeurIPS).*

Wainwright, M. J., and M. I. Jordan. 2008. Graphical models, exponential families, and variational inference. *Foundations and Trends in Machine Learning* 1 (1-2): 1–305.

Walker, M. A. 2000. An application of reinforcement learning to dialogue strategy selection in a spoken dialogue system for email. *Journal of Artificial Intelligence Research* 12: 387–416.

Walker, M. A., J. E. Cahn, and S. J. Whittaker. 1997. Improvising linguistic style: Social and affective bases for agent personality. In *Proceedings of the First International Conference on Autonomous Agents.*

Wang, C., N. Xue, and S. Pradhan. 2015. A transition-based algorithm for AMR parsing. In *Proceedings of the North American Chapter of the Association for Computational Linguistics (NAACL).*

Wang, H., T. Onishi, K. Gimpel, and D. McAllester. 2017. Emergent predication structure in hidden state vectors of neural readers. In *Proceedings of the 2nd Workshop on Representation Learning for NLP.*

Weaver, W. 1955. Translation. In *Machine Translation of Languages*, eds. W. N. Locke and A. D. Booth, Vol. 14, 15–23. Cambridge, MA: MIT Press.

Webber, B. 2004. D-LTAG: Extending lexicalized TAG to discourse. *Cognitive Science* 28 (5): 751–779.

Webber, B., and A. Joshi. 2012. Discourse structure and computation: Past, present and future. In *Proceedings of the ACL-2012 Special Workshop on Rediscovering 50 Years of Discoveries.*

Webber, B., M. Egg, and V. Kordoni. 2012. Discourse structure and language technology. *Journal of Natural Language Engineering* 18 (4): 437–490.

Wei, G. C., and M. A. Tanner. 1990. A Monte Carlo implementation of the EM algorithm and the poor man's data augmentation algorithms. *Journal of the American Statistical Association* 85 (411): 699–704.

Weinberger, K., A. Dasgupta, J. Langford, A. Smola, and J. Attenberg. 2009. Feature hashing for large scale multitask learning. In *Proceedings of the International Conference on Machine Learning (ICML)*.

Weizenbaum, J. 1966. Eliza–A computer program for the study of natural language communication between man and machine. *Communications of the ACM* 9 (1): 36–45.

Wellner, B., and J. Pustejovsky. 2007. Automatically identifying the arguments of discourse connectives. In *Proceedings of Empirical Methods for Natural Language Processing (EMNLP)*.

Wen, T.-H., M. Gasic, N. Mrkšić, P.-H. Su, D. Vandyke, and S. Young. 2015. Semantically conditioned LSTM-based natural language generation for spoken dialogue systems. In *Proceedings of Empirical Methods for Natural Language Processing (EMNLP)*.

Weston, J., S. Bengio, and N. Usunier. 2011. Wsabie: Scaling up to large vocabulary image annotation. In *Proceedings of the International Joint Conference on Artificial Intelligence (IJCAI)*.

Wiebe, J., T. Wilson, and C. Cardie. 2005. Annotating expressions of opinions and emotions in language. *Language Resources and Evaluation* 39 (2): 165–210.

Wieting, J., M. Bansal, K. Gimpel, and K. Livescu. 2016a. CHARAGRAM: Embedding words and sentences via character n-grams. In *Proceedings of Empirical Methods for Natural Language Processing (EMNLP)*.

Wieting, J., M. Bansal, K. Gimpel, and K. Livescu. 2016b. Towards universal paraphrastic sentence embeddings. In *Proceedings of the International Conference on Learning Representations (ICLR)*.

Williams, J. D., and S. Young. 2007. Partially observable Markov decision processes for spoken dialog systems. *Computer Speech & Language* 21 (2): 393–422.

Williams, P., R. Sennrich, M. Post, and P. Koehn. 2016. *Syntax-Based Statistical Machine Translation*, Vol. 9. San Rafael, CA: Morgan & Claypool.

Wilson, T., J. Wiebe, and P. Hoffmann. 2005. Recognizing contextual polarity in phrase-level sentiment analysis. In *Proceedings of Empirical Methods for Natural Language Processing (EMNLP)*.

Winograd, T. 1972. Understanding natural language. *Cognitive Psychology* 3 (1): 1–191.

Wiseman, S., A. M. Rush, and S. M. Shieber. 2016. Learning global features for coreference resolution. In *Proceedings of the North American Chapter of the Association for Computational Linguistics (NAACL)*.

Wiseman, S., S. Shieber, and A. Rush. 2017. Challenges in data-to-document generation. In *Proceedings of Empirical Methods for Natural Language Processing (EMNLP)*.

Wiseman, S. J., A. M. Rush, S. M. Shieber, and J. Weston. 2015. Learning anaphoricity and antecedent ranking features for coreference resolution. In *Proceedings of the Association for Computational Linguistics (ACL)*.

Wolf, F., and E. Gibson. 2005. Representing discourse coherence: A corpus-based study. *Computational Linguistics* 31 (2): 249–287.

Wolfe, T., M. Dredze, and B. Van Durme. 2017. Pocket knowledge base population. In *Proceedings of the Association for Computational Linguistics (ACL)*.

Wong, Y. W., and R. J. Mooney. 2006. Learning for semantic parsing with statistical machine translation. In *Proceedings of the North American Chapter of the Association for Computational Linguistics (NAACL)*.

Wong, Y. W., and R. Mooney. 2007. Generation by inverting a semantic parser that uses statistical machine translation. In *Proceedings of the North American Chapter of the Association for Computational Linguistics (NAACL)*.

Wu, B. Y., and K.-M. Chao. 2004. *Spanning Trees and Optimization Problems*. Boca Raton, FL: CRC Press.

Wu, D. 1997. Stochastic inversion transduction grammars and bilingual parsing of parallel corpora. *Computational Linguistics* 23 (3): 377–403.

Wu, F., and D. S. Weld. 2010. Open information extraction using Wikipedia. In *Proceedings of the Association for Computational Linguistics (ACL)*.

Wu, X., R. Ward, and L. Bottou. 2018. WNGrad: Learn the learning rate in gradient descent. *arXiv preprint arXiv:1803.02865*.

Wu, Y., M. Schuster, Z. Chen, Q. V. Le, M. Norouzi, W. Macherey, M. Krikun, Y. Cao, Q. Gao, K. Macherey, J. Klingner, A. Shah, M. Johnson, X. Liu, Łukasz Kaiser, S. Gouws, Y. Kato, T. Kudo, H. Kazawa, K. Stevens, G. Kurian, N. Patil, W. Wang, C. Young, J. Smith, J. Riesa, A. Rudnick, + O. Vinyals, G. Corrado, M. Hughes, and J. Dean. 2016. Google's neural machine translation system: Bridging the gap between human and machine translation. *CoRR* abs/1609.08144.

Xia, F. 2000. The part-of-speech tagging guidelines for the Penn Chinese Treebank (3.0), Technical report, University of Pennsylvania Institute for Research in Cognitive Science.

Xu, K., J. Ba, R. Kiros, K. Cho, A. Courville, R. Salakhudinov, R. Zemel, and Y. Bengio. 2015. Show, attend and tell: Neural image caption generation with visual attention. In *Proceedings of the International Conference on Machine Learning (ICML)*.

Xu, W., X. Liu, and Y. Gong. 2003. Document clustering based on non-negative matrix factorization. In *Proceedings of the ACM SIGIR Conference on Research and Development in Information Retrieval*.

Xu, Y., L. Mou, G. Li, Y. Chen, H. Peng, and Z. Jin. 2015. Classifying relations via long short term memory networks along shortest dependency paths. In *Proceedings of Empirical Methods for Natural Language Processing (EMNLP)*.

Xuan Bach, N., N. L. Minh, and A. Shimazu. 2012. A reranking model for discourse segmentation using subtree features. In *Proceedings of the Special Interest Group on Discourse and Dialogue (SIGDIAL)*.

Xue, N. 2003. Chinese word segmentation as character tagging. *Computational Linguistics and Chinese Language Processing* 8 (1): 29–48.

Xue, N., H. T. Ng, S. Pradhan, R. Prasad, C. Bryant, and A. T. Rutherford. 2015. The CoNLL-2015 shared task on shallow discourse parsing. In *Proceedings of the Conference on Natural Language Learning (CoNLL)*.

Yamada, H., and Y. Matsumoto. 2003. Statistical dependency analysis with support vector machines. In *Proceedings of the 8th International Workshop on Parsing Technologies (IWPT)*.

Yamada, K., and K. Knight. 2001. A syntax-based statistical translation model. In *Proceedings of the Association for Computational Linguistics (ACL)*.

Yang, B., and C. Cardie. 2014. Context-aware learning for sentence-level sentiment analysis with posterior regularization. In *Proceedings of the Association for Computational Linguistics (ACL)*.

Yang, Y., and J. Eisenstein. 2013. A log-linear model for unsupervised text normalization. In *Proceedings of Empirical Methods for Natural Language Processing (EMNLP)*.

Yang, Y., and J. Eisenstein. 2015. Unsupervised multi-domain adaptation with feature embeddings. In *Proceedings of the North American Chapter of the Association for Computational Linguistics (NAACL)*.

Yang, Y., M.-W. Chang, and J. Eisenstein. 2016. Toward socially-infused information extraction: Embedding authors, mentions, and entities. In *Proceedings of Empirical Methods for Natural Language Processing (EMNLP)*.

Yang, Y., W.-t. Yih, and C. Meek. 2015. WikiQA: A challenge dataset for open-domain question answering. In *Proceedings of Empirical Methods for Natural Language Processing (EMNLP)*.

Yannakoudakis, H., T. Briscoe, and B. Medlock. 2011. A new dataset and method for automatically grading ESOL texts. In *Proceedings of the Association for Computational Linguistics (ACL)*.

Yarowsky, D. 1995. Unsupervised word sense disambiguation rivaling supervised methods. In *Proceedings of the Association for Computational Linguistics (ACL)*.

Yee, L. C., and T. Y. Jones. 2012. Apple CEO in China mission to clear up problems. *Reuters*. March 27.

Yi, Y., C.-Y. Lai, S. Petrov, and K. Keutzer. 2011. Efficient parallel CKY parsing on GPUs. In *Proceedings of the 12th International Conference on Parsing Technologies*.

Yu, C.-N. J., and T. Joachims. 2009. Learning structural SVMs with latent variables. In *Proceedings of the International Conference on Machine Learning (ICML)*.

Yu, F., and V. Koltun. 2016. Multi-scale context aggregation by dilated convolutions. In *Proceedings of the International Conference on Learning Representations (ICLR)*.

Zaidan, O. F., and C. Callison-Burch. 2011. Crowdsourcing translation: Professional quality from non-professionals. In *Proceedings of the Association for Computational Linguistics (ACL)*.

Zaremba, W., I. Sutskever, and O. Vinyals. 2014. Recurrent neural network regularization. *arXiv preprint arXiv:1409.2329*.

Zeiler, M. D. 2012. ADADELTA: An adaptive learning rate method. *arXiv preprint arXiv:1212.5701*.

Zelenko, D., C. Aone, and A. Richardella. 2003. Kernel methods for relation extraction. *The Journal of Machine Learning Research* 3: 1083–1106.

Zelle, J. M., and R. J. Mooney. 1996. Learning to parse database queries using inductive logic programming. In *Proceedings of the National Conference on Artificial Intelligence (AAAI)*.

Zeng, D., K. Liu, S. Lai, G. Zhou, and J. Zhao. 2014. Relation classification via convolutional deep neural network. In *Proceedings of the International Conference on Computational Linguistics (COLING)*.

Zettlemoyer, L. S., and M. Collins. 2005. Learning to map sentences to logical form: Structured classification with probabilistic categorial grammars. In *Proceedings of Uncertainty in Artificial Intelligence (UAI)*.

Zhang, C., S. Bengio, M. Hardt, B. Recht, and O. Vinyals. 2017. Understanding deep learning requires rethinking generalization. In *Proceedings of the International Conference on Learning Representations (ICLR)*.

Zhang, X., J. Zhao, and Y. LeCun. 2015. Character-level convolutional networks for text classification. In *Neural Information Processing Systems (NeurIPS)*.

Zhang, Y., and S. Clark. 2008. A tale of two parsers: Investigating and combining graph-based and transition-based dependency parsing using beam-search. In *Proceedings of Empirical Methods for Natural Language Processing (EMNLP)*.

Zhang, Y., and J. Nivre. 2011. Transition-based dependency parsing with rich non-local features. In *Proceedings of the Association for Computational Linguistics (ACL)*.

Zhang, Y., T. Lei, R. Barzilay, T. Jaakkola, and A. Globerson. 2014. Steps to excellence: Simple inference with refined scoring of dependency trees. In *Proceedings of the Association for Computational Linguistics (ACL)*.

Zhang, Z. 2017. A note on counting dependency trees. *arXiv preprint arXiv:1708.08789*.

Zhao, J., T. Wang, M. Yatskar, V. Ordonez, and K.-W. Chang. 2018. Gender bias in coreference resolution: Evaluation and debiasing methods. In *Proceedings of the North American Chapter of the Association for Computational Linguistics (NAACL)*.

Zhou, J., and W. Xu. 2015. End-to-end learning of semantic role labeling using recurrent neural networks. In *Proceedings of the Association for Computational Linguistics (ACL)*.

Zhu, J., Z. Nie, X. Liu, B. Zhang, and J.-R. Wen. 2009. StatSnowball: a statistical approach to extracting entity relationships. In *Proceedings of the Conference on World-Wide Web (WWW)*.

Zhu, X., and A. B. Goldberg. 2009. *Introduction to Semi-Supervised Learning*. San Rafael, CA: Morgan & Claypool.

Zhu, X., Z. Ghahramani, and J. D. Lafferty. 2003. Semi-supervised learning using Gaussian fields and harmonic functions. In *Proceedings of the International Conference on Machine Learning (ICML)*.

Zipf, G. K. 1949. *Human Behavior and the Principle of Least Effort*. Reading, MA: Addison-Wesley.

Zirn, C., M. Niepert, H. Stuckenschmidt, and M. Strube. 2011. Fine-grained sentiment analysis with structural features. In *Proceedings of the International Joint Conference on Artificial Intelligence (IJCAI)*.

Zou, W. Y., R. Socher, D. Cer, and C. D. Manning. 2013. Bilingual word embeddings for phrase-based machine translation. In *Proceedings of Empirical Methods for Natural Language Processing (EMNLP)*.

Index